Law in Context

D1335061

Law in Context

Third Edition

Stephen Bottomley
BA, LLB, LLM
Professor of Law, The Australian National University

Simon Bronitt
LLB, LLM
Professor of Law, The Australian National University

THE FEDERATION PRESS
2006

Published in Sydney by

The Federation Press
    PO Box 45, Annandale, NSW, 2038
    71 John Street, Leichhardt, NSW, 2040
    Telephone (02) 9552 2200 Fax (02) 9552 1681
    E-mail: info@federationpress.com.au
    Website: http://www.federationpress.com.au

1st edition   1991
2nd edition   1997
3rd edition   2006

National Library of Australia Cataloguing-in-Publication
    Bottomley, Stephen
    Law in context.

    3rd ed
    Includes index.
    ISBN 1 86287 341 0

    1. Law – Philosophy. 2. Law – Australia. 3. Sociological jurisprudence. I. Bronitt, Simon. II.
    Title.

340.115

Typeset by The Federation Press, Leichhardt, NSW.
    Printed by McPherson's Printing Group, Maryborough, Vic.

Foreword to the Third Edition

What is 'law'? I asked this question in the first law article I ever wrote, published in the *Jaipur Law Journal* in 1969, and I am still struggling with the answer.

Part of the problem lies in the perennial issue of whether law is best understood as an autonomous body of abstract rules, precepts, and doctrines, or rather as a phenomenon that is intelligible only by reference to the cognate disciplines of history, philosophy, psychology, sociology, economics, and political science.

In truth, neither view is satisfactory. The idea of law as an autonomous body of rules is not only enigmatic and inscrutable. It is also potentially an instrument of injustice, with embedded but outdated values that can oppress a later and more enlightened generation. Those values – characteristically hidden under a cloak of apparent neutrality – can be exposed, and the supposedly neutral laws that embody them subjected to the processes of deliberate change, only if law is understood in a broader context, especially as a product of social forces and an instrument of social control.

Yet, at the same time, law cannot simply be equated to its social context. Legal doctrine does have a life of its own, and a real world impact. Those who practise it practise a craft of the highest order. And just as it entrenches values and policies that become ill-adapted to social needs over time, so it simultaneously vindicates enduring values that we may think are essential to a free society. The final sentence of the second edition of this book (unfortunately omitted from this edition) nicely captured the dilemma: 'Law cannot be understood without its context, but law is not reducible to that context'.

There is a parallel pedagogical dilemma. To introduce students to law as a system of abstract rules is to court the danger that they will be seduced by the search for elegance and coherence and lose sight of the ends which the law is intended to serve. Yet to present doctrine as an artificial construct of illusory certainty that is in reality a product of social forces, hidden values and open-ended discretions is to court the opposite danger that students will lose interest in, and even capacity for, that careful and rigorous analysis that is the necessary underpinning of professional competence. The trick is to promote insight without compromising craft, or, to put it conversely, to teach craft without inhibiting insight.

There is a related tension between two different conceptions of legal education: law as training for professional practice, and law as an intellectual discipline. In my view, these competing conceptions of legal education are in fact profoundly consistent. The legal professional without an understanding of legal history, legal theory, the forces that shape the law, and the role of law in society, will be a mere technician, deprived of insight into current and future legal development and incapacitated from making a meaningful contribution to the continuous improvement of the law and the operation of the legal system. At the same time, legal insight demands that abstract theory be tested in the crucible of unforgiving empiricism and down-to-earth practicality.

Life is full of dilemmas, tensions, and competing guideposts. 'Look before you leap', clamours one proverb; 'he who hesitates is lost', responds another. The antinomy is not trivial. Like law in isolation versus law in context, or law as a profession versus law as an intellectual discipline, neither guidepost can tell the whole story. Neither is true; yet both are true. Ultimately, we must exercise judgment and choose that which is appropriate in the circumstances.

This excellent book will help you make that choice. It will give you many ways to think about law – many ways to conceptualise it, contextualise it, and criticise it. The authors are two of my most valued colleagues, and they are not afraid to express a point of view. Yet, if you take the real message of this book, you will not necessarily agree with them. You will apply your own mind to the issues. You will expose their predilections and challenge their points of view. You will begin to supply your own answer to the question, 'what is law?'

Professor Michael Coper
Dean of Law and Robert Garran Professor of Law
The Australian National University
1 February 2006

Contents

Preface to the Third Edition

'In law context is everything'

R (Daly) v Secretary of State for the Home Department
[2001] 2 AC 532 at 548 per Lord Steyn

The 'Law in Context' movement unsurprisingly has its own context. In Australia, contextual legal scholarship has flourished since the 1970s, stimulated by a period of social change that intensified sociological critique and the contextual examination of law. This process was undoubtedly aided by new law schools, such as those at the University of New South Wales and Macquarie University, that self-consciously adopted new contextual approaches to the study of law and new publications that overtly addressed the wider social, political and economic contexts of law. A significant impetus was the creation of the 'Law in Context' series in the United Kingdom, which sought to depart from traditional textbook orthodoxy by placing legal doctrine in its wider context.[1]

Australia and the United Kingdom were relative slow-comers to the 'Law in Context' movement – an approach that has a longer history in the United States traceable to the scholarship of American legal realists in the 1940s such as Roscoe Pound and Karl Llewellyn. By contrast, Australian legal scholarship was less developed, with few full-time academics, and fewer still who were prepared to explore sociological dimensions of law. A towering exception was Julius Stone at the University of Sydney whose theorising about precedent and legal reasoning laid the foundation for many lawyers, judges and scholars to be more honest and open about the political and social influences shaping law. Notwithstanding these few developments, available contextual perspectives remained largely a theoretical or 'scientific' exercise, doing little to penetrate core law subjects or furthermore influence the way in which law was taught or even practised. The Pearce Report into legal education in 1987 painted a dismal picture of Australian law schools as largely trade schools – unlike the LLB in the United Kingdom, legal theory was not even a prerequisite for a university degree in law!

Fast forward more than two decades, and things look different. Context is no longer something set apart from the 'core of law' – some judges are prepared to acknowledge its relevance (and the contribution of academic scholarship) in development of the common law and role in statutory interpretation. No longer is it a form of legal heresy to expose and critique 'law's truths': indeed, as we see in this book, more than two decades of feminist scholarship has exposed law's 'hidden gender',[2] permitting masculinist assumptions about sexuality and gender roles to be challenged and fundamental legal concepts like reasonableness,

---

1   The first and highly influential volume of this new series was Patrick Atiyah's, *Accidents, Compensation and the Law*, 1st ed, Weidenfeld & Nicolson, 1970. Although focused on English law, the textbook drew heavily on Australian and American sources, and was completed during Atiyah's tenure as a member of the ANU Law Faculty. For a discussion of the significance of these approaches, see W Twining, *Law in Context*, Clarendon Press, 1997, 60ff.

2   R Graycar and J Morgan, *The Hidden Gender of Law*, 2nd ed, The Federation Press, 2002.

relevance and autonomy to be normatively reconstructed. Neither is context confined to local settings, with judges and legislatures increasingly prepared to recognise the international context within which domestic law develops, particularly in relation to human rights.

'Law in Context' should be viewed neither as a distinctive legal theory nor an academic orthodoxy.[3] Rather it is better viewed as a cluster of methodologies, perspectives or orientations towards law and its study. Significantly, it draws scholars across the philosophical spectrum – liberal theorists, neo-Marxists, and critical and feminist theorists have all sought to expose the wider political, social and economic context of legal doctrine. The approach is also distinctive in its disciplinary pluralism: contextual studies draw from an infinite range of disciplines, deploying insights from history, the social sciences, psychology and literary and cultural studies, and so on.

Such pluralism can often be disconcerting and bewildering for students and scholars who are attuned to focus on what the law is (or should be), and on how to become proficient lawyers. A legitimate concern about contextualism is that it can neglect or downplay the importance of legal doctrine. We believe that contextual approaches must take legal doctrine seriously – however, the focus must move beyond the formal legal rules and principles stated in the higher courts or statute books to examine how the law works in practice and wider society.

This empirical approach to the 'law in books' is highly revealing. It can demonstrate that the law and judicial rhetoric in the higher courts can be subverted or reconfigured by lower court practice – it also reveals how law is also used as a negotiating and bargaining tool outside the courtroom and the context of litigation. Empiricism also reveals the limits of law reform – while looking good on paper, changes to the common law and statute books may not always be effective in achieving the desired outcome; worse still, sometimes reform can be counterproductive or have unintended effects. Looking beyond the formal expression of laws found in statutes and law reports ensures that these failures do not pass unnoticed. Responding to these concerns, law reform itself has changed significantly over the past 30 years both in Australia and the UK. Comparing law reform reports then and now reveals a fundamentally different approach: laws are no longer reviewed and remodelled exclusively from the 'technical' perspective of clarity, coherence and predictability. Today law reform is characterised by a much stronger commitment to inter-disciplinarity in developing legal policy.[4]

Legal education in Australia has followed these broad trends. Legal educators have developed pedagogical approaches, as well as educational materials, that promote a contextual study of law. With an increasing array of books and courses proclaiming a critical and contextual orientation, it might be said that a primer on 'law in context' may have had its day. However, the problem, as we see it, is that the contextual critique is often applied in specialist elective courses and is not itself contextualised within the particular fields of legal doctrine and practice. In our view, the application of critique and context for law students and lawyers must

---

3   Twining, n 1, 62.

4   As a subject of intellectual study itself, law reform has been largely neglected by legal scholars. A recent exception exploring the history, trends and potential of law reform in Australia and wider common law world is B Opeskin and D Weisbrot (eds), *The Promise of Law Reform*, The Federation Press, 2005.

proceed from an internal rather than external perspective – it must be focused on how law is actually used as a *process*. The location of legal rules and principles here requires an examination of how law operates on the streets, as much as in lawyers' offices and corporate suites. We believe that a book of this type, which is aimed at first year law students, remains crucially important – laying the foundations of law requires more than grasping the rules of precedent, understanding of various legal sources and techniques of legal reasoning and statutory interpretation. There are many ways to lay a contextual foundation to the study of law – one approach is to examine the traditions of law, using historical and comparative material to illuminate the distinctive features of our system of law and ideas about justice. Other approaches explore foundational law through the perspective of legal culture.

This book shares some similarities with these other approaches, though our aim, as in previous editions, is to expose the assumptions and liberal values underlying our laws and legal system and to anchor and illustrate our critique within current controversies. Law is deeply normative, projecting a vision of how the state should relate to individuals, and how individuals should relate to each other – it is a vision that has been shaped by 19th century ideas of liberalism and it reflects a socio-cultural, economic and political world-view based on the importance of individual autonomy and rights such as liberty, fairness, equality and privacy. That is not to say that law is a perfect blueprint of liberalism. As many chapters here illustrate, liberal ideas regularly collide with morality and other competing public policies – indeed, the dialogue between the interests of individual liberty and the communal right to security, reviewed in Chapter 14, is symptomatic of how these values often operate in tension. As this book reveals, these values imprint themselves on law and our ideals of justice in a variety of ways. The authors' intention, following previous editions, is not to trash liberalism, but rather to expose its limits and to offer competing perspectives on how these fundamental ideals can be understood and reconstructed.

This new edition brings a new team of authors, new chapters added, old ones deleted or revised. This edition sees the departure of Stephen Parker from the team of authors. Stephen was one of the original authors and was a driving force behind the first two editions of the book. This new edition relies on many of his insights, carries much of his scholarship and owes a great deal to his commitment to progressive and contextual legal education. The previous editions of this book also contained a chapter on law and race written by our colleague Jennifer Clarke. She was not able to continue her involvement into this edition, and we thank her for her rich contribution to the earlier editions.

While much has changed in the third edition, some things have not. Particularly, there are ideas and themes about law that we have persisted with and, consequently, other ideas and themes that we have abandoned or not picked up. For example, there is little mention of post-modernism, post-structuralism, or post-liberalism in this edition. This is for two reasons. First, notwithstanding the useful or intriguing insights that these theories can offer, our view is that liberalism is still the 'main game' in our legal system, and has proven to be a resilient blueprint for law. Given this, we have also stuck with some of the 'classic' responses to liberal thinking (such as Marxist and feminist analyses of law). The second reason for these changes is that the book is intended primarily as an undergraduate text, for use in introductory courses in the typical law curriculum. Our hope is that the ideas and information presented in the book will help to open up students' understanding of law and legal issues, and to prompt inquiry that looks beyond the usual boundaries of a law syllabus. No doubt students will encounter many different critiques of the liberal ideology that we describe, and we leave it to other texts, typically written for other advanced theory courses, to assist students in that regard.

Like all good legal texts, our preface contains a disclaimer. The views expressed here are ours alone and we bear responsibility for the inevitable errors and inaccurate glosses. We remain thankful for the many inputs from previous co-authors, our colleagues and students that have shaped our view of law over the many decades of working at ANU. Special thanks to our research assistants, Cath Kelso, Prita Jobling, Christine Feerick, and to Wendy Kukulies-Smith (who generously shared her research expertise on discrimination to develop the gender questions). Special thanks to Prita, Christine and Wendy for their huge effort on the index and page proofs under the tightest of deadlines. Thanks also to Professor Michael Coper for making time in his busy decanal schedule to write such a thoughtful and thought-provoking Foreword.

Authorship is often a hazardous exercise. The vicissitudes of scholarly and family life have an tendency to waylay the best plans and rash promises to publishers. Deadlines always press. The mutual understanding between authors and our publishers at Federation Press (Chris Holt and Kathy Fitzhenry) have smoothed the way, as has our shared vision and objectives for the book. Bottomley and Bronitt share many similarities – not only a strong commitment to the ideals behind Law in Context and promoting legal education that combines theoretical and applied perspectives on law, but also a questionable sense of humour, irritatingly congruent fashion sense and most unhelpfully even our initials.

The law is current, to the best of our knowledge, as at 16 January 2006.

SB1 and SB2
Canberra
February 2006

To our families,
who put everything into context

Acknowledgments

The authors wish to thank the following for granting permission to use materials included in the text:

Basil Blackwell for N Lacey, "Legislation Against Sex Discrimination: Questions from a Feminist Perspective" (1987) 14 *Journal of Law and Society* 411.

Blackwell Publishing for M Galanter, "Why the Haves Come out Ahead: Speculations on the Limits of Legal Change" (1974) 9 *Law and Society Review* 95 and "Delivering Legality: Some Proposals for the Direction of Research" (1976) 11 *Law and Society Review* 225; A Sarat and WLF Felstiner, "Law and Strategy in the Divorce Lawyer's Office" (1986) 20 *Law and Society Review* 93.

Butterworths Ltd for W Twining, "Taking Facts Seriously" in N Gold (ed), *Essays on Legal Education*, 1982.

The Carswell Co (a division of Thomson, Canada) for A Hutchinson, *Dwelling on the Threshold*, 1988.

Ross Cranston QC for *Law, Government and Public Policy*, Oxford University Press, 1987.

Frank Easterbrook for "The Inevitability of Law and Economics" (1989) 1 *Legal Education Review* 3.

Harvester-Wheatsheaf for Frank H Stephen, *The Economics of Law*, 1989.

Doreen McBarnet for *Conviction, Law, the State, and the Construction of Justice*, Macmillan, 1981.

Sir Robert Megarry for "Law as Taught and Law as Practised" (1967) 9 *Society of Public Teachers of Law Journal* 176.

Ngaire Naffine for *Law and the Sexes*, Allen and Unwin, 1990.

Richard Posner for *Economic Analysis of Law*, 2nd, Little Brown, 1977 and 1986.

Carol Smart for *The Ties that Bind*, Routledge & Kegan Paul, 1983; and *Feminism and the Power of Law*, Routledge, 1990.

Margaret Thornton for "The Public/Private Dichotomy: Gendered and Discriminatory" paper delivered to the Australasian Law Teachers Association Annual Conference, September 1990, The Australian National University.

Dr Cento Veljanovski for *The New Law and Economics*, Oxford University Press, 1982.

Virginia Law Review Association and Fred B Rothman for AA Leff, "Commentary – Economic Analysis of Law: Some Realism about Nominalism" (1974) 60 *Virginia Law Review* 460.

Yale Law Journal for A Sarat and WLF Felstiner, "Lawyers and Legal Consciousness: Law Talk in the Divorce Lawyer's Office" (1989) 98 *Yale Law Journal* 1663.

While every care has been taken to establish and acknowledge copyright, the authors and publishers tender their apologies for any accidental infringement.

PART A

Law in a
Political Context

Chapter 1

Introduction

[T]o treat the law as a discrete set of principles in a vacuum and without a context is to misconceive its dynamic and ubiquitous nature and, more importantly, to undervalue or even to overlook the manner in which it contributes to the fundamental fabric of modern society.

Sir Anthony Mason, Chief Justice of Australia, 19 February 1991.[1]

(a)   Introduction

A central theme in this book is that, as the former Chief Justice says, law cannot be treated as a discrete set of principles without a context. In the chapters which follow, we seek to examine and evaluate the context of Australian law. Since the first edition of this book was published in 1991, many law schools have introduced subjects into their curriculum, or revised existing subjects, so that law can be evaluated critically in its theoretical and practical contexts. To appreciate the significance of this, and to introduce the book generally, some account of traditional legal education in Australia is helpful.

(b)   Traditional legal education and its assumptions

Australian legal education has its origins in English[2] methods for the training of lawyers. In recent times some distinctively local educational practices have emerged, and North American teaching styles and degree schemes have become more influential,[3] but the starting point is England.[4]

Legal training in England, until a relatively late stage, was left largely in the hands of the profession, conducted though apprenticeships and informal lectures offered through the Inns of Court in London. It was not until the endowment of Sir William Blackstone's chair at the University of Oxford in the mid-18th century that the teaching of English common law began in earnest. This initiative was aided by Blackstone's attempt to reduce and systematise the body of common law found in law reports into a four-volume *Commentaries on the Laws of England*

---

1   Inauguration of the Faculty of Law at the University of Wollongong.

2   In fact, the *institutional structure* of many Australian universities and degree schemes originates more from Scottish than English higher education but the content of law degrees is dominated by the classifications found in English law schools.

3   CM Bradley, "Legal Education in Australia: An American Perspective" (1989) 14 *Journal of the Legal Profession* 27.

4   A convenient summary can be found in J Disney, P Redmond, J Basten and S Ross, *Lawyers*, Law Book Co, 1986, 21-22 and this account relies upon it.

(first published, 1765).[5] It took nearly 80 years before the first Chair in Law was created in 1831 at Kings College, London. Before these developments, the only law taught at university was Roman and Canon law, which had provided the core curricula for universities across Europe since the rediscovery of key Roman law texts in the 13th century.

Throughout the 19th century the hold of universities over legal education was fragile, however, and the dominant method remained apprenticeship. In 1846 a House of Commons Select Committee on Legal Education had reported that reform was urgently needed but it had also recommended that university legal education should not lead directly to the right to practise. The Select Committee Report is credited with stinging the professions into action to provide some systematic training. The Council of Legal Education was established in 1852 to oversee the training of barristers and in 1877 the Law Society was given statutory powers over the training of solicitors. From that time, university education has existed *alongside* professional education, providing an alternative way of obtaining *initial* training in law,[6] but it has not provided what is regarded as vocational training. Until recently, the majority of the English legal profession possessed no university degree at all and it is even more recently that the *law* degree has become the normal tertiary qualification.

The long tradition of apprenticeship and the persistence of beliefs that it is a more appropriate method of training lawyers than university study have arguably had an important effect on the content and objectives of university syllabi. One theory, espoused by David Sugarman, is that "academic law" was shaped by a continuing concern for legitimacy amongst both the academic and professional community.

Sugarman argues that there is a particular common law frame of mind which still overshadows the way the English teach, write and think about law.[7] He claims that that frame of mind derives from the efforts of academic lawyers in the period 1850-1907 to establish a place for themselves, both in the eyes of university colleagues and of the profession. Initially, the universities were sceptical of the need for academic training in the common law (bearing in mind that for centuries training had been in the hands of the profession[8]) and so law dons had to establish their legitimacy in the academic world. Equally, law dons had to persuade the *profession* of their usefulness in order for their graduates to prosper. Few of the profession's leaders would themselves have been law graduates (or perhaps graduates at all) and there was obvious sensitivity about claims regarding the value of a university education. Sugarman argues that the dons created a "narrow ledge" for themselves in their attempt to appease both sides. Within the academy, the dons argued that law was not the chaotic jumble of rules and decisions that might first appear. It was, in fact, internally coherent and grounded on a few

---

5   Later published as *Commentaries on the Laws of England* in 1765.
6   Overwhelmingly today, however, would-be lawyers obtain exemption from the initial stage of professional qualification by obtaining an approved law degree or by passing a number of law subjects in another approved degree scheme.
7   D Sugarman, "Legal Theory, the Common Law Mind and the Making of the Textbook Tradition" in W Twining (ed), *Legal Theory and Common Law*, Blackwell, 1986, Ch 3.
8   This was also the belief of the head of Australia's first university, the University of Sydney. Weisbrot quotes John Wooley, himself a lawyer, as saying that the "soundest lawyers come forth from schools in which law is never taught, the most accomplished physicians are nurtured where medicine is but a name". See D Weisbrot, *Australian Lawyers*, Longman Cheshire, 1990, 121.

general principles. The scholar's task was to tease out those general principles, to teach them and to systematise them in text books. The teaching method consistent with this self-image was the "problem method"; of setting fact situations and encouraging students to analyse those facts in a way which invoked the relevant legal principles. The facts were therefore handed down to the students and used as a vehicle for explicating the principles (which the law dons themselves were engaged in divining from the chaos of court decisions).

With regard to the profession, the law dons presented themselves as performing a useful complementary role in shaping and preparing the legal mind, but without aspiring to monopolise legal training. A sharp division between "law" and "facts", between "academic" and "vocational", was maintained. The profession's task was to deal with the empirical dimension of training; pleadings, dealing with lay people and so forth. The academics' task was exclusively about extracting internal coherence from the law at a safe distance from "reality". As Sugarman says, "the dominant tradition of classical legal education and scholarship had the pre-eminent merit of being cheap".[9]

One consequence of the "narrow ledge" was that (unlike in many civil law countries) the study of law at university has not been seen to involve the great questions of philosophy, politics and morality. As we shall see below in Chapters 2 and 3, a common refrain of liberalism is the claim that law should be *separate* from both politics and morality. To the extent that any "philosophy" was regarded as useful it was of a confined analytical kind that addressed itself to the meaning of key legal concepts or theories of adjudication. The academy both in England and the United States has been preoccupied with codification of law, and its restatement into a coherent and principled legislative form. As we explore in Chapter 3, this formed an important part of liberalism's campaign to constrain judicial creativity and place law reform, somewhat unrealistically, in a technocratic realm beyond politics.[10]

Moving now to Australia, we see a similar, although not identical, story.[11] Chesterman and Weisbrot have argued that the main difference between Australian and English legal education is the closer links between the profession and the law schools here.[12] The involvement of the profession meant that, unlike in England, the professional bodies were prepared to recognise law degrees as one way of satisfying *all* the substantive law training.[13] They did not initially require

---

9   Note 7, 50.

10   See J Horder, "Criminal Law" in P Cane and M Tushnet (eds), *Oxford Handbook of Legal Studies*, Oxford UP, 2003, Ch 12, 227.

11   See, for example, L Martin, "From Apprenticeship to Law School: A Social History of Legal Education in Nineteenth Century New South Wales" (1986) 9 *University of New South Wales Law Journal* 111; D Pearce, E Campbell and D Harding, *Australian Law Schools*, AGPS, 1987, Ch 1; and Weisbrot, n 8, Ch 5. One possible difference of significance may be that statute law has always assumed a more central role in Australian law than in English law, and this centrality may be reflected in legal education here.

12   M Chesterman and D Weisbrot, "Legal Scholarship in Australia" (1987) 50 *Modern Law Review* 709.

13   One obvious reason *why* university legal education was regarded as sufficient non-clinical preparation for legal practice here was simply the absence of any long-standing tradition of apprenticeship training in Australia or professional training institutes. The universities were therefore asked to fill the gap. Disney et al, n 4, 254 note that law teaching was sponsored by the universities but in response to the demands of the legal professions and not as a result of university initiatives.

supplementation by courses at a professional training establishment. Accordingly, law degrees, to be recognised for admission purposes, had to contain more of the "practitioner" subjects, such as Evidence and Procedure, than their English counterparts.[14] This may have maintained Australian law schools even nearer to the "trade school" role than in England.

The consequence of all this is that for much of their history Australian law schools have seen their primary task as preparing students to practise law in their particular State or Territory. As with the provincial universities in England, many of the lecturers were part-time practitioners. Until the 1960s, there were few full-time legal academics in Australian law schools, with teaching regarded as a part-time activity of practitioners.[15] Furthermore, the *kind* of education carried out was based on the narrow ledge tradition of English legal training with its emphasis on pragmatic, inductive reasoning.[16] In fact, until the 1970s English textbooks were regularly set as prescribed texts in some common law subjects.

Certainly there has been change in recent years, and this book is a symptom of it. There is, in Le Brun and Johnstone's words, a "shifting paradigm in legal education".[17] Probably all law schools are now conscious of a need to break away from tradition, even if they have done so to varying extents.[18] The introduction of "contextual" material into law degrees has led to some resistance from the profession, however, as Chesterman and Weisbrot show. They quote a former President of the NSW Bar Association in 1983 as saying:

> In the whole of Australia ... there are only one or two academic teachers of any real value in real property, in contracts or in torts ... There are, to be sure, multitudes of academic homunculi who scribble and prattle relentlessly about such non-subjects as criminology, bail, poverty, consumerism, computers and racism. These may be dismissed from calculation: they possess neither practical skills nor legal learning. They are failed sociologists.[19]

Responding to this jibe in an essay titled "Failed Sociologists in the Market-place: Law Schools in Australia",[20] Andrew Goldsmith and Christine Parker conclude that the "failed sociologist model" is important because it brings the perspectives of other disciplines to bear in the study of law. They conclude that the debate about legal education circulates around an unhelpful polarity between

---

14 University education was not, however, a prerequisite for entry to the profession and apprenticeship through articles was for a long time the dominant alternative. Only in 1968 in New South Wales, for example, did the annual admission tip in favour of university graduates and even in 1978 nearly one third of entrants were without university degrees. Furthermore, we should not be understood as saying that Evidence and Procedure are unworthy of academic study. It depends on how they are taught.

15 A Goldsmith and C Parker, "Failed Sociologists in the Marketplace: Law Schools in Australia" (1998) 25(1) *Journal of Law and Society* 33 at 34.

16 Inductive reasoning involves inferring general laws from particular instances and is the hallmark of legal reasoning in the common law tradition. Deductive reasoning involves inferring from the general to the particular. The difference is discussed further in Chapter 11 when we look at differences in the methods of economists and lawyers.

17 M Le Brun and R Johnstone, *The Quiet Revolution*, Law Book Co, 1994, 26.

18 This consciousness exists amongst those who are not educational radicals, as Sampford and Wood note: see C Sampford and D Wood, "'Theoretical Dimensions' of Legal Education – A Response to the Pearce Report" (1988) 62 *Australian Law Journal* 32.

19 Note 12.

20 Goldsmith and Parker, n 15.

"academic" and "practical" objectives. The aim of their essay is to sketch a "transformative vision of legal education" in which the tension between academic and practical objectives, which daily confronts law students, teachers, practitioners and judges, should be embraced positively rather than negatively. They suggest that Australian law schools should reconstitute themselves by embracing and entrenching the following features:

- A broad conception of the legal knowledge which we are responsible for passing on, a knowledge based on a variety of disciplines from the humanities, social sciences and elsewhere, that allow law students to study the diverse meanings and consequences of law as a social and human variable in everyday life; and:

- An expanded conception of the field of legal practice for which we prepare our students so as to integrate a critically and ethically oriented understanding of how lawyers and others carry law and legal institutions into the communities in which they live and work.[21]

Understanding the legal system as a complex social phenomenon rather than simply as a set of legal rules requires engagement with a wide array of perspectives. Indeed, this advocacy for a new model of legal education can be seen in some, though not all of the recommendations of the 1987 Pearce Report, which emphasised the importance of "curricular and scholarly integration of theoretical and practical concerns".[22]

One way of promoting contextualisation of law and legal practice is to introduce clinical legal education and skills teaching. These are evidence of significant advances in thinking about the *methods* by which law should be taught and assessed. Such advances, in turn, will have some effect on how law in universities is conceptualised. We may now be entering a phase where syllabus content and teaching method progressively interact. As an illustration, assessable client interviewing, whether in a clinical or simulated setting, may enhance awareness of the difficulties that certain groups face in engaging with the legal system, perhaps because of their culture, poverty or language difficulties. Issues of culture and gender are also beginning to feature in the syllabi of individual subjects.[23] Provided that skills initiatives integrate perspectives from external disciplines, such as social psychology, gender studies, ethics and sociology, this is a helpful development. On the other hand, while the life of law is experience, skills exercises that contextualise legal practice through anecdotes and untested *perceptions* of what "works" are likely to perpetuate an unreflexive approach to law and lawyering.

The purpose of this discussion of the history of legal education, apart from the intrinsic interest of the subject, is to suggest reasons why a particular conception of the law and its study is still prominent in many law schools today. Sugarman's thesis is that the tradition of cautious systematising, which avoids the big philosophical and sociological questions but which fails also to track the processes and

---

21   Ibid 47.
22   Ibid 37.
23   A boost to this was provided by consultancies issued by the federal government in 1994 and 1995 to prepare materials for the law curriculum on gender and cross-cultural issues. The impact of these materials is discussed further in Chapter 8.

practices of law, stems partly from the "narrow ledge" that university law lecturers carved out for themselves in the search for legitimacy amongst both the academic and professional communities and partly from considerations of financial cost. Nevertheless, it is the case that many legal academics are stepping off that "narrow ledge", embracing a wider range of perspectives in their own research and teaching activities. Indeed, this change in scholarly environment led one senior lawyer to claim that "the dominant model of academic study and legal analysis now involves an attack on the social and political underpinnings of the law".[24] We should not overstate the impact of critical and contextual scholarship, nor understate the continuing influence of the profession on law and legal education – the senior lawyer making this claim teaches law part time in a leading law school, as well as actively contributing to scholarly discussion through his many legal publications. It is true, however, that an increasing number of scholars, judges and practitioners are recognising that contextual perspectives and other disciplines open fresh perspectives on law and legal change. Though unfamiliar and somewhat alien, they are not necessarily subversive supplements to law or legal education.[25]

We can add a further suggestion to this. Anglo-Australian law teaching took its shape in the late 19th century during the emergence of the Diceyan conception of the rule of law. A growing awareness of the practical and political importance of predictable judicial decision-making in liberal democratic states added impetus to the search for formalism.[26] In this sense, the traditions of modern legal education and legal culture are fundamentally liberal. A similar phenomenon took place in the United States, particularly at Harvard Law School under the Deanship of Christopher Langdell in the 1870s.[27] Led by Langdell, the academy came to focus increasing attention on "leading cases" as a vehicle for educating lawyers and as an object of academic analysis.[28] This methodology spawned the emergence of a self-conscious American "realist" movement, which introduced the realities of procedure and decision-making into the understanding of law.[29] This development was not paralleled in England or Australia.

In sum, all these forces have led, we believe, to the still prominent "laboratory" view of law in legal education[30] which rests on three assumptions.

---

24 S Odgers, "Book review: Principles of Criminal Law by S Bronitt and B McSherry" *Bar News NSW* Summer 2001, 2002, 66.

25 Roger Cotterrell in "Why Must Legal Ideas Be Interpreted Sociologically" (1998) 25 *Journal of Law and Society* 171 at 183 suggests that a socio-legal approach requires an appreciation of the political, social and cultural contexts of legal development, as well as a commitment to theorising law as a social phenomenon. Such sociological perspectives are not merely a "desirable supplement but an essential means of legal understanding": 192.

26 See Chapter 3 below for a discussion of formalism and the rule of law. The argument briefly is that courts should not make law, because that is the preserve of the legislature, but they should apply law in a predictable way so that people can plan their lives rationally. Formalistic legal reasoning is supposed to assist because it reduces the choices that are presented to judges.

27 See R Gerber, *Lawyers, Courts and Professionalism*, Greenwood, 1989, Ch 2 for a discussion of Langdell and subsequent developments in American legal education.

28 See AWB Simpson, *Leading Cases in the Common Law*, Oxford UP, 1995, 4-7 on the "invention" of the leading case.

29 For a cutting review of Langdell by one of the leading realists, see J Frank, "A Plea for Lawyer-Schools" (1947) 56 *Yale Law Journal* 1303.

30 Langdell once declared that the law library is "what the laboratory is to the chemist or the physicist and what the museum is to the naturalist"; see Frank, n 29, 1304.

The first assumption is that law is only about litigation. This is a convenient assumption because it is only from litigation that academics can easily obtain any data to systematise. In fact, much work done by lawyers is not about litigation at all. It is about "non-contentious" matters, such as drafting deeds and wills, property transactions and contractual negotiations.

The second assumption is that litigation means a trial or hearing. In fact, as we will see in Chapter 5, most civil disputes never reach a contested hearing. They are settled, abandoned or won by default. In those cases where court orders are actually made, many involve the mere rubber-stamping of settlements reached by the parties. It is commonly thought that less than 10 per cent of all cases go through to trial. In the criminal context, trials are a similar rarity, especially before a jury. Most matters are resolved by a guilty plea following "charge-bargaining" between the prosecutor and the defence.[31] As a result the legal rules (encapsulated in procedural, evidential and substantive legal definitions) operate primarily as "bargaining chips" for the police, prosecution and defence lawyers in negotiating charges and pleas.

One might go even further and suggest that law schools are preoccupied with *appeal* cases; a small minority of the minority of cases that reach the courts. This is partly so because appellate decisions are more likely to be reported and the only chemicals used in the laboratory are law reports (and statutes). A further virtue for the law school of what the American realists called "appellatitis" is that in appeal cases the "facts" are settled and only the principles of law – the workings of formalism – are in dispute. Many practitioners, even those who specialise in litigation, would say this is a reversal of the position in their working life. A good illustration of this is in an address given by RE Megarry, then a leading English barrister and subsequently an eminent judge, to the Society of Public Teachers of Law (a professional association for law lecturers). His theme was the difference between law as taught and law as practised and the extract below concerns the relationship between law and fact:

RE Megarry, "Law as Taught and Law as Practised"
(1967)

Put as a proposition, law as taught is mainly law, whereas law as practised is mainly facts. This proposition has five main aspects.

(a) There is a vast difference as regards to certainty. In the law school, the facts are always certain; any uncertainty is in the law. A problem question in an examination paper sets out the facts explicitly: the candidate merely has to wrestle with the law. In daily practice, the position is usually the reverse. So often the law is perfectly clear; the only question is what happened. If all the witnesses are to be believed, at the moment of impact both cars were stationary, each on its proper side of the road and displaying all the requisite lights. Once find the facts, and the law gives little enough trouble; but facts are the devil.

---

31   The term "plea bargaining" has been described as misleading in the Australian context where judges are not involved in brokering and approving the terms of these agreements. "Charge negotiation" better describes the common practice by which the prosecution may withdraw a charge on the promise that an accused will plead guilty to other charges: K Mack and S Anleu, "Reform of Pre-Trial Criminal Procedure: Guilty Pleas" (1998) 22 *Criminal Law Journal* 263. See also J Bishop, *Prosecution Without Trial*, Butterworths, 1989.

Many a solicitor has found that the extensive and detailed study of the law which, quite rightly, he had had to make in order to be admitted to the Rolls has set him free to live a life in which over 90 per cent of his time is devoted to facts and people and being business-like, with the law standing in the background, mute though omnipresent. If I may exaggerate a little, one may say that in law as taught the facts are clear and the law uncertain, whereas in law as practised the law is clear and the facts uncertain.

(b) There is also a difference as to the importance of the facts. In teaching law, the facts serve as a mere background for the law. One can roam at will, taking any convenient set of facts that will illustrate the operation of the law. Sometimes a simple set of imaginary facts illuminates a doctrine far better than the obscure complexities of the actual facts in the leading case. In practice, on the other hand, many cases are merely cases on fact; they alone matter. In other cases, the actual facts determine what rule of law will apply; every little fact must be cherished if it can by possibility affect the legal consequences.

(c) There is an important difference quoad relevance. In law as taught, the facts stated are nearly always all relevant. Most examiners play fair; usually all the facts stated in a problem question in an examination are relevant to the solution of the problem. Occasionally some wicked examiner will include some irrelevant fact, and watch the weaker candidates (and not them alone) in full pursuit of his red herring; but most examiners are benign. Text-books and lecturers alike normally refrain from a display of irrelevant facts; and even though some law reports take a generous view of what is relevant, the wind blows strongly against irrelevance. The student is thus nurtured in an atmosphere of unconscious assumption that what is stated is relevant; and this assumption is of a validity which is cousin to that of assumptions such as the ancient rule that anything which appears in print must be true.

The practitioner, on the other hand, spends a large part of his life in identi-fying and provisionally discarding the irrelevant. The client in his solicitor's chair tells all; and the solicitor takes perhaps a quarter of what he says as having some possible degree of relevance. In essence, much of the practice of law con-sists in provisionally throwing away most of the facts, examining the remainder with a microscope, and then erecting an imposing structure on the best-favoured of the residue. I say "provisionally" because every now and then a discarded fact is suddenly seen to be of great value in meeting some new or ill-perceived difficulty. But broadly speaking the precept "cut down and build up" is of the essence. Of all the qualities that a practitioner needs, a highly developed sense of relevance claims pride of place.

(d) A further distinction lies in completeness. The student can usually rely upon finding all the relevant facts stated in his examination question, by his lecturer, or in his text-book or report. There are, of course, examiners who some-times deliberately omit one vital fact from a question, so as to call for an "It depends" answer; and I would applaud. But this is the exception rather than the rule. Practitioners, on the other hand, would be delighted to feel assured that no more than one important fact is missing, instead of half a dozen or more. Often it is not until one is enmeshed in the thickets of cross-examination that one begins to suspect that ahead lie riches. At earlier stages, the solicitor will often find that one witness or document serves mainly to lead him on to others; and the tally of facts is not finally closed until judgment, and occasionally not even then.

(e) Lastly under this head, there is the element of time. The student lives in a world of ascertained facts. He has to apply his law to the complete and relevant facts stated by the question, lecture, text-book or report beyond the peradventure of argument. The work has been done before he begins. The practitioner, on the other hand, often lives in a world of provisional facts. The advocate in a trial court must prepare himself to argue his case not merely on the basis of the facts for which he contends, but also on the basis of those facts for which his adversary is contending, as well as on the basis of any selection of the facts put forward by each side which the judge might conceivably find. The student always argues a known set of facts, the practitioner often on a variety of possible sets of facts. Put another way, the student leads an appellate life, free from the uncertainties of a hearing at first instance. In saying this I leave out of account some of the actual facts of appellate life, such as finding at the last minute that an appeal set down for hearing before Lords Justices A, B and C is to be transferred to Lords Justices D, E and F (before whom a case has collapsed), leaving counsel for the appellant to reflect that the type of approach which he had hoped would commend itself to A, B and C, LJJ is likely to sit pretty sourly on the stomachs of D, E and F, LJJ.[32]

In the above extract Megarry refers to the practitioner living in the world of provisional facts. William Twining, amongst other things a leading scholar of the law of evidence, has for many years been arguing that we should take facts seriously. In the extract below he tells the fictional story of the establishment of a new law school which decides to call its graduates "Doctors of Facts", because that is what lawyers essentially are.

W Twining, "Taking Facts Seriously"
(1982) (footnotes omitted)

Once upon a time, on the eastern seaboard of Xanadu, a brand new law school was established. An innovative, forward-looking, dynamic young dean was appointed and he quickly recruited a team of innovative, forward-looking dynamic young colleagues in his own image. At the first faculty meeting – there were as yet no students to complicate matters – the only item on the agenda was, naturally, curriculum. The dean opened the proceedings: "Persons", he said, "there is only one question facing us today: What can we do that is new, creative, innovative, path-breaking ...?" His colleagues nodded assent; being young and forward-looking they had not yet learned that even in legal education there is nothing new under the sun. Suggestions followed quickly: law and the social sciences; a clinical program; psycho-legal studies; eco-law; computer-based instruction; law and development; and many of the fads, fashions, follies, and frolics of the 1970s and 1960s, and even some from the 1950s (for how far back does the history of legal education stretch?), were all quickly rejected as old hat. They were, in Brainerd Currie's phrase, "trite symbols of frustration". For our subject is governed by a paradox: in general education there is no reported example of an experiment that has ended in failure; in academic law no movement or program has ever achieved success.

Eventually the Oldest Member spoke up. He had actually looked backward into past numbers of the Journal of Legal Education and other forgotten sources:

"It was once suggested that 90 percent of lawyers spend 90 percent of their time handling facts and that this ought to be reflected in their training. If 81 percent of lawyer-time is spent on one thing, it follows that 81 percent of legal education ought to be devoted to it. There have been some isolated

32 RE Megarry, "Law as Taught and Law as Practised" (1967) 9 *Society of Public Teachers of Law Journal* 176.

courses on fact-finding and the like, but no institution has had a whole program in which the main emphasis was on facts. I propose that we base our curriculum on this principle and that we call our degree a Bachelor of Facts".

Opposition to this proposal was immediate and predictable.

"We do it already".

"Illiberal!"

"It's only common sense, therefore it is unteachable".

"Fact-finding can only be learned by experience".

"None of us is competent to teach it".

"There are no books".

"You cannot study facts in isolation from law".

"It would not be law; law schools should only teach law".

"The students would not find it interesting or easy".

"The concept of a fact is a crude positivist fiction".

"Who would want to go through life labelled a BF?"

The Oldest Member was an experienced academic politician; he had studied not only the Journal of Legal Education but also Cornford's Microcosmographica Academica which, as you know, is our special supplement to Machiavelli's The Prince. Adapting the tactic of the Irrelevant Rebuttal, he seized on the objection to the title of the degree and made a crucial concession: "It need not be a bachelor's degree", he said, "there are good American precedents for calling the undergraduate law degree a doctorate. To call our graduates Doctors of Facts will not only attract students and attention, it will also signal that we are well aware that reality is a social construction and not something out there waiting to be found".

The opposition having been routed, a curriculum committee was set up to work out the details. To their surprise they learned that the range of potential courses was virtually limitless and, what is more, that there already existed an enormous, if scattered, literature. They submitted a detailed plan for the curriculum, including a full range of options, and added a recommendation that the length of the degree should be increased to five years.[33]

The third assumption on which the laboratory view of legal education rests is that lawyers are mere neutral agents and not worthy of study in their own right. The limited amount of research carried out on how lawyers relate to their clients, however, suggests that lawyers are more than mere alter egos of their clients. The culture, organisation and behaviour of lawyers may actually affect outcomes. Perhaps one should begin with the proposition "that law is not what judges say in the reports but what lawyers say – to one another and to clients – in their offices".[34]

(c) The approach of this book

Many of the above ideas are taken up in one way or another in subsequent chapters. In Part A we look at "Law in a Political Context". Chapter 2 sets out the core elements of liberalism as a political theory and is intended as a foundational

---

33   W Twining, "Taking Facts Seriously" in N Gold (ed), *Essays on Legal Education*, Butterworths, 1982, 51-52.

34   M Shapiro, "On the Regrettable Decline of Law French: or Shapiro Jettet Le Brickbat" (1981) 90 *Yale Law Journal* 1198 at 1201.

chapter. Since about the 18th century the formal law of countries like America, Australia, Britain and Canada has been shaped by certain powerful ideals. These liberal ideals, which are not shared by all nations, nor even by all citizens in those countries, involve particular conceptions of individual liberty, equality and rationality: conceptions that are interwoven in laws and procedures.

The coherence and desirability of liberalism came under attack in the 1980s from radical legal scholars associated with the Critical Legal Studies (CLS) movement.[35] Not surprisingly for a movement within law schools, their immediate targets were legal reasoning and the rule of law. They purported to show that legal reasoning does not proceed in the predictable formal fashion that liberal legalists supposedly claim. This in turn is said to undermine the more general ideal of the rule of law – that judges impartially apply pre-given norms in a way that one can rationally anticipate – and from there we are led into more profound problems of liberalism as a way of ordering and evaluating the world. A leading exponent of CLS, American criminal lawyer Mark Kelman typified this approach by exposing, through close textual analysis, the internal "politics" of legal discourse. His internal (or "immanent") critique unmasked the indeterminacy and contradictions of "general principles" in the criminal law. It may be fairly said that the movement paid insufficient attention to developing an "external critique", or to engage in normative reconstruction within the structures of the law. As Lacey concludes, developing an internal critique requires engagement with a broader set of "historical, political, and social questions about the conditions and existence and efficacy of particular doctrinal arrangements".[36] While it presents challenges to master so many disciplines, recent critical scholarship has begun to challenge this much more seriously. In Chapter 3 we consider "Formalism and the Rule of Law", not particularly because it was a CLS focus, but because an understanding of legal reasoning and the central role of law in liberal societies is an essential part of legal education.

Whereas Part A tends to look at law through the prism of political theory, Part B, The Processes of Law, has concerns which are also sociological. In Chapter 4, we consider problems of access to justice. Who uses law in practice? What barriers are there to accessing the legal system? Should we be seeking to remove these barriers in an effort to promote access to justice, or can justice be promoted partly by side-stepping the formal legal system altogether? The questions in this chapter lead us into an examination of Litigation, in Chapter 5. Rather than focus on the law reports of appellate cases, this chapter considers what we know about the realities of using the court system; whether in criminal or civil matters. These realities give us a rather different view of the "adversarial system" than we might have acquired from some introductory legal texts. Whether or not the system is truly adversarial, it is clear that lawyers are its "gatekeepers". Only to a limited

---

35   For a bibliography of CLS writing up until 1984, see A Hunt, "Critical Legal Studies: A Bibliography" (1984) 47 *Modern Law Review* 369 and, for a more recent guide, see RW Bauman, *Critical Legal Studies: A Guide to the Literature*, Westview Press, 1996. For general discussions, see A Hunt, "The Theory of Critical Legal Studies" (1986) 6 *Oxford Journal of Legal Studies* 1 and "The Critique of Law: What is 'Critical' about Critical Legal Theory?" (1987) 14 *Journal of Law and Society* 5; and M Tushnet, "Critical Legal Studies: An Introduction to its Origins and Underpinnings" (1986) 36 *Journal of Legal Education* 505.

36   N Lacey, "Legal Constructions of Crime" in M Maguire, R Morgan and R Reiner (eds), *The Oxford Handbook of Criminology*, 3rd ed, Oxford UP, 2002, 277.

extent can a citizen or corporate body make effective use of the law without calling on the assistance of a lawyer. Chapter 6 studies lawyers as actors in the legal system in their own right. What do we know of their relationship with clients? How do they portray the legal system to their clients? What ethical principles are they supposed to obey? Are these principles adequate?

In Part C of the book, Law and Power, we move away from the law courts and ask some larger questions about law and where it comes from. In Chapter 7 we note that, whilst political scientists regard issues of power as central to their discipline, legal education has tended to take a rather two-dimensional approach to power. Power is something that is constrained by law, even though particular powers, in the plural, are created by law. More adventurous scholarship has suggested that the relationship between law and power is more complex and we seek to introduce that scholarship here. From here the Chapter moves on to ask what it is that prompts the introduction of laws? Are they simply the disinterested product of parliamentarians and public servants, following informed debates about the public interest? Or are other forces at work? Because it is impossible to give an answer that can account for each and every law, scholars have tended to adopt models or theories of society which, they say, best fit the facts. For example, the more one believes that societies are made up of conflicting groups and classes, the more likely one is to regard the production of laws as bound up in the conflict. At the most extreme, law is seen as a tool of the ruling classes which is used to perpetuate their dominance. Even after a law is enacted, there is no reason to suppose that it will operate in the manner intended; nor that it will have a non-discriminatory impact. In Chapters 8 and 9 we pursue these questions of inequality, particularly by reference to scholarship about gender and indigenous peoples.

Part D, Law and Regulation, picks up some of the themes raised in Chapter 7 and looks directly at the relationship between law and regulation in modern society. Chapter 10 introduces the general themes and issues, drawing on recent sociological and political theory about regulation. Because we have dealt more extensively with sociological perspectives earlier in the book, the remaining chapters in this Part focus on what economists have had to say about the role of law as a regulatory mechanism. We ask questions about the extent to which contract and tort law can be seen to promote the efficient allocation of liability. We consider whether the common law system of case-by-case development is a singularly good way of promoting efficient outcomes in changing circumstances. In Chapter 13 we return to questions which have a more obvious political character. We introduce the reader to some economic theories about how and why government regulation comes about.

A recurrent method of the book is to take an ideal and contrast it with what appears to be the reality. For example, in Chapter 2 we look at philosophical underpinnings of law, and how liberalism emphasises, in particular, the central importance of liberty and liberal values (relating to autonomy, privacy and equality etc). Liberal is not a perfect blueprint for law and, as we outline in Chapter 2 and subsequent chapters, the law does not always live up to its liberal rhetoric. This use of empiricism is a common enough method in the social sciences as a way of explicating the complexity of social life but it has a particular pedigree in the analysis of law, broadly falling under the banner of socio-legal methodology. Law can be seen as a collection of prescriptions about what *ought* to happen (although this is only one way of seeing law) so it is not surprising that some scholars have asked whether it *does* happen. And, of course, these questions are not asked simply out of idle curiosity. They are intensely practical ones for a society's government and bureaucracy. One particularly famous formulation of this contrast is that of the American sociological jurist Roscoe Pound (1870-1964) who talked of the gap between "law in the books" and "law in action".[37] The resurgence of "socio-legal studies" in the 1960s brought with it a renewed interest in the nature of this gap, but a reaction then set in as the limitations of "gap theory" became apparent. Because our method is largely one of investigating gaps between law and practice, or the rhetoric and reality, if only as a device to expose law students to other views, it is appropriate that we acknowledge two of these limitations in particular.[38]

The first criticism of this approach challenges the *significance* attached to the gap. Rather than constituting a legal "con-trick", the gap may be viewed as simply an acknowledgement that law operates in a real world context. To identify a gap between law and practice is merely to acknowledge that the world is an imperfect place, which is hardly news. Law projects a normative ideal, which is rarely perfected in practice, honoured more in the breach than the observance. Whilst we acknowledge the force of this argument, the point we make is that the "gap" is not a failing or deficiency, but rather says something about how law is constituted. Focusing on this deviation reveals the complex moral, social and political values that are in contestation when people debate "the law question".[39] On a practical level, an empirical approach to law can produce better policy-making and law reform – it serves to counteract the belief of lawyers, judges as well as legislators, that significant social and cultural change can be effected through legal inter-vention.[40] An empirical orientation necessarily focused attention on what happens "on the streets" and in the lawyer's office, as well in the lower courts. Since much legal education ignores questions of the "law in action" we believe empirical perspectives provide a critical antidote to the implicit message that law is what happens in the appellate courts. Silbey and Sarat have said that "the law and society movement began as an attempt not to be deceived".[41] This book is designed to help readers decide whether legal discourse is engaged in a deception or, put more positively, is not providing the full story.

The second criticism of socio-legal studies is that it takes a simplistic view of "law". Law is taken to be an identifiable thing that can be used instrumentally to achieve certain goals. Taking this view makes it easier for the gap theorist to find out whether "it" works in the manner intended. The criticism, however, is that law is much more complex than that. A perennial question within legal philosophy and

---

37 See, for example, "Law in Books and Law in Action" (1910) 44 *American Law Review* 12.

38 Useful discussions of the limitations of gap theory can be found in D Nelken, "The 'Gap Problem' in the Sociology of Law: A Theoretical Review" (1981) 1 *Windsor Yearbook of Access to Justice* 35 and A Sarat, "Legal Effectiveness and Social Studies of Law: On the Unfortunate Persistence of a Research Tradition" (1985) IX *Legal Studies Forum* 23.

39 A term we borrow from M Davies, *Asking the Law Question: The Dissolution of Legal Theory*, 2nd ed, Law Book Co, 2002.

40 A Ashworth, "Editorial – The Value of Empirical Research in Criminal Justice" [1997] *Crim Law Review* 533.

41 SS Silbey and A Sarat, "Critical Traditions in Law and Society Research" (1987) 21 *Law and Society Review* 165 at 166.

the sociology of law is the definitional one: what *is* law? Where does it begin and end? Is there an "it" to be described, or should we be talking about the divergent practices of lawyers, judges, police and officials? William Twining requires his first year law students to read a single issue of a non-tabloid newspaper and mark every passage which deals directly with law or is law-related.

> The newspaper exercise is intended as an eye-opener. It should serve to convey a number of simple messages about their subject to first year law students: about the pervasiveness of law in society, its dynamism, its international character, its diversity and its potential interest.[42]

We approach "law" in this spirit. We hope to have avoided an unduly static view of it but we have been conscious also that this is an introductory text. Our aim is to alert newcomers to some of the difficult but fascinating issues in studying law rather than to attempt a full resolution of them. We are conscious that the very title of the book "Law in Context" implies a separation of law from its context and that this is a debatable proposition. We hope the material that follows will help the reader engage in an informed debate about the answer.

Questions

1. Read a newspaper and mark every passage which deals directly with law or is law-related. What images of law are being projected in these reports?

2. An increasing number of law students are engaged in combined degrees, or pursuing law degrees after completing another degree. What influence, if any, should students' other courses bring to their study of law?

---

42   W Twining, *Blackstone's Tower*, Stevens & Sons, 1994, 9.

Chapter 2

Law's Blueprints:
The Political and Philosophical
Foundations of Law

(a) Introduction

This chapter traces how political philosophical ideas have shaped the development of modern law and legal traditions in countries such as Australia, Canada, New Zealand, the United Kingdom and the United States of America. While the law has developed differently in each of these jurisdictions, some of the fundamental values between them are shared. At the forefront of these legal cultures have been the political values of "liberalism".

Liberalism at its heart posits the view of rational person or legal subject – perhaps famously embodied in the standards imposed by the "reasonable person" that inhabits the law of negligence and criminal law doctrine. These ideas, however, were forged in an era where law was constructed around a set of liberal values – certainty, coherence and rationality being vaunted as fundamental legal principles. They also underlie the rule of law, with its strong commitment to legality which is further explored in Chapter 3. In addition to the values of legality, a distinctive aspect of liberalism is that it views certain interests, such as personal autonomy and property, as paramount.

The impact of liberal theory (and the particular values and interests it protects) is felt in many compartments of law – they are imprinted on parts of the criminal law, contracts and torts, as well as administrative and constitutional law. Students reading law for the first time must be conscious that the impact and influence of liberal theory may not be explicit. Indeed, theoretical perspectives are often downplayed in legal analysis, both in conventional academic and judicial writing. When these fundamental values are acknowledged they are represented being timeless, universal truths, packaged either as "commonsense" or "conventional legal wisdom". This approach denies the historical specificity and cultural contingency of these ideas, most of which, as we explore below, were forged in the writings of 19th century theorists.

Liberalism may pervade law and legal culture, but it is rarely beyond contestation, either morally or politically. Indeed, a significant portion of critical scholarship and "law in context" studies has been devoted to exposing those instances where law fails to live up to its liberal rhetoric – typically revealing "the gap" between "law in the books" and "law in action". Liberal scholars regard "the

gap" as a failure in the law, characterised as "exceptions" or remediable deroga-
tions. Critical scholars, by contrast, regard this tension as something constitutive
of law *itself*.[1] Indeed, the tension exposes the wider range of political and moral
interests at play. In many fields, such as criminal law, individual interests relating
to property and personal autonomy are much vaunted in legal doctrine. Upon
closer doctrinal scrutiny we discover that in many instances these values are
balanced or traded against competing moral values and the public interest. Indeed,
the clash of political and moral ideals around liberalism, the contested definitions
and interests at stake, will be explored through our case study on the legal
regulation of pornography below

In sum, there are at least four benefits in critically analysing liberal ideas. The
first is to help students appreciate the extent to which modern common law
systems are built around ideas which are historically and culturally specific. The
second is to show, in this and later chapters, that these ideas may still be hotly
contested and that the contests affect law as well as everyday political debate. The
third is to enable us to contrast the ideal of the law with its actuality and thus
introduce students to literature on the actual workings of law and the legal system.
Finally, an analysis of liberalism and its limitations exposes students to at least
some of the concerns of legal and political philosophy; subjects they may
encounter later in their studies. At the outset we should say that there is nothing
wrong with striving for a law that promotes liberal values such as certainty or
freedom. Indeed, we shall explore below how republican theorists have set out to
rehabilitate liberalism as a normative guide for the criminal law and criminal
justice reform, though these new blueprints have been modelled around a new idea
of social freedom that is less individualist, and more conscious of the structural
inequalities facing citizens, particularly from disadvantaged communities. Liberal
values may be represented as universal truths – upon closer scrutiny, we reveal
that they are really normative ideals or models which are politically and morally
contestable.

The relationship between liberalism, or any political philosophy, and law is a
complex one. The danger in introducing it at all is that some readers might take
the exercise too literally. To be clear, we do not claim that an understanding of
liberal thought will enable one to understand all the branches and details of laws.
Liberalism itself, as we will see, comes in many versions or mixes. It does not
necessarily lead to any specific set of laws. Other ideologies, for example
socialism and feminism, feature in the societies we are considering and some laws
are the product of gains by these movements. Nor are we saying that merely
because a law might contradict liberal thinking that it is somehow invalid (in the
sense that it would not be enforced in the courts). The exercise we are embarking
upon is one at a high level of generality and is designed to throw light upon law
rather than offer a theory of it.

---

1   P Fitzpatrick, "Law and Societies" (1984) 22(1) *Osgoode Hall Law Journal* 128.

(b) What is liberalism?

The political philosopher Alan Ryan has said that it is easy to list famous liberals but harder to say what they have in common.[2] In this chapter we attempt to list what we regard as key elements of liberalism. Although there are undoubtedly major differences between liberal thinkers over some of them, most would agree that these are the elements which, in some version or another, go to make up the liberal view of the world. Our exercise is similar to constructing a photo-fit picture of a wanted person. A limited number of features are accentuated for the purposes of recognition, although no one would argue that it is a portrait that captures the fine lines of the subject, and there may be disagreement as to the accuracy of the likeness.

"Liberalism" is the label given to the dominant ideology of modern western society dating from about the 17th century,[3] although it was only in the early 19th century that people sharing the ideology came to be described as liberals. Since then a variety of labels have been used to describe different kinds of liberals and it is as well to be on one's guard. In the United States, for example, the term "liberal" is often reserved specifically for the left-leaning person who favours government intervention in order to correct social inequalities. The word "libertarian" is then applied to the right-leaning person who places more emphasis on individual freedom from government action than on equality. In Australia, Britain and some other western countries, the picture is further confused because there are political parties who have taken the name liberal in their title and there can be considerable differences of policy between them. There may also be an historical dimension. For instance, the Liberal Party of 19th century Britain had a significantly different view about the proper sphere of state action than their successors, now called the Liberal Democrats.

Liberalism can be contrasted with ideologies like "absolutism" – a belief in unlimited government[4] – and "socialism" – a belief in collective ownership of productive assets. Increasingly today it is also possible to describe certain kinds of feminism as ideologies which are opposed to liberalism.

In the Australian context, all the main political parties represented in the federal legislature can be described as liberal in the sense that we are using the term, although there are individual members of these parties whose views may cross the boundaries of liberalism. We see liberal beliefs as spanning a continuum from conservatism[5] at one end through libertarianism to social democracy at the

---

2 A Ryan, "Liberalism" in R Goodin and P Pettit (eds), *A Companion to Contemporary Political Philosophy*, Blackwells, 1993, 291.

3 The word "liberal" as a social distinction seems to have come into English in the 14th century to differentiate free men (sic) from others. In the European revolutions from the mid-17th to mid-19th centuries social orders based on privilege and hierarchy were purportedly overturned by those based on liberty and equality.

4 Words like dictatorship and totalitarianism could also be used in place of absolutism. They too carry implications of government controlling everything.

5 Provided, at least, that it falls short of endorsing entrenched hierarchy and inequality. Literature in the United States tends more often to differentiate conservatives from liberals but that may be because the term "liberal" is given a specific application there. In Anglo-Australian political culture many conservatives have standard liberal beliefs about the economy but are prepared to countenance greater state authority on moral and social issues such as religion and the family. For a clear discussion, see R Leach, *Political Ideologies*, 2nd ed, Macmillan, 1993, Ch 2.

other end.[6] Whilst this is inevitably rather vague, when we look at some elements of liberalism below things should come into clearer focus.

Liberalism is normally taken to include some form of market-based or capitalist economy and some form of political democracy, although early forms of liberalism were neither capitalist nor democratic in the modern sense and even today there is considerable diversity in economic and political structure between liberal societies.[7] The so-called New Right governments of Ronald Reagan in the United States and Margaret Thatcher in the United Kingdom, for example, were said to be neo-classical[8] liberal governments in that they aspired to bring about modern versions of 19th century liberalism and overturn half a century or more of social democratic policies and attitudes. Even then, there were significant differences between the policies pursued by the two governments (and many of those policies were a long way from 19th century ones).[9]

If we turn our attention to law, it is probably easier to identify those matters over which there is stronger consensus. All liberals unite on the rule of law ideal even if, as we will see in Chapter 3, there is some disagreement about everything that it entails. The rule of law expresses, amongst other things, the liberal's suspicion of state authority by requiring that government takes place under law and through law. Furthermore, as we will also see in Chapter 3, law is to be applied in a formalistic way so that its use can be predicted in advance and its justifications challenged later.

All liberals also unite on the need for law to preserve the liberty of the individual from the encroachments of others. On the other hand, the differences between liberals over the permissible *scope* of law and the appropriate method of legal reasoning can be quite marked. Is law to be used only to provide a neutral framework within which individuals can peacefully pursue their separate ends? Or is law to be used as a tool of social engineering towards certain collective ends? These theoretical choices reflect an important difference within liberal philosophy which we will touch upon below when we discuss the competing values of rights and utility.

We hope to show in the sections that follow that whilst certain beliefs and attitudes can usefully be grouped together and described as liberalism, there is no pure or correct version. Many would acknowledge that there are tensions within liberalism. Others, notably the Critical Legal Studies movement, would say that there is a fundamental contradiction within it: that it is incapable of generating a

---

6   Provided, at least, that collective ownership and control is in the context of a mixed economy. In the Anglo-Australian context one stops being a liberal when social democracy shades into democratic socialism. See generally, N MacCormick, *Legal Right and Social Democracy*, Oxford UP, 1982.

7   Liberalism and democracy are conceptually distinct in that liberalism is a total ideology (in the sense defined earlier in this chapter) whereas democracy is a political system. Most socialists would argue that a socialist society would be democratic, although it would obviously not be liberal. Indeed, many socialists claim that liberalism and democracy are a contradiction in terms. Even liberal democrats themselves recognise that liberalism and democracy are not only distinct but can come into conflict. Thus a democratic state could decide to infringe individual liberties in a way that could not be countenanced by a liberal; see C Kukathas, DW Lovell and W Maley, *The Theory of Politics: An Australian Perspective*, Longman Cheshire, 1990, 4 and I Berlin, "Two Concepts of Liberty" in *Four Essays on Liberty*, Oxford UP, 1969, 118 at 129.

8   "Classical" here meaning pure, or of its class.

9   See DS King, *The New Right*, Macmillan, 1987, Ch 2.

coherent code by which we should live.[10] Our aim is not to play down these differences. In fact, one might say that the undoubted gap between law as it appears in the books and the law as it happens in practice can partly be explained by the uncertainties of liberalism itself. At any rate, this thought throws light on questions such as how the law in liberal societies can manifestly fail to correct sexual and racial inequality.

Whatever position one takes on these issues, there is little doubt that the structure of modern law in countries like Australia – its divisions between contract and tort and crime, its notions of responsibility and excuse, and so forth – were crucially formed during the middle part of the 19th century and the heyday of classical liberalism.[11] By approaching the context of law through the prism of liberal philosophy we obtain insights into orthodox legal thought and practices and into the ways that they might be changing.

(c) Elements of liberalism

In this section we list some key elements of liberalism. It is appropriate to begin with three ideals which were prominent historically in Europe and North America in the struggles to break away from a traditional social order based on hierarchy, privilege and status: the ideals of liberty, individualism and equality.

(i) Liberty

All liberals believe that people are by nature free. The word "liberal" itself derives from the notion of liberty (in the sense of being unenslaved). A working assumption in liberal thought is that people owe no obligations unless they have freely entered into agreements with each other. Any obligations which are said to flow other than from agreement, therefore, need to be carefully justified. These propositions can only operate as starting points, however, because liberty or freedom means different things to different people.

(ii) Negative liberty

In classical liberalism, freedom is the absence of external constraint; in particular, constraints imposed by the State, groups or powerful people. This idea of negative liberty ("freedom from") is often seen to be in conflict with that of positive liberty ("freedom to").[12] With negative liberty the State is not seen to be under an obliga-

---

10 See, for example, RM Unger, "Liberal Political Theory" in A Hutchinson (ed), *Critical Legal Studies*, Rowan and Littlefield, 1989, Ch 2. In *Crime, Reason and History*, 2nd ed, Butterworths, 2001, Alan Norrie uses legal history to critique the modern principles of criminal responsibility. His study reveals that the criminal law's commitment to subjectivism, rather than being a timeless and universal principle of "mens rea", was formed in the crucible of social and political forces in the 19th century, which remains, in the 21st century, the site of continuing struggle and contradiction.

11 See WR Cornish and G de N Clark, *Law and Society in England 1750-1950*, Sweet and Maxwell, 1989, especially 60-74. See also PS Atiyah, "Contracts, Promises, and the Law of Obligations" in *Essays on Contract*, Clarendon, 1986, Ch 2.

12 The classic discussion of these two conceptions of liberty is that of Sir Isaiah Berlin, see n 7. For a collection of essays which explores liberty and its relationship with law, see S Ratnapala and G Moens, *Jurisprudence of Liberty*, Butterworths, 1996.

tion to give positive *assistance* to the individual to help them realise their aims, but it is obliged to refrain from interfering in the individual's own attempts to do so and it should help protect the individual from the interference of others. Historically, however, liberal societies have moved from the mere protection of negative liberties to the promotion of positive ones. The notion of a welfare state can be seen to represent the belief that concrete assistance may be necessary to help people exercise their freedom.

The social philosopher LT Hobhouse in 1911 described the "Liberalizing Movement" as assailing the old order by advancing various spheres of liberty.[13] These included civil liberty, fiscal liberty, personal liberty, social liberty, economic liberty, domestic liberty and local, racial and national liberty. Demands for the first two of these (civil and fiscal liberty) were instrumental in bringing about the significant political revolutions that shaped the modern western world.

The idea of "civil liberty" was a demand to be freed from arbitrary control by government. It is reflected in the "rule of law", a phrase coined by English constitutional law scholar, AV Dicey, writing in the late 19th century.[14] The concept secures legitimation of state power by purporting to constrain its arbitrary exercise in a number of ways. A key idea is that no person should be punished except for a breach of law established in the ordinary manner before the courts. Another important component is that no person is above the law – that every person is subject to these laws without exception, thus ensuring equality before the law. Judges are required to do justice according to the law, rather than by reference to arbitrary and discretionary notions of fairness, morality or "the good". Many of these ideas are now bundled together in the rule of law ideal, which is further discussed in Chapter 3.

The modern conception of civil liberties involves a longer list of individual rights. These include the right to liberty and security of the person, rights to property and privacy, right to a fair trial and the rights to free speech and peaceful assembly, and many more. These civil and political rights, now framed as "human rights", are protected by numerous international treaties, including the *International Covenant on Civil and Political Rights* (ICCPR) to which Australia is party.

Unlike Canada, New Zealand, the United Kingdom and the United States of America, Australia has not yet adopted a national Bill of Rights. Even the United Kingdom, which traditionally had a deep scepticism towards Bills of Rights, has adopted the *Human Rights Act 1998*. The Australian Capital Territory is the only local jurisdiction to adopt this model of human rights protection.[15] Rather than constitutionally entrench human rights as overriding, this path-breaking legislation

---

13   *Liberalism*, 1911.

14   See AV Dicey, *Introduction to the Study of the Law of the Constitution*, 10th ed, Macmillan, 1959, 202-203. The idea of rule by law rather than by men has an older lineage traceable to the Magna Carta (1215), the Glorious Revolution (1688) and the United States Declaration of Independence (1776) and Constitution (1787). For an essay examining the rule of law, see D Clark, "The Many Meanings of the Rule of Law" in K Jayasuriya (ed), *Law, Capitalism and Power in Asia*, Routledge, 1999.

15   *Human Rights Act 2004* (ACT); in December 2005 the Attorney-General of Victoria announced the State Government would enact a charter of human rights and responsibilities in 2006, following the recommendations of the Human Rights Consultation Committee in *Rights, Responsibilities and Respect*, Victoria, 2005.

requires the courts to adopt an interpretation of existing laws that is consistent with the human rights (drawn from the ICCPR) and, if this is not possible, to make a declaration of incompatibility: ss 30 and 32 respectively. Like the UK Act, the ACT *Human Rights Act* does not permit the courts to invalidate legislation that is inconsistent with human rights but, consistent with parliamentary supremacy, places the responsibility for amending the law upon the ACT Legislative Assembly.

The idea of "domestic liberty" has a number of components. From the earliest liberal philosophers there came the belief that social life was to be seen as divided into public and private spheres. The private, or domestic, sphere was an area that should be none of the "law's business", where "the King's writ did not run". In relation to the legal protection conferred on property, this is captured in the famous aphorism that an "Englishman's home is his castle". It extended to domestic relationships within the family, to servants and other affective relationships such as friendship. Thus it was not sufficient that a government act lawfully (or "constitutionally" as we might now say) because there are certain matters in which it should not act at all, on which there should be no laws.

Some definitions of the "private sphere" have included the market as well[16] and this leads us to economic liberty. The history of liberalism in England and the United States until well into the 19th century was one of attacks on government intervention in economic activity. Beginning with attacks on state-provided monopolies and culminating with the partial (and in England almost complete) removal of tariffs and other forms of protectionism, classical liberalism came to be associated with the belief that people (or at least, men) were to have equal liberty to trade goods, services and labour within the framework of a minimal set of laws to protect property and so forth. Beyond that, the state should have no role.

Finally, Hobhouse's list included local, racial and national liberty. Although liberalism has historically been a liberating movement at the national level, it has certainly not always been egalitarian as between peoples. Hobhouse expressed the liberal uncertainties of his age:

> A specious extension of the white man's rights to the black may be the best way of ruining the black ... Until the white man has fully learnt to rule his own life, the best of all things that he can do with the dark man is to do nothing with him. In this relation, the day of a more constructive Liberalism is yet to come.[17]

When we look at questions of law and race in Chapter 9 we will be asking how it is that an apparently liberal society such as Australia could tolerate past and present treatment of Aborigines. One possible answer lies in the liberal attitude to race in the first place and its assumption that the higher liberties were to be reserved for those with certain moral and mental capabilities.

A key principle for protecting the negative sphere of liberty outlined above is the "harm principle". This principle addresses the proper province of government action in a range of fields, most prominently criminal law. The idea is that individual liberty should not be curtailed simply to promote public morals, the welfare of the majority or the interests of the state. As a principle of political philosophy,

---

16   See F Olsen, "The Family and the Market: A Study of Ideology and Law Reform" (1983) 96 *Harvard Law Review* 1497.

17   Note 13, 27.

this idea was championed in the mid-19th century by John Stuart Mill (1806-79) in *On Liberty*.[18] The relevant passage from the first chapter of *On Liberty* is this:

> The object of this essay is to assert one very simple principle, as entitled to govern absolutely the dealings of society with the individual in the way of compulsion and control, whether the means used be physical force in the form of legal penalties or the moral coercion of public opinion. That principle is that the sole end for which mankind are warranted, individually or collectively, in interfering with the liberty of action of any of their number is self-protection. *That the only purpose for which power can be rightfully exercised over any member of a civilized community, against his will, is to prevent harm to others.* His own good, either physical or moral, is not a sufficient warrant.[19]

As Alan Norrie notes in *Crime, Reason and History*, the harm principle is a product of 19th century liberalism, reflecting a view that the social world is founded upon individual self-interest and rights.[20] It aims to accommodate the principal concerns of the state whilst respecting individual freedom and autonomy. This principle has been used to justify in some cases, or to rule out in others, state intervention in many social controversies. The decriminalisation of homosexual activities and prostitution between consenting adults, for example, has commonly been justified on the basis that it is an exercise of sexual liberty that causes no harm to others.[21] It has also provided the philosophical framework for debating law reform relating to pornography, discussed below.

Of course there is plenty of room for questioning the meaning and scope of "harm", including the following:

- What types of harm should be included (physical, psychological, economic or environmental harm)?
- To what extent, if at all, does the principle accommodate conduct involving potential harm?
- Does it extend to indirect harm?

As we shall explore below, this argument is often used by feminists to justify tighter criminal regulation of pornography – such material is claimed to cause harm indirectly by increasing the likelihood of sexual assault or perpetuating discrimination against women. Other scholars have argued for the criminalisation of racial vilification on the ground that it is necessary to prevent harm in the form of "psychic injury".

The difficulty from a liberal perspective is that these expanded notions of harm significantly weaken the harm principle as a means of maximising individual freedom and curbing state power. Harm seems to be both indeterminate and highly elastic. It seems hard to escape from the fact that the concept of harm is "morally loaded", as Neil MacCormick noted in *Legal Right and Social Democracy*,[22] with

---

18   Penguin, 1974, first published 1859.

19   JS Mill, *On Liberty*, 1859, Ch 1, emphasis added.

20   2nd ed, Butterworths, 2001, 19.

21   The Wolfenden Committee in the UK in the 1950s adopted the harm principle, concluding that acts in private between consenting adults should be none of the law's business. This led to the extensive reform of homosexual and prostitution offences: see Report of the Committee on Homosexual Offences and Prostitution, HMSO, Cmnd 247, 1957.

22   Oxford UP, 1982, 29.

the effect that the designation of a consequence as a "harm" involves a societal judgment with moral dimensions.[23]

The idea of making the avoidance of harm to others the litmus test for justifiable state intervention into negative liberty underpinned much classical tort and criminal law. It suggests why tort law was held back in the 19th century and contract law was more prominent. Tort law involves the state saying that someone should not do something (albeit indirectly through the threat of civil liability). Thus it was confined to cases of harm through proven fault. Contract, however, is supposedly the *exercise* of freedom (the liberty to bind oneself where advantage is subjectively perceived) and the law on that developed much more. It may be that a more expansive view of harm and a stronger promotion of *positive* liberty account for the expansion of modern tort law and for much of the blurring that has taken place recently at the boundary between contract and tort.[24]

The idea of fiscal freedom can be seen as part of the sanctity which liberals have traditionally attached to private property generally and there are today still libertarian liberals who regard taxation as a form of theft. In one way or another the English Civil War, the American War of Independence and the French Revolution were triggered by controversies over taxation. The cry "No taxation without representation" from the 18th century onwards illustrates how democratic controls over fiscal matters were demanded some time in advance of demands for democracy as a general form of government.

The liberal's attachment to social liberty, of more recent origin than the attachment to civil and fiscal liberty, is well captured by the modern idea of social mobility. In more or less accentuated forms, traditional societies were caste societies in that certain offices and positions were open only to people of particular ranks or families. The history of liberal societies has involved a stripping away of monopolistic and caste privileges and a focus upon formal equality before the law (see below). On the other hand, inequalities based upon social class, gender and race still persist in liberal societies (as they do in all other societies). At various parts of this book we will note the law's limited response to these inequalities and suggest that they are caused in part by an ambivalence within liberal ideas as to how they should be eradicated, if at all.

(iii) Liberalism and the Protection of Morals

Liberalism offers limitations on state powers. The harm principle operates as an *exclusory* guide. It dictates that activities should *not* be restrained by the state unless they cause harm to others, but, as MacCormick noted above, it does not tell us what should counts as "harms" and whether those are sufficient reasons for the state to limit those activities. Liberalism dictates what the state should *not* be doing, but offers limited guidance on what it should be doing, except promoting and protecting liberal values through law. Liberalism's rejection that law should embody a particular conception of morality or the "good life" for individuals, as noted above, is deliberate. Individuals should be at liberty to pursue their own

---

23   See further P McCutcheon, "Morality and the Criminal Law: Reflections on Hart-Devlin" (2002) 47 *Criminal Law Quarterly* 15 at 22.

24   See Atiyah, n 11.

conception of what is good for them, provided it does not cause harm to others or unreasonably interfere with the liberty of others.

Liberalism is challenged by those who believe that the function of law is to protect morality. The tension between liberalism and morality emerged in the 1950s, precipitated by the movement to liberalise offences criminalising homosexual activity between consenting adults. In the United Kingdom, the report of the influential Wolfenden Committee advanced the harm principle, and the classical liberal view, that homosexuality should fall within a zone of privacy – a sphere of private immorality – that should be none of the state's business.[25] Lord Devlin, a distinguished judge and jurist, subsequently delivered a set of public lectures as a counter-offensive against the gathering political momentum to "liberalise" offences against homosexuality and prostitution.

The general thesis of these lectures were published in *The Enforcement of Morals* where Devlin argued that, as a sociological fact, there existed a common positive morality that binds members of a society together.[26] Morality was critically important to the functioning of society and consequently "society may use the law to preserve morality in the same way as it uses it to safeguard anything else that is essential to its existence".[27]

But what is this "morality"? Where does it come from? In Devlin's view, moral standards were not eternal truths that had force because they derived from God. Rather morality was simply a reflection of those particular moral values held by most people, which, in England, he took to be based broadly on Christian teachings. A common morality could be determined by inquiring into what "every right-minded person" presumes to consider immoral.[28] This hypothetical subject is similar to the reasonable person who inhabits the law of torts and criminal law. Tying morality to established religion conferred stability on the concept of morality, though it is debatable whether Christian teachings, explicitly or implicitly, guide and inform the common morality in a broadly secular society like Australia, or indeed Britain, in the 21st century.

The image of a reasonably harmonious society bound by shared moral values sits uncomfortably with the realities of modern secular, pluralistic and multicultural societies within which moral disagreement rages over issues such as abortion, genetic research, euthanasia, pornography, prostitution, drug use and the like. The stability of a common morality is questionable even in relation to apparently uncontroversial crimes, such as murder, which purport to uphold the most fundamental of moral principles – the sanctity of life. Later in this chapter we discuss the limits of this moral principle in relation to the defence of necessity, and whether the law ever justifies murder of one person (outside the confines of self-defence) in order to save the lives of others.

Devlin's thesis is often presented as morally conservative, as an attempt to entrench religious dogma into law. This is unfair. For Devlin, Christian morals held no special significance other than reflecting the common morality in England in the late 1950s. In different places, at different times, morality could draw its normative foundations from other sources. Moreover, Devlin's moralism was

---

25   *Report of the Committee on Homosexual Offences and Prostitution*, HMSO, Cmnd 247, 1957.
26   *The Enforcement of Morals*, Oxford UP, 1965.
27   Ibid 11.
28   Ibid 15.

infused with liberalism. While he argued that the morality had a place in debates about the proper direction of law, he remained avowedly committed to fundamental liberal principles and values. Devlin proposed that laws adopted to protect core moral values had to conform to a set of "loose principles", that assumed the following:

- the practical difficulties of removing such laws once moral attitudes had changed;
- the importance of respecting personal privacy as far as possible; and
- most importantly in his view, that the criminal law should be concerned with established minimum rather than maximum standards of conduct.[29]

Paul McCutcheon, a leading Irish legal scholar, has recently brought fresh perspective to Devlin's theories.[30] He points out that it would be wrong to conclude that a moral theory of criminal law *necessarily* supports the enactment of repressive and discriminatory sexual offences. Liberal theorists, like HLA Hart, who opposed Devlin, proceeded with the implicit assumption that morality would necessarily condemn homosexual conduct between consenting adults, a condemnation that liberalism would avoid by deeming such behaviour to be within the realm of private immorality that is none of the law's business. As McCutcheon points out, this assumption is contestable in light of the significant shifts in community attitudes to homosexuality in recent years.[31] An approach to morality which is more secular than Devlin's, grounded in contemporary public opinion and community standards, remains vulnerable to capture by "law and order" populism. Indeed, there are signs that criminal justice reforms in Australia, increasingly driven by "moral concern" about crime, have produced an "uncivil politics of law and order".[32] Popular morality, whether measured through opinion polls or views expressed on talk-back radio, promotes a cycle of ever more repressive and harsh laws. When confronted with this prospect, liberalism – with its suppression of contentious political and moral values – appears as a safe refuge for law reformers!

In sum, law rarely evolves by reference to a perfect blueprint of liberalism. Liberalism is always engaged in an intellectual tussle with competing values and ideas. Even those who favour a strong role for morality in law, such Devlin and McCutcheon, accept the reality, indeed necessity, of theoretical pluralism. As McCutcheon concluded:

> [T]he limits of the criminal law cannot be set by reference to a "simple principle", be it harm, individual liberty or whatever. Instead the boundaries of the law are shaped by a variety of forces that operate as broad guidelines rather than as clear-cut criteria. Once this is acknowledged it must be accepted that it is legitimate and appropriate to take moral considerations into account in determining the contents of the criminal law. In short, the law-maker may properly justify a prohibition on an appeal to moral reasons.[33]

---

29 These principles are critically reviewed in N Bamford, *Sexuality, Morals and Justice*, Cassell, 1997, 181.

30 McCutcheon, n 23.

31 Ibid 36.

32 R Hogg and D Brown, *Rethinking Law and Order*, Pluto Press, 1998, Ch 1.

33 Ibid 16.

(iv)   Individualism

Individualism is so deeply rooted in our thought that it is hard to understand. A great part of the difficulty lies in imagining a different principle that might help define it by contrast.[34]

Although liberalism as a term derives from the notion of liberty, all liberals would assert that it is liberty *of the individual* that they seek to protect. Liberals are sometimes described as "atomistic". They see society as comprised merely of individual human beings (atoms) who come to society with fully formed identities.[35] Society is an association no greater than the sum of its individual parts. Margaret Thatcher is reported as saying once that there is no such thing as "society" and this reflects an extreme individualism which can see no purpose in importing a meaningless concept like "society" into debates.

Roberto Unger in his book *Law in Modern Society*[36] puts the rise of individualism in an historical and anthropological context.[37] He says that one way to distinguish, for example, a tribal society from a liberal one is to look at the associations which people have and their sense of insiders and outsiders.[38]

Take now a society that stands at the opposite pole from the tribal and call it liberal. In such a society, every individual belongs to a large number of significant groups, but each of these groups affects only a limited part of his life. Thus, personality is carved up into a long list of separate or even conflicting specialized activities. The reverse side of this specialization is that the whole person comes to be seen and treated as an abstract set of capabilities never tied together in any one context of group life.

Such a mode of association undermines, though it does not abolish, the tribal contrast of strangers and insiders. As significant groups grow in number, they intermesh more and more. Hence, the frequency with which men who are insiders for some purpose become strangers for another increases. The extent to which a subject can define himself and his fellows by reference to their shared experience in a group diminishes. At the same time, as individuals interact more often in impersonal contexts, like markets and bureaucracies, the position of the stranger is itself robbed of much of the foreignness, hostility and fear with which it is connected in tribal society. Thanks to these convergent trends, impersonal respect and formal equality edge out communal solidarity to some and suspicious

---

34   Unger, n 10, 25.

35   In the words of C Geertz, the western conception of the person is as a "bounded, unique, more or less integrated motivational and cognitive universe, a dynamic centre of awareness, emotion, judgment and action organized into a distinctive whole and set contrastively against a social and natural background". See "From the native's point of view: On the nature of anthropological understanding" in P Rabinow and WM Sullivan (eds), *Interpretive Social Science*, U of California Press, 1979, 229.

36   Free Press, 1976.

37   Unger's book is perhaps more safely read as a theoretical than a descriptive text. There is a line of thought that the seeds of individualism in England (and therefore the societies deriving from it) were actually sown considerably before the rise of capitalism and "modernity"; see A Macfarlane, *The Origins of English Individualism*, Blackwell, 1978 and L Rosen, "Individualism, Community, and the Law: A Review Essay" (1988) 55 *U of Chicago LR* 571.

38   He acknowledges that his analysis is close to, although not identical with, a conventional distinction between gemeinschaft societies based on "community" and gesellschaft societies based on "association".

hostility toward others. In place of the insider and the stranger, there emerges the abstract other to whom one shows neither love nor hate.[39]

In a liberal society, then, impersonality, formal equality (explained below) and indifference are hallmarks. People associate with others in complex and inter-secting ways (families, work-places, social organisations, business ventures etc) and the sense of identity with a particular large group diminishes.

The common law, in the shape that it took during the middle of the 19th century in England and the United States, reflected this world of unconnected individuals who come together at different times for different purposes and then go their separate ways. Classical contract law in the second and third quarters of that century was, and often still is, regarded as the quintessence of the common law. It was seen as the state providing a framework which facilitated the spon-taneous association of monadic individuals as they pursued their own ends but at the same time expressing no judgment on those ends. Tort law, however, rejected any general legal duty to avoid foreseeable harm to others until 1932 with the famous case of *Donoghue v Stevenson*.[40] This was despite the fact that the components for such a concept (the duty of care, the reasonable man etc) had been available in the case law since at least the second half of the 19th century.[41] Some scholars, whether or not they are influenced by the work of Unger, see the changing relationship between, and content of, contract and tort law as evidence that western common law countries are becoming post-liberal or at least embracing liberalism of a radically new kind.[42]

A critical dimension of law's impersonality is that legal doctrine evaluates an individual's conduct, not by examining reference to subjective capacities of the parties, but rather through applying objective hypothetical standard. This standard for modern legal doctrines (both in criminal, contract and tort law) is what the "reasonable man" would have done, known or foreseen. This standard emerged in the mid-19th century and persists across a range of areas including criminal law, contract and tort law, though it is now framed as the genderless "reasonable person". The "neighbour principle", famously established in *Donoghue v Steven-son* above, employed the hypothetical reasonable man to determine when the duty of care applied, and what precise standard of care should be expected. The emergence of the hypothetical legal subject in both the civil and criminal law projects a strongly liberal viewpoint of reasonableness: it is said to be the fictive embodiment of the rational, self-interested person against whom the conduct of ordinary people will be judged.[43] The challenge for critical scholars, particularly feminists, has been to expose how gender shapes law's normative standards, though packages them in gender neutral language and concepts.[44]

---

39 Note 36, 143-144.

40 [1932] AC 562.

41 See, for example, *Heaven v Pender* (1883) 11 QBD 503. This argument is developed further in S Parker and P Drahos, "Closer to a Critical Theory of Family Law" (1990) 4 *Australian Journal of Family Law* 159 at 171-172.

42 See, for example, the work of Hugh Collins in *The Law of Contract*, Weidenfeld and Nicolson, 1986 and "The Decline of Privacy in Private Law" (1987) 14 *Journal of Law and Society* 91; and PS Atiyah, *Essays on Contract*, Clarendon, 1986.

43 A Norrie, *Crime, Reason and History*, 2nd ed, Butterworths, 2001, 20-24.

44 R Graycar and J Morgan, *The Hidden Gender of Law*, 2nd ed, The Federation Press, 2002.

(v)   Positive Liberty and Republicanism

Liberalism is not beyond challenge, and within political and moral philosophy, particularly in North America, the rise of "communitarian" theory offers a serious challenge to the liberal view of the isolated self.[45] During the 1980s and 1990s a number of scholars have sought to identify a non-socialist alternative to liberalism. One of the key points of difference between communitarianism and liberalism has been whether people can indeed stand back from their culture and social roles and make choices as individuals. According to communitarians such as Michael Sandel and Alasdair MacIntyre, the self is embedded in existing social practices: our identity is defined by certain ends that we did not choose.[46] The consequence is that there is a legitimate role for the state, as the political representation of the community, to take steps which support cultural diversity and community values.

Although communitarian writing has certainly forced liberals to re-examine some of their assumptions, there is an argument that communitarianism offers little that was not already conceivable within liberalism. There has long been a strand of liberal thought that views individuals as being held together by certain bonds. This is often called social contract theory. In its classical form,[47] societies or governments were seen as the product of a contract between (some[48]) individuals. The terms of the contract may have been those that happily suited possessive individuals,[49] in that they involved a limited "nightwatchman" government whose main tasks were to provide external defence and preserve negative liberty and property rights, rather than to redistribute wealth. Nevertheless, social contract thinking has remained important as a general ideology that legitimates a particular form of government and which does not depend on Mill's harm principle. In recent years the idea has been revived in a form which does provide for redistribution of wealth and which rests upon a stronger conception of equality than many liberals have hitherto favoured.[50]

Another approach, recognising the limitations of classical liberalism, has been to reconstruct the concept of liberty. We saw above that negative liberty ("freedom from") has been contrasted with positive liberty ("freedom to"), usually from the point of view that the state's obligation is only to protect the former. In recent years, some liberals have taken a broad approach to the promotion of positive liberty and have preferred to use the term "autonomy". Individuals, in other words, have some claim on the state to the advancement of their autonomy.

The idea of autonomy captures not only the notion of positive liberty but also some modern ideas about individualism and equality (elements which we have yet to discuss). Joseph Raz has described it like this:

---

45   For a good discussion of liberalism and communitarianism, see M Sandel (ed), *Liberalism and its Critics*, New York UP, 1984 and W Kymlicka, *Liberalism, Community and Culture*, Clarendon, 1989.

46   See M Sandel, *Liberalism and the Limits of Justice*, Cambridge UP, 1982 and A MacIntyre, *After Virtue: A Study in Moral Theory*, Duckworth, 1981.

47   For example, in John Locke's *Second Treatise on Government* (1690), J-J Rousseau's *The Social Contract* (1764) and Immanuel Kant's *The Foundations of the Metaphysics of Morals* (1785).

48   For an extended feminist critique of the kind of people that social contract theorists had (and still have) in mind, see C Pateman, *The Sexual Contract*, Polity, 1988.

49   See CB MacPherson, *The Political Theory of Possessive Individualism*, Oxford UP, 1962.

50   The most illustrious example is John Rawls whom we discuss below under the sub-heading of Justice.

The ruling idea behind the ideal of personal autonomy is that people should make their own lives. The autonomous person is a (part) author of his own life. The ideal of personal autonomy is the vision of people controlling, to some degree, their own destiny, fashioning it through successive decisions throughout their lives.[51]

To write one's life-lines, however, one must have some *real* and not just theoretical choices. Furthermore, to be autonomous requires that one be given more than *a* choice. One must have an adequate *range* of choices. Raz's two imaginary cases illustrate this well.[52] The Man in the Pit is unable to climb out or to summon help. He has just enough food to keep him alive without any suffering, once he gets used to it. He has choices. He can eat now or later. He can sleep now or later. He can scratch his left ear or desist. But he is not autonomous. He is not the author of his own life. The Hounded Woman on a desert island is perpetually hunted by a fierce carnivorous animal. Her various inner resources of mental stamina, will power and physical fitness enable her to keep away from the animal but she never has the chance to do or think of anything except escape. She (like many woman today who are trapped in violent relationships) is not the author of her own life. Neither has an adequate range of options to choose from.

This approach to liberty, when combined with substantive rather than formal notions of equality (see below), can and has been used to justify certain supposed interferences by the modern state in the liberty of the citizen even where the Millian justification is either unavailable on the grounds that it would be paternalistic[53] or only tortuously available. Compulsory education, for example, can be defended by an argument based on improving the range of young people's choices. Yet at the time of its introduction in liberal societies in the late 19th century it was seen by those attached only to the idea of negative liberty as either socialist or as stretching liberalism in an unacceptable new direction.[54] Arguments in favour of the legal recognition of children's rights today are also often couched in terms of the promotion of children's autonomy when they become adults.[55]

In the 1990s, some theorists attempted to rehabilitate liberalism, by developing a republican model based on the concept of social freedom. According to these scholars, the system of justice should be directed to the promotion of freedom,

---

51   J Raz, *The Morality of Freedom*, Clarendon, 1986, 369. Kleinig has described autonomy as a "personality ideal", see J Kleinig, *Paternalism*, Rowman & Allanheld, 1984, 19. The term "autarchy" has also been coined to express government of oneself through a developed capacity for rational choice, see S Benn, "Freedom, Autonomy and the Concept of a Person" (1975-6) *Proceedings of the Aristotelian Society*, NS, 76, 109.

52   Ibid 373-374.

53   According to Barry, n 7, 158: "At the heart of traditional liberal theory is an objection to *paternalism*". See also Kleinig, n 51, 9. For an argument that Raz is a moderate paternalist, see L Green, "Un-American Liberalism: Raz's 'Morality of Freedom'" (1988) 38 *University of Toronto Law Journal* 317 at 325.

54   See, for example, Hobhouse, n 13, 25: "[T]he State control of education gives rise to some searching questions of principle, which have not yet been fully solved. If, in general, education is a duty which the State has a right to enforce, there is a countervailing right of choice as to the lines of education which it would be ill to ignore, and the mode of adjustment has not yet been adequately determined either in theory or in practice". Barry, n 7, 160 notes how adherents of positive liberty justify social legislation which is designed to increase the opportunities of individuals because it is said to increase liberty and not merely reduce inequalities.

55   See, for example, JM Eekelaar, "The Importance of Thinking that Children have Rights, in P Alston, S Parker and J Seymour, *Children, Rights and the Law*, Clarendon, 1992, 231.

though this freedom is not the atomistic, individualistic and asocial model envisaged by classical liberalism. Republican theory reconceives freedom in *social* and *relational* terms. As Braithwaite and Pettit note in *Not Just Deserts – A Republican Theory of Criminal Justice*:

> Republicans differ from classical liberals … in arguing for a different inter-pretation of what the ideal of negative liberty is more or less bound to involve. According to the classical liberal interpretation, the sort of condition required is that of being left alone, a condition exemplified *par excellence* in the solitary individual. According to the republican interpretation, it is the condition of citizenship or equality before the law.[56]

The authors coin the phrase of freedom as dominion or freedom as non-domination:

> Dominion is a republican conception of liberty. Whereas the liberal conception of freedom is the freedom of an isolated atomistic individual, the republican concep-tion of liberty is the freedom of a social world. Liberal freedom is objective and individualistic. Negative freedom for the liberal means the objective fact of individuals' being left alone by others. For the republican, however, freedom is defined socially and relationally. You only enjoy republican freedom – dominion – when you live in a social world that provides you with an intersubjective set of assurances of liberty. You must subjectively believe that you enjoy these assurances, and so must others believe. As a social, relational conception of liberty, by definition it also has a comparative dimension. To fully enjoy liberty, you must have equality-of-liberty with other persons. If this is difficult to grasp, think of dominion as a conception of freedom that, by definition, incorporates the notions of liberté, égalité, and fraternité; then you have the basic idea.[57]

Using these ideas, Braithwaite and Pettit set out a new blueprint for the criminal justice system where promoting dominion was the principal goal. It has impli-cations across the legal system, with some constitutional scholars advocating this model to protect a wider range of constitutional and human rights, including freedom of protest.[58] Other scholars have similarly argued that the overriding purpose of the criminal justice system should be the maximising of freedom: see, for example, the "freedom model" developed by Sanders and Young.[59]

Like liberal scholarship generally, these ideas view utilitarianism, a theory that aims to maximise the happiness or the welfare of the majority, as a profound threat to individual freedom. Utilitarianism additionally renders rights unstable: "[I]t fails to provide the criminal justice authorities with reason to take the rights seriously, attaching moral as well as legal force to them".[60] Utilitarian approaches are dangerous because they subscribe to penalisation of the innocent, prevention-ism and overcriminalisation (or more generally, over-regulation).

---

56 Clarendon Press, 1990, 58.

57 J Braithwaite, "Inequality and Republican Criminology" in J Hagan and R Peterson (eds), *Crime and Inequality*, Stanford UP, 1995, 279.

58 For a review of the implications of republican theory for reshaping constitutional law, see G Williams, *Human Rights under the Australian Constitution*, Oxford UP, 1998, Ch 1. See also S Bronitt and G Williams, "Political Freedom as an Outlaw: Republican Theory and Political Protest" (1996) 18(2) *Adelaide Law Review* 289.

59 A Sanders and R Young, *Criminal Justice*, 2nd ed, Butterworths, 2000.

60 Ibid 44.

(vi)   Equality

At various points in the preceding discussion reference has been made to equality. For example, we have seen that individuals should have equal liberty (at least in the public sphere). It is a fundamental liberal precept, embodied in the idea of equality before the law. [61]

Yet the concept of equality, like liberty, is deeply contested. Under the rule of law, as we will see, everyone is equal before the law, but what does "equal" mean here? The purpose of much anti-discrimination law in Australia is to bring about a position of equality between disadvantaged and dominant groups, but what kind of equality? The main task of the welfare state is usually said to be the reduction, if not the elimination, of inequalities in matters such as disposable income, health care, housing, education and access to justice: but to introduce precise policies one needs some idea of what *equality would be*. We cannot in a few paragraphs do justice to the literature on this subject and our purpose is simply to introduce some basic ideas and distinctions which will recur in discussions later in the book, for example about topics such as legal aid, gender and race.

In a crude sense, the definition of, and importance attached to, equality differ according to the political complexion of the liberal. On the libertarian end of the spectrum, the attachment is very much to a purely formal or procedural equality – equal *treatment* of individuals before the law is directed to procedural rather than substantive ends. As formal or strict equality promotes sameness of treatment, it may conceal the substantive political, social and economic inequality of disadvantaged groups or individuals. This is captured in famous line in Anatole France's *Le Lys Rouge* (1894) that the poor must "labour in the face of the majestic equality of the law, which forbids the rich as well as the poor to sleep under bridges, to beg in the streets, and to steal bread". The equality being derided there is purely formal: the law applies to everyone equally but it totally ignores substantive differences between people. Only the poor need to sleep under bridges, beg or steal food. Measures to take us nearer to substantive equality would be those which reduced the necessity for people to sleep under bridges in the first place.

Two writers who epitomise opposing positions on equality are Friedrich Hayek and Ronald Dworkin. Hayek advocates the ideal of equality prominent amongst classical liberals in the mid-19th century.

> It was a demand that all man-made obstacles to the rise of some should be removed, that all privileges of individuals should be abolished, and that what the state contributed to the chance of improving one's conditions should be the same for all. That so long as people were different and grew up in different families this could not assure an equal start was fairly generally accepted. It was understood that the duty of government was not to ensure that everybody had the same prospect of reaching a given position but merely to make available to all on equal

---

61   Equality before the law is a fundamental principle ensuring that individuals are not subject to discrimination in the enjoyment of their legal rights or entitlements. The *Universal Declaration of Human Rights* (adopted and proclaimed by the General Assembly resolution 217A (III) of 10 December 1948) provides that: "All are equal before the law and are entitled without discrimination to equal protection of the law": Art 7. The *International Covenant on Civil and Political Rights* contains a similar provision in Art 26, which states that "the law shall prohibit any discrimination and guarantee to all persons equal and effective protection against discrimination on any ground such as race, colour, sex, language, religion, political or other opinion, national or social origin, property, birth or other status".

terms those facilities which in their nature depended on government action. That the results were bound to be different, not only because the individuals were different, but also because only a small part of the relevant circumstances depended on government action, was taken for granted.[62]

This passage describes neatly the formal conception of equality: there should be no state-provided *obstacles* to the equal enjoyment of rights by all citizens. If, however, other forces are responsible for blocking the equal enjoyment of rights, such as wealth or natural ability, the state through its laws and policies should not seek to interfere. Apartheid in South Africa was indefensible, according to this perspective, because it was a case of the state imposing formal barriers on particular groups, not because of any particular consequences. Laws that disentitled married women from holding property in their own name have been dismantled since the 1870s in common law countries on liberal as well as feminist grounds because they were instances of the state putting legal obstacles in the way of a subset of individuals.[63]

There are obviously close connections between negative liberty and formal equality, although they are not altogether the reverse sides of the same coin. Undoubtedly, formal equality requires that everyone have the same negative liberties protected in the same manner. On the other hand, there is nothing in the idea of formal equality that prescribes the *content* of those liberties. Their content is determined by the particular theory of negative liberty itself, which in turn must involve a rule, like Mill's harm principle, to justify encroachments into that liberty. Some *stronger* conceptions of equality, however, have been put forward as determining the content of liberty itself.

Ronald Dworkin's argument, in shortened form, is this.[64] If a new state were being established and an initial distribution of goods, resources and opportunities were being made, then a liberal government would have to make a roughly equal distribution between citizens because it would have no justification for treating some more favourably than others. Imagine first that all citizens are the same in all material respects. Each has the same talents and the same theory of the good life (and hence exactly the same scheme of preferences) as others. Then, says, Dworkin, the government would arrange for production that maximised the mix of goods, including jobs and leisure, that everyone (unanimously) favoured, distributing the product equally.

Now relax the assumptions so that the only difference between people was their theory of the good, and therefore their preferences. In this case the liberal would introduce a market economy and a democratic polity. These are the best mechanisms available, says Dworkin, for collective decisions about what goods should be produced, how they are to be distributed and what conduct should be prohibited or regulated. The market will determine a price that reflects the cost in

---

62   F Hayek, *The Constitution of Liberty*, Chicago UP, 1960, 92.

63   As Lee Holcombe says, "In demanding reform of the married women's property law, feminists of the 19th century were fortunately not battling adverse intellectual elements. Rather, they were identifying themselves with some of the most important intellectual themes of the period": L Holcombe, *Wives and Property*, Martin Robertson, 1983, 5. See also DM Stetson, *A Woman's Issue*, Greenwood, 1982 and J Scutt, *Even in the Best of Homes*, Penguin, 1983, Ch 2.

64   For clear accounts, see R Dworkin, "Liberalism" in S Hampshire (ed), *Public and Private Morality*, Cambridge UP, 1978 (reprinted in Sandel, n 45) and *A Matter of Principle*, Harvard UP, 1985, Ch 9.

resources of material, labour and capital that could have been applied in the production of something else that others want. In this way, a figure is arrived at which can be debited from the citizen's (initially equal) distribution. Over time, citizens have unequal amounts in their account but this reflects their own preferences: some want large houses, some want smaller ones, some want to work more whilst others prefer leisure, and so forth. On these restrictive assumptions the founder of this imaginary state would choose the market rather than centrally planned distribution (call it socialism) because the state would simply have to mimic the market anyway. That would be costly in researching people's preferences and the wrong answer might still be produced. The state could not have a role in fixing non-market prices because it would be interfering with people's preferences and the state is supposed to be neutral.[65] Furthermore such interference would be inegalitarian because it involves a redistribution of resources which had initially been distributed equally and which had only come to be shared unequally as a result of individual choices.

Now the point of this model is, of course, to relax the assumptions further and approximate to reality. As Dworkin says:

> In the actual society for which the liberal must construct political institutions, there are all the other differences. Talents are not distributed equally, so the decision of one person to work in a factory rather than a law firm, or not to work at all, will be governed in large part by his [sic] abilities rather than his preferences for work or between work and leisure. The institutions of wealth, which allow people to dispose of what they receive by gift, mean that children of the successful will start with more wealth than the children of the unsuccessful. Some people will have special needs, because they are handicapped; their handicap will not only disable them from the most productive and lucrative employment, but will incapacitate them from using the proceeds of what-ever employment they find as efficiently, so that they will need more than those who are not handicapped to satisfy identical ambitions.[66]

Dworkin, unlike Hayek, finds it "obviously obnoxious" to the liberal that someone should have more than what the community as a whole has to distribute simply because of superior skill, luck or family. The liberal can only accept inequalities that reflect the true differential costs of goods and opportunities rather than those that follow from differences in ability, inheritance and so on. What one does to correct these latter inequalities is a complex question and we will return to it in the discussion of justice below. One might leave the pricing system intact but introduce a scheme of welfare rights financed by redistributive measures like taxation. Or one might believe that this would be more inefficient than going further and simply substituting socialist for market decisions. In either event,

---

65 This assertion is qualified below in the discussion of rights and utility. As we will see, some liberals believe there are at least some things that can be said about the good life and that it is permissible for the state to promote it.

66 Dworkin in Sandel, n 45, 68. Dworkin does not add in social class and ethnicity which, to some, are much more powerful causes of inequality; see Chapters 8 and 9 below. Bellamy has criticised Dworkin (and Rawls) for their methodological individualism and parochial standards of rationality, describing them as "sociologically misconceived when the increasing complexity of modern societies is calling such assumptions into question": R Bellamy, "Defining Liberalism: Neutralist, Ethical or Political?" in R Bellamy (ed), *Liberalism and Recent Legal and Social Philosophy*, ARSP, 1989, 23 at 41.

according to Dworkin, the liberal will choose a mixed economic system and be either a reluctant capitalist or a reluctant socialist in order to achieve "the best practical realisation of the demands of equality itself".[67]

We find in Dworkin a much stronger conception of equality than the purely formal equality espoused by Hayek. Although other ways of distinguishing between versions of equality can be formulated, and we will touch on them later in the text, this basic dichotomy between formal and substantive equality, and the relationship between this dichotomy and that between negative and positive liberty, are sufficient for present purposes. In many areas of law we can see the uneasy compromise between these different views. The classical rules of contract, for example, contained few escape routes for those who repented of their bargain because it worked on the assumption of formally equal contractors with whose preferences the state should not interfere. As a stronger notion of equality developed from about the third quarter of the 19th century protections were added, usually by statute and usually aimed at particular kinds of parties – employees, borrowers, tenants, purchasers of consumer goods and so forth. Each of these changes no doubt had its own history and immediate causes but they can be seen generally as part of a movement in the law and political process towards correcting what were now seen as material inequalities of bargaining power. At the least, it is difficult to imagine them occurring in a polity committed to the principles of Hayek. Whether such measures survive the deregulatory climate of Australia and the particular theories of economic efficiency currently in vogue waits to be seen.[68]

Acknowledging the limitations of formal or procedural equality has fostered remedial versions of equality, such as substantive equality and equality of opportunity.[69] Yet, both formal and these remedial conceptions of equality have been criticised from a feminist perspective. Nicola Lacey has summarised the feminist critique as follows:

> In the case of equality, it has been argued that liberal notions of equality are fundamentally premised on the idea of sameness: equal treatment is due to all who are similarly situated to the full liberal subject. Hence, if the subject is implicitly marked as masculine – is understood in terms of bodily and psychic characteristics which have been culturally understood to be associated with men – then the strategy of equality amounts to the assimilation of women to a norm set by and for men.[70]

---

67 Dworkin in Sandel, n 45, 69.

68 The law and economics movement, many of whose exponents are neoclassical liberals, has paid particular attention to legal measures designed to correct inequality; measures such as rent control laws. Their criticisms have exerted some influence on legal change in America and Britain. See generally, Part C below.

69 Nicola Lacey lists "equal concern and respect", "equal consideration of interests", "equality of welfare", "equal counting in the utilitarian calculus", "equality of resources", "equality as the exclusion of irrelevant reasons" and "equality of opportunity"; see "Punishment and the Liberal World" (1987) 11 *Bulletin of the Australian Society of Legal Philosophy*" 70 at 77.

70 *Unspeakable Subjects – Feminist Essays in Legal and Social Theory*, Hart Publishing, 1998, 240.

(vii) Justice

Justice is also a foundational value in liberal thought. From a philosophical perspective, justice has been conceived in a number of different ways, with distinctions drawn between formal and substantive conceptions of justice. Liberal theorists have conceived justice in terms of "fairness", equality of treatment and respect for individual rights.[71] The centrality accorded to individuals and their rights within this conception of justice has attracted substantial criticism. As with the concept of equality, feminist legal theorists have exposed how liberal concep-tions of justice have only a limited ability to address structural and group-based discrimination that lies beyond the public sphere.

A formal conception of justice tends to identify justice closely with legal process, in particular the concept of "due process". As long as a court has observed the proper rules of procedure in the course of properly applying the law then the decision can be regarded as just.[72] There is psychological evidence to support this emphasis on procedural justice: a person will accept an adverse legal judgment relating to a law that they do not personally support if the processes are judged to be fair and just.[73]

Lawyers are often described as being attached only to formal ideas of justice if they refuse to take a stance on the outcome of a case. To ascribe the label "formal" to this idea of justice can be misleading, however, because "the law" being applied in a case may well itself embody more substantive ideas about what is a just state of affairs. The real criticism of lawyers might be that they are agnostic about the substantive approach to justice reflected in the outcome. This criticism is allied to a criticism of legal formalism as a method of legal reasoning, which we discuss in Chapter 3. In a criminal context, appellate review seems less concerned with corroborating the innocence or guilt of the accused, but rather whether trial had been conducted according to law. The law is not, however, unconcerned with procedural justice, which underlies specific rights such as the right to a fair trial. As Brennan J pointed out in *Jago v District Court (NSW)*, justice is an ideal that is pursued in law, though it is not an absolute:

> If it be said that judicial measures cannot always secure perfect justice to an accused, we should ask whether the ideal of perfect justice has not sounded in rhetoric rather than in law and whether the legal right of an accused, truly stated, is a right to a trial as fair as the courts can make it. Were it otherwise, trials would be prevented and convictions would be set aside when circumstances outside judicial control impair absolute fairness.[74]

From a legal procedural perspective, the question is not whether the trial achieved justice in the abstract, but whether the trial was unfair by reference to specific

---

71   See J Rawls, *A Theory of Justice*, Harvard UP, 1971; R Dworkin, *Taking Rights Seriously*, Duckworth, 1977 respectively. For a review of the competing conceptions of justice, see T Campbell, *Justice*, 2nd ed, Macmillan, 2001, and S Wojciech (ed), *Justice*, Ashgate, 2001.

72   For a brief but clear discussion of justice intended for beginner law students, see AWB Simpson, *Invitation to Law*, Basil Blackwell, 1988, Ch 2.

73   T Tyler, *Why People Obey the Law*, Yale UP, 1990. As Ashworth has noted "there is ample evidence that people place great emphasis on the fairness of procedures, even when they disagree with the outcome": "Crime, Community and Creeping Consequentialism" [1996] *Crim LR* 220 at 228.

74   (1989) 168 CLR 23 at 49.

legal standards.[75] A quick review of the case law reveals that it is easier to identify processes which are "unfair" (and therefore may amount to a miscarriage of justice), than to enumerate positively the attributes of a "fair trial". We examine the issues around access to justice and the right to a fair trial further in Chapters 3 and 4. There is some uncertainty from whose perspective justice is to be measured: the standpoint of the accused, victim or wider community. For this reason, retributive justice is being challenged by restorative justice, where community-based initiatives such as conferencing offer the prospect of reintegration and restoration for offenders, victims and communities affected by crime.[76]

Modern lawyers are called upon more frequently to comment on the "justice" of the situation. One reason is that many laws give a court discretion to decide what is "just" or "equitable". The lawyer therefore needs to be equipped to make relevant arguments. Another reason is that lawyers are increasingly involved in the reform and criticism of law. It is important, therefore, to be able to identify some of the competing positions on justice. Substantive conceptions of justice tend to centre on three particular ideas:

- justice as equality;
- justice as desert; and
- justice as entitlement or rights.

These are not mutually exclusive – indeed, there are significant overlaps – but most substantive theories of justice give priority to one or another of them.

Justice as equality is based on the belief that like cases should be treated alike. People should be treated equally unless there is some significant and relevant difference between them. Liberals, and many non-liberals, assent to this proposition in a general way. The difficulty is that we are forced back on to the problematic nature of equality in order to do anything concrete with it. More specifically, we need some theory which will help us decide which differences are to be regarded as significant and in need of correction. Many legal distinctions, past and present, can seem reasonable to some and unreasonable to others precisely because of disagreement over the relevance of the distinction. If, for example, one takes the view that there are relevant and significant differences between racial groups, perhaps between the Indigenous and the Europeans, then one can adduce arguments in support of different legal treatment of them.[77] One of the significant claims against recognition of Aboriginal law and jurisdiction outside Australian law has been that it would violate the standards of equality. As Mason CJ observed in *Walker v New South Wales*, denying that customary law may have survived British settlement:

---

75 S Bronitt and B McSherry, *Principles of Criminal Law*, 2nd ed, Lawbook Co, 2005, 101ff, for a discussion of the fair trial principle in *Dietrich*.

76 H Strang and J Braithwaite (eds), *Restorative Justice: Philosophy to Practice*, Ashgate, 2000; D Roche, *Restorative Justice*, Ashgate, 2000; J Braithwaite, *Restorative Justice and Responsive Regulation*, Oxford UP, 2002.

77 We will return to this in Chapter 9 below when we deal with the harsh discriminatory treatment of Aboriginal people by the legal system.

It is a basic principle that all people should stand equal before the law. A construction which results in different criminal sanctions applying to different persons for the same conduct offends that basic principle.[78]

Justice as desert or "just deserts" is an idea of wide appeal both within and outside the law. In historical terms, according to Tom Campbell, the idea that people should get what they deserve "is perhaps the most common and tenacious conception of justice".[79] Although it long pre-dates liberalism, classical liberals from Adam Smith to John Stuart Mill were desert theorists and it is not surprising that deserts theory was highly influential in economic and legal thought from the end of the 18th to the end of the 19th century. For example, the analysis of contracts as exchanges of things or promises led to the view that contracts were almost sacred because each side had given something up and deserved the other party's performance in return.[80] Moral intuitions that voluntary conduct might also give rise to legal liability where it had been detrimentally relied upon were either expunged from the law or masked in apparently peripheral rules.[81] In the criminal field, just deserts justifies punishment proportionate to the harm caused and the individual's blameworthiness or guilt. There is no further purpose behind punishment, such as prevention or rehabilitation. As a consequence, retribution is said to be "backward-looking" because it focuses exclusively on the criminal act and the offender's criminal responsibility – hence the question and degree of the accused's fault (or to use the Latin, "mens rea") is critical to the severity of punishment. Its revival in the late 20th century, and reintroduction of determinate and mandatory sentencing, coincides with widespread dissatisfaction with deterrent and rehabilitative goals. It continues to be highly influential in some criminal justice systems, most notably in the United States.

Deserts theory has never found favour as an exclusive theory of justice. This is perhaps because human behaviour, especially criminal offending, rarely conforms to a model based on individual rational free-choice. That is not to say that, conversely, human behaviour is purely a matter of individual pathology, psychology, genetics or socio-economic exigency as some social scientists and criminologists might suggest. Human behaviour is multifaceted and, unsurprisingly, our system of justice embodies these multiple, sometimes contradictory, assumptions. The criminal law, influenced by liberalism, wants to project the image of rational and voluntary actors. Unfortunately, this model confronts the hard empirical truth that the bulk of offending occurs while individuals are impaired through drugs and alcohol. The law necessarily adopts a pragmatic compromise between promoting individual justice, the prevention of crime and protection of the public.

The third main substantive conception of justice is justice as entitlement or rights. "A just system of laws", says Simpson, "is one which distributes good things, of one kind or another, so that they are in the hands of those who are entitled to them, who have the best claim to them, who, as we often say, have a right to them".[82] Clearly a rights theory can embrace deserts theory (people have a

---

78   (1994) 182 CLR 45 at 50.
79   Campbell, n 71, 149.
80   See generally, Collins, n 42, Ch 2.
81   Atiyah, n 11.
82   Simpson, n 72, 36.

right to what they deserve) but it goes wider than that. Early liberal philosophers in the 17th and 18th centuries developed a conception of *natural* rights as a basis for challenging the old social order.[83] A prominent modern successor is Robert Nozick and we will discuss his work below when we look at the importance of property rights in liberal thought.

All three concepts of justice mentioned above have their attractions for the liberal at an intuitive level. That does not mean, however, that they offer a concrete way of deciding how goods and entitlements should be distributed in the real world. In other words, a variety of distributions is compatible with each theory. John Rawls, a modern liberal philosopher, has put forward a *mechanism* for deciding the institutional means under which distributions can take place; in his case pursuant to a theory of justice as equality.[84]

Rawls develops standard social contract theory by asking what contract would free and rational people concerned to further their own interests accept in an initial position of equality as defining the fundamental terms of their association.[85] The negotiators of this hypothetical social contract are hidden behind a veil of ignorance so that they do not know their place in society, their class position or social status, their fortune in the distribution of natural assets and abilities, intelligence, strength and so on.

The reason for the veil of ignorance is to ensure that no one is able to design principles of justice which favour their particular position. Rawls argues that people would choose two principles of justice. The first requires equality in the assignment of basic liberty compatible with a similar liberty for others. The second provides that social and economic inequalities are just *only if they result in compensating benefits for everyone*, and in particular for the least advantaged members of society. Rawls develops his argument at great length.[86] Our purpose in mentioning it here is to suggest one method for arriving at a just distribution: a method which allocates certain basic substantive rights equally and then justifies inequality beyond that point by reference to the effect that this inequality has on the least advantaged. When we look at the ethical basis of the economic analysis of law in Part C, an analysis which deals with the distribution of legal rights in conditions of scarcity, we will look further at this kind of argument.

Critics of liberalism attack both the primacy given to justice in liberal thought and the way that justice is conceptualised. Some Marxists and feminists see a preoccupation with justice as only necessary because liberal societies are full of conflicting interests and accordingly need some mechanism to keep the conflict within bounds and maintain the legitimacy of the system. Communitarians, in contrast, have acknowledged the importance of justice as a social virtue but have attacked the individualism implicit within liberal ideas of justice. Justice, say communitarians, is not some abstract ahistorical idea, but something embedded in particular communities. Some argue that the quest for a universal theory of

---

83   Although the notion of justice as entitlement can be traced back to Aristotle.

84   Rawls, n 71.

85   Ibid 11.

86   See, however, Campbell, n 71, Ch 3; SM Okin, "Justice and Gender" (1987) 16 *Philosophy and Public Affairs* 42 and "Reason and Feeling in Thinking about Justice" (1989) 99 *Ethics* 2; and C Kukathas and P Pettit, *Rawls – A Theory of Justice and Its Critics*, Polity Press, 1990.

justice is misguided: a society is just if it acts in accordance with the shared understandings of its members. To identify the principles of justice one engages in interpretation of a particular culture rather than in philosophy.[87] Rather similar criticisms have been directed at liberals beliefs in rights, to which we now turn.

(viii)   Rights

We have seen that in the 17th and 18th centuries the idea took hold in a small number of countries that people had natural rights to life, liberty and property – a powerful rhetorical political foundation for the French and American revolutions. This phenomenon was arguably a precondition of liberalism because it gave a basis for attacking despotic government and traditional privilege. In the 19th century, however, the idea of natural rights seemed to give way. People were said to derive their rights not from "nature" or religion but simply from the fact that those rights had been laid down (or posited) in law.

This positivist view, that rights are socially or institutionally constructed rather than naturally or divinely derived, is often associated with a strand of liberalism that dominated much of the 19th century called Utilitarianism, which is discussed separately below. One prominent utilitarian, the English lawyer, and philosopher Jeremy Bentham (1748-1832), rejected the rhetoric of natural rights as "nonsense upon stilts".[88] He suggested that the principle of utility was instead the criterion by which the content of laws should be decided – this theory is described below.

The mid-20th century and the horrors of Nazism led to a revival of natural law and natural rights thinking, albeit embodied in the language of universal human rights. Students of law need to understand something of the opposition between rights and utility in order to understand what is at stake in many legal controversies, and in public policy-making generally. Arguably, many of the hard questions in law boil down to a conflict between the protection of individual rights and the promotion of collective utility.

Liberals who have a notion that rights exist irrespective of the content of law at any one time fall within the category of "deontological liberals" (deriving from the Greek word "deon", meaning duty). They may draw inspiration from the German philosopher Immanuel Kant (1724-1804) who argued that individuals are ends in themselves and should not be used merely as means to an end. A deonto-logical liberal gives priority to the *right* over the *good*. Thus certain things are right regardless of their consequences. According to Michael Sandel, a communi-tarian writer, the core thesis of deontological liberalism is that:

> [S]ociety, being composed of a plurality of persons, each with his own aims, interests and conceptions of the good, is best arranged when it is governed by principles that do not *themselves* presuppose any particular conception of the good; what justifies these regulative principles above all is not that they maxi-mize the social welfare or otherwise promote the good, but rather that they

---

87   See, in particular, the work of Michael Walzer, *Spheres of Justice: A Defence of Pluralism and Equality*, Blackwell, 1983.

88   See J Waldron (ed), *"Nonsense upon Stilts", Bentham, Burke and the Rights of Man*, Methuen, 1987.

conform to the concept of *right*, a moral category given prior to the good and independent of it.[89]

The last part of the above quotation shows that a deontological liberal does not seek to evaluate an act in terms of *consequences*, such as the maximisation of social welfare, but in the right of the actor to do the act. At a collective level, the state should be neutral about the good life and simply protect the rights of people to pursue their *own* idea of the good life. This is in contrast to a "teleological liberal" (deriving from the Greek word "telos", meaning goal) who does have a particular conception of the good: that is, a goal to be aimed at. Such a liberal does evaluate acts in terms of their consequences for reaching that goal.

The kind of teleology that has dominated liberal thought is utilitarianism which, as we will see, holds broadly that the good life is one that promotes the greatest happiness for the greatest number. A utilitarian therefore defines the morally right as simply that which maximises the good.[90] Put crudely, a Kantian objects to utilitarianism because under it individuals can be used as means to an end beyond themselves.

This division between deontological and teleological liberalism is reflected in everyday legal controversies. On the one hand, the liberal lawyer is tempted by the idea that certain things are in the nature of moral absolutes; principles like one should not kill, steal or break one's promise.[91] On the other hand, there is a feeling that sometimes wrongs must be committed to bring about a greater good; that the big picture must also be borne in mind. An example of this tension between the right and the good relates to the whether the defence of necessity, which falls outside the immediate bounds of threat of unlawful violence that could legitimately justify self-defence, should be recognised. This has particularly troubled the courts in relation to the application of necessity to cases of intentional killing. The conflict between the individual rights and the collective good was brought into sharp relief by the infamous 19th century English case dealing with cannibalism on the high seas, *R v Dudley and Stephens*.[92] In accordance with established maritime custom,[93] shipwrecked sailors would often choose one from their number, usually by drawing lots, to be killed and consumed in order to permit the survival of the remainder. The Court of Crown Cases Reserved established that this would be murder – the common law drawing its line in favour of the right to life rather than utility. Lord Coleridge CJ, in delivering the judgment of the court, held that the accused were guilty of murder and sentenced them to death. This mandatory penalty was later commuted by the executive to six months' imprisonment. In holding that the defence of necessity was not available to a charge of murder, Lord Coleridge CJ stated:

> To preserve one's life is generally speaking a duty, but it may be the plainest and the highest duty to sacrifice it. War is full of instances in which it is a man's duty

---

89 Note 46, 1 (original emphasis).

90 See A Buchanan and D Mathieu, "Philosophy and Justice" in RL Cohen, *Justice*, Plenum Press, 1986, 11 at 22.

91 For a Kantian analysis accessible to students of contract law, see C Fried, *Contract as Promise*, Harvard UP, 1981.

92 (1884) 14 QBD 273.

93 For an engaging legal historical analysis of this case, see A Simpson, *Cannibalism and the Common Law*, University of Chicago Press, 1984.

not to live, but to die ... It is not correct, therefore, to say that there is any absolute or unqualified necessity to preserve one's life ... It is not needful to point out the awful danger of the principle which has been contended for. Who is to be the judge of this sort of necessity? By what measure is the comparative value of lives to be measured? Is it to be strength, or intellect, or what? It is plain that the principle leaves to him who is to profit by it to determine the necessity which will justify him deliberately taking another's life to save his own ... it is quite plain that such a principle once admitted might be made the legal cloak for unbridled passion and atrocious crime.[94]

In Chapter 6 we will see that legal ethics provides another example. One feels that clients should have a right to confide in their lawyer in the absolute certainty that the communication will be kept confidential.[95] However, we can also see the antisocial, even unjust, consequences that this can have if the court is deprived of true information and an innocent person suffers as a result. Recognising that these dilemmas are illustrations of more fundamental divisions within liberal thought may not generate a particular solution to them but it does provide a theoretical framework for balancing these competing interests.

Two prominent deontological liberals today are Ronald Dworkin and Robert Nozick.[96] The former's *Taking Rights Seriously*[97] has been one of the most acclaimed and disputed texts on legal philosophy in recent times. To Dworkin, rights are trumps which cannot be made to give way to the wishes of the majority or to policies aimed at promoting the good of "society".[98] We have already seen Dworkin's strong conception of equality. When combined with his rights theory we have what appears to be a powerful theory of justice.

Dworkin argues that, in addition to positive rights enshrined in legal rules, there are background rights and these, or their derivatives, are to be found, inter alia, in entities called legal principles. The ultimate or basic background right is the right to "equal consideration and respect" and from this a scheme of egalitarian moral rights is deduced. Legal *principles* are invoked in the so-called hard case where there is no legal *rule* unambiguously available.

The ambitious nature of this theory lies in two aspects. First, to Dworkin the law can always produce a right answer. Unlike the modern legal positivist who usually acknowledges that rules can run out in unusual cases and that a judge simply has to exercise discretion, Dworkin says that the judge must retreat to principles to find the answer: for example, the principle that no man should profit from his own wrong. Second, Dworkin's thesis attempts to bridge the gap between law and morality; a gap upon which legal positivists insist. Instead of a sharp disjunction between law and morality, we have legal principles which are vehicles for

---

94　Note 92, 287-288.

95　For a Kantian analysis, see C Fried, "The Lawyer as Friend: The Moral Foundations of the Lawyer-Client Relation" (1976) 85 *Yale Law Journal* 1060. See generally D Luban, *Lawyers and Justice*, Princeton UP, 1988, Ch 5.

96　One could add John Rawls' entitlement theory of justice, already discussed. A contrast between Rawls and Nozick highlights the divisions within liberal thought in that, from some shared premises, they arrive at opposite conclusions regarding the extent of free contract and the redistributive role of the state; see J Cassels, "Liberal Presuppositions" (1988) 38 *University of Toronto Law Journal* 378 at 395.

97　Duckworth, 1978.

98　For a clear critical discussion of Dworkin's rights theory, see Campbell, n 71, Ch 4.

conveying moral principles into the courtroom. To use a distinction that we drew earlier, Dworkin suggests a way of bringing substantive justice (in this case a rights theory) into formal justice. We will return to Dworkin's ideas when we look at the rule of law and formalism in Chapter 3. At this stage we need only note that Dworkin provides an intriguing, if controversial, argument in support of left-leaning welfare policies and rules that is grounded in deontological rather than teleological theory.

One reason why Dworkin's approach is intriguing is that rights theories are often associated with the political right rather than the political left.[99] They are commonly portrayed as theories for resisting utilitarian policies that place the collective's good over the individual's rights. A celebrated example of this can be found in Robert Nozick's *Anarchy, State and Utopia*[100] and we mention him here both for contrast with Dworkin but also because of his attachment to property rights specifically.

Nozick argues that the most extensive state that can be justified is the minimal, or "nightwatchman", state. Such a state is limited to the functions of protecting all its citizens against violence, theft and fraud and to the enforcement of contracts. Any state more extensive violates people's rights. Nozick describes his theory as an historical entitlement theory of justice. A distribution of goods is just if the property in question was *acquired in the correct way*. The distribution is not to be evaluated in terms of the resulting patterns of distribution in society. In very much summary form, he argues that holdings are acquired in the correct way if the transferor freely chose to part with them, either by gift or contract (exchange) or if the holder mixed her or his labour with an unowned object. It follows, therefore, that a state which takes away the holdings to which people are entitled, for example by taxing them, for purposes other than to fulfil the night-watchman role, is acting unjustly because it is interfering with their rights. It further follows that taxation is a form of theft, at least in a non-legal sense.[101]

Nozick is undoubtedly on the libertarian "right" wing of modern liberalism. Many liberals acknowledge that the state has a much more extensive role in redistributing wealth by raising taxes for education, health, roads and income support for the needy. On the other hand, the Nozick strand of liberalism is reflected in diffuse forms, for example in the differing social attitudes to social security fraud and tax evasion. The former is often seen as the immoral scrounging from others whilst the latter, though illegal, is regarded more leniently and often seen as a failed but valiant attempt by citizens to keep what is theirs.[102]

Nozick's thesis also illustrates the general attachment that liberals have to rights of ownership. Honore describes what he calls "the liberal concept of ownership" as "the greatest possible interest in a thing which a mature system of law recognizes".[103] The owner of a thing can, in the simple uncomplicated case,

---

99 For a discussion of whether this association is justified, see T Campbell, *The Left and Rights*, RKP, 1983.

100 Basic Books, 1974.

101 See, for example, B Bracewell-Milnes, *Tax Avoidance and Evasion: The Individual and Society*, Panopticum Press, 1979.

102 See M Sawer, "Philosophical Underpinnings of Libertarianism in Australia" in M Sawer (ed), *Australia and the New Right*, Allen & Unwin, 1982, 24.

103 T Honore, "Ownership" in A Guest (ed), *Oxford Essays in Jurisprudence*, Oxford UP, 1961, 108.

use it, stop others from using it, lend it, sell it or leave it by will. This notion of ownership is not peculiar to liberal societies in the modern world, of course. What is distinctive is that the liberal begins with an assumption that *all* things can be subject to ownership by an individual unless there is a justifiable reason to the contrary. A liberal, particularly a deontological liberal, therefore tends not to draw distinctions between different classes of things. The owner is free to act on a whim and close down a profitable factory on which a whole community depends. This would contrast with, say, a socialist system where productive assets such as land and businesses are withdrawn from private ownership, even if there remain ownership rights in personal property.

We mentioned above that the *assumption* is that all things can be subject to ownership. All modern liberal states have laws preventing the ownership of particular dangerous items. A common justification for prohibiting ownership is JS Mill's harm principle which we discussed earlier in the chapter. The case of flick-knives is illustrative. The liberty to manufacture, sell, hire, offer for sale or hire, lend or give a flick-knife was prohibited in most jurisdictions and the prohibition may be justified on the Mill principle. In the case of *Fisher v Bell*,[104] well known to first year law students, the Divisional Court drew the distinction in contract law between an offer for sale and an invitation to treat when overturning the conviction of a shopkeeper who had displayed such a knife in his shop window. An invitation to treat was not specifically prohibited by the Act, although it subsequently became so.[105] The decision illustrates the principle that if the state is to interfere with the liberty of the subject then it must do so in unambiguous terms: any ambiguity being decided in favour of the individual.[106]

In Australia, there is a presumption that penal provisions are strictly construed, which operates so as to allow resolution of any ambiguity or doubt raised by the language of the statute in favour of the accused. There is also a presumption that coercive powers would be interpreted in a way that protects private property rights. In *Coco v The Queen*,[107] the High Court examined the legal powers of the police in Queensland to enter private premises (in effect, trespassing) in order to install a listening device. The High Court stressed that any interference with the ordinary rights of ownership is justified only where it has been authorised or excused by law.[108] The High Court held that, in the absence of an express provision in the Queensland Act authorising such trespass, a warrant could not be issued in such broad terms. The primacy of property rights, and the reluctance to authorise what otherwise amounts to a trespass, means that the legislation governing the use of listening devices is narrowly construed. The legislation was quickly amended to permit the lawful installation, maintenance and removal of these devices. The basic liberal principle is that subjects may do what they please with their property unless specifically prevented by law.

The harm to others principle tends to be invoked within utilitarian thought as a justification for interfering with liberty and Mill was himself a utilitarian of sorts. Although it can be similarly invoked within deontology to justify the

---

104 [1961] 1 QB 394.
105 *Restriction of Offensive Weapons Act 1961* (UK) s 1.
106 *Beckwith v R* (1976) 12 ALR 333 at 339 per Gibbs J.
107 (1994) 68 ALJR 401.
108 Ibid 403.

interference with rights, at least if the "harm" being caused to others amounts to an interference with *their* rights, there is some general alignment between deontological societies and devotion to freedom of property. Hostility to gun control and taxation in the United States, for example, is partly founded on a strong attachment to property rights, although culture, folk-lore and vested interest no doubt also contribute.[109]

There is a strong tendency in liberal discourse to fetishise rights. Legal rights are considered as self-executing, taking no account of the social and cultural disadvantage of individuals who theoretically possess particular rights, a concern which we identified above. Dissatisfied with the privileging of liberalism within conventional legal discourse, some critical and feminist scholars have rejected the concept of rights entirely.[110] Valerie Kerruish in *Jurisprudence as Ideology* rejects the prevailing politico-morals ideas for using rights, claiming it is wrong to support rights as "claims of liberal ideals of liberty, equality and democratic community, or of justice or human rights or whatever".[111] Rather, she argues that rights should be construed as "claims by people bearing the heaviest burdens of our way of life, which express resistance to the established order of things". This approach recognises the empowering effect of the language of rights within legal and political discourse. As Hilary Charlesworth concludes:

> The assertion of rights can have great symbolic force for oppressed groups within a society offering a significant vocabulary to formulate political and social grievances which is recognised by the powerful.[112]

(ix)   Utilitarianism

Modern liberal philosophy has offered utilitarianism, a teleological theory, as the main alternative to Kantian deontology. Utilitarianism takes many forms but, as David Lyons says, "the central idea of many of its most common and traditional forms is that acts and institutions must be judged solely by their effects on human *welfare*, where the welfare of an individual is understood to be determined by facts about that individual's interests, wants and needs".[113] "Utility", to Jeremy Bentham, was the greatest happiness of the greatest number and its maximisation the proper end of humankind. Thus the basic principle for testing the adequacy of any law or act of administration is a calculus of pain and pleasure. Maximising the happiness of the maximum number lies at the core of this theory. Alan Norrie in *Crime, Reason and History* has summarised the theory as follows:

> In England, the utilitarian reformer Bentham wrote that mankind was placed under two sovereign masters, pain and pleasure, and possessed an innate tendency to avoid one and seek the other. The ability to calculate rationally the

---

109   For a general discussion, see K Ahern, "The Right to Shoot" (1988) 7 *Australian Society* 62.

110   For a review of this debate, see H Charlesworth, "Taking the Gender of Rights Seriously" in B Galligan and C Sampford (eds), *Rethinking Human Rights*, Federation Press, 1997, 32-35; and J Morgan, "Equality Rights in the Australian Context: A Feminist Perspective" in P Alston (ed), *Towards an Australian Bill of Rights*, CIPL and HREOC, 1994, 123-131.

111   Routledge, 1991, 145.

112   H Charlesworth, "The Australian Reluctance About Rights" in Alston, n 110, 49. See also Charlesworth, "Taking the Gender of Rights Seriously", n 110, Ch 3.

113   D Lyons, *Ethics and the Rule of Law*, Cambridge UP, 1984, 111.

consequences of action combined with the pain/pleasure principle to enable the individual to maximise his [sic] self interest.[114]

The impact of this central assumption was manifold. To be able to guide conduct, laws must be laid down in advance and knowable to all, which favoured the adoption of legislation and codes over the continued dominance of judge-made common law which Bentham despised.[115] The impact of these liberal utilitarian values on law has been significant and enduring. The modern law continues to pursue codification in many areas (with limited success) and is stamped throughout with liberal assumptions about "free will" and "rationality". The emphasis on subjective fault as a measure of culpability, and prevention and deterrence as principal objectives of the criminal law, are testament to the enduring power of these ideas.

As an ethical theory, utilitarianism can be contrasted with "prudence", which evaluates actions or decisions in relation to the *agent's* own good or welfare, because utilitarianism evaluates actions or decisions in relation to the *general* welfare.[116] Thus, although utilitarianism is an individualistic theory (in that it is only the sum of individual preferences that matters), it is also an altruistic theory in that it resolves a conflict of individual interests in the manner which serves the greater aggregate interest. It is also egalitarian in a limited way because each person's interests count equally when they are put into the aggregate; no one's can be discounted. It is not fully egalitarian, however. If, for example, a particular proposal is in the general interest (calculated by the sum of individual interests) but will benefit people unequally, the utilitarian may favour it whilst the egalitarian may favour an alternative that spreads the benefits equally even if less benefit results overall.

This contrast with egalitarianism leads us into some criticisms of utilitarianism. By and large, liberal moral and political philosophers in the past two decades have moved away from what HLA Hart has called "the old faith that some form of utilitarianism must capture the essence of political morality" to a new faith that "the truth must lie with a doctrine of basic human rights, protecting specific basic liberties and interests of individuals".[117] Numerous examples have been proffered where utilitarianism seems to lead to unjust results: for example, the death of an innocent person in order to save a greater number of innocent lives, as in the graphic case of survivalist cannibalism discussed above. Another difficulty with the utilitarian calculus is determining how pleasure and pain can be quantified and how the intensity of one person's preferences can be measured against the intensity of another's. Furthermore, scepticism has been expressed about utilitarianism's psychological premise that human beings do, as a matter of fact, all seek to maximise their own pleasures and minimise their own pains.

---

114 Note 43, 18.

115 Bentham called common law "dog law", "for it condemned individuals after the event, in the way that a person punishes his [or her] dog. The dog only learns after the punishment that what it has done is wrong": Norrie, n 43, 19. Bentham's preference for legislation over common law stood in stark contrast to the earlier views of Blackstone who eulogised the common law in *Commentaries on the Laws of England*, 9th ed, Garland, 1978 (first published, 1765).

116 Lyons, n 113.

117 "Between Utility and Rights" in A Ryan (ed), *The Idea of Freedom*, Oxford UP, 1979, 77.

Various reformulations of utilitarianism have been produced in response to these criticisms[118] but its philosophical appeal has waned. It may be that the new challengers to rights-based liberalism are communitarianism and republicanism, which place greater emphasis than many rights theories do on the individual's membership of a community and which stress that "the individual" is partly constituted by the community: he or she is not a fully formed person before participating in social life.[119] Such theories can lead to results which are similar to modern utilitarianism – for example, the endorsement of a welfare state – but they claim to do so without the right-ward tugging of libertarian considerations. One might add that environmentalism may emerge as a separate body of theory that challenges both utilitarian concerns with majority interests and economic growth, and also Kantian concerns with individual rights.

Outside the world of political and moral philosophy, and particularly in the worlds of law and economics, utilitarianism remains powerfully attractive, however. As Tom Campbell says:

> Utilitarianism – in some shape or form – has been, in recent times, a working hypothesis for most western economists and constitutes a fair reflection of the concentration on economic growth as the central policy goal in modern politics. Present-day utilitarianism is, perhaps, best exemplified by "welfare economics" which adopts as the basic economic norm the maximization of human utility or "welfare", an approach which has also been applied to democratic theory and, more recently, to the common law.[120]

More commonly in law, utilitarian and liberal approaches are engaged in a dialogue that is often reduced to conflict between individual rights and collective welfare.[121] In this way, welfare is not conceived as an overriding principle but rather as a rival to the harm principle that mediates and limits arguments based on individual autonomy.

(x)   The assumption of rationality

Rationality has been a central theme in over 2000 years of philosophy because of a conviction that it is the power to reason which distinguishes human beings from other sentient beings. Liberalism, however, is said to be particularly based upon an assumption of rationality, both of individuals and governments. An adequate definition of rationality for these purposes is notoriously elusive but a standard one is along the following lines. Rationality describes thought and action which

118   For contemporary discussions, see JCC Smart and B Williams, *Utilitarianism: For and Against*, Cambridge UP, 1973; P Singer, *Practical Ethics*, Cambridge UP, 1979, Ch 1; and RE Goodin, *Utilitarianism as a Public Philosophy*, Cambridge UP, 1995.

119   The differences between communitarian and republican positions do not concern us here but, for a brief discussion, see P Pettit, "Liberalism and Republicanism: Variation on a theme from Roberto Unger" (1987) 11 *Bulletin of the Australian Society of Legal Philosophy* 190.

120   Campbell, n 71, 124-125. Jules Coleman, however, has argued that alternative ethical bases to utilitarianism can be supplied for various definitions of economic efficiency: see J Coleman, "Efficiency, Utility and Wealth Maximization" in *Markets, Morals and the Law*, Cambridge UP, 1988, Ch 4.

121   N Lacey has advocated the principle of welfare, as a means for reconstructing the criminal law and punishment around a different set of collective goals. Her principle of welfare includes "the fulfilment of certain basic interests such as maintaining one's personal safety, health and capacity to pursue one's chosen life plan": *State Punishment*, Routledge, 1986, 104.

are conscious, in accordance with rules of logic, based on factual knowledge and aimed at objectives which are coherent, mutually consistent and to be achieved by the most appropriate means.[122]

The social theorist Max Weber (1864-1920) argued that the most important trend in modern western society has been towards formal rationality. This involves the subjection of social life to precise regulation, the extension of exact calculation in the economy and the application of scientific methods to production. The authority of rulers in modern societies stems not from a belief in the exceptional qualities (or "charisma") of a particular person, nor from the mere fact that it has always been done this way ("tradition"), but because the rule is bureaucratic and proceeds along formally rational lines. In Weber's ideal type, a formally rational legal system is procedurally logical. The legal system has long abandoned the *irrational* systems of proof such as immersing litigants in water or subjecting them to some other ordeal, or using trial by battle where champions fought on the parties behalf. This might be contrasted with a *substantively* rational legal system which bases its decisions on some general principles drawn from outside the legal system.[123] Rationality, however, is deeply historically contingent. From an earlier perspective, trial by ordeal made perfect sense since the parties were leaving it for God to intervene to determine the rightful party. The process of determining outcomes logically from principles *within the law itself* took many centuries to establish. Indeed the modern law of evidence, and the rational system of proof upon which it is based, emerged at a relatively late stage of legal development – indeed, notwithstanding claims of an ancient pedigree, the presumption of innocence and burden and standard of proof date are entrenched only in the early 20th century.[124]

Weber used terms more commonly found today in sociology than in philosophy but the ideal type of a formally rational legal system seems to resemble most closely the legal systems of European liberal states in the late 19th and early 20th centuries. As one might expect of a social theorist, Weber was concerned with *institutional* arrangements in modern societies and this explains his emphasis on rationality in government and law. Liberal philosophers have tended to begin with the rationality of the individual and then extrapolate to the collective level. The liberal believes that individuals are all endowed with the capacity to reason; that they are essentially rational beings. They can calculate the consequences of various lines of action and make their choices. This assumption of fact about the rational capacities of individuals is related to the normative belief in personal autonomy. In other words, human beings are innately capable of reasoning and should do so in becoming authors of their own lives.

Simmons notes that "[a] powerful strand of thinking which has tended to support utilitarian theories is the idea that rationality is almost entirely a matter of fitting means to ends in an instrumental way".[125] According to the 18th century Scottish utilitarian David Hume, reason cannot tell us what we ought to pursue but

---

122 See the entry by M Albrow for "Rationality" in GD Mitchell, *A New Dictionary of Sociology*, RKP, 1979.

123 For clear introductions to Weber's sociology of law, see EM Schur, *Law and Society*, Random House, 1968, 108-110 and A Hunt, *The Sociological Movement in Law*, Macmillan, 1978, Ch 5.

124 Bronitt and McSherry, n 75, Ch 2.

125 NE Simmonds, *Central Issues in Jurisprudence*, Sweet and Maxwell, 1986, 22.

only how to attain ends we have already chosen. Ultimately our moral beliefs, such as that promises ought to be kept, are based on preferences which are neither reasonable nor unreasonable. The one thing that we all desire, however, is happiness (says the utilitarian). The rational way of acting morally, and therefore of arranging laws to promote moral actions, is accordingly to aim for the maximum happiness.

Standing opposed to the utilitarian disjunction between reason and morality is the Kantian view that there is a basic moral requirement to act with respect for persons. A Kantian believes there *are* ways of reasoning towards correct moral positions from this premise of respect for persons. A moral theory, to Kant, must be a universalisable theory, that is, the fundamental test of the morality of action is whether one could consistently will that the principle of one's actions should become a *universal law* of human nature (the so-called "categorical imperative"). Thus one can ask whether a proposed action shows a respect for the person which is capable of being elevated into a rule applicable *to all persons*. Charles Fried, for example, has written a Kantian analysis of contract law which purports to show rationally that it is wrong to break one's promise in particular circumstances. Respect for the promisee, and all other promisees, requires that the promise be kept:

> There exists a convention that defines the practice of promising and its entailments. This convention provides a way that a person may create expectations in others. By virtue of the basic Kantian principles of trust and respect, it is wrong to invoke that convention in order to make a promise, and then to break it.[126]

Although this difference over morality and reason is as major as other differences between utilitarian and Kantian liberalism, there are nevertheless similarities in psychological assumptions. Both theories are based on individualistic premises and both assume that people are capable ordinarily of making rational decisions. Both reject strong forms of determinism that suggest individuals are conditioned or programmed to behave in certain ways.

This is important for an analysis of law because so much of the common law works on an assumption of rational decision-making as the basis for responsibility for actions. The criminal law, for example, is slow to excuse people from the consequences of their acts merely on the grounds that their family background, class, drug addiction, race or gender had given them no choice. This is not to suggest that these external factors that influence behaviour (an account that is often labelled as "determinism") never play a role in assessing responsibility. Rather, we are suggesting that liberalism focuses legal and doctrinal attention on freewill and voluntariness, pushing other constraining factors to the margins, usually to be considered as an "exceptional" excuse or mitigating factor relevant to the sentencing. Another example is contract law, which classically requires strict performance of promises and, with a few exceptions, only excuses the promisor if the promisee has played some part in the problem (such as contributed to a mistake or wrongfully taken advantage). The utilitarian, at least a modern one, might be prepared to take a more lenient line in certain categories of cases than a Kantian, but the utilitarian would still argue that the greatest happiness is ordinarily served by the enforcement of promises.

---

126 Fried, n 91, 17.

We will return to the liberal assumption of rationality at various points. In particular, we will be looking at a version of feminist jurisprudence which argues that the law in liberal societies is constructed with the thought patterns and behaviour of middle class men of the market in mind. Both the substantive rules and the procedures of law therefore tend to exclude women, the poor and those from other cultures.

(d)   A case study on the limits of liberalism

The above account of liberalism aims to draw out many of its key elements. As a principle of political philosophy, liberalism has implications for contemporary debates about the proper direction of law reform, as well how legal doctrine is (or rather should be) constructed. The following case study illustrates how many of these values apply to a specific area – the legal regulation of pornography – and how many of the key elements and assumption of liberalism remain hotly contested.

Pornography and the challenges to liberalism

> I shall not today attempt further to define the kinds of material I understand to be embraced within that shorthand description [hardcore pornography]; and perhaps I could never succeed in intelligibly doing so. But I know it when I see it ...[127]

The law governing obscenity, which regulates the production, supply and possession of pornography, has not developed according to a coherent theoretical blueprint. Before the 20th century, the law in Australia was largely bound up with state efforts to curb press freedom and impose censorship on political and literary radicals.[128] As political censorship of the theatre and novels became increasingly untenable, the focus of obscenity laws shifted to the regulation of pornography in the 20th century. In the early part of that century, the law was primarily concerned with upholding morals, particularly enforcing a conception of Christian morality. The legal test was whether the materials exhibited a tendency to "deprave and corrupt morals". Change came in the 1960s, a period when Australia underwent significant social upheaval. The law relating to obscenity shifted away from applying Christian moral standards to a wider "community standards" test.[129]

This was not just a semantic change that repackaged the protection of public morals into more acceptable secular form. The idea of community standards, as incorporated into legal doctrine and now underpinning the federal classification scheme, incorporates a set of liberal values, such as the right to privacy. Balanced against these interests is the right not to harmed by such material. Indeed, these

---

127 *Jacobellis v Ohio* (1964) 387 US 184 at 197 per Stewart J.

128 M Pollak, *Sense and Censorship – Commentaries on Censorship Violence in Australia*, Reed, 1990.

129 *Crowe v Graham* (1968) 121 CLR 375, discussed in A Blackshield, "Censorship and the Law" in G Dutton and M Harris (eds), *Australia's Censorship Crisis*, Sun Books, 1970, 23. See also S Bronitt and H Mares, "Sex" in T Blackshield, M Coper and G Williams (eds), *Oxford Companion to the High Court of Australia*, Oxford UP, 2001, 620-622.

values are expressed as "principles" in the federal *National Classification Code*, which are intended to guide the classification of materials under the *Classification (Publications, Films and Computer Games) Act 1995* (Cth) Act (see Schedule). This Code provides that classification decisions are to give effect, as far as possible, to the following principles:

(a) adults should be able to read, hear and see what they want;

(b) minors should be protected from material likely to harm or disturb them;

(c) everyone should be protected from exposure to unsolicited material that they find offensive;

(d) the need to take account of community concerns about:

    (i) depictions that condone or incite violence, particularly sexual violence; and

    (ii) the portrayal of persons in a demeaning manner.

From a liberal perspective, interference with privacy in order to protect morals in the absence of any harm to others is simply unacceptable. Liberalism rejects the idea that the criminal law should be used to enforce a particular conception of private morality, and legal philosophers, such as Ronald Dworkin, have argued that there is a right to pornography as an exercise of the freedom of moral responsibility.[130] While the first principle contained in the *National Classification Code* above demonstrates some commitment to *individual* freedom, classification (and hence legal availability) is also determined by looking at relevant *community* standards of morality, decency and propriety.

The legal definition of obscenity is notoriously elusive raising many objections from a liberal perspective. Justice Stewart's famous dictum on hardcore pornography – the "know it when I see it" approach – typifies the definitional difficulty confronting judges. This fundamental indeterminacy not only affects the common law. Many key statutory concepts in statutory offences are left to judges and juries with only limited guidance in the legislation or caselaw.

Like Justice Stewart, Barwick CJ in *Crowe v Graham* doubted the wisdom of defining terms like "indecent" or "indecency", concluding simply that material that offended "the modesty of the average man or woman in sexual matters" would be an indecent article for the purpose of the *Obscene and Indecent Publications Act 1901* (NSW).[131] As Windeyer J held in *Crowe v Graham*, considerations of liberty, such as freedom of speech, were not relevant to the task of determining the community standard of decency.[132] From a liberal perspective, there is difficulty in determining the permissible limits of obscenity as the inherently conservative values of judges (which can exert considerable influence on the jury) may operate to discriminate against individuals or groups that hold unconventional views on sexual matters. While key definitions remain hazy, the law in a pragmatic way "regulates" obscenity through the classification scheme. Indeed, the uncertainty surrounding the scope of obscenity crimes encourages publishers and suppliers of potentially obscene or indecent material to submit to a "voluntary" *National Code of Classification*, compliance with which confers immunity from prosecution. As a result obscenity prosecutions are

---

130 R Dworkin, "Is There a Right to Pornography" (1981) 1 *Oxford Journal of Legal Studies* 177.

131 (1968) 121 CLR 375 at 379.

132 Ibid 398-399.

increasingly rare. The concept of regulation and its relationship to law is further explored in Chapter 10.

Under the existing legal framework, the classification scheme exhibits strong liberal hues: privacy interests of adults combine with the importance of preventing harm, especially to minors. Moral and communal standards also intervene in a number of ways: decision-makers must reflect community standards in applying standards of morality, decency and propriety of "reasonable adults": s 11. The federal Act requires that members of the Classification Board be "broadly representative of the Australian community": s 48(2). Indeed, the harm principle implicitly applied by the Board extends beyond curbing conduct that causes physical injury (sexual violence) to others and includes protection from "offensive" and "demeaning" depictions. Liberalism would reject restrictions on materials consumed in private simply because they were offensive to others. While some regulation of pornography would be justifiable to protect the autonomy rights of those individuals involved in the sex industry and those members of the general public who did not wish to view such material, the prohibition of sexual material on the ground that it causes offence to the moral standards of a hypothetical "reasonable person" would not be justifiable.[133]

There is considerable disagreement over whether such offensive material, whether directly or indirectly, causes "harm to others". Liberal theorists have struggled with the accommodating offensiveness within the harm principle. Joel Feinberg in *The Moral Limits of the Criminal Law: Harm to Others* explored this aspect of the harm principle, proposing a broader conception of the harm principle that encompassed any "setback to a person's interest".[134] In his later work, Feinberg refines these ideas through the development of the "offense principle", which would permit the use of criminal prohibitions in order to prevent serious offence or hurt to other persons.[135]

The federal Act and *National Classification Code* offer no guidance on how conflicting liberal and communal interests should be reconciled. Presumably, the tribunal determining the matter must engage in some form of a balancing exercise. This tension between individual liberal and communal morals is apparent in the European Court of Human Rights (ECHR) decision of *Handyside v United Kingdom*, where the court held that the freedom of expression may be justifiably restricted in order to protect "public morals".[136] Anne Orford has noted that a review of international and comparative jurisprudence in this area reveals that the liberal principles of free speech and privacy are held not to be infringed by obscenity laws based on "community standards".[137] However, as Orford points out the process of building "community" in legal discourse continues to exclude women's interests:

---

133 J Braithwaite and P Pettit, *Not Just Deserts*, Clarendon Press, 1990, 96.

134 Oxford UP, 1984, 215; see also J Schonsheck, *On Criminalisation: An Essay in the Philosophy of the Criminal Law*, Kluwer, 1994.

135 *Offense to Others*, Oxford UP, 1985.

136 (1976) Series A, No 24, 1 EHRR 737.

137 "Liberty, Equality, Pornography: The Bodies of Women and Human Rights Discourse" (1994) 3 *Australian Feminist Law Journal* 72.

The silencing of the voices of women enables the construction of "community consensus" in liberal theory, of a false universal which assimilates all difference in the public sphere. The idea of moral consensus has been used by liberal theorists and judges, both to uphold or propose regimes for criminalising or regulating "obscenity", and to argue that anti-pornography ordinances based on feminist perspectives are an infringement of individual freedom.[138]

Leading US feminist Catharine MacKinnon has noted that obscenity laws in the United States have rarely operated to prohibit the publication, sale and supply of sexually explicit material. She concludes that persistent judicial refusal in the case law to define obscenity is systematic and determinate. It is part of an epistemological process by which the legal standard of obscenity "is built on what the male standpoint sees".[139]

While liberals object to the breadth and arbitrariness of legal definitions of obscenity, feminists and critical legal scholars raise concern that the legal standards of indecency operate in discriminatory ways against women and sexual minorities such as gays and lesbians. The debate about the regulation of pornography is deeply implicated in questions about gender, in particular the role of the public/private dichotomy. Feminist anti-pornography arguments are confronted with the assertion of both public and private rights. As Nicola Lacey has observed:

> The liberal analysis which constructs pornography as a matter of private sexual preference in one breath constructs it as a matter of public right to free expression in the next. In what might be called a "no-lose situation" for the producers and consumers of pornography, the production of pornography is seen as a matter of public right, and hence protected, whilst its consumption is constructed as a matter of private interest, and hence also protected.[140]

Debates over the legal regulation of pornography can produce strange coalitions of conservative moralism and radical feminism.[141] While both desire restrictions on the availability of obscene material, the justifications for so doing are dramatically different. Rather than focus on the perceived immoral quality of pornography, the feminist critique conceives it as a harmful social practice which expresses and causes the subordination of women. The question of harm to women generally is problematic, raising once again the fundamental indeterminacy and elasticity of the concept of "harm to others" discussed above. The correlation between the wider availability of pornography and levels of sexual violence and discrimination remains contentious and inconclusive. Rather than enter this discussion, some feminist have argued that pornography *itself* constitutes a form of gender discrimination. This approach deftly avoids establishing whether pornography causes harm or contributes to violence against women in society.

By focusing on discrimination and inequality, only certain forms of sexually explicit materials need be censured. Indeed, in the United States, Indianapolis

---

138 Ibid 97-99.

139 *Towards A Feminist Theory of State*, Harvard UP, 1989, 197.

140 Lacey, n 69, Ch 3, 88.

141 For a review of the conflicting perspectives – moral, feminist and liberal – on pornography, see H Potter, *Pornography*, Federation Press, 1996.

enacted an anti-pornography ordinance based on a model law drafted by leading feminist law professors, Andrea Dworkin and Catharine MacKinnon. This model conceptualised pornography as sex discrimination, creating a wide range of civil causes of action to individuals harmed by pornography. Ultimately, the law was held to be constitutionally invalid for unduly interfering with freedom of speech protected by the First Amendment.[142] A more successful outcome from a feminist perspective was achieved in Canada, where the Supreme Court of Canada held that depictions of degrading and dehumanising stereotyping of women constituted an interference with the right to equality and therefore could be justifiably restricted by obscenity laws.[143] Such strategies require the law to distinguish between types of porn: between discriminatory sexual imagery and material which promotes positive images of female sexuality. Admittedly, such a vision of pornography seems remote, bearing in mind the prevailing genre that sexualises dominance and violence.

Equality, as noted above, is not without its limitations. Liberal conceptions of equality, particularly the idea of equality *as sameness*, fail to address the structural disadvantage of marginalised and disempowered groups. Mindful of this, some feminists have doubted that embracing liberal constructs, such as the right to equality, is likely to be an effective legal strategy. Nicola Lacey, for example, has expressed doubts about the value of reforms of pornography laws based on equality, noting that this discourse can have counterproductive effects, often working against legislative reforms designed to alleviate disadvantage. This is because of the individuated nature of the anti-discrimination laws and their limited ability to redress group-based harms.[144]

Modern debates about legislative reform, including much feminist critique, seem trapped within a liberal dichotomy drawn between private and public interests. Rather than accept this dichotomy, Nicola Lacey argues that the dichotomy needs to be reconceptualised. While feminists have sought to relocate sexual harms against women from the private/unregulated sphere to the public/regulated sphere, they have largely overlooked the potential of privacy to maximise human autonomy through positive regulation. Privacy, like liberty generally, may be reconstructed as a positive right to personal and emotional development, rather than a negative right to be free from unjustified interference by others, in other words, the right to be left alone. Lacey's perspective provides the platform from which feminists may challenge serious autonomy-reducing sexual practices ranging from rape to violent pornography. She doubts the value of pursuing the legislative strategies of the sort adopted in the United States, placing greater emphasis on the power of feminist critique to transcend the public/private dichotomy and to raise consciousness.[145] Carol Smart, while recognising the importance of such feminist strategies, argues that "consciousness

---

142 *American Booksellers v William Hudnutt III, Mayor, City of Indianapolis* (1985) 771 F 2d 323 (7th Cir). The background to the ordinance and the constitutional challenge are reviewed in Graycar and Morgan, n 44, 375-390.

143 See *R v Butler* [1992] 1 SCR 452; discussed in A Orford, "Liberty, Equality, Pornography: The Bodies of Women and Human Rights Discourse" (1994) 3 *Australian Feminist Law Journal* 72 at 97.

144 Lacy, n 69, 92-97.

145 Ibid 96-97.

raising is a starting point not the finishing post".[146] Law's truths about women and female sexuality must be confronted within the legal as well as political and social arena.

In conclusion, the present law seems ill-equipped to deal with the controversy around pornography. As we have demonstrated in this case study, the legal evaluation of obscene material can be attempted without a coherent or consistent set of political philosophical principles. Yet, at some levels, the system seems to work. The existing regulatory strategy promotes a range of liberal values through the principles guiding classification. These are balanced by other countervailing ideas that exhibit a stronger moral and utilitarian orientation. Perhaps the most powerful constraint on achieving theoretical coherence for law is the political context of law-making. Like the regulation of the sex industry generally, modern lawmakers approach pornography with a high degree of pragmatism. According to some, this pragmatism is elevated to a distinct philosophy of public policy called "harm minimisation".[147] This strategy, which has been applied to the regulation of illicit drugs, aims to minimise the harms that follow from particular behaviours, including the unintended consequences that flow from strict prohibition. It has been influential in the reform of some drug laws, leading to the decriminalisation of the personal possession of cannabis in some jurisdictions and the introduction of safe-injection rooms from drug users. By creating a lawful market for obscene and indecent material, the state minimises the involvement of organised crime, corruption and threats to public health. It also profits through the imposition of substantial taxes on pornography and classification fees.

The law regulating pornography in Australia and other "liberal" democracies lacks a clear, coherent and consistent philosophical basis. The law incorporates a wide range of conflicting interests: welfare, communal and moral interests must be balanced against individual interests relating to privacy and freedom of choice. All of the key liberal ideas such as freedom, autonomy, equality and privacy remain deeply contested, capable of interpretation and reconstruction in ways that are more or less protective of the interests of women. Feminists would conclude that the consistent position across liberal discourse is that women's perspectives and interests presently struggle to be recognised, especially in legal discourse.

(e)   Conclusion

In this chapter we have tried to orientate the reader to what we see as the dominant philosophical context within which law in Australia[148] and comparable societies is debated and understood. To state it in this way can be misleading – the structure and content of law, and indeed academic critique, may be shaped by liberal beliefs, although not necessarily wholly determined by them. Some of the theories

---

146 "Law's Truth/Women's experience" in R Graycar (ed), *Dissenting Opinions*, Allen and Unwin, 1990, 13.

147 Bronitt and McSherry, n 75, Ch 14, 786ff.

148 Although we have not sought to describe the specifically Australian manifestations of liberalism. See, however, H Collins, "Political Ideology in Australia: The Distinctiveness of a Benthamite Society" in S Graubard (ed), *Australia: The Daedalus Symposium*, Angus and Robertson, 1985, 147 and Leach, n 5, 101-110. For an historical account of Australian liberalism, see S MacIntyre, *A Colonial Liberalism*, Oxford UP, 1991.

outlined in this chapter relate to protecting classical liberal values, such as the liberty protected by Mill's harm principle, and the importance of autonomy and the necessity of imposing limits on the power of the state. But liberalism is not beyond contestation and there is scope for adopting alternative blueprints for law. This might involve reconstituting liberalism around positive liberty or republican liberty. Or it might involve abandoning liberalism in favour of alternative communitarian or welfare theories. In the end, a search for a single grand theory that can explain or guide the law is probably pointless. Accepting the inherent theoretical pluralism of law we believe is an important starting principle to students reading law for the first time.

Of greater significance is the need to recognise that the law can espouse the values of liberal philosophy in its legal rhetoric, while systematically denying them in practice. In later chapters we will explore the gap between theory and practice. First, however, we need to examine further the central role that the rule of law has in liberal thought, and the related question of how legal reasoning should be conducted. Such a messy beginning is hardly satisfying for the new student. The idea of stating law in rational and principled terms is essential to the notion of legality and the rule of law. This liberal aspiration directs much of our disciplinary effort to "tidying up" the uncertainty and indeterminacy of law. However, resolving incoherence through "better" doctrinal analysis often serves only to mask the internal political and moral contradictions within the law. It also conceals the normative choices available for reform or judicial development. Legal scholarship is deeply implicated in this process of constructing and reconstructing law. An approach that draws only on a narrow brand of (liberal) moral and political philosophy severely inhibits the potential to imagine the criminal law and its organising principles differently.

Discussion Questions

1. Imagine that your class is shipwrecked on a desert island with limited food and water. You know that there is a scheduled visit to the island in two months time by a survey team, and a nutritionist in the group believes that there is only food and water for one month. Among the possessions washed ashore is a copy of *Law in Context*. The book is passed around and read by most of the group. The group accept that the chances for survival of all is remote, and that cannibalism is the only option for survival of some.

   Divide the class into groups. Each team is assigned with the task of addressing one of the following perspectives:

   - **The Liberal Perspective:** What are the liberal values threatened by the proposed course of action? Are these values absolute? Assuming this action will be taken, what measures need to taken to protect these values to the maximum extent?

   - **The Moral Perspective:** What moral values are threatened by taking such action. Are these values absolute? Assuming this action will be taken, what measures need to taken to protect these values to the maximum extent?

- **The Utilitarian Perspective**: How would a utilitarian approach the dilemma? What does the welfare of the majority demand? In the balancing of interests, how should the competing interests be weighed?

- **The Pragmatic Perspective**. Your team is to move around the groups and identify the difficult practical consequences (either intended or unintended consequences) of any measures under consideration.

After 20 minutes, convene in a large group to discuss the differing perspectives. There are of course no right answers!

2. In our "War on Terror", liberal democracies are threatened with large scale terrorist attack. Faced by such large threats, which are possibly nuclear and biochemical, it is now said that liberal values must give way to utilitarian considerations. A leading criminal lawyer from Harvard, Professor Alan Dershowitz, is a long time civil libertarian who famously assisted the OJ Simpson's Defence Team. In his book, published shortly after the 9/11 attacks, Dershowitz argued that torture, as a last resort, might be necessary to obtain intelligence to avert such catastrophic attacks, albeit torture administered under judicial warrants: Dershowitz, *Why Terrorism Works: Understanding The Threat, Responding To The Challenge*, New Haven and London: Yale UP, 2002. Can torture ever be justified?

3. Imagine that your class is a group of legal policy officers in the Commonwealth Attorney General's Office. Each team has been assigned the task of developing a new policy and draft provision on pornography. Each group is asked to approach the topic from a different philosophical perspective. (We have included some questions to start discussion – your task, however, is to produce a policy statement on the approach to pornography and an outline of what new legislation might look like.)

- **The Liberal Perspective:** What are the liberal values threatened by pornography and restrictions on pornography? How should the harm principle apply here? How should we address the arbitrary and discretionary aspects of regulation? How should we reconcile the rights of potential consumers, individuals involved in the industry, and the wider community?

- **The Utilitarian Perspective**: How would a utilitarian approach the dilemma? What does the welfare of the majority demand? In the balancing of interests, how should the competing interests be weighed?

- **The Feminist Perspective:** How does feminism approach pornography? What values are threatened? How can abuse of power be addressed? From a feminist, rather than classical liberal perspective, how should legal regulation address equality, privacy and autonomy?

- **The Pragmatic Perspective:** Your team is to move around the groups and identify the difficult practical consequences (either intended or unintended consequences) of any measures under consideration.

Chapter 3

Formalism and the Rule of Law

(a) Introduction

One of the early challenges faced by new students of law is the expectation that they "think like a lawyer". Explicitly or implicitly, introductory courses on legal method or legal process attempt to induct or acculturate first year students into legal reasoning. Learning these skills involves not simply the acquisition of a method of arguing, it also involves developing a sense of the *range* of permissible arguments. Legal reasoning has traditionally been described as formalistic and is to be distinguished from more open-ended forms of reasoning which one might find in political debate or ethics.

The question whether legal reasoning is indeed distinctive is a controversial one in legal theory. Some critical scholars argue that law is indeterminate; that is, that legal reasoning is capable of producing a wide range, and perhaps an infinite range, of plausibly correct outcomes. Law and politics are separated more by language styles than by underlying methods of reasoning. Others argue that law is a closed system which generates unique correct answers. This may seem a rather technical argument, but there is a considerable amount at stake. For example, in the context of a democracy where judges are not elected, the decisions of courts acquire political legitimacy precisely because judges are believed to be constrained by rules as to what they may decide: the function of the courts should be confined to the interpretation and application of existing rules or principles.[1] Questions of what the law *is* are primarily technical legal matters for the courts. Questions of what the law *should* be are political matters for the legislature.[2] If those constraints are shown to be illusory, the whole business of judging faces disrepute. More fundamentally the idea of rule by laws rather than rule by people is challenged. To appreciate the significance of debates about formalism, therefore, we need to look first at the rule of law and its political justifications.

---

1   HLA Hart, *The Concept of Law*, Clarendon Press, 1961; R Dworkin, *Law's Empire*, Fontana, 1986.

2   This ideal is strongly promoted in Tom Campbell's *The Legal Theory of Ethical Positivism*, Dartmouth Publishing Co, 1996. This explicitly normative theory of law emphasises the importance of democratic institutions and separation of powers with the effect of imposing strict limits on judicial law-making. Ethical positivism, however, is open to the same criticisms that have been levelled at its ancestors: it adopts a narrow conception of legal and political power and denies the relevance of external disciplinary perspectives on law: N Lacey, "Feminist Perspectives on Ethical Positivism" in T Campbell and J Goldsworthy (eds), *Judicial Power, Democracy and Legal Positivism*, Ashgate, 2000.

(b) The rule of law

Official adherence to the rule of law ideal is a hallmark of all liberal societies but, as with many other components of liberal thought, there are differing conceptions of the ideal. In the most general terms the rule of law requires that government should be in accordance with rules.[3] This principle is commonly taken to have two broad consequences; first, that there should be no arbitrary use of power and, secondly, that any government discretion should be limited and exercised within the limits imposed by general laws.

This formulation may surprise some because in everyday use "the rule of law" is often taken to mean simply "law and order", that is, people should obey the law. While law and order might be an aspect of some versions of the rule of law, it is not really at the heart of it. For the liberal, the rule of law is more to do with duties on *governments* than on citizens. It obliges governments to rule only by way of laws. In fact, some philosophers argue that the rule of law actually justifies *disobedience* if governments do not govern in accordance with certain norms which are at the real core of the ideal. This issue has exercised the minds of natural lawyers, like Lon Fuller, who claimed that particular violations of the rule of law by a government have the consequence that the government's rules are not laws at all (indeed, they might not even be rules) and so there is no moral obligation to obey them.[4]

The rule of law is valued by many liberals for at least three reasons. First, it is thought to curb the power of government; to prevent it from becoming absolute. Second, it is thought to protect the rights, and particularly the liberties, of the citizen. Third, it promotes personal autonomy in that individuals can predict the circumstances when governments will interfere with their lives and thus plan their lives accordingly. So, as an ideal, it may be seen as an expression of the liberal's commitment to liberty, individualism, equality and rights. Although a utilitarian theorist judges acts and rules by their consequences for welfare, many utilitarians regard the rule of law as so likely to be productive of overall individual happiness that it falls only slightly short of being an absolute value.

Those writers who take a narrow definition of the rule of law say that it can theoretically exist in a range of political systems and has no *necessary* connection with liberal societies. Tyrants can govern by rules just as much as democratically elected polities, they say. Indeed, the new Constitution of the People's Republic of China has been amended to guarantee the "Rule of Law". The Constitution does contain formal guarantees of most of the rights one would normally find in a Bill of Rights, it is just that they are offset by countervailing duties and they are not enforced or implemented in practice.[5] Thus in practice, while encouraging, this amendment does not necessarily import into that system the bundle of liberal constitutional values and rights forged over many centuries in western democracies.[6]

---

3   See, for example, FA Hayek, *The Road to Serfdom*, Routledge, 1944, 54: "stripped of all technicalities this means that government in all its actions is bound by rules fixed and announced beforehand".

4   *The Morality of Law*, Yale UP, 1964, Ch 2.

5   Ann E Kent, *Between Freedom and Subsistence: China and Human Rights*, Oxford UP, 1993.

6   Within developing Asian economies, the rule of law is primarily used as a means of legitimating strong government rather than protecting democratic, liberal values: K Jayasuriya (ed), *Law, Capitalism and Power in Asia*, Routledge, 1999. British colonial powers have not been averse to supplying legal rights in lieu of democracy: C Jones, "Politics Postponed: Law as a Substitute for Politics in Hong Kong and China" in Jayasuriya, ibid, 45.

There is a danger that the concept is understood simply as "rule by law", which overlooks the specific constraints on state power outlined below.[7]

There is, however, an *historical* connection between liberalism and the rule of law, and by understanding this we can see more clearly the relationship between the rule of law and other liberal beliefs. Roberto Unger argues that emerging liberal societies had to construct a legal order that could co-exist with the new values and be seen as legitimate.[8] Thus as society was increasingly regarded as the voluntary association of formally equal, rational individuals with their own interests and differing conceptions of the good, who conferred on the state only the minimum powers necessary for the preservation of liberty, then particular institutional arrangements were desired. These involved a commitment to generally applicable rules that were openly promulgated and operated prospectively. Also required was a system where law-making and law-application were treated as separate. One of the merits of this arrangement was that no single group could gain ascendancy and impose its own conception of the good life.

Some writers argue that the rule of law is a narrow idea and is only one virtue of a legal system. Others argue that the rule of law ideal entails a long list of consequences so that it is almost coterminous with "a just legal system".[9] A clear formulation of the narrow view is that by Joseph Raz.[10] He says that the rule of law is not to be confused with the rule of good law. It is therefore a virtue that might be possessed by a legal system but distinct from other virtues such as democracy, justice, equality or human rights.

> It is evident that this conception of the rule of law is a formal one. It says nothing about how the law is to be made: by tyrants, democratic majorities or any other way. It says nothing about fundamental rights, about equality or justice.[11]

Raz's approach can be contrasted, for example, with the formulation of the International Commission of Jurists in 1959:

> The function of the legislature in a free society under the Rule of Law is to create and maintain the conditions which will uphold the dignity of man as an individual. This dignity requires not only the recognition of his civil and political rights but also the establishment of the social, economic, educational and cultural conditions which are essential to the full development of his personality.[12]

In Australia, Geoffrey De Q Walker has put forward a definition of the rule of law which contains not only formal attributes (such as certainty, generality and an independent judiciary, discussed below) but also some requirements about substantive content.[13] Thus, he claims, the laws themselves must prohibit private

---

7   For discussions of the Rule by Law in China, see Randall Peerenboom (ed), *Asian Discourses of Rule of Law: Theories and Implementation of Rule of Law In Twelve Asian Countries, France and the U.S.*, Routledge, 2004 and Randall Peerenboom, *China's Long March Toward Rule of Law*, Cambridge UP, 2002.

8   *Law in Modern Society*, Free Press, 1976, 166-192.

9   For a discussion of "procedural" and "substantive" approaches to the rule of law, see R Beehler, "Waiting for the Rule of Law" (1988) 38 *University of Toronto Law Journal* 298.

10   "The Rule of Law and its Virtue" (1977) 93 *Law Quarterly Review* 195.

11   Note 10, 198.

12   Quoted in Raz, n 10, 195.

13   *The Rule of Law: Foundation of Constitutional Democracy*, Melbourne UP, 1988, 23-42. See also G de Q Walker, "Rule of Law and the Democratic World Order" in S Ratnapala and G Moens, *Jurisprudence of Liberty*, Butterworths, 1996, Ch 13.

violence and coercion, must be generally congruent with social values and ensure accessibility of the courts. Justice Heydon of the High Court of Australia recently emphasised the symbolic, as well as the instrumental, aspects of the Rule of Law:

> The purpose of the rule of law is to remove both the reality of injustice and the sense of injustice. It exists not merely because of the actual remedies it provides for damages, injunctions and other specific remedies, and criminal sanctions. It exists also to prevent a damaging release of uncontrollable forces of disorder and primal urges towards primal revenge against wrongdoers by assuaging the affront to human dignity experienced by wrongdoers. ... The rule of law channels potentially destructive energies into orderly courses.[14]

Because our present purpose is to outline the political context of Australian law rather than engage in detailed jurisprudential issues, we set out below the components which are uncontroversially included in most lists. As we go along we will mention instances where the requirements of the rule of law tend to conflict with the practices of, and demands upon, modern governments. We present the list uncritically and then discuss separately some criticisms which have been levelled at the rule of law.

(i) Constitutionality

The modern notion of constitutionality is often connected with the English jurist AV Dicey (1835-1922), although its contours had been developing since at least the English Civil War in the mid-17th century. Dicey argued that the rule of law involves more than simply government *through* laws. It also involves government *under* laws. There must therefore be laws, or at least conventions, about how laws are to be made. Constitutionality means that there are some superior rules (the constitution), above the political arena, which say how the governors are to govern. Individually, members of the governments, officials and police are subject to the same laws as all other citizens.

An institutional device to maintain constitutionality in liberal societies is the theory of the separation of powers. Power should not be concentrated in any one part of the state and each part acts as a check or balance on the other. For our purposes, the most important aspect of the separation of powers between legislature, executive and judiciary is the requirement of an independent judiciary which can decide constitutional and other legal questions uninfluenced by powerful people and groups, whether within or outside government.[15] A necessary prop for the independence of the judiciary is generally thought to be security of tenure so that a judge can only be dismissed for misconduct by a vote in the legislature. This is intended to immunise judges from covert pressure by the executive. The

---

14 JD Heydon, "Judicial Activism and the Death of the Rule of Law" (2003) 23 *Australian Bar Review* 110 at 112.

15 Ironically, Britain (from where many of these ideas come) does not obviously apply the theory in its fullest sense because parliament (rather than the courts) is supreme there, even on constitutional questions, and the senior judge, the Lord Chancellor, is a member of cabinet. Australia, however, took certain parts of the American Constitution at Federation and the High Court is the ultimate authority on constitutional questions. A standard text on the separation of powers is MJC Vile, *Constitutionalism and the Separation of Powers*, Clarendon Press, 1967; see also I Holloway, *Natural Justice and the High Court of Australia: A study in Common Law Constitutionalism*, Ashgate, 2002.

preservation of judicial independence is very much a topical issue. For example, there is currently concern in Australia at the growth of specialist tribunals which perform judicial functions but whose members are not so immunised from pressure. Another example is the decision by the High Court in *Wilson v Minister for Aboriginal and Torres Strait Islander Affairs*[16] where the majority of the High Court held that the appointment of a Federal Court judge by the Commonwealth Government to report on matters connected with the construction of a bridge to Hindmarsh Island was invalid as being incompatible with her role as a judge. Similarly, the High Court has held that the issuing of surveillance warrants[17] is an exercise of executive power with respect to both telecommunication interceptions and listening devices.[18] The involvement of judges in clandestine investigations by the police and the executive threatens the perceived legitimacy and independence of the judiciary. For this reason federal interception warrants are now issued by Administrative Appeals Tribunal members, who are clearly exercising administrative rather than judicial power. In cases like these, the demand for strict separation of powers is discordant with the need for "checks and balances" and the desirability of independent judicial officers maintaining a "watching brief" over the use of covert surveillance by state officials.

In theory, the separation of powers system imposes restraints on judges in return for their independence. Judges are required to apply laws in the manner intended by the legislature. The rules are supposed to come to them pre-formed. Legal formalism, therefore, is a theory that can be traced back to liberal concerns to disperse state power and, more problematically, to democratic theory.[19]

(ii) Formal legality

This element describes some of the general characteristics of the laws by which governments should rule. Laws should be general, promulgated, clear, specific, prospective, practicable and stable. We deal with each of these characteristics in the succeeding paragraphs.

The requirement of *generality* dictates that laws must be addressed to classes or groups of people *equally* and provide for *types* of situation; in other words, they must be impersonal. Lon Fuller equated the requirement of generality with the very requirement that *there be rules*.[20] An order to someone concerning a unique event, analogous to a direction by an employer to an employee to do something, is not a rule at all. A law concerning a particular person for a specific occasion, for example, abrogates this requirement. The capricious tendency of despotic British

---

16   (1996) 138 ALR 220.

17   Surveillance warrants allow the lawful use of surveillance devices by law enforcement or security and intelligence officers under conditions outlined in the warrant. Section 6 of the *Surveillance Devices Act 2004* (Cth) defines a "Surveillance device warrant" to include the use of surveillance devices, listening devices, optical surveillance devices or tracking devices.

18   *Grollo v Palmer* (1995) 184 CLR 348 at 359; *Hilton v Wells* (1985) 157 CLR 57; *Coco v The Queen* (1994) 179 CLR 427; *Love v Attorney-General (NSW)* (1990) 169 CLR 307; see S Bronitt and J Stellios, "Telecommunications Interception in Australia: Recent Trends and Regulatory Prospects" (2005) 29 *Telecommunications Policy* 878 at 882.

19   For a contemporary examination of the implications of judicial review for democracy, see D Feldman, "The Rule of Law, Judicial Review and Democratic Values" (1991) 19 *Federal Law Review* 1.

20   Note 2, 46.

monarchs to dispense with the law for favoured subjects precipitated many constitutional conflicts, culminating in the outlawing of grants of prospective immunity by the Crown: *Bill of Rights* 1689 (UK) states that "power of suspending of laws or execution of laws by regal authority without the consent of Parliament is illegal".[21] For this reason, the executive is bound by the law, and can only be exempted where Parliament confers a specific immunity. This principle of constitutionalism was affirmed by the High Court in *Ridgeway v The Queen*,[22] which held that federal police officers involved in the importation of heroin as part of controlled operation have no immunity from the federal offences prohibiting unlawful importation or possession and that the "permission" by the executive under a Ministerial Agreement did not alter this legal position. The federal Parliament subsequently legislated extensively to permit the granting of authorisation certificates, conferring criminal and civil immunity, for police and civilians involved in these undercover operations: *Crimes Act* 1914 (Cth) s 15I.

The requirement of generality is often linked to the idea of equal respect for persons. A law addressed only to one person in circumstances where there is no relevant difference between her and another person has treated the persons unequally as well as failed the test of generality. As we have seen in the preceding chapter, however, debates over the meaning of equality are often also debates over the relevance of differences. This is a matter to which we will return when we look at sex discrimination and affirmative action legislation in Chapter 8.

The requirement of *promulgation* means that governments must not act according to secret laws, for everyone must be able to know what is required of them and what they may do. The principle underlying this requirement accords well with liberal notions of individual rationality and responsibility. One cannot plan one's life if one cannot know the laws, nor can one justly be held responsible for breaching them. Nevertheless, effective promulgation is easier said than done in complex societies. No one can reasonably be expected to know the detail of all legislation governing him or her, even when most of them are now available through the Internet!

As for *clarity* and *specificity*, the requirement is that a law should be intelligible and give guidance to citizens and state officials alike. A prescription "Do not injure others" will not suffice because it is too vague. It does not say what is to count as an injury or anything about context. Is the rule breached, for example, by the surgeon making an incision during a routine operation? There has long been debate about the clarity of language in legislation and the balance to be struck between the value of achieving precision through technical terminology and the value of easy intelligibility. More recent is a concern about the increasing use of less specific rules outside the criminal law, such as prohibitions on misleading and deceptive conduct or on contract terms which are not fair and reasonable. At its core here is a concern about vagueness conferring too much power on state officials or indeed judges. The criminalisation of using offensive language is another example where the vaguely drafted offences confer too much discretionary power on the police and magistrates to define what is a threat to "good order" in an ad hoc fashion. Empirical research suggests that these laws, which are

---

21   See D Kell, "Immunity From Prosecution for Prospective Illegal Conduct" (1997) 71 *Australian Law Journal* 553.

22   (1995) 184 CLR 19.

commonly used, are applied unfairly and harshly against young people and Aboriginal people. The common denominator in many cases is that the powers are invoked against individuals who challenge or disrespect police authority on the streets.[23] We will return to these issues of race and discrimination in Chapter 9.

The requirement of *prospectivity* is broadly that a law should only operate on events that take place subsequent to its enactment. From the viewpoint of the individual, a wholly retrospective law is impossible to comply with and it is usually regarded as unjust to punish or disadvantage anyone who has breached it. According to Fuller:

> Taken by itself, and in abstraction from its possible function in a system of laws that are largely prospective, a retroactive law is truly a monstrosity. Law has to do with the governance of human conduct by rules. To speak of governing or directing conduct today by rules that will be enacted tomorrow is talk in blank prose. To ask how we should appraise an imaginary legal system consisting exclusively of laws that are retroactive and retroactive only, is like asking how much air pressure there is in a perfect vacuum.[24]

There are some circumstances where retrospective legislation is considered acceptable, for example, to correct a mistake or to confer benefits, and there is no doubt that in Australia it can be enacted. There is, nevertheless, a presumption of statutory interpretation that an Act does not operate retroactively.[25]

In the field of criminal law, the presumption against retrospectivity is regarded as fundamental and absolute. Reflecting provisions in Art 15(1) of the *International Covenant on Civil and Political Rights*, the *Human Rights Act 2004* (ACT) is the only local jurisdiction to enshrine this principle in legislation. Section 25 provides:

25 Retrospective criminal laws

(1) No-one may be held guilty of a criminal offence because of conduct that was not a criminal offence under Territory law when it was engaged in.

While there are deep concerns about retrospective criminal laws from a rule of law and human rights perspective, Australia has applied offences retrospectively, including some of the most serious. In the aftermath of the Bali Bombings, the federal parliament inserted a new offence into the *Criminal Code*, s 104 "Harming Australians", which created a range of extraterritorial offences dealing with the murder, manslaughter and causing of serious harm to Australian citizens or residents.[26] These are expressly intended to operate retrospectively. The political imperative to bring the offenders to justice in Australia justifies these exceptional retrospective measures: the Indonesian Constitutional Court overturned the Bali

---

23   D Brown, D Farrier, S Egger and L McNamara, *Brown Farrier Neal and Weisbrot's Criminal Laws*, 3rd ed, Federation Press, 2001, 962-967; S Bronitt and B McSherry, *Principles of Criminal Law*, 2nd ed, Lawbook Co, 2005, Ch 13, 756ff.

24   Note 2, 53.

25   See *R v Kidman* (1915) 20 CLR 425 and *Yrttiaho v Public Curator (Queensland)* (1971) 125 CLR 228.

26   These four offences carry severe penalties ranging from life imprisonment for murder to 15 years for recklessly causing serious injury. The provisions are specified to apply retrospectively, from 1 October 2002, as the drafters intended to use them to prosecute those involved with the 12 October Bali Bombings: The Parliament of the Commonwealth of Australia House of Representatives, *Criminal Code Amendment (Offences Against Australians) Bill 2002: Second Reading*.

bombers convictions in July 2004 on the ground that the terrorist laws under which they had been convicted, enacted six days *after* the Bali Bombings, were retrospective and hence unconstitutional! Of course, the bombers could be charged with murder, an offence which was clearly on the statute book at the time of the bombings. Paradoxically, there is no similar expression of liberal values in the Australian Constitution, and consequently little that our own courts, including the High Court, could do to prevent a prosecution and conviction under retrospective criminal laws here.[27]

The requirement of prospectivity is arguably part of a more general requirement of *practicability*. A law that requires the impossible is unjust and, to some, not a law at all. Thus a rule such as "no sneezing" would breach this requirement because, in most circumstances, the rule cannot practicably be complied with. To disadvantage someone in this situation, therefore, is unjust because he or she bears no true responsibility for what occurred. The concept of the reasonable person in tort law and criminal law might be justified by reference to this component of the rule of law because it controls what is to count as practicable. If the reasonable person would have acted in a particular way then there is usually no negligence.

Last, the requirement of *stability* involves a belief that a law which continually changes might as well not exist. It would offend the requirement of practicability, in that people cannot reasonably be expected to comply with it, and it disables people from making long-term plans for their lives because legal change (whether by judicial or legislative means) might subsequently frustrate their purposes. Complaints about the instability of laws have increased in most modern liberal societies. This importance of stability presents a peculiar challenge for legal rules: owing to the process of common law adjudication or statutory interpretation, the scope of the law is sometimes moved in a novel and unexpected direction. It is trite to say that settled wisdom in law is rarely beyond contestation and is always a "work in progress". These demands for stability in law are clearly not absolute. They are better understood as demands for *reasonable* stability.

This tension between stability and development in law is aptly illustrated in the history of the marital rape immunity. At common law husbands could not be prosecuted for the rape of their wives, and this was settled law from the 18th century. In *R v R*, this was challenged when a trial judge in England refused to recognise that the immunity existed in the modern law.[28] The accused pleaded guilty and appealed. The House of Lords, affirming the conviction, agreed with the Court of Appeal, that the immunity was a "common law fiction which has become anachronistic and offensive".[29] The decision to abolish the marital rape immunity was widely welcomed, although it raised questions about the limits of

---

27 The constitutional compatibility of retrospective and extraterritorial war crimes offences was challenged before the High Court in *Polyukhovich v Commonwealth* (1991) 172 CLR 501. The High Court upheld the validity of the *War Crimes Act 1945* (Cth) as a proper exercise of the Commonwealth's external affairs power in the Constitution pursuant to s 51(vi), (xxiv). The majority concluded that the legislation was a valid exercise of these powers, notwithstanding the fact that it had extraterritorial effect, and applied to past conduct of persons who at the relevant time had no connection with Australia.

28 [1992] 1 AC 599.

29 Ibid 623. Although the immunity had been abolished by statute in every Australian jurisdiction, the High Court held that the immunity had never in fact formed part of the common law of Australia: *R v L* (1991) 174 CLR 379.

judicial law-making: indeed, the abolition of the immunity may be viewed as the creation of a new crime of marital or spousal rape that previously did not exist, therefore raising legitimate concerns about retrospectivity in the criminal law.[30] This question was subsequently considered by the European Court of Human Rights in *SW v United Kingdom; CR v United Kingdom*.[31] The court noted that the common law doctrine of precedent legitimately facilitated legal development, and that offences may be broadened and defences narrowed through judicial interpretation. This would not violate the principle against retrospectivity, provided that the development of the law is consistent with the "essence" of the offence and could have been "reasonably foreseen".

(iii) Procedural legality

If formal legality is about the *characteristics* of a law that satisfies the requirements of the rule of law, procedural legality is about the *procedures* under which those laws are put into operation. Terms which tend to be used interchangeably with procedural legality are "due process" and "natural justice".

In essence, procedural legality requires that trials be conducted by unbiased and disinterested tribunals which hear both sides of the case and expose themselves to public scrutiny. These principles are implemented by specific rules concerning, for example, advance notice of the issues to be decided, adjournments, the assistance of a lawyer and the examination of witnesses.[32] There is, however, considerable scope for variations in detailed arrangements over procedure. Legal systems that stem from liberal societies on the continent of Europe, in particular from France and Germany, justify quite different rules by reference to the demands of procedural legality and we will return to this when we contrast adversarial and inquisitorial procedures in Chapter 5.

The foregoing account of the components of the rule of law idea was largely conventional and uncritical. The Diceyan conception of the rule of law[33] has been attacked since as early as the 1920s however,[34] and there now exists a range of criticisms. Some concern the very *idea* of the rule of law whilst others concern its appropriateness in modern western conditions.

One vigorous debate was sparked by the socialist historian EP Thompson in the late 1970s. In the final chapter of his analysis of draconian criminal laws in 18th century England, he announced an unexpected conclusion. Despite overwhelming evidence that the law had been used by a powerful minority to oppress the powerless majority, he said:

> But the rule of law itself, the imposing of effective inhibitions upon power and the defence of the citizen from power's all-intrusive claims, seems to me to be an unqualified human good. To deny or belittle this good is, in this dangerous

---

30 M Giles, "Judicial Law Making in the Criminal Courts: The Case of Marital Rape" [1991] *Criminal Law Review* 407.

31 (1996) 21 EHRR 363.

32 See RA Macdonald, "A Theory of Procedural Fairness" (1981) 1 *Windsor Yearbook of Access to Justice* 3 at 5.

33 As expressed, for example, in AV Dicey, *The Law of the Constitution* in 1885.

34 See W Robson, *Justice and Administrative Law*, Stevens, 1928.

century when the resources and pretensions of power continue to enlarge, a desperate error of intellectual abstraction.[35]

Thompson's conclusion seemed to contradict much of the text that preceded it and also some earlier work by him and his colleagues.[36] His critics claimed that he had made too little of the ideological nature of law (using ideology in the sense of deception). The rule of law was said to bolster conservative cultural practices[37] and to make an unjust social system appear legitimate by persuading people that the advantaged were under the same rules as the disadvantaged.[38] The poor are encouraged by the ideology of legality to look for reasons outside the social system itself to explain their position. According to Horwitz, for example:

> [The rule of law] creates formal equality – a not inconsiderable virtue – but it *promotes* substantive inequality by creating a consciousness that radically separates law from politics, means from ends, processes from outcomes. By promoting procedural justice it enables the shrewd, the calculating, and the wealthy to manipulate its forms to their own advantage. And it ratifies and legitimates an adversarial, competitive, and atomistic conception of human relations.[39]

The extent to which the rule of law actually operates to constrain the exercise of arbitrary state power, or conversely legitimates the power of the ruling elite, is a matter of continuing debate in the Australian context. Colonial history can be presented as robust independent judges, such as Chief Justice Forbes, imposing limits on the exercise of executive excess.[40] The courts also delivered some form of access to justice, for at least some of the time, to both convicts and Aboriginal people. The fact that the first civil action in NSW was brought by a convict is presented as a testament to the legality and affirmation of the rule of law. Yet from the strict perspective of legality rather than justice, the common law should have denied the convicted felon legal standing to sue under the established doctrine of attainder. Clearly, legality and the rule of law remain deeply contested notions.

Common to many of these criticisms is the idea of an inevitable and exclusive connection between the rule of law and liberalism. One cannot have one without the other.[41] Because liberal-capitalism is said to be an undesirable form of political and economic organisation then the rule of law is also undesirable. Participants in the debate inspired by Thompson have tended to be socialists. More recently, however, feminist writers have also begun to doubt whether the commitment to

---

35 EP Thompson, *Whigs and Hunters*, Penguin, 1977, 266.

36 See, D Hay, P Linebaugh, J Rule, EP Thompson and C Winslow, *Albion's Fatal Tree*, Penguin, 1977 and in particular the essay by Hay, "Property, Authority and the Criminal Law", 17.

37 M Kelman, *A Guide to Critical Legal Studies*, Harvard UP, 1987, 26.

38 See P O'Malley, *Law, Capitalism and Democracy*, Allen & Unwin, 1983, 24-25.

39 M Horwitz, "The Rule of Law: An Unqualified Human Good?" (1977) 86 *Yale Law Journal* 561 at 566. See also P Anderson, *Arguments within English Marxism*, Verso, 1980, 197-202; Beehler, n 9, 302; S Hall and P Scraton, "Law, Class and Control" in M Fitzgerald, G McLennan and J Rawson (eds), *Readings in History and Theory*, RKP, 1981, 490; and B Fine, *Democracy and the Rule of Law*, Pluto Press, 1984, 169-189.

40 D Neal, *The Rule of Law in A Penal Colony*, Cambridge UP, 1991, Ch 3; B Kercher, *An Unruly Child: A History of Law in Australia*, Allen & Unwin, 1995; G Woods, *A History of Criminal Law in New South Wales*, Federation Press, 2002.

41 Although many non-Marxist socialists support the notion of constitutionality as a restraint upon state authority: see, for example, PQ Hirst, *Law, Socialism and Democracy*, Allen & Unwin, 1986, Ch 4.

generality implied by the rule of law can be justified. As we will see in Chapter 8, the argument is that men and women are in substantively different positions in society. By ignoring these differences, the law perpetuates and exacerbates them.

A second strand of criticism, that the rule of law idea is no longer appropriate for modern western societies, tends to acknowledge the correctness of the connection between the Diceyan view of the rule of law and *classical* liberalism. Now that more substantive notions of liberty and equality are widely held, however; now that the state is acknowledged to have a greater role in social and economic affairs; and now that technological complexity[42] makes it unrealistic to expect a rule system to cope with all contingencies, a different relationship between government and law is called for, it is said.[43] This leads to demands for increased specialisation, with special courts and procedural rules adapted to suit the particular subject-matter under consideration. Family and commercial disputes require different procedures, levels of formality and expertise. The late 20th century witnessed an increase in the number of specialised courts and tribunals (including drug and family violence courts). At the same time, there is increased emphasis on diverting matters way from formal adjudication – governed by legal rules – to alternative dispute resolution processes.

Roberto Unger takes the argument further and suggests that changes to law in western countries actually indicate the arrival of *post*-liberalism.[44] He notes a rapid expansion in the use of open-ended standards and general clauses in legislation, administration and adjudication:

> For example, the courts may be charged to police unconscionable contracts, to void unjust enrichment, to control economic concentration so as to maintain competitive markets, or to determine whether a government agency has acted in the public interest.[45]

He also notes a move away from formalistic towards purposive or policy-oriented styles of legal reasoning and this is a convenient link into the last section of the chapter.

An illustration of this trend is the emergence of what may be termed post-liberal forms of criminalisation. One of the most common legal procedures in Australia is the process to obtain a protection order from a magistrate – these are variously called restraining orders, apprehended violence (AVO) or domestic violence orders (DVO); and antisocial behaviour orders in the UK. Thousands of these orders are obtained each year in Australia and seek to restrain a wide range of antisocial nuisance-type behaviours, as well as prevent serious family violence. Protection orders, unlike criminal offences, are granted on the traditional civil standard of "balance of probabilities" by a magistrate. They are issued in cases

---

42   For a critique, see P O'Malley, "Technocratic Justice in Australia" (1984) 2 *Law in Context* 31.

43   See J Jowell, "The Rule of Law Today" in J Jowell and D Oliver (eds), *The Changing Constitution*, 2nd ed, Clarendon, 1989, Ch 1.

44   Unger, n 8, 192-216. The view is shared by those with quite different political positions. FA Hayek, for example, argues for a turning away from the institutions and practices of the administrative/welfare state because they infringe the principles of liberalism and the rule of law. For a discussion of Hayek's work, see AI Ogus, "Law and Spontaneous Order: Hayek's Contribution to Legal Theory" (1989) 16 *Journal of Law and Society* 393. For a contrary view, see RA Belliotti, "The Rule of Law and the Critical Legal Studies Movement" (1986) 24 *University of Western Ontario Law Review* 67.

45   Note 3, 194.

where the person engages or threatens to engage in defined conduct, such as intimidation, harassment, stalking and molestation. The problem from a liberal perspective is that these concepts are open-ended and vaguely defined. From a policy perspective, employing highly context-dependent concepts is essential to their efficacy, enabling them to be tailored to the subjective character, sensitivities and perceptions of both parties. Breach of these orders is made a discrete criminal offence, therefore expanding the regulatory reach of the criminal law and displacing the use of criminal assault charges in the domestic violence context. From the liberal perspective, the danger is that these hybrid legal processes or quasi-criminal laws provide inadequate protection against the exercise of arbitrary state power – in some cases, the restrictions placed on individual freedom, in relation to conduct which is not always distinctly criminal, is hard to reconcile with a commitment to classical liberal values. We explore these new forms of social control in Chapter 10 dealing with law and regulation.

(c)   Formalism

A year or so ago, a swimming meet took place at the University of Toronto. Most of the races proceeded as planned. But, at the end of one race, there was a challenge to the winner of the race. The appropriate group of officials convened. The deliberations were lengthy and tense. After much argument and poring over the rules, a decision was announced: the winner had been disqualified and the second swimmer was acclaimed the victor. The referee took the unusual course of offering a brief justification of the committee's decision – "the rules were clear ('The winner is the first swimmer to touch the side of the pool with both hands') and, if this regrettable outcome is to be avoided in the future, it will be necessary to change the rules". The winning swimmer had only one arm.[46]

With the story of the one-armed swimmer Allan Hutchinson, a Critical Legal Studies exponent, opens his discussion of formalism, a topic that has been vigorously debated in legal theory since at least the American Legal Realist movement in the 1920s.

At its most general, formalism is a method of reasoning and can be contrasted with substantive reasoning.[47] The basic idea behind *legal* formalism is that it is possible to learn and apply the law as if it were a self-contained system. In its strictest version formalism involves a claim that the decision-maker should not (and need not) refer to "external" considerations such as her own values, social consequences or the justice of the outcome in making a decision. The rules come to the decision-maker pre-formed. It might be a skilled job to learn what they are, but once they have been learned the rules can be applied in this mechanical manner. Formalism, as Frederick Schauer says, is the way in which rules achieve

---

46   AC Hutchinson, *Dwelling on the Threshold*, Carswell, 1988, 23.

47   Formalism is often used synonymously with words like legalism and literalism. There are actually semantic differences between them in that legalism is usually regarded as the tendency to reduce relations to rules and literalism is an approach to the interpretation of rules. Nevertheless, one can see how the ideas fit together. A formalist may well also have a preference for rule-based solutions in all spheres because he or she believes that rules are a way of constraining arbitrary decisions. A formalist may also have a preference for the literal interpretation of rules as a way of providing further, predictable constraints. The relationship between formalism, legalism and literalism should become clearer in the text that follows.

their ruleness by "screening off from a decisionmaker factors that a sensitive decisionmaker would otherwise take into account".[48]

Formalism has had a bad press in recent years. Critical scholars have attacked it on a number of grounds. To some, it is simply wrong to adhere to a system which compels one to make a decision that is otherwise unjustifiable. (Only in a world where swimming was easier with one arm than two could a reasonable person be happy about disqualifying a one-armed swimmer.) Whatever value there might be in having a system that is predictable and efficient – formalism should cut down a potentially infinite range of disputes – this value is outweighed by the need to do justice in the particular case.

To others, the objection is that formalism involves deception. Language is incapable of constraining choice to the extent that formalists claim (or even at all), the argument goes. It follows that value judgments are just being dressed up in the language of rules so as to create the illusion that there is some gap between law and politics, law and morality and so forth.[49] So this second objection to formalism is that it amounts to the hoodwinking of those on the receiving end of decisions, and perhaps even those on the giving end.

A third objection is that formalism is based on the Rationalist tradition; the belief that social existence can be reduced, through rational reflection, to a series of eternal verities and that knowledge and truth can be objectively grounded. Once we doubt the possibility of adequately capturing, say, the meaning of "intention", "free will", "foresight" and all the other key concepts in liberal legal thought, then formalism loses its rationale. Ultimately, it seems all down to the subjectivity of the decision-maker.

As Allan Hutchinson points out below, it is rare now to come across a belief in the kind of formalism that is said to lead to "slot-machine justice". That said, until relatively recently Anglo-Australian legal education did routinely involve a conception of law as a gapless system of rules with logically integrated parts. The fictional case of *R v Ojibway* is presumably designed to show the ludicrous results that such a conception can lead to.[50] Here a Canadian Indian, Fred Ojibway, shot his pony after it had broken its leg. Fred had been using a downy pillow rather than a leather saddle. He was charged under the *Small Birds Act 1960* with killing a small bird. "Bird" was defined in the Act as a two legged animal covered with feathers. He was convicted on the basis that the pillow amounted to a covering of

---

48 F Schauer, "Formalism" (1988) 97 *Yale Law Journal* 509 at 510.

49 The presidential age-rule, for example, requires a person to be aged at least 35 to be eligible for the US presidency. One might have thought that this is a rule about which there could be little choice yet it has been the subject of much dispute between traditional legal scholars (for want of a better term) on the one hand and both critical scholars and economic analysts on the other. For a collection of the arguments, see A D'Amato, "Aspects of Deconstruction: The 'Easy Case' of the Under-Aged President" (1990) 84 *Northwestern University Law Review* 250. Those who claim the rule is ambiguous have a range of grounds. For example, when the Constitution was framed people had shorter life expectancies. Thus the right age could now be 50 (being the same percentage of average life expectancy) or 30 (being the same number of years after puberty). Alternatively, the purpose of the rule could be identified as ensuring the maturity of the candidate. On this basis, the Supreme Court could uphold the nomination of a mature 34 year old. The debate might seem sterile to the newcomer but it does have some importance for legal theory. If an apparently unambiguous rule can be made out as indeterminate (in other words as not determining a unique result) then the determinacy of all other rules is thrown into doubt.

50 See (1975) 94 *Law Notes* 331 and (1966) 8 *Criminal Law Quarterly* 137. It has apparently been cited in American cases in ignorance of its fictional origins.

feathers. The requirement of two legs was satisfied because it was construed as a minimum requirement only. The court reasoned that a horse with feathers on its back must be a bird within the Act and therefore a pony must be a small bird.

The point of this story (and others such as the surgeon rendering emergency assistance who was convicted of spilling blood on the streets) is presumably that formalism can descend into the mindless application of rules which *appear*, in a crude literal sense, to be relevant to the dispute.[51] The story points up the need for other values to be invoked in legal reasoning to control the actual outcome.

Most lawyers would agree that legal rules are reasonably determinate, though they would acknowledge that there always exist cases for which the rules run out or over which there is a choice as to which rule to apply or how to interpret that rule. Here the judge must exercise discretion and to this extent values from outside the system are permitted to enter.[52] Those minded actually to *praise* the denial of choice inherent in formalism today tend to be forced to justify their position by asserting the justice or the morality or the "immanent rationality" of the *rules themselves*. In other words, the "right" answer is produced by the system anyway and so the exclusion of other answers should cause us no concern.[53]

Our discussion here crosses into the wider debate in the community, often between judges themselves, on the proper role and limits of judicial activism. In the late 1980s and 1990s, senior judges in Australia and New Zealand predicted the decline, even death, of narrow kinds of legal formalism.[54] Decisions like *Mabo* in 1992[55], which recognised native title and overturned settled legal doctrines of *terra nullius*, revived once again concerns over the legitimate limits of judicial law-making. Members of the current High Court display a more cautious approach to activism. Justice Heydon in a recent essay acknowledges that law does need to change, but locates the responsibility for radical legal change with the legislature:

> In short, radical legal change is best effected by professional politicians who have a lifetime's experience of assessing the popular will, who have been seasoned by much robust public debate and private haggling, who have all the resources of the executive and legislature to assist, who can deal with mischiefs on a general and planned basis prospectively, not a sporadic and fortuitous basis retrospectively, and who can ensure that any changes made are consistent with overall public

---

51 See Schauer, n 48, 522.

52 This is broadly the position of the leading positivist legal philosopher HLA Hart: see, for example, "Positivism and the Separation of Law and Morals" (1958) 71 *Harvard Law Review* 593 at 608-612 and generally *The Concept of Law*, Clarendon, 1961.

53 Ronald Dworkin's identification of background "principles" which can be invoked to supplement rules is an example of an attempt to justify formalism by showing its capacity to do substantive justice, see the discussion in Chapter 1. See also EJ Weinrib, "Legal Formalism: On the Immanent Rationality of Law" (1988) 97 *Yale Law Journal* 949.

54 See, for example, M McHugh, "The Law-Making Function of the Judicial Process" (1988) 62 *Australian Law Journal* 15 (Part 1) and 116 (Part 2); A Mason, "The Role of the Courts at the Turn of the Century" (1993) 3 *Journal of Judicial Administration* 156; A Mason, "The Courts as Community Institutions" (1998) 9(2) *Public Law Review* 83; Sir R Cooke, "The New Zealand National Identity" (1987) 3 *Canterbury Law Review* 171. In the latter article, Sir Robin Cooke noted that for an appellate judge "hearing cases day by day it seems more than a decade since the pretence of legal formalism was abandoned". For a general discussion of what the author calls "legalism", see B Galligan, *The Politics of the High Court*, Queensland UP, 1987.

55 *Mabo v Queensland (No 2)* (1992) 175 CLR 1.

policy and public institutions. Professional politicians may not be an ideal class, but they are better fitted than the courts to make radical legal changes.[56]

Judicial creativity is confined not only by legal conventions, principles and rules governing precedent and the interpretation of statutes, but also by judicial *beliefs* about the appropriate constitutional limits of judicial law-making. Thus formalism, though seeking to deny the relevance of external political factors shaping the law, is *itself* a distinct political viewpoint about law-making. A commitment to formalism denies the political context of adjudication, and suppresses judicial creativity, for a purpose. As Justice Heydon recently noted, judges who abrogate legislative function ultimately threaten judicial independence, a value that lies at the heart of the rule of law:

> The more the courts freely change the law, the more the public will come to view their function as political; the more they would rightly be open to vigorous and direct public attack on political grounds; and the greater will be the demand for public hearings into the politics of judicial candidates before appointment and greater judicial control over judicial behaviour after appointment. So far as these demands were met, judicial independence would decline... [57]

To bring together some of the forgoing arguments we return to Allan Hutchinson and the one-armed swimmer. The extract below touches on many of the concerns of this Part of the book. The extract is a difficult one in some respects and not all of the ideas and authors mentioned by Hutchinson have been introduced in earlier pages of this book.

Allan Hutchinson, Dwelling on the Threshold
(1988) (footnotes omitted)

This episode [of the one-armed swimmer] offers many insights. An interesting and revealing observation, but one that I will not pursue here, is the hold that rule-formalism has on the public imagination: it is not only a feature of the legal mentality. When thrust into the role of decision-maker, an assumed responsibility is to take the rules very seriously. They are felt to place a very real constraint on the type and range of permissible decisions that can be made. While each of the officials most likely wanted to circumvent the rule and reach a "fairer" result, they seemed to believe that the moral force of following the rules laid down took precedence over their own moral intuitions, no matter how strongly held or shared. The rules existed and operated as a palpable check on their official power. To ignore the rules would be to indulge in "palm-tree justice" with all its attendant dangers; the long-term benefits of rule-following outweighed any temporary costs. While obviously disappointed, the winner would understand the predicament and solution of the committee.

While I will not explore the extent or force of this rule-formalism in quasi-legal or extra-legal settings, I do intend to explore its operation in the legal community. The immediate response from lawyers will be that, although there may be a few Neanderthals still around who subscribe to such a slot-machine version of rule-formalism, such an unsophisticated and mechanical version of decision-making cannot be foisted on today's lawyers – "we are all realists now" is the

---

56 Note 14, 93.
57 Ibid 93.

chorused response. They argue that, while rules are dominant and deserving of close respect, they are necessarily open-textured. In "hard cases", when the facts fall within their penumbral margins, the rules will give unclear guidance. It will be necessary to consult the more general maxims and broad principles that stand behind the rules. In combination, these norms provide a more coherent scheme for resolving disputes in a flexible and just fashion. For these lawyers, rules are bare bricks that have to be laid in accordance with the architectural plans of the whole legal order.

When the swimming rules were made, the possibility of a one-armed swimmer was clearly not in the rule-makers' contemplation. One solution is to assume that, if they were confronted with such a situation, the rule-makers would agree that there was an implicit qualification or exception to the rule. Another solution is to ignore these counter-factual speculations and to read the rule against the existing body of equitable principles that inhere within the legal order. The moral structure of the common law demands that "each person can only do the best they can and no more; they cannot be expected to do the impossible". In light of this maxim, the rule is illuminated to read that "the winner is the first swimmer to touch the side of the pool with as many hands as they have". Such an interpretation and application of rules not only makes sense and does justice in the particular circumstances, but is consistent with the officials' general respon- sibility to resolve the dispute in accordance with the laws of swimming and not their own personal code of morality.

Yet, for all this so-called sophistication and sensitivity, modern lawyers remain enthusiastic practitioners of a pervasive formalism: enthusiastic in that their power and prestige is dependent for legitimacy upon it and pervasive in that their professional lives are thoroughly dominated by its demands. However, their's is not a crude rule-formalism; that represents only a sub-species of a grander genus. While they draw upon the full range of doctrinal materials, modern lawyers rest their claims to authority on the two major components of formalism: that there is a defensible and workable distinction between legal reasoning and open ideological debate and that such legal reasoning itself repre- sents a defensible and workable scheme of social justice. In this sense, although appearing to be at odds, the reasoning of the swimming officials and the critical response of modern lawyers are fundamentally the same; the latter is simply operating at a higher and more abstract level of formalism than the former.

First, both recognize and consider realizable the responsibility of the decision-maker to eschew personal preference and to be guided by the dispositive force of the law: each defers to and feels bound by the appropriate legal norm.

Secondly, both defend any decision by reference to an implicit vision of social justice. The swimming officials look to a standard of formal justice or legality: society will work best when people can rely on an established and uniformly applied set of general norms that act as a skeleton for each person to flesh out with their own substantive muscle. To avoid arbitrary government, it is especially important that officials entrusted with decision-making power strictly adhere to the declared rules until they are publicly changed. On the other hand, modern lawyers adopt a more substantive vision of social justice. As well as being sceptical about the actual possibility of performing a thoroughly formal and value-free application of rules, they maintain that such an ideal compromises the decision-maker's responsibility rather than fulfils it. Justice can be frustrated by the blind application of individual rules; each person is entitled to a decision in line with the overall scheme of justice that the total body of rules embodies. In this way, legal reasoning and decision-making is claimed to satisfy the political need for decisional objectivity and the popular demand for social equity. Of course, the difference between these two approaches is not trivial and it does result in a considerably divergent set of decisions. Nonetheless, both share the same general theoretical justification for their account and the decisions it preserves. That justification is the worth and efficacy of formalism – an attitude and a technique of reasoning that is separate from political haggling, expresses a coherent and neutral blueprint for human relations and, as such, is deserving of institutional allegiance and obedience.

Throughout this book, I attack the plausibility of formalism and reject its legitimacy ...

In this essay, I will attempt to sketch out the deep premises and commitments of my own theoretical position. Although often implicit and frequently denied, everyone has to have some theoretical beliefs about the nature of human existence and social life. Without such rudimentary beliefs, daily existence would be profoundly meaningless and incomprehensible. The only difference between "a person without a philosophy and someone with a philosophy is that the latter knows what [his or her] philosophy is". By emphasising this, my aim is not to make jurisprudence even more abstruse or arcane. My rationale for subjecting the reader to the rarefied environment of metaphysical debate is concrete and practical. Immersion in epistemology and ontology is only justified if it can lead to an improved understanding of our present predicament. By exploring the theoretical basis of contemporary jurisprudential practice, it might be possible to redirect and redeploy the massive energy and resources invested in the legal project. Informed by a fresh theoretical self-appreciation, law and legal theory might develop a greater relevance and a rigour in the struggle to achieve social justice. There is nothing so practical and so necessary as good theory. Without the ability to theorise a problem, we are destined to reinscribe its debilitating pattern within the fabric of any proposed solution. In theorising about practice, we practise theory. Theory can never free itself from practice nor practice escape theory. They are the flip sides of the philosophical coin ...

As troubling a condition as formalism is, it is only a symptom of a much more profound malaise. The villain of the piece is the Rationalist tradition which has dominated our thinking (and our thinking about thinking) for so long. We have never managed to shake off the effects of the Platonic contagion. Indeed, so accustomed have we become to its presence that we consider its metaphysical malady to be the natural and proper condition of human endeavour and thought. This is all the more debilitating because it is venerated as the universal solvent for social conflict and moral disharmony. As the embodiment of rational wisdom and thinking, law has not surprisingly come to occupy a sacred position in this culture and its thinking; the Rule of Law is venerated, even by many on the political left, as an "unqualified human good".

Resuscitated in the 17th and 18th centuries by Descartes, Kant, Locke, and others, it is now more commonly and conveniently referred to as the Enlightenment Project. It is the attempt to escape our finitude and its thoroughly contingent contexts and to establish a body of principles that are unconditionally valid for all persons at all times. Philosophy saw and still sees the road to respectability and success in the faithful lepidopterists [a person who studies and collects moths and butterflies]. The challenge was, armed with a small number of rudimentary insights into human nature, to capture the precious and eternal butterflies of Truth and Justice as they flitted through history, to press them flat in the heavy tomes of philosophical learning and to exhibit them for people's temporary gratification and edification. In this way, although history is always on the move, we might better be able to distil its enduring essence and withstand its continuing vicissitudes.

To understand what would otherwise be another intellectual indulgence, it is necessary to appreciate the belief and ambition of such a tradition. It is founded on the notion that, in order to command any moral authority or intellectual allegiance, there must be a solid epistemological foundation on which to build moral theory. Without such a base, people cannot be expected to live in and be bound by its ethical maxims. In a world in which the voice of God no longer commanded the necessary attention or respect, some alternative ground or origin of authority had to be established for obedience to be expected or enforced. Without an objective grounding, knowledge and truth would become prey to a radical scepticism, behind which lurks the spectre of social chaos and tyranny. As Kant put it:

> [This domain of pure understanding] is an island, enclosed by nature itself within unalterable limits. It is the land of truth – enchanting name! – surrounded by a wide and stormy ocean, the native home of illusion, where many a fog bank and many a swiftly melting iceberg give the deceptive appearance of farther shores, deluding the adventurous seafarer ever anew with empty hopes, and engaging him in enterprises which he can never abandon and yet is unable to carry to contemplation.

Separate from myth and religion, human reason must and can transcend vulgar political debate and ideological struggle. For the rationalist, the solution lies in letting Nature speak for itself. Although it might speak in an unrecognizable tongue, its utterances will be translated and popularized by the philosophical cyphers.

Despite its regular incantation that "the life of the law has not been logic, but experience", modern legal scholarship remains firmly within the rationalist tradition. Abstract reflection is given priority over experiential engagement. Human reason remains the touchstone for valid knowledge about ourselves, our socio-historical situation and the legal order. Law is still packaged and promoted as a scientific study. Although the Kelsenian search for methodological purity is exceptional, the rationalist dream retains a tenacious hold on the juristic imagination. More often implicit, Posner's work is devoted to discovering the knowable rationality of the observable world:

> As biology is to the living organisms, astronomy to the stars, or economics to the price system, so should legal studies be to the legal system: an endeavour to make precise, objective and systematic observations of how the legal system operates in fact and to discover and explain the recurrent patterns in the observations – the "laws" of the system.

Many thought that legal rationalism/formalism had been laid to rest by the realist critique of the 1920s and 1930s. Posner and others were engaged in a morbid form of intellectual necrophilia. However, realism was, at best, only an interlude in the long-running drama of legal formalism. At its height, realism toppled the regnant rule-formalism only to pave a better path to a full political realization of the formalist ideal. Ideologically and practically wedded to the reform programme of New Deal liberalism in the United States, the realists effected a pragmatic shift of institutional focus rather than a thoroughgoing rejection of formalism: they wanted to replace judge-dominated legal science with bureaucracy-wielded policy science. As such, realism's attacks were never intended to amount to more than a palace revolution. Smothering the truly radical insights and implications of the Realist critique, contemporary scholars have served up a thin gruel of neo-formalism and returned it (for it was never expunged, but only relocated) to the adjudicative arena.

While any faith in a crude reliance on some mechanical algorithm has been abandoned, there is still a fervent commitment and aspiration to the possibility of developing a theory of legal interpretation that is built around an impersonal and determinate application of immanent rationality. As Ronald Dworkin puts it, "law ... is deeply and thoroughly political ..., [b]ut not a matter of personal or partisan politics". The task of scholars is to uncover the political morality that runs deep within the common law. To do that, theorists have begun to step outside the legal arena and to search for formal allies in other disciplines. The role of this inter-disciplinary study is not to supplant legal reasoning nor to provide a substitute for legal wisdom, but to locate and understand better the formal threads that tie together the legal blanket in which society is wrapped. Like Coke, they all reaffirm their urgent and traditional belief that "the artificial reason and judgment of law ... requires long study and experience". As always, Truth only reveals itself to the initiated few and remains forever elusive to those unlearned in professional ritual and acumen: it is truly an acquired taste.[58]

(d)   Conclusion

We have outlined something of the substantive debates about formalism and the rule of law but we do not pretend to have exhausted the various perspectives that exist. Formalism has been at the heart of the common law system from its very inception, though it has not been beyond challenge. The stricture of the common law formalism (with its inflexible system of writs and procedures) was soon supplemented by a parallel system of equity. Rooted in the power of the sovereign to dispense justice to subjects, a distinct court applying distinct maxims and principles developed in the shadow of the common law. Equitable principles considered the matter from the perspective of fairness, conscience and morals, providing a curative to remedy a defect or deficiency in the common law. In *The Earl of Oxford's Case*, Lord Ellesmere described the relationship between law and equity thus:

> [M]en's actions are so diverse and infinite that it is impossible to make a general law which may aptly meet with every particular and not fail in some circum-stances. The office of chancellor is to correct men's consciences for frauds, breaches of trust, wrongs and oppressions of what nature soever they be, and to soften and mollify the extremity of the law.[59]

By the 19th century, equity itself had become excessively expensive, technical and formalistic – all the attributes of the common law it had originally sought to address.

Formalism is no relic of the past, and this cursory review of our legal history reveals that it has rarely stood unchallenged. Our immediate purpose here has been to suggest that a belief in some kind of formalism is a necessary part of a liberal legal system, given the centrality of the rule of law idea. If, as many new law students are, the reader has been struck by the strangeness of legal discourse and its detachment from other styles of argument, then at least that sensation can

---

58   Hutchinson, n 46, 23-30.
59   (1615) 21 ER 485.

be put into some kind of political context. An understanding of the relationship between formalism and liberalism is also important for an appreciation of critical and feminist jurisprudence which has begun powerfully to challenge the orthodoxy in many law schools.

Discussion Questions

1. Consider some cases you have read so far where you think that the outcome was "wrong". Give reasons for your answer.
2. Do you think that judges are constrained in the decisions that they can make?
3. What is the relationship between formalism and the rule of law?
4. What criticisms have been made of the rule of law? Suggest some reasons why it might still be an important concept.

PART B

The Processes of Law

Chapter 4

Access to Justice

(a)   Introduction

In this chapter we explore a number of questions which are fundamental to a contextual understanding of law, such as: Who uses law? How is it used? What are the impediments to its use? For what purposes is it used? These questions can be grouped under a general concern about "access to justice".

Why worry about access to justice? Part of the answer lies in the continuing influence of liberal ideals on western legal ideology. We have seen that liberalism places particular value on certain key ideals – equality, liberty, individual rights, and notions of justice being most relevant here. For these reasons, liberal thought seeks to separate the private realm of our lives as individuals from the public realm of governmental and judicial decision-making. Liberal theorists also favour certain means of access to public decision-making forums for private individuals. Access to the court system is both formally guaranteed and structured by rules of standing and procedure. Access to justice has come to be regarded as synonymous with, or crucially dependent on, ideals of due process or the rule of law:

> The right to one's day in court, the right to be heard, the right to take part in procedures through which one's fate is determined all provide the basic substance of due process, which is, in turn, at the heart of our conceptions of fairness and justice.[1]

Additionally, as Sarat reminds us, the liberal view is that access to the courts is necessary not just to ensure that individual rights are protected but also to control and limit the exercise of power by public agencies and officials. Thus we can conclude, with Sarat, that "the right to participate in the legal process is funda-mental to liberal theory".[2] Conversely, evidence that some citizens are under-represented in court processes or, worse, not represented at all (because of insuf-ficient resources or inadequate laws), threatens the legitimacy of this liberal theory.

There are, of course, considerable differences amongst liberal thinkers about how these ideals should be interpreted and protected, and which of them is to be regarded as more significant. At the risk of oversimplifying those differences, the strict classical liberal may not regard unequal access to the legal system as a problem in itself. The notions of formal equality and negative liberty do not

---

1   A Sarat, "Access to Justice: Citizen Participation and the American Legal Order", in L Lipson and S Wheeler (eds), *Law and the Social Sciences*, Russell Sage Foundation, 1986, 527.

2   Ibid 528.

require that the state should actively assist or ensure that citizens actually have their day in court. To take one example, we have seen that Nozick, a strong libertarian, objects to any action by the state to redistribute social goods other than in accordance with the limited scope of his entitlement theory of justice.[3] Presumably Nozick's opposition to redistributive measures such as taxation would also extend to state-sponsored attempts to guarantee equal use of the legal system.

In contrast, some modern liberals aspire to notions of substantive equality and positive liberty. Rawls, for example, argues that in order for rational people to fulfil their plans they must be guaranteed access to certain primary goods, natural and social.[4] In a similar vein, Raz argues that the ideal of personal autonomy cannot be realised where individuals are unable to take advantage of the options which are offered to them.[5] In other words, the ideal of substantively equal access to justice is an important part of modern liberal beliefs. To the extent that society falls short of this ideal then modern liberals perceive a problem. However, to some it seems inevitable that equal access will remain unattainable in practice, as Katz has argued. This, he explains, is because of the very nature of our legal system – the law does not stand still: "law is not a static distribution of rights but a process of arguing what the law is".[6] As new claims are made so new precedents are set which generate new legal arguments, and so on. In the end, Katz argues, equal access can only work as an empirically unattainable benchmark by which we can assess the moral worth of our legal system.

(b) Problems of access to justice

(i) Problems of definition

Studying the problems of access to justice has been one of the major areas of inquiry for socio-legal research since the 1970s.[7] Much of the early work was formulated as an examination of the "gap" that is said to exist between "the law in the books" and "the law in action".[8] As Roshier and Teff have pointed out, the inspiration for this work "derives from the liberal ideals of due process and equality of treatment before the law".[9] The general functions of law in society tend to be assumed rather than examined in this kind of work.

As we noted, most of the work in defining and studying the problems of access to justice began in the 1970s.[10] In Australia the main impetus for this work was the Federal Government's Commission of Inquiry into Poverty, especially its "Law and Poverty" inquiry headed by Professor Ronald Sackville (later a Judge of

---

3   R Nozick, *Anarchy, State and Utopia*, Basic Books, 1974; see Chapter 2 above.

4   J Rawls, *A Theory of Justice*, Belnap Press, 1971, 90-95; see Chapter 2 above.

5   J Raz, *The Morality of Freedom*, Clarendon, 1986, 373; see Chapter 2 above.

6   J Katz, *Poor People's Lawyers in Transition*, Rutgers UP, 1982, 1-3.

7   For an early and influential discussion of the distinction between socio-legal research and the sociology of law, see C Campbell and P Wiles, "The Study of Law in Society in Britain" (1976) 10 *Law and Society Review* 13.

8   A phrase given currency by Roscoe Pound, "Law in Books and Law in Action" (1910) 44 *American Law Review* 12.

9   Roshier and Teff, *Law and Society in England*, Tavistock, 1980, 3.

10   See, for example, the four-volume survey, M Cappelletti and B Garth (eds) *Access to Justice*, Giuffre/Sijthoff, 1978.

the Federal Court of Australia).[11] The problem of access to justice has continued to occupy the attention of politicians and law reformers. Nearly 20 years after the Law and Poverty inquiry, Sackville chaired another federal inquiry into access to justice which published a 500-page "action plan" for the federal Attorney-General in May 1994.[12] In the same year, the Australian Law Reform Commission produced two reports under the heading *Equality Before the Law*, which focused particularly on problems of access to the legal system for women.[13] Just before this, in 1993, the Senate Standing Committee on Legal and Constitutional Affairs published two reports as a result of its inquiry into the cost of justice.[14] In 2000 a major report by the Australian Law Reform Commission focused on questions of "the cost, timeliness, efficiency and accessibility of the federal justice system".[15] That report documents many more of the reports and inquiries into access problems.[16] More recently still, indicating the depressingly resilient nature of these problems, the Senate published a further report on its inquiry into legal aid and access to justice.[17]

In the 1970s, the catch-cry of socio-legal research into access problems was that many underprivileged groups in society had "unmet legal needs", a problem which could be remedied by strategies aimed at improving their access to the legal system. Much of the research then and since has been concerned to identify the nature of those unmet needs and to design and assess effective means of access. Today the main legacies of that work – legal aid schemes and a diversity of alternative dispute resolution forums – are established (although frequently under-resourced) features of most modern western legal systems.

Curiously, despite the volumes that have been written under the heading of "access to justice" it remains a vague concept within which many assumptions and perspectives are buried.[18] The 1994 Access to Justice Action Plan, produced by the Sackville Committee, argued that the concept of access to justice involves three key elements:

> All Australians, regardless of means, should have access to high quality legal services or effective dispute resolution mechanisms necessary to protect their rights and interests. ...

---

11 See, for example, R Sackville, *Law and Poverty in Australia: Second Main Report of the Australian Government Commission of Inquiry into Poverty*, AGPS, 1975; *Legal Aid in Australia*, AGPS, 1975; M Cass and R Sackville, *Legal Needs of the Poor*, AGPS, 1975.

12 Access to Justice Advisory Committee, *Access to Justice – an Action Plan*, Cth of Australia, 1994.

13 Australian Law Reform Commission, *Equality Before the Law: Women's Access to the Legal System*, Report No 67 (Jan 1994); *Equality Before the Law: Justice for Women*, Report No 69 (Parts I and II) (April 1994).

14 Senate Standing Committee on Legal and Constitutional Affairs, *The Cost of Justice: Foundations for Reform* (Feb, 1993); *The Cost of Justice Second Report: Checks and Imbalances* (August, 1993)

15 Australian Law Reform Commission, *Managing Justice: A Review of the Federal Civil Justice System*, Report No 89, January 2000, para 1.69.

16 Ibid para 1.77.

17 Senate Legal and Constitutional References Committee, *Legal Aid and Access to Justice*, June, 2004.

18 As Sackville commented in 1980, phrases like "access to law" or "access to justice" "are not self evident in their meaning": R Sackville, "Summary", in J Goldring et al (eds), *Access to Law: The Second Seminar on Australian Lawyers and Social Change*, ANU Press, 1980, 315.

> All Australians, regardless of their place of residence, should enjoy, as nearly as possible, equal access to legal services and to legal services markets that operate competitively. ...
>
> All Australians should be entitled to equality before the law.[19]

This definition highlights one of the main assumptions which has permeated research in this area – access to "justice" is usually taken to mean access to formally constructed, politically impartial courts and administrative agencies. It necessarily involves using the legal/administrative system and the services of lawyers in some way.

To the reader who is (or is becoming) immersed in the law and legal culture this may not be surprising, but it leads us to an important point. To use O'Malley's words:

> The identification of a social problem as a legal need rather than as some other sort of problem altogether is dependent on the place that law occupies in the society concerned, and especially the extent to which legalism permeates social consciousness. To identify a problem as a legal need is to make a particular judgement about appropriate solutions to that problem and then to recast the conception of the problem to accord with the nature of the proposed solution.[20]

In other words, when considering this literature it is important to bear in mind that the problems of unequal access to the law have been constructed out of a legal ideology. Lack of access is regarded and defined as a problem by people who accept the dominance of that ideology.

(ii)   Identifying problems of access

Having examined the way in which the concept of access to justice has been constructed, we now turn to look in more detail at the factors which create problems of access.

The information available from studies in Australia and overseas clearly suggests that the process of deciding to deal with a problem by invoking the legal system (sometimes described as "mobilising the law"[21]) is not the same for all people and can be a complex one. Much depends upon the nature of the particular problem, its social and cultural context, who the parties are (access can be particularly problematic for women, especially Aboriginal and Torres Strait Islander women[22]), the nature of the relationship between the parties, each party's prior experience in using the law, each party's perception of the likelihood that their case will be successful, and the organisation and distribution of the local legal profession. To use a simple contrast, the decision by a large corporation to seek legal advice in the face of a threatened takeover is likely to be much more immediate than the decision by a single mother faced with a violent ex-partner or a troublesome landlord.

---

19   Access to Justice Advisory Committee, n 12, xxx.

20   P O'Malley, *Law, Capitalism and Democracy*, Allen and Unwin, 1983, 104.

21   See, for example, R Lempert, "Mobilizing Private Law: An Introductory Essay" (1976) 11 *Law and Society Review* 173.

22   See Australian Law Reform Commission, *Equality Before the Law: Justice for Women*, Report No 69 (Part I) (April 1994) 117ff; *Legal Aid and Access to Justice*, n 17, Ch 4.

Early research into these issues in Australia focused on two interrelated questions: what work do lawyers do and what matters do clients take to lawyers? In the late 1970s and early 1980s surveys were made of lawyers, to determine what type of matters predominate in their everyday legal practice and of clients (or potential clients) to see what cross-section of the community engages the services of lawyers. Though the findings may seem unexceptional today, it is necessary to bear in mind that at the time relatively little was known about the actual work practices of the profession. This evidence was thus an important part of the process of defining access to justice as a problem. It is also likely that the evidence produced by these studies helped to foster an assumption that finding legal "solutions" to legal "problems" equates with the provision of justice.

Studies of the legal profession in Australia found that lawyers' work was concentrated on particular areas. In Victoria, Hetherton found that more than three-quarters of solicitors and over a third of barristers performed what she labelled "economic" work – property, probate, estate and tax planning, and commercial and company matters.[23] In New South Wales, Tomasic found that approximately 50 per cent of lawyers' work concerned such matters.[24] More recently, the Australian Bureau of Statistics has produced figures which show that in 2001-02 commercial work accounted for 36 per cent of income for solicitors' practices with six or more partners, with property work (including conveyancing) accounting for a further 14 per cent. In smaller practices property work represented 28 per cent and commercial work 11 per cent of income.[25]

Surveys of potential clients have produced data which support the idea that much legal work is oriented towards property-related matters. An early study, reported in 1978, found that home owners were much more likely than non-home owners to seek the assistance of lawyers, and to do so more regularly.[26] Approximately 80 per cent of respondents to that survey reported that conveyancing was the reason that they contacted a solicitor.[27] If we define the poor as those who have less property, then these findings seem to confirm what many have long suspected, that the poor have less access to the legal profession. This finding was repeated in studies in the United Kingdom and the United States.[28] The picture is not as simple as this, however. A 1980 Australian survey found that "those who need legal advice and do not seek it include many who are not poor, and those who seek advice include many who are poor".[29] The Australian Law Reform Commission makes a similar observation about civil proceedings in federal courts, noting that "contrary to the popular view, parties

---

23   M Hetherton, *Victoria's Lawyers. The Second Report of a Research Project on "Lawyers in the Community"*, Victorian Law Foundation, 1981, 205.

24   R Tomasic, "The Functions of the Legal Professions in Australia", monograph, 1982, cited in O'Malley, n 20, 97-98.

25   Australian Bureau of Statistics, *Legal Practices*, (2003) Cat No 8667.0. For details of an earlier ABS survey, see F Regan, "Some Revelations about the Legal Industry" (1990) 15 *Legal Services Bulletin* 206.

26   R Tomasic, *Lawyers and the Community*, Allen and Unwin, 1978, 59.

27   Ibid 53.

28   See the survey of studies in M Zander, *Legal Services for the Community*, Temple Smith, 1978, 276-288.

29   M Cass and J Western, *Legal Aid and Legal Need*, Commonwealth Legal Aid Commission, 1980 58; Zander uses the same words, n 28, 288.

include, but are not limited to, the very poor and the very wealthy".[30] It may be more accurate to conclude that the poor do have substantial contact with lawyers, but, first, this is often in circumstances where they have little or no choice about becoming involved in legal proceedings;[31] secondly, when they do seek advice it is for different types of matters than wealthier clients; and, thirdly, they seek this advice from a different set of legal service providers. As to the second point, Cass and Western referred to data from various legal aid agencies in Australia and found that the bulk of legal work for the poor consisted in giving advice (as opposed to court-room representation) on family law, criminal law and motor vehicle accident matters.[32] On the third point, O'Malley concluded from the available Australian studies that "lawyers working for the poor generally occupy the lower regions of the legal profession".[33] Again, while these statistics and conclusions may seem trite today, the significance of this research at the time was to provide empirical support for the view that the overall structure and delivery of professional legal services results in a legal system that is skewed against a large section of the community. More recent evidence supports this. A study of cases in the Common Law Division of the Supreme Court of New South Wales in 1992 found that, compared with the NSW population in general, plaintiffs had "a smaller proportion of lower incomes and a higher proportion of middle and higher incomes".[34]

How, then, do we account for the relationship between poverty and inequality in access to and use of legal services that is suggested by the research data? This has been an important question for policy makers and law reformers, because the answer determines the type of response that is made to the access problem. One way of approaching this issue is to regard poverty primarily as a matter of an individual's economic status. Seen this way, access to law becomes similar to a consumer problem, and an appropriate response is to lower the cost of legal services.

There are three main sources of expense for a person contemplating either commencing or defending a civil action in court. First, there are the "opportunity costs", that is, the costs to the person of the lost opportunities when they use their time and resources to commence and continue the litigation. These costs may include items such as lost wages, child care costs, missed business opportunities and so on. These costs cannot be recovered through the court rules relating to the awarding of costs.

Secondly, there are court costs. These are the fees which are charged by courts and tribunals for things such as issuing subpoenas, filing documents to commence a claim, or searching and obtaining court documents. The historical reason for imposing such fees was to "discourage trivial, vexatious or unmeritorious claims".[35] The fees vary from one court to another. As an example, the charge for filing a document to commence a proceeding in the ACT Supreme

---

30 ALRC, n 15, para 4.15.

31 Ibid para 1.49.

32 Cass and Western, n 29, 74, and see Zander, n 28, 287-288 for a similar conclusion.

33 O'Malley, n 20, 103.

34 T Matruglio, *So Who Does Use the Court? A Profile of the Users of the Common Law Division of the Supreme Court of New South Wales*, Civil Justice Research Centre, 1993, 25.

35 ALRC, n 15, para 4.100.

Court is $589; in the ACT Magistrates Court the cost is $341 for claims of more than $10,000 and $98 for claims less than that amount.[36] There is mixed evidence about the effect of court fees on restricting access to the court system, although a Senate Committee noted in 1993 that between 1965 and 1985:

> [T]he total amount collected through court fees in the NSW Supreme Court rose by almost 750% and in the NSW District Court by more than 640%. Over the same period, in the Queensland Supreme and District Courts the amount rose by more than 900%.[37]

The third source of costs are the professional fees associated with obtaining legal advice and representation, together with disbursements (eg, fees for expert witnesses, or the costs of medical reports). According to the Australian Law Reform Commission these costs easily outweigh court charges and other costs of litigation.[38] Consequently, legal fees are a major deterrent for people contemplating legal action. Further uncertainty for potential litigants arises from the fact that there are different methods for calculating the charge for a legal service, including charging for prescribed items (such as preparing a letter), charging for the amount of time spent on the legal work, charging a flat fee for the total work done, and calculating the charge according to the value of the subject of the legal work.[39] In a litigious matter, a solicitor may charge according to a scale of fees, but he or she is also free to reach an agreement with the client about the charge. Some idea of the magnitude of legal costs can be gained from a study in 1993 of a sample of 259 civil matters commenced in the District and Supreme Courts in NSW, which found that the median solicitor's fee paid by plaintiffs was $6000, with an average fee of just over $10,600.[40]

The problem of costs is compounded by rules which govern the awarding of costs in a litigated dispute. The Law Reform Commission of Victoria describes the situation in its paper on *The Cost of Litigation*:

> Although costs are awarded in the discretion of the court, the general rule that is followed is that the loser pays not only his or her own costs but also those of the winner. However, this rule – the "costs indemnity rule" – does not require the loser to pay the full costs ("solicitor-client" costs) incurred by the winner. It only requires payment of reasonable costs ("party-party" costs) incurred by the winner. These are calculated on the basis of scales of costs set by the relevant court.[41]

There are several rationales for this rule. According to the ALRC, the basic rationale is fairness: "it is unfair for a party to be out of pocket as a result of pursuing a valid claim or defending an unjustified suit".[42] The rule is said to give

---

36   These figures represent charges effective at 10 January 2005.

37   Senate Standing Committee on Legal and Constitutional Affairs, *The Cost of Justice Second Report: Checks and Imbalances*, 1993, 77 (footnotes omitted).

38   Australian Law Reform Commission, *Costs Shifting – Who Pays for Litigation?* Report No 75, 1995, 32.

39   Access to Justice Advisory Committee, n 12, 151.

40   D Worthington and J Baker, *The Costs of Civil Litigation*, Civil Justice Research Centre, Sydney 1993, 12.

41   Law Reform Commission of Victoria, *Access to the Law: The Cost of Litigation*, Issues Paper, May 1990, 7.

42   ALRC, n 38, 52.

people who do not have adequate resources the opportunity to commence litigation. It is also said to deter frivolous claims and to encourage settlement of disputes before a court decision. Against these alleged advantages, however, it can be argued that the risk of bearing the other party's costs acts as a major deterrent to poor people pressing their claims. In its report on costs, the ALRC noted that the rule

> will provide less assistance in cases where the outcome is uncertain and the litigant is risk averse. The rule is also of less assistance in proceedings which do not involve a monetary award as the costs that may be recovered are usually insufficient to meet the reasonable costs of the litigation.[43]

Moreover, because the rule only relates to the reasonable costs incurred, the successful party may still have to bear a significant portion of their own costs.[44] The Commission listed the types of cases which are likely not to be pursued because of the impact of the costs rules. These include: cases involving small claims or non-monetary relief, professional negligence, mortgagors defending themselves against action by mortgagees, environmental challenges and employees' termination payments.[45]

One way of mitigating the impact of the costs rules is through the use of arrangements in which the payment of fees to the lawyer is contingent on a successful outcome for the client. In some instances – typically personal injury or workers compensation cases – plaintiffs and their lawyers may agree to an arrangement whereby the lawyer only receives remuneration if the litigation is successful. In theory this might take one of three forms: a speculative fee arrangement – if the action is successful the lawyer receives his or her normal fee; an uplift fee arrangement – on a successful action the lawyer receives the normal fee plus a further amount which is calculated as a percentage of the normal fee; or a percentage fee arrangement – the lawyer receives the normal fee plus an agreed percentage of any *damages* which are awarded to the plaintiff. Percentage fee arrangements are not permitted in any Australian jurisdiction. Speculative fee arrangements are permitted in all Australian jurisdictions, while uplift arrangements are permitted (but not for criminal matters) in NSW, Victoria, Queensland (for barristers only) and South Australia.[46] The latter two arrangements are usually called "contingency fees" and they aim to compensate the lawyer for the risk of not being paid if the action is unsuccessful. One effect of a contingency fee arrangement is that the lawyer acts like an insurance company – subsidising work for unsuccessful litigants out of the premiums which are gained from successful litigants.[47]

So far we have been considering the relationship between poverty and lack of access to legal services as though it were mainly a problem of lack of resources. An alternative perspective is to argue that poverty is more than a lack of sufficient

---

43 Ibid 52.

44 It is commonly thought that this portion is about one third of their legal costs.

45 ALRC, n 38, 44.

46 ALRC, n 15, para 5.21. The situation in NSW will be affected by s 324(1) of the *Legal Profession Act 2004* (not in force at the time of writing) which prohibits uplift fees in relation to claims for damages.

47 D Luban, "Speculating on Justice: The Ethics and Jurisprudence of Contingency Fees" in S Parker and C Sampford (eds), *Legal Ethics and Legal Practice*, Clarendon Press, 1995, 89 at 110.

purchasing power, that it is also the product of complex social and political relations. This indicates that a more detailed explanation of the relationship between poverty and access to the law is required. One possibility is the "social organisation thesis" put forward by the American sociologists Mayhew and Reiss in 1969.[48] In essence their argument was that just as access to income and other resources is stratified in the community, so too there are parallels in the stratification and specialisation of legal practice. As they put it:

> The usual interpretation placed on the association between income and the use of legal services is that income *enables* the citizen to make use of legal services. Might the influence be more indirect? Income brings one into participation in the institution of property, and property as an institution is socially organised so as to bring its participants into contact with attorneys.[49]

Thus the unequal social organisation of wealth in society results in a legal profession which is predominantly structured to serve property interests. "Out of this convergence emerges a pattern of citizen contact with attorneys that is heavily orientated to property".[50]

In his review of access studies, Zander argued that although it is fruitful, this theory does not explain the evidence that many people do not use lawyers even though their place in the social organisation would indicate a strong pattern of contact with lawyers.[51] To explain this, Zander suggested that a crucial determinant in seeking legal advice is the informal networks of "lay intermediaries" (neighbours, friends, work colleagues and so on[52]) who can persuade an individual to take the often difficult step of contacting a lawyer. Early research found that approximately 50 per cent of survey respondents contacted a lawyer following advice from such intermediaries.[53]

"Access" studies have also shown that there are often considerable personal or psychological barriers to using a lawyer. In their review of Australian surveys of potential clients, Cass and Western note that:

> [S]ome respondents were fearful of taking the step of entering a solicitor's office. Migrants often expressed concern with the problems of communicating with solicitors who spoke only English. Unfavourable social attitudes to lawyers were expressed too, by a substantial proportion of respondents.[54]

In its report on *Justice for Women* the ALRC noted that women who are victims of domestic violence face particular difficulties in contemplating whether or not to use the court system to obtain protection. These include "the fear that legal action will exacerbate the problem of violence", "intimidation by or lack of faith in the court process", and concern about the lack of follow up. The report went on to

---

48   L Mayhew and A Reiss, "The Social Organisation of Legal Contacts" (1969) 34 *American Sociological Review* 309.

49   Ibid 312 (emphasis in original).

50   Ibid 313.

51   Zander, n 28, 291, citing studies in London, Oxford and the United States.

52   Ibid 293-294.

53   Tomasic, n 26, 244-245; see also Cass and Sackville, n 11, 78.

54   Cass and Western, n 29, 65. In this light it is also worth noting a 1990 Draft Report on *Access to Interpreters in the Australian Legal System*, which found that in the Federal Court, the Family Court, and a sample of Magistrates Courts, the usage of interpreters was either infrequent or extremely low: Commonwealth Attorney-General's Dept, AGPS, 1990, 10-13.

comment that many women find the masculine culture of the courtroom alienating. The Commission noted that:

> Most judges, prosecutors, lawyers and court officials are men. Room layout is formal and intimidating. Courts also have many legal formalities and rituals, such as wearing of wigs and gowns. While these are matters that affect all people coming to court, it was suggested they have traditional and patriarchal connotations which subtly deter many women.[55]

Finally, another important determinant in the process of legal mobilisation is the structure and organisation of the legal profession. For example, the professional division between barristers and solicitors which still exists in most Australian States is said to contribute to increased costs and delays in the legal system.[56] It also seems that the distribution of lawyer's firms around the country does not match the spread of population. In 2001-02 approximately 60 per cent of the Australian population lived in New South Wales and Victoria, and yet nearly 77 per cent of barristers practices and 70 per cent of solicitors practices in were located in these States. Moreover, 79 per cent of all solicitors practices were located in capital cities.[57]

As we have summarised them so far, access studies have focused on why it is that not every person who encounters a "legal" problem takes steps towards mobilising the law in relation to that problem. We have seen that this is because of a variety of personal, social and economic factors, including biases inherent in the organisation and structure of the legal system itself. Those who do take such steps usually want to achieve some quite specific end; "access to justice" has come to be regarded as an instrumental exercise in pursuing or defending individual claims at law.

Access to the legal system does not necessarily mean access to equal treatment in that system, however. The party who has more money, power, or experience will likely enjoy an advantage in any legal contest. As one judicial commentator has noted:

> [F]undamental aspects of our existing procedural system are substantial causes of excessive cost, delay and unfairness. It is too cumbersome and labour intensive to allow disputes to be resolved at an affordable cost; it unfairly disadvantages the poorer of the two litigants.[58]

This point was explored in detail by Marc Galanter in his 1974 article, which we extract below. Though it was based on American data, Galanter's argument has been extremely influential in subsequent analyses of the problem of access to justice elsewhere. Indeed it has become one of the most cited law review articles of all time.[59]

---

55   ALRC, n 55, 129 and 150. See also *Legal Aid and Access to Justice*, n 17, Ch 5 "Women and Family Law".

56   J Disney, *Improving the Quality and Accessibility of Legal Services*, Centre for International and Public Law, ANU, 1994.

57   Australian Bureau of Statistics, n 25; *Year Book Australia*, 2004.

58   Justice GL Davies, "A Blueprint for Reform: Some Proposals of the Litigation Reform Commission and their Rationale" (1996) 5 *Journal of Judicial Administration* 201 at 201.

59   Fred R Shapiro, "The Most Cited Law Review Articles Revisited" (1996) 71 *Chicago-Kent Law Review* 751, Table 1.

Marc Galanter, "Why the 'Haves' Come Out Ahead: Speculations on the Limits of Social Change"

(1974) (footnotes omitted)

Most analyses of the legal system start at the rules and work down through institutional facilities to see what effect the rules have on the parties. I would like to reverse that procedure and look through the other end of the telescope. Let's think about the different kinds of parties and the effect these differences might have on the way the system works.

Because of the differences in their size, differences in the state of the law, and differences in their resources, some of the actors in the society have many occasions to utilize the courts (in the broad sense) to make (or defend) claims; others do so only rarely. We might divide our actors into those claimants who have only occasional recourse to the courts (one-shotters or OS) and repeat players (RP) who are engaged in many similar litigations over time. The spouse in a divorce case, the auto-injury claimant, the criminal accused are OSs; the insurance company, the prosecutor, the finance company are RPs. Obviously this is an oversimplification; there are intermediate cases such as the professional criminal. So we ought to think of OS-RP as a continuum rather than as a dichotomous pair. Typically, the RP is a larger unit and the stakes in any given case are smaller (relative to total worth). OSs are usually smaller units and the stakes represented by the tangible outcome of the case may be high relative to total worth, as in the case of injury victim or the criminal accused. Or, the OS may suffer from the opposite problem: his claims may be so small and unmanageable (the shortweighted consumer or the holder of performing rights) that the cost of enforcing them outruns any promise of benefit. See Finklestein (1954: 284-86).

Let us refine our notion of the RP into an "ideal type" if you will – a unit which has had and anticipates repeated litigation, which has low stakes in the outcome of any one case, and which has the resources to pursue its long-run interests. [...] An OS, on the other hand, is a unit whose claims are too large (relative to his size) or too small (relative to the cost of remedies) to be managed routinely and rationally.

We would expect an RP to play the litigation game differently from an OS. Let us consider some of his advantages:

(1) RPs, having done it before, have advance intelligence; they are able to structure the next transaction and build a record. It is the RP who writes the form contract, requires the security deposit, and the like.

(2) RPs develop expertise and have ready access to specialists. They enjoy economies of scale and have low startup costs for any case.

(3) RPs have opportunities to develop facilitative informal relations with institutional incumbents.

(4) The RP must establish and maintain credibility as a combatant. His interest in his "bargaining reputation" serves as a resource to establish "commitment" to his bargaining positions. With no bargaining reputation to maintain, the OS has more difficulty in convincingly committing himself in bargaining.

(5) RPs can play the odds. The larger the matter at issue looms for OS, the more likely he is to adopt a minimax strategy (minimize the probability of maximum loss). Assuming that the stakes are relatively smaller for RPs, they can adopt strategies calculated to maximize gain over a long series of cases, even where this involves the risk of maximum loss in some cases.

(6) RPs can play for rules as well as immediate gains. First, it pays an RP to expend resources in influencing the making of the relevant rules by such methods as lobbying. (And his accumulated expertise enables him to do this persuasively.)

(7) RPs can also play for rules in litigation itself, whereas an OS is unlikely to. That is, there is a difference in what they regard as a favorable outcome. Because his stakes in the immediate outcome are high and because by definition OS is unconcerned with the outcome of similar litigation in the future, OS will have little interest in that element of the outcome which might influence the disposition of the decision-maker next time around. For the RP, on the other hand, anything that will favorably influence the outcomes of future cases is a worthwhile result. The larger the stake for any player and the lower the probability of repeat play, the less likely that he will be concerned with the rules which govern future cases of the same kind. Consider two parents contesting the custody of their only child, the prizefighter vs. the IRS for tax arrears, the convict facing the death penalty. On the other hand, the player with small stakes in the present case and the prospect of a series of similar cases (the IRS, the adoption agency, the prosecutor) may be more interested in the state of the law.

Thus, if we analyze the outcomes of a case into a tangible component and a rule component, we may expect that in case 1, OS will attempt to maximize tangible gain. But if RP is interested in maximizing his tangible gain in a series of cases 1 … n, he may be willing to trade off tangible gain in any one case for rule gain (or to minimize rule loss). We assumed that the institutional facilities for litigation were overloaded and settlements were prevalent. We would then expect RPs to "settle" cases where they expected unfavorable rule outcomes. Since they expect to litigate again, RPs can select to adjudicate (or appeal) those cases which they regard as most likely to produce favorable rules. On the other hand, OSs should be willing to trade off the possibility of making "good law" for tangible gain. Thus, we would expect the body of "precedent" cases – that is, cases capable of influencing the outcome of future cases – to be relatively skewed toward those favorable to RP. [...]

In stipulating that RPs can play for rules, I do not mean to imply the RPs pursue rule-gain as such. If we recall that not all rules penetrate (ie, become effectively applied at the field level) we come to some additional advantages of RPs.

(8) RPs, by virtue of experience and expertise, are more likely to be able to discern which rules are likely to "penetrate" and which are likely to remain merely symbolic commitments. RPs may be able to concentrate their resources on rule-changes that are likely to make a tangible difference. They can trade off symbolic defeats for tangible gains.

(9) Since penetration depends in part on the resources of the parties (knowledge, attentiveness, expert services, money) RPs are more likely to be able to invest the matching resources necessary to secure the penetration of rules favorable to them.

It is not suggested that RPs are to be equated with "haves" (in terms of power, wealth and status) or OSs with "have-nots". In the American setting most RPs are larger, richer and more powerful than are most OSs, so these categories overlap, but there are obvious exceptions. RPs may be "have-nots" (alcoholic derelicts) or may act as champions of "have-nots" (as government does from time to time); OSs such as criminal defendants may be wealthy. What this analysis does is to define a position of advantage in the configuration of contending parties and indicate how those with other advantages tend to occupy this position of advantage and to have their own other advantages reinforced and augmented thereby. This position of advantage is one of the ways in which a legal system formally neutral as between "haves" and "have-nots" may perpetuate and augment the advantages of the former. [...]

We may think of litigation as typically involving various combinations of OSs and RPs. We can then construct a matrix such as Figure 1 and fill in the boxes with some well-known if only approximate American examples. (We ignore for the moment that the terms OS and RP represent ends of a continuum, rather than a dichotomous pair.)

Figure 1

A Taxonomy of Litigation By Strategic Configuration of Parties

Defendant	***Initiator, Claimant*** — One-Shotter	***Initiator, Claimant*** — Repeat Player
One-shotter	Parent v Parent (Custody) Spouse v Spouse (Divorce) Family v Family Member (Insanity Commitment) Family v Family (Inheritance) Neighbor v Neighbor Partner v Partner OS v OS I	Prosecutor v Accused Finance Co v Debtor Landlord v Tenant IRS v Taxpayer Condemnor v Property Owner RP v OS II
Repeat player	Welfare Client v Agency Auto Dealer v Manufacturer Injury Victim v Insurance Company Tenant v Landlord Bankrupt Consumer v Creditors Defamed v Publisher OS v RP III	Union v Company Movie Distributor v Censorship Board Developer v Suburban Municipality Purchaser v Supplier Regulatory Agency v Firms of Regulated Industry RP v RP IV

On the basis of our incomplete and unsystematic examples, let us conjecture a bit about the content of these boxes:

Box I: OS vs. OS

The most numerous occupants of this box are divorces and insanity hearings. Most (over 90 per cent of divorces, for example) are uncontested. A large portion of these are really pseudo-litigation, that is, a settlement is worked out between the parties and ratified in the guise of adjudication. When we get real litigation in Box I, it is often between parties who have some intimate tie with one another, fighting over some unsharable good, often with overtones of "spite" and "irrationality". Courts are resorted to where an ongoing relationship is ruptured; they have little to do with the routine patterning of activity. The law is invoked

ad hoc and instrumentally by the parties. There may be a strong interest in vindication, but neither party is likely to have much interest in the long-term state of
the law (of, for instance, custody or nuisance). There are few appeals, few test
cases, little expenditure of resources on rule-development. Legal doctrine is
likely to remain remote from everyday practice and from popular attitudes.

Box II: RP vs. OS

The great bulk of litigation is found in this box – indeed every really numerous
kind except personal injury cases, insanity hearings, and divorces. The law is
used for routine processing of claims by parties for whom the making of such
claims is a regular business activity. Often the cases here take the form of stereotyped mass processing with little of the individuated attention of full-dress
adjudication. Even greater numbers of cases are settled "informally" with
settlement keyed to possible litigation outcome (discounted by risk, cost, delay).

The state of the law is of interest to the RP, though not to the OS defendants.
Insofar as the law is favorable to the RP it is "followed" closely in practice (subject to discount for RP's transaction costs). Transactions are built to fit the rules
by creditors, police, draft boards and other RPs. Rules favoring OSs may be less
readily applicable, since OSs do not ordinarily plan the underlying transaction, or
less meticulously observed in practice, since OSs are unlikely to be as ready or
able as RPs to invest in insuring their penetration to the field level.

Box III: OS vs. RP

All of these are rather infrequent types except for personal injury cases which are
distinctive in that free entry to the arena is provided by the contingent fee. In auto
injury claims, litigation is routinized and settlement is closely geared to possible
litigation outcome. Outside the personal injury area, litigation in Box III is not
routine. It usually represents the attempt of some OS to invoke outside help to
create leverage on an organization with which he has been having dealings but is
now at the point of divorce (for example, the discharged employee or the
cancelled franchisee). The OS claimant generally has little interest in the state of
the law; the RP defendant, however, is greatly interested.

Box IV: RP vs. RP

Let us consider the general case first and then several special cases. We might
expect that there would be little litigation in Box IV, because to the extent that
two RPs play with each other repeatedly, the expectation of continued mutually
beneficial interaction would give rise to informal bilateral controls. This seems
borne out by studies of dealings among businessmen and in labor relations.
Official agencies are invoked by unions trying to get established and by
management trying to prevent them from getting established, more rarely in
dealings between bargaining partners. Units with mutually beneficial relations do
not adjust their differences in courts. Where they rely on third parties in dispute-
resolution, it is likely to take a form (such as arbitration or a domestic tribunal)
detached from official sanctions and applying domestic rather than official rules.

However, there are several special cases. First, there are those RPs who seek
not furtherance of tangible interests, but vindication of fundamental cultural
commitments. An example would be the organizations which sponsor much
church-state litigation. Where RPs are contending about value differences (who is
right) rather than interest conflicts (who gets what) there is less tendency to settle
and less basis for developing a private system of dispute settlement.

Second, government is a special kind of RP. Informal controls depend upon
the ultimate sanction of withdrawal and refusal to continue beneficial relations.
To the extent that withdrawal of future association is not possible in dealing with

government, the scope of informal controls is correspondingly limited. The development of informal relations between regulatory agencies and regulated firms is well known. And the regulated may have sanctions other than withdrawal which they can apply; for instance, they may threaten political opposition. But the more inclusive the unit of government, the less effective the withdrawal sanction and the greater the likelihood that a party will attempt to invoke outside allies by litigation even while sustaining the ongoing relationship. This applies also to monopolies, units which share the government's relative immunity to withdrawal sanctions. RPs in monopolistic relationships will occasionally invoke formal controls to show prowess, to give credibility to threats, and to provide satisfactions for other audiences. Thus we would expect litigation by and against government to be more frequent than in other RP vs. RP situations. There is a second reason for expecting more litigation when government is a party. That is, that the notion of "gain" (policy as well as monetary) is often more contingent and problematic for governmental units than for other parties, such as businesses or organized interest groups. In some cases courts may, by proffering authoritative interpretations of public policy, redefine an agency's notion of gain. Hence government parties may be more willing to externalize decisions to the courts. And opponents may have more incentive to litigate against government in the hope of securing a shift in its goals.

A somewhat different kind of special case is present where plaintiff and defendant are both RPs but do not deal with each other repeatedly (two insurance companies, for example.) In the government/monopoly case, the parties were so inextricably bound together that the force of informal controls was limited; here they are not sufficiently bound to each other to give informal controls their bite; there is nothing to withdraw from! The large one-time deal that falls through, the marginal enterprise – these are staple sources of litigation.

Where there is litigation in the RP vs. RP situation, we might expect that there would be heavy expenditure on rule-development, many appeals, and rapid and elaborate development of the doctrinal law. Since the parties can invest to secure implementation of favorable rules, we would expect practice to be closely articulated to the resulting rules.

On the basis of these preliminary guesses, we can sketch a general profile of litigation and the factors associated with it. The great bulk of litigation is found in Box II; much less in Box III. Most of the litigation in these Boxes is mass routine processing of disputes between parties who are strangers (not in mutually beneficial continuing relations) or divorced – and between whom there is a disparity in size. One party is a bureaucratically organized "professional" (in the sense of doing it for a living) who enjoys strategic advantages. Informal controls between the parties are tenuous or ineffective; their relationship is likely to be established and defined by official rules; in litigation, these rules are discounted by transaction costs and manipulated selectively to the advantage of the parties. On the other hand, in Boxes I and IV, we have more infrequent but more individualized litigation between parties of the same general magnitude, among whom there are or were continuing multi-stranded relationships with attendant informal controls. Litigation appears when the relationship loses its future value; when its "monopolistic" character deprives informal controls of sufficient leverage and the parties invoke outside allies to modify it; and when the parties seek to vindicate conflicting values.[60]

---

60   (1974) 9 *Law and Society Review* 95 at 97-114. The work referred to in Galanter's text is H Finklestein, "The Composer and the Public Interest – Regulation of Performing Rights Societies" (1954) 19 *Law and Contemporary Problems* 275.

In reflecting on Galanter's argument it is useful to consider the following points. First, the article is concerned mainly with which parties do well in court. As we will see later in this chapter, since the mid-1970s (when the article was written) there has been a much greater emphasis on non-court based dispute resolution and on systems of private justice. A question to consider, then, is whether Galanter's thesis applies in these non-court settings. Secondly, not all repeat players will enjoy the systemic advantages identified in the article. For example, repeat offenders in the criminal court system will more likely come out worse than first-time offenders.[61] This reminds us that the advantages described by Galanter have as much to do with economic power and socio-political advantage as with a person's frequency of contact with the court system. But, thirdly, it does not necessarily follow that rich or stronger parties will necessarily gain favourable outcomes in court. This was tested by Wheeler et al in a survey of nearly 6000 American State Supreme Court decisions between 1870 and 1970.[62] By looking at the overall pattern of the results in those cases they found limited support for the argument. There was no strong pattern of advantage enjoyed by the stronger parties (governments and business organisations); indeed Wheeler et al comment that "[n]o broad type of party, either 'have' or 'have not', consistently won or lost, with the exception of state and large city governments".[63] Nevertheless they observe that "parties with greater resources – relatively speaking, the 'haves' – generally fared better than those with fewer resources", while also noting "the comparatively strong showing of individual parties".[64] Research findings such as these are a reminder that the "repeat player/one shotter" typology, while a powerful analytical tool for suggesting hypotheses about the way in which our legal system operates, requires empirical verification.

Notwithstanding these points, Galanter's argument continues to provide a useful platform from which to explore the contrast between legal ideals and procedural reality which is suggested by the access to justice surveys.[65]

(c) Responses to problems of access

Having looked at the nature and extent of problems in achieving access to justice, we now look at the range of possible and actual responses to it. Under the first of these headings we note that individuals confronted with the difficulties of access may well respond to a "legal" problem by taking steps that do not involve the legal system at all. For want of a better term we describe these as "non-legal" responses. Under the subsequent sub-headings we consider responses that might be made from within the legal system ("legal responses"). Because the provision of legal aid services has been the most common such response in Western legal

---

61 R Lempert, "A Classic at 25: Reflections on Galanter's 'Haves' Article and Work it Has Inspired" (1999) 33 *Law and Society Review* 1099 at 1103.

62 S Wheeler, B Cartwright, R Kagan, and L Friedman, "Do the 'Haves' Come Out Ahead? Winning and Losing in State Supreme Courts, 1870-1970" (1987) 21 *Law and Society Review* 403.

63 Ibid 438.

64 Ibid 438 and 441.

65 Indeed, the continued importance of Galanter's article 25 years after it was published was explored in a symposium issue of the *Law and Society Review* ((1999) vol 33 no 4). See also H Kritzer and S Silbey (eds), *In Litigation: Do the 'Haves' Still Come Out Ahead?*, Stanford UP, 2003.

systems, we deal with it separately from other legal responses. We stress, though, that our division of the material under these headings is simply for ease of discussion. In what follows, it will quickly become apparent that in practice there are no simple distinctions between what is "legal" and "non-legal".

(i) Non-legal responses[66]

One set of options available to the individual who is confronted with a "legal problem" involves either ignoring or by-passing the legal system altogether. Several commentators have pointed out that merely because a problem can be defined in legal terms or shown to have a legal dimension, it does not necessarily follow that a legal response will be appropriate or effective.[67]

The interests which draw individuals together in modern "technologically complex rich societies" are often characterised by one-sided, single-instance transactions. The purchase of consumer goods is an everyday example.[68] For the modern consumer, the process of instigating formal steps to have a complaint dealt with will often be seen as too complex, time-consuming and expensive. Dissatisfied consumers may thus decide to minimise their losses and take their business elsewhere rather than take action against a dishonest trader. In the language of studies of complaint behaviour this is described as the "exit" or "avoidance" option.[69] Where the avoidance option is not realistic – where, for example, the trader has a monopoly over that product – another realistic response might be simply to put up with the situation (described in the literature as "lumping it"). Whereas avoidance involves terminating (or at least redefining) the relationship between the parties, "lumping it" refers to the decision to continue the relationship in spite of the differences between the parties. This may be the experience of women or migrant workers faced with discriminatory work practices. Felstiner's work suggests that strategies of avoidance or lumping it are likely to be common in these types of situations.[70]

Of course many relationships between individuals are not "one-off" events but continue for indefinite periods. Relations between neighbours or family members are examples. Often the knowledge that the relationship between the parties is likely to continue will constrain the use of legal remedies. A classic illustration of this comes from an early, and still influential, study of the role of contract law in business relations by Stewart Macaulay.[71] In many commercial settings a contract

---

66   The following discussion assumes situations in which an person has to decide whether to activate the legal system in some way in order to bring it to bear on a problem. There are, of course, many instances when a person has no effective choice in the matter – a person charged with a criminal offence is one example.

67   P Lewis, "Unmet Legal Needs" in P Morris et al (eds), *Social Needs and Legal Action*, Martin Robertson, 1973 was an early contribution on this point.

68   See W Felstiner, "Influences of Social Organization on Dispute Processing" (1974) 9 *Law and Society Review* 63.

69   So named by A Hirschman, *Exit, Voice, and Loyalty: Responses to Declines in Firms, Organisations and States*, Harvard UP, 1970; and Felstiner, n 68.

70   Felstiner, n 68.

71   S Macaulay, "Non-Contractual Relations in Business: a Preliminary Study", originally published in (1963) 28 *American Sociological Review* 55. An abridged version appears in V Aubert (ed), *Sociology of Law*, Penguin, 1977, 194. Further references are to the version in Aubert. See also S Macaulay, "An Empirical View of Contract" (1985) *Wisconsin Law Review* 465.

forms only one part of a continuing series of transactions between the parties (eg, arrangements between a manufacturer and the supplier of raw materials). Macaulay found that contractual disputes were "frequently settled without reference to the contract or potential of actual legal sanctions".[72] As one business person said, "You don't read legalistic contract clauses at each other if you ever want to do business again".[73] Although his study concerned relations between "haves" (in Galanter's terminology) and thus falls outside the usual parameters of the "access to justice" literature, it nevertheless makes a clear point about the dangers of simply assuming that pursuing legal remedies *via* formal processes is the key to achieving "justice".

The Macaulay study shows that even if a decision is made to act upon a grievance there are often methods available other than resort to the legal system. In the 1980s considerable effort was put into creating forums in which disputants could avoid relying on the legal system. This became known as the alternative dispute resolution (or ADR) movement. In its early formulations, the idea behind ADR was to offer disputants an alternative to the adjudicative legal system which would deal with disputes in a manner which was relatively inexpensive, voluntary, controlled by the parties, relatively informal, and facilitated by a skilled third-party acting as an intermediary.

In its broadest sense, ADR encompasses a diverse range of dispute-processing methods and institutions. In the ADR literature it is common for different dispute-processing methods to be arranged along a scale according to a number of criteria, including: whether the process is voluntary; whether a third party is involved; whether that third party imposes a decision on the parties or facilitates an agreement by the parties; the degree of formality in the process; how broadly or narrowly the issue in dispute is defined; whether the resulting decision is binding on the parties; whether the proceedings are private or public; and the overall intrusiveness of the process.[74] Following this approach, we might place court-room adjudication at one end of the scale. In its "pure" form this is characterised by a win-or-lose, binding decision that is imposed on the parties by a neutral third party (the judge), and which concerns a narrowly defined issue (eg, whether one party has breached a duty of care).[75] At the other end of the scale there are methods such as private voluntary negotiation between disputants with no third party being involved. There is no consensus about where ADR is to be placed along this scale. Some commentators define ADR to exclude any process that involves a third party who imposes a decision on disputants. Others take a wider view and translate ADR to mean any alternative to adversary litigation.[76] In part, this lack of consensus is due to the fact that in practice many dispute-processing forums are hybrids, using a variety of methods.[77]

---

72   Macaulay, "Non-Contractual Relations in Business" n 71, 200.

73   Ibid 200.

74   See the longer list in S Golberg, E Green, and F Sander, *Dispute Resolution*, Little, Brown and Co, 1985, 8-9. See also J Effron, "Alternatives to Litigation: Factors in Choosing" (1989) 52 *Modern Law Review* 480 at 482.

75   The nature of court-based litigation is discussed in Chapter 6 below.

76   See the various definitions discussed in H Astor and C Chinkin, *Dispute Resolution in Australia*, Butterworths, 2nd ed, 2002, 77-81. See also M Fulton, *Commercial Alternative Dispute Resolution*, Law Book Co, 1989, 14-15.

77   Astor and Chinkin provide a thorough overview of the different types of ADR: n 76, 82-104.

Whilst there are no agreed definitions, the main method of dispute-processing which is commonly discussed in the ADR literature is mediation. Mediation is a broad term which usually refers generally to non-compulsory processes in which a neutral third-party mediator facilitates the negotiation of a dispute by the parties.[78] Some commentators distinguish mediation from conciliation, but there is no clear agreement on what necessarily distinguishes the two.[79] Depending on the context, the mediator may take a strictly passive role, merely bringing the parties together and facilitating discussion. Alternatively, the mediator may be more active, suggesting (but not imposing) possible solutions to the dispute.[80] In either instance the discussion is not limited to narrow issues of fault or legal liability. Indeed, a major claim of the ADR movement is that it is more flexible than traditional litigation, allowing the parties to "get to the root of the problem".[81] Mediation thus stands towards the opposite end of the scale from the adversary court trial and it has been the focal point of the ADR movement in Australia.

Prominent among the early ADR institutions were the Community Justice Centres in New South Wales, which were the first State-backed forums to provide for the mediation of "neighbourhood" disputes by trained mediators.[82] In 1986, the Australian Commercial Disputes Centre (ACDC) was established by the NSW Government as a forum for commercial disputes. Again, the intention was to remove some of the costly and time-consuming disputes from the courts.[83] To this picture we can add the work of the various government ombudsmen in dealing with disputes between citizens and government. More recently a number of independent ombudsmen offices have been created in certain industries and sectors to facilitate the handling of consumer complaints, for example the Banking and Financial Services Ombudsman, the Telecommunications Industry Ombudsman, the Credit Ombudsman Service, and the Energy and Water Ombudsman (in NSW and Victoria).

The ADR movement not only covers a variety of methods and institutions, it is also supported by a disparate range of justifications which can be categorised as either negative or positive.[84]

The negative justifications call attention to both the inability of legal rules and the inefficiency of the court system in dealing with disputes between parties in continuing relations, such as neighbours:

> ADR proponents espouse a larger and less traditional view of lawyering skills, criticize the physical and financial barriers to justice, and focus attention upon the drawbacks of the judicial process, the seemingly needless complication of issues,

---

78 As we note later, mediation is increasingly becoming compulsory in some settings, raising issues of whether a person can be forced to mediate a dispute.

79 Fulton, n 76, 75. In this discussion we subsume both processes under the label "mediation".

80 Mediators usually undertake some form of training for their job.

81 See R Danzig and M Lowy, "Everyday Disputes and Mediation in the United States: A Reply to Professor Felstiner" (1975) 9 *Law and Society Review* 675 at 691.

82 See the *Community Justice Centres Act 1983* (NSW).

83 For more detail on these ADR forums, see W Faulkes, "The Modern Development of Alternative Dispute Resolution in Australia" (1990) 1 *Australian Dispute Resolution Journal* 61.

84 R Matthews, "Reassessing Informal Justice" in Matthews (ed) *Informal Justice?*, Sage Publications, 1988, 2.

the unidimensional character of adversarial representation, the excessive cost and interminable delays.[85]

ADR has been advocated as one response to these shortcomings. Amongst the many virtues claimed for mediation are the speed and lower cost involved in dealing with disputes.

The positive justifications for ADR forums have sought to highlight the value of informalism. The premise is that formal systems of legality are not necessary to achieve justice. The absence of the trappings and ritual of the court room, and of procedural rules, is said to give greater access to justice by opening up forums for people who would not otherwise use or benefit from the courts.

> Formal legal procedures have been eschewed in the family courts, consumer and small claims tribunals, juvenile courts and "equal opportunities" tribunals. In particular contexts, formality has been deemed to be unnecessarily expensive, slow and intimidating, as well as inefficient and counter-productive.[86]

It is also claimed that mediation permits a broader consideration of different types of problems from those catered for by the formal legal system.

The source of these different arguments in favour of ADR is varied. Often these arguments rest on a pluralistic view of society,[87] that is, they regard power as being spread more or less evenly throughout society which is seen as being made up of a multiplicity of competing individuals and groups. ADR forums are promoted as a non-coercive means of managing this competition. However, ADR has also been advocated by people who reject the pluralist view, who see much deeper divisions and inequalities in society. Some feminist legal scholars, for example, have argued that:

> [C]onciliation represents a step towards a caring, communal and co-operative form of dispute resolution reminiscent of a past age, hailed as a welcome move in light of the anomie and alienation generated by the combative litigation of capitalist society ... Thus, a growing communitarian consciousness has heightened the idea that there might be an homology between women and conciliation, on the one hand, and between men and the aggressive, competitive, Anglo-Saxon style of adjudication, on the other.[88]

It is also interesting to consider that in some ways the ideals espoused by the ADR movement echo concerns raised by modern economic theories of law, which we examine in Part C of this book. ADR envisions a world of more-or-less self-sufficient individuals who, in seeking to maximise the satisfaction of their own needs, meet together to negotiate their own voluntary, mutually beneficial agreements. Since in practice this cannot always be done, ADR promotes itself as a

---

85 T Carbonneau, *Alternative Dispute Resolution: Melting the Lances and Dismounting the Steeds*, University of Illinois Press, 1989, 4.

86 B Dunne, "Community Justice Centres: A Critical Appraisal" (1985) 10 *Legal Services Bulletin* 188. See also P O'Malley, "Technocratic Justice in Australia" (1984) 2 *Law in Context* 31 at 35.

87 Matthews, n 84, 3.

88 M Thornton, "The Public/Private Dichotomy: Gendered and Discriminatory", paper delivered to the Australasian Law Teachers' Association Conference, ANU, 1990, 17. See also Thornton, "Equivocations of Conciliation: The Resolution of Discrimination Complaints in Australia" (1989) 52 *Modern Law Review* 733. Not all feminist legal writers agree: see, for example, A Bottomley, "Resolving Family Disputes. A Critical View" in MDA Freeman (ed), *State, Law and the Family: Critical Perspectives*, Tavistock, 1984, 293.

relatively cost-free forum for such bargaining. In the language of economists, ADR seeks to reduce the transaction costs involved in that bargaining process. The assumption is that "a settlement derived from a consensus based alternative process is likely to be more efficient than a coerced decision by an adjudicator or an arbitrator".[89]

Critics of ADR[90] have challenged most of the assumptions underlying claims about its virtues.[91] In particular they have warned about over-reacting against formalised dispute resolution forums such as the courts. Critics argue that formality is often necessary to protect individuals from procedural abuse:[92]

> Formal justice can offer three crucial things. Firstly, it gives substantive rights, although these are frail and can be as easily taken away as given. Secondly, it offers procedural safeguards. Rules in relation to the collection and evaluation of evidence, for instance, and rights to appeal against decisions do go some way towards a notional equality in presenting cases before the law. Thirdly, a formal justice involves lawyers who can again mitigate the power imbalance between the parties. Whether in bargaining or the presentation of cases in court, particularly in an adversarial court, what is being confirmed is that there are different interests. Informality, conciliation and an inquisitorial mode of justice, even with remnants of the adversarial mode, offer less protection for weaker or more vulnerable parties and particularly for those who do not conform to prevailing social values.[93]

In other words, although informality in procedures may make mediation seem more "user friendly" it can also disguise or fail to account for power inequalities between the disputants (eg, husband and wife).

This leads to a further criticism – that informal justice may simply *reinforce* prevailing relations of power and authority by defusing conflict and thus the possibility of social change.[94] Typically, ADR proceedings are conducted in private. This, combined with the absence of formal procedures and legal rules, challenges concepts which are basic to the rule of law, such as the idea that the law and its processes should be visible. Thus, in relation to cases of violence and abuse against women and children, Jocelynne Scutt argues that the public nature of court procedures has its advantages:

> Having these cases heard publicly means that those of us who do take such matters seriously are alerted to their incidence; to the way in which courts deal

---

89   Fulton, n 76, 86.

90   See the two-volume collection by R Abel (ed), *The Politics of Informal Justice*, Academic Press, 1982, and the collection edited by Matthews, n 84.

91   See R Tomasic, "Mediation as an Alternative to Adjudication: Rhetoric and Reality in the Neighborhood Justice Movement" in R Tomasic and M Feeley (eds), *Neighborhood Justice: Assessment of an Emerging Idea*, Longman, 1982, 215 for a critique of 18 different assumptions associated with the ADR movement.

92   A point made in R Abel, "Conservative Conflict and the Reproduction of Capitalism: The Role of Informal Justice" (1981) 9 *International Journal of the Sociology of Law* 245. EP Thompson makes a similar claim about the value of the rule of law; see Chapter 2 above.

93   A Bottomley, "What is Happening to Family Law? A Feminist Critique of Conciliation" in J Brophy and C Smart (eds), *Women in Law: Explorations in Law, Family and Sexuality*, Routledge and Kegan Paul, 1985, 162 at 184. See also R Delgado et al, "Fairness and Formality: Minimising the Risk of Prejudice in Alternative Dispute Resolution" [1985] *Wisconsin Law Review* 1395 at 1389.

94   See R Abel, "The Contradictions of Informal Justice" in Abel, n 90, 267.

(or fail to deal) with them; to the lamentable way in which women are treated by the "justice" system. And the failure of formal, public justice to deal appropriately with these cases is not answered by providing even less satisfactory, private systems.[95]

Abel makes similar observations about the tactical use of small claims tribunals by merchants to the overall disadvantage of consumers.[96] In other words, whilst we need to be aware of the limitations in seeking justice through formalised processes, we should not simply assume that informalism necessarily guarantees better results.

Another aspect of ADR considered here is the claim that ADR helps the speedy resolution of disputes in society by reducing court congestion.[97] This is because ADR supposedly channels minor disputes away from the court system. Four criticisms have been made about this claim. The first is an empirical point. Evidence in Australia and overseas indicates that the availability of ADR has had little impact on court case-loads at any level of the court system.[98] The second criticism is that, in concentrating on so-called "minor" disputes, ADR thereby helps to preserve an image that these matters are somehow less significant and less in need of formal attention than the more "serious" matters left to the courts. In short, the concern is that ADR represents a form of "second-class justice" for those parties.[99] The third criticism highlights another aspect of the second-class justice argument. As we have seen, ADR favours dispute settlement over dispute litigation. There is an economic argument that a settlement necessarily means that the plaintiff will receive less than what their case is worth.[100] ADR thereby institutionalises this disparity. It may be sensible for a litigant to agree to settle, but that is because of the costs, delays and uncertainty of the litigation, not because of the intrinsic merits of ADR. Fourthly, there is a legitimate question about the extent to which ADR is an *alternative* to the legal system. Various types of conciliation or mediation processes are now formally part of the dispute resolution processes in many courts and statutory systems, such as those governing family law, anti-discrimination, consumer, land and environment cases, and retail tenancies.[101] Many courts, including the Federal Court, and the Supreme, District and Local Courts in NSW, have the power to make orders with the consent of the parties to refer a case to a mediator.[102] It appears that in the Federal Court over 90

95 J Scutt, "Privatisation of Justice: Power Differentials, Inequality and the Palliative of Counselling and Mediation" in J Mugford (ed), *Alternative Dispute Resolution*, Australian Institute of Criminology, 1986, 195; and see Delgado et al, n 81, 1398; and O Fiss, "Against Settlement" (1984) 93 *Yale Law Journal* 1073.
96 Abel, n 90, 295.
97 See F Sander, "Varieties of Dispute Processing" in Tomasic and Feeley, n 91, 26, for one version of this claim.
98 ALRC, n 15, para 6.59; Tomasic, n 91, 239-240.
99 This is reminiscent of the argument that the lower court system trivialises cases: see D McBarnet, *Conviction: Law, the State and the Construction of Justice*, Macmillan, 1981, discussed in Chapter 6 below.
100 R Posner "An Economic Approach to Legal Procedure and Judicial Administration" (1973) 2 *Journal of Legal Studies* 399 at 442.
101 See, for example, *Family Law Act 1975* (Cth); *Anti-Discrimination Act 1977* (NSW) s 92; *Consumer, Trader and Tenancy Tribunal Act 2001* (NSW) Part 5; *Land and Environment Court Act 1979* (NSW) s 34; *Retail Leases Act 2003* (Vic) ss 85-88.
102 See *Courts Legislation (Mediation and Evaluation) Amendment Act 1994* (NSW).

per cent of these cases involve consumer protection matters.[103] Under these various systems of "mandated" conciliation or mediation, parties may be under considerable pressure to use ADR-type processes. Ingleby observes that:

> Mandation [sic] in relation to mediation may take a number of forms. The clearest is a requirement that parties attend mediation before they are entitled to a court hearing. Less directly, it may be the financial compulsion constituted by the withholding of legal aid if mediation is not attempted; or the inability to afford any other form of dispute resolution.[104]

This underlines the point that there is no clean distinction to be drawn between ADR and the court system, nor between non-legal and legal responses to the problems of access. In their review of ADR, Astor and Chinkin note that the acronym ADR could now stand for Additional Dispute Resolution:

> [T]he current trend towards mainstreaming ADR by bringing it within the court system or incorporating it within government decision-making makes it seem that "additional" is becoming an appropriate label.[105]

The debate about ADR has been conducted in terms of a series of dichotomies such as formalism versus informalism, coercion versus volition and idealised notions of mediation versus adjudication. The term "alternative" quite likely has encouraged this. Despite this terminology, arguments about ADR are a useful reminder of the limitations in simple preconceptions about what constitutes "the law" or "the legal system". No matter what set of arguments we eventually agree with, the value of the debate is that it moves us away from a purely court-centred, professionally defined view of justice.[106]

(ii)   Legal responses

By "legal responses" we mean responses to issues of unequal access that rely on practices and reforms within the legal system. Again, while this is a convenient way to divide up the discussion, we stress that there is no neat division between "non-legal" and "legal" responses, as the discussion about ADR has shown.

Galanter summarises four possibilities in the following extract.

Marc Galanter, "Delivering Legality: Some Proposals for the Direction of Research"

(1976) (footnotes omitted)

> I would like to address myself to some of the alternative strategies for performing the functions which, it has sometimes been assumed, could only be performed by legal services. For purposes of this analysis, I shall make some gross simplifying assumptions about the legal system (including the assumption that such a "system" can be meaningfully isolated from its social context). Let us think of that system as comprised of four elements or levels
> - a body of authoritative normative learning – for short, RULES

---

103   Access to Justice Advisory Committee, n 12, 280-281.

104   R Ingleby, "Court Sponsored Mediation: The Case Against Mandatory Participation" (1993) 56 *Modern Law Review* 441 at 443.

105   Astor and Chinkin, n 76, 70.

106   See, for example, S Henry, *Private Justice*, Routledge & Kegan Paul, 1983.

- a set of institutional facilities (courts, administrative agencies, etc) within which the normative learning is applied to specific cases – for short, INSTITUTIONS
- a body of persons with specialized skill in dealing with the above – for short, LEGAL SERVICES
- persons or groups with claims they might make to the courts with reference to the rules – for short, PARTIES.

Consider some of the ways in which each of these components might be transformed so as to enhance the access of individuals to the benefit of legality. (Of course, increasing the access of some may reduce the legality benefits of others, but we shall ignore this for the moment.)

(1) One may in various ways change legal services. One may seek changes in the recruitment, training, or ideology of the professionals rendering such services; one may seek changes in the organization of the delivery of those services; and one may seek changes in the character of the services being offered. [...] I want to talk not about legal services per se but about the way in which the other elements interact with legal services to amplify or diminish access possibilities.

(2) Another way to improve access is to change the rules. Changes at the level of rules can provide greater (or reduced) access. For example, a shift from individuated "fault" rules to "no-fault" or "strict liability" can provide access by diminishing the complexity and technicality of a claim, eliminating the need for difficult showings of fact, employment of experts, use of professional advocates, etc. Again, access to facilitative rules might be provided by the development of preformed standardized packages ("canned transactions"), which can be used with little or no professional advice. Most dramatically, rules can be changed to reduce the need for professional services by abandoning regulation of an area of activity. These are examples of rule-changes that deliver legality by reducing the need for legal services. Most rule-change, it hardly needs to be said, is not of this kind. Typically, rule-change involves an increase in the complexity of the law and its remoteness from popular understanding and thus entails greater dependence on professionals to deliver its benefits.

Legal professionals have tended to overestimate the benefits that could be delivered through obtaining rule-changes from eminent institutions, especially from courts. A vast literature has documented the constantly rediscovered and never-quite-believed truths that judicial (or legislative) pronouncements do not change the world; that the benefits of such changes do not penetrate automatically and costlessly to their intended beneficiaries; that often they do not benefit the latter at all. We have some notion of why rule-changes produced by courts are particularly unlikely to be important sources of redistributive change (Friedman, 1967; Hazard, 1970; Galanter, 1974). Like everything else, favorable rules are resources and those who enjoy disproportionate shares of other resources tend also to reap the benefit of rules. The basic question is how to supply the resources that enable parties to secure the benefit of favorable rules.

(3) There is a great variety of proposals for providing greater access through changes at the level of institutions. These might be sorted out in a number of ways. Let me suggest some of the major categories in terms of the departures they make from the model of our ordinary courts.

A. One classic response is to provide "small claims" courts – that is, courts with lower costs and simpler procedures, overcoming barriers of cost, locational accessibility, intimidation, and incomprehensibility.

B. One might instead attempt to provide institutions that are mediative and conciliatory, rather than judgmental, imposing a win/lose outcome.

C. One might attempt to change the character of courts by creating tribunals that are more "popular", responsive and participatory, less professional and alien, thereby reducing the cultural and psychological distance between tribunal and parties.

D. One might instead encourage the development of tribunals in the private sector – such as the consumer forums operated by the dry cleaners, the carpet industry, and the home appliance manufacturers, or by the Better Business Bureaus. More of these may be spawned by the new FTC rules under the Magnuson-Moss Warranty-Federal Trade Commission Improvement Act of 1975.

E. Related to these are various devices that are not tribunals but champions – something halfway between a dispute processing institution and an institution that provides representation. The ombudsman (Anderson, 1969; Rowat, 1973) and the media ombudsman (Action Line, etc) are the prime examples.

F. Coming full circle, one may think of supplying institutions that are more "active" – ie, that depart from the passive umpire role of courts to take investigatory initiative to secure, assemble, and present proof, and to monitor performance, etc. Such proactive institutions would reduce the advantages conferred by the differential competence of parties or their representatives. Advocacy of an unrepresented interest may be built into the tribunal itself, as it was, for example, in early workman's compensation boards. The possibilities here commend themselves to observers like Whitford and Kimball (1975), who suggest that effective processing of numerous complaints involving small amounts may require abandonment of adversary processes and substitution of inquisitorial adjudication.

(4) Finally, one may think of changes at the level of the parties. I submit that the fundamental problems of access to legality are to be found at this level and can best be visualized as problems of the capability of parties. That is, lack of capability poses the most fundamental barrier to access and correspondingly, upgrading of party capacity holds the greatest promise for promoting access to legality. Party capability includes a range of personal capacities which can be summed up in the term "competence": ability to perceive grievance, information about availability of remedies, psychic readiness to utilize them, ability to manage claims competently, seek and utilize appropriate help, etc.[107]

Under Galanter's first category (changing the way in which lawyers perform legal services) we can include pro bono legal work. The term "pro bono" is taken from the Latin "pro bono publico", meaning "for the public good". Pro bono legal work therefore means the provision of legal advice or representation for no fee, or for a substantially reduced fee, to assist the poor, the disadvantaged or persons who

---

107 (1976) 11 *Law and Society Review* 225 at 227-231. The works referred to in Galanter's text are: S Anderson, *Ombudsman Papers: American Experience and Proposals*, U of California Press, 1969; L Friedman, "Legal Rules and the Process of Social Change" (1967) 19 *Stanford Law Review* 786; M Galanter, "Why the 'Haves' Come Out Ahead: Speculations on the Limits of Social Change" (1974) 9 *Law and Society Review* 95; G Hazard, "Law Reforming in the Anti-Poverty Effort" (1970) 37 *University of Chicago Law Review* 242; D Rowat, *The Ombudsman Plan*, McCleland and Stewart, 1973; W Whitford and S Kimball, "Why Process Consumer Complaints? A Case Study of the Office of the Commissioner of Insurance of Wisconsin" [1975] *Wisconsin Law Review* 639.

otherwise deserve public support.[108] This can include the continued provision of legal services by a lawyer after a client has run out of money to pay for those services, and voluntary work in community legal centres. Pro bono work may be organised within a law firm or legal practice, by professional law associations (eg, local Law Societies), or by specialised organisations such as the Public Interest Advocacy Centre or the National Pro Bono Resource Centre. While pro bono work is encouraged by Law Societies and other professional associations, it is not mandatory. Nevertheless the evidence suggests that the practice is well supported in the legal profession: 63 per cent of private solicitors practices reported that they had undertaken pro bono work in 2001-02, involving nearly 1.7 million hours of work; 78 per cent of barristers reported having done pro bono work, involving 614,100 hours of work.[109] These figures should be read subject to two qualifications. First, because there is no generally accepted definition of what counts as pro bono work, it is not possible to be precise about the actual extent of pro bono activity and, secondly, the figures say nothing about the areas of law in which pro bono work is being done. There is evidence that there may be "a mismatch of available legal skills and unmet community need in pro bono service provision".[110]

Relevant to Galanter's second set of reforms (changing the rules) is the *form* in which legal rules are expressed and utilised. In its paper on *The Cost of Litigation*, the now defunct Law Reform Commission of Victoria identified three factors which it saw as contributing unnecessarily to high costs in the legal system. The Commission pointed to the obscure and inaccessible style, and the complexity, of much legislation:

> There can be no doubt that the style in which much legislation has been drafted adds substantially to the cost of giving legal advice and litigating. Much of the legislation in force in Victoria [and, we would add, elsewhere in Australia] is written in an unnecessarily obscure style which appears to value prolixity above communication. Even the most expert lawyers find it extremely difficult to understand. Other factors include the volume of legislation, its proliferation over recent years, and inaccessible and voluminous subordinate legislation.[111]

---

108 This definition is adapted from Stephen Parker, "Why Lawyers Should Do Pro Bono Work" in C Arup and K Laster (eds), *For the Public Good: Pro Bono and the Legal Profession in Australia*, Federation Press, 2001, 5.

109 Australian Bureau of Statistics, *Legal Practices*, (2003) Cat No 8667.0.

110 *Legal Aid and Access to Justice*, n 17, para 9.42.

111 Law Reform Commission of Victoria, *Access to the Law: The Cost of Litigation*, Issues Paper, May 1990, 30. The following figures give some indication of the volume of Commonwealth legislation:

Years	Commonwealth Acts passed
1960-1969	1182
1970-1979	1684
1980-1989	1731
1990-1999	1742
2000-2004	800

(figures updated from a table in R Tomasic (ed), *Legislation and Society in Australia*, Allen and Unwin, 1979, 11.)

The Commission went on to make similar comments about the even greater inaccessibility and inconsistency of the common law.[112] Finally, it also referred to the cumbersome nature of many established court procedures, such as the reliance on oral argument and examination of witnesses, and the formally neutral role of the judge.[113] These and other aspects of procedural legality are perceived as impediments to the cost efficient operation of the legal system.

Galanter's third category, reforming legal institutions such as courts and tribunals, raises issues that we have discussed already when looking at the role of ADR.

Finally, in considering Galanter's fourth set of reforms (changes to the capacity and capability of parties) it is relevant to consider two issues: the rules that determine a person's right to begin legal proceedings in the first place (their "standing to sue"), and the position of the party who has no legal representation.

With regard to a person's standing to sue, the Australian Law Reform Commission has argued that:

> [T]he laws concerning standing ... should ensure that access to the courts is available for a sufficient range of plaintiffs and other participants to ensure that the public interest is properly protected in the courts.

The Commission goes on to state that:

> [T]hese rules are an essential element in
> - ensuring that a party with a legitimate cause of action has access to the courts to pursue that action in accordance with the proper administration of justice
> - ensuring that the validity of government decisions and legislation can be tested and that other "public rights" can be protected
> - enhancing the amount and nature of the information courts possess when making a decision that has implications beyond the parties to the proceedings.[114]

Representative actions are one way in which standing rules can improve access to the courts. Representative actions are appropriate where a number of individuals each have small claims against the same defendant but each claim is not economically viable on its own. All Australian jurisdictions provide for representative actions. These allow a person to commence a court action as a representative of a large number of people where all persons have the same interest in the proceedings. For many years, the courts interpreted the idea of "same interest" in a narrow way, thereby restricting the availability of these actions. In 1995, the High Court held that a broad approach should be taken in deciding what constitutes having "the same interest", saying that it means having a significant common interest in a question of law or fact to be decided in the case.[115] This approach is similar to the representative action which is available in the Federal Court in cases

---

112 Law Reform Commission of Victoria, n 111, 31-33. Scholars within the Critical Legal Studies movement have argued that internal inconsistency and incoherence is the very nature of our liberal legal system: see P Drahos and S Parker, "Critical Contract Law in Australia" (1990) 3 *Journal of Contract Law* 30.

113 Law Reform Commission of Victoria, n 111, 33-38. We examine adversarial practices in more detail in Chapters 6 and 7 below.

114 ALRC, *Beyond the Door-Keeper: Standing to Sue for Public Remedies*, Report No 78, 1996, 23-24.

115 *Carnie v Esanda Finance Corporation Ltd* (1995) 127 ALR 76.

where seven or more people have a substantial common issue of law or fact arising from the same, similar or related transactions.[116]

The availability of legal representation is another factor that shapes the capability of a person to use the court system. Although there is no comprehensive data, the available evidence suggests that a growing number of litigants are appearing in court and conducting their cases without legal representation. For example, 38 per cent of matters in the Federal Court of Australia during 2002-03 "involved at least one party who was unrepresented at some stage of the proceedings".[117] On one estimate, nearly half of litigants in the Family Court are unrepresented at some stage of proceedings.[118] In 2003-04, the High Court reported that 48 per cent of the applications for leave or special leave to appeal and 46 per cent of the matters heard by a single Justice involved self-represented litigants.[119] Obviously, there can be consequences for a person who represents themselves in court. One study reports that in the Federal Court a self-represented litigant is less likely to be successful, more likely to discontinue the case and more likely to be ordered to pay costs.[120] There are also consequences for the other party and the court. Self-represented litigants require more of the court's time (and the time of registry staff) in explaining procedures and providing assistance, slowing the progress of a case and adding to its costs. As Kirby J noted in *Cameron v The Queen*, "where an applicant is not legally represented, a heavy burden is cast on the Justices of this Court to scrutinise often voluminous and ill-expressed materials against the risk that an error of law or miscarriage of justice has occurred".[121]

There are many reasons why a person may choose to represent themselves in court. The Australian Law Reform Commission notes that:

> Many cannot afford representation, do not qualify for legal aid or do not know they are eligible for legal aid, and are litigants in matters which do not admit contingency or speculative fee arrangements. They may believe that they are capable of running the case without a lawyer, may distrust lawyers, or decide to continue unrepresented despite legal advice that they cannot win.[122]

Of these reasons, the restricted availability of legal aid is regarded as a major cause of the rise in self-represented litigants.[123]

---

116 *Federal Court of Australia Act 1976* (Cth) Pt IVA.

117 *Legal Aid and Access to Justice*, n 17, para 10.8.

118 Ibid.

119 High Court of Australia, *Annual Report 2003-04*, 2004, 7.

120 H Gamble and R Mohr, *Litigants in person in the Federal Court of Australia and the Administrative Appeals Tribunal – A Research Note*, 1998, cited in Law Council of Australia, *Erosion of Legal Representation in the Australian Justice System*, February 2004, 15.

121 (2002) 187 ALR 65 at 90.

122 ALRC, n 15, para 5.147.

123 J Dewar, J Giddings, S Parker, *The Impact of Changes in Legal Aid on Criminal and Family Law Practice in Queensland*, Griffith University, Faculty of Law, 1998; J Dewar, B Smith, C Banks, *Litigants in Person in the Family Court of Australia*, Research Report No 20, Family Court of Australia, 2000.

(iii)   Legal aid

Legal aid has been the most commonly used method of providing access to the law for those with "unmet legal needs".[124] Under this heading we describe, in general terms, the different methods by which legal aid can be made available. Then, we look at the limitations on, and criticisms of, legal aid as a response to the problem of unequal access.

There is little precision in usage of the term "legal aid". Some legal aid services simply provide financial assistance to enable people to litigate specific matters; others give legal advice and assistance which may not necessarily lead to litigation; still others may add law reform, lobbying and community legal education to their functions.

Over time in different countries three major methods of providing legal aid have evolved. To use the accepted labels, they are the judicare, the public salaried lawyer, and the combined models.[125] These are general labels, and the precise structure of legal aid services varies in different places. Each has its own advantages and disadvantages, both for the intended beneficiaries and for those who provide and fund the service.

Under the judicare approach, legal aid services are provided by the private legal profession while the state pays the bill. Provided that a legal aid client falls within the state-determined eligibility criteria, they then consult a private practitioner as any other client would. Judicare schemes thus depend upon the potential legal aid client's ability to perceive that her problem might be a legal one, and her capacity and preparedness to seek out a lawyer in the first place. As we have seen, there can be considerable hurdles in contacting a lawyer.

The public salaried lawyer model involves the government directly employing the lawyers who perform the legal aid work. Such schemes often espouse broader aims than the judicare model. Along with the provision of basic legal services these include community legal education, law reform on poverty-related issues, as well as providing legal services via non-lawyers (eg paralegals).

The combined model, as its name implies, has elements of both of the previous approaches. This is the model found in Australia. In the States and Territories, the bulk of legal aid work is organised by Legal Aid Commissions.[126] Legal aid is funded jointly by the Commonwealth and State governments, with some funding also derived from interest earned on solicitors' trust accounts. The Commonwealth provides funds only for legal aid matters that involve federal law; the States and Territories fund matters involving State or Territory law. According to the report of a Senate inquiry into legal aid, the level of Commonwealth funding has declined in real terms between 1996-97 and 2003-04.[127] As we note later on, there are different eligibility criteria for Commonwealth and State or Territory matters. There are differences between States and Territories in the range and level of legal aid services that are provided.

---

124   See Cappelletti and Garth, n 10; and B Garth, *Neighbourhood Law Firms*, Sijthoff and Noordhoff, 1980.

125   See Cappelletti and Garth, n 10, 24-33.

126   In addition to the legal aid schemes mentioned in the text, it should be noted that Law Societies may also provide legal advice and referral services. For a review of the history of legal aid in Australia, see J Basten, R Graycar and D Neal, "Legal Centres in Australia" (1983) 6 *University of New South Wales Law Journal* 163.

127   *Legal Aid and Access to Justice*, n 17, para 2.9.

Under the combined model the Legal Aid Commissions provide legal aid both by "in-house" salaried lawyers and by referral to private practitioners. The Commissions also employ public solicitors (or roster private practitioners as "duty solicitors") to attend local courts and appear for people who are eligible for legal aid. Governments do not pay the same amount to the private practitioner as would a private client. This means that the discounted rate of payment for legal aid work can act as a deterrent for some practitioners to take on legal aid work. In its "Managing Justice" report, the Australian Law Reform Commission noted that there has been a "noticeable exit from legal aid work by private practitioners".[128]

In addition to legal aid schemes staffed by salaried lawyers there are approximately 190 community and specialist legal centres (or CLCs) throughout Australia.[129] They offer either referrals or general legal advice to defined geographic populations, or specialist legal services for particular groups (for example, psychiatric patients, social security recipients and tenants). CLCs are independent of the Legal Aid Commissions, although they rely on the Commissions as one source of funds. They employ a mix of lawyers, social workers and paralegals. The CLCs have deliberately sought to adopt a broad view of what constitutes legal aid. This is summed up in the claim that:

> [T]o limit legal aid to the provision of individual casework in the form of traditional legal representation is to fail to address the broader economic, social and political inequalities which create and perpetuate many of our society's injustices and hardships.[130]

Finally, the particular problems and concerns of Aboriginal and Torres Strait Islanders when they confront white social and legal culture have led to the establishment of indigenous legal services in all States and the Northern Territory, providing legal aid and other support services.[131] These services employ both lawyers and "paralegal" field officers, the latter acting as a link with local Aboriginal communities. Most of the advice and representation work is done by the services themselves, although some work is referred to private practitioners. These legal services exist independently from the State and Territory Legal Aid Commissions, drawing their funding from federal sources. We look more closely at the problems that white Australian law poses for Aboriginal and Torres Strait Islanders in Chapter 9.

Legal aid is perhaps the most prominent response to the issue of unequal access to the law. Whilst the work of those involved in delivering legal aid services is both necessary and often undervalued, it is also appropriate to devote some time to a general assessment and critique of legal aid. We do this by considering three broad claims that have been made about legal aid.[132]

---

128 ALRC, n 15, para 5.113.

129 Information about CLCs can be found at <http://www.austlii.edu.au/au/other/clc/>.

130 P Kellow, "NLAAC Review of Legal Aid – The Community Legal Centres' Response" (1989) 14 *Legal Services Bulletin* 180.

131 These include the Aboriginal and Torres Strait Islander Legal Services, the Aboriginal and Torres Strait Islander Women's Legal Services, and the Family Violence Prevention Legal Services.

132 These broad claims are found throughout the legal aid literature and consequently no attempt is made to attribute each of them to a particular source.

The first claim proposes a fairly narrow vision for legal aid. Legal aid, it is said, is necessary to ensure equality of access to the legal system.[133] Often, this claim simply amounts to a "day in court" philosophy in which legal aid means little more than the provision of financial assistance to allow people to conduct litigation. The equality referred to here lies somewhere between the poles of formal and substantive equality identified in Chapter 2. It can be thought of as an "equality of starting point",[134] that is, the concern is to ensure that all individuals have the opportunity to pursue or defend claims in court. In this way, it is argued, legal aid helps to guarantee procedural equality, to foster a view of the court proceeding as "a contest between equals [where] the outcome of such a contest *is* justice".[135]

It is interesting to consider this argument in the light of judicial decisions about the importance of legal representation and the availability of legal aid. The principal authority in Australia is the High Court's decision in *Dietrich v R*.[136] Dietrich was convicted of importing heroin into Australia after a trial at which he had no legal representation. Before the trial he had made an unsuccessful application for legal aid. The Legal Aid Commission would only provide representation for a plea of guilty, something which Dietrich did not want to do. He also made applications for legal assistance through other channels – all were unsuccessful. He sought leave to appeal against his conviction, one of his grounds being that a person without means who is charged with an indictable offence is entitled to legal representation at the expense of the state. A further ground was that the failure of the trial judge to appoint a lawyer was a miscarriage of justice and that the conviction should therefore be quashed. The Court of Criminal Appeal in Victoria refused leave to appeal and Dietrich then sought special leave to appeal to the High Court. By a majority, special leave was granted, the appeal was allowed and a new trial was ordered.

All of the judges agreed that there is no right of an accused person to be provided with legal representation at public expense.[137] The court listed a number of reasons against such a right. For example, it would entail the courts in deciding what constituted *effective* legal representation; the allocation of public funds must be decided by the government, not the courts; and it would carry the implication that an absence of representation necessarily meant an unfair trial.

But although there is no right to publicly funded legal representation, the High Court did affirm that an accused person has a right to a fair trial and that, depending on the circumstances, lack of representation might mean the absence of a fair trial. The court noted that a person charged with a serious offence who, through no fault on his or her part, is unable to obtain legal representation, can request an adjournment or stay of proceedings. According to the joint judgment of Mason CJ and McHugh J:

---

133 R Abel, "Socializing the Legal Profession: Can Redistributing Lawyers Services Achieve Social Justice?" [1979] *Law and Policy Quarterly* 5 at 6.

134 See B Gaze and M Jones, *Law, Liberty and Australian Democracy*, Law Book Co, 1990, 400, discussing equality of opportunity.

135 Abel, n 133, 7 (emphasis in original). Abel describes this as a concern to achieve "formal equality".

136 (1992) 109 ALR 385.

137 Ibid 386 (Mason CJ and McHugh J), 401 (Brennan J), 411 (Deane J), 421 (Dawson J) and 438 (Gaudron J).

> In that situation, in the absence of exceptional circumstances, the trial in such a case should be adjourned, postponed or stayed until legal representation is available.[138]

Deane J agreed, putting the general proposition that:

> [I]n the absence of exceptional circumstances, a trial of an indigent person accused of serious crime will be unfair if, by reason of lack of means and the unavailability of other assistance, he is denied legal representation.[139]

The 1994 Access to Justice Action Plan commented that the *Dietrich* decision "effectively puts an obligation on governments to fund the defence in certain serious cases".[140] While this result may be applauded, it is important to note the limitations of *Dietrich*.

One practical limitation is that the decision may have entrenched the priority which criminal matters have in legal aid budgets, to the detriment of other areas of law. In a later decision, the High Court affirmed that its decision in *Dietrich* should not be extended to civil proceedings, committal hearings or non-serious criminal cases, and that it applies only to courts (referring to the exercise of their inherent jurisdiction to adjourn cases) and not to tribunals (which must find this power in their enabling statute).[141] This leads to a second limitation. Note that the High Court's decision focuses on the question of legal representation for an accused charged with a "serious" crime. The decision raises the question whether the fair trial principle is dependent on the gravity of the offence.

The role of legal aid in ensuring some level of substantive equality between parties can also be questioned by looking at who actually receives legal aid.

Eligibility for legal aid varies between different States and Territories. Generalising, in non-criminal matters eligibility usually depends upon the application of a means test (on the assessable income and assets of the applicant; a successful applicant may be asked to pay a contribution to the Legal Aid Commission); a merits test (to determine whether the case has a reasonable chance of success);[142] and on whether the application falls within the guidelines set by each Legal Aid Commission to determine which matters have priority for legal aid funding. Because the combined model of legal aid is heavily reliant on continued government funding, one important function of these eligibility criteria is to enable the Legal Aid Commissions to ration the availability of scarce legal aid resources.

The diversity in eligibility criteria in different jurisdictions, combined with the lack of comprehensive data, makes it difficult to obtain a complete picture of who the beneficiaries of legal aid in Australia actually are. The available data indicates that:

---

138 Ibid 399.

139 Ibid 417.

140 Note 12, 241. In doing this, the High Court overcame the narrow implications of some of the majority judgments in its earlier decision in *McInnis v The Queen* (1979) 143 CLR 575. But *Dietrich* did not go as far as Murphy J's dissenting judgment in the *McInnis* case, where it was argued that the right to a fair trial "includes the right to counsel in all serious cases" (at 583).

141 *New South Wales v Canellis* (1994) 181 CLR 309 at 328.

142 Different merits tests apply for State/Territory matters than for Commonwealth matters. The Commonwealth test asks, additionally, whether an "ordinarily prudent self-funding litigant" would risk funds on the action, and whether the use of scarce legal aid funds is warranted by the likely benefit to the applicant or, in some instance, the community.

- Grants of legal aid tend to be restricted to the very poor. In 1990 the New South Wales Legal Aid Commission found that:

   > The profile of the typical legal aid applicant thus amounts to one of extreme income impoverishment and indicates that grants of legal aid are being directed to the poorest section of the general community.[143]

   This is still an accurate description. In 1993-94, 54.5 per cent of legal aid applicants had no weekly net disposable income after allowable deductions were made under the various Legal Aid Commission means tests; 16 per cent had a net disposable income of $51-100 per week. In 2003-04, over 90 per cent of applicants for legal aid in Victoria were unemployed and 70 per cent were in receipt of government benefits.[144] The result is a gap between those who meet the means test and are therefore eligible to receive legal aid, and those who are able to afford their own lawyer.

- The majority of legal aid applications concern criminal matters. The Australian Law Reform Commission noted in 1994 that Legal Aid Commissions have "a strong culture which sees criminal work as the major priority".[145] This continues to be the case. For example, in 2003-04 legal aid grants in criminal matters made up 75 per cent of all legal aid grants in NSW and 59 per cent in Victoria. For family law matters the figures were 22 per cent (NSW) and 29 per cent (Victoria), and for civil matters 2 per cent (NSW) and 12 per cent (Victoria).[146]

- Women receive a smaller share of the overall legal aid budget than men. A 1994 study concluded that in Australia "there is an overall bias towards men in legal aid approvals".[147] A 2004 Senate Committee inquiry into "Legal Aid and Access to Justice" heard evidence that "women do not have equal access to legal aid, nor to the legal system in general, and ... there is an indirect gender disparity in the way that legal aid is granted".[148] A key explanation for this is that a large portion of legal aid resources is consumed by criminal law cases, where most defendants (and most of the legal aid applicants) are men.[149] As was noted above, legal aid is not as widely available for the types of problem for which women are more likely to seek assistance (such as family law and civil matters).

It is reasonable to conclude from this evidence that even the narrow claim that legal aid can produce equality of access would not seem to be fulfilled for many in the community.

The second claim that has been made about legal aid is slightly broader than the first. This is the hope that comprehensive legal aid schemes will expose the

---

143 *Who Gets Legal Aid? A Survey of Legal Aid Applicants in New South Wales*, April 1990, Policy and Research Section, NSW Legal Aid Commission, 4.

144 Victoria Legal Aid, *Annual Report 2003-04*, 1.

145 Note 22, 95-96.

146 Figures taken from Annual Reports for 2003-04 of NSW Legal Aid Commission and Victoria Legal Aid.

147 Legal Aid and Family Services, *Gender Bias in Litigation Legal Aid*, Issues Paper, Attorney-General's Department, 1994, 36 and 37.

148 *Legal Aid and Access to Justice*, n 17, para 4.18.

149 ALRC, n 22, 95.

legal system to new types of claims and claimants (such as pressure to introduce class or representative actions against the manufacturers of harmful products[150]), and also to increase the frequency of claims which are otherwise given insufficient voice (for example, actions by tenants or social security recipients). As we have already noted, there is some indication that some legal aid services have developed in this way (for example, the Public Interest Advocacy Centre in New South Wales, and other legal services specialising in work for groups such as women, Aborigines, welfare recipients and the mentally disabled). Nevertheless, it can also be argued that these are exceptions to the mainstream of legal aid services, and that the overall effect of large-scale legal aid schemes has been to reinforce, rather than reform the legal system. This is said to be due to the major role played by the private legal profession in legal aid delivery.

It has been argued that the scope of legal aid in judicare or combined schemes ultimately tends to be restricted to those problems already being serviced by the legal profession. The referral of legal aid to the private profession accounts for the majority of legal aid work in Australia. For example, in 1993-94 approximately 53 per cent of all legal aid cases in Australia were referred to the private profession.[151] The rate of referrals is also a reflection of the type of matters involved and the different specialisations of private and public lawyers. In the same period, 82 per cent of family cases and 61 per cent of civil cases were referred to private practitioners, while 43 per cent of criminal cases were referred.[152]

So, as Cappelletti and Garth comment, "the poor tend to utilize judicare systems mainly for legal problems with which they are already familiar – criminal and divorce matters – rather than to pursue their new rights as consumers, tenants, and the like".[153] An additional criticism is that most legal aid is provided in a manner defined in terms of traditional legal practice; the concentration is on adversarial modes of litigation, with social workers and paralegals often occupying an ancillary role. There seems to be little scope for public legal education or law reform work, despite the fact that this sort of work is a legislative requirement of most of the Legal Aid Commissions.[154]

This tends to support the claim made by Johnson in his sociological study of professions that "the effect of state intervention may be to support for a time at least, existing institutions of professionalism".[155] The conclusion is, then, that the scope and style of large-scale legal aid schemes has been conditioned by the established practices of the private profession.

The third and final claim that we consider about legal aid takes a wider view of substantive equality than either of the previous claims. Here, the legal system is viewed as a forum within which wider ideals such as political democracy and social and economic equality can be achieved. Social reform is thus added to law

---

150 The Dalkon Shield litigation is an example. See P Cashman, "The Dalkon Shield" in P Grabosky and A Sutton (eds), *Stains on a White Collar*, Federation Press, 1989, 92.

151 Legal Aid and Family Services, *Legal Aid in Australia 1993-94 Statistical Yearbook*, June 1995 There are significant variations in referral patterns between the different Legal Aid Commissions.

152 Ibid.

153 Cappelletti and Garth, n 10, 27.

154 See, for example, s 10(2) of the *Legal Aid Act 1977* (ACT), which is similar to provisions in the relevant legislation in most other Australian States.

155 T Johnson, *Professions and Power*, cited in Z Bankowski and G Mungham, *Images of Law*, Routledge and Kegan Paul, 1976, 65.

reform as an aim of legal aid. This type of argument was prominent in the 1970s when the first major publicly funded legal aid schemes were being established in Australia. For example, the *Second Main Report* of the Commission of Inquiry into Poverty argued that:

> [F]or the legal system to realise fully the goal of equality before the law it must become more responsive to the needs of poor people and a positive force for the elimination of poverty,

adding later that:

> Legal aid services are the means by which the goal of equality before the law will be transformed from an ideal into a reality.[156]

Such arguments are based more explicitly on utilitarian and redistributive themes than the claims considered earlier.

Commentators have identified two limitations which stand in the way of achieving this ideal. First, as we have already seen, legal aid has been restricted to the very poor. It is then argued that on the whole the poor have shown themselves to be "unusually reluctant and reactive litigants".[157] For them, resort to law is a last resort, to be used only in relation to a limited range of matters. Secondly, critics have asked "even if the legal system was used more vigorously and frequently, is it capable of effecting substantial redistributions?" Different commentators have suggested different reasons why this cannot happen. Some argue that in a legal system that emphasises values of neutrality and procedural fairness there is caution, even opposition, towards using the legal system (especially the courts) as a mechanism of social change.[158] Other criticisms go further and argue that, since the law is built upon and engenders inequalities in social relations, then it is unlikely to be able to remedy those inequalities.[159] In this way, it is argued, legal aid, like other welfare measures, is significantly constrained by the very structures of which it is a part.

(d) Conclusion

There are many complex and intriguing questions which are subsumed within the idea of access to justice. Although we have not been able to examine them all in detail in this chapter, we have affirmed the value of moving beyond a simple picture of the legal system as a neutral purveyor of rights and remedies. Mauro Cappelletti, one of the doyens of the access to justice movement, has argued that by studying questions of access we create a three-dimensional picture of law. The first dimension directs our attention to "the societal problem, need or demand that prompts a legal intervention or the creation of a legal institution".[160] In the second dimension we examine the legal response or solution (including norms,

---

156 Sackville, *Law and Poverty in Australia*, n 11, 2 and 9. See also Sackville, *Legal Aid in Australia*, n 11, 2-4.

157 R Abel, "Law without Politics: Legal Aid under Advanced Capitalism" (1985) 32 *UCLA Law Review* 474 at 596.

158 See, for example, Abel, n 133, 27.

159 This is a theme explored in Bankowski and Mungham, n 155, Ch 3.

160 M Cappelletti, "Alternative Dispute Resolution Processes within the Framework of the World-Wide Access-to-Justice Movement" (1993) 56 *Modern Law Review* 282 at 283 (emphases deleted).

institutions and processes) which are intended to deal with the problem. The third dimension assesses the results or impact of the legal response. As Cappelletti sees it:

> [T]he result of the access-to-justice approach is a 'contextual' conception of the law.... The role of legal scholarship, and indeed the role of lawyers generally, thus becomes much more complex, but also much more fascinating and realistic. To exemplify, it does not limit itself to describing the rules, forms and procedures applying to the acts of initiating a judicial proceeding or an appeal; it must also consider the *costs* to be borne, the *time* required, the *difficulties* (including psychological ones) to overcome, the *benefits* to be obtained, etc.[161]

Discussion Questions

1. How should we define the concept of "access to justice"? Is access to justice the same thing as access to law? Is access to lawyers a part of the solution or part of the problem?

2. Where should the primary responsibility lie for responding to the problems of access to justice – with the parties? the legal profession? the courts? governments? the economy? some other group or system?

3. In 1995 the Australian Federation of Consumer Organisations published its Consumer Justice Charter. Clause 2 of the Charter is headed "Universal Access to Justice" and it states:

   i. Everyone should be able to assert their rights and the rights of every person should be protected.
   ii. Universal access to justice should be a measure against which progress is assessed.

   How effective is the ideal of "universal access to justice" as a benchmark by which we can assess "progress"?

4. What does Galanter's analysis of repeat players and one shotters tell us about "law and power"? (refer back to Chapter 4 in answering this question).

5. In *McInnis v The Queen* (1979) 143 CLR 575, the late Murphy J made the following argument:

   > The right to counsel derives from the disadvantage of being unrepresented in a judicial system which claims to dispense equal justice in accordance with the rule of law.... [I]t is fundamental to the administration of justice in serious cases ... that an accused has the right to legal representation. Counsel is necessary for the protection of an accused and desirable for assistance to a court in the administration of justice. (at 586)

   Compare this view with the High Court's decision in *Dietrich*. Which view do you prefer? Which view is the more workable?

6. Are ADR mechanisms appropriate responses to the problems of access to justice, or do they merely avoid the problems?

---

161 Ibid 283 (emphasis in original).

Chapter 5

Litigation

(a)   Introduction

One implication that can be drawn from the analysis of liberalism presented in Chapter 2 is that it promotes a court-centred view of the legal system. This is partly because properly constituted courts are regarded as the primary sites of legal authority in society. Furthermore, the trial process, as traditionally imagined, symbolises the ideals embedded in the rule of law. As we will see shortly, the trial process is formally depicted as one of public accountability and of "checks and balances" against the unbiased exercise of power; the principle of separation of power and "checks and balances" is discussed in Chapter 3. These values are central to the rule of law ideology. Given this link, an examination of the litigation process offers an important vantage point from which to assess the actual effect of liberal ideals on the operation of our legal system. Do those ideals determine the way in which courts actually operate, or do they work more as symbols of how courts *should* operate?

We begin by discussing the traditional ideal of litigation in the Anglo-Australian (and American) legal systems – the adversarial trial – and some of its alternatives. The adversarial system is typically understood by contrasting it with inquisitorial systems, derived from Roman-canonical procedure. These systems place less emphasis on the trial as a contest between the parties, with greater judicial involvement in the role of fact-finding.[1] In much the same way as our description of liberalism in Chapter 2 was only a generalised picture, so too our description of the adversarial process will be an approximation. This is because "pure" examples of that process are rare.[2] Instead, as we shall see, the daily life of our courts more often involves routine departures from the adversarial ideal: a fact which is tacitly accepted by the participants in the process. We will look at some studies of the actual operation of courts. These are not studies about the substance of judicial decisions – that type of inquiry already receives sufficient attention in law curricula. Rather, these studies look at the behaviour of courts and at the processes which shape the types of decisions that are made. For the sake of clarity our discussion is divided between the criminal and civil court processes,

---

1   Under this model there is an increased reliance on written rather than oral evidence. The inquisitorial judge has the primary responsibility for investigation and evidence-gathering. For a useful review of these distinctive features of inquisitorial systems, see Independent Commission Against Corruption (ICAC), *Inquisitorial Systems of Criminal Justice and the ICAC: A Comparison*, November 1994, <www.icac.nsw.gov.au>. See also J Hunter and K Cronin, *Evidence, Advocacy and Ethical Practice*, Butterworths, 1995, 25ff.

2   Australian Law Reform Commission (ALRC), *Managing Justice: A Review of the Federal Civil Justice System*, Report No 89, 2000, para [1.116].

although we will see that there are many things they share in common – in both areas administrative routine is the order of the day.

It will be apparent that we take up the story from the previous chapter on access to justice. We have already seen that for a variety of reasons many people are excluded from full participation in the legal process; now we look more closely at what that process offers those who are able to participate in it.

(b) The adversarial model

(i) Key features of the adversarial model

Liberal legal rhetoric and popular culture provide a very definite image of the litigation process. Both tell us that litigation centres on the court-room, and that in the Australian court system, as in the United Kingdom and the United States, trials are formally structured on an adversarial model.

The ideal of the adversarial trial assigns particular and separate functions to the participants in the trial, especially the judge, the parties and the lawyers.[3] The implication is that when each participant fulfils his or her assigned function, then objective and unbiased results will be achieved. We will address each of these three roles in turn.

The adversarial model prescribes a non-interventionist role for the judge. Judges themselves have frequently re-asserted this. For example, in a much-quoted passage from *Jones v National Coal Board*, Lord Denning argued that:

> In the system of trial which we have evolved in this country, the judge sits to hear and determine the issues raised by the parties, not to conduct an investigation or examination on behalf of society at large, as happens, we believe, in some foreign countries. Even in England, however, a judge is not a mere umpire to answer the question "How's that?" His object, above all, is to find out the truth, and to do justice according to law; and in the daily pursuit of it the advocate plays an honourable and necessary role. Was it not Lord Eldon LC who said in a notable passage that "truth is best discovered by powerful statements on both sides of the question"? see *Ex parte Lloyd* (1822) Mont 70, 72n. And Lord Greene MR who explained that justice is best done by a judge who holds the balance between the contending parties without himself taking part in their disputations? If a judge, said Lord Greene, should himself conduct the examination of witnesses, "he, so to speak, descends into the arena and is liable to have his vision clouded by the dust of conflict": see *Yuill v Yuill* [1945] P 15, 20; 61 TLR 176; [1945] 1 All ER 183.[4]

Other judges have been less hesitant in applying the metaphor of "the umpire". Lawton LJ (in *Laker Airways Ltd v Dept of Trade*) stated quite simply that:

---

3   We have not included the jury in this list. Eggleston has argued that features of the adversary system can be distinguished from those that owe their origin to the jury system, for example the oral, question and answer format of examining witnesses, and the rule against hearsay evidence: Sir Richard Eggleston, "What is Wrong with the Adversary System?" (1975) 49 *Australian Law Journal* 428. For a good general summary of the adversary system, albeit with an emphasis on civil litigation, see N Andrews, *Principles of Civil Procedure*, Sweet and Maxwell, 1994, Ch 3. See also J McEwan, *Evidence and the Adversarial Process*, Blackwell, 1992, Ch 1.

4   [1957] 2 QB 55 at 63.

I regard myself as a referee. I can blow my judicial whistle when the ball goes out of play; but when the game restarts I must neither take part in it nor tell the players how to play.[5]

And whilst Lord Denning expressed an aspiration to "find out the truth", the High Court of Australia has noted that there are limitations. Dawson J in *Whitehorn v R* stated that:

> A trial does not involve the pursuit of truth by any means. The adversary system is the means adopted and the judge's role in that system is to hold the balance between the contending parties without himself taking part in their disputations. It is not an inquisitorial role in which he seeks to remedy the deficiencies in the case on either side. When a party's case is deficient, the ordinary consequence is that it does not succeed. If a prosecution does succeed at trial when it ought not to and there is a miscarriage of justice as a result, that is a matter to be corrected on appeal. It is no part of the function of the trial judge to prevent it by donning the mantle of prosecution or defence counsel.[6]

These statements not only require judicial detachment from "the dust of conflict",[7] but also from the substantive legal rules that are relied upon to decide the case. Hand in hand with the belief in procedural neutrality goes a belief in formalism:

> The judgment, though pronounced or awarded by the judges, is not their determination, but the determination and sentence of the law. It is the conclusion that regularly follows from the premises of law and fact ...[8]

Griffith puts the point bluntly in his study *The Politics of the Judiciary*, when he describes the traditional view as one in which the judge "must act like a political, economic, and social eunuch, and have no interest in the world outside his court when he comes to judgement".[9] This traditional view is reflected in the convention prescribing judicial reticence, known as the "Kilmuir Rules" in the United Kingdom. It is increasingly challenged in Australia, with judges routinely prepared to contribute to public debate, delivering speeches and addresses on a wide variety of topics of contemporary political and social relevance.[10]

---

5   [1977] 2 All ER 182 at 208.

6   (1983) 152 CLR 657 at 682 cited with approval by the Full Bench of the High Court in *R v Apostelides* (1984) 154 CLR 563.

7   See the full quotation at Eggleston, n 3. The ALRC notes the common use of battle and sporting imagery in descriptions of the court system: n 2, para 1.119. This is also a noticeably masculine imagery – a point we make in Chapter 8.

8   Sir William Blackstone, cited in J Eisenstein et al, *The Contours of Justice*, Little, Brown and Co, 1988, 6.

9   J Griffith, *The Politics of the Judiciary*, 3rd ed, Fontana Press, 1985, 193.

10 The Kilmuir rules are derived from a letter written by Lord Chancellor Kilmuir in 1955 to the Director General of the BBC, which noted the overriding importance that judges should be insulated from controversy: "So long as a Judge keeps silent his reputation for wisdom and impartiality remains unassailable: but every utterance which he makes in public, except in the actual performance of his judicial duties, must necessarily bring him within the focus of criticism". The extent to which Australian judges have departed from this convention is explored in a paper by Justice Keith Mason in "Should Judges Speak Out?" *Bar News*, Spring 2000. The extensive extra-curial speeches and papers of our current High Court may be found at <http://www.hcourt.gov.au/publications_05.html>.

Turning to the role of the parties, the adversarial model prescribes that trials are bipolar contests in which only one party can succeed.[11] In the language of economists, a trial is a "zero-sum" game. Each party is responsible for initiating, defining and presenting his or her own case in the most favourable light. Thus the parties decide when to bring the action, what legal issues to raise, what evidence to present, and what witnesses to call. As one writer has put it, the trial is regarded as:

> [A] competitive struggle between two formally equal parties. The grounds for the struggle and the materials used are decided upon by the competing interests who select evidence, witnesses and examination strategies with minimal intervention from the judge.[12]

Furthermore, the trial is regarded as a self-contained event. The formal effect of the court's judgment is restricted to the parties and, once the decision is handed down, the involvement of the court ends.[13]

Of course the parties are not entirely unconstrained in their control of the case. For one thing, the substantive law that is to be argued will often determine the range of arguable issues, what defences are available, what type of evidence must be led, and so on. Furthermore, the process and progress of the trial is governed by rules of evidence and procedure (allowing the judge to determine when "the ball goes out of play"). These factors alone mean that the adversarial model guarantees a role for lawyers in the court process.

While it is generally accepted that a person has a right to self-representation in civil or criminal proceedings, and the courts have discretion to allow non-lawyers as representatives, legal practitioners nevertheless have an effective monopoly over the representation of litigants in court.[14] Despite this, the formal view of the trial process insists that it is the parties who put the arguments – the lawyers, acting on instructions from their clients, simply facilitate this process. Yet, as we will see in the next chapter, lawyers in court are more than mere representatives of the parties; they become players.[15] Because the judge is supposed to be passive, lawyers, by virtue of their professional expertise, have considerable influence in the conduct of a case, over both facts and law. Many regard the role of the lawyer as the exact opposite of that of the judge: "The lawyer is active, the judge passive. The lawyer partisan, the judge neutral. The lawyer imaginative, the judge reflective".[16] It is important "to distinguish between the adversarial system

---

11 A Chayes, "The Role of the Judge in Public Law Litigation" (1976) 89 *Harvard Law Review* 1281 at 1282.

12 P O'Malley, *Law, Capitalism and Democracy*, Allen and Unwin, 1983, 122.

13 See Chayes, n 11, 1283.

14 In *Dietrich v The Queen* (1992) 177 CLR 292, the High Court of Australia held that there is no right to legal representation at public expense. Nevertheless, the court held that a trial in which an indigent accused charged with a serious offence was not legally represented may be rendered unfair, imposing on the trial judge a duty to stay the legal proceedings as an abuse of process. The fair trial jurisprudence is further explored in S Bronitt and B McSherry, *Principles of Criminal Law*, 2nd ed, Lawbook Co, 2005, 93ff.

15 A point made by Jerome Skolnick, "Social Control in the Adversary System" (1967) 11 *Conflict Resolution* 52 at 65; Vago argues that lawyers are repeat players, in Galanter's sense, in the adjudication process: see S Vago, *Law and Society*, Prentice-Hall, 1981, 73.

16 Justice Peck, describing a view with which he disagrees, cited in M Frankel, "The Search for Truth: An Umpireal View" (1975) 123 *University of Pennsylvania Law Review* 1031 at 1035.

itself and behaviour of lawyers or their clients [that may be] described as 'adversarial'".[17] Because of the risk that the lawyer's partisanship may lead to the intentional distortion of evidence, the adversary model is supplemented by rules prescribing that the lawyer not only has a duty to her client but also to the court. The lawyer is not regarded simply as an agent of his or her client but also as an officer of the court. We explore this idea in more detail in Chapter 6.

Many commentators have noted the tension between the claim that judges are supposed to "find out the truth" and the insistence that they must rely solely on the evidence put before them by the parties.[18] It is not immediately apparent that the truth will necessarily emerge from the presentation of partisan and self-interested arguments.[19] A frequent observation is that the adversarial process is not so much concerned with determining "the truth" as its principal purpose, but rather on ensuring a "fair fight".[20] As one American judge has put it, "the truth and victory are mutually incompatible for some considerable percentage of the attorneys trying cases at any given time".[21] A milder view assumes that justice lies in the pursuit of proper procedures. Thus the American legal theorist Lon Fuller once observed that the essence of the judge's function in the adversarial process does not lie in the substantive conclusion reached in a given case, but "in the procedures by which that substance is guaranteed".[22]

These features of the adversarial system have led many commentators to draw a parallel with the philosophy of laissez-faire, free-market economics.[23] In Jerome Frank's words:

'Classical' laissez-faire economic theory assumed that, when each individual, as an economic man, strives rationally, in the competitive economic struggle or 'fight', to promote his own self-interest, we attain public welfare through the wisest use of resources and the most socially desirable distribution of economic goods. The 'fight' theory of justice is a sort of legal laissez-faire. It assumes a 'litigious' man, it assumes that, in a law suit, each litigious man, in the court-room competitive strife, will, through his lawyer, intelligently and energetically try to use the evidential resources to bring out the evidence favourable to him and unfavourable to his court-room competitor; that thereby the trial court will obtain all the relevant evidence; and thus, in a socially beneficial way, the court will apply the social policies embodied in the legal rules to the actual facts, avoiding the application of these rules to a mistaken version of the facts. Legal laissez-faire theory therefore assumes that the government can rely on the "individual enterprise" of the individual litigants to ensure that the court orders will be grounded on all the practically available relevant facts.[24]

---

17 ALRC, n 2, para 3.41.

18 See, for example, Eggleston, n 3, 429; Hunter and Cronin, n 1, 5-9.

19 D Rhode, "Ethical Perspectives on Legal Practice" (1985) 37 *Stanford Law Review* 589 at 596.

20 This claim has been made by journalist Evan Whitton, who concluded that the adversarial system should be abandoned in favour of inquisitorial modes of proof: *Trial by Voodoo: Why the Law Defeats Justice and Democracy*, Random House, 1994. For a more balanced view of the strengths and weaknesses of inquisitorial systems, see ICAC, n 1.

21 Frankel, n 16, 1037.

22 Lon Fuller, cited in Skolnick, n 15, 669.

23 Noted in O'Malley, n 12, 122-123.

24 J Frank, *The Courts on Trial*, Princeton UP, 1973, 92.

In court it is assumed that the lawyers for each party are equally competent; the onus is on each party to secure the best representation. Roshier and Teff make a similar observation, drawing the conclusion that in the adversarial system:

> [J]ustice is unattainable, because the ability to win reflects the respective resources of the parties, which are mobilized to advance each side of the case to the limits allowed by the rules ... success may reflect the resources brought to bear and the proficiency of legal advisers as much as the apparent merits of the case.[25]

The economic analogy must be treated cautiously. There is no *necessary* l ink between a society's form of economic organisation and its mode of court process. As O'Malley points out, many capitalist countries (particularly in continental Europe) have evolved a quite different system of adjudication – based on the inquisitorial model discussed below – from that in Australia, England or the United States.[26] It is possible that the mode of court process tells us more about a society's attitude to the state and the political process than about its economic system.[27] Liberal societies in the English rather than the continental tradition have tended to be more suspicious about the power of the state as a threat to individual liberty. This may have been reflected particularly in criminal matters, where the adversarial system is designed to make the prosecutor (ie in most modern cases the Crown) make all the running.

The adversarial system is not just about putting the prosecutor at some (theoretical) disadvantage in criminal proceedings, it is also about limiting *judicial* power, remembering that the judiciary is seen as the third arm of government. The insistence on the passivity of the judge reflects liberal ideals of a neutral and non-interventionist state, of limited government, and the separation of the judiciary from other arms of government: of "checks and balances". The state, in the guise of the judge, can only decide those issues put before it by the parties. Recall too that liberalism argues that legality, procedural fairness or due process is an essential component of the rule of law. Thus litigation must be conducted within a complex framework of rules of evidence and procedure that are designed to promote the fairness of the process. In criminal trials these rules should also work to protect the individual's liberty against unwarranted intrusion from the state, a rationale that is evident in many of the rules of evidence such as the judicial discretion to exclude illegally or improperly obtained evidence.[28] In civil trials the adversarial model reinforces notions of individual "autonomy, dignity and responsibility".[29] It is the parties who, via their lawyers, run the case. These notions are, in turn, reinforced by the perpetuation of the sporting metaphor, with its easily digested messages about winners and losers, and the importance of individual initiative.

---

25   B Roshier and H Teff, *Law and Society in England*, Tavistock, 1980, 162.

26   O'Malley, n 12, 123.

27   See M Damaska, *The Faces of Justice and State Authority*, Yale UP, 1986.

28   See *Bunning v Cross* (1978) 141 CLR 54 at 75 where the High Court held that the rationale for excluding illegally obtained evidence related to society's right to insist those who enforce the law themselves respect it, "so that a citizen's precious right to immunity from arbitrary and unlawful intrusion into the daily affairs of private life may remain unimpaired".

29   J Handler, *The Conditions of Discretion*, Russell Sage, 1986, 123.

(ii)   Criticisms and alternatives

There is a well-rehearsed list of problems in the day-to-day operation of the adversarial court system that have caused concern. The list includes:

- delays caused by excessive court caseloads, lengthy hearings or inefficient procedural rules;[30]
- the costs of conducting litigation (discussed in Chapter 4);
- difficulties in ensuring the ready availability of legal advice and representation (also discussed in Chapter 4);
- the lack of judges with experience in areas requiring technical or expert knowledge;[31] and
- disparities in matters of granting bail and sentencing.[32]

The list of suggested solutions is equally varied, ranging from streamlining the procedural rules, revising the methods and criteria for the selection of judges, to establishing specialist courts for particular types of cases, and the use of alternative dispute resolution forums (as we discussed in Chapter 4). In the United Kingdom, an inquiry headed by Lord Woolf recommended in 1996 sweeping changes to the way that civil cases are dealt with in England and Wales, in particular by diminishing the passive role of the judiciary and empowering it to "manage" cases through the system.[33]

Much of the literature on court reform has seemingly accepted the formalist view that court-based litigation is central to the recognition and protection of individual rights. The task of court reform is to improve the practical application of that ideal by identifying its shortcomings and implementing procedural changes. Often the search for solutions has led commentators to consider aspects of the inquisitorial (or investigative) systems found in continental Europe.[34]

---

30   The cause and extent of court delay (or "waiting time") varies between courts and between civil and criminal jurisdictions. See R Callinan, "Court Delays in NSW: Issues and Developments", *NSW Parliamentary Library Briefing Paper 1/2002*. For earlier studies, see R Cranston, P Haynes, J Pullen, and I Scott, *Delays and Efficiency in Civil Litigation*, Institute of Judicial Administration Inc, 1985; M Feeley, *The Process is the Punishment*, Russell Sage, 1979, Ch 8: "The Myth of Heavy Caseloads".

31   This problem has been noted particularly with regard to legislation such as the *Trade Practices Act 1974* (Cth); see J Starke, "Proposal for a specialist court with economic experts" (1990) 64 *Australian Law Journal* 379.

32   G Zdenkowski, "Sentencing trends: past, present and prospective " in D Chappell and P Wilson (eds), *Crime and the Criminal Justice System in Australia: 2000 and beyond*, Butterworths, 2000, Ch 10, critically surveys the literature on sentencing disparities, and the various policies adopted to address these problems including mandatory sentencing, guideline judgments and sentencing grids.

33   Lord Chancellor's Department, *Access to Justice*, The Stationery Office, 1996, or <http://criminalsolicitors.com/puhead/woolf.htm>. Many of the recommended reforms had already been introduced in Australia. See also ALRC, n 2, Federal Justice. On case management in the criminal justice system in Australia, see J Willis, "The processing of cases in the criminal justice system" in D Chappell and P Wilson (eds), *Crime and the Criminal Justice System in Australia: 2000 and beyond*, Butterworths, 2000, Ch 9.

34   See, for example, Eggleston, n 3, 433; Frankel, n 16. Galanter lists the use of more investigatory procedures in his survey of reform proposals: M Galanter, "Delivering Legality: Some Proposals for the Direction of Research" (1976) 11 *Law and Society Review* 225, extracted in Chapter 4 above. See also ICAC, n 1.

(iii)   The inquisitorial model

To Anglo-Australian eyes the main distinguishing feature of the inquisitorial process is that the judge has general control of the proceedings. Although each case, civil or criminal, is initiated by parties, the judge is not restricted to either the facts or the legal issues put by them. Thus, within the general boundaries of the case defined by the parties, the judge can call and examine witnesses and suggest further points of law as appropriate. The case may unfold in stages, with the judge being involved along the way. The contrast with the adversarial model has been described as follows:

> While the English judge is an umpire sitting at the sidelines watching the lawyers fight it out and afterwards declaring one of them the winner, the German judge is the director of an improvised play, the outcome of which is not known to him at first but depends heavily on his mode of directing.[35]

In adversarial systems, the purpose of procedure during "interlocutory stages" or the pre-trial phase is to refine the issues in readiness for a climactic trial, where considerable emphasis is placed on oral evidence as a way of proving the case. In inquisitorial systems, there is no such sharp distinction between the interlocutory and trial stages. The inquisitorial model might more accurately be called an "inquiry model" or an "investigatory model", since the usual justification for the interventionist judicial role is that it aids the court's inquiry into the truth that lies behind the case. The role of the lawyer is supplementary to that of the judge. For example, once the judge has examined a witness, a lawyer may ask additional questions, but there is little occasion for lengthy cross-examination. Contrast this with adversarial procedure, where lawyers have the central role; to the extent that a judge who seeks to take over the role of lawyer risks a successful appeal for a re-trial.

As with the adversarial model, these descriptions of the inquisitorial model refer to an "ideal type".[36] It is difficult to find "pure" examples of either model in practice. Moreover, with regard to the inquisitorial model, there are significant differences between, say, the German, French and Italian systems, as well as emerging hybrid systems that meld inquisitorial and adversarial features.[37] Neither is it possible to claim that one or other of the adversarial or inquisitorial models is definitively "better" than the other. Both systems are capable of delivering fair, just and efficient outcomes. It is important to recognise that these systems developed with specific socio-historical, political and economic contexts. For another, what counts as "better" depends upon which objective one thinks a court system should pursue. We might, for example, draw different conclusions depending on whether we think that courts should pursue "truth" as opposed to

---

35   W Zeidler, "Evaluation of the Adversary System: As Comparison, Some Remarks on the Investigatory System of Procedure" (1981) 55 *Australian Law Journal* 390 at 394. See also B McKillop, *Anatomy of a French Murder Trial*, Hawkins Press, 1997.

36   See Damaska, n 27, 3-6.

37   See McEwan, n 3, 8-11. For a useful summary of these differences between the European civil law systems see the ICAC Report, n 1. The Japanese legal system is an example of a hybrid system. It was based originally on German Civil code and legal concepts but, following the Second World War, with growing US influences, has moved to allow greater party control over the conduct and pace of litigation: H Oda, *Japanese Law*, 2nd ed, Oxford UP, 1999, 30, 413-416.

"justice".[38] There is, however, research that has compared how people perceive the results of cases decided in these different systems. A classic American empirical study by Thibaut and Walker in 1975, found that adversarial procedures were considered by participants to be fairer and more satisfactory than inquisitorial procedures *regardless of the trial outcome*.[39] The suggestion is that perceptions of fairness are related to the level of control that a litigant feels they have in the process. When people feel that "they have had a hand in the decision" they are more likely to accept the outcome, even if the decision goes against them.[40]

(iv) Merging the models in practice

Even in legal systems which are thought to belong predominantly to one tradition or the other, there are hybrid features. Indeed, there is considerable evidence of a convergence between the two models.[41] For example, in Australia many court proceedings are marked by a greater degree of overt judicial intervention than is envisaged by the adversarial ideal. It is now an accepted part of the judge's role to manage the business of the court, rather than sitting as a detached "umpire". This has developed in response to the length and cost of both civil and criminal cases. Justice Rogers of the NSW Supreme Court described the problem this way:

> Complex commercial cases were assuming the proportions of medieval battle trains. The trolleys of photocopied documents in arch lever [file]s, the battery of partners, employed solicitors and paralegals with their portable telephones to call for reinforcements, the lap top computers to spew out even more information, were not only stretching court accommodation to the point where a usually spacious courtroom was insufficient to provide the necessary elbow room but where both cost and character were transforming a complex commercial case into a major Hollywood production.[42]

This shift in the judicial role has been formalised throughout court systems in Australia as part of what is termed "case management". The underlying purpose of case management is to utilise court resources (including time resources) "more efficiently and effectively".[43] The ALRC has summarised these developments as follows:

> Case management involves a deliberate transfer of some of the initiative in case preparation from the parties to the court, with the aim of controlling costs and ensuring the timely resolution of cases, without compromising the quality and fairness of the process. To support case management objectives, practice and

---

38 Thibaut and Walker argue that there is a "fundamental dichotomy" between the dispute resolution objectives of "truth" and "justice": J Thibaut and L Walker, "A Theory of Procedure" (1978) 66 *California Law Review* 541 at 565.

39 J Thibaut and L Walker, *Procedural Justice: A Psychological Analysis*, Lawrence Erlbaum, 1975. A subsequent study found that even French and German participants also favoured adversarial systems over inquisitorial systems: EA Lind, BE Erickson, N Friedland, and M Dickenberger, "Reactions To Procedural Models For Adjudicative Conflict Resolution: A Cross-National Study" (1978) 22 *Journal of Conflict Resolution* 318, discussed in M Nolan, "The Adversarial mentality versus the inquisitorial mentality" (2004) 16(3) *Legal Date* 7.

40 T Tyler, *Why People Obey the Law*, Yale UP, 1990, 163.

41 ALRC, n 2, para 1.126.

42 Justice Rogers, "The Managerial or Interventionist Judge" (1993) 3 *Journal of Judicial Administration* 96 at 101.

43 ALRC, n 2, para 6.2.

procedure rules have in turn been significantly modified so that pleadings, discovery, evidence presentation and settlement facilitation are subject to court control and supervision.[44]

The actual mechanisms of case management vary from jurisdiction to jurisdiction; some schemes are based in legislation, while others are governed by the administrative practices and policies of the particular court. They also vary according to the type of dispute (civil or criminal) before the court. They may include the use of mandatory disclosure, pre-trial conferences and directions hearings,[45] the imposition of time limits on the presentation of cases, and greater reliance on written – rather than oral – evidence during the pre-trial phases.[46] The dominant rationale for these reforms has been to promote efficiency, though there is concern that some of these processes may impinge negatively on the right to a fair trial, in particular, the extent to which the mandatory disclosure rules imposed on the defence threaten the presumption of innocence by requiring individuals to furnish evidence of their own guilt.

These developments are not limited to Australian courts. In United Kingdom and the United States case management is widely accepted. For example, Lord Roskill in the House of Lords has stated that:

> [I]t is the trial judge who has control of the proceedings. It is part of his duty to identify the crucial issues and to see they are tried as expeditiously and as inexpensively as possible. It is the duty of the advisers of the parties to assist the trial judge in carrying out his duty.[47]

This adversarial evolution has led the ALRC to conclude that "processes such as case management, court or tribunal connected ADR processes, and discretionary rules of evidence and procedure, have modified the adversarial nature of the system".[48] However, a note of caution is appropriate here. While the trend towards case management clearly represents a move away from the "pure" adversarial model, it does not mean a shift to the full inquisitorial model. Rather:

> While it is unlikely that the case management approach adopted by courts in the modern adversarial system will become like the intensive supervisory approach of the inquisitorial system, it is likely that further incremental modifications to the traditional adversarial system which was designed for a different world will continue, in order to adapt to the changing environment within which courts operate.[49]

There is also a growing number of decision-making forums that depart from the traditional model altogether and which operate either alongside or in conjunction with the conventional court system. Examples include restorative justice

---

44   Ibid para 6.3.

45   For a review of these innovations, see R Refshauge, "Frankenstein's Monster – Creating a Criminal Justice System for the 21st Century" (2000) 9(4) *Journal of Judicial Administration* 185; Willis, n 33, Ch 9. A directions hearing involves both parties and the judge, and gives the judge the opportunity to review the progress of a case and to give directions to the parties as required.

46   G Flatman and M Bagaric, "Accused Disclosure – Measured Response or Abrogation of the Presumption of Innocence" (1999) 23 *Criminal Law Journal* 327.

47   *Ashmore v Corp of Lloyds* [1992] 2 All ER 486 at 488.

48   ALRC, n 2, para 1.129.

49   Commonwealth Attorney-General's Department, *Federal Civil Justice Strategy Paper*, 2003, 188.

conferencing and alternative dispute resolution processes,[50] coronial inquests, parole board hearings, and the use of royal commissions to inquire into a diversity of matters (ranging from Aboriginal deaths in police custody, the maltreatment of psychiatric patients or the collapse of large corporations).[51]

Perhaps the most significant Australian legal institution to depart from the adversarial model is the administrative tribunal. Tribunals are another key and indispensable feature of the decision-making processes and dispute-processing apparatus of the modern bureaucratic state. Although there is no prototypical form of tribunal, in general they combine aspects of both adversarial and inquisitorial models. On the one hand, tribunals may be perceived to act like courts – they are sometimes headed by judicial officers, and receive evidence, hear representations from the parties and make determinations about their disputes. On the other hand, tribunals are a noticeable departure from the traditional model of the courts. Commonly encountered features of tribunal practice are the absence of formal rules of procedure and evidence, the possible absence of legal representation, and the power of the tribunal to "inform itself on any matter relevant to a review of a decision in any manner it considers appropriate".[52] Tribunals often develop special expertise; for example, the decisions about a defendant's fitness to plead in criminal trials or to be involuntarily detained in a psychiatric institution for assessment or treatment may be made by an interdisciplinary team of decision-makers sitting on a mental health review tribunal.[53]

Tribunals do not, therefore, conform neatly to the classical liberal view of law.[54] Under the doctrine of the separation of powers,[55] tribunals, which are established by statute, are said to be a part of the executive, rather than the judicial arm of government. Yet tribunals in areas such as social security law make large numbers of decisions in cases that usually involve disputes between government (that is, executive) agencies and individual citizens (for example, appeals against the withdrawal of social security benefits). That is, while they exercise an apparently adjudicative role, at the same time they operate within a context of governmental administration; they are part of an overall system by which the government seeks to implement particular policies (for example, a policy to monitor more closely the range of beneficiaries to whom social security payments are made).

The criticisms of the adversarial model that have been considered so far share a broad reformist aim. The existence of "gaps" between the adversarial ideal (the law in the books) and everyday practice (the law in action) can be treated as a sign that repairs are needed to enable the courts to live up to their ideals.[56] The "gaps"

---

50 Discussed in Chapter 4.

51 For example, the several reports issued by the Royal Commission of Inquiry into Aboriginal Deaths in Custody; the report of the New South Wales Royal Commission into Mental Health Services (investigating, inter alia, deaths of patients at the Chelmsford Private Hospital in Sydney), and the report of the Royal Commission into the HIH collapse.

52 See, for example, *Social Security (Administration) Act 1999* (Cth) s 167(2).

53 For a collection of articles on this institution, see "Special issue: mental health tribunals and decision-making" (2003) 10(1) *Psychiatry, Psychology and Law*.

54 For a brief resume of the issues, see P Bayne, "Dispute about tribunals" (1990) 64 *Australian Law Journal* 493.

55 See the discussion on "Constitutionality" in Chapter 3.

56 The term "gaps" is qualified as a reminder of the difficulties inherent in gap research, outlined in the introductory chapter to this book.

are regarded as problems because, by and large, the court system is assessed *in terms of the ideal*. We turn now to critiques of a different kind. At the risk of over-generalisation, they can be described as sharing a sociological perspective. They see evidence of "gaps" as providing important clues to the nature of our legal system.[57] In broad terms, these socio-legal perspectives have yielded three important insights.

The first insight points out that the traditional model of litigation is based on a "top-down" view of the courts. That is, it presumes that appellate or higher courts can (or should) be regarded as representative of the whole court hierarchy. Undoubtedly this is reflected in assumptions about the effect of the doctrine of precedent on the behaviour of lower courts. In contrast, many sociological studies have taken a "bottom-up" view of the court system, concentrating on the work of the lower courts.[58] This work has shown that there are significant differences between the practice and the traditional ideal of the adversarial system. The majority of work performed by lower courts involves routine administrative processing of cases rather than anything approaching the vigorous contest suggested by the adversarial model.

The second insight provided by empirical studies of courts is that the adversarial model provides only a partial picture of the litigation process. That model defines litigation in terms of a trial which follows specific procedures.[59] The traditional model thereby under-emphasises the importance of informal pre-trial practices (such as negotiation), and ignores the great range of factors which, as we have seen, determine whether, when and what type of people become litigants. A trial is only one part of a process of negotiation and planning that goes on between lawyer and client, and between lawyers. In many instances this pre-trial process is far more significant in deciding the outcome of a case than the trial. This is what Skolnick meant when he observed that:

> [A]djudication does not define the adversary system, but is instead the outcome of a failure of pre-trial negotiation, perhaps as frequently a failure of negotiation between attorney and client as between defence and prosecution.[60]

Thirdly, even if we adopt the limited focus on the trial, the ideal of the adversarial model is rarely realised in practice. This insight takes us beyond the reforms introduced by "case management". We will look at evidence that the business of running a court inevitably produces compromises and departures from the formally defined roles. Moreover, the way in which this occurs varies from one court to another. For example, one study in the United States found that "[j]udges applying the same substantive and procedural law – and sometimes sitting in adjacent court-rooms – dispense justice in radically different

---

57   As Peter Fitzpatrick has observed the gap revealed between the "law in the books" and "law in action" is not "some vague, but remediable derogation from the efficacy of law; rather, there is something constitutive of law itself": "Law and societies" (1984) 22 *Osgoode Hall Law Journal* 116 at 128.

58   The "top-down/bottom-up" dichotomy is taken from R Tomasic, *The Sociology of Law*, Sage Publications, 1985, 79-80.

59   For example, the exchange of pleadings between the parties (a process by which the parties in a civil action define the issues of fact and law which will be disputed in court). As noted above, case management in the criminal process is intended to perform at similar function.

60   Skolnick, n 15, 70.

ways".[61] The point here is that the traditional adversarial model is based on a monolithic concept of *the court-room* as an arena in which players have definite and discrete roles. Sociological studies present an alternative view of *courts* as varied and complex organisations, made up of interactions between people and institutions (such as the legal profession or the magistracy) fulfilling often quite indefinite functions.[62]

To explore these points further it is helpful to look separately at studies of criminal and civil cases.

(c) Criminal litigation

One influential contribution to this area is Doreen McBarnet's study of criminal cases in lower courts.[63] Her thesis is that in practice the criminal courts have produced two tiers of justice. The upper tier (consisting of superior or appellate courts) provides the public image of justice – this is where "the ideology of justice is put on display".[64] It produces images of a criminal justice system constrained by due process values such as the right to silence, the presumption of innocence, and the prosecution bearing the burden of proving its case "beyond reasonable doubt". In this legal arena, criminal trials are presided over by a superior court judge sitting with a jury, with defendants represented by legal counsel. The visibility of these legal processes may be contrasted with the lower tier of justice (typified in Australia by the Local Court or Magistrates' Court), which is where the bulk of offenders are processed. At this lower tier McBarnet notes that an "ideology of triviality" pervades the summary jurisdiction.[65] The ideology sustains the view that the summary offences and penalties meted out are "minor". Yet summary offences are not insignificant in punitive terms: many offences can carry significant fines or periods of imprisonment. They are also numerically significant. In Australia, as in the United Kingdom, it is the lower courts which handle the vast majority of cases processed by the legal system. Recent Australian data demonstrate that magistrates' courts handled 97 per cent of the criminal matters that were finalised in 2003-04; the remaining 3 per cent were dealt with by higher courts (that is Supreme Courts and intermediate courts).[66]

---

61 J Conley and W O'Barr, "Fundamentals of Jurisprudence: An Ethnography of Judicial Decision Making in Informal Courts" (1988) 66 *North Carolina Law Review* 467 at 504.

62 For example, a sociologically inspired view of the courts might ask whether a duty solicitor's main allegiance lies with the client (the traditional view), the legal aid bureaucracy, or to the particular local court in which she must appear everyday. Note that use of an organisational model to understand the courts is only one of a number of approaches evident in the literature: see Tomasic, n 58, 55-81.

63 *Conviction: Law, the State and the Construction of Justice*, Macmillan, 1981. Her study was conducted in Glasgow, but the arguments generated by her findings are applicable to the English and Australian context. McBarnet's work has been influential in a range of studies of Australian law and practice, including the law relating to pre-trial investigation and legal responses to entrapment: see D Dixon, *Law in Policing: Legal Regulation and Police Practices*, Clarendon Press, 1997; S Bronitt and D Roche, "Between Rhetoric and Reality: Sociolegal and Republican Perspectives on Entrapment" (2000) 4 *International Journal of Evidence and Proof* 77.

64 McBarnet, n 63, 153.

65 Ibid, especially chs 7 and 8.

66 Australian Bureau of Statistics, 4513.0 *Criminal Courts, Australia*, 2003-04.

To cope with this huge volume of cases, it is said that the lower courts have evolved informal procedures and practices that better conform with ideas of bureaucratic processing than with the formalities of the rule of law or due process. McBarnet points out that the purpose of this informality is not to benefit the many defendants who are processed through these courts, but to ensure "fast, easy and cheap" court administration: "conveyor-belt" or "assembly line" metaphors are often used to describe this model of justice.[67] Since McBarnet's study further system efficiencies have been promoted through the wide-scale adoption of infringement notice schemes (sometimes called "on the spot fines") in Australia and the United Kingdom. The offender who is issued an infringement notice has the choice of paying the fine – essentially pleading guilty to the commission of the offence but with no conviction recorded – or disputing the matter in court. These offences are no longer confined to minor traffic infringements, but extend to offences such as the possession of small quantities of drugs and some public order offences.[68]

The criminal cases that do reach the lower courts occupy relatively little of the legal profession's time. Both the offences and the penalties with which these courts deal are regarded (except by the accused) as less serious and less deserving of detailed attention than those dealt with in the higher courts. This is what McBarnet means when she refers to the "ideology of triviality".[69] Lower court cases tend to be regarded by the relatively few lawyers who appear there as "straightforward", requiring little skill.[70] This is reflected in the fact that, in Australia, such work will often be done by public or duty solicitors, while the bulk of the profession reserves its skills for work associated with the upper tier, or on property-related matters. Hence, the view that lower court work is "straight-forward" becomes self-perpetuating: the cases are seen as simple because of the lack of lawyers. McBarnet goes on to suggest that the ideology of triviality may ultimately derive from the perceptions held about the people who appear in these courts – the poor, the unemployed, the homeless etc.[71] Lawrence Friedman, writing in an American context, sums up the prevalent attitude as follows:

> The average or typical criminal trial is no trial at all; it is an administrative procedure or a deal hammered out by lawyers. Some deals are elaborate, some

---

67   McBarnet, n 63, 140, where she also notes that magistrates will sometimes resort to formalism, particularly as a means of defining the defendant's role in the process. H Packer, *The Limits of the Criminal Sanction* Stanford UP, 1968, 159 coined the "assembly line" metaphor. Packer's theory of criminal justice, and McBarnet's critique, is explored below.

68   Infringement notices have been described by the Australian Law Reform Commission as a tool to divert offenders in minor cases away from the criminal courts, which "results in an 'opt-in' criminal process where the criminal burden of proof will only need to be met by the prosecution if the alleged offender elects to contest the offence in court": ALRC, *Securing Compliance: Civil and Administrative Penalties in Australian Federal Regulation* Discussion Paper No 65 2002, 397. These diversionary schemes offer, at first glance, significant savings in terms of system costs since there is no hearing and the "penalty" paid covers enforcement costs: RG Fox, *Criminal Justice on the Spot: Infringement Penalties in Victoria* Australian Institute of Criminology, 1995. There are concerns that such systems create unfair pressures on defendants not to contest their guilt, and effectively "de-moralise" breaches of the criminal law: see Bronitt and McSherry, n 14, 44-46 for a discussion of cannabis offence notices.

69   McBarnet, n 63, 143.

70   Ibid 147.

71   Ibid 146.

are perfunctory. An important case means a carefully crafted bargain. A dull, ordinary case – a 19 year-old from a slum neighborhood caught holding up a gas station – gets perfunctory treatment, especially if an overworked public defender handles the case ... Careful sifting of evidence, meticulous concern for defendants' rights – this was and is saved for the big case, the exceptional case. On the other hand, it is from these big cases that the public gets its idea of what criminal trials are "really" like. The information is decidedly misleading. The everyday case was and is buried in obscurity.[72]

The routine processing of criminal cases through the lower courts is made possible by the fact that in the great majority of cases the defendant pleads guilty. In 2003-04, 96 per cent of defendants in adjudicated matters in magistrates' courts in Australia pleaded guilty.[73] One study has concluded that as a consequence:

Magistrates are rarely called upon to determine a defendant's guilt or innocence, and are concerned primarily with sentencing defendants who have pleaded guilty.[74]

Nor is this phenomenon restricted to the lower courts. Even though the higher courts handle a comparatively much smaller criminal caseload, 84 per cent of defendants in adjudicated matters in Supreme and intermediate courts pleaded guilty in 2003-04.[75] The incidence of guilty pleas in Australian courts is similar to that overseas. For example, a UK report published in 2002 showed that 95 per cent of defendants in magistrates' courts, and 74 per cent in the Crown Court, pleaded guilty.[76]

How can the high rate of guilty pleas be explained? One answer may be that the vast majority of defendants are in fact guilty of the charge laid and that these statistics simply chronicle the efficiency of the criminal justice system both at the police investigation and prosecution stages. Whilst this is undoubtedly true of some percentage of the cases, there are several other factors that must be taken into account.

For one thing, such an explanation relies on a formalistic premise: that each case involves an undisputable set of facts that can be matched to an unambiguous legal rule proscribing that conduct. But neither facts nor laws are necessarily like this; indeed, if they were there would be little justification for the adversarial model. Given the technical language in which many criminal laws are expressed, and the confusion that court procedures can create for the uninitiated, it is quite likely that some defendants plead guilty in the mistaken belief that they have no defence to the particular charge they face. Other defendants may simply wish to minimise the costs that accompany involvement in the criminal justice process. It is important to note that a guilty plea need not always result in a conviction for the accused: indeed, for minor matters it is not uncommon for defendants to plead

---

72 L Friedman, "Courts over Time: A Survey of Theories and Research" in K Boyum and L Mather (eds), *Empirical Theories About Courts*, Longman, 1983, 9, 39.

73 Australian Bureau of Statistics, n 66.

74 M Lippmann, "Magistrates' Courts: A Game for Several Players" (1979) 4 *Legal Service Bulletin* 109.

75 Australian Bureau of Statistics, n 66.

76 UK Secretary of State for the Home Department, *Justice for All*, 2002, CM 5563, 67. This confirms the results of an earlier study, A Bottoms and J McLean, *Defendants in the Criminal Process*, Routledge and Kegan Paul, 1976, which found that 93 per cent of defendants in lower courts pleaded guilty.

guilty but request through their lawyers that the sentencing court exercise its discretion not to record a conviction: see, for example, *Crimes (Sentencing Procedure) Act 1999* (NSW) s 10. Malcolm Feeley has observed the strong pressures on defendants to plead guilty; considerations such as the risk of losing wages or, worse, one's job through prolonged absence from work undoubtedly promote guilty pleas.[77] It has also been suggested that a plea of guilty may be prompted by a desire to avoid prolonging the traumas of appearance in the court-room. Pat Carlen's 1976 classic study of magistrates' courts in Britain found that factors such as the physical design and layout of the court-room,[78] poor acoustics, unfamiliarity with the niceties of court behaviour (addressing the magistrate as "Your Worship", knowing when to stand up, and so on) can confuse and even degrade an inexperienced defendant.[79] Whilst the ideals of due process assume that a defendant is a rational, competent individual who is well versed in the Anglo-Australian legal culture, the operation of the system frequently negates these values.

Criminologists have pointed to a further factor that is critical in the pro-duction of guilty pleas. The process by which a particular charge is laid against an accused is not the automatic result of their having committed some act that might attract criminal penalties. This process is determined substantially by *discretionary police decisions*. Police exercise discretion on a range of issues: the types of behaviour that warrant police attention in the first place (for example, concen-trating on minor public order offences of offensive language rather than, say, domestic violence), whether an arrest should be made in any particular case, who should be arrested and what, if any, charge(s) will be laid. They may also divert offenders from the court system by administering a caution or referring the matter to a restorative justice conference. (In Chapter 9 we will examine the role of police discretion in the overpolicing of Aboriginal communities, which produce disproportionately high rates of arrest and imprisonment.) There is little external scrutiny or judicial review of the legal basis for these decisions – which are have been described as "low visibility decisions".[80] The result is that the police act as "gatekeepers" of the criminal justice system; their decisions constitute a hidden dimension of the statistics about the rate of guilty pleas.

The final factor that we consider is the role of negotiation between the prosecution and the defence in criminal matters. The term "plea-bargaining" covers a variety of practices that can occur throughout the court hierarchy. They all have the aim of obtaining a guilty plea from the accused who hopes in return to

---

77   Feeley, n 30, 30.

78   In the Australian context, Russell Hogg describes the "high ceilings, elevated windows, wholly enclosed physical and visual space, sombre furnishings, distinctive spacial hierarchies and carefully ordered rituals" of 19th century courthouses in NSW, many of which still exist: R Hogg, "Law's Other Spaces" (2002) 6 *Law, Text, Culture* 29 at 36-37.

79   P Carlen, *Magistrates' Justice*, Martin Robertson, 1976, Ch 2. Aboriginal defendants, in particular, experience difficulties in coping with the question-and-answer technique of court-room interrogation, because of different cultural perceptions about what constitutes appropriate interpersonal behaviour. See J Kearins, "Factors Affecting Aboriginal Testimony" (1991) 16 *Legal Services Bulletin* 3.

80   J Goldstein, "Police Discretion not to Invoke the Criminal Process: Low-Visibility Decisions in the Administration of Justice" (1960) 69 *Yale Law Journal* 543. On police discretion generally, see O'Malley, n 12, Ch 4; and Bronitt and McSherry, *Principles of Criminal Law*, n 14, 750ff in the context of policing public order.

receive some concession in sentencing. These practices range from negotiations between the prosecution and the defence about withdrawing a particular charge laid in return for a plea of guilty to a less serious charge, to seeking some prior indication from a judge of the likely sentence if the accused pleads guilty.[81] These practices, where conducted secretly and informally, have attracted judicial criticism: the High Court expressing concern that judicial involvement in such negotiations represents the administration of justice "behind closed doors".[82] A system of sentence indication was introduced as a pilot scheme in New South Wales by legislation in 1992, though it was subsequently discontinued after an evaluation found that the scheme had not led to the reduction in workload for the courts.[83] That said, there remain high levels of support for promoting discussion between the prosecution and the defence. In its 1980 Interim Report on *Sentencing of Federal Offenders* the Australian Law Reform Commission stated that in a survey of Australian judges 56.7 per cent approved of plea bargaining between the defence and the prosecution. The ALRC commented that "such bargaining is certainly part of the criminal justice system in all Australian jurisdictions".[84]

The term "plea bargaining" has been described as misleading in the Australian context where judges, unlike in the United States, are not responsible for brokering and sanctioning the terms of these agreements. "Charge negotiation" better describes the common practice by which the prosecution may withdraw a charge on the promise that an accused will plead guilty to other charges; the effect of an early plea of guilty will operate as a significant mitigating factor or "discount" leading to a less harsh sentence. Take, as an example, the comments in *R v Winchester*[85] of Hunt CJ of the NSW Supreme Court:

> A plea of guilty is always a matter which must be taken into account when imposing sentence. The degree of leniency to be afforded will depend upon many different factors.

After listing factors such as when was the plea entered, and whether the plea is evidence of contrition or indicates co-operation in saving time and cost, he continued:

> The leniency is afforded in order to encourage early pleas of guilty so that the criminal list is more expeditiously disposed of and so that other cases, in which there is a genuine issue to be determined, will be brought on for hearing without delay.[86]

The pressures and incentives to plead to a lesser charge, however, can lead to injustices from both a victim and defence perspective, though in Australia, DPP Guidelines and Policies have been adopted aimed at ensuring that the prosecution

---

81 P Sallmann, *Report on Criminal Trials*, Australian Institute of Judicial Administration, 1985, 135-136.

82 *Bruce v R* (unreported, May 1976). See also *R v Marshall* [1981] VR 725 in which the Court of Criminal Appeal in Victoria similarly condemned this practice.

83 D Weatherburn, E Matka and B Lind, *Sentencing Indication Scheme Evaluation – Final Report*, NSW Bureau of Crime Statistics and Research, 1995.

84 Australian Law Reform Commission, *Interim Report on Sentencing of Federal Offenders*, 1980, 81.

85 (1992) 58 A Crim R 345 at 350.

86 In *Cameron v The Queen* (2002) 209 CLR 339 the High Court reviewed the appropriate discount applicable to the sentences where the accused pleads guilty at the first reasonable opportunity.

achieve a charge agreement that not only procures a guilty plea but adequately represents the criminality revealed by the facts.[87]

Research in the United States, the United Kingdom and Australia has shown that plea or charge bargaining is sufficiently prevalent to be an integral part of court processes in those countries.[88] One estimate has it that approximately 90 per cent of guilty pleas in the United States are negotiated.[89] The English Court of Appeal has, subject to certain limitations, given approval to plea bargaining that involves consultation between the trial judge in chambers and both defence and prosecution lawyers.[90] According to a study of plea bargaining in higher courts commissioned by the Australian Institute for Judicial Administration in 1995, private meetings in chambers are now very rare in Australia, although plea bargaining in other forms (that is, charge bargaining) was found to be wide-spread.[91]

There is less publicly documented evidence of plea bargaining practices in lower courts in Australia, though it has been noted that "these negotiations are regarded by those involved in them as an integral, albeit little discussed, aspect of the practice of Australian criminal law".[92] A 1980 study by the Legal Studies Department at La Trobe University in Victoria concluded that, although it may not be as overt a practice as in other countries, there is evidence that plea bargaining does occur. The study also suggested that these practices are more common in courts where legal representation of defendants is more frequent. Hence, its impact is likely to be less in the lower courts.[93]

Plea bargaining can be understood as one factor in a process which is seem-ingly geared towards "the automatic production of guilty pleas".[94] It is a process which has developed in response to demands for bureaucratic efficiency this is felt by courts at all levels, though especially by the lower courts. In turn, those demands are reinforced by the daily operation of this process. To highlight the contrast between this and the adversarial ideal it is useful to ask whose interests are served by these practices and in what ways.

Lippmann argues that plea bargaining works because all parties involved in the criminal courts, for their own reasons, see some value in it.[95] Magistrates are concerned to achieve high conviction rates but at the same time to exercise control and discretion in the court process. A high rate of guilty pleas allows court resources to be concentrated on sentencing decisions in which magistrates can

---

87   N Cowdrey, "Negotiating with the DPP especially under the Samuels Report" (2003) <http://www.odpp.nsw.gov.au/speeches/speeches.html>.

88   See J Baldwin and M McConville, *Negotiated Justice*, Martin Robertson, 1977, for a major UK study. See also K Mack and S Anleu, "Reform of Pre-Trial Criminal Procedure: Guilty Pleas" (1998) 22 *Criminal Law Journal* 263; J Bishop, *Prosecution Without Trial* Butterworths, 1989.

89   Sallmann, n 81, 140.

90   *R v Turner* (1970) 54 Cr App R 352.

91   See K Mack and SR Anleu, *Pleading Guilty: Issues and Practices*, AIJA, 1995, 136. This research is discussed in Mack and Anleu, n 88.

92   Sallmann, n 81, 142.

93   Legal Studies Department, La Trobe University, *Guilty, Your Worship: A Study of Victoria's Magistrates' Courts*, 1980, 40-41.

94   O'Malley, n 12, 130. There are many other factors, including the availability of legal represen-tation, the nature of the charge, and the defendant's experience as a repeat player in the court process.

95   Lippmann, n 74, 110.

demonstrate their sense of fairness and mercy.[96] Lippmann's study found that a greater proportion of the court's time was spent on sentencing decisions than on the determination of guilt.[97] A study of the operation of magistrates' courts in Victoria commented that "conviction is so far from the norm as to suggest that their main function is to decide on sentence".[98]

There are apparent benefits for other court personnel and officials in producing guilty pleas. Lippmann argues that the police prosecutors bear the burden of managing high caseloads and maintaining a steady turn-over of cases. The defence lawyers who appear in the lower courts (predominantly public or duty solicitors) have similar considerations to deal with, as well as the knowledge that they must work with other court personnel on a repeat basis. The purpose of plea bargaining and the processes associated with producing guilty pleas is to minimise, if not eliminate, the need for a trial.[99] In other words, the majority of criminal cases that go through the court system do not involve the use of full adversarial procedure.[100] If the great majority of defendants plead guilty, then the processing of criminal cases becomes more predictable and manageable for all concerned. As one example, when court administrators prepare the court lists they can make more accurate assessments about how much time to allocate to each case. Carlen has highlighted the significance of control over time in the court process. She found that:

> During judicial proceedings in magistrates' courts the timing of events is mono-polised by the police. They are the ones who set up the proceedings; it is their responsibility to see that all defendants arrive at court; it is their job to ensure that all relevant documents are in the hands of the clerk of the court. And policemen are very jealous of their competence in programming the criminal business. ...
>
> Policemen are well aware that concern with time-saving can influence their decision concerning the nature of the charge in the first place: "Most of them you just charge with being drunk, because if you say 'drunk and disorderly' they don't plead guilty. It's a waste of time". (policeman, Court A) And at the hearing both solicitors and defendants experience police pressure to save time.[101]

Finally, as already indicated, it is generally assumed that the defendant will be attracted towards a guilty plea because of the prospect of a lighter sentence (known as a sentence discount) for having pleaded guilty, and particularly for having done so at an early stage. The sentence discount is believed to exist in all jurisdictions, but its effect and formal status is not uniform. In most jurisdictions it is now explicitly provided for in sentencing legislation.[102] A study done by La

---

96 The importance of mercy in justifying the legal and social order has deep historical roots. See D Hay, "Property, Authority and the Criminal Law" in D Hay et al, *Albion's Fatal Tree: Crime and Society in Eighteenth Century England*, Penguin, 1977.

97 Lippmann, n 74, 109.

98 Legal Studies Department, La Trobe University, n 92, 39.

99 See J Willis, "Pre-Trial Decision Making" in G Zdenkowski, C Ronalds, and M Richardson (eds), *The Criminal Injustice System*, Vol 2, Pluto Press, 1987, 59. See also Willis, n 33, Ch 9.

100 Although, as Willis points out, plea-bargaining between lawyers "is clearly consistent with the adversarial system, with both parties, prosecution and defence, seeking what is in their best interest": Willis, "Pre-Trial Decision-Making", n 99, 86. See also M Feeley, "Plea Bargaining and the Structure of the Criminal Process" (1982) 7 *Justice System Journal* 338, arguing that plea bargaining in the United States is a consequence of increased adversariness.

101 Carlen, n 79, 25-26.

102 For a full discussion, see Mack and Anleu, n 91, 161.

Trobe University, before the trend towards formal statutory recognition of sentence discounts, found that there was not as strong a link as might be assumed between pleading guilty and receiving a lighter sentence, and that much depended on the type of case.[103] The difficulty in determining this correlation is further compounded by the trend in some jurisdictions, including Victoria, for judges to adopt an "instinctive synthesis" approach to sentencing in which the "discounts" for early pleas of the guilt are not disaggregated from the overall sentence.[104] The problem is the lack of transparency involved in "instinctive" approaches, which ultimately will undermine the public interest in promoting early pleas of guilty as defendants and their lawyers will not be able to see the benefits that are flowing from that early decision to plead guilty.[105]

All this gives us some idea about how the roles and expectations of different participants in the criminal court process differ from the traditional adversarial ideal. We need to go further than this, however. In seeking an adequate explanation to replace that ideal we must broaden our inquiry beyond the concerns of the individuals involved. Sociologists and criminologists have advanced a range of different theoretical frameworks to explain the empirical evidence.

In what has become a standard reference, American criminologist Herbert Packer in 1968 put forward two models of the criminal process.[106] As he expressed them, these models are ideal types. Criminal justice systems in different places and at different times will draw nearer to one or other of these models, depending upon the values pursued by that system.

First, there is the "due process model". Packer's argument has been summarised as follows:

> The due process model … enshrines the assumption that an accused is legally innocent until proven guilty. Throughout the [criminal justice] process it privileges formal procedures for safeguarding the rights of the accused. The testing of fact at the trial takes precedence over the informal fact-finding processes of the police. Efficiency is subordinated to reliability and control over the exercise of official power. Legal representation of the accused is crucial in the due process model.[107]

---

103 In traffic cases guilty pleas were found to attract more severe sentences, while in theft and violence cases milder sentences resulted: see Legal Studies Department, La Trobe University, n 92. Note that this study was conducted before s 4 of the *Penalties and Sentencing Act 1985* (Vic) was enacted.

104 There is no authoritative resolution of which approach should be followed, though support for instinctive synthesis can be found in *Pearce v The Queen* (1998) 194 CLR 610 at 624 [46] per McHugh, Hayne and Callinan JJ; *AB v The Queen* (1999) 198 CLR 111 at 156 [115] per Hayne J and at 120-123 [13]-[19] per McHugh J. The competing models of sentencing decision-making are discussed in S Traynor and I Potas, "Sentencing Methodology: Two-tiered or Instinctive Synthesis" (2002) 25 *Sentencing Trends and Issues* <http://www.judcom.nsw.gov.au/st/st25/>.

105 In *Cameron v The Queen* (2002) 209 CLR 339 the majority did not decide whether instinctive synthesis was the correct approach. McHugh J (dissenting) was strongly in favour. Kirby J, by contrast, was highly critical of the instinctive synthesis approach on the grounds that it lacked transparency, defeated the public interest in promoting early guilty pleas and was ultimately unfair to defendants: at 362 per Kirby J.

106 Packer, n 67.

107 R Hogg, "Perspectives on the Criminal Justice System" in M Findlay, SJ Egger and J Sutton (eds), *Issues in Criminal Justice Administration*, Allen and Unwin, 1983, 3, 4.

This model expresses the traditional ideal of a court system operating according to the dictates of the rule of law, including the presumption of innocence. The image that is often used in explaining this model is to liken the court system to an obstacle course made up of a succession of clear and precise rules and procedures designed to test out the state's case against the accused.[108]

At the other end of the continuum lies the "crime control model". As its name suggests, this model sees the primary role of the criminal justice process as the repression or containment of criminal activity. Using Russell Hogg's synopsis of Packer's argument once more:

> In the crime control model the repression or control of criminal conduct is seen to be the central function of criminal justice. Effective repression of crime is understood to be a necessary condition of individual liberty. The focus is upon efficiency, speed, finality and uniformity. An administrative model of criminal justice takes priority over the demands of the criminal justice system. The system is weighted towards the initial processes of apprehension and investigation so that those who are "probably guilty" are rapidly processed through the system. A presumption of guilt thus operates from an early stage in police investigation.[109]

Not surprisingly, this model stresses the importance of guilty pleas, since they minimise the need for time consuming court-room argument. For this reason it is sometimes called the "Plea-Bargaining" model.[110]

Although Packer's two-model analysis does draw attention to competing demands and tensions in the criminal justice system, it is somewhat limited. Whilst it is sometimes described as a continuum, it seems to assume that the due process end of the scale is the basic reference point or normative ideal, while the crime control model is depicted as a deviation from that ideal. On the one hand, we revere due-process protections such as the right to silence, the standard of "beyond reasonable doubt", the rule against admitting evidence of prior convictions etc. On the other hand, we are told that the system operates in such a way that the police, court officials, lawyers and the judiciary have considerable discretion in negotiating their way around those protections. In this way Packer's argument reproduces the normative framework of the "law in the books/law in practice" dichotomy, and therefore suffers from the same problems.[111]

In particular, we might ask how great the difference between the two models really is. It can be argued that the ideas of "due process" and "crime control" simply express competing values *within* a broad liberal framework.[112] For example, we would expect deontological liberals to sympathise with the due process model, evaluating the criminal justice system in terms of what is right, rather than in terms of consequences (an attitude summed up in the legal aphorism that it is better that 10 guilty people go free than that one innocent person be convicted.[113] Conversely, those we described earlier in the book as teleological liberals would presumably

---

108 Packer uses this imagery himself: n 67, 163.

109 Hogg, n 107, 4.

110 For example in Feeley, n 30, 27.

111 See the discussion of gap theory in Chapter 1 above.

112 A point also made by Hogg, n 107, 5.

113 See *R v Hobson* (1823) 1 Lew CC 261.

find the crime control model, with its concern for ends rather than means, more appropriate.[114]

Other researchers have sought to elaborate on Packer's approach by developing alternative models to explain the workings of the criminal justice system. We consider some of these below. In many cases these alternatives can be seen as attempts to explain more adequately the tensions that exist between different liberal views of that system.

One set of alternative models draws our attention to the managerial and efficiency-oriented aspects of modern court systems. We take, as an example, the model suggested by Bottoms and McLean in the conclusion to their empirical study of the decisions which defendants must make as they are processed through the criminal justice system.[115] They argue that, taken separately, neither of Packer's models gives us a full explanation of the criminal court process. They suggest a third paradigm, which they call the "liberal bureaucratic model". This model is distinguished, first, from a strict crime control model, because:

> The Liberal Bureaucratic Model holds ... that the protection of individual liberty, and the need for justice to be done and to be seen to be done, must ultimately override the importance of the repression of criminal conduct.[116]

The liberal bureaucratic model is also said to differ from a pure due process approach:

> The liberal bureaucrat is a practical man; he realises that things have to get done, systems have to be run. It is right that the defendant shall have substantial protections; crime control is not the overriding value of the criminal justice system. But these protections must have a limit. If it were not so, then the whole system of criminal justice, with its ultimate value to the community in the form of liberal and humane crime control, would collapse. Moreover, it is right to build in sanctions to deter those who might otherwise use their "Due Process" rights frivolously, or to "try it on"; an administrative system at State expense should not exist for this kind of time-wasting.[117]

Bottoms and McClean thus recognise that both of Packer's models play a part, but that in practice each is compromised by the competing demands of the other. Their liberal bureaucratic model is, in many ways, an amalgamation of these other models; it is an attempt to explain how and why that process of compromise works.[118]

Bottoms and McLean argue, for example, that their model helps us to understand the role of publicly provided defence lawyers in the criminal process.

114　See the discussion on "Rights" in Chapter 2 above.

115　Bottoms and McClean, n 76; another example is developed in M King, *The Framework of Criminal Justice*, Croom Helm, 1981.

116　Bottoms and McClean, n 76, 229.

117　Ibid.

118　It is appropriate at this stage to note Galanter's warning that whilst the term "bureaucracy" is used frequently "as a code word to refer to the slide from individualized treatment into stereotyped routines, and from adversary combat to collaborative negotiation", it is nevertheless inaccurate to label the courts as bureaucracies. This is because courts lack many key features of modern bureaucracies, such as close hierarchical control and supervision between participants in the system. See M Galanter, "Adjudication, Litigation and Related Phenomena" in L Lipson and S Wheeler (eds), *Law and the Social Sciences*, Russell Sage, 1986, 151, 172-173.

Although the provision of legal representation reinforces a central tenet of due process ideals, Bottoms and McLean found that these lawyers commonly advised clients who were "possibly innocent" to plead guilty. This is because the lawyers knew that if the client pleaded not guilty a trial would be required. If the outcome of that trial was a guilty verdict, the lawyers reasoned that the subsequent sentence may be harsher than if the client simply pleaded guilty. In short, argue Bottoms and McLean, the provision of defence lawyers reinforces the liberal bureaucratic model.[119]

Another attempt to provide a theoretical framework within which to understand the operations of the criminal courts comes from Doreen McBarnet, whose arguments introduced this section. Like Bottoms and McLean, McBarnet concludes her study by considering, and then questioning, the two-model approach suggested by Packer. As we have already noted, one consequence of applying Packer's models is an image of the lower courts as failing to fulfil the promises of the law about liberty, rights and justice. That image implicitly accepts the upper tier ideal of the courts; it suggests that practices in the lower courts occur *in spite of* the law. McBarnet argues, to the contrary, that lower court practices occur *because they are permitted* by the law. In effect, the law gives licence to magistrates and police to deviate from the rhetoric of due process legality.[120] Her empirical analysis of the criminal process revealed Packer's models as drawing a "false distinction": to understand properly the lower criminal courts we need to explore the gap, not between "the law in the books" and "the law in action", but between the ideology of the law (respect for individual rights etc) and the substance of the law:

> If the practice of criminal justice does not live up to its rhetoric one should not look only to the interactions and negotiations of those who put the law into practice but to the law itself. One should not look just to how the rhetoric of justice is subverted intentionally or otherwise by policemen bending the rules, by lawyers negotiating adversariness out of existence, by out-of-touch judges or biased magistrates: one must also look at how it is subverted *in the law*. Police and court officials need not abuse the law to subvert the principles of justice; they need only use it. Deviation from the rhetoric of legality and justice is institutionalised in the law itself.[121]

In the following extract from McBarnet's book, she develops an argument to explain how it is that the legal system can routinely depart from the rule of law and yet at the same time preserve the rhetorical power of that ideology. Much of the answer, she suggests, lies in the idea of making law through cases. She goes on to discuss the connections between the case law method and the rule of law.

---

119 See Bottoms and McClean, n 76, 231. Similarly, Doreen McBarnet argues that the provision of legal aid is not likely to have any impact on lower court practice: "even with a lawyer the defendant in the lower court would have the odds weighted against him". This, she argues, is because the lower courts are performing a different social role to the higher courts: "they are simply in the business of summary justice", McBarnet, n 63, 138.

120 See D Brown's review of McBarnet's book in *Australian Society*, 1 September 1983, 33.

121 McBarnet, n 63, 155-156, emphasis in original.

Doreen McBarnet, *Conviction: Law, the State and the Construction of Justice* (1981)

(footnotes omitted)

A legal system based on case law (and even the states that boast codified law also use case law in a modified form) operates at the level of the concrete case: is highly particularistic. Hence the justification of excepting the specific case from the application of the general rule without destroying the general rule *per se*. The rhetoric and the law operate at two different levels, the abstract and the concrete, and the contradiction is operationally negated and a clear clash prevented by each being pigeon-holed out of the other's realm of discourse. The rhetoric is rarely actually denied, it is simply whittled away by exceptions, provisos, qualifications.

Law in this form is rather like a Russian doll. You begin with the rhetoric and a single, apparently definite, condition which on closer inspection turns out to contain another less clear condition which in turn opens up to reveal even more ifs and buts and vaguenesses, reducing so often to the unpredictability of "it all depends on the circumstances" – what criteria we use in your case depends on your case. This form provides an extremely potent way of maintaining the facade of civil rights ideology – the first doll – while in fact allowing extensive *legal* police powers. Cases can readily accommodate both statements of general principle and the exceptions of particular circumstances. Thus an appeal on the grounds of abuse of a legal right can be rejected because of the circumstances of the particular case, while at the same time a grand statement reiterating that right is made. The conflicting rhetoric of due process and practical demands for crime control are thus both simultaneously maintained and the gap between rhetoric and practice is managed out of existence. Lawyers may boast of the flexibility and individualised treatment afforded by case law but it also plays a potent role in maintaining the ideology of justice. ...

THE CASE LAW FORM AND THE RULE OF LAW
The principles of justice are part of the ideology of the democratic state not only in their substance but in a much more fundamental way, in the very idea that there should be principles at all, that those who wield the power of the state should not do so arbitrarily but should themselves be governed by law. The idea of legality itself is an essential ideological form of the democratic state; its rule is the rule of law.

The idea of the rule of law is central not just to the arena of criminal justice, perhaps the most explicitly coercive aspect of state-individual relations, but to sociological theories of law in general in capitalist society. One strand, epitomised by Weber (1954) and Neumann (1957) emphasises dependability or certainty as its one essential element; the rule of law is the rule of *known* law. Concerned more with civil than criminal law, they relate the development of law in capitalist society to the need for commerce to operate in a situation of certainty, in the knowledge that contracts could be relied on to be fulfilled or enforced. Second, EP Thompson has sparked off debate by challenging the crude Marxist notion that the rule of law is merely a mask for the rule of the dominant class. Though he qualified his argument as being only certainly applicable to 18th-century England, it has been generalised in debate to the question of the function of law in capitalist society in general. He argues that the ideology of justice is no mere mask but also a potential for genuine transcendence of class interests: "The law may be rhetoric but it need not be empty rhetoric" (EP

Thompson, 1975, p 263). There are two reasons for this. Class relations are expressed in law "*through the forms of law*" (*Ibid*, 262). These are independent of class interests and Thompson implies, a constraint upon them. What is more, people are not, says Thompson, mystified by the first man to put on a wig. The principles of justice, once declared, take a force of their own in that they have to be lived up to if their ideological functions are to succeed. The rulers thus become "prisoners of their own rhetoric" (*ibid*, 263). The essential issue here is the autonomy of law, the idea of the rule of law above man as of theoretical as well as ideological validity.

For both these strands of theorising and debate on the rule of law the form of case law must raise serious questions, questions which have indeed been raised at various historical moments in the politics and ideology of Common Law. Certainly one can find quotations from judges on the need for certainty in the law. In 1754 Lord Hardwicke noted: "I think authorities established are so many laws and receding from them unsettles property; and uncertainty is the unavoidable consequence" (cited in Holdsworth, 1934, p 188). But such statements jar so clearly not just with the practice of judges but with the *form* of the case law method, that one cannot help but speculate that Weber's description of a move to "rational" law for the sake of certainty traces the development of an ideology of law rather than a description of either its practice or its form.

Case law is discretionary and particularistic; it does not operate at the level of general rules. What is more, … it only operates *post hoc* – it does not make law until *after* a dispute has made it into an issue. Of course there are precedents to constrain judgements. But they need only constrain the justification of the decision rather than the decision itself. Indeed the discretion invested in judges, and the fact that the case comes before them only after dispute, only because "informed lawyers disagree" and can make out a case for both sides, means "a judge's decision either way will not be considered a failure to perform his judicial responsibilities" (Greenawalt, cited in R Cross, 1977, p 221). What Hart (1961) calls the open texture of law allows wide scope in the use and application of precedent. Indeed precedents can be employed to do the exact opposite of their original use, as examples in this study show. The meaning attached to precedent deserves attention too. Holdsworth argues that the method of making law by precedent was only accepted historically by the judiciary on condition that it was not an overbearing constraint (Holdsworth, 1934, p 180). This was accomplished by developing their own ideology of law. Coke, Hale, and Blackstone were all firm exponents of the view that decisions and precedents were not law but merely "evidence of what the law is". The result is that: "The courts must decide what weight is to be attached to the evidence in different sets of circumstances. Holdsworth concludes:

> The manner in which they have decided this question has left them many means of escape from the necessity of literal obedience to the general rule that decided cases must always be followed. (ibid, p 185)

Structurally indeed there *could* not historically have been a systematic following of precedents quite simply because there was no systematic reporting of cases until the end of the 19th century, a matter which provided further justification for the judges to ignore precedent on the basis that reports were not authoritative. Cross suggests that with more systematic law reporting and restructuring of the courts, by the 19th century the idea of binding precedent had become more rigid (R Cross, 1977, 23). but it did not last long, for he also observes that the English doctrine of precedent is *currently* in a state of flux (ibid, 6). Though the Court of Appeal is still in theory bound by its own and the House of Lords' decisions, there are several well-known cases in which it has not followed them, while in 1966 the House of Lords stated quite explicitly it need not be bound by its own precedents. This is not to say that precedent is never followed in the making of case law; it may even *usually* be followed. It is merely to say that it *need* not be a rigid constraint. Indeed the very degree of constraint involved is, it would seem, subject to the changing decisions of the judges themselves, the people it is supposed to constrain. The doctrine of precedent may thus be placed more aptly in the rhetoric rather than the actual procedure of justice. The doctrine of precedent may tell us where the ideology of the rule of law is grounded and how it is maintained, but it tells us very little about the practice of case law – not just because of judicial techniques to used and avoid precedent but because of the nature of the ideology of precedent and the *post hoc* discretionary particularistic form of the case law method.

The result is that the law is so far from being certain as to be almost impossible to pin down. This study would never have taken the shape it has if I had been able, as an observer in courts unread in law at all, to get a precise answer from the lawyers I eagerly asked what the law of search, or arrest, or the right to silence, actually was. The answer was a list of cases all with different specific lines – in *R v Green* the decision of X but of course in *R v Brown* it was Y, – and so on. The textbooks offered the same, noting sometimes that the law on that point may be so and so. And soon it became clear that it was not my lack of legal learning that made the law so elusive: that was the nature of the law, a will-o'-the-wisp pausing but a moment before the next decision, and then only "clear" for the particular circumstances of that particular case.

When law takes such a form there *can be* no fixed or certain rule of law. The Weberian thesis of the bourgeois need for certain law must be challenged by even a perfunctory analysis of the form of law, especially in the common law systems of both the first capitalist society, Britain, and the most advanced, the United States, which illustrate the case law method *par excellence*. But it is not just common law that is based on cases; modern law *per se*, however codified in general, comes down in the end to application to concrete situations, to case law. Law in modern society, far from being certain, is as elusive and as adaptable as a chameleon.

This elusiveness also plays its part in the mystique of law. What can be more mystical than a statement of what the law is which is not only veiled by the need to know where and how to look for it, but which turns out when you find it to be provisional, particular, and only really ascertainable for your specific question if you take it to court? The portrayal by Thompson – and others – of the mystique of law is too simple. People may not be bamboozled by the wigs and ceremony and jargon of the law, but they are quite likely to be bamboozled by the law itself. It is not just that they are in their ignorance puzzled by the law, it is also quite simply that the law is a puzzle. Its particularistic *post hoc* form inevitably makes it so.[122]

Although we have not attempted to present all of the competing models that have been advanced to explain the criminal court system, the above sample should impress upon the reader the importance and role of theory in that endeavour.

---

122 Ibid 162-165. The works referred to in the extract are: R Cross, *Precedent in English Law*, Oxford UP, 1977; HLA Hart, *The Concept of Law*, Oxford UP, 1961; W Holdsworth, "Case Law" (1934) 50 *Law Quarterly Review* 180; F Neumann, *The Democratic and Authoritarian State*, Collier Macmillan, 1957; EP Thompson, *Whigs and Hunters*, Allen Lane, 1975; M Weber, *On Law and Economy in Society* (M Rheinstein, ed), Harvard UP, 1954.

Empirical study is only an important first step in opening up our view of the courts. It is important to understand how the legal rules shape and respond to criminal justice practices. Socio-legal research like McBarnet's is important because it "encourages deeper reflection on the structure and functions of law in the criminal process and the apparent tensions and contradictions within legal doctrine and its fundamental principles".[123] The role of the theoretical models is to put this information together, to construct possible explanations and to suggest new avenues of inquiry.

(e) Civil litigation

In comparison with criminal cases, there has been relatively little research done on the operation of the civil courts, particularly in Australia. This may be because civil cases lack the impact and drama that is promised (but, as we have seen, rarely provided) by the criminal justice system. Another reason may be that the area of civil litigation is less able to be defined succinctly. The category "civil cases" is a residual one, referring generally to cases that are non-criminal. Civil cases include claims for personal injury, debt recovery (which, in turn, includes mortgage recovery, hire purchase and other forms of consumer credit), landlord and tenant matters, defamation, family law (including dissolution, custody, access, main-tenance matters), actions for damages or other relief in both tort and contract, and company law, bankruptcy and administrative law matters. Along with this diversity of cases there is a diversity of claimants and defendants: individuals, corporations, governmental agencies and departments, covering all of the repeat player/one shotter combinations identified by Galanter and discussed in Chapter 4.[124] In short, the category of "civil cases" may not be as susceptible to the development of overarching models or explanations as is the case with criminal law.

One attempt to do this is found in Kenneth Scott's two models of the civil process.[125] First, Scott proposes a "conflict resolution model" according to which the purpose of civil process is to achieve an orderly and peaceful settlement of private disputes. The state supplies the mechanisms for achieving this, in the form of the court system and the rules of process and procedure. The state also supplies the substantive rules (for example, tort or contract law) which determine the scope of a party's claim. This model does not, however, dictate the content of these rules beyond the idea that they should be seen as "fair".[126] As Scott describes it, under this model the purpose of civil procedure is to serve the concerns of the *plaintiff* and to avoid more disorderly or violent methods of dealing with grievances.

The alternative model is described as the "behaviour modification model". Here the purpose of civil process is to change the behaviour of *defendants* by ensuring that they bear the costs of their wrongful actions. Faced with the prospect of having to pay compensation for a negligent action or a contractual breach a

---

123 Bronitt and McSherry, n 14, 40. Hogg, n 107, provides an overview and critique of these and other theoretical models. See also Feeley, n 30, 28-33; Bronitt and McSherry, n 14, 36-41.

124 See M Galanter, "Why the 'Haves' Come Out Ahead: Speculations on the Limits of Social Change" (1974) 9 *Law and Society Review* 95, extracted in Chapter 4 above.

125 K Scott, "Two Models of the Civil Process" (1975) 27 *Stanford Law Review* 937.

126 Ibid 937.

person (so it is assumed) will modify their behaviour and take the necessary precautions. This model sees the law as an instrument that can be used to bring about pre-determined outcomes or patterns of behaviour. The model has a strong resonance with economic theories of the common law which are discussed in Chapter 12.

Some idea of the overall pattern of civil litigation can be gained from the small amount of available data which details the types of matters which feature more prominently in the civil court process. It is worth emphasising here that there is very little recent empirical data on civil litigation in Australia. This is remarkable, given the comparatively rich variety of information that is available on the criminal litigation system. Turning to the data on civil litigation that is available, a study published by the Australian Institute of Judicial Administration contains figures of the types of civil cases commenced in New South Wales, Victoria and the ACT Supreme Courts between 1977-80.[127] Combining the figures for those jurisdictions provides the following sample of percentages: personal injury cases – 25.75 per cent; liquidated claims for money owing – 26.25 per cent; mortgage default and landlord/tenant matters – 18.1 per cent.

The distinctions between civil and criminal litigation may seem obvious, having to do with the role of the state in criminal trials, and the differences in outcome (for example, penalty versus compensation).[128] Beyond these factors, however, there are important ideological themes that are employed to distinguish civil from criminal cases. One theme derives from the way in which liberal thought divides social life into public and private spheres.[129] Whereas criminal law is regarded as dealing with public concerns, civil law is said to be concerned (for the most part) with the private rights and duties of individuals. Secondly, in contrast to the coercive nature of the criminal justice system, the instigation of civil proceedings is said to be a voluntary matter. One of the consequences of characterising civil actions as private and voluntary is that the conduct of these cases is regarded as being in the hands of both parties. Whilst there are detailed procedural rules governing the various steps in the civil litigation process (for example, service of documents, answering inquiries etc) the court traditionally has had no formal role in the preparation or the progress of the matter. The theory is that the state simply provides a means whereby knowledgeable and adequately resourced individuals can resolve their private disputes if they so choose. Civil law is regarded, generally speaking, as facilitative rather than mandatory. That the courts are taking an increasing role in the conduct of civil cases may tell us something about changing ideas to do with privacy, although it is too early to say at this stage.

---

127 Cranston et al, n 30, 25 Table 3.9. See also T Matruglio, *So Who Does Use the Court?* Civil Justice Research Centre, Law Foundation of New South Wales, 1993.

128 The increased use of "civil penalties" in Australian legislation (eg *Corporations Act 2001* (Cth), *Trade Practices Act 1974* (Cth), *Environment Protection and Biodiversity Act 1999* (Cth)) blurs this distinction. A civil penalty is a monetary penalty imposed as a consequence of the contravention of a designated legislative provision. These penalties have a punitive purpose, but do not involve a criminal conviction, and the case is argued on the civil standard of proof. See Australian Law Reform Commission, *Principled Regulation: Federal Civil and Administrative Penalties in Australia*, Report 95, 2002.

129 See the discussion on "Liberty" in Chapter 2 above.

Given all this, it should come as no surprise that the law also permits the possibility that one or both of the parties may discontinue or settle their action at any time, right up until the stage when the court makes a final decision on the case. (Indeed, there are increasingly financial and procedural incentives to settle.) The following extract by Ross Cranston elaborates on this, and also the question of judgments in default of the defendant entering a defence, which may or may not indicate a settlement.

Ross Cranston, *Law, Government and Public Policy* (1987)
(footnotes omitted)

Formal adjudication of civil law cases is atypical. Australian civil courts dispose of the bulk of cases by routine administration or by providing a forum in which cases are settled. Characterized in this way, the civil courts parallel other organizations in society to a greater extent than if focus were to be, as it often is, on adjudication alone. Whether handling cases by routine administration or by facilitating settlement is desirable is a separate issue from that of describing the manner in which courts actually work in practice. However, the normative question inevitably arises, just as it does in the criminal courts, where the counterparts of routine administration and settlement are the routine sentencing of those pleading guilty in lower courts on the one hand, and plea bargaining on the other.

Routine administration
Much of what the courts do in disposing of cases involves routine administration – approving outcomes agreed elsewhere or determined by structural factors. A court order might be desired to guarantee compliance with those outcomes or because it is a precondition to further action. One aspect of routine administration is the consent judgment, where parties have settled a case and simply entered judgment. With routine processing, court officials undertake a limited inquiry to ensure that an application fits established categories (often, this only involves checking that documents are correctly completed) and then give their imprimatur by entering judgment. There are no contested issues, as where both parties want a divorce and have agreed on custody and property. (Divorce is an example of a court order being a legal prerequisite to persons taking certain action, in the particular case, remarrying.) As with divorce, a court might order an individual's bankruptcy or the winding up of a company in a routine manner when there are no disputed matters. Nonetheless, such orders have profound consequences – a change in a person's status in the case of bankruptcy (similarly with divorce) and the end of a company's existence in the case of a winding up.

Debt collection and mortgage default are well recognized as areas where the civil courts frequently engage in routine processing of cases. As noted, such claims typically result from institutions such as business, banks and building societies taking action against individuals. While not legally necessary, a judgment might be valuable to a creditor or mortgagee taking further action such as seeking the insolvency of a debtor or writing off the debt to tax. Although individuals might have a defence or cross-claim in relation to debt and mortgage claims, these are not always raised because of the cost – the very fact of a debt or possession action indicates a lack of financial resources – or because of social factors such as ignorance. Of the commenced cases in the survey mentioned above, [referring to the survey of Supreme Courts in NSW, Victoria, and the ACT] default judgments were entered in 14.9 per cent of the cases in the New South Wales Supreme Court, 23.1 per cent of cases in the Victorian Supreme

Court and 25.4 per cent of cases in the Australian Capital Territory Supreme Court. A survey of the Victorian County Court found that default judgments occurred in over a quarter of cases commenced, and official figures from the Melbourne Magistrates' Court show that over 95 per cent of the summons issued annually are default summons. Much default work involves debt collection and mortgage default on family homes.

Greater procedural safeguards ought to be introduced in the routine processing of cases, especially default work, since plaintiffs' cases are not always unassailable. One approach would be to require a plaintiff to establish a prima facie case as a precondition to obtaining a default judgment. At present plaintiffs who obtain a default judgment are in a strong position, because of the difficulties of having it set aside. The costs of legal action can be added to the original claim, and if judgment is entered an order for costs can be obtained. Even if there is no defence to a claim for debt or for possession, it is desirable to have a procedure whereby the possibility of assisting individuals to repay by instalments and over a longer period is always properly explored. ...

Adjudication

The attrition of cases means that it is relatively rare that the courts give authoritative rulings after a completed adjudication. Even cases which obtain a date for hearing might have settled by the hearing, or at the door of the court. In addition, cases sometimes settle after the hearing has commenced, which might occur because the weaknesses of a party's case are exposed or because the partial hearing resolves important issues, with the result that the parties are able to agree on the others.

Cases where there is a completed adjudication do not always match the adversary model of the conventional wisdom. It might be that there is only an applicant, and no defendant, as where a party obtains an ex parte injunction, an executor seeks an authoritative construction of a will, a company applies for its winding up, or a liquidator wants a ruling on how he (or she) ought to proceed. Moreover, adjudications do not necessarily involve a judge. Masters now perform work which in the past was the responsibility of judges. In New South Wales, for example, the Masters in the Common Law division of the Supreme Court try claims for damages for personal injuries in running down cases in the non-jury list. The Master in Equity in New South Wales, and the Master in Queensland, have not insignificant functions in company law and have delivered reported judgments in this area.

A further qualification is that where there is a jury trial, a completed adjudication will obviously not involve a final ruling on the case by the trial judge, although he or she rules on the evidence, instructs the jury on the relevant law and makes observations to them on the facts. Although jury trial for civil cases is uncommon or non-existent in other Australian jurisdictions, it is still firmly entrenched in New South Wales and Victoria. In New South Wales jury trial is confined mainly to personal-injury claims involving industrial accidents. Juries are common in Victoria in personal injury claims for both industrial and motor vehicle accidents. Jury trial in civil cases is said to have advantages such as enabling community participation in the administration of justice, providing a means by which community values are taken into account, acting as a check on judges and reducing appeals. By contrast it is said that juries in civil cases are costly, cause inconvenience and possibly monetary loss to jurors, require the retention of rigid, technical rules of evidence, and introduce irrationality into decision-making which cannot readily be appealed against.

Even if these qualifications are taken into account, adjudication is still far removed from the world of most jurisprudents. Delays, expense, and tactics all distort the ideal model. Outcomes may reflect the nature, interests and representation of the parties, rather than the legal merits. Llewellyn described the position neatly in relation to the right to sue for damages for breach of contract:

> [T]he right could rather more accurately be phrased somewhat as follows: if the other party does not perform as agreed, you can sue, and if you have a fair lawyer, and nothing goes wrong with your witnesses or the jury, *and* you give up four or five days of time and some ten to thirty percent of the proceeds, and wait two to twenty months, you will *probably* get judgment for a sum considerably less than what the performance would have been worth – which, if the other party is solvent, and has not secreted his assets, you can, in further due course, collect with six percent interest for delay.[130]

The few and, as we noted earlier, dated figures that are available give support to the picture described by Cranston. According to Crawford:

> In the Victorian County Court, half the cases commenced in 1981 were for debt (ie liquidated claims): of these 51 per cent led to default or summary judgements, and less than 3 per cent were listed for trial.[131]

Similarly, the survey of Supreme Courts in three Australian jurisdictions, referred to above, found that during the survey period only 7.8 per cent of civil cases commenced in NSW were heard to completion (the corresponding figures for Victoria and the ACT were 2.7 and 3.3 per cent respectively).[132]

The points made by Cranston are echoed in a study of a civil court in London conducted by Maureen Cain.[133] In her sample of cases, Cain found that default judgments were entered in 59.5 per cent of cases. Her conclusion was that in civil cases "the court settles disputes between two actively participating parties in only one quarter of the non-familial cases with which it deals".[134] Cain notes that bureaucratic processing is thus a feature of both civil and criminal courts, but she argues that there is an important difference: in criminal courts the routinisation of justice is not openly publicised (as shown by McBarnet), whereas in civil courts it is "intended and public":

> It happens explicitly and openly, usually by means of a formal default procedure in which there is little scope for either judicial or administrative discretion. The procedure is based on the assumption that there will be no defence in most cases. And with matters being set down for two months ahead it is plain that the court could not function if a full adversary procedure were in operation.[135]

If we combine the points made by Cranston and Cain, and read them together with the earlier discussion on "non-legal" responses to legal problems,[136] we can

---

130   R Cranston, *Law, Government and Public Policy*, Oxford UP, 1987 63-64; 66-68. The final quote comes from K Llewellyn, "A Realistic Jurisprudence – The Next Step" (1930) 30 *Columbia Law Review* 431 at 437-438.

131   J Crawford, *Australian Courts of Law*, 2nd ed, Oxford UP, 1988, 108.

132   Cranston et al, n 30, Table 3.13.

133   M Cain, "Where are the Disputes? A Study of a First Instance Civil Court in the UK" in M Cain and K Kulcsar (eds), *Disputes and the Law*, Akademiai Kiado, 1983, 119. Note that the civil jurisdiction of the court in the study was limited to claims for amounts up to £2000.

134   Cain, n 133, 121.

135   Ibid.

136   See Chapter 4 above.

develop a broad picture of the processing of civil disputes. Despite the paucity of statistics, it can be asserted confidently that only a very small proportion of civil disputes make it as far as a judicial decision at the end of a fully contested trial. A useful image which captures this is that of a "leaky hose", where most disputes are diverted from the formal justice system before reaching the end of the process.[137] At the risk of some over-simplification we can represent the process as follows:[138]

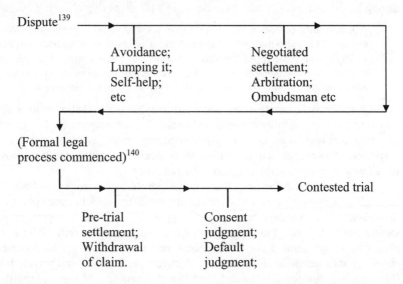

Dispute[139]

Avoidance;
Lumping it;
Self-help;
etc

Negotiated
settlement;
Arbitration;
Ombudsman etc

(Formal legal
process commenced)[140]

Contested trial

Pre-trial
settlement;
Withdrawal
of claim.

Consent
judgment;
Default
judgment;

This diagram illustrates the point that the settlement of disputes before they become cases, and of cases before they reach the stage of a contested trial, is an integral part of the civil process:

> [T]he negotiated settlement of civil cases is not a marginal phenomenon; it is not an innovation; it is not some unusual alternative to litigation. It is only a slight exaggeration to say that it *is* litigation.[141]

---

137 A metaphor suggested by Roman Tomasic.

138 This diagram is a compilation of various analyses, but in particular see M Galanter, "The Radiating Effects of Courts" in Boyum and Mather, n 72, 118-119.

139 W Felstiner, R Abel and A Sarat, in "The Emergence and Transformation of Disputes: Naming, Blaming, Claiming ..." (1980-81) 15 *Law and Society Review* 631, argue that disputes are social constructs. That is, a dispute is defined as such as a result of complex social processes by which a person identifies an experience as injurious (naming), transforms it into a grievance (blaming), and then communicates that grievance to the person(s) believed to be responsible (claiming).

140 It is appropriate to note here that the courts are only one of the forums in which official decisions are made. Indeed, as Wexler has commented, "[m]ost of the decisions which affect a person's legal rights and duties are not made in courts". They are made by a diversity of non-judicial officials. To choose one example, staff in the local social security office make many decisions each day (eg eligibility for unemployment benefits) that have considerable impact on the lives of many people. Our legal tradition can produce a rather one-sided account of the nature and the sites of decision-making in our society. See S Wexler, "Non-Judicial Decision Making" (1975) 13 *Osgoode Hall Law Journal* 839.

141 M Galanter, "'... A Settlement Judge, not a trial Judge:' Judicial Mediation in the United States" (1985) 12 *Journal of Law and Society* 1 (emphasis in original).

The point at which a dispute leaves the system is affected by many factors, two important ones being the type and setting of the dispute, and the relative power and experience of the parties.

As to the first of these factors, Marc Galanter has suggested that some cases may be fully adjudicated because one of the parties sees particular value in having a judicial pronouncement on the matter – there may be a "premium placed on having an external agency make the decision". He gives the following examples:

> [A]n insurance company functionary may want to avoid responsibility for a large payout ... Or there may be value to an actor in showing some external audience (a creditor or the public) that no stone has been left unturned ... Or external decision may be sought where the case is so complex or the outcome so indeterminate that it is too unwieldy or costly to arrange a settlement.[142]

Alternatively, in some cases one party may consider that a judicial decision will lead to "unacceptably harsh or calamitous"[143] consequences. For example, a governmental regulatory body may prefer to negotiate a solution with a business suspected of improper activity, rather than seeking to apply statutory provisions which would jeopardise the positions of employees.

As to the second factor – the relative power of the parties – Cain's study highlights cases in which there were significant differences between plaintiffs and defendants. Her findings add further support to Galanter's repeat player/one shotter analysis.[144] She found that private individuals formed only 10.9 per cent of plaintiffs. In her sample the civil process was used mainly (in 86.3 per cent of cases) by state agencies (for example, electricity authorities) and private business (for example, finance companies), and that the majority of these plaintiffs were repeat players. The defendants in these actions were mainly private citizens (in 83.9 per cent of cases). Where "central state agencies" were the plaintiffs, private citizens were defendants in 98.5 per cent of cases. Other types of plaintiffs brought actions against private citizens in the following proportion of cases: local authorities – 100 per cent; private business – 69.4 per cent; and private citizens – 73.7 per cent.

Cain found that over 80 per cent of these cases were debt recovery actions. The organisational plaintiffs regarded use of the court process as an important mechanism in securing general compliance with loan obligations. They argued that:

> [U]npaid bills had to be "chased" because if it got known that their company or agency did not take defaulters to court, then nobody would pay. *They were concerned with general deterrence.*[145]

Given this attitude, the high proportion of debt cases, when combined with the disparity between the parties in most of these cases (that is, repeat player versus

---

142 Galanter, n 118, 203, citing H Ross, *Settled out of Court: The Social Process of Insurance Claims Adjustment*, Aldine, 1970.

143 Galanter, n 141, 2.

144 Again, some caution is needed in using these labels. As Galanter warns, not all businesses are repeat players, nor are all individuals necessarily one shotters; see the extract from Galanter in Chapter 4 of this book.

145 Cain, n 106, 130 (emphasis added).

one shotter), calls into question the dominant image of civil cases as private and voluntary forums for the resolution of disputes.[146]

It is interesting to compare the results from Cain's study with figures from the survey of Australian Supreme Courts, referred to earlier.[147] In the latter, during the three-year survey period it was found that approximately one-half of all civil actions were commenced by individuals (about half of these cases being personal injury claims). The proportion of individual plaintiffs increased as cases proceeded further along the litigation process; according to Cranston, more than four fifths of cases listed for trial had individuals as plaintiffs (again, most of these were personal injury cases).[148] Conversely, the proportion of cases in which individuals were defendants declined as cases proceeded through the litigation process. Cranston reports that the majority of these cases were debt or mortgage default matters, and many were either settled or dealt with by default judgment.[149] The contrast with Cain's study, then, lies in the higher proportion of individuals as plaintiffs found in the Australian study. The explanation for this difference may well lie in the different levels of courts being studied (a first instance civil court in Cain's study, and Supreme Courts in the Australian study) and, consequently, the different type and monetary value of case involved (debt matters as opposed to personal injury claims).

Thus far we have concentrated on civil cases between different types of parties. We conclude this section by considering briefly disputes between parties with more or less equal bargaining power (for example, business against business, which represented 11.5 per cent of cases commenced, and 3.2 per cent of cases listed in the NSW Supreme Court between 1977-80).[150] In the previous chapter we referred to studies in the 1960s and 1970s which examined how business people dealt with contract disputes. It was found that such disputes were frequently settled without reference to express contractual rights or legal sanctions. The attitude of the disputants was that it would be "poor form" to resort to heavy-handed legal tactics. Since the parties anticipated future dealings with each other, their concern was that use of the law would put future commercial relationships in jeopardy, and possibly create an adverse business reputation.

However, while it may be infrequent for such disputes to involve the full trial process, it has been argued that the courts do exert an influence over the processes of settlement and negotiation between disputants. These negotiations are said to be conducted "in the shadow of the law".[151] That is, the mere existence of court decisions and court rules (especially those dealing with the awarding of costs) can shape and constrain the process of negotiating disputes outside the courts. Indeed, it has been argued that one of the significant roles played by courts in modern society is to send out signals which can restrain or elicit, legitimate or stigmatise

---

146 We should, of course, be wary of extrapolating the results of one study to other courts in other jurisdictions. Nevertheless, findings such as these should alert us to the type of questions that need to be asked when we assess our own court system.

147 The following information is taken from Cranston, n 130, 51-54.

148 Ibid 51.

149 Ibid 51.

150 Ibid 56.

151 R Mnookin and L Kornhauser, "Bargaining in the Shadow of the Law: The Case of Divorce" (1979) 88 *Yale Law Journal* 950.

certain behaviours and courses of conduct, long before any court involvement in an actual dispute.[152]

Although the "shadow of the law" image is powerful we should be careful to avoid generalisations. In recent years there is some indication that in some types of civil case the image may not be accurate. In Australia, parties in company takeover battles have increasingly resorted to the use of court proceedings.[153] Even here, though, this use of the courts is only intended to serve limited purposes. Directors seeking to defend their company against the takeover bid of an unwelcome corporate raider are likely to initiate court action automatically as a method of delaying the takeover, effectively buying some time while further defensive tactics are finalised.[154] These court cases typically involve quite narrow technical issues, such as a challenge to some aspect of the formal documentation that is required by the legislation on takeovers. The fact that so few of these cases ever go on to the appeal courts reinforces the view that what is important to the parties is the tactical advantage that is gained, rather than settling the legal issue in the dispute. Again, the image of the courts as dispute resolution forums does not adequately capture actual practice.

(e) Conclusion

In this chapter we have seen that the traditional view of the courts – a view that underlies much legal writing – seems out of place in daily court practice. Whether we refer to the type of court (upper or lower tier), or to the type of case (criminal or civil), the traditional ideal of the litigation process is scarcely evident in practice. In its place we find bureaucratic routine and the administrative processing of cases. We have seen that there are many factors which must be taken into account to explain this, including the type of dispute and its social setting, who the parties are, what their experience with the courts has been or is likely to be, and the varying nature of the court structure. In the next chapter we go on to look at one factor which so far has only been referred to briefly: the role of the legal profession in the operation of the legal system and in the conduct of litigation.

As a final point, it should be stressed that none of the empirical evidence that has been summarised in this chapter requires us to conclude that the traditional image of the courts is irrelevant. Whilst we have concentrated on comparing the "reality" of the court system with the image, it remains true that the adversarial ideal retains considerable ideological and normative significance for lawyers and others involved in that system. As was suggested at the beginning of this chapter, the adversarial ideal operates as an important symbol of how the courts *should* operate in a liberal world.

---

152 Marc Galanter has described this as "the radiating effects" of litigation – n 118, 215. See also D Trubek, "The Construction and Deconstruction of a Disputes-Focused Approach: An Afterword" (1980-81) 15 *Law and Society Review* 727.

153 See R Tomasic and B Pentony, "Litigation in Takeovers – the Decision-Making Process" (1990) 6 *Australian Bar Review* 67.

154 Ibid 71.

Exercise and questions

1. Divide the class into small groups of 4-5 students. Half of these groups should visit a Magistrates' Court, Local Court/Divisional Court or Tribunal. The remainder should visit a Supreme Court or Court of Appeal. It is advisable to contact the Court first, to obtain advice about a suitable case for you to attend. You should make some discussion notes about your experience (Note: it is always advisable to ask for permission from a court usher to take notes when entering the public gallery, explaining that you are a law student undertaking a class assignment.)

    In undertaking this exercise, your groups should consider the following questions.

    *   What was the nature of the dispute – civil or criminal? (Could you tell, if so how?)
    *   What type of judge/judicial officer/tribunal member presided over the proceedings?
    *   What type of proceeding (pre-trial or trial) and what was its function?
    *   Was there a jury? How many jurors were used and what was their make-up (likely age, gender, ethnicity, occupation). What did the judge say about their role in the proceeding?
    *   Were the parties present? If so, what role did they play? Did they give evidence? From your position, what was their attitude to the process?
    *   Were the parties legally represented or self-represented? Did this present any difficulties for parties presenting their cases? How did the judge or magistrate respond to the lack of representation?
    *   What role, if any, did the victim(s), lawyers, witnesses play in the proceedings?
    *   How interventionist was the court in managing and controlling the process?
    *   What features of the proceedings would you say were adversarial? Were there any inquisitorial elements evident?
    *   Did you understand the legal arguments being made? What were they?

    After visiting the court, reconvene into your groups to discuss your experiences.

    *   What was your overwhelming impression of the process?
    *   Was it fair to all parties?
    *   What role did the judges, judicial officers and lawyers play in ensuring the process was fair? Were they effective?
    *   Was cross-examination effective at getting to the truth?
    *   Were there any cross-cultural issues at play (interpreters etc)?

    Reconvene as a single group and consider the following:

    *   Do you agree with the view that there are distinct (upper and lower) tiers of justice? Did you detect an "ideology of triviality" in the lower courts – if so, how did it manifest itself. Compared with the lower courts, could you detect any significant differences in terms of a judicial system's

commitment to values of legality and due process in the higher courts? Do you believe that due process routinely fails to live up to its claims?

- What reforms would you make to the system to improve the quality of justice?
- What are the strengths and weakness of our adversarial system?

2. A current driver of reform in both the civil and criminal litigation system is efficiency. This has led to much innovation and experimentation, such as case management, charge bargaining and wider use of diversionary schemes. The problem with these trends is that fundamental legal values – such as the right to a fair trial – can be severely compromised. Discuss.

3. The statue that symbolises justice, found outside many courts, depicts a woman wearing a blindfold and holding a set of scales and a sword. What does this say about the process by which justice is administered in the courts? Is it an accurate metaphor?

4. "So few disputes get to court that it is difficult to see why courts matter". Discuss.

Chapter 6

Lawyers, Clients and Ethics

Practising lawyers are gatekeepers between the law and the citizen:[1] assuming, of course, that the citizen has the admission money with which to pass through the gate and can overcome the other obstacles to the justice system that were discussed in Chapter 4. Therefore, the way that lawyers deal with their clients, each other and the courts is potentially very important. If, to put it rather loosely, lawyers have their own agenda, individually or collectively, then the ideals of law may be distorted in practice. This chapter is an examination of only two important concerns to do with the legal profession. We begin by looking at some sociological literature on the relationship between lawyers and their clients. We challenge the orthodox picture of the lawyer as a mere mouthpiece who "takes instructions" and does what he or she is told. The situation is seen to be more complex than that. We then consider the principles of legal ethics which are meant to govern lawyers' conduct, concentrating on the particular issue of how the duty of confidentiality affects the flow of information, maybe even of truth, to a decision-maker.

For reasons of space we do not attempt to deal with many other interesting questions about lawyers. This means we do not look at literature on the structure and organisation of the profession,[2] the monopolies or protected markets that lawyers enjoy,[3] the quality of legal services,[4] the question of what *is* a profession,[5] the economic, political and social role of lawyers[6] and the social composition of the legal profession.[7] To an extent, therefore, we might be criticised for adopting

---

1   F Zacharias, "Lawyers as Gatekeepers" (2004) 41 *San Diego Law Review* 1387 discusses some of the ways in which the gatekeeper role is performed.

2   See generally D Weisbrot, *Australian Lawyers*, Longman, 1990, and Y Ross, *Ethics in Law*, 4th ed, Butterworths, 2005, Ch 4. Nor do we discuss moves towards national regulation of the legal profession in Australia: see Law Council of Australia, *Towards a National Profession*, October 2005.

3   See, however, the Trade Practices Commission Report on the *Legal Profession*, 1994; G Sturgess, "Lawyers and the Public Interest" in R Albon and G Lindsay (eds), *Occupational Regulation and the Public Interest*, Centre for Independent Studies, 1984, 99; and information available on the National Competition Council website: <www.ncc.gov.au>.

4   See N Harris, "Do Solicitors Care for Their Clients?" [1994] *Civil Justice Quarterly* 359.

5   For an interesting collection of essays on this theme, see R Dingwall and P Lewis, *The Sociology of the Professions*, Macmillan, 1983. See also Ross, n 2, Ch 3.

6   See generally M Cain and CB Harrington (eds), *Lawyers in a Postmodern World*, Open UP, 1994; RL Nelson, DM Trubek and RL Solomon (eds), *Lawyers' Ideals/Lawyers' Practices*, Cornell UP, 1992; R Abel, *English Lawyers Between Market and State: The Politics of Professionalism*, Oxford UP, 2003.

7   See Weisbrot, n 2, Ch 4.

lawyers' own image of themselves as professionals. On the other hand, we hope to present some material and arguments on which critical evaluation in other law courses can build.

(a) How lawyers deal with their clients

The topic of how lawyers deal with their clients has received close attention within literature on legal skills. The purpose there is to improve communication between lawyer and client, and thereby the quality of representation that a lawyer can offer. Our concern here is different. We take one step back and analyse the lawyer-client relationship within which those communications take place.

Implicit in much of the sociological and critical literature is an assumption that a power imbalance exists between lawyer and client which works to the disadvantage of clients.[8] Lawyers have the upper hand, if only because their superior knowledge of rules and procedures gives them an advantage. This "information asymmetry" leads to conclusions that clients are poorly equipped to evaluate the quality of the legal services they receive. The assumption therefore contradicts the standard professional image that lawyers "take instructions" from their clients and it suggests instead a different relationship. The literature is not, however, all one way. The empirical evidence suggests that lawyer-client relations vary between different areas of legal practice. For example, Maureen Cain's research indicates that lawyers with middle-class clients often *are* mere translators of their clients' wishes, turning those wishes into legal language.[9] The clients simply say what they want and the lawyers comply. Furthermore, one would expect the relationship between lawyers and large corporate clients to be different again. The corporate manager might well have sufficient knowledge to evaluate the lawyer's advice, and the lawyer might be reliant on the client for financial survival. The power balance might therefore be reversed. It follows that one must be careful when seeking to generalise from specific pieces of research. In addition, even within one area of legal practice, it is clear that there are different *styles* of client-handling or client-management.[10]

The extract from Ngaire Naffine's pathbreaking book on law and the sexes provides a clear summary of some of the literature on lawyer-client relations. Naffine's concern is with the way that law is constructed with a model person in view. That person is male, moneyed, educated and middle-class and thrives in the competitive marketplace. This is a theory to which we will return when we look at the feminist jurisprudence in Chapter 8 but it may help to bear it in mind when reading the following passage. The consequence of the theory is that law is able to mask or legitimate substantive inequalities between people because it seems to cater for someone – the man of law – who is (just) recognisable.[11] In the context of lawyers and clients, the rhetoric of "taking instructions" may be appropriate

---

8   See R Moorhead, A Sherr and A Paterson, "What Clients Know: Client Perspectives and Legal Competence" (2003) 10 *International Journal of the Legal Profession* 5 and S Ellman, "Lawyers and Clients" (1987) 34 *UCLA Law Review* 717.

9   See M Cain, "The General Practice Lawyer and the Client: Towards a Radical Conception" (1979) 7 *International Journal of Sociology of Law* 331 and "The Symbol Traders" in Cain and Harrington, n 6, Ch 1.

10 See G Davis, S Cretney and J Collins, *Simple Quarrels*, Clarendon, 1994, Ch 4.

11 Similar arguments have been made in criticism of the rule of law idea: see Ch 3.

where the client is the man of law who knows what he wants and how to get it, the kind of client whom Maureen Cain observed, but the rhetoric also operates for those in less fortunate positions. As we will see, there is a considerable body of literature which suggests that lawyers face imperatives other than their clients' "instructions".

N Naffine, *Law and the Sexes*
(1990)

The basic principle of legal practice is that the lawyer must obey the directions of the client. The lawyer must not "substitute his own judgement for the specific instructions of his client", even if he believes his own judgement is more likely to operate in the client's best interests (Disney et al, 1986:637). Discussions between lawyers and their clients are therefore referred to as "the taking of instructions". The general idea is that the client explains the nature of his problem to the lawyer, receives advice about its legal implications, and then instructs the lawyer about how he would like to proceed in the light of this advice. When the lawyer appears in court he (as we have seen, the lawyer is more likely to be a man) is said to act on behalf of his client and repeatedly refers to "his instructions". If it should transpire during the course of a case that the lawyer is unsure of the wishes of his client, he is required to obtain further instructions, not to proceed independently. In theory, then, the lawyer is the servant of the client. He is there to interpret the law and represent the client's interests, to act according to the client's view of the matter, not his own.

The idea that the lawyer is the professional servant of the paying client, that the lawyer is the one who takes orders, meshes well with the ideal of the man of law. It assumes that the client is a sentient, rational being who knows his own mind and, with the assistance of a legal expert, will be able to defend his interests. It vests control of the vital decisions in any legal proceeding with the client, not the lawyer. The lawyer is to explain the law and may advise on tactics, but the wishes and intentions represented in court are said always to be those of the client.

The notion that the lawyers are in the service of their clients may also be seen to accord with the legal profession's idea of itself – as impartial, neutral and dispassionate in its legal dealings. The lawyer does not take sides or express a moral or personal view of the matter. In fact, it can be a breach of ethics to do so. He does not act in his own interests, or according to his personal convictions; rather he acts in the interests of his client according to the client's view of things and according to the client's instructions. The lawyer's sole concern is to provide the best advice possible and to represent the client's version of events in court.

What is wrong with the service model of the lawyer-client relationship is that, in many instances, it does not accord with legal practice. Indeed, as we shall see, there is evidence to suggest that when it comes to representing people in the criminal jurisdiction – who are, in the main, the socially disadvantaged – many lawyers regard their clients as incapable of making sensible decisions and so proceed to take control of the case. There is also evidence that lawyers do not always present themselves in court in a neutral fashion, as the client's representative, but seek to establish a social distance between themselves and the individuals who hire their services. Indeed, it has been observed that lawyers in the criminal courts seem at times to identify not with their clients, their social inferiors, but with the other members of the court (Blumberg, 1967; Carlen, 1976; Bankowski and Mungham, 1976).

One can point to a number of reasons why lawyers might not grant their clients the full status of the legal person. One is the implicit acceptance among many lawyers that their superior knowledge of the law makes it only sensible that they should take the reins. As Tomasic (1978a) has shown in his study of New South Wales lawyers, the dominant legal cultural value is one of cynical realism in that lawyers acknowledge that their clients are powerless. Though the service ideal is meant generally to guide the work of legal practitioners, one can find professional support for the view that lawyers should at times assume full command of their client's cases, particularly when those clients are thought incapable of acting wisely.

In a recent Australian publication directed at practitioners, for example, clear recognition is given to the lawyer-client relationship which employs the "lawyer-control" model, as opposed to the "client-control" or the "co-operative" model. Its justification, we are told, is that "the lawyer has the training and the expertise to assess what is in the client's best interests". The acknowledged cost of the lawyer assuming full control of the relationship, however, is that it may fail to preserve "the autonomy, responsibility and dignity of both parties" (Basten, 1986:23). In other words, it sacrifices the ideal of the legal subject as an intelligent and independent individual.

A recent appraisal of the American lawyer-client relationship also stresses the value of the more participatory model, but notes its limitations. Based on a study of New York City practitioners, it observes that when clients are allowed to take an active role in their case, more satisfactory results are achieved. The same writer, however, concedes the professional problems of giving clients too much control. Notably, the lawyer may lose the ability "to restrain clients from taking immoral, illegal or simply unfortunate actions". In other words, there are times when the lawyer knows best and should secure his authority over the wayward client (Rosenthal, 1974). Moreover, it is not always possible for the client to grasp "the complexities of technical language" nor to deal with "uncertain multifaceted decisions". The service ideal which vests authority in the client as a rational legal subject, it seems, is fine in theory but not always feasible.

Other commentators on the lawyer's role believe that, from the outset, authority should be wrested from the client. Such lawyers suffer no illusions about the autonomy or intellectual faculties of the client. Simply, the client is perceived to be a dependent person with little command of the situation. For example, the perceived ineptitude of the client is described in the most candid of terms in the following opinion of a Canadian Queen's Counsel on lawyers in the criminal jurisdiction (who, by nature of their work, deal mainly with the less privileged members of the community). Defending counsel, we are told, should assume "total control and responsibility over the defence". This should be done kindly but firmly since the defendant is likely to be "a rather frightened and bewildered man [who] is looking for help". Thus "some time, quite early in the process, you should tactfully let him know that you are in charge" (Martin, 1969:282).

Clearly, some members of the legal community defend their right to take full charge of their clients' cases. Others favour a more egalitarian relationship. Though the lawyer-dominated model of legal practice tends to cast the client in a dependent relationship, it is not regarded by the legal community as inappropriate behaviour. Witness Halsbury:

When counsel is instructed, then, subject to his duties to the court, and subject to his right to advise another course of action, he must accept and adhere to the instructions given by or on behalf of his client, but counsel is entitled to insist, and as a general rule, ought to have complete control over how those instructions are carried out and over the actual conduct of the case. (Quoted in Disney et al, 1986:639)

Indeed if one looks closely at the ethics laid down for advocates one can see that they are a bundle of contradictions. Though lawyers must take instructions, they are also expected to be in control. Though they must obey the wishes of their client, they must not identify with their client's claims. In fact the case law shows that lawyers are more in danger of "professional misconduct" if they go too far when criticising other lawyers than if they assume too commanding a role in the lawyer-client relationship (Disney et al, 1986).

Where lawyers have attracted criticism, however, is in those instances where they have been observed to treat the client as purely incidental to the business of the court, or, more worrying still, when they have been thought to act more in their own than in their client's interests. In such cases, the threat to the client extends beyond his autonomy as legal subject.

A swingeing critique of the treatment of defendants by English lawyers has been advanced by Bankowski and Mungham (1976). In their volume, *Images of Law*, they characterise the treatment of defendants in English magistrates' courts as a "degradation ceremony". This expression is borrowed directly from Garfinkel (1955:420), who defines it as "any communicative work between persons, whereby the public identity of an actor is transformed into something looked on as lower in the local scheme of social types". The purpose of such courtroom degradation, according to the authors, is to subdue and pacify the defendant so that he will cause as little difficulty as possible.

The "arcadian sketch" of the courtroom, in which "skilled and articulate advocates" protect the interests of their clients, is therefore expressly challenged in this analysis of English justice. Instead, the situation described by Bankowski and Mungham is one in which lawyers co-opt the identity of their clients, refer in open court to the intimate details of their private lives, without reference to the clients themselves, who are treated as the non-participating objects, not the subjects, of the legal process. Lawyers, they claim, speak in a technical language which specifically excludes the layperson. What is more, little effort is made to involve or engage the client, to ensure that he knows what is happening to him. Rather, it is simply assumed that he is neither able nor inclined to understand. Consistently, he is seen to be the recipient of whatever is deemed by the court to be appropriate for him (Bankowski and Mungham, 1976:89).

The English criminologist Pat Carlen (1976:91) presents a similar view of the treatment of accused persons. Indeed her observations of the operation of a magistrates' court led her to conclude that the dominant attitude to defendants was that they were "'pretty dim', 'rather pathetic creatures' who had 'never had a chance'". The lawyer's response to this sorry assessment of the defendant was to make him over, to tell the accused, before he got into the courtroom, what he should say and how he should say it.

This finding again puts paid to the traditional notion that it is the client who invariably informs the lawyer what he wants done for him in the form of "instructions". While clients may well call the lawyer's tune in the lucrative sphere of commercial law, ..., in the criminal courts, where the poor predominate, the reverse would seem to be true. It is more a matter of the lawyer instructing the client than the client instructing the lawyer. As another commentator on English justice describes this process:

> The lawyer takes down those facts that he considers relevant to the client's case; he tells him how to plead; he decides what aspects of the defendant's character and background to emphasise before the magistrates, whether to challenge the police or probation officer and what sentence to propose to the court. In most cases it is clear that the lawyer is in charge. Defendants tend to follow advice and obey instructions. (King, 1981:118)

To make matters worse, there is a variety of ways in which the status and contribution of the defendant can be further diminished once he enters the court, to the point that he ultimately becomes, according to Carlen (1976), merely a "dummy player". All professional members of the courtroom, Carlen informs us, use signals, gestures, language as well as legal procedures to ensure that the defendant does not take an active part in proceedings. A bad defendant, from the point of view of all professional players in the legal drama, lawyers included, is one who steps out of line and attempts to offer an independent and unorchestrated challenge to the court. But it is not difficult to quell the recalcitrant defendant, according to Carlen, by ruling his comments inappropriate and inadmissible.

The Canadian criminologists Ericson and Baranck (1982:3) present a view of North American justice which meshes well with that offered by the English critics. In the course of an ambitious longitudinal study of accused persons, from encounter with the police to court disposition, they interviewed 100 defendants about their experiences of the law and also, where possible, spoke to their legal counsel. Their general conclusion was that the accused was a dependant in the criminal process. He was caught up in a legal web not of his own design, subject to the orders of others, his freedom to make choices that might serve his own interests "clearly circumscribed, and often foreclosed".

The common opinion of lawyers interviewed in this study was that the lawyer should make the main decisions affecting the case because the accused did not appreciate the processes of the law. As one lawyer put it: "No, I really have a tendency to decide myself which is better for the client and I don't say, well, these are the avenues, because I don't think they understand enough of what I'm talking about. I don't think they're capable of me explaining everything to them because it took me a long time to learn what the different avenues meant too" (Ericson and Baranck, 1982:96). To another legal representative, a precondition of his defending an accused person was that the client should fully surrender control of his affairs. In the opinion of this learned counsel, "any lawyer who's worth his salt tells his client how to dress, how to have his hair cut, how to have it combed, how to behave, how to answer questions" (Ericson and Baranck, 1982:98). Again, there is little evidence here of our knowing and assertive man of law who calls the shots.

Though writers such as Bankowski and Mungham and Carlen have been highly critical of lawyers who dominate their clients, other writers have at times found more noble motives informing just this sort of lawyer-client relationship. Eve Spangler (1986:167-68), for example, writing about members of the American profession who provide services to the poor, has observed that "in taking over the decision-making process, lawyers are trying to honour the intentions of their clients". Thus:

> When people come to us, they're in immediate crisis. They literally come in, "My God, what is going to happen to me and my four-year old [who] is lead poisoned, and me, who has emphysema and 85 per cent over-weight and can't walk up the stairs?" We're people who have a lot of clients die on

us. There are all these questions and choices they have to make, and they're crying during the whole time that you talk to them and they just say, "Will you please do what you think is best? You're the lawyer, I don't want to have to do this. You do it". So you take the cue from them.

Good intentions, however, can also work against the client, when they lead to the lawyer supplanting the client's wishes for his own. Spangler (1986:168), for example, remarks on the practices of certain legal aid lawyers whose personal opinion of what is best for their clients, what is in their clients' own good, may lead them to use their superior knowledge to subvert their clients' goals.

Whatever the intentions of legal counsel, whether they be altruistic or self-interested, it is possible to observe a clear distinction between their relations with the indigent client ... and their dealings with the wealthy ... In the former case it is the lawyer who is in a position to make the critical decisions while in the latter case, the client assumes command (Heinz and Laumann, 1982; Spangler, 1986). The degree of fit between the social location of the client and the social character of the man of law therefore makes a difference to his treatment by the legal profession. Wealthy, commercial clients closely approximate the legal model of the person and accordingly retain control of the legal process. Socially disadvantaged clients depart from the model in most respects and so have little say over what is done to them in the courts.[12]

In the above extract Naffine deals with the idea that lawyers in the criminal courts seem at times to identify not with their clients but with the other members of the court. She refers to work by Blumberg, whose article in 1967, "The Practise of Law as Confidence Game", has become a classic in socio-legal studies.[13] Blumberg was an experienced criminal defence lawyer in the United States who began to question whether the traditional conception of the defence lawyer as the zealous hired gun of the defendant actually squared with reality. We have already seen in Chapter 5 that the image of criminal proceedings as adversary contests is an unreliable one, given the negotiations and guilty pleas that pervade the process. Blumberg's article deals with the role of criminal lawyers, at least in the United States.

AS Blumberg, "The Practise of Law as Confidence Game"
(1967) (Footnotes omitted)

Accused persons come and go in the court system schema, but the structure and its occupational incumbents remain to carry on their respective career, occupational and organizational enterprises. The individual stridencies, tensions and conflicts a given accused person's case may present to all the participants are overcome because the formal and informal relations of all the groups in the court setting require it. The probability of continued future relations and interaction must be preserved at all costs.

This is particularly true of the "lawyer regulars" ie, those defense lawyers who, by virtue of their continuous appearances on behalf of defendants, tend to represent the bulk of a criminal court's non-indigent case workload, and those lawyers who are not "regulars", who appear almost casually on behalf of an

---

12   N Naffine, *Law and the Sexes*, Allen & Unwin, 1990, 125-131.

13   AS Blumberg, "The Practise of Law as Confidence Game" (1967) 1 *Law and Society Review* 15. For an abridged version, see V Aubert (ed), *The Sociology of Law*, Penguin, 1969, Ch 27. References here are to the version in Aubert.

occasional client. Some of the "lawyer regulars" are highly visible as one moves about the major urban centres of the nation, their offices line the back streets of the courthouses, at times sharing space with bondsmen. Their political "visibility" in terms of local club house ties, reaching into the judge's chambers and prosecutor's office, are also deemed essential to successful practitioners. Previous research has indicated that the "lawyer regulars" make no effort to conceal their dependence upon police, bondsmen, jail personnel. Nor do they conceal the necessity for maintaining intimate relations with all levels of personnel in the court setting as a means of obtaining, maintaining, and building their practise. These informal relations are the sine qua non not only of retaining a practise, but also in the negotiation of pleas and sentences.

The client, then, is a secondary figure in the court system as in certain other bureaucratic settings. He becomes a means to other ends of the organization's incumbents. He may present doubts, contingencies, and pressures which challenge existing informal arrangements or disrupt them; but these tend to be resolved in favour of the continuance of the organization and its relations as before. There is a greater community of interest among all the principal organizational structures and their incumbents than exists elsewhere in other settings. The accused's lawyer has far greater professional, economic, intellectual and other ties to the various elements of the court system than he does to his own client. In short, the court is a closed community.[14]

Having located the regular defence lawyer within the court community, Blumberg goes on to talk about the variety of stratagems which are employed to dispose of caseloads which are often too large:

A wide variety of coercive devices are employed against an accused client, couched in a depersonalized, instrumental, bureaucratic version of due process of law, and which are in reality a perfunctory obeisance to the ideology of due process. These include some very explicit pressures which are exerted in some measure by all court personnel, including judges, to plead guilty and avoid trial. In many instances the sanction of a potentially harsh sentence is utilized as the visible alternative to pleading guilty, in the case of recalcitrants. Probation and psychiatric reports are "tailored" to organizational needs, or are at least responsive to the court organization's requirements for the refurbishment of a defendant's social biography, consonant with his new status. A resourceful judge can, through his subtle domination of the proceedings, impose his will on the final outcome of a trial. Stenographers and clerks, in their function as record keepers, are on occasion pressed into service in support of a judicial need to "rewrite" the record of a courtroom event. Bail practises are usually employed for purposes other than simply assuring a defendant's presence on the date of a hearing in connexion with his case. Too often the discretionary power as to bail is part of the arsenal of weapons available to collapse the resistance of an accused person. The foregoing is a most cursory examination of some of the more prominent "short cuts" available to any court organization. There are numerous other procedural strategies constituting due process deviations, which tend to become the work style artifacts of a court's personnel. Thus, only court "regulars" who are "bound in" are really accepted; others are treated routinely and in almost a coldly correct manner.[15]

---

14   Aubert, n 13, 323-324.
15   Ibid 325-326.

One response to Blumberg's thesis, assuming it to be well-founded in the first place, is that the lawyers nevertheless do act in their clients' interests. It may objectively be the case that a guilty plea *is* the most prudent course of action. One immediate point to be made here is that one cannot *know* that this is so. As Blumberg says, the lawyer is not like a plumber whose work one can inspect and evaluate:

> In the practise of law there is a special problem in this regard, no matter what the level of the practitioner or his place in the hierarchy of prestige. Much legal work is intangible either because it is simply a few words of advice, some preventive action, a telephone call, negotiation of some kind, a form filled out and filed, a hurried conference with another attorney or an official of a government agency, a letter or opinion written, or a countless variety of seemingly innocuous, and even prosaic procedures and sanctions. These are the basic activities, apart from any possible court appearance, of almost all lawyers at all levels of practise. Much of the activity is not in the nature of the exercise of the traditional, precise professional skills of the attorney such as library research and oral argument in connexion with appellate briefs, court motions, trial work, drafting of opinions, memoranda contracts, and other complex documents and agreements. Instead, much legal activity, whether it is at the lowest or highest "white shoe" law firm levels, is of the brokerage, agent, sales representative, lobbyist type of activity, in which the lawyer acts for someone else in pursuing the latter's interests and designs. The service in intangible.[16]

Applying this idea to the context of criminal defence, one never knows whether the client who has been persuaded to plead guilty would actually have been found guilty had the case gone to trial.[17] But leaving aside this particular problem of knowledge, one should note that Blumberg is describing the criminal lawyer as a double agent and, of course, a double agent does actually perform services for both sides:

> In effect, in his role as double agent, the criminal lawyer performs an extremely vital and delicate mission for the court organization and the accused. Both principals are anxious to terminate the litigation with a minimum of expense and damage to each other. There is no other personage or role incumbent in the total court structure more strategically located, who by training and in terms of his own requirements is more ideally suited to do so than the lawyer.[18]

Finally, although Herbert Kritzer's later analysis of the role of lawyers in ordinary civil litigation shows considerable similarities,[19] Blumberg himself admits that some of his observations may be peculiar to the practice of criminal law (and, for our purposes, they relate also to the United States of the 1960s):

> Criminal law practise is a unique form of private law practise since it really only appears to be private practise. Actually it is bureaucratic practise, because of the legal practitioner's enmeshment in the authority, discipline, and perspectives of the court organization. Private practise, supposedly, in a professional sense,

---

16 Ibid 327.

17 Although the reverse might be true in that a defendant who is convicted after a trial may be told by the judge that the sentence takes into account the fact that the defendant had not admitted her or his guilt.

18 Aubert, n 13, 329.

19 H Kritzer, *The Justice Broker*, Oxford UP, 1990, 17.

involves the maintenance of an organized, disciplined body of knowledge and learning; the individual practitioners are imbued with a spirit of autonomy and service, the earning of a livelihood being incidental. In the sense that the lawyer in the criminal court serves as a double agent, serving higher organizational rather than professional ends, he may be deemed to be engaged in bureaucratic rather than private practise. To some extent the lawyer-client "confidence game", in addition to its other functions, serves to conceal this fact.[20]

More recently in the United States, empirical research has been carried out on the way that divorce lawyers deal with their clients.[21] The conclusions reached from this work seem to be consistent with those of Blumberg and Kritzer. Sarat and Felstiner observed and tape-recorded 115 lawyer-client conferences in divorce matters and they have written a series of articles dealing with the data from different angles.[22] Again, it is a matter of speculation how applicable their observations are to the Australian context and to different kinds of work with different kinds of clients.

The most common kind of case that Sarat and Felstiner observed was where the lawyer persuaded a reluctant client to try and settle the case. In one article, they focus on a single example of this and they concentrate on three issues: first, how the lawyer and client have different views of law and the legal process; second, how these differences are "resolved" or handled; and, third, how this process affects the client's eventual decision about what to do.[23]

As to the first issue, clients are likely to expect the legal system to be predictable and rational. In contrast, the lawyer presents it as hurried, routinised and accident-prone. The lawyer stresses how one has to be inside the system and know the local scene in order to succeed.

As to the second issue, the lawyer persuades the client that the law is not about justice as she, the client, sees it. It is not about vindicating rights or redressing wrongs. It is about achieving an outcome where the benefits exceed the costs; the lawyer sees both sides of the equation primarily in money terms.

As to the third issue, the client is by now relatively powerless because the lawyer is the insider and has defined what the system is about. The lawyer's preference for settlement then comes out. As Sarat and Felstiner say, the lawyers are supreme in the world of settlements but not in the courts. They note, however, that the relationship is not all one-way. Lawyers must rely on the client's perception and version of events and, to that extent, the client can shape the direction that is taken by the case.[24]

The factual background to the next extract is as follows. The lawyer acts for the wife, Jane. There are no children of the relationship and the major asset is the matrimonial home. The house is an unconventional building to which the husband was especially attached. Housing in the area is very expensive. The husband had

---

20   Aubert, n 13, 330.

21   In addition to the work of Sarat and Felstiner, discussed below, see L Mather, RJ Maiman and CA McEwen, " 'The Passenger Decides on the Destination and I Decide on the Route': Are Divorce Lawyers 'Expensive Cab Drivers'?" (1995) 9 *International Journal of Law and the Family* 286.

22   The research was subsequently written up in full in A Sarat and WLF Felstiner, *Divorce Lawyers and Their Clients*, Oxford UP, 1995, but the sources used here are more convenient for extracting.

23   A Sarat and W Felstiner, "Law and Strategy in the Divorce Lawyer's Office" (1986) 20 *Law and Society Review* 93.

24   See Moorehead, n 8, 8.

refused to leave the home and the wife had reluctantly moved out so as to facilitate mediation. She visited the house occasionally, primarily to check on plants and pets, and she said that she was careful to warn the husband before a visit. The husband then hired what he described as "the meanest son-of-a-bitch in town" as his lawyer to obtain an ex parte restraining order. This is an order obtained without the wife's knowledge which prevents her from coming to the property.[25] Not surprisingly, this ended any prospect of mediation and the wife instructed the lawyer who appears in the extract. A second judge subsequently upheld the ex parte order. We are omitting those passages where the lawyer re-orients the client's expectations of the legal system and establishes himself as one with the necessary inside knowledge and we take up the story at the stage where the client must decide whether to fight or to settle.

A Sarat and W Felstiner, "Law and Strategy in the Divorce Lawyer's Office"

(1986)

Generally the question is whether the client should attempt to negotiate a settlement or insist on resolution before a judge. This question is sometimes posed issue by issue and sometimes across many issues.

While many clients think of the legal process as an arena for a full adversarial contest, most divorce disputes are not resolved in this matter. Although not all lawyers are equally dedicated to reaching negotiated agreements, most of those we observed advised their clients to try to settle the full range of issues in the case. This is not to say that these divorces were free of conflict, for the negotiations themselves were often quite contentious. Although some of our lawyers occasionally advised clients to ask for more than the client had originally contemplated or to refuse to concede on a major issue when the client was inclined to do so, most seemed to believe that it is generally better to settle than contest divorce disputes. Thus, we are interested in the ways in which lawyers get their clients to see settlement as the preferred alternative.

The conference we are examining revolves around two major issues: (1) whether to ignore or contest the restraining order; and (2) what position to take concerning disposition of the family residence. Much of the conference is devoted to discussing the restraining order – its origins, morality, and legality; the prospects for dissolving it; the lawyer's stake in contesting it; and the client's emotional reaction to it. Substantively the order is not as important as the house itself, which received much less attention and generated much less controversy. Both issues, however, force the lawyer and client to decide whether they will retain control of the case by engaging in negotiations or cede control to the court for hearing and decision. The lawyer definitely favors negotiations.

Lawyer: Okay. What I would like your permission to do then is to meet with Foster, see if I can come up with or negotiate a settlement with him that, before he leaves ... I leave his office or he leaves my office, he says, we've got something here that I can recommend to my client,

---

25   Such orders are possible in Australia, either under the *Family Law Act 1975* (Cth) s 114 or under State legislation. An ex parte order excluding a spouse from the home is supposed to be made only in exceptional circumstances because, of course, it violates ideas of due process in that the spouse should have the chance to argue a case. An ex parte order preventing return visits by a spouse who has already moved out is, however, an order that is more likely to be made.

and I can say, I've got something here that I can recommend to my client. My feeling is, Jane, that if we reach that point, both lawyers are prepared to make a recommendation on settlement to their respective clients, if either of the clients, either you or Norb, find something terribly disagreeable with the proposal that we have, the lawyers have come to between themselves, then the case just either can't be settled or it's not ripe for settlement. But we would have given it the best shot. But I wouldn't ... as you know, I'm very concerned about wasting a lot of time and energy trying to settle a case where two previous attempts have been dismally unsuccessful.

The major ingredient of this settlement system is the primacy of the lawyers. They produce the deals while the clients are limited to initial instructions and after-the-fact ratification. The phrase "we would have given it our best shot" is crucial. The "we" seems to refer to the lawyers. Indeed, their efforts could come to nothing if either client backs out at the last minute. The settlement process as described thus has two dimensions – a lawyer to lawyer phase, in which an arrangement is worked out, and a lawyers versus clients phase, in which the opposing lawyers join together to sell the deal to their clients (see Blumberg, 1967). If the clients do not accept the settlement as a package, the only alternative is to go to trial. Furthermore, if the professionals are content with the agreement they have devised, dissatisfied clients not only have nothing to contribute but also had perhaps better seek psychotherapy:

> Lawyer: And if we have to come down a little bit off the 10 percent to something that is obviously a real good loan – 9 percent – a percentage point on a one-year, eighteen-month, $25,000 loan does not make that much difference to you. And that's worth settling the case, and I'll say, Jane, if we're going to court over what turns out to be one percentage point, go talk to Irene some more. So that's the kind of a package that I see putting together.

The client in this case is reluctant to begin settlement negotiations until some attention is paid to the restraining order. While she acknowledges that she wants a reasonable property settlement, she reminds her lawyer that that is not her exclusive concern:

> Client: Yes, there's no question in my mind that that [a property settlement] is my first goal. However, that doesn't mean it's my only goal. It's just my first one. And I have done a lot of thinking about this and so it's all this kind of running around in my head at this point. I've been looking very carefully at the parts of me that want to fight and the parts of me that don't want to fight. And I'm not sure that any of that ought to get messed up in the property settlement.

The lawyer responds by acknowledging that he considers the restraining order to be legally wrong and that he believes it could be litigated. Thus, he confirms his client's position and inclination on legal grounds. Yet he dissents from her position and opposes her inclination to fight on other grounds. First, he states that the restraining order, although legally wrong, is "not necessarily ... completely wrong" because it might prevent violence between spouses. This complicated position is a clear example of a tactic frequently used by lawyers in divorce cases – the rhetorical "yes ... but". The lawyers we observed often appeared to be endorsing the adversarial pursuit of one of the client's objectives only to remind the client of a variety of negative consequences associated with it. In this way lawyers present themselves as both an ally and an adviser embracing the wisdom of a long-term perspective.

164

Second, the lawyer is worried that an effort to fight the restraining order would interfere with the resolution of the case, that is, of the outstanding property issues. Although the lawyer considers the restraining order to be a legal mistake, its effect would end upon final disposition of the house. In the meantime, the client can either live with the order or pay for additional hearings. He believes that it would be unwise for her to fight further not only because the contest would be costly but also because it would postpone or derail entirely negotiations about the house and other tangible assets. Thus when the client asks whether the issue of the restraining order has been raised with her husband's lawyer, her lawyer says:

> Lawyer: Well, I've talked to him. My feelings are still the same. They're very strong feelings that what has been done is illegal, that I want to take it to the Supreme Court. I told Foster off. I basically told him the contents of the letter. I said that I think that Judge Cohen is dead wrong, and I would very much like to litigate the thing. On the other hand, I have to be mindful of what Irene said, which is absolutely correct, does that move us toward or away from the ultimate goal, which is the resolution of the case and what you told me when we started off now in very certain terms.

The lawyer's position in this case can be interpreted as a preference for negotiations over litigation based on his determination that this client has more to lose than gain by fighting the restraining order and for the house. In this view the lawyer is neutral about settlement in general and is swayed by the cost-benefit calculation of specific cases. Thus there is a conflict between the client's desire for vindication on what the lawyer perceives to be a peripheral issue and the lawyer's interest in reaching a satisfactory disposition on what for him is a much more important issue. Time and again in our study we observed lawyers attempting to focus their client's attention on the issues the lawyers thought to be major while the clients often concentrated on matters that the lawyers considered secondary. While the disposition of the house in this case will have long-term consequences for the client, the restraining order, as unjust as the lawyer understands it to be, is in his view a temporary nuisance. His sense of justice and of the long-term best interests of his client lead him to try to transform this dispute from a battle over the legality and morality of the restraining order to a negotiation over the more narrow and tangible issue of the ultimate disposition of the house and other assets, which he believes can and should be settled.[26]

Sarat and Felstiner's work tends to support a conception of law that is becoming more common in the social sciences and is probably a commonplace in legal anthropology. This is that one should be sensitive to the existence of *local* legal systems constructed by practitioners and partially detached from "the law on the books" emerging from superior courts in contested cases. Such are the findings of Carol Smart who carried out research on solicitors in Sheffield (UK), again concerning family law. Smart found that the values of solicitors came through in their settlement patterns. The extract below deals with just one issue; solicitors' views about social security and marriage breakdown. She asked solicitors whether they took into account the availability to the wife of "supplementary benefit"[27] when negotiating maintenance payments by the husband. If the wife's entitlement

---

26   Sarat and Felstiner, n 23, 109-12.
27   Supplementary benefit (or income support) was reduced by one pound for every pound in income. Thus the more a husband paid in maintenance then the more that the wife lost in benefit.

to benefit *was* taken into account then she was treated in negotiations as already having some income and pressure was taken off the husband. If her entitlement to benefit was ignored, however, then she may have no income and the demands upon the husband would be greater. The question is therefore an important one of public policy about who should support a sole parent – the state or the absent parent? Smart's research showed that the majority of the solicitors placed primary emphasis on state support, for a variety of reasons.

C Smart, The Ties that Bind
(1984)

When solicitors are representing clients who are on low incomes they are immediately faced with a dilemma over principles. They will know that once two separate households are established, the wage or wages of the ex-couple will no longer be as adequate as they were, especially if the man adopts new financial responsibilities. If this separation places the ex-spouses on or around the poverty line the solicitor must decide whether or not to be influenced in his or her nego-tiations by the availability of public funds. If he or she does consider them then he or she is condoning the principle that the state has a responsibility to provide support even though marriage is essentially a matter of private law and redress. If he or she ignores state provision it generally indicates a rejection of the role of the state in these family matters.

My first enquiry of the solicitors on this matter concerned whether or not they took account of the availability of supplementary benefit when negotiating on maintenance payments where the spouses were on low incomes. Three-quarters of the solicitors (74 per cent) said they did and the remaining one-quarter said they did not. This is not to imply that the majority of solicitors treated supple-mentary benefit as if it was the equivalent of a wage for the wife which would then reduce her husband's liability. But the fact that a husband could not afford to pay as much as the basic subsistence level obviously influenced some solicitors who saw no point in squeezing more out of him especially when his wife would not benefit as the money would just reimburse the state. But there were also other considerations to be taken into account when supplementary benefits became involved, for example the possible advantage to a wife of signing over her book to the DHSS so that she would receive regular payments. In other instances of course such a move might be undesirable, especially if the woman might be able to start work in the near future, in which case she would not be entitled to supple-mentary benefit although she might still have some entitlement to maintenance. Consequently there were more considerations to be taken into account than the one of saving the taxpayers' money by requiring the husband to pay as much as possible.

It is interesting to look initially at the minority of solicitors who argued that they did not take the availability of supplementary benefits into account when they were negotiating over maintenance payments. It should perhaps be pointed out that these solicitors did not ignore its existence altogether but their concern was mainly that husbands should not avoid their responsibilities or that the tax-payer should be protected. The following quotes are representative of this point of view.

> Take it into account … not really. It seems to me that you've got to look at the available income of the parties as a result of their legitimate earning capacity and not as a state handout. I'm not in the job of encouraging the

state to pay more and letting husbands off, which is so often what it comes down to. No, I think you disregard that, I always do. It may well be that the state will then top up the amount, but that isn't a consideration you should take into account to start off with.

No I don't, I think it is wrong to because I think that supplementary benefits should be ignored. In taking the one-third line, gross income what-have-you, I think it is wrong to say the wife's income, well I'm quite sure that it is wrong and the courts would agree it is wrong, to say that she has got so much supplementary benefits because after all that is the taxpayers' money. So I think that in those circumstances you shouldn't take it into account. I mean obviously it can't practically be ignored but I think that as far as actually setting maintenance is concerned it would work far too much in favour of the husband if it was taken into account.

To the extent that we do as far as possible try to make sure that the husband takes them off it, if that's possible. But we don't actually take it into consideration, I mean it is not a factor which the magistrates are prepared to or which the registrar is prepared to take into consideration. You know the fact that the order that the husband is going to have to pay is still going to leave the wife on SB is irrelevant as far as the courts are concerned. So we do tend to ignore it, but if there is a possibility of taking them off it then we like it to happen simply because we all pay a lot of tax and we tend to feel that husbands should maintain their dependants rather than the state.

These solicitors clearly saw it as their duty to relieve the taxpayer of as much expenditure as possible – at least where it came to poor families. They viewed state benefits not as a form of insurance policy to which people had a right but as a form of charity or handout. Arguably these solicitors, in adopting the duty of helping the taxpayer, were abrogating their duty to act in the interests of their clients. Arguably also, if it is anyone's task to protect the public purse, it is the court's duty and not that of individual solicitors.

The following comments from solicitors who worked according to a very different set of principles not only reveals the ideological disparity between some solicitors but also the different level of practical care and concern provided.

Yes [I do take state benefits into account]. [How?] Quite a few different ways. For a start assuming that the wife, when she comes to see you, is already on supplementary benefit which she often will be, then generally speaking if she gets an order for maintenance from her husband then there's a very good chance that he's not going to be able to keep her at higher than SB rate anyway ... If she gets an order that's just for slightly less than she's getting from social security, she can sign it over to them ... so she's got no hassle, you know that at the top end of the scale we'll be advising people on how to get the maximum tax advantage, then up to a point at the other end you can do the same, but obviously there's not so much scope for it as there is at the top end.

A similar position was adopted by another solicitor who did mainly legal aid work and was therefore very familiar with the intractable problems caused by the combination of poverty and family breakdown. He said,

Yes very much so. With low-income families I think you start off on a completely different basis, as I say the whole calculation about maintenance is a bit of a joke in most cases, what we are talking about is their ability to survive, not maximising their financial position. The whole thing turns then on what benefit they are going to be entitled to, or what their chances of work are and I think you start off really by considering, right this woman is going to leave on Friday … low-income family, she is going to be leaving or, either hopefully husband is going to be chucked out of his house early part of next week, we then have to sort out what is going to happen about maintenance and the first thing is to get her to go down to social security. I already arrange that, [it's] the first step before you ever do anything else. You then have to consider what other benefits they may be entitled to or whether they might be better off finding a part-time job, if one's available, and claiming, you know, FIS because of the enhanced ability to claim that as a single parent …

It might be tempting to identify solicitors who were against state benefits as being classically "right-wing" and solicitors like the two quoted above as far more "left-wing". Although this is probably accurate, in fact the views of the solicitors were more complex than this and were not simply a reflection of traditional political ideologies. For example a difference was perceived on the level of whether the solicitors chose to speak for the interests of women or men. Solicitors who prioritised the needs of women did not automatically see state provision as in their interests. Moreover some solicitors who did not hold particularly liberal views were none the less in favour of state benefits, not because they might improve the financial position of the parties, but because they worried that depressing a man's income too low would encourage him to give up work altogether and thus become more of a burden on the state. Two solicitors expressed their concern over incentives as follows:

You have got to leave him with an incentive and I'm very keen on this incentive factor because if you take too much off the husband then he'll just mutter under his breath and give his notice in. And one has a deal of sympathy particularly if he's got a wretched wife who hasn't played fair and done her job in the home.

and

Yes experience shows that if you push a man too far he stops paying altogether and doesn't work so the court has to decide in each case how far it thinks it is fair to push any given man. He's got to have some beer money at the end of the week otherwise he won't work.[28]

Before moving to a final question we stress again that the amount of empirical research on lawyers and clients is small and that any findings should be treated with caution when applied to the Australian context and to different kinds of legal matters. Nevertheless enough has been said to suggest that the law school conception of law as the outcome of contested cases, usually decided on appeal, is at best a partial one. In so far as law is also the outcomes that lawyers negotiate with other lawyers and with court personnel then there is evidence that lawyers have some autonomy from the law on the books and that there is scope for their own values and interests to affect the result.

Our final question under this heading involves the relationship between these differing conceptions of law. Where precisely do rules come in? In Chapter 3 we saw that formalism is a method of legal reasoning which is justified (perhaps demanded) by the rule of law and certain other liberal values. The question therefore has important ramifications. If doubt is cast on the existence of a formal rule structure in the mass of cases which do not reach a court, then doubt is also

---

28   C Smart, *The Ties that Bind*, RKP, 1984, 181-184. The author's emphasis has been omitted.

cast upon the attainability of a central plank of liberalism; namely a relatively stable, clear and predictable legal system.

Sarat and Felstiner in a separate article from that extracted above consider the significance of rules for the way that lawyers deal with their clients. They say that lawyers begin with formalism and open their advice with some account of the applicable rules. After that, "formalism fades rather quickly as the interaction progresses" and further reference to rules is only in response to questions from clients. In addition, the answers they give to these questions are often incomplete, giving the client no chance to comment upon them or judge them. Generally, the lawyers being studied were cynical about the role of rules. As one of them says, "there are no rules here, just people, the judge, the lawyers, the litigants".

A Sarat and W Felstiner,
Lawyers and Legal Consciousness: Law Talk in the Divorce Lawyer's Office
(1989)

How do lawyers describe the law, particular laws, or legal processes to their clients? What characteristics are attributed to law and the legal system? Before addressing these questions it is important to note that there is a rather regular progression in law talk – a constant narrative structure. Almost all divorce cases start with the lawyer's brief explanation of divorce procedures as they are laid out in statutes. This law talk is full of explicit references to rules. Lawyers begin, if you will, with formalism. They describe the rules that frame the process, establish its limits and provide alternative routes. However, the written law is only a starting point. Formalism fades rather quickly as the interaction progresses. Descriptions and characterizations of the legal system now occur mainly when clients ask why a particular result occurred or what results might be predicted. In response to these unsolicited inquiries, lawyers rarely make explicit reference to rules. Rules and their relevance are taken for granted by lawyers who generally act as if clients already shared their empirical understanding of the legal process. As a consequence, at this point in the interaction, lawyers do not take the time to introduce their clients to the subtle manner in which rules penetrate and permeate the legal process.

Lawyers often talk about what can or cannot be done or what is or is not likely to happen without explicitly noting that their views are shaped by statutes or court decision, although the trained ear would recognize that their formulations are clearly rooted in an understanding of rules. Typical of such implicit rule references is the response of a lawyer to a client's inquiry about what would happen to child support if his income were reduced:

> You should keep in the back of your mind ... that if your financial situation changes in the future the judgment can be modified. That's not a problem. It is not etched in stone ... Anything to do with a child is always modifiable by the court.

How and why judgments in court "can be modified" is not explained. The client is not told whether that possibility is a result of the ease with which lawyers escape from earlier agreements, or of the sympathy that judges display toward children, or of the rules governing support, custody, and visitation. This failure to identify rules and highlight their relevance prevents clients from having access to law's public discourse and the resources for argument provided by an understanding of rules. In addition, it helps lawyers maintain a monopoly of those resources and focuses client concerns on the professional skills and capacities of their particular lawyer.

Lawyers, in fact, talk to clients in much the same way that they talk to each other. There is no acknowledgement that clients may not already understand the salience of rules. The normal conventions of lawyer-to-lawyer discourse are not translated for divorce clients, who most often bring an incomplete and unsophisticated understanding to their encounters with the legal process. There is no concerted effort to bridge the gap between professional and popular culture.

Even when rules are explicitly noted, there are few references to or discussions of their determining power. Lawyers do not describe the legal process of divorce as rule driven or rule governed. Nor do they usually provide an explicit evaluation of the rules themselves. However, when rules do at times emerge as part of the explicit conversational foreground, they are generally disparaged; contrary to the assumptions of both the organized bar and critical scholars, lawyers rarely defend the rationality, importance, or efficacy of legal rules.

For instance, it is common for lawyers to mock rules as irrelevant or useless in governing the behaviour of legal officials involved in the divorce process. Rules according to one California lawyer, do not give "clear-cut answers. If they did we wouldn't even have to be talking". A Massachusetts lawyer spoke more generally about the irrelevance of rules in describing the way the local court system operated: "There really are no rules here, just people, the judge, the lawyers, the litigants". Another maintained that the scheduling of cases reflected the virtually unchecked power of the bailiff:

> When you get heard is up to the court officer ... he's the one who controls the docket. They don't have a list prepared and they don't start at the top and work down. They go according to his idea of when people should be heard.

Other lawyers extended the argument about the ambiguity or irrelevance of rules to more important aspects of the legal process of divorce. Several suggested that judges refuse to be guided by rules of evidence and that such rules therefore have no bearing on the way hearings are conducted. One Massachusetts lawyer explained that he would not be able to prevent the opposing spouse from talking about his client's alleged adultery even though such testimony would be technically inadmissible according to the literal rules:

> I think we just have to realize that it is going to come out. We just have to take that as a given. You know, they teach you in law school about how to object to that kind of testimony: "I object, irrelevant", "I object hearsay". But then when you start to practice you realize that judges, especially in divorce cases, don't pay any attention. They act as if there were no rules of evidence.

Other lawyers expressed frustration about the ineffectiveness of rules governing filing periods, establishing times in which responsive pleadings are to be submitted or governing the conduct of discovery.

Moreover, statutes concerning property division are, as lawyers tell it, often irrelevant to actual outcomes. Lawyers in both Massachusetts and California regularly criticized judges for failing to pay attention to those statutes or to the case law interpreting them. As one Massachusetts lawyer told her client in a case involving substantial marital property,

> [i]n this state the statute requires judges to consider fifteen separate things, things like how long you were married, what contributions you and Tom made, whether you have good prospects. It is a pretty comprehensive list,

but I've never seen a judge make findings on all of those things. They just hear a few and then divide things up. Things generally come out roughly even, but not because the rules require it.

Thus, what lawyers do make visible as they respond to their clients' questions are the personalities and dispositions of actors within the legal process and the salience of local norms rather than legal rules. Emphasizing people over rules, law talk acquaints clients with a process in which judges exercise immense discretionary power. The message to the client is that it is the judge, not the rules, that really counts. What the judge will accept, what the judge will do is the crucial issue in the divorce process. With respect to property settlements, Massachusetts clients are reminded that since all agreements require judicial approval there is, in effect, "nothing binding about them. The judge will do what he wants with it". Another lawyer explained that in dividing the marital property, "the judge can do with it as he chooses to do". Still another lawyer informed his client of what he called the "immense amount of power and authority" which judges exercise and suggested that the particular judge who would be hearing his case would use that power "pretty much as he deems fit".

A second way in which lawyers denigrate rules is by characterizing them as unnecessarily technical. They claim that, as a result, even judges and lawyers frequently do not know what they mean. For example:

Client: Tell me the mechanics of this.

Lawyer: You should know. It's your right to know. But whether or not I'm going to be able to explain this is questionable... . It's sort of simple in practice, but its very confusing to explain. I've an awful lot of really smart people who've ... who've asked me after the divorce is over, now what the hell was the interlocutory judgment?

A third criticism of rules focuses on their weakness in guiding or determining behaviour outside the legal process. Lawyers identify the limits of law. They acquaint their clients with the limited efficacy of legal rules and caution them not to rely too heavily on rules or court orders. This is particularly the case when a lawyer is trying to discourage his client from pursuing a certain course of action. Thus, in one California case, where the client was very disturbed by her husband's continuing refusal to obey a restraining order [restricting contact with the spouse], the lawyer's response was to stress the futility of going to court to obtain a contempt order:

Lawyer: Okay. So what you would like is what? You'd like phone calls if he needs to ...

Client: Limited to the concern of the children or medical bills, and, you know, never mind giving me all his heartache trouble.

Lawyer: You know, he's in violation of the court order [restricting contact with the spouse], but to take him to court, it can be done, I'm not saying that we won't do it or anything, it's a matter of proving contempt. We can prove it, but then what do you get out of that. You don't get anything... .

"You don't get anything" suggests that since rules and orders are not self-executing, they do not necessarily govern behaviour or resolve problems. This lawyer is schooling his client in what has been called the "gap" problem, the extremely loose coupling between legal rules and social behaviour.

The same emphasis on the limited efficacy of rules is conveyed in the following discussion of joint legal custody, where a Massachusetts lawyer talks to his client about the irrelevance of joint legal custody. The client brings substantial preconceptions about the meaning of joint custody to this exchange. The lawyer's effort is to disabuse him of those preconceptions, to emphasize that what matters is the ongoing relationship between spouses rather than the posture of official arrangements:

> Client: The custody order I would like to be requested is joint custody. That means, and correct me if I'm wrong, that I shall be aware and informed and be able to have input in my daughter's life as well as she would have the right to be aware, informed and have input in my daughter's life whether my daughter is there with her or here with me.
>
> Lawyer: There's no such thing as court ordered joint custody. In a realistic sense, real sense of joint custody. You are thinking of it as if there is. Just like it's a court ordered step. You get custody and she has visitation rights. That means definite things. You have the custody and you control the child's life: She becomes a visitor. On joint custody that's something that is worked out between the two individuals who right from the start are able to deal with the child with at least no major problems. They would deal with the child in a normal manner...

This lawyer's comparison of court orders and what really happens suggests a parallel between the ineffectiveness of rules governing the behaviour of those who are part of the legal apparatus. Lawyers, court officers, judges – and the limited power of rules to control the behaviour of people outside the legal process.[29]

We mentioned above that doubts about the application of formalism in practice cast doubt in turn on the attainability of certain liberal values. They may also make us cautious about the economic analysis of law, which we look at later in this book. A major strand in economic analysis is transaction costs economics. Here the assumption is that in the absence of transaction costs (like the time and cost of bargaining and litigating) parties would reach the most efficient outcome by themselves. Since in the real world transaction costs do seriously impede or prevent bargaining, a major purpose of law is said to be to "mimic the market". Law should simulate the result that the parties would have arrived at if they could have bargained costlessly. The law should try to by-pass transaction costs by enabling the parties to "bargain in the shadow of the law".[30] The law is supposed to provide information on which parties can predict the outcome of litigation. They can therefore build these predictions into their bargaining and arrive at settlements with lower costs.[31] Central to this view, of course, is the empirical claim that legal rules do perform this function of assisting predictions. Work like Sarat and Felstiner's makes one suspicious of such a claim. At the least it suggests that the rules providing the shadow are more localised and difficult to identify than scholars normally admit.

---

29 A Sarat and W Felstiner, "Lawyers and Legal Consciousness: Law Talk in the Divorce Lawyer's Office" (1989) 98 *Yale Law Journal* 1663 at 1671-1676.

30 The phrase is usually attributed to R Mnookin and L Kornhauser, "Bargaining in the Shadow of the Law: The Case of Divorce" (1979) 88 *Yale Law Journal* 950. See back to Chapter 4.

31 Although it has been argued that the picture is more complex and that reducing the costs does not necessarily increase the probability of an agreement; see R Cooter and S Marks with R Mnookin, "Bargaining in the Shadow of the Law: A Testable Model of Strategic Behavior" (1982) 11 *Journal of Legal Studies* 225. Relatively little work seems to have been done on lawyers' ability to predict outcomes; see, however, EF Loftus and WA Wagenaar, "Lawyers' Predictions of Success" (1988) 28 *Jurimetrics* 436. This study found that lawyers are over-confident about the prospects for their clients.

One set of rules that lawyers are less likely to dismiss publicly as irrelevant are the rules of professional ethics. Arguably, the existence of ethical rules is an important prop to the legitimacy of the adversarial system of justice. Furthermore, the reality (as opposed to the rhetoric) of ethical practices can make a fundamental difference to the outcome of litigation.

(b) Legal ethics

The word "ethics" tends to be used differently according to the context. Sometimes it is used interchangeably with the word "morals".[32] At other times it is used to refer to the morals of a particular organised group and distinguished from morals at large. Thus, it is said, professions have a code of ethics, meaning that they are required to behave in a way that non-members are not. Some usages also distinguish between ethical and legal obligations. Here an ethical obligation is one which the law does not require a person to discharge but for which there are nevertheless compelling moral reasons why the person should. This distinction between legal and ethical obligations is a difficult one to sustain in the case of lawyers, as legal sanctions are sometimes available against lawyers for behaviour which would be lawful by others. This is partly because in the common law world lawyers are "officers of the court" and can be disciplined by the Supreme Court in which they are admitted.

In this chapter we take ethics to be the legal and professional rules which govern lawyers' behaviour *by virtue of the fact that they are lawyers*. We do not, therefore, examine the ordinary rules of contract, tort or criminal law, although they do of course apply to lawyers,[33] because they apply to people generally. We are interested in the rules which professional bodies like Law Societies enforce against their members (often pursuant to statutory powers) or which courts enforce under their inherent jurisdiction to discipline their own officers or under specific statutory powers. We are also interested in some legal rules which are not strictly unique to lawyers but which only apply to a small class[34] of "fiduciaries"; that is, people who owe special obligations of fidelity because of the position they hold. Examples include company directors and trustees as well as lawyers.

Lawyers in Australia are admitted to the Supreme Court of a particular jurisdiction and there are some differences between the ethical rules amongst the eight different jurisdictions and between barristers and solicitors in some of those jurisdictions. Because our purpose is to deal with important general issues these differences need not concern us greatly here.[35]

---

32 As Peter Singer does in *Practical Ethics*, Cambridge UP, 1979, 1. See also L Payne, "Moral Thinking in Management: An Essential Capability" in D Rhode (ed), *Ethics in Practice: Lawyers' Roles, Responsibilities, and Regulation*, Oxford UP, 2000, 59.

33 There are actually some qualifications to be made here. A barrister cannot sue for her or his fees at common law. There is also some immunity from negligence suit when it comes to advocacy. This was reaffirmed by the High Court in *D'Orta-Ekenaike v Victoria Legal Aid* [2005] HCA 12.

34 Although the categories of fiduciary relationship are often said not to be closed and in some jurisdictions there is considerable pressure to extend them: see P Finn, "Contract and the Fiduciary Principle" (1989) 12 *University of New South Wales Law Journal* 76.

35 Indeed, there is a move towards a national set of rules governing admission and legal practice; see, for example, the Law Council of Australia's *Model Rules of Professional Conduct and Practice*, March 2002.

Our starting point, therefore, is that legal practitioners are supposed to comply with ethical rules, derived from a number of sources, and applied to them because they are lawyers and fiduciaries. Indeed, it is commonly said by sociologists and by those actually claiming the social status of being a professional that the *existence* of a code of ethics is one of the traits of a profession which distinguishes it from a mere occupation.[36] Opinions differ, however, about the true role and effect of professional ethics.

At one end of the debate, supporters of the legal profession believe that the existence of ethical rules preserves standards of honesty and integrity that make lawyers act, at times, contrary to their own interests.[37] Furthermore, ethics are said to make lawyers act against the interests of their *clients* when the normatively higher interests of "justice" are at stake. Defenders of the profession might say that if liberal ideals are to be translated into reality through law, particularly in an adversary system where judges have a largely passive role, then we need a principled legal profession which is not governed purely by market considerations and the general law.

At the other end there are critics who take a quite different view. They say that ethical rules are rarely enforced in practice, partly because the profession closes ranks in all but the most serious cases of dishonesty and partly because the layperson has an uphill struggle in making a complaint. In any event, the rules are often expressed in such vague terms that they give plenty of leeway at the borderline of impropriety. Ethics, say some critics, is too frequently reduced to a set of technical rules the main function of which is to maintain the privileged and autonomous status of the profession rather than to encourage lawyers to be socially responsible, to take account of wider justice concerns, or to be "curators of the public frameworks that sustain our common existence".[38]

Most of the scholarly work on legal ethics comes from the United States, although there are examples in Australia[39] and Britain.[40] The involvement of American lawyers in the Watergate scandal of the 1970s (the bugging of the Democrats' headquarters which led to the resignation of President Nixon) prompted a great deal of research into legal ethics there and the requirement that all accredited law schools provide courses on "professional responsibility". In broad terms the ethical rules are the same in the United States as here, although they are spelt out in considerably more detail in codes. At the same time, however, they operate in particular professional and cultural contexts. For example, American lawyers often work on a contingency fee basis in civil cases (that is, they take a percentage of the plaintiff's winnings but little or nothing if the case is lost) and

---

36   For a discussion of the "traits" approach in the sociology of professions see Weisbrot, n 2, Ch 1.

37   And, of course, one purpose of moral and legal rules is to guide people away from a course of action which self-interested prudence would otherwise suggest.

38   R Gordon "Why Lawyers Can't Just be Hired Guns" in D Rhode (ed), *Ethics in Practice: Lawyers' Roles, Responsibilities, and Regulation*, Oxford UP, 2000, 42 at 47; see also C Parker, "Regulation of the Ethics of Australian Legal Practice: Autonomy and Responsiveness" (2002) 25 *University of New South Wales Law Journal* 676.

39   See Ross, n 2; S Parker and C Sampford (eds), *Legal Ethics and Legal Practice*, Oxford UP, 1995; and C Parker, "A Critical Morality for Lawyers: Four Approaches to Lawyers' Ethics" (2004) 30 *Monash University Law Review* 49.

40   See R Cranston, *Legal Ethics and Legal Responsibility*, Oxford UP, 1995 and R O'Dair, *Legal Ethics: Text and Materials*, Butterworths, 2001.

this might be an inducement to misconduct.[41] There is no shortage of critical literature in the United States but the extract below from Schnapper is a good introduction.

E Schnapper, *The Myth of Legal Ethics*
(1978)

At the Watergate hearings, John Dean, noting the profession of the principal characters in the Watergate scandal, thought it "incredible" that ten of the fifteen men involved were lawyers. That surprise apparently was shared by the legal community, which vigorously assured itself and the public that the willingness of those lawyers to trifle with the law and the truth was an aberration. The organized bar adhered to its traditional article of faith that lawyers maintain ethical standards far higher than ordinary citizens and expressed its confidence that the grievance committees established to enforce those standards could and would, subject perhaps to some mild renovation, continue to do so.

Both the public opinion polls and our own experience, however, tell us that the public probably was not the least surprised to find a group of lawyers up to their ears in unethical or illegal activity. On the contrary, samplings reveal that now, as in the past, the public regards lawyers as among the least trustworthy of people. Lawyers are often viewed as clever and devious people who, using all sorts of technicalities and double talk, trick honest working men and women out of their hard-earned money and property.

Although popular experience is a more plausible gauge than the bar's self-esteem, no reliable test of comparative honesty of lawyers has been made or is necessarily possible. There are, however, a variety of factors which suggest that, human nature being what it is, lawyers are not certain to be the pinnacle of morality.

Lawyering is within the relatively narrow category of occupations where borderline dishonesty is fairly lucrative. In most jobs nothing short of outright theft – usually with an acceptably high danger of apprehension – will increase the workers' real income appreciably, although less risky species of laziness may reduce the effort required for the same yield. To the extent, often substantial, to which lawyers increase the odds of prevailing in litigation, negotiations, or otherwise by less than puritanical means, they will tend to increase the amount of business they receive or, in a contingent fee relationship, their immediate income. In contingent fee litigation in particular the potential reward for success, however achieved, is often quite disproportionate to the investment, in costs or time, the lawyer has made or to the lawyer's normal income.

Unlike the situation in virtually every other profession or occupation, in law a resort to sharp practices does not tend to threaten continued employment. For a doctor, carpenter, or merchant, the victim and customer are one and the same; even if dissatisfied customers cannot prove illegality, they can punish and thus deter unfair practices by withholding their patronage. This system tends to break down when, for example, the purchases are so infrequent, as with used cars, that the vendor has little interest in repeat sales. For unethical lawyers the victim and customer are different individuals. If lawyers resort to high-handed tactics to protect their clients, the clients will usually be pleased with the result and continue the lawyer in their employ.

---

41   For a general discussion, see D Luban, "Speculating on Justice: The Ethics and Jurisprudence of Contingency Fees" in Parker and Sampford, n 39, Ch 5.

In many instances the very art of the lawyer is a sort of calculated disregard of the law or at least of ordinary notions of morality. The job of a good tax lawyer is often to find a loophole that will enable the client to evade the purpose of federal law. The job of a good criminal lawyer is frequently to persuade a judge or jury to set free a man the lawyer may have every reason to believe is guilty. If, as a former federal judge has urged, legal justice is a special type of truth finding, legal advocacy – urging a decision with knowledge of contrary facts hidden behind a claim of privilege – is, to coin a euphemism, a special type of truth telling. It is a valuable skill to be able to fashion a sentence that the other side, judge, or jury will take as having one meaning but which, if the truth later emerges, can be explained away as not having such a meaning at all, or to dress up in innocuous language a statement of damning content. That skill was in great demand among defenders of the presidency prior to August of 1974.

This aspect of lawyering is not unlike the work of an advertising agency, except that, in the long run, misleading advertising can tend to hurt the credibility and business of the client, while misleading lawyering generally has no such consequence. It is hard to imagine, in the legal arena, a more one-sided fight than that in which one party is represented by counsel and the other is not, but that is the stock in trade of a substantial proportion of all lawyers, including those involved in debt collection, representing landlords, and many instances of practice before administrative agencies.

The Code of Professional Responsibility, as the Canons of Professional Ethics before it, is a treasure trove of moral platitudes. If taken seriously, they would steel the most weak-willed lawyer against the daily temptations of his or her profession. The code enjoins lawyers to assist in maintaining the integrity of the profession, to improve the legal system, to avoid even the appearance of impropriety, to assist the profession in fulfilling its (not his or her?) duty to make legal counsel available, to be "temperate and dignified", to avoid "all illegal and morally reprehensible conduct", to refrain from actions involving "dishonesty, fraud, deceit, or misrepresentation", to encourage and participate in educational programs concerning our legal system, and in general to conduct themselves so as "to inspire the confidence, respect, and trust" of the public.

Virtually none of this inspirational material, however, has anything to do with legal ethics as actually enforced by the courts and bar associations. As was confirmed last year by the report on the grievance system by the Ad Hoc Committee on Grievance Procedures of the Association of the Bar of the City of New York, disciplinary proceedings are almost exclusively limited to three abuses: attorneys who steal the funds of their clients, attorneys who accept fees but fail to pursue their clients' cases, and lawyers who commit felonies. One who is guilty of this misconduct runs a significant, although declining, danger of being suspended or, in a rare case, disbarred.

But disciplinary actions for any of the other myriad forms of misconduct forbidden by the code are largely unheard of. One searches in vain for a lawyer disciplined for failing to give free legal assistance to the indigent, for failing to disclose legal precedent contrary to his client's interests, for misrepresenting facts to judges, juries, or opposing counsel, or for using political office or connections to attract clients, although the frequency of these occurrences is common knowledge. The code sets wondrous standards beyond the reach of most mortals. As enforced, it is intended solely, and somewhat erratically, to protect the few individuals rich enough to hire a lawyer from misconduct, although not from incompetence.

Why the Dissimilarity?

There are several reasons for this dissimilarity between the code as written and as enforced.

First, the standards are enforced by lawyers who will themselves be subject to whatever limitations they treat as enforceable. Few attorneys choose to steal from or neglect their clients, if only because doing so tends, in the long run, to be unprofitable. But to the extent that the enforced rules punish overzealousness on behalf of a client, they conflict with the interest of the client and thus with that of the attorney who wishes to retain that client as a customer. To be sure, the members of a grievance committee are likely to be more conscientious than the least scrupulous lawyer in their area, but they are also astute enough to understand the precedent that would be set if the bar were to look beyond the traditional areas of concern.

Second, the traditional sanctions – disbarment and suspension – are so drastic that no one wants to use them except in the most extreme cases. A punishment that strips the offender, permanently or for a limited period of time, of the ability to make a living is one from which even the most vindictive judge would ordinarily shrink. That reluctance must be all the greater when those who must decide whether to rescind that license depend for their own livelihood on possession of the same license.

Third, the traditional, if not exclusive, source of complaints to grievance committees are disgruntled clients, who may object to pelf or incompetence, if they can detect it, but are hardly likely to protest that their attorney, although successful, used unworthy means. The people most likely to perceive this misconduct, and to be able to distinguish it from the ordinary arbitrariness of any legal system, are judges and opposing counsel, both of whom are properly reluctant to see the grievance machinery become another forum for or weapon of litigation. Lawyerless individuals who may have been undone by an overreaching opposing counsel are unlikely to protest their treatment to another group of lawyers or to possess the knowledge necessary to frame a nondemurrable grievance.[42]

In broad terms, there are two classes of professional ethical duties. The first concerns duties to the client. The second concerns duties to the administration of justice. In the event of a conflict between the two, the duties to the administration of justice are supposed to prevail.

Ethical duties to the client can mostly be attributed to one or other of two principles: principles of partisanship and zealousness. Thus, the principle of partisanship generates a duty that lawyers must act only in the client's interests and not have a conflicting obligation to anyone else. It also generates a duty that their own undeclared interests must not intrude.[43] The duty of confidentiality,

---

42   E Schnapper, "The Myth of Legal Ethics" (1978) 64 *American Bar Association Journal* 202.

43   The authority for these propositions lies in several sources. In some jurisdictions there is an express professional rule. In any event, equitable duties stemming from the fiduciary nature of the lawyer-client relationship apply. There are also statutory provisions dealing with certain aspects of the principle. For example, there is commonly a requirement that money being held by a solicitor for a client must be kept in a separate account from the solicitor's own money and recorded against the client's name. The "trust account" or "client account" (the terms differ between jurisdictions) must be audited annually. The arrangement is supposed to remove the temptation for a solicitor to make temporary use of a client's money for her or his own purposes or for the purposes of another client and also to make it easier to detect breaches. Acting as a backstop in all these cases are powers given to professional bodies to discipline their members for professional misconduct and the inherent powers of the Supreme Court.

which prevents a lawyer from disclosing a client's communications without the client's consent, can also be regarded as stemming from the principle of partisanship.[44] The principle of zealousness is premised on the idea that individual rights should be protected against abuse, especially the abuse of state power. The principle leads to duties that require a lawyer to do all that is legally permissible and consistent with the lawyer's duties to the administration of justice on behalf of her or his client. This means that the lawyer's own views on the client's instructions should not enter the picture. Furthermore, the lawyer should voluntarily undertake distasteful courses of action if they are in the client's interests and do not contradict other legal or ethical obligations. We will discuss below the *Lake Pleasant* case where the lawyers searched for and found the bodies of three murder victims but did not tell the relatives of the deceased. The theory is that the lawyer is not the judge of the client's cause, nor of its consequences, and the lawyer's choice is to be zealous or, where permitted, to resign.[45]

The role of the lawyer in the adversary system is often likened by critics to that of a "hired gun";[46] a mercenary whose own conscience is irrelevant (except within the limits already mentioned). A growing number of American legal ethicists argue, however, that there should be a permitted level of ethical discretion so that the lawyer can follow his or her own conscience in certain cases.[47] An example commonly given is the lawyer who acts for a large corporation which is embarking on action that the lawyer considers anti-social. Some ethicists believe that "whistle-blowing" should be allowed here. A topical application of this concern might be the situation where a lawyer believes that her or his client is inflicting damage on the environment or on consumers, but of a kind which is not necessarily unlawful.

In order to take a position on these issues one has to take into account the wider context in which the theory of legal ethics is supposed to operate. We mentioned above that the duties to clients give way to duties to the administration of justice. Although the term "administration of justice" is a conventional one, it might be more accurate to refer to "duties to the adversary system of adjudication". Ethical rules which would otherwise be morally repugnant might become

---

44 Again, however, the authority for the rule can be found in a mixture of sources. In equity, an injunction can be obtained to restrain the breach of confidences. In practical terms the boundaries of the confidentiality principle have been worked out in some detail. Attempts are frequently made to call solicitors as witnesses or to force them to produce documents from their clients' files. A defence to these demands, called legal professional privilege, exists in the case of certain confidential communications and cases on this privilege are a useful source of authority on the extent of the duty of confidentiality.

45 There are usually ethical restrictions on resigning once a case has been taken on, quite apart from any contractual position; see, for example, *Professional Conduct Rules* (WA) r 17.3 .

46 See MH Freedman, "The Lawyer as a Hired Gun" in A Gerson (ed), *Lawyers' Ethics*, Transaction Books, 1980, 63.

47 See Gordon, n 38; and D Luban, *Lawyers and Justice*, Princeton UP, 1988 for his conception of lawyers and moral activism. See also the debate between him and Stephen Ellman in (1990) 90 *Columbia Law Review* 116 and 1004. In addition, see WH Simon, "Ethical Discretion in Lawyering" (1988) 101 *Harvard Law Review* 1083: "Lawyers should have ethical discretion to refuse to assist in the pursuit of legally permissible courses of action and in the assertion of potentially enforceable legal claims". It is as well to remember that in practical terms lawyers have what Geoffrey Hazard has called "pervasive marginal discretion" anyway, because legal ethics are not a "rule-determined domain"; see G Hazard, "Ethical Opportunity in the Practice of Law" (1990) 27 *San Diego Law Review* 127 at 128.

acceptable if they are necessary to preserve the adversary system. As we have seen, the adversary system is supposed to pit one party against the other in combat under certain ground rules so that an impartial umpire can decide which is the better argument. The principles of partisanship and zealousness are supposed to interlock with the adversary system by requiring each combatant to be represented by a loyal gladiator. Indeed, these principles are said to be defining features of the adversarial system.[48] The duties to the administration of justice are supposed to impose some minimum restraints (for example, that lawyers must not knowingly collude with perjury by the client or themselves actively mislead the court) so that in some way the fight is a "clean" one.

Analogies with the theory of the free market operating within a framework of neutral laws or the boxing contest under the Marquis of Queensbury's rules might spring to mind.[49] One does not ordinarily condone punching someone for a living but there are those who regard it as acceptable in boxing. At the same time, however, seeking to justify behaviour by reference to role morality (that is, the roles of court actors, business people or sports people) may simply move the problem somewhere else. At the end of the day one must take a view on the *system that gives rise to the roles*. The reader already has some information on which to evaluate the adversary system, both in its ideal forms and its everyday workings, and in the remainder of this chapter we supplement that information by looking at one important issue – the duty of confidentiality and the impact that this might have on the determination of truth.

Before doing so, two preliminary points need to be made. The first is that we have no reliable information on the extent to which ethical rules are actually complied with.[50] Opinions abound but there is little in the way of empirical data. What we say here tends therefore to assume compliance with the duties in the first place. Secondly, legal ethics are often presented as a formal coherent system, rather like the traditional law school image of the common law. On the other hand, as with the common law, one could characterise legal ethics as a series of indeterminate, ambiguous and confused prescriptions. William Nelson, for example, has argued that lawyers face a crisis of thought about ethical issues:

> Most analyses of standards of professional responsibility [a synonym for legal ethics] assume, quite wrongly, that a single, coherent set of ideas derived from the adversary system of adjudication undergirds the field. My claim, in contrast, is that at least three different and unrelated conceptual approaches are salient. Standards of professional responsibility are affected first, by concepts of moral ethics; second, by the need to keep the adversary system of litigation operational; and third, by a hope that sound political values will motivate lawyers when they find themselves clothed with coercive, governmental power. When a question about a lawyer's professional duty arises, an analyst must consider not only which of the three approaches should control the outcome, but in addition the outcome that the chosen approach demands. So understood, the task of deciding professional responsibility questions becomes as complex as that of deciding any

---

48   See C Menkel-Meadow, "The Limits of Adversarial Ethics" in Rhode, n 38, Ch 7.

49   And, of course, there may be ideological connections between them all. As we will see, some recent feminist jurisprudence draws links between law on the one hand and the market, maleness and aggression on the other.

50   For one example of empirical work, see D Lamb, "Ethical Dilemmas: What Australian Lawyers Say About Them" in Parker and Sampford, n 39, Ch 10.

other legal question, and it is no wonder that confusion abounds when the complexity is not even appreciated.[51]

We turn, then, to the duty of confidentiality. Its function can be assessed against the background of rule of law ideals. We saw in Chapter 3 that the rule of law requires the judge to apply impartially a pre-given rule on the basis of facts proved or admitted in the case. The outcome of a case in the adversary system is obviously sensitive to the flow of information that comes through to the judge because he or she will rarely do any investigation of the facts personally. The lawyers are therefore in a key position to decide what that information should be, but their choice is hedged by ethical rules. The duties to the administration of justice impose certain positive obligations to bring particular information to the court.[52] On the other hand, the duties to the client restrict other kinds of information which would otherwise seem to be relevant. Lawyers cannot (without the client's consent) volunteer information that harms the client because that would breach the principle of partisanship. Nor can they divulge directly to the court or to prospective witnesses the client's communications (again, without the client's consent).

It can be seen, then, that the rationale for the rules about confidentiality is similar to the rationale for the adversarial system in general. That is, the effective protection of individual rights requires that a client can trust their lawyer in the confidential disclosure of information that can be used in partisan and zealous advocacy on their behalf.

To make this a little more concrete, here are two illustrations. The first is a civil case. Pauline is injured in an accident and sues Don. Don denies liability. It looks like Pauline's word against Don's and Pauline is likely to lose because she will presumably fail to establish Don's liability on the balance of probabilities. Don tells Larry, his lawyer, that there *is* a witness, Wendy, whose evidence would help Pauline, but Pauline could not possibly know about Wendy's existence because Pauline was unconscious at the relevant time. The duty of confidentiality (and, for that matter, the duty of loyalty) prevents Larry from disclosing the existence of the witness to Pauline. It is Pauline's misfortune that the court is deprived of the information.

The second is a criminal case. Darius is accused of murder. He admits to his lawyer, Liz, that he did it in cold blood and in full control. Liz may continue to act for Darius, albeit in a limited way. She can probe the prosecution's case and argue for an acquittal on the grounds that the case has not come up to the required

---

51 WE Nelson, "Moral Ethics, Adversary Justice, and Political Theory: Three Foundations for the Law of Professional Responsibility" (1989) 64 *Notre Dame Law Review* 911 at 911-912. See also DB Wilkins, "Legal Realism for Lawyers" (1990) 104 *Harvard Law Review* 468.

52 The duties of candour, as they are often called, are discussed in Ross, n 2, Chs 14 and 15 and G Dal Pont, *Lawyers' Professional Responsibility in Australia and New Zealand*, 2nd ed, Lawbook Co, 2001, Part IV. For example, there are obligations to inform the court of legal authorities directly on the point, whether or not they help the client, and there are duties to correct previous evidence which is discovered to be untrue. In addition, in most civil litigation there is an obligation of "discovery" or "disclosure" of documents. The rules now vary around the jurisdictions but generally a lawyer should ensure that the client discloses the existence of all documents which relate to the issues in dispute. Some of these documents need not, however, be made available for inspection if they are covered by legal professional privilege. This privilege covers similar ground to the duty of confidentiality: the upshot is that pertinent information may properly be withheld from the opposing party and the court.

standard of proof beyond a reasonable doubt.[53] This means that she can try to discredit prosecution witnesses who are actually telling the truth.[54] In fact, Liz can do everything except become a mouthpiece for Darius to assert positively his innocence. To do that would count as misleading the court. If Liz feels she is being drawn in too far, she might be allowed to resign[55] but she must never reveal what Darius has said to her. Authority for this proposition, if authority is needed at all, can be found in the High Court decision in *Tuckiar v the King* in 1934. In that case Tuckiar was accused of murdering a police officer. He was convicted and sentenced to death. Tuckiar's lawyer then made a public statement about what Tuckiar had said to him because he wanted to clear the reputation of the dead officer. Tuckiar's conviction was quashed, on this and other grounds. The High Court of Australia resoundingly upheld the duty of confidentiality. Gavan Duffy CJ, Dixon, Evatt and McTiernan JJ said:

> The subsequent action of the prisoner's counsel in openly disclosing the privileged communication of his client and acknowledging the correctness of the more serious testimony against him is wholly undefensible. It was his paramount duty to respect the privilege attaching to the communication made to him as counsel, a duty the obligation of which was by no means weakened by the character of his client, or the moment at which he chose to make the disclosure.[56]

The dilemma that Tuckiar's counsel presumably found himself in was between preserving confidences and avoiding harm to others (in this case the distress of the dead constable's relatives). The famous *Lake Pleasant* case is a further illustration of such a dilemma.[57] In 1973 Garrow was charged with the murder of a man. He was represented by two lawyers and a defence of insanity was entered. Garrow told his lawyers that he had also murdered two women and told them where the bodies were. The lawyers found the bodies but did not disclose the fact to the authorities. They attempted to make a plea bargain, in a confidential discussion with prosecuting lawyers, so that the insanity plea would be accepted in return for clearing up the murders of the three missing women. Various approaches were made by the police and the father of one of the missing women for information about the cases but the lawyers said they had nothing to tell. The plea bargain was rejected and the case went to trial. In the witness box, Garrow confessed to the murders and said that his lawyers already knew about them. The lawyers then informed the authorities of the whereabouts of the

---

53 See, for example, the *NSW Barristers' Rules*, r 33(b) of which says that a barrister must not falsely suggest that some other person committed the offence charged and must not set up an affirmative case inconsistent with the confession, but may argue that the evidence taken as a whole does not prove that the accused is guilty of the offence charged or that for some reason of law the accused is not guilty.

54 This statement needs some qualification. Making unsupported allegations and asking insulting questions may be unethical. As for discrediting truthful witnesses in other ways, there is a disagreement amongst legal ethicists about its permissibility. However, an ethical rule which is expressed vaguely or is disputed may itself be a problem and allow considerably leeway to practitioners.

55 There are ethical restrictions on refusing to act, particularly at a late stage in a serious case. See, for example, *NSW Barristers' Rules* r 33(a). On the other hand, concern is regularly expressed at the frequency with which barristers do "return briefs" at a late stage.

56 (1934) 52 CLR 335 at 346.

57 For contrasting views of this case, see Gerson, n 46, Part IIE.

bodies.[58] There followed a public outcry about the actions of the lawyers; actions which, according to Luban, "wreaked havoc on their own law practices and peace of mind, caused agony to the families of the murder victims, damaged the economic life of the tourism-centered area (no-one likes to camp when they think there's a killer on the prowl), and did not help the client at all".[59] Legal ethicists and the local Bar Association, however, supported the lawyers saying that their ethical rules had required them to remain silent.

Again, to evaluate this case one must return to the adversary system. As Luban says:

> Everything rides on the argument. Lawyers have to assert legal interests unsupported by moral rights all the time – asserting legal interests is what they do, and everyone can't be in the right on all issues. Unless zealous representation could be justified by relating it to some larger social good, the lawyer's role would be morally impossible. That larger social good is supposed to be the cluster of values – procedural justice and the defense of rights – that are associated with the adversary system.[60]

We have been assuming so far that the arguments for or against the adversary system and its ethics are the same in criminal and civil proceedings. In theory, the prosecutor in criminal proceedings is simply one of the adversaries in the case. The theory does provide for exceptions, however. In the Anglo-Australian tradition, there are said to be special duties upon lawyers acting for the prosecution, at least when it is the Crown prosecuting rather than a private party.[61] The lawyer is not to be as zealous as the lawyer for a plaintiff in civil proceedings. For example, the prosecuting lawyer should try to ensure that the jury has before it the whole of the relevant facts in intelligible form and should not press for a conviction beyond putting the case for the Crown fully and firmly.[62] Furthermore, the prosecution lawyer should inform the defence of the existence, identity and whereabouts of any witness that he or she does not propose to call but whose evidence he or she considers is relevant to the defence case.[63]

One reason why the Crown is in a different position can be traced back to liberal concerns about limiting the powers of the state. The state normally has greater resources to collect evidence and present it to a court than a defendant. The liberal perspective is concerned to boost the position of the individual in such a situation. Furthermore, the consequences to a defendant of a conviction are commonly thought to be more serious than a judgment in civil proceedings. The power of the state to remove a person's liberty therefore needs particular scrutiny. This might also justify the application of special rules to private prosecutors as well as the Crown because the penalties are the same no matter who prosecutes.

One might continue the theme and argue that protections for defendants in criminal cases, such as the confidentiality surrounding communications with their lawyers, are more easily justified than in civil cases. Take, for example, another

---

58   They believed that the client had waived the confidentiality attaching to the communication by making a public announcement.

59   D Luban, *Lawyers and Justice*, Princeton UP, 1988, 53-54.

60   Ibid 54.

61   See K Crispin, "Prosecutorial Ethics" in Parker and Sampford, n 37, Ch 8.

62   See, for example, the *NSW Barristers' Rules* rr 62 and 63.

63   *NSW Barristers' Rules* r 66.

American case, *Spaulding v Zimmerman*.[64] Here Spaulding, when aged 20, had been injured in a road accident. The case against the driver, Zimmerman, was settled and the court approved the settlement. Spaulding had been examined by Zimmerman's medical expert Dr Hannah and the doctor discovered a heart problem, an aorta aneurysm, which had been caused by the accident. Spaulding's own doctor, however, had not spotted the aneurysm and the case was settled for a lower sum than it warranted. In other words, Spaulding was more seriously injured than he and his own advisers thought. Dr Hannah informed Zimmerman's lawyers who did not pass on the information (for fear of inflating the damages payable). The first instance court set aside the settlement, thus enabling Spaulding to claim extra damages, and this was upheld on appeal to the Supreme Court of Minnesota. The point to note, however, was that the Supreme Court agreed that there was no legal or ethical obligation on Zimmerman's lawyer to pass on the information (and, in fact, it would have been a breach of the duty of loyalty if he had done so without Zimmerman's consent). The Supreme Court upheld the setting aside of the settlement on other, and rather confusing, grounds. In some way it seems that Spaulding's being under 21, and thus technically a minor at that time in that jurisdiction, made a difference. Whilst the case ended well, it need not have done so. The aneurysm was life threatening and only came to light when Spaulding was required by the army reserve to have a medical check-up. Furthermore, the condition was operable. Had things gone differently, Spaulding could have died from a curable complaint of which he was ignorant but which was known to Zimmerman's lawyer. How does one justify the concealment of relevant truth in a civil case like this? Could there be a justification as strong as the one that operates within criminal law (that the power of the state needs to be kept in check)? As Luban says:

> No one is accused of a crime in this case. Uncharitably put, the basis of confidentiality here is the need to save money for the defendant or his insurance company. Charitably put, it is that the adversary system is weakly justified[65] – justified simply because it is there. That may be a reason to risk one's own life on a mountain, but it is no reason to risk Spaulding's life in a law office.[66]

The facts in Spaulding's case are dramatic, but bluff and reticence are commonplace in settlement negotiations. This was acknowledged by Young J in the Supreme Court of New South Wales:

> It would be extremely common, especially in common law settlements, for a plaintiff's barrister to negotiate out a settlement well knowing that the plaintiff has no memory at all of the accident and if the matter is called onto court would not be able to prove his case. The defendant, fearing that if the plaintiff does run his case the verdict will be a large one, thinks he has done well because he has settled for a moderate amount. Plaintiff's counsel on the other hand knows that he has done well because had the matter gone to court he would have failed.[67]

---

64   116 NW 2d 704 (1962), Sup Ct of Minnesota.

65   By which Luban means the argument that because nothing obviously better is on offer we should stick with what we have.

66   Luban, n 59, 150.

67   *Easyfind (NSW) P/L v Paterson* (1987) 11 NSWLR 98 at 106. The finding in this case was that the compromise by legal advisers of litigation is not voidable for unilateral mistake where a legal adviser, though knowing of the other's mistake, neither induced it nor deliberately cloaked it.

We do not pretend to be presenting all the issues here for an informed judgement on these questions. There are many other dimensions, not the least of which is the danger of accepting uncritically a dichotomy between criminal and civil proceedings.[68] Our purpose in this chapter is simply to rescue legal ethics from being regarded as the vocational component of a lawyer's training and demonstrate how legal ethics and the adversary system need to be brought into any doctrinal, let alone philosophical or sociological, understanding of law. Virtually all the cases studied in a law degree have been through the funnel of the legal profession, their ethics and practices. What we learn as the "facts of the case" are actually the story that has survived the process.

Whatever position one takes, there still remains the practical matter of changing anything. Arguably, lawyers have a vested interest in the current structure of legal ethics and would resist any change. The current structure offers a convenient way of screening off troubling questions by shifting responsibility elsewhere.[69] The legal profession has certainly resisted community involvement in the regulation of its affairs.[70] Although it has not always been successful in this resistance, there is no doubt about its power in public issues. As one writer put it:

> Professions are a very hard thing to take on. They are very well organised. They are powerful. They can use their muscle. They've got lots of money for advertising and they really are a form of very strong, untouchable union. We found ... that the lawyers are the worst of the lot. The accountants, architects and dentists weren't so bad, although they weren't so wonderful. I'd rank them as lawyers worst, doctors next, then dentists and accountants.[71]

Finally, as we said in opening this chapter, we do not wish to suggest that legal ethics is the only interesting topic to do with lawyers. More mundane matters

---

68   The power of repeat players like insurance companies might be regarded as raising the same kinds of problems as the power of the state. Criminal cases need not be categorised simply as the Crown versus a defendant. Other important interests are sometimes represented. It is commonly said that in rape cases the victim is also on trial. Are the arguments for protecting the defendant as strong there? If not, how does one distinguish between cases where the defendant's interests need to be balanced against those of another person and cases where no such interests arise?

69   As Nancy Lee Firak says: "In return for conforming conduct, a professional code insulates the individual in the professional role from responsibility for his or her conduct. It creates a framework within which the professional can act out that role without ethical accountability". See NL Firak, "'Ethical Fictions as Ethical Foundations': Justifying Professional Ethics" (1986) 24 *Osgoode Hall Law Journal* 35 at 44. See also D Rhode, "Ethical Perspectives on Legal Practice" (1985) 37 *Stanford Law Review* 589 at 595-601.

70   See, for example, the submission of the NSW Law Society to the NSW Law Reform Commission on the *General Regulation of the Legal Profession*, quoted in J Disney, P Redmond, J Basten and S Ross, *Lawyers*, 2nd ed, Law Book Co, 1986, 220: "In order to fulfil this necessary function [of expressing views on the actions of government] there must exist independence for the profession as a body as well as independence for the individual legal practitioner. Loss of independence of the profession as a body limits the ability of the profession to fulfil the functions which society demands of it, particularly the function of impartial consideration by commenting upon and making representations in relation to proposed government legislation and regulation with a view to ensuring that the rights and interests of the individual members of the public are both protected and fairly treated". For a review of the arguments concerning lawyers' independence, the rule of law and liberalism, see RW Gordon, "The Independence of Lawyers" (1988) 68 *Boston University Law Review* 1.

71   Dr J Nieuwenhusen, former Research Director, Committee for Economic Development, Melbourne quoted in the third submission of the Federation of Community Legal Centres (Victoria) to the Senate Cost of Justice Inquiry.

like the quality, cost and punctuality of the services of even the most ethical lawyers are of great concern to the citizen. As with ethics compliance, however, one's opinions on these matters are based largely on anecdotal evidence in the absence of anything more reliable.

Discussion Questions

1. Bearing in mind the difficulties in having access to the justice system (see Chapter 4) and the fact that the majority of cases are settled or abandoned without a trial (see Chapter 5), do you think the adversary system of justice provides a complete justification for legal ethics?

2. You act for an insurance company. You are told that the company recently arranged for a routine medical examination in connection with a proposal for life assurance. They discovered that the proposer is HIV positive, although the proposer is unaware of this. The company is about to refuse the life cover but is not going to give its reasons, for fear of public criticism that it is discriminating against people who are HIV positive. Assuming that its proposed action is not unlawful (for example, because there is no relevant anti-discrimination legislation in that jurisdiction), what would you do? In particular, if your client will not change its decision, would you contact the proposer and make her or him aware of the condition?

3. Earlier in this book we looked at the idea that "law is not what the judges say in the reports but what lawyers say to one another and to clients – in their offices". In the light of the material in this present chapter, do you agree with this view?

4. Do the professional conduct rules for lawyers serve the cause of justice?

5. In this chapter lawyers have been described variously as gatekeepers, hired-guns, double agents, or translators. Which, if any, of these labels do you think is accurate? Which do you disagree with? Are there other labels you would choose?

Chapter 7

The Politics of Law-Making

(a)   Introduction

In this chapter we explore, primarily through a number of case studies, the relationship between law and power in the formation of law. We focus here primarily on the "emergence" of legislation, although the role of both judicial and non-legal actors in the interpretation, implementation and enforcement of legislation is also considered.

Many of the theories that we examine in this chapter rely, at least to some extent, on claims about power – that there are inbuilt inequalities within modern societies like Australia based on wealth, gender, race and so on. Whether these claims are valid, and whether concepts such as social class, power elites or interest groups best advance them, are questions for sociology and political science and fall outside the scope of an introductory text for law students.[1] That said, in the first part of this chapter, we preface our case studies with a short excursion into the various theories of power and its relationship with making, breaking and enforcing law. To some it may seem obvious that law and power are interrelated in some way – not least since statutes are forged through the overtly political dynamics and institutional party politics of the legislative process. Yet lawyers do not seem to be too concerned to inquire very deeply into the connection between law and power. Perhaps this is because the connection is so complex and difficult to define. The insularity that law has traditionally maintained from other disciplines has left it poorly equipped for such analysis. Other reasons, however, might lie in the liberal underpinnings of law.

First, a key liberal assumption is that the only significant actors in society are individuals (to be favoured) and governments (to be watched). This has the effect of diverting attention away from other kinds of group-based identities, such as those based on gender, wealth or race. Indeed, one of the criticisms that could be levelled at orthodox legal scholarship is that it has failed to address properly the imbalances of power within the legal system that affect an individual's capacity to assert their rights and to obtain access to justice. The significance of these power imbalances in relation to legal representation was considered in Chapter 4.

---

1   See, however, M Western, "Class and Stratification" in JM Najman and JS Western (eds), *A Sociology of Australian Society*, 2nd ed, Macmillan, 1993; S Encel, "Class and Status" in S Encel and MJ Berry (eds), *Selected Readings in Australian Society: An Anthology*, Longman Cheshire, 1987, 136; J Higley, D Deacon and D Smart, *Elites in Australia*, Routledge and Kegan Paul, 1979 and RW Connell, "The Money Measure: Social Inequality of Wealth and Income" in The Social Justice Collective, *Inequality in Australia*, Heinemann, 1991, 129, and the references cited therein.

Secondly, another liberal tenet is that the state should be neutral between people, which has the effect that the kinds of distinctions important to an analysis of power (such as gender, wealth, or race) are deemed irrelevant. Fundamental liberal principles, such as equality before the law, rule out the making of non-relevant distinctions. The blind-folded figure holding the scales of justice symbolises the neutrality and impartiality of law. Once law's neutrality between groups is treated *as a fact*, certain inquiries are closed off for judges, lawyers and legal scholars, even if they remain open for others.

Thirdly, since freedom of the individual is paramount and must be protected by law, the law is constructed as the *antithesis* of power. It is the law and its institutions that *control* the exercise (and abuse) of power by others. Indeed, a significant rationale behind the rule of law is that it confers legitimacy on the state institutions and public officials who exercise power over individuals. Liberal constitutional ideas, such as the "separation of powers" and "checks and balances" are attempts to place limits on the power of state institutions, principally the legislature and executive.

(b) Law and power

The relationship between law and power, although its full significance may be suppressed within liberal theory, is a crucial part of the political context of law. In the following sections, we can only provide an introduction to, and an overview of, the different issues and perspectives which are relevant to analysing law and power.

We suggested above that, despite a liberal disinclination to examine law and power, there are some obvious relationships. Roger Cotterrell, a lawyer and sociologist, suggests three ways of approaching the relationship between law and power.[2] First, there is the idea that law makes power available for people to use in their everyday lives – law as a tool of *empowerment*. For example, we can commence legal action to recover damages from, or to restrain the actions of, another person; we can use contract law to facilitate commercial relationships; or we can use family law to re-order our domestic relationships. The idea of having *a* power in law is often linked with having a right. Thus a standard theory on the nature of rights is that rights involve the power to have one's will predominate over that of another. A clear example is "a power of appointment" which might be created under a will or trust deed where the power-holder can decide on the destination of the trust funds, irrespective of the wishes of the potential beneficiaries. As Cotterrell puts it, law gives the person:

> [T]he ability to coerce, influence, make things happen, and get things done; ... [we can] invoke the aid of the state or, at least, ... make use of certain procedures, practices, or circumstances of state agencies to further or protect one's interests.[3]

Secondly, we can take the reverse point of view and think of law as a tool of *disempowerment*. People often experience law as power being exercised over them. This experience:

---

2   R Cotterrell, *Law's Community: Legal Theory in Sociological Perspective*, Clarendon Press, 1995. These are not exhaustive. For example, according to Hindess, the 17th century English political theorist John Locke defined political power as a right to make laws and to enforce them: B Hindess, *Discourses of Power: From Hobbes to Foucault*, Blackwell, 1996, 52 and 62.

3   Cotterrell, n 2, 4.

involves feelings of vulnerability and insecurity, of being subject to official control or interference. It is often an experience of being threatened in precise, calculated, and complex ways by other individuals, agencies or collectivities, which are able to invoke law against the person ... It may also be an experience of being made helpless by the technicality and obscurity of regulations and practice, which one does not understand but which nevertheless envelop and entrap the individual.[4]

So, when we alter our behaviour because of the likelihood or threat of being punished we experience the power of law as much as when that threat is actually realised. Thirdly, Cotterrell points out that law and power are seen to be related in a more general way, which he describes as the experience of *legal security*:

This experience is one of social peace, or of dangers held at bay; the sense, for example, of safe streets and secure homes, reliable transactions with others, and of plans and investments in which reasonable expectations will not be frustrated. The experience of legal security is based on the belief that power is being used in unseen ways to protect the citizen from unknown others (individuals, corporations, groups of various kinds) who might pose threats through unpredictable or irresponsible action, and from political or military authorities that might otherwise seem uncontrolled or unaccountable.[5]

This conception of the relationship between power and law is particularly pertinent in the wake of the 9/11 attacks in the United States, and the need to enact new powers and offences to reassure citizens that the law is protecting them. These reforms, as we shall explore in Chapter 14, were hastily enacted, though the claims of inadequacy of existing powers are hotly debated. Indeed, many of the reforms passed as a package after 9/11 had their genesis in initiatives years earlier.[6]

We see that the idea of power can be used in different ways. Power is variously seen as something which individual social actors use to achieve specific goals, as a characteristic of particular social relations, or as part of the broad social fabric. The exact nature of the relationship between law and power also varies. For example, law is seen as a means of exercising or achieving power, as a way of controlling power, or as a system of power in itself. In relation to the latter, the power of law is manifest not merely in law's connection with state coercion, whether actual or threatened. It also expresses itself conspicuously in those decisions *not* to punish those who have broken the law. The power of the state to grant mercy to the law-breaker, by sentence mitigation or issuing pardons, expresses the power of law over the individual. The liberal use of the royal prerogative of mercy in the 18th century tempered the harshness of English criminal law, expressing symbolically the awesome power and beneficence of law simultaneously.[7] This is

---

4   Cotterrell, n 2, 4-5.

5   See, Cotterrell, n 2, 5.

6   S Bronitt and B McSherry, *Principles of Criminal Law*, 2nd ed, LBC, 2005, 877-882, explores the political opportunism around many of the reforms enacted in the aftermath of the 9/11 attacks.

7   A similar thesis can be supported from reviewing the "contradictions" surrounding the use of English law by convicts in the early colonial period: B Kercher, *The Unruly Child: A History of Law in Australia*, Allen and Unwin, 1995, Ch 2. It has been suggested, more generally, that law replaced monarchy as the principal legitimating ideology for the state in the 18th century: D Hay, "Property, Authority and the Criminal Law" in D Hay, P Linebaugh, J Rule, EP Thompson and C Winslow (eds), *Albion's Fatal Tree: Crime and Society in 18th Century England*, Pantheon, 1975.

further explored through a review of Douglas Hay's work later in this chapter. So, while there are some obvious ties between law and power, we need to go beyond the obvious if we are to gain a better understanding of that relationship.[8]

Suppose that law does not check all kinds of power. Suppose that law *perpetuates* some kinds of it. Suppose, even, that law is the *prize* of the powerful: it is something for which groups might struggle. Suppose further that law and power are not independent or merely overlapping concepts, and that law *is* power, or that law *defines* power. By exploring these (and related) suppositions we can see law in a wholly new light.

In the next section we look at some of the ways in which power has been analysed in the social sciences. Of necessity this will be a selective overview. Then, in the subsequent sections, we look at some ways in which the relationship between law and power can be applied to illuminate how laws "emerge" and are applied (or *not* applied) in practice.

(c) Perspectives on power

The concept of power is a central one in the social sciences.[9] Although particular disciplines tend to focus upon different aspects of power, some common questions are being explored in this vast literature. These include questions such as: Is power a property or a relationship? Is it *possessed* or is it *exercised*, and by whom or what – individuals, collectivities, structures or systems? Does the exercise of power by one person or group necessarily reduce the power of another person or group?[10] Does power always involve unequal or dependent relationships, or can it be shared and collective?

(i) Political, philosophical and sociological perspectives

We deal with these three disciplinary perspectives under the one heading because their treatments of power tend to overlap, especially in the subdisciplines of political philosophy and political sociology. Perhaps even more than with law, there is an intuitive link between politics and power. For some political scientists power is the defining concept of their discipline: politics is simply the study of institutionalised power.

There is an important distinction to be drawn between having "power over" another person and having "power to" do something. The "something" might be persuading others to change their position, or granting benefits to others. This latter perspective treats power as a resource which can be used to achieve results, whether by coercion or consensus. In this view power is what money is to the economist: it is the medium via which transactions are observed and measured.[11]

---

8   Cotterrell, n 2, 6.

9   For a review of the role of power in political theory and the social sciences, see S Lukes, "Power and Authority" in T Bottomore and R Nisbet (eds), *A History of Sociological Analysis*, Heinemann, 1978, Ch 16, and Hindess, n 2.

10   In the literature, the idea that as power accrues to one side of a relationship it also is diminished on the other side is called a "zero-sum game".

11   JD Singer, "Inter-Nation Influence: A Formal Model" (1963) 57 *American Political Science Review* 420. For a modern discussion, see DA Baldwin, *Paradoxes of Power*, Blackwell, 1989, Ch 2.

This is usually described as a structural or systemic perspective on power.[12] This has been the domain of political sociology, and it directs our attention to power within social organisations, rather than within interpersonal relations. Political sociologists, such as C Wright Mills, Robert Nisbet and Karl Marx, have, in different ways, studied power in the context of political and social movements, bureaucracies, social stratification, and race relations. Questions considered here include whether power is exercised predominantly by social classes, by elites or simply by groups who come and go, rise and fall, within a pluralist polity.

For their part, philosophers have engaged in more detailed semantic analyses in an attempt to distinguish "power" from a whole host of related terms like influence, control, persuasion, manipulation, domination, authority and force. Such analyses are important pre-conditions to much philosophical work, in particular to subjects like justice.

(ii) Economics

On the whole, economists have not developed any well-structured theory of power.[13] Of course the idea of power does feature in economic writing. For example, in neo-classical and "new institutional" economics (two of the main schools of contemporary economic thought[14]) one finds express references to the power which monopolists have to control and restrict the operation of otherwise free markets, or to the relative bargaining power of parties where both are seeking to maximise their own benefits. But more often than not in this literature the idea of power is either expressly ignored[15] or it is submerged. An example of a "submerged" power argument is found in the neo-classical presumption against the state regulation of private economic activity. Here the presumption is that the exercise of private power is always preferable to public power and that there is some clear distinction which can be drawn between the two.

Some schools of economic thought deal with power more openly. Some economists see the economy as a system of power. The focus of this approach is summed up as follows:

> The society's economic wellbeing depends finally on how power, public and private, is acquired and used. What goals are sought? Whose interests matter? What criteria of judgment are reflected in private and public power decisions and choices? How can power, public and private, be held accountable?[16]

Marxist economists, on the other hand, see their very subject matter, "the economy", as a locus of struggle between more or less powerful classes.

---

12 Quite different examples of this perspective are found in the structural functionalism of Talcott Parsons and Marxist analysis of Nicos Poulantzas, extracts from which are in S Lukes (ed), *Power*, Blackwell, 1986, Chs 6 and 7.

13 R Bartlett, *Economics and Power*, Cambridge UP, 1989, 3.

14 See Chapter 12 of this book for a description of these two schools.

15 For example, Oliver Williamson, the founder of "new institutional economics", urges us to put aside considerations of power and justice in favour of looking at the economy of transaction costs (we discuss Williamson's approach in Chapter 12): O Williamson, *The Mechanisms of Governance*, Oxford UP, 1996, 7-8.

16 M Tool and W Samuels, "Introduction", in Tool and Samuels (eds), *State, Society and Corporate Power*, 2nd ed, Transaction Publishers, 1989, viii.

In the light of the voluminous literature on the meaning of "power", we do not pretend to resolve these debates over its proper definition here. Indeed, because of the seeming intractability of these debates, a position has emerged in the social sciences that power is an "essentially contested" concept.[17] There is no single objective meaning capable of rational verification: there is no essence that can be uncontroversially captured. Instead, one has to accept that a particular theory within a particular discipline generates its own meaning useful for its own purposes. This is the position that we take here.

(d)   Perspectives on law and power

Although analysis of law and power has not been a prominent feature of liberal legal scholarship, other theoretical perspectives have offered some useful insights.

(i)   Marxist approaches

Whilst Marx did not have a lot to say about law, legal theorists have subsequently applied his theories to the study of law and legal phenomena. Alan Hunt has summarised the major themes in Marxist writings on law. Those relevant to our present discussion argue that "law is inescapably political", that "law is always potentially coercive or repressive" and that "the content and procedures of law manifest, directly or indirectly, the interests of the dominant class(es) or the power bloc".[18]

Early Marxist theory depicted a straightforward relationship between law and power – laws were created and enforced by the state in order to further the interests of the dominant class. The dominant class is the one that controls access to the means of production, and is also able to gain political control. In this theory – known as class instrumentalism – law is reduced to a single dimension – a means of maintaining economic power. As Collins describes it, "the economic base determines the legal superstructure, not instantaneously and mechanically, but through a process of class rule in which the participants further their interests through the legal system".[19] Subsequent Marxist work on law abandoned this rather simplistic view, recognising instead that law (here meaning legal rules, legal systems and processes) is too complex and inconsistent to be described as a blunt tool of the dominant class.

The adoption of Marxist and Leftist perspectives challenged many other disciplines, challenges which had direct implications for law. Revolutionary shifts in disciplines like criminology reshaped views on criminal behaviour and how legal responses to crime should be understood. The "New Criminology" emerging in the 1970s viewed criminality and criminalisation as essentially *political* acts of resistance and control respectively.[20] Criminal behaviour, it was proposed, was normal and natural, merely an assertion of human diversity in a society of

---

17   See, for example, S Lukes, *Power: A Radical View*, Macmillan, 1974 and KI Macdonald, "Is 'Power' Essentially Contested?" (1977) 7 *British Journal of Political Science* 418. For an argument that power is not "essentially contested", see T Ball, "Power" in R Goodin and P Pettit (eds), *A Companion to Contemporary Political Philosophy*, 1993, Blackwell, 548.

18   A Hunt, *Explorations in Law and Society*, Routledge, 1993, 249-250.

19   H Collins, *Marxism and Law*, Oxford UP, 1982, 29.

20   I Taylor, P Walton and J Young, *The New Criminology*, Routledge and Kegan Paul, 1973.

inequality of wealth, power and property. Criminality, on the other hand, was merely a social construct invented by the powerful to protect the interests of capital. The idealism evident in this scholarship was the contention that crime, being a function of existing unequal social, economic and political arrangements, would disappear when these inequalities were eradicated.

The modern law can and does operate in an oppressive fashion against the poor and disadvantaged members of society. This is further explored in Chapter 9 in relation to the police use of public order laws, especially minor charges like offensive language, to exercise power over Aboriginal communities, a development that has replaced earlier "welfare" laws with "criminalisation" as the predominant instrument of social control.[21] Welfare "cheats" are more aggressively pursued through the criminal law than predominantly middle class "tax cheats".[22] This approach has also exposed the differential response to "crime on the streets" and "crime in the suites". The crimes of the powerful, by white collar criminals or corporations, have become a significant object of study in both criminal and corporations law.[23] That said, there are many ways in which law *benefits* the poor and the working class (for example, social security laws, legal aid and compulsory superannuation). Also the law's commitment to formalism and legality provides sympathetic courts with resources to detect defects in how laws are enforced against minorities. While the courts are rarely in a position to challenge the underlying fairness of the substantive law, they can demand that the conduct of law enforcement officials in gathering evidence is lawful and proper. In Chapter 9 we explore how some courts have tempered the overzealous enforcement of offensive language charges in Aboriginal communities through the application of the judicial discretion to exclude improperly obtained evidence.

Many further examples could be found where laws are invoked to prevent discrimination or oppression of disadvantaged groups by the state or its officials, often successfully. For this reason, Marxist legal theory began to explore the idea that the state (and its laws) are neither wholly separate from ruling class interests, nor are they mere instruments of repression. Instead, the state is said to be "relatively autonomous" from ruling class interests. Collins sums up one view of the role of law within this system of relative autonomy:

> Where the job of articulating and developing law is handled by a distinct caste of lawyers, who are not identical in their composition to the ruling class, it is much easier to suppose that they reason without concern for the material interests of the dominant class, and furthermore that not all their ideas are derived from the dominant ideology.[24]

We return to this idea later in this chapter.

---

21   See generally C Cunneen, *Conflict, Politics and Crime – Aboriginal Communities and the Police*, Allen and Unwin, 2001.

22   The majority of tax and Medicare fraud is dealt with by civil and administrative measures to recover losses, rather than by criminal prosecution. Welfare fraud, by contrast, seems much more likely to be prosecuted. See D Brown and R Hogg, *Rethinking Law and Order*, Pluto Press, 1998, 95-98.

23   C Wells, *Corporations and Criminal Responsibility*, Oxford UP, 2001. B Fisse and J Braithwaite, *Corporations, Crime and Accountability*, Cambridge UP, 1993.

24   Collins, n 19, 63.

(ii)   Foucault

More recently a different approach to power has emerged from the writing of the late French philosopher, Michel Foucault.[25] Foucault's work was concerned more with power than with law. Indeed, one of his basic arguments was that if we are to have a proper understanding of power in modern society, law should not be the centrepiece of our study. In his words, we should "try to rid ourselves of a juridical and negative representation of power, and cease to conceive of it in terms of law, prohibition, liberty and sovereignty".[26] This is because in modern society the locus of power has shifted and has become diffuse. Foucault's theory was that other disciplines, or other forms of power, have come to de-centre law in modern societies. Thus social control is as much a product of new bodies of knowledge such as the "psy" disciplines (psychiatry, psychology and psychoanalysis) as of traditional instruments of the state, such the courts and the police. Law interacts with these disciplines, seeking to "recode" them in the form of law. A good example of this is found in the role of expert psychiatric judgments in legislation which authorise the involuntary hospitalisation and treatment of persons defined as mentally ill.[27] Another example is how medical and scientific discourse came to conceptualise drug use as a pathology and therefore as a treatable disease. Before the scientific discovery of "addiction" in the late 19th and early 20th centuries,[28] drug use was primarily viewed as an immoral practice, which in Australia was associated with the Chinese (see the discussion later in this chapter). The medicalisation of drug use is consistent with Foucault's analysis, where the new diagnosis of social as well as biological "diseases" empowered medical science and the medical profession as the appropriate disciplinary authority over subjects.[29]

Foucault argued that we should not think of power as something which is concentrated in the hands of certain individuals, groups or classes, or as something which is exercised by the "haves" over the "have-nots". Nor is the exercise of power restricted to official or formal mechanisms. Instead, Foucault's concern was more with the *mechanisms* of power than with who exercises it. Power is an essential feature of all aspects of social life. In his words:

> It is never localised here or there, never in anybody's hands, never appropriated as a commodity or piece of wealth. Power is employed and exercised through a net-like organisation. And not only do individuals circulate between its threads; they are always in a position of simultaneously undergoing and exercising this power. They are not only its inert or consenting target; they are always also the

---

25   Foucault's major works include *Discipline and Punish*, Allen Lane, 1979; *Madness and Civilization*, Tavistock, 1979; and *The History of Sexuality*, Allen Lane, 1979. An analysis of Foucault's approach to power can be found in Hindess, n 9, Ch 5.

26   Foucault, cited in Hunt, n 18, 268.

27   See S Bottomley, "The Concept of Mental Illness in New South Wales: A Critical Argument" (1989) 12 *UNSW Law Journal* 284.

28   The concept of drug and alcohol "addiction" as a disease emerged in the late 19th century, see H Levine, "The Discovery of Addiction: Changing Conceptions of Habitual Drunkenness in America" (1978) 39(1) *Journal of Studies on Alcohol* 143. The medical profession conceptualised drug use as a progressive disease, the principal symptom of addiction being the loss of control over usage which could only be cured by abstinence. A similar process was applied to the discovery of alcohol addiction, which generated new laws and powers for dealing with habitual drunkenness.

29   These developments are explored in M Foucault, *The Birth of the Clinic: An Archaeology of Medical Perception*, Vintage Press, 1975.

elements of its articulation. In other words, individuals are the vehicles of power, not its points of application.[30]

So, power is constantly being created and exercised by and within social institutions such as universities, prisons and corporations, as well as courts and the police. Power is not simply a legal phenomenon.

Foucault's efforts were directed toward exploring the governance of subjects, a concept which had both external and internal disciplinary dimensions. In *Discipline and Punish – The Birth of the Prison*,[31] Foucault traced the transformation of disciplinary technologies from their initial focus on the "corporeal" (such as capital punishment and flogging), to the "carceral" (the rise of the penitentiary in the 19th century) and, finally, to the emergence of "risk management" in the late 20th century. He examined the new surveillance technologies, such as Jeremy Bentham's blueprint for a model prison that incorporated "The Panopticon", that were developed to produce "docile bodies". The Panopticon's circular design, based around a central watch-tower, subjected prisoners to the constant but invisible threat of surveillance from a central observation point.[32] The penitentiary model emerged as an instrument of "carceral" discipline directed to training the mind or soul of the offender. The penitentiary incorporated the pervasive surveillance technology of Bentham's Panopticon and social isolation of prisoners as a means of achieving "reform through suffering". This new architecture of penality was supported by the emerging disciplines of criminology and penology, which offered scientific explanations for offending that progressed from crude pathological or biological accounts, to more complex psychological explanations.

Feminist scholars have shown a greater scepticism toward Foucault. Whilst Foucault predicted the displacement of law by discourses with greater claims to being scientific, feminists like Carol Smart are not so sure. In her book, *Feminism and the Power of Law*,[33] Smart has examined the power that lies within the idea of law. She has argued that law has power because it can lay claim to the truth. If a particular issue becomes regulated by law then the legal depiction of the situation disqualifies other perspectives on it. If, for example, foetuses are seen to have legal rights then the abortion debate changes significantly, even though the moral and political arguments are unchanged. Another instance is rape. The law's definition of rape, its version of consent and its insistence on the relevance of the victim's previous sexual history have a more powerful claim to the truth about rape than the woman's truth.[34] The law's view as to "the best interests of the child"

---

30   M Foucault, *Power/Knowledge*, Harvester Press, 1980, 98.

31   M Foucault, *Discipline and Punish — The Birth of the Prison*, Pantheon Books, 1977.

32   We refer to the Panopticon again in Chapter 10. In his famous essay "The Panopticon versus New South Wales" (1802) Bentham trumpeted the model of prison reform as a preferable solution to transportation to Australia. Mark Finnane has traced these shifts through the demise of transportation and the emergence of "model prisons" in Australia: *Punishment in Australian Society*, Oxford UP, 1997.

33   C Smart, *Feminism and the Power of Law*, Routledge, 1990.

34   Smart's research explored how substantive legal definitions of consent and the rules of evidence in rape trials construct a legal truth about sexuality – a "phallocentric" discourse – that does not conform with women's experience: see C Smart, "Law's Truth/Women's Experience" in R Graycar (ed), *Dissenting Opinions – Feminist Explorations in Law and Society*, Allen and Unwin, 1990, and C Smart, *Law, Crime and Sexuality*, Sage, 1995.

in custody cases has more power than the psychologist's or social worker's view. Unlike Foucault, Smart suggests that there is little evidence that the power of law has waned. Arguably more areas of life are becoming legalised, with the effect that other versions of the truth about these areas are disqualified.

Law remains a "closed system" to other disciplines. Alternate truths about "human behaviour", particularly those that contradict the liberal ideas of individual autonomy and freewill, find it difficult to obtain a foothold. This is apparent in trials of women who kill their abusive spouses. While these killings could be explained in terms of legitimate self-defence, women are rarely able to speak for themselves about the necessity of their actions. To count legally, the experiences of battered women are typically mediated through psychological and psychiatric expert testimony, which tends to support a finding of insanity or diminished responsibility. These accepted scientific narratives, however, conceal important perspectives on the gendered nature of harm; they also downgrade the significance of expertise that is acquired through "experience", rather than scientific research or formal training.[35]

The implications of Foucault's work, as adapted to law by writers like Smart, are still being worked out. At the least, however, these ideas illuminate some of the issues in the following chapters. We will see in Chapter 8 how some feminists believe that legal rules, reasoning and processes are imbued with maleness and that they disempower the woman's voice on many issues. We will see in Chapter 9 that common law theory about property and ownership is a discourse which runs counter to Aboriginal customary ideas about land-holding. The "truth" that Australia was unowned at the time of British "settlement" – *terra nullius* – was one, although only one, factor in disempowering the original inhabitants.

(iii) Law as culture

Another way of examining the relationship between law and power, related to Foucault's work, is to begin by thinking about law as a system of ideas. Cotterrell points out that from this perspective, law's power lies in the way it shapes and influences how people think and act. Law shapes the way in which we view the world and the possibilities which we see as being available in organising our lives. One important implication of this is that law can affect the way in which we think of power itself. It does this

> by shaping the very concepts (for example, property, contract, ownership, fiduciary relationship, responsibility, liability, rights, and duties) which citizens use in describing and explaining (to themselves and to others) social reality and the nature and significance of social relationships.[36]

As a general example, consider what happens when a person enters the legal system for the first time, either to bring an action or to defend a claim. She will likely find that her own ideas of what is just and fair, of what is an appropriate outcome, are reshaped. Court personnel (this includes the registry staff, the lawyers and the magistrate) are able to impose their perceptions of what is "legal" onto the case. This is done in many ways, including advice about what are the

---

35   The pros and cons of using expert evidence in cases of femicide are explored in Bronitt and McSherry, n 6, 312-315.

36   Cotterrell, n 2, 7.

"relevant" legal issues, what is the "best" strategy, what is a "realistic" outcome, whether the evidence "supports" the case and so on. Barbara Yngvesson, an American legal sociologist, has observed that all of this activity "silences some interpretations and privileges others, constructing the official definition of what constitutes order and disorder in the lives of local citizens".[37]

Understanding law *as culture*, rather than as a set of formal rules, is an important aspect of the critical and socio-legal perspective on law.[38] This perspective has been aided by developments in legal history over the past two decades. Legal historians are increasingly aware that formal legal sources – embodied in the surviving fragments of common law and statute – can only be understood by studying the characters, history, prevailing ideas and values of the legal profession who applied these laws. Brian Simpson, a leading English scholar of 19th century English legal history, has attempted to articulate this into a general theory of law. Disputing the positivist model of law as a "rule-book" or "system of rules", Simpson offers an alternative concept in which "the common law is best understood as a system of customary law, that is a body of traditional ideas received within a caste of experts".[39]

Focusing attention on the cast of experts – which includes lawyers, judges and legal scholars – exposes the wider role of legal culture in understanding how law is applied and developed over time. To be sure, traditional ideas are embedded in formal legal rules. But they are also found in customs, conventions, education and ethics of the legal profession. Some of these ideas will be universal – ideas about justice, the rule of law, formalism and liberalism that we have explored above in Chapter 2. Others may be highly localised to specific jurisdictions or courts, such as how judges should be addressed, how legal argument should be advanced, court dress and etiquette etc. We have examined the implications of this idea of law and legal culture in the three previous chapters when we looked at "access to justice", litigation and the role of lawyers.

It is important to be clear about the implications of the "law as culture" perspective. Rather than law being something separate from social structures and practices, it sees law as part and parcel of those structures and practices. So, law regulates social behaviour not as a set of rules which are imposed from the "outside", but by being internalised in that behaviour – we see ourselves as law sees us, and the demands which law makes come to seem obvious and natural to us.[40]

This approach therefore emphasises the ideological and expressive nature of law, and the ways in which law is important in shaping and reinforcing certain social, economic and political relationships. Following Foucault, this approach also recognises that law is not the only ideological force at work in society – it is simply one of the more institutionalised ways in which ideas are expressed.

---

37 B Yngvesson, "Making Law at the Doorway: The Clerk, the Court, and the Construction of Community in a New England Town" (1988) 22 *Law & Society Review* 409 at 410.

38 One of the few introductory legal textbooks to adopt this approach is K Laster, *Law as Culture*, 2nd ed, Federation Press, 2001.

39 AWB Simpson, *Legal Theory and Legal History – Essays on the Common Law*, Hambledon Press, 1987, 362.

40 A Sarat and W Felstiner, *Divorce Lawyers and Their Clients – Power and Meaning in the Legal Process*, Oxford UP, 1995, 12.

Thus far in this chapter we have encountered several explanations of the law-power relationship: law is an instrument for exerting power; law is a check upon power; law legitimates power; law is a source of power; law is a product of power; law *is* power; and law is but one aspect of power. Many of these explanations overlap to some extent with the others. Each tells us something about law and power, but none tells us everything. The point is not to become too immersed in any one explanation; we must be prepared to consider the relationship between law and power from a variety of perspectives.

In the remainder of this chapter we begin to examine the process of law-making and the various social, moral and economic forces that shape the "reform" of law. Power and politics are never far from this analysis. Law-making is not simply the domain of the legislature, as the fate of new statutes lie in the hands of those who are required to interpret and apply them. Socio-legal scholars point out that rule interpretation is not merely the domain of the judiciary. In some areas, where litigation supplies little or no authoritative guidance, *administrative* interpretations of the rules by regulators and public officials become paramount. What is significant is that some of these "interpretations" are highly novel, demonstrating how statutes may be operationalised administratively, often in ways unintended by the legislature. In the criminal context, David Dixon in his empirical study of English and Australian policing concluded that the law from the police perspective is not conceived as a "rule book" to be either followed or ignored, but rather as a "tool" or normative resource used by police in advancing their diverse roles of maintaining order, crime prevention and detection.[41] This reveals yet another dimension to the gap between the "law in the books" and the "law in action".

The following analysis is divided into three parts. First, we describe and assess some broad models that might be of use in understanding how and why laws are made and applied. Secondly, we examine how statutes have come about ("emergence studies"). Then, thirdly, we examine the fate of some statutes after enactment ("implementation studies"[42]). Whilst, from a formalist perspective, only the emergence studies are accounts of law-*making*, it is important to remember that the real effects of law lie in its implementation. Laws which come about ostensibly for one purpose might have quite different effects in reality. What follows may be seen as a useful corrective to the liberal image of law as somehow removed from the fray of competition in political life. It will become clear that an understanding of legislation does not begin with a Bill's first reading in parliament nor end with its proclamation.

(e) Consensus, conflict and beyond

(i) The use of models

We begin with a word on method. In what follows we look at examples of how social scientists build conceptual models so that they can bring under control a

---

41 D Dixon, *Law in Policing: Legal Regulation and Police Practices*, Oxford UP, 1997. More generally see S Corcoran and S Bottomley (eds), *Interpreting Statutes*, Federation Press, 2005.

42 A more common term is "impact studies". The sociology of law is replete with studies of the impact of legislation on social change. Because these studies have considerable limitations, we have used the term "implementation" to indicate that our focus is more on the impact of group behaviour on the *legislation* than the impact of the legislation on "society".

potentially infinite amount of data. A model is a useful way of organising thought, of dividing phenomena into manageable portions, and of isolating key variables from which to develop generalisations and testable propositions. Models are starting points for inquiry, ways of filtering an otherwise incoherent jumble of information, ways of making sense of the world.

A distinction is drawn between this type of *explanatory* model, and *normative* models. While some theorists use models to explain how the law works, other models are concerned with how it *ought* to be. Importantly, as John Braithwaite has noted, "sound policy analysis involves a combination of explanatory and normative theory".[43] The difficulty with this binary classification is that explanatory analysis is invariably founded upon an implicit normative model. The model one adopts will influence what one looks for, what one sees (and does not see) and how one's observations are fitted into a broader explanation.[44] As noted in Chapter 2, liberalism and its values provide the implicit normative blueprint for law and legal critique by the academy. Students must be aware that the subtle slippage from the "is" to the "ought", and vice versa, is a powerful rhetorical strategy of persuasion used by lawyers, judges and academics alike.

For most social science and economic research, a model is best viewed as a kind of "ideal type". Ideal types express those variables which the theorist takes to be crucial, "put together in a pattern whose form derives not from detailed data (for gathering data constitutes the purpose of the research), but from logical inferences based upon preliminary excursions into the domain of study".[45] While ideal types are unlikely to be found in the real world (take, for instance, the "perfect market") their value is to identify possible explanations, outcomes, causative factors and conditions and to articulate how these logically connect with each other.[46]

The analysis of the emergence of laws and of their implementation can be structured along a continuum of models. At one end is the consensus model, and at the other is the conflict model. Before looking at the graduated positions in between, it is helpful to have some idea of what the two extremes entail.

The consensus model stresses the cohesion, solidarity, integration, co-operation and stability in society, and presents it as united by a shared culture and by agreement on the norms and values that underpin it. Although consensus theory does not deny *some* level of disagreement, this is seen to be resolved through agreed processes. Power represents legitimate authority, upholding commonly held beliefs and sentiments. In this model, both the law-in-the-books and the law-in-action reflect the shared "core" values of society.

In complete contrast, the conflict model sees society as an unstable system involving continuous political struggle between sometimes hostile groups with different goals and values. The maintenance of power requires inducement and coercion. Law is an instrument of repression for perpetuating the interests of the powerful at the expense of alternative interests, norms and values.

---

43   J Braithwaite, "Introduction" in K Hazlehurst (ed), *Crime and Justice: An Australian Textbook in Criminology*, LBC, 1996, 5.

44   W Chambliss (ed), *Sociological Readings in the Conflict Perspective*, Addison-Wesley, 1976, 2.

45   W Chambliss and R Seidman, *Law, Order and Power*, Addison-Wesley, 1982, 56.

46   Ibid 56.

Dissatisfaction at being forced to make a clear-cut choice between consensus and conflict models led to the development of intermediate models which introduced ideas of pluralism. The basic positions along the continuum can be presented like this:

"Pure"	Consensus	Conflict	"Pure"
Consensus	Pluralism	Pluralism	Conflict

To understand the strengths and weaknesses of each model's depiction of law, we need to investigate them in more depth. Before doing so it must be made clear that the continuum notion, whilst an advance on the simplistic consensus-conflict dichotomy, has its own limitations. It is still predicated on the idea that conflict and consensus are the fundamental alternatives. As we will see, however, some Marxist theory suggests that power is exercised through the *manufacture* of consent. Such an approach therefore emphasises consent but has quite a different analysis to that of pure consensus theory. Another critical perspective on the continuum is the idea that consensus and conflict models can plausibly apply simultaneously; that a single piece of legislation may cohere to seemingly contradictory models. The legal framework for the regulation of pornography, for example, contains elements of consensus and conflict in its attempt to accommodate the various interests shaping the reform of law, whether informed by liberal, moral, feminist or pragmatic concerns.[47] If its limitations are borne in mind the continuum notion is, nevertheless, a useful way of making a start of giving some topography to competing theories.

(ii) "Pure" consensus theories

"Pure" consensus theories assert that law is the product of societal values which transcend the immediate interests of individuals or groups. In the past two centuries, this view has found considerable support from social theorists. Law has been variously described as emanating from the "collective consciousness", as "deriving from a source equally authoritative for all mankind" and as

> represent[ing] a sustained effort to preserve important social values from serious harm and to do so not arbitrarily but in accordance with rational methods directed toward the discovery of past ends.[48]

Within classical social theory, the consensus view is closely associated with Emile Durkheim (1858-1917). For Durkheim, primitive societies comprised a unified whole, with a common culture, a collective conscience, agreed values and aims, and consensus on the content of the criminal law. Even in modern societies which are characterised by a complex division of labour and the *collapse* of a collective conscience, Durkheim did not regard conflict as endemic. It is clear from the "organic" model he employed in analysis that he regarded society rather as a natural system based on consensus.

Twentieth century versions of pure consensus theory can be identified. For example, some theorists see legal change as closely influenced by "public opinion" and indeed regard the political processes of liberal democracy as geared to achieve precisely this result. As Wolfgang Friedmann put it:

---

47 See the case study in Chapter 2 of this book.
48 J Hall, *General Principles of Criminal Law*, 2nd ed, Bobbs-Merrill, 1960, 608, 613.

In a democracy, public opinion on vital social issues constantly expresses itself, not only through the elected representatives in legislative assemblies, but through public discussion in the press, radio, pressure groups and, on a more sophisticated level, through scientific and professional associations, universities and a host of other channels.[49]

On this view, legislation reflects, at the very least, the opinions of the majority of society. Indeed Friedmann goes further and concludes that criminal law reflects the social consciousness of society: the kind of conduct an organised community considers sufficiently condemnable to warrant the imposition of official sanctions. It is, for him, "a barometer of the moral and social thinking of a community".[50]

Both in its 19th and 20th century variants, pure consensus theory represents the orthodox liberal view of law. Law is neutral and protects individuals equally. It should not, and does not, reflect or promote the interests of any powerful group. Indeed, the methodological individualism which characterises much of this work[51] tends to preclude an analysis of group power in the first place. Groups are defined out of the picture by virtue of the premises used. In its "law as public opinion" version, pure consensus theory can be closely associated with classical utilitarianism. Law should be geared to maximise the satisfaction of aggregated individual wishes or needs.

This pure form of consensus theory has commonly been accused of naivety for failing to recognise the way in which powerful interests influence the law, for downplaying the extent of conflict involved in society generally and in law-making particularly, and for its lack of empirical support. Critics have countered that there may be no consensus on what is to be regarded as a vital social issue in the first place, nor on how the issue is to be resolved. Moreover, for an issue to become a vital social issue often depends upon its being seen subjectively as a social problem. As we will see, this in turn may depend largely upon the abilities of various "moral entrepreneurs" or vested interests to impose their definitions on the situation.

At best, proponents of the pure consensus perspective, as Cohen suggests, must retreat to a position whereby they claim that only the *general character* of the body of laws in existence at any time reflects the values of the period, without requiring that every single law does so to the same degree.[52] As Tomasic puts it, where popular consensus exists regarding legislation, it does so only at the level of rhetorical or normative pronouncements.[53]

(iii) *Consensus pluralism*

These problems have led to the development of a more sophisticated version of the consensus model: consensus pluralism. This model acknowledges the existence of

---

49   W Friedmann, *Law in a Changing Society*, Harmondsworth, 1972, 24-25.

50   Quoted in R Quinney, "The Social Reality of Crime" in RL Akers and R Hawkins (eds), *Law and Control in Society*, Prentice Hall, 1975, 73. For similar views, see also G Sawer, *Law and Society*, Oxford UP, 1965. Today, consensus is more commonly an unarticulated assumption in a research agenda than it is a coherent theory. See A Hunt, "Perspectives in the Sociology of Law" in P Carlen (ed), *The Sociology of Law*, Sociological Review Monograph, 1976, 29.

51   See the discussion of individualism in Chapter 2.

52   AK Cohen, *Deviance and Control*, Prentice Hall, 1966.

53   R Tomasic, "The Sociology of Legislation" in R Tomasic (ed), *Legislation and Society in Australia*, Allen and Unwin, 1980, 23.

competing groups and interests (hence its "pluralism"). It acknowledges th. modern societies are stratified in complex ways along the lines of social class and status but these groupings are said to follow from legitimate criteria. Social class is determined primarily by reference to occupation and income levels within the context of a system of values. On the basis of equal opportunities, some people have reached positions which are rewarded more highly than others because they have superior abilities or have made greater effort.

In crucial respects, however, this pluralist model retains the essential element of consensus which is at the core of the pure version. First, the state itself is viewed as providing a value-neutral framework within which the struggle of competing but balanced interests is contained. Instead of assuming that society has a set of shared values, this perspective acknowledges that there is a plurality of norms and values, and that the population is heterogeneous. Underlying this pluralism and heterogeneity, however, the model detects consensus on how conflict is to be resolved. Thus, while different groups may have different interests, it is in *everyone's* interests to maintain a political apparatus which permits the peaceful resolution of conflicts. On this view, the state, through law, establishes the general framework within which social and economic life is conducted and also serves to reconcile the conflicting claims made by different groups. Although there may be a ruling party at any one time, so that the personnel of the state are not all value-neutral, this is simply a consequence of the framework of elections, and that framework itself is value-neutral.

The second tenet of consensus pluralism is that power is more or less equally divided between different groups and interests. No group can become a ruling class or power elite (whose control over the instruments of power enables it to oppress its opponents) because power is scattered among a *number* of groups and associations. If one group starts to become too powerful, the others combine to restrain it. Even if it is not stalemated by other groups, the electorate or constitution will achieve the same effect. In this system of checks and balances, even the weakest interest group is assumed to have enough power to force some kind of exchange with more powerful groups. Thus consensus pluralism implies that "everyone, including those at the end of the line, gets served".[54]

While the pure consensus model might be regarded as the idealised version of how liberal democracies operate, consensus pluralism can be seen as an attempt to describe how liberalism *actually works* in modern western democracies. By the same token, however, consensus pluralist models have been seriously criticised. They are said to ignore a considerable amount of evidence that some groups *do* "win" more frequently than others, and that, far from operating neutrally, the state and law commonly function so as to *reinforce* class, racial and sexual inequalities. Critics have argued that there is no equality of power because groups which are at the centre of power are better able to reinforce their interests than those at the periphery. In addition, the majority of people are often apathetic about or unaware of an issue, and even when they *are* concerned they are frequently unable to organise and impose their opinion on the legislature.

Consensus pluralism has been further attacked by Chambliss and Seidman who contend that:

---

54   R Miliband, *The State in Capitalist Society*, Merlin, 1969, 2.

Far from a value-neutral framework within which conflict finds peaceful resolution, state power itself rewards the successful in the endless social conflict. The legal order in fact constitutes a self-serving system to maintain power and privilege.[55]

Chambliss and Seidman reject the value-free model of the state because the activities of government are not confined merely to the application of fixed rules to facts. They consist in large part of the exercise of discretion in deciding to create (or not to create) rules. Such rules are normative and are consequently value-laden.

It is largely in response to these perceived shortcomings of the consensus-based models that conflict models were developed. They have at their core the belief that society is built on fundamental conflict about both means and ends and that certain groups have a disproportionate amount of power which they use to ensure that their interests prevail.

(iv) Conflict pluralism

One version is conflict pluralism, which is consistent with various forms of elite or interest group theory. Conflict pluralism, like its consensus-based counter-part, sees power in society as being divided between a range of groups and interests. However, some groups have more power than others. They may have it because inevitably some people are in strategically useful positions (power elites) or because they have successfully combined to promote collective ends (interest groups) or because they happen to be members of particular family networks (dynasties). Furthermore, contrary to the consensus models, power is not seen as held more or less equally among many different groups. Rather, it is held dispro-portionately by a few, such as "big business". It is for this reason, they say, that despite the emergence of labour and social reform movements there has been relatively little redistribution of wealth or income from the rich to the poor.[56]

Similarly, conflict pluralism challenges the assumption that the state is a value-neutral framework. This, as we have seen, is the position taken by Chambliss and Seidman, who were leading proponents of the conflict pluralist perspective, at least in their early work.[57]

In sum, conflict pluralism differs from its consensus counterpart in asserting that particular groups are disproportionately advantaged in the law-creation process; in claiming that there exist strong links between such groups and the state; and in arguing that the legal system is "not a set of neutral techniques available to anyone who could seek control of its levers and pulleys, but a game heavily loaded in favour of the wealthy and powerful".[58]

In emphasising the asymmetry of power between interests, and the crucial role played by a limited number of groups in the law-making process, conflict pluralism has considerable empirical support.[59] On close examination, however, it

---

55 Chambliss and Seidman, n 45, 8.

56 Connell, n 1, 131.

57 Chambliss and Seidman, n 45.

58 R Gordon, "New Developments in Legal Theory" in D Kairys (ed), *The Politics of Law*, Pantheon, 1982, 284.

59 See the discussion below, and Chambliss and Seidman, n 45 and C Reasons and R Rich, *The Sociology of Law: A Conflict Perspective*, Butterworths, 1978. However, it must be acknowled-ged that there are also some reform movements which do not fit comfortably within this perspec-tive. See, for example, the discussion in R Tomasic, *The Sociology of Law*, Sage, 1985, 101-102.

also has limitations. In particular, "it has never developed beyond a case by case indictment of self-serving interest groups into a *systematic* analysis of conflicting claims and the order in which they are likely to be resolved".[60] Specifically, it does not develop any coherent explanation of when one particular interest group will succeed rather than another, nor why this is so. That is, it lacks any developed concept of the basis of power.[61]

To the extent that conflict pluralism *has* tried to explain who the powerful are, it has often lapsed into tautology. Quinney, for example, claims that laws "are formulated according to the interests of those segments of society which have the power to translate their interests into public power".[62] Such arguments are circular, for it is true by definition that groups who change the law have power to do so.[63] Simply to assert that law X serves the interests of group Y, and therefore Y is powerful, is to ignore the possibility that far more complex forces may be at work and that Y might have had little to do with the passage of that legislation.

The limitations of conflict pluralism have pushed some theorists to look for a more sophisticated theory that can relate the question of power to broader social processes within an historical perspective. An early attempt to do this, which some American sociologists sought to locate at the "pure conflict" end of the continuum, was instrumental Marxism. This perspective (that law is an instrument in the hands of the capitalist ruling class) is examined further below. It has the seeming virtues of identifying who the powerful are, explaining why they rose to power, what their interests are and what goals they might be expected to pursue through legislation.

(v)   Reviewing the consensus-conflict paradigm

It is appropriate to review the contribution and limitations of the consensus-conflict paradigm. There can be no doubt that this paradigm has provided considerable insights into the law-creation process and each model can usefully be "tried for size" to aid our understanding of the emergence, and implementation, of any new law. The conflict model, in particular, has been helpful in challenging the myths about consensus.[64] It invites us to ask whether the state is indeed a value-neutral framework within which conflicts are resolved peacefully; whether the competing forces *are* evenly balanced or whether one wins disproportionately; and whether there is indeed an elite or ruling class. It sensitises us to any gap between liberal ideals and the reality of liberal societies, and it exposes the distinction between the law in the books and the law in action. Above all else, it sharpens our focus and extends our understanding of the relationship between law and power.

However, these models cannot claim to represent the reality of law creation in every case. Rather, each provides a way of seeing, a means of focusing attention, a way of conceptualising the world, and of unravelling its complexity. Thus it is

---

60   SD Stein, "The Sociology of Law" (1980) 20 *British Journal of Criminology* 99.

61   For example Quinney maintains that any interest group's ability to influence public policy depends on that group's position in the political power structure, but he never indicates where power comes from or why certain interests arise in certain periods or circumstances. See generally O'Malley's critique of Quinney's early work in P O'Malley, *Law, Capitalism and Democracy*, Allen and Unwin, 1983, 18-19.

62   R Quinney, *The Social Reality of Crime*, Little Brown, 1970, 11, quoted in O'Malley, n 61, 19.

63   This point is made by Tomasic, n 59, 102.

64   Chambliss and Seidman, n 45, 7-8.

hardly surprising to find that each model contains some truths about the emergence of legislation:

> [T]he "public interest" model, in suggesting that the state, or at least parts of it, can be motivated by a conception of the public interest; the [consensus] "pluralist" model, in recognizing how different interests can have a hand in the emergence of laws; the "private interest" [conflict] model, in underlining the crucial role that powerful interests, their surrogates in the state, and dominant ideology, can play; and Marxist models, in emphasizing that legislating occurs within the limits set by the larger economic and social forces of a society. But none accounts fully for the process by which legislation emerges.[65]

Secondly, the concept of power implicit in the conflict model is inadequate in that it is instrumental and uni-dimensional. For example, most conflict studies tacitly assume that A is powerful if she or he succeeds in affecting what B does. The focus is on behaviour in the making of decisions and on issues as observable conflicts of interests.[66] But as we saw earlier in this chapter, there are other, more subtle, and perhaps more important, faces of power. Steven Lukes, for example, has suggested that power is at its greatest when it is unrecognised, and it is most effectively and insidiously used to *prevent* conflict from arising in the first place.[67]

Finally, to emphasise a point made earlier, conflict theory fails to consider the possibility that consensus itself might be forced or manufactured, or, more broadly, the result of ideology. If this is so, then consensus and conflict are *not* necessarily dichotomous variables or contradictory characteristics of law. Rather, it can be argued, the legal and social order are secured by legitimacy and consent as well as by coercion, but this is a state of affairs achieved by dominant groups whose interests are in almost inevitable conflict with those of the group they dominate.[68]

(vi) Marxist theories

In an attempt to overcome some or all of these shortcomings in the consensus-conflict dichotomy, some social theorists turned to Marxism.[69] Although it is often thought of simply as a (failed) revolutionary program, Marxism is also a philosophy and an economic and social theory that has had a noticeable influence on the understanding of law.

The Marxist methodology is usually described as historical materialism.[70] At its core is the claim that the source of social change lies in the "material" conditions of life (which, very provisionally, we can call "the economy"). The underlying impulse for change does not come from changes in ideas or from some transcendental force.

---

65   R Cranston, *Law, Government and Public Policy*, Oxford UP, 1987, 6.

66   Occasionally, this is taken one step further. For example, Chambliss' study of vagrancy imports the idea of mobilisation of bias in changing the contents of the agenda for decision-making, but still stops short of the broader approach discussed in the text below.

67   Lukes, *Power: A Radical View*, n 17.

68   O'Malley, n 61, 4. See also A Hunt, "Dichotomy and Contradiction in the Sociology of Law" (1981) 8 *Brit Journal of Law and Society* 47. For further criticisms of the consensus-conflict dichotomy, see D Dickson, *From Prohibition to Regulation: Bookmaking, Anti-Gambling and the Law*, Clarendon Press, 1991, 24.

69   Another perspective, which we do not have space to deal with in the present context, is corporatism. For a useful summary, see PJ Williamson, *Corporatism in Perspective: An Introductory Guide to Corporatist Theory*, Sage, 1989.

70   For a good introduction, see M Rader, *Marx's Interpretation of History*, Oxford UP, 1979.

Marx developed the notion that the history of societies has been a history of changing "modes of production": for example, primitive, slave, feudal and capitalist. According to its revolutionary agenda, the socialist mode of production would be a transitional stage towards the end state of communism.

Any mode of production can be seen as comprised of two basic elements: the forces of production and the relations of production. The forces of production can be broadly described as the skills and resources in a society (the "technology"). The relations of production are the relationships that people enter into (willingly or otherwise) in the course of producing goods and services.

In capitalist society, the relations of production are based on a specific class structure where the number of classes has been reduced to two. The fundamental distinction is drawn between the owners of the means of production (the bourgeoisie), such as factory-owners, and those who only have their labour power to sell (the proletariat). These two classes have irreconcilably conflicting interests.

Historical materialism holds that the catalyst behind the evolution of societies lies in contradiction between the forces of production and the relations of production. In rather crude terms, technological change brings with it changes to the relations of production. For example, industrialisation in many western societies broke down the more graduated social stratification appropriate to an agricultural economy, leading to the rise of the bourgeoisie, the emergence of a distinctive proletariat and the demise of an aristocracy. From time to time, the tension between the state of the technology and the relations of production appropriate to earlier technology is so extreme that a social revolution occurs. The 19th century, during which Marx lived, was the century of European revolutions.

The materialist nature of Marxist theory calls for an explanation of social phenomena that are not patently to do with the mode of production; for example, culture, laws and political organisation. Even more fundamentally, because we *feel* that we are acting as a result of ideas that we have adopted with at least some degree of voluntariness, Marxism needs to account for the apparent role that ideas have in bringing about change.

A common metaphor to describe this relationship is that of the base and the superstructure. The forces and relations of production are the base. Social, political and cultural practices are the superstructure. One major area of controversy about Marxism concerns the extent to which (if at all) the former "determines" the latter. It is at this stage that we can introduce the place of law in Marxist theory.

Marx himself had relatively little to say about law directly. Most of his later work concerned the operations of capitalism, principally as he saw it in 19th century England, and the nature of class conflict. Nevertheless there are scattered references to laws in his writing[71] and these were developed into what might be called a Marxist jurisprudence. Hugh Collins' description of it, which possibly exaggerates its dynamism, serves to capture the main goals:

> The principal aim of Marxist jurisprudence is to criticize the centrepiece of liberal political philosophy, the ideal called the Rule of Law. Although this undertaking constitutes a mere fragment of the Marxist tradition of critical social theory, today it is regarded as a vital element. Never before have Marxists devoted so much energy to the investigation of the nature and functions of

---

71 See in particular M Cain and A Hunt, *Marx and Engels on Law*, Academic Press, 1979, and P Phillips, *Marx and Engels on Law and Laws*, Martin Robertson, 1980.

legal systems. Their efforts merge into the general purpose of Marxism which is to mount a sustained offensive against the existing organizations of power in modern society. By exposing the structures of domination and subverting the beliefs and values which sustain them, Marxists seek to pave the way towards a revolutionary social transformation. Within this programme, the theory of law assumes an important place. Marxists examine the real nature of law in order to reveal its functions in the organizations of power and to undermine the pervasive legitimating ideology in modern industrial societies known as the Rule of Law.[72]

Pausing here, we can see that Marxist jurisprudence places law within what seems to be an all-embracing conflict theory, a total ideology. It offers the prospect of overcoming some of the limitations of conflict pluralism by enabling a *systematic* account to be constructed of the way that powerful groups (in orthodox Marxism, the owners of the means of production) use law. As we will now see, however, that prospect has not obviously been realised. The patent difficulties with a crude materialist conception of law led to various attempts to develop more subtle versions which remain faithful to some basic Marxist principles but which are more plausibly consistent with the way that we sense modern societies actually work.

The version that has received most attention is known as "class instrumentalism",[73] according to which laws "emerge" because the ruling class wants them.

> Instead of laws being described as a reflection of the mode of production, they were explained as creations of the state apparatus to further the ends of the ruling class.[74]

To take a simple example, criminal laws are seen by instrumentalists as ways of protecting private property (which mainly benefits the ruling class because they monopolise the possession of wealth) and as generally maintaining an obedient working class that would otherwise revolt. Indeed, the history of modern policing can be understood in this way. The "New Police", established in early 19th century in England and subsequently in its colonies, were constituted primarily to prevent disorder and protect property. With its mandate emphasising prevention and deterrence through visible presence and the protection of private property, the new police served the interests of the propertied and middle classes.[75] As Finnane pointed out this mandate translated into a mission of civilising manners: a major function of the police was the demarcation of the "respectable" from the "rough" classes, thereby "reproducing inequalities in society or even in enhancing them".[76] Taking action against intoxicated persons, pimps, prostitutes, Aboriginals and other "disorderly" subjects has formed the focus of uniformed policing from its

---

72   Collins, n 19, 1.
73   For a modern defence within British legal scholarship, see Z Bankowski, "Anarchism, Marxism
 .   and the Critique of Law" in D Sugarman (ed), *Legality, Ideology and the State*, Academic Press,
      1983, 267 at 273.
74   Collins, n 19, 27.
75   In Australia, colonial police forces established in early 19th century Australia were not confined
      to preventing crime and protecting property. Unlike their English counterparts, colonial police
      assumed a wide range of governmental responsibilities including prosecution and administering
      punishment: see M Finnane, *Police and Government: Histories of Policing in Australia*, Oxford
      UP, 1994, Ch 1.
76   M Finnane, "Larrikins, Delinquents and Cops: Police and Young People in Australian History" in
      R White and C Alder (eds), *The Police and Young People in Australia*, Cambridge UP, 1994,
      103.

very inception and continues today in the form of "zero tolerance" policing on our streets. The mandate to discriminate between different classes was not simply an expression of police culture. It is also grounded expressly in positive law. Until 2000 in New South Wales, the statutory regulations required police officers to enforce the law with strict impartiality, though with the following significant rider:

> Police officers must be strictly impartial in the discharge of their duties towards all persons. While required to zealously carry out their duties, officers must exercise forbearance and discretion in dealings with minor offences committed inadvertently or in ignorance, or without evil intent, by respectable and law abiding citizens. A caution or warning is all that is necessary on many occasions.[77]

This Regulation emphasises the importance of equality before the law, while it simultaneously institutionalises departures from this standard through promoting diversionary justice (though cautions etc) for "respectable" rule-breakers. Although now removed from the official "rule book", there is plenty of empirical research suggesting that police discretion, especially in relation to cautions, continues to operate in a similar manner. We explore this in the context of Aboriginal people's experiences of policing in Chapter 9 below.

One criticism of the class instrumentalist position is that it does not take account of the complexity of social class. Although one might, from a distance, characterise owners of the means of production all as "the ruling class", we are of course talking about owners of finance capital, of land, of factories and so on. They may well have some broad interest in maintaining the capitalist system, but may also have conflicting interests in a more immediate sense. Even within the same sector of the economy there are conflicting interests. For example, there is evidence of big business favouring legislative regulation precisely so that small competitors will be driven out. The instrumentalist position, therefore, offers little to explain how such a diverse group as "the ruling class" can act with sufficient unity to produce and maintain a complete legal order.

Another, related, criticism is to do with class consciousness. Inadequate information, pressure of time and lack of sophisticated analysis makes it unlikely that the owners of the means of production can formulate a clear view of their common interests and then protect those interests with any degree of accuracy. A class instrumentalist might respond to this criticism by saying that the bourgeois state is there precisely to act as some kind of management committee. The function of the state, through its various officials (judges, bureaucrats, legislators etc), is to stop mistakes from happening. It is situated so that it can see the overall picture and take the co-ordinated measures which individual capitalists cannot do. As we will see, however, this tends merely to push the problem somewhere else. An account has to be offered of why the *state* should be seen as merely the tool of the ruling class.

Another problem lies in the either/or nature of social class which underpins instrumentalism. Whilst the English industrial society which Marx observed might have been starkly divided between bourgeoisie and proletariat (after allowing for anomalous groups like professions and survivors from previous eras), modern societies seem to be stratified in a more graduated way and the distinction between owner and non-owner is less easy to draw. Many large businesses are owned by a range of shareholders who take little active part in day-to-day affairs. The

---

77   *Police Service Regulation 1990* (NSW) cl 7.

shareholders in turn may be other businesses. Ultimately, of course, ownership must be traced to human beings but the direct nexus between ownership and control, implicit in orthodox Marxism, is broken. On a similar note, the kind of people whom one observes to have power in a large organisation might own nothing except their salary.

Finally, from what could have been a longer list of criticisms, the instrumentalist position cannot account for the large body of law which has no obvious economic aspect. There are laws about road safety, witnessing of wills and so on which are undoubtedly predicated on a particular kind of *society* (it must have roads and heritable property) but to describe these as devices of a ruling class would require a more sophisticated argument than class instrumentalism.

Attempts have, however, been made to develop such an argument. Marxists (and many non-Marxists too) claim that people make sense of their world by using ideological frameworks, although by and large they are unaware of doing so. They think they are seeing the world "as it is". The ideas that make up that framework are constructed through practical activities and day-to-day encounters with people. Thus it is possible to discern, say, a different outlook between white collar and blue collar workers, between those who live in rural areas and urban areas, and so on.

In the same way, those who own the means of production have a view of the world which is shaped by their position, their interactions with others, and their perception of their own interests. The factory owner is not likely to claim that a particular kind of family law is essential to the survival of her or his business, for example. The far-sighted owner might, however, have a broad view on what kind of family system produces a stable and healthy labour force and such a labour force quite possibly *is* essential for the survival of a business. In this way, family law and the factory owner can be connected.

The point to be made, therefore, is that one does not have to be conscious of one's membership of a group in order to have preferences which are, objectively, common to that group. Those preferences need not be directly related to one's immediate interests but they may be related to a view of the world which *suits* one's interests generally.

This brief sketch of Marxist theories enables us to add in a further idea: the notion of hegemony. Literally, the word hegemony means a position of supremacy. In Marxist use it implies more than supremacy through force or coercion. It includes the power to make people see their world in a particular way so that they think they are observing a natural and inevitable state of affairs.

One institution for establishing hegemony is the law. If, for example, a legal system seems to provide what people want then they are more likely to regard the social order as legitimate and blame their disadvantaged position on other causes. At the same time, that legal system embeds particular values which form part of the dominant ideology. Thus, for example, the criminal law, whilst providing defences to charges and mechanisms for leniency, also encodes specific notions of individual responsibility and rationality. It also encodes specific ideas about equality before the law, that the poor and rich, black and white, men and women all have equal access to the law, and be treated in like fashion before the courts. In Chapter 2 we looked at the elements of liberalism and illustrated how they are (or at least ought to be) reflected in the law. Notwithstanding the central place of these normative values in legal rhetoric, as subsequent chapters on access to justice, gender and race and multiculturalism demonstrate, the law in practice often fails to deliver the goods!

We have now come some distance from the crude claim that law is a reflection of the economic base. We now have a position that law is used as an instrument of the ruling class but that it operates at an ideological level as well as a material one. Laws which might not obviously be connected with the pursuit of profit and the protection of property can nevertheless be explained by a broad strategy of legitimating the social order and imposing a general world view upon the subordinate class.

This approach has shown up the limitations of too rigid a dichotomy between conflict and consensus in the search for a theory of social power.[78] Rule by the powerful few might be quite consistent with a kind of consensus.

But there are still some gaps. In particular we have not established that the hands of the ruling class are actually on the levers of law-making at all; whether law is seen in instrumental or ideological terms. The kind of law-making activity which looks most fruitful for empirical inquiry is the passage of legislation. The activities of legislators are presumably more open to inquiry than the closed deliberations of judges. We will see shortly that emergence studies provide an element of support for the proposition that legislation is under the control of a ruling class. But, as we will also see, the evidence is by no means overwhelming.

This absence of a clear connection between ownership of the means of production and the enactment of law has been one factor in a theoretical departure for Marxism; the idea that the state might be *relatively autonomous* from the relations of production.

The relative autonomy idea amounts to a break with the base-superstructure metaphor. Only in the final instance, say some Marxists, are superstructural forms like the state, politics, law and culture determined by the base. There is plenty of scope for variation and inconsistency. Thus it is possible for the state, which is conceived here as relatively autonomous from the ruling class, to enact laws that favour subordinate classes, such as laws protecting consumers from unfair trade practices or protecting the rights of workers or tenants. Such laws do not have to be seen as deliberate attempts to legitimate capitalism, although they might be, on the facts. Rather they may be the product of a state in which the interests of the powerful compete with the interests of the less powerful over the proper direction of law reform. This directly impacts on the law-making process since political interest groups representing employers and farmers compete for political influence with social justice groups and labour organisations.

The relative autonomy thesis brings its own problems. Once the *direct* linkage is lost between forces of production, relations of production and the state, then Marxism begins to look like just another approach, to be set alongside elite theory or a radical interest group analysis. Its proclaimed virtue of being a systematic, historical and predictive theory of power is potentially weakened. Furthermore, unless a sub-theory can be developed to explain the *conditions* which determine how autonomous the state will be at any particular time, then we have no reason to take the thesis seriously in theoretical terms. The most one can say is that it accords more with what appears to be reality than does orthodox class instrumentalism.

---

78   For a review of the inadequacies of the conflict/consensus dichotomy, see Hunt, n 18, 47.

Much the same kind of remarks can be made about judge-made law. No doubt it is possible to mount a sociological thesis that judges come from privileged classes and therefore approach issues from a particular perspective. Their lack of exposure to certain ways of life may lead them to decisions which work against particular groups. On the other hand, there are many decisions which protect the rights of the under-privileged and which act as a check on power. Furthermore, the idea of rule-following does seem to constrain decision-makers (see back to Chapter 3 and our discussion of legal formalism) even if, as Legal Realists and Critical Legal Studies scholars have claimed, there are more "lee-ways of choice" than are openly acknowledged.[79]

This leads us to wonder whether there is not at least some autonomy of legal *thought*, and not just legislative process, from the demands and interests of a ruling class. Again, this means losing the distinctiveness of Marxism as against pluralist theories of society. After all, pluralism posits the existence of value-neutral institutions like the courts, even if they might be captured by certain groups from time to time. To retain some kind of class-based Marxism, and yet acknowledge a role for autonomous legal thought, requires considerable care.

There are many more arguments and counter-arguments concerning Marxist jurisprudence than we have had space to develop. We should have done enough, however, to have isolated some different approaches that can be brought to bear on the creation and implementation of legislation. We hope to have given a fair coverage of the strengths and weaknesses of a conflict-consensus approach and of an alternative rooted in ideology.

(f) Studies of the emergence of legislation

There have been numerous studies of the emergence of particular pieces of legislation. These studies, individually or collectively, do not point conclusively to the "correctness" of any particular model of the relationship between law, class and power, but they do provide significant insights into the politics of law-making.

Some of the "classic" studies are described below. Our selection does not purport to be comprehensive, but it serves to indicate, and to give concrete examples of, some of the most important ways in which law, class and power are connected. Moreover, these studies can readily be related to the various paradigms described in the previous section.

Almost all the studies confirm that laws do not just happen when they are "needed". Rather, someone or some group must have a strong enough interest in their creation to press for their enactment and to *make* them happen. This raises a further question: what sorts of factors will determine the success or failure of such legislative initiatives?

(i) Moral entrepreneurs

According to the American sociologist Howard Becker, whether an individual (or group) is successful in bringing about legislative change will depend on their success in bringing the problem to the attention of others, in convincing them that

---

79 See Julius Stone, *Precedent and the Law: The Dynamics of Common Law Growth*, Butterworths, 1985.

the situation is dangerous enough to require public action, in defending particular definitions against those of others, and on access to the instruments of publicity and political power. The key participants in the process of law creation, according to Becker, are "moral entrepreneurs": those individuals who unite in order to eliminate social evils from society.[80] To be successful, these people must persuade others that the proposed law serves some recognised value in society, and they must neutralise the objections of others whose interests will be adversely affected by the law.

Becker uses the United States *Marijuana Tax Act 1937* (an Act which effectively criminalised marijuana use) to illustrate this. He shows that sustained and large scale moral enterprise, provoked by the activities and ideology of the Federal Bureau of Narcotics rather than the spontaneous recognition by Congress of self-evident evil, created the "awareness" of a major social problem and forced the subsequent legislation. Becker emphasised the critical role of the Chief of the Federal Bureau of Narcotics, Harry J Anslinger, who shaped drug law enforcement policies in the US from the 1920s to the 1960s. Becker maintained that deviance is always the result of such enterprise:

> [B]efore any act can be viewed as deviant, and before any class of people can be labelled as outsiders for committing the act, someone must have made the rule which defines the act as deviant. Rules are not made automatically. Even though a practice may be harmful in an objective sense to the group in which it occurs, the harm needs to be discovered and pointed out. People must be made to feel that something ought to be done about it. Someone must call the public's attention to these matters, supply the push necessary to get things done, and direct such energies as are aroused in the proper direction to get a rule created.[81]

An alternative view of the *Marijuana Tax Act* is that of DJ Dickson, who explains the emergence of the Act in terms of the needs of a bureaucracy under severe pressure.[82] He points out that by 1936 the Narcotics Bureau was experiencing low morale, a shortage of funding and was losing its status as a government agency. It had a strong interest in persuading others that marijuana was a dangerous substance that should be made illegal, because it could then offer itself as the most appropriate agency to deal with such a new moral hazard, thereby gaining both an increased budget and increased prestige.

Accordingly, the Narcotics Bureau embarked upon a campaign to ban marijuana; a drug which until then had only been the subject of a few, infrequently enforced, State laws. It contacted other organisations with similar interests and made systematic efforts to draw the problem to the attention of the public:

> These included the diligent promotion of an image of marijuana use as vicious, debilitating, and a major threat to the general welfare. This promotion entailed the use of the Bureau's already considerable prestige as an authority in the field of drugs, and the dissemination, under its own name and through persons and organisations to whom it freely provided prepared materials, of its message to the mass media. This *publicity* effort led to five days of hearings by the Congressional committee that was considering the aforementioned anti-marijuana bill.

---

80   H Becker, *Outsiders: Studies in the Sociology of Deviance*, Collier McMillan, 1963.

81   Ibid.

82   DJ Dickson, "Bureaucracy and Morality: an organisational perspective on a moral crusade" (1968) 16 *Social Problems* 143.

Having prepared the bill, the Bureau was of course the principal witness at these hearings ("reefer" smokers sent no delegation). The only potentially troublesome obstacles to passage of the bill were the objections of the hemp seed oil and birdseed industries, who feared that their business operations might be hampered by the proposed legislation, and these were neutralized by minor changes in the bill, which swiftly became law.[83]

This analysis has much in common with the literature on "Public Choice", examined in Chapter 13, particularly its predictions about the self-interested behaviour of bureaucracies.

Significantly, on neither Becker's nor Dickson's view, was the law initiated by the mass of society. Rather, a small group in an influential position was able to manipulate the media, create a demand for legislation and see that it was enacted. Public opinion, almost non-existent on the marijuana issue in 1935, was "manufactured" in order to lend support to the legislative campaign.

As we have seen, Becker maintains that the key players in the law-creation initiatives are "moral entrepreneurs" who "make it their business to sew another patch on the moral fabric of society".[84] However, while the concept of moral enterprise may be useful in explaining the "softening up" before legislation is enacted, it ignores the potentially crucial role played by personal, financial and other material interests. Indeed, such interests may have played a far greater role in the enactment of the *Marijuana Tax Act* itself than either Becker or Dickson concede. Thus Galliher and Walker, in a subsequent reinterpretation, argue that drug laws generally are passed to help control specific ethnic, economic or racial minorities, and that this Act in particular was designed to control Mexican-Americans at a time of economic downturn when minorities compete for scarce jobs.[85] This argument is supported by the history of drug laws in Australia. While there was undoubtedly a moral crusade dimension to the movement to limit the sale and supply of opium in the 19th century in Australia, the community's negative attitude to opium-smoking was related to wider perceived threats from the Chinese migrant community, threats which coalesced around a range of political, economic and scientific/public health interests. As Desmond Manderson observes:

> There is no simple or overarching reason for the development of drug laws in Australia. But there is one clear message: no matter what we are told, "drug laws" have *not* been about health or addiction at all. They have been an expression of bigotry, class, and deep-rooted social fears, a function of Australia's international subservience to other powers, and a field in which politicians and bureaucrats have sought power. Drugs have been the subject of our laws, but not their object.[86]

The moral entrepreneur hypothesis places too much emphasis on the moral dimensions of reform, and on the role of charismatic individuals. In truth, it is groups, which are politically and economically more powerful, that have a greater chance of success in the large majority of issues, than have individual moral entrepreneurs.

---

83   Cohen, n 52, 35.

84   Ibid 35.

85   See JF Galliher and A Walker, "The Politics of Systematic Research Error: the Case of the Federal Bureau of Narcotics as a Moral Entrepreneur" (1978) *Crime and Social Justice* 29.

86   D Manderson, *From Mr Sin to Mr Big – A History of Australian Drug Laws*, Oxford UP, 1993, 12.

(ii) Instrumental uses of economic and political power

Other emergence studies have also emphasised the centrality of economic and financial (rather than moral) interests in influencing the shape of the law. Some of the best of these have been historical, one of the most eminent being Chambliss' analysis of the history of vagrancy laws.[87] Chambliss' central argument is that the English vagrancy laws were mobilised differentially in different periods of history. The content of the laws varied depending on which groups were powerful at the time; and the way the laws were interpreted and enforced was also affected by group interests.

Chambliss recounts how, in 1348, the bubonic plague (the Black Death) killed almost half of England's population. One result was a severe shortage of labour, which generated an economic crisis. Given that there was now a serious imbalance between the supply and demand for labour, it might be anticipated that wages would have risen substantially. However, this could only happen if there was some sort of "market" for labour; that is, if workers were able to reject offers of low wages in one place and seek out higher offers elsewhere. Had this occurred, it would have spelt disaster for the politically dominant feudal ruling class. This class was already threatened by the growth of new industries which were attracting many peasants away from agricultural labour and into the freer and more prosperous urban areas. The greater scarcity of labour following the Black Death, coupled with a further movement of agricultural labour in search of higher wages, threatened their interests fundamentally.

One partial solution for the feudal overlords was to curb the mobility of labour. It is here that the vagrancy laws came to be of use. Such laws had existed since 1274, at which time an Act was passed designed to give the religious houses financial relief from providing food and shelter to travellers. However, by a statute of 1343, it became a crime to give alms to any person who was unemployed while of sound body and mind. Moreover, able-bodied persons were required by the statute to work at pre-plague wage rates, and workers were forbidden to seek higher pay. This measure, Chambliss argues, was an attempt by the feudal over-lords to curtail the mobility of serfs, inhibiting them from deserting their masters to find free labour elsewhere. As he puts it:

> [V]agrancy statutes were designed for one express purpose: to force labourers (whether personally free or unfree) to accept employment at a low wage in order to insure the landowner an adequate supply of labour at a price he could afford.[88]

Chambliss' story does not end there. He goes on to show how, after a period in which the vagrancy laws fell into disuse, they were resurrected by newly power-ful social groups as a means of furthering their perceived economic interests. This is most strikingly illustrated by their use in the 16th century. By this time feudalism had decayed, and commerce and industry had become increasingly successful. Trade between England and Continental Europe was now important but was threatened by the activities of thieves, highwaymen and vagabonds. Unless merchants transporting goods could be protected from being preyed on by such persons, then the merchant class could not thrive. Again, the vagrancy laws were invoked in aid of the dominant economic interests of the day.[89] In particular,

---

87   WJ Chambliss, "A Sociological Analysis of the Law of Vagrancy" (1964) 12 *Social Problems* 67.
88   Ibid 69.
89   Ibid 59.

these laws were extended to include "ruffians who shall wander, loiter or idle use themselves and play the vagabonds", with the result that the law could be used to restrain persons of dubious character even if they could not be proved to have actually committed a crime. As a result, it was possible to clear the trade routes for the furtherance of commerce.

This study has frequently been cited in support of "interest group" theory, and located within the "conflict pluralist" framework discussed above: different groups, in different historical periods, gained disproportionate amounts of political power which they then used to establish favourable economic conditions supportive of their own interests. However, Chambliss' analysis can more compatibly be absorbed within a Marxist interpretation of English class relations and social change: it was, after all, the dominant *economic* group (or ruling class) in each historical period, which was able to manipulate the law to serve its own economic and class purposes.[90]

Subsequently, Chambliss has both extended his analysis to vagrancy laws in the 19th and 20th century,[91] and reinterpreted his own data to develop a more sophisticated Marxist-inspired theory of law creation.[92] He now argues that:

> [T]he emergence of vagrancy law, in common with other laws, is the result of a process in which lawmakers attempt to deal with the contradictions, conflicts and dilemmas inherent in the political, economic and social relations of a particular historical period.[93]

That is, major legislative changes are seen as a response to contradictions within capitalism (eg, the means of production are privately owned but the process of production is public). Such contradictions lead to conflicts and create dilemmas for law-makers who "must decide what laws are needed to resolve or at least ameliorate the conflicts".[94] However, since the basic contradictions still remain they are likely to give rise to further conflicts at a later date.

One particular criticism of Chambliss' initial study of the vagrancy laws, and indeed of many of the earlier studies of the emergence of legislation, is their "instrumental" nature. That is, they assume that some individual or group wished to achieve some concrete, identifiable (usually economic) goal, and utilised legislation as a mechanism ("instrument") to achieve it. While no doubt a substantial number of laws are, at least in part, instrumental in nature, such studies fail to recognise the extent to which law commonly fulfils other functions. That is, legislation's primary function is often symbolic rather than instrumental.

(iii)   Symbolic legislation

To be fair, a few studies did recognise this. Both Arnold's book, *The Symbols of Government*, and Gusfield's description of the American Prohibition laws, entitled *Symbolic Crusade*, emphasise how "the proclamation and maintenance of symbols

---

90   This point has been made by O'Malley in an unpublished paper. See generally the critique of Chambliss by J Adler, "A Historical Analysis of the Law of Vagrancy" (1989) 27 *Criminology* 209. See also Chambliss' reply at 231.

91   WJ Chambliss, "The Law of Vagrancy" in WJ Chambliss (ed), *The Criminal Law in Action*, Wiley, 1984.

92   Ibid 140-63.

93   Ibid 233.

94   Ibid 233.

– values, ideals and ways of thinking about government and society",[95] is a fundamental task of law. Gusfield's argument is that those who supported the legislation outlawing alcohol use (an abstinent, Protestant middle class) were far more concerned with what the law symbolised (the moral superiority of that group over the Catholic "drinking classes") than with whether the law could be enforced. In Gusfield's words:

> Legal affirmation or rejection is ... important in what it symbolises as well as or instead of what it controls. Even if the law is broken, it was clear whose law it was.[96]

However, such studies are in danger of falling into a similar trap to their instrumentalist counterparts: namely they assume that laws are *either* instrumental *or* symbolic (or "expressive", or whatever). They do not countenance the possibility that, within the highly complex emergence process, there may be found more than one of these elements.

A useful and sophisticated corrective to this dichotomous view of law-making is Carson's study of the emergence of the 1833 English Factory legislation.[97] The context of Carson's study is the early industrial revolution which created considerable prosperity for manufacturers, but brought physical squalor and long working hours for the newly urbanised working class. The *Factories Act 1833* was the first legislative measure seriously to address these problems.

Pressure for legal protection (in the form of shorter working hours) came not only from the machine operatives themselves, but also from a number of High Tories. Traditional accounts stress their humanitarian motives, but there may also have been deeper reasons for their taking the side of the workers against the Whig manufacturers on the issue of factory reform. Carson suggests that the conflict had symbolic overtones for the Tory landed gentry striving to reaffirm traditional values and their power over the middle class manufacturers. According to EP Thompson, the views of the Tory reformers "reveal deep sources of resentment and insecurity among traditionalists before the innovations and the growing power of the moneyed middle-class".[98]

In 1832, an uneasy alliance was forged between a number of High Tories and the workers' organisations, and a factory reform Bill was introduced in parliament. Although the manufacturers wholeheartedly opposed this Bill, Carson shows that this was more because of its unpalatable symbolic connotations than because of its instrumental content. The larger manufacturers, at least, recognised the value of legislation which would compulsorily restrict the hours worked by children and young persons. Enlightened self-interest suggested the value of having a "moral, sober, well-informed, healthy and comfortable body of workmen" and that such legislation would further this objective. Moreover, many larger manufacturers, whose technology and methods of production were more advanced than that of their smaller rivals, understood that factory legislation might give them a compe-

---

95 R Cotterrell, *The Sociology of Law*, 2nd ed, Butterworths, 1992, 102.

96 J Gusfield, *Symbolic Crusade*, U of Illinois Press, 1963, 178. See also T Arnold, *The Symbols of Government*, Harcourt Brace, 1935.

97 WG Carson, "Symbolic and Instrumental Dimensions of Early Factory Legislation" in RG Hood (ed), *Crime, Criminology and Public Policy*, Heinemann, 1974, 107-138.

98 EP Thompson, *The Making of the English Working Class*, Penguin, 1968, 377, quoted in Carson, n 97, 124.

titive advantage. Specifically, they would more readily be able to comply with its provisions than would their smaller competitors.

In its original form, however, the Bill (and the Parliamentary Select Committee to which it was referred) had unpalatable symbolic connotations for the manufacturers and these made it impossible for them to support it. Manufacturers as a class were stigmatised as cruel, greedy and callous. As the Select Committee put it:

> Before this Committee there files a long procession of workers – men and women, girls and boys. Stunted, diseased, deformed, degraded, they pass across the stage, each with the tale of his wronged life, a living picture of man's cruelty to man, a pitiless indictment of those rulers who, in their days of unabated power, had abandoned the weak to the rapacity of the strong.[99]

Moreover, the intention was to impose severe fines and imprisonment on all owners who breached the proposed law, thereby effectively "criminalising" the activities of such persons.

Understandably, many manufacturers "saw the reformers' allegations as a reprehensible attack upon the manufacturers as a group, and upon the factory system as a whole".[100] To have accepted the Bill would have been to acknowledge that the reformers' accusations were justified. Even those manufacturers with a strong material interest in new legislation could not accept that.

Carson shows that, had it not been for the passing of the Reform Bill in June 1832, the Tory-worker alliance, armed with the Committee's report, might have succeeded both in achieving the 10-hour working day and, symbolically, "in publicly affirming the cultural and moral inferiority of the manufacturing class".[101] Instead, the Reform Bill produced a dramatic change in the political climate. By substantially increasing the parliamentary representation of the manufacturing districts at the expense of the landowners, it gave the Whigs the means of victory over the Tories.

In the reformed parliament, the manufacturers took advantage of their greater numbers to establish a Royal Commission "to clear their reputation from the aspersions of the Select Committee". This the Commission largely did, blaming the worst abuses on the older, smaller and more remote mills, and mainly vindicating the large manufacturers. Its report was "a great triumph for the influential segment of the manufacturing interest".[102] It rid the issue of factory legislation of its "unpalatable symbolic connotations",[103] thereby enabling the larger manufacturers to pursue their competitive self-interest through legislation without accepting any of the symbolic denigration or imputations of moral inferiority which accompanied the earlier Bill. Legislation was duly enacted to restrict the length of the working day in such a manner as to disadvantage competitively their politically weaker, and smaller rivals.

> That legislation ... by restricting the hours worked by children and juveniles (who carried out many vital ancillary tasks) was expected either to reduce the total hours worked by smaller factories, or to make it more difficult for them to

---

99 *Report from the Select Committee on the Bill to Regulate the Labour of Children in the Mills and Factories of the United Kingdom*, London, 1832.

100 Carson, n 97, 132.

101 Ibid 125.

102 Ibid 136.

103 Ibid 134.

undercut their larger competitors (because more expensive adult labour would have to be used to do the work formerly done by the protected classes).[104]

Thus the 1833 Act, far from being the simple outcome of working class pressure, or of growing humanitarian concern, also contained a strong element of self-interest on the part of certain influential manufacturing interests. It was more the result of conflict *within* a class, based on a struggle over competition, than the result of conflict *between* classes. This suggests that the power of the working class was still clearly subordinate to that of the capitalists, who were only prepared to accede to legislation if they (or their most powerful sections) perceived it as within their economic interests to do so.

Carson's analysis not only emphasises the complex interconnections between symbolic and instrumental dimensions of legislation, it also emphasises how it is necessary "to portray symbolic meaning as an *emergent property* of the inter-actional sequences occurring in connection with particular pieces or types of legislation".[105] That is, symbolic overtones emerged only in the course of the debate, serving for a time to inhibit the manufacturers from pursuing their instrumental objectives. As we have seen, only when the unpalatable symbolic element was neutralised were they able to return to the original instrumental agenda.

(iv) Legislation as ideology

Under the previous heading we considered the symbolic role that legislation can have. It is also important to recognise that law can be important ideologically.[106] The difference between law's symbolic and ideological role may not always be stark. For present purposes we say that legislation has a symbolic role when it *reflects* certain values, ideals or ways of thinking about social, economic and political relations. The ideological role of legislation arises from its status as an authoritative source of those values and ideals. When we consider legislation as ideology we look at how it constitutes those values, and gives them legitimacy and meaning. Again, some of the best empirical work on this theme has been historical and there is no better example than Douglas Hay's powerful and eloquent analysis of 18th century English criminal law.[107]

Hay focuses on a well known peculiarity of the criminal justice system of that period. Compared with previous centuries, the legislature in the 18th century enacted, in what came to be known as the "Bloody Code", an increasing number of felonies punishable by death. These new offences dealt mainly with property offences, such as poaching etc. While the statute book of crimes grew more repressive, in practice, a lesser proportion of persons convicted of felony were executed in the 18th century than in the two preceding centuries. So why was there a decline in the "penal death rate" at the same time as the legislature was actually increasing the number of capital offences?

---

104 WB Creighton, *Working Women and the Law*, Mansell, 1979.

105 Carson, n 97, 113.

106 For a clear discussion of the strengths and weaknesses of the ideological analysis of law, see A Hunt, "The Ideology of Law: Advances and Problems in Recent Applications of the Concept of Ideology to the Analysis of Law" (1985) 19 *Law and Society Review* 11. See also C Sumner, *Reading Ideologies: An Investigation into the Marxist Theory of Ideology and Law*, Academic Press, 1979.

107 D Hay, "Property, Authority and the Criminal Law" in D Hay et al, *Albion's Fatal Tree*, Allen Lane, 1975, 17-62.

To answer this question, Hay locates the criminal law in the context of political events of the period. He argues that the English ruling class of the 18th century faced a serious problem in maintaining order. The "divine right of kings" was no longer a credible means of maintaining the status quo. Political agitators were on the increase. Riots were prevalent and, in 1789, the French Revolution gave a hint of what might follow if order were to break down. Yet there was no police force and standing armies were not only expensive to maintain, but had been known to turn against their paymasters. Repression, then, did not seem to be a particularly viable or attractive option.

The alternative, according to Hay, was to manipulate the ideology of law, to use it as "an instrument of authority and a breeder of values" to maintain the legitimacy of the existing social order. That is, while terror alone could not establish deference to the law, the structures of the law itself might be used ideologically, to establish deference without force, to legitimate the class structure, and to maintain the domination of the holders of property. Hay emphasises how the elements of majesty, justice and mercy, embodied in the practices of the criminal law, served these ends.

The *majesty* of the law was encapsulated in the spectacle and elaborate ritual that surrounded public trials. According to Hay:

> The assizes were a formidable spectacle in a country town, the most visible and elaborate manifestation of state power to be seen in the countryside, apart from the presence of a regiment. The town was crowded, not only with barristers and jurors, but with the cream of county society, attending the assize ball and county meetings, which were often held in the same week. Tradesmen and labourers journeyed in to enjoy the spectacle, meet friends, attend the court and watch the executions. In the court room the judges' every action was governed by the importance of spectacle. Blackstone asserted that "the novelty and very parade of … [their] appearance have no small influence upon the multitude": scarlet robes lined with ermine and full-bottomed wigs in the seventeenth century style, which evoked scorn from Hogarth but awe from ordinary men. The powers of light and darkness were summoned into the court with the black cap which was donned to pronounce sentence of death, and the spotless white gloves worn at the end of a "maiden assize" when no prisoners were to be left for execution.[108]

Judges used the trial as a platform for addressing "the multitude". The charge to the grand jury, for example, was frequently used "as a statement of central policy, as well as a summary of the state of the law and the duties of gentlemen … it was often a secular sermon on the goodness of whatever Hanoverian chanced to be on the throne, the virtues of authority and obedience, the fitness of the social order".[109] Similarly, before passing sentence of death ("the moment of terror around which the system revolved") the judge rarely missed an opportunity of emphasising the enormity of vice, and the fatal consequences to which it led. The aim, says Hay, "was to move the court, to impress the onlookers by word and gesture, *to fuse terror and argument into the amalgam of legitimate power in their minds*".[110]

---

108 Ibid 27.
109 Ibid 28.
110 Ibid 29 (emphasis added).

The ideology of *justice* was also important, particularly the theory that, once in court, all men were equal and that even the poorest was assured of fair treatment. This seeming even-handedness of the law did much to legitimise existing power arrangements in the eyes of the populace. As Hay puts it:

> When the ruling class acquitted men on technicalities they helped instil a belief in the disembodied justice of the law in the minds of all who watched. In short, its very inefficiency, its absurd formalism, was part of its strength as ideology.[111]

Finally, there was the element of *mercy*, whereby the ferocity of the criminal law, its harsh and brutal penalties, were mitigated by the widely exercised discretion to pardon the offender. By granting mercy to the weak, through an elaborate hierarchy of patronage leading to pardons, it was possible to disguise much of the class interest of the law (which primarily protected property and the propertied classes) and to make it appear as a humane force, a paternalistic structure, operating in the interests of all.

In sum:

> [T]he extremely harsh formal punishments provided an important backdrop of terror which helped to endow the law with its quality of majesty, while at the same time providing the judiciary with the opportunity to temper justice with mercy. It was the manipulation of these qualities of the law ... which enabled the ruling class to legitimize their position in the eyes of the ruled; to command the deference and establish the authority which constituted the basis of their successful hegemony throughout the eighteenth century.[112]

It was these elements that helped to create a spirit of consent and submission, so important in maintaining social order and the socio-political status quo. It would never have been possible to maintain the interests of the propertied class by force alone. Law as ideology superseded law as repression and terror, and had the effect of the many submitting to the few with a minimum of bloodshed. Law as ideology legitimised the entire class structure of 18th century England.[113]

It is appropriate to end this section with an Australian study which explores the complex connections between instrumental and ideological elements of the law emergence process. Carson and Henenberg have examined the political economy of Victoria's *Occupational Health and Safety Act 1985*, an Act intended to reduce substantially the level of occupational injury and disease. They seek to "make sense" of that legislation by "linking its enactment and import to the wider social structures, processes and developments within which it is embedded".[114]

Their starting point is the:

> [T]raditional hegemonic ideology of occupational health and safety, the way in which, historically, certain ways of perceiving and responding to issues of health and safety at the workplace came to be taken as "natural" and the subject of acquiescence ...

---

111 Ibid 32.

112 B Roshier and H Teff, *Legislation and Society in England*, Tavistock, 1980, 23.

113 For criticisms of Hay's analysis, see A Hyde, "The Concept of Legitimation in the Sociology of Law" (1983) *Wisconsin Law Review* 379; JH Langbein, "Albion's Fatal Flaws" (1983) 98 *Past and Present* 96.

114 W Carson and C Henenberg, "The Political Economy of Legislative Change: Making Sense of Victoria's New Occupational Health and Safety Legislation" (1988) 6(2) *Law in Context* 1 at 2.

Stated very briefly, what used to be called "factory legislation" appears to have accomplished two crucial and related things: it signalled an ideological separation of occupational health and safety issues from the war-torn terrain of industrial relations, and it achieved this not insubstantial feat by indicating that these matters were now the business of the state. Even if the business in question was only ever half-heartedly taken on and was certainly less than enthusiastically conducted, the clear legislative message was that these issues need no longer be canvassed as ones of conflictual class relations or of class domination. To be sure, it is important to acknowledge that the organised labour movement may never have been completely taken in, but there is no doubt that the ideological thrust of historical development was away from viewing the prevention of occupational health and safety hazards as central to industrial relations. The state could be and frequently was criticised for the inadequacy of its attention, but even such indictment of deficient practice conceded and underlined a responsibility assumed.[115]

In part, this ideological impact was by default, for trade unions have traditionally been preoccupied with more basic issues like wages. To the extent they considered health and safety, it was usually in the context of compensation rather than prevention, and as a lever to be used in negotiating "dirt" or "hazard" money. In part also, the practices of the State occupational health and safety inspectorates reinforced the same ideological message. Visits by inspectors emphasised the perception that regulatory responsibility lay with the State, while the fact that the inspectors almost invariably consulted with management and not with workers supported the view that safety was "a matter for managerial prerogative on the one hand and for the State on the other".[116]

Even where workers *were* involved in the inspectors' practices, the emphasis was usually on the "careless worker syndrome". That is, it was implied that what needed to be fixed up was the worker, not the workplace. This way, any conflict between worker safety and corporate profitability was conveniently side-stepped. Moreover, any suggestion that some management practices which caused industrial injury or death were actually criminal was also avoided by virtue of inspectoral practices. As Carson and others have documented, the inspectorates operated on the basis of consultation, education and cooperation with management. Prosecutions were extremely rare and only resorted to when advice, persuasion and other methods had failed completely. These practices, too, had an important ideological effect. Carson and Henenberg suggest that:

> [T]he Victorian inspectorate's always ready embrace of advice as its major *modus operandi*, coupled with its more than slightly ambivalent attitude to prosecution, ... perpetuated the perception of most occupational health and safety violations as customary, conventional and not really to be regarded as criminal.[117]

Against that background, Carson and Henenberg then examine some of the institutional and structural factors which led to a partial loosening of this hegemonic grip and to the very different approach and assumptions that underpin the *Occupational Health and Safety Act 1985*. They trace the efforts of the more

---

115 Ibid 2-3.
116 Ibid 5.
117 Ibid 6.

active unions and the left of the Victorian branch of the Australian Labor Party to embed a quite far-reaching legislative reform program into party policy, and to secure support in Cabinet. They also identify these developments with wider economic issues in the period in question, in particular, concern to increase the competitiveness of sectors of Victorian industry and concern with the high costs to industry of occupational injury and disease. Reforms to occupational health and safety legislation apparently offered to mitigate both these problems. Finally, they note that in 1983 the federal Labor government reached an "accord" with the unions on pay, with the result that the latter had more scope to devote energy to other issues, such as occupational health and safety.

The result of these and other social forces was to produce new legislation, which in significant respects challenged the hegemonic framework of occupational health and safety. First, provisions in the new Act for worker participation included rights to establish safety representatives and committees. The former, at least, were given powers to challenge management, including the right to stop dangerous work in certain prescribed circumstances. These provisions clearly threatened the concepts of managerial prerogative and of the necessary separation between occupational health and safety, and industrial relations. Secondly, the legislation's central concern to facilitate and encourage self-regulation by workers and management threatened the "received orthodoxy which would define occupational health and safety as a matter for state regulation".[118]

However, Carson and Henenberg caution against exaggerating the significance of these changes. The basic power structure of society does not shift that easily. The 1985 legislation perhaps promised far more than it actually provided. For example, in practice worker-elected safety representatives have rarely used the more far-reaching of their powers under the Act. Safety committees may also function as a means of diverting attention away from enforcement and into the committee room,

> there to be buried under the procrastinatory propensities for which such rooms are famed … Such committees still operate within the milieu of the broader hierarchy of power relations operative at the workplace.[119]

Moreover, a partial return to direct bargaining over wages has meant that scarce union resources may now be redeployed away from occupational safety while, at the same time, Federal government funding, a prerequisite to effective training programs for union representatives, is also likely to diminish.

These predictions are supported by Perrone's empirical study of work-related fatalities in Victoria, which revealed how even the most extreme injuries to workers – those resulting in death – have continued to be constructed as "accidents". Of the 353 work-related deaths studied, 203 occurred in a corporate context and 25 of those were related to an "extreme level of company negligence" sufficient to establish criminal culpability to sustain a conviction of manslaughter.[120] Corporations continued, however, to be prosecuted, if at all, for breaches of provisions of the *Occupational Health and Safety Act 1985* (Vic).

---

118 Ibid 13.

119 Ibid 16.

120 S Perrone, "Workplace Fatalities and the Adequacy of Prosecutions" (1995) 13(1) *Law in Context* 81 at 87; see also R White and S Perrone, *Crime and Social Control*, Oxford UP, 1997, 102-105.

These charges would result in modest fines on companies and directors, which could easily be incorporated into "the costs of doing business".

There is now much empirical evidence demonstrating how workers are exposed to risk of death and serious injury, and corporate cultures accept and condone these risks.[121] Undoubtedly the under-use of the criminal law against corporations is hampered by the technical difficulties of pinning criminal liability on the board of directors.[122] However, many of the difficulties with the substantive law have been addressed, and doctrinal inadequacy cannot explain the scale of apparent immunity conferred upon industrial manslaughter. The limited use of the criminal law is more related to a lack of police interest in industrial deaths (which may be contrasted with their active role in investigating road-related deaths and injuries). From a regulatory perspective, such deaths are "OHS matters" rather than police business. To address the under-utilisation of criminal law in relation to industrial "accidents", the Australian Capital Territory has enacted a distinct offence of "industrial homicide", with the effect that employers/senior officers may be held personally responsible for the death of an employee if the employee dies or is injured during the course of employment and the employer "substantially contributes" to the employee's death by a reckless or negligent act: *Crimes Act 1900* (ACT).[123] The legislation is designed to express symbolically that industrial deaths are homicide, deserving the label, and that corporate directors and senior executives cannot hide behind the corporate veil to avoid responsibility. While some of these reforms to the law could have been effected by changes to the general law and principles governing corporate liability, the Legislative Assembly marshalled the symbolic and regulatory promise of criminalisation, especially the stigmatic label of "homicide", to deal with this problem.

In summary, the above research sensitises us to the instrumental and symbolic properties of law-making in areas such as occupational health and safety. The studies demonstrate how, in certain political and economic circumstances, there is potential for challenge to the status quo. They also leave us with the caution that "reform" may be limited by the context of substantively unequal power relations between workers and their employer, as well as the political priority attached to the issue by the state and its officials. Such studies are a valuable counterbalance to earlier, cruder, law emergence studies, which all too often saw law creation purely in instrumental terms, often with clear winners and losers. The reality, they demonstrate, is far more complex.

Many of the studies we have just examined focus principally on the enactment of legislation. However, it is important to realise that the struggle for power does not end once a Bill is proclaimed. The "emergence process" is just one battle, not the entire war. It may be that groups, who are unable to prevent legislation being passed, can nevertheless assert their power at a later stage.

---

121 P Grabosky and A Sutton (eds), *Stains on A White Collar: Fourteen Studies in Corporate Crime or Corporate Harm*, Federation Press, 1989; C Wells, *Corporations and Criminal Responsibility*, Oxford UP, 1993.

122 See further S Chesterman, "The Corporate Veil, Crime and Punishment: *The Queen v Denbo Pty Ltd and Timothy Ian Nadenbousch*" (1994) 19(4) *Melbourne University Law Review* 1064.

123 Sections 49A-49E. There is, of course, a story to be told about the emergence of this legislation. For a discussion of these reforms, see M Addison, "Industrial Manslaughter: A Necessary Evil?" (2004) 184 *Lawyers Weekly* 12; K Lorric and R Morgan, "Directions in OHS: The Year in Review" (2004) 94 *Australian Construction Law Newsletter* 51.

Even at the legislative stage itself, they may be successful in introducing clauses which weaken the Bill, which provide defences and loopholes, and which render it incapable of effective enforcement. For example, Gunningham has documented how, in the case of early British anti-pollution legislation, "well-nigh impregnable barriers" were built into the legislation which, as one parliamentarian noted at the time, made it "nearly impossible to prosecute the recalcitrant industrialist who is still largely responsible for black and dark smoke".[124]

Again, in a well-known study of a Norwegian statute passed to regulate the conditions of women working as housemaids, Vilhelm Aubert showed how it was possible for the legislation to satisfy competing group interests (reformists who wanted to protect housemaids, and conservatives who resisted such change). This was achieved by setting up a reformist ideal but ensuring that the legislation (in the absence of any provision for the creation of a viable enforcement agency) would not be enforced.[125] In the modern context, all that is necessary to neutralise protective legislation is to decimate the enforcement agency's budget, to remove its offices to undesirable areas, to dislocate and demoralise its bureaucrats and enforcement agents. The point, then, is that the story of law, class and power does not end with the enactment of legislation. In the following section we develop this theme by demonstrating the equally crucial role of the implementation process.

(g) The implementation of legislation

(i) How can we assess implementation?

Australian liberalism is arguably characterised by utilitarian motives.[126] The modern utilitarian view tolerates some degree of state intervention into the private lives of individuals in order to maximise the general welfare of society. In Australia, there has been a marked reliance on legislation to achieve this. This relatively modern emphasis on the public regulation of social and economic activity, and on "reform through legislation", makes an important assumption: that law can be used to achieve pre-determined results in social and economic arenas. It is assumed that law in general, and legislation in particular, is an effective instrument of social engineering.

In turn, this instrumentalist view assumes a relatively straightforward progression from the emergence stage of legislation to the implementation stage, and then to the achievement of a desired end-result (be it fewer road deaths, increased income tax revenue for government, or fairer employment and promotion processes). Laws, once enacted, are thus regarded as somehow independent of their political and social contexts. This is sometimes reinforced in legal education which tends to focus on teaching the legal rules (their meaning and scope), and overlooking the context of their enforcement.

It should be apparent by now that there are serious difficulties with this view. We have already seen that the *emergence* of legislation is influenced in various ways by dominant relations of power in society. Another difficulty with the

---

124 G Nabarro quoted in N Gunningham, *Pollution, Social Interest and the Law*, Martin Robertson, 1974, 61.

125 See V Aubert, "White Collar Crime and Social Structure" (1952) 58 *American Jo Sociology* 263.

126 See H Collins, "Political Ideology in Australia: The Distinctiveness of a Benthamite Society" in S Graubard (ed), *Australia: The Daedalus Symposium*, Angus and Robertson, 1985.

instrumentalist view lies in defining the criterion by which it can be said that a legislative rule has been *effective*.[127] This difficulty has been highlighted by Griffiths, who distinguishes between four different effects which a legal rule might have.[128]

Direct effects occur either when the primary audience at whom the rule is directed conforms with the letter of the rule ("primary direct effects"), or when the officials responsible for enforcing or implementing the rule carry out that function ("secondary direct effects"). For example, the primary direct effect of a rule that prohibits drink driving would be that people do not drive with more than the prescribed concentration of alcohol in their blood. Griffiths argues that, whilst there is little doubt that legal rules do produce some direct effects, these vary considerably and their extent is often exaggerated. After all, he argues, it is usually not direct compliance that is interesting, but the consequences of that compliance.

Griffiths includes these consequences under the heading *indirect effects*. For example, whereas the primary direct effect of legal rules against drink driving may be that fewer people drive whilst over the prescribed concentration of alcohol limit in breath or blood (PCA), the hoped for indirect effect will presumably be fewer automobile fatalities. An unwanted indirect effect of the same legal rules may be higher unemployment in the liquor industry.[129] According to Griffiths, when people talk about using the law to achieve certain aims, they are usually concerned with indirect effects, yet these are much more difficult to predict or measure than direct effects.

The third category described by Griffiths are the *independent effects* of legal rules. These are "effects which occur independently of any conforming behaviour".[130] For example, laws which prohibit unsafe work practices might not succeed in prompting factory owners to revise their production processes, nor might they lead to a reduction in workplace injuries – that is, these laws might have few direct or indirect effects. Nevertheless, these laws might allow a government to promote itself to the voters as concerned with the important social issue of occupational safety, as in the case of the recent adoption of industrial homicide laws, noted above, and the uninformed general public might also be comforted by "the idea that the law is rational and up-to-date".[131] In other words, as indicated earlier, laws may be important for what they symbolise as much as, or even instead of, what they achieve directly. As Griffiths says, "[i]t would be sociologically silly to describe a law as ineffective just because it is not obeyed".[132]

Finally, Griffiths suggests, laws may also have *unintended effects*. For example, in the United States laws were passed in the 1920s to prohibit the sale of alcohol; what resulted, however, was widespread evasion of the law and the scope for organised crime to prosper from an underground industry in manufacturing and supplying "bootleg liquor". This category overlaps with those mentioned previously, in that all three such effects may lie outside those that the law-maker

---

127 Tomasic notes, for example, that effectiveness might be measured by reference to the degree to which the new rule is compatible with existing values, or the enforceability of the law, or extent to which the law is actually enforced. See "The Sociology of Legislation", n 53, 35.

128 J Griffiths, "Is Law Important?" (1979) 53 *New York University Law Review* 339.

129 An example used in Griffiths, n 128, 352-353.

130 Ibid 354.

131 Ibid 355.

132 Ibid 355.

has foreseen. Griffiths suggests, in fact, that most indirect effects are likely to be unintended. If this is correct, then the idea that law is an important means of achieving social change becomes problematical. Griffiths' conclusion is that the implementation process is so variable and subject to pressure from competing interests that, for the most part, legal rules – considered as instruments of social change – are not very important.[133]

Griffiths' argument about the results of legislation highlights the point that, contrary to the instrumentalist image, the process of social change via legislation is far from straightforward. In particular the implementation of legislation is crucially affected and shaped by what an instrumentalist would regard as extraneous conflicts and pressures. As Bardach points out:

> A single governmental strategy may involve the complex and interrelated activities of several levels of governmental bureaus and agencies, private organisations, professional associations, interest groups, and clientele populations.[134]

In other words, the implementation of legislation usually requires input from a wide range of interests. Moreover, these disparate interests and groups will quite often act independently of, and sometimes in outright opposition to, each other. It is hardly surprising, then, that the original purposes behind the legislation (insofar as they can be accurately determined) are likely to become deflected, modified, thwarted or just simply ignored.

The point, therefore, is that political processes are important in determining and conditioning the implementation of law. Indeed, as we have stressed throughout this book, law is not just a body of abstract rules that are imposed on society. It is, *in addition*, comprised of the variety of processes, practices and conventions whereby those rules are implemented, interpreted, used and/or avoided. Law is "intimately related"[135] to those social processes and practices rather than existing independently of them. These processes and practices are as much a function of power relations as those which lead to the passing of legislation in the first place. Accordingly, as with emergence studies, the implementation process can be analysed by reference to the continuum of political models identified earlier in this chapter.

(ii)   Implementation and the consensus-conflict paradigm

Bardach provides one example of this in the following passage (in which he refers to the emergence of legislation as the "adoption of policy mandates"):

> The goals embodied in a policy mandate typically undergo some change during the implementation phase. They might have been ambiguous and therefore might have required, or at least permitted, further definition. Or they might have been based on a very weak consensus, hastily, and perhaps insincerely, contrived during the contest surrounding the adoption of the mandate. Indeed, interests opposed to the goals of the mandate might have stayed quiet during the adoption contest precisely because they counted on subsequent opportunities to achieve

---

133 Ibid 344.

134 E Bardach, *The Implementation Game: What Happens after a Bill becomes a Law?*, MIT Press, 1977, 5.

135 Tomasic, n 53, 105.

more decisive, and less publicized, victories during the struggle over implementation.... *[I]mplementation is the continuation of politics by other means.*[136]

The politics that Bardach refers to in this passage is the politics of consensus pluralism, of power struggles between more-or-less equally powerful competing interest groups. But whether one takes a consensus pluralist or a conflict perspective the same general conclusion applies: the implementation of legislation is about politics and power.

It is relatively easy to suggest why implementation processes are important in shaping our legal system.[137] It is much more difficult to go further and create a general theory of implementation which can explain why some legal rules seem to produce intended outcomes while others do not, and how this connects with issues of politics and power. There are a number of reasons why this is so. First, there are significant methodological problems in studying the implementation of legal rules. As we have seen from Griffiths' work, there are problems in defining what constitutes a "successful outcome"; the intention behind a particular law may often be obscure. Secondly, even where a legal rule does have direct effects (to use Griffiths' terminology) there is the problem of establishing causation. It is one thing to point to the introduction of a new legal rule, and then point to a change in people's behaviour; it is another thing to say that the former caused the latter. Can we be certain that behaviour which appears to be in compliance with a particular rule is *brought about* by that rule? Changes in drink-driving behaviours may be the result of massive public education campaigns about deaths on the road, not law enforcement: indeed the modern media advertisements reinforce the self-interest in modifying behaviour, as much as the legal consequences of being caught. Other factors may explain the conduct – religious beliefs, moral pressure, habit, custom, or self-serving interests – all of which may simply be reinforced by the rule in question.[138] Finally, and crucially, it is unlikely that any single theory of implementation could account adequately for the variety of groups and interests which can affect the process of implementation in any given instance.

Nevertheless some *general* observations can be made about the relationship between implementation and power.[139] Many legal rules must be actively enforced or applied by some agency or group, such as the police or a government body. It follows that the actions (and inactions) of these rule enforcers can be crucial in determining the extent and manner to which a rule is "successful" (in instrumental terms). In explaining the behaviour of such agencies one significant factor is the difference in power between the agency itself and those with whom it deals (the "target population").[140] When dealing with the relatively powerless, some regulators both seek to expand their sphere of regulatory control (as with the entrepreneurial activities of the Federal Bureau of Narcotics regarding marijuana use, discussed earlier) and also adopt a more punitive approach to the target population.

---

136 Bardach, n 134, 85 (emphasis added).

137 This is not to suggest that all writers conceive of that process in the same way. Bardach, for example, depicts it as a loosely connected set of strategies or "implementation games"; see n 134.

138 See RL Kidder, *Connecting Law and Society: An Introduction to Research and Theory*, Prentice-Hall, 1983, 119-123.

139 The following discussion strays into the literature on "law and regulation" which is discussed in more detail in Chapter 10 of this book.

140 See Roshier and Teff, n 112, 26-27.

Conversely, many studies of regulatory behaviour suggest that when the target population is able to exert some power over the rule enforcers, the latter are likely to adopt a more compliant and restrictive approach to enforcement. We can see some clear examples of this in the regulation of business and industry.

This is an area that is populated by a variety of specialised governmental regulatory agencies, ranging from statutory bodies like the Australian Competition and Consumer Commission or the Australian Securities and Investments Commission to inspectorates charged with the task of enforcing a variety of laws dealing with occupational health and safety. Different theories have been advanced to explain why it is that regulators are so often unable to apply the laws in question effectively.[141] Since our purpose here is to illustrate the ways in which different groups can exert power in the process of implementing legislation, we do not intend to survey all of these theories. Instead, we have selected one that has been both widely espoused and criticised; the so-called "capture theory".

Proponents of this theory argue that the enforcement practices of some regulatory agencies tend, over time, to be "captured" by the ideals and interests of those whom they are supposed to regulate. In blunt terms, the regulated are able to control how and when the regulators do their work. This process of capture may come about in a number of ways depending on the context. For example, a lack of technical knowledge amongst the regulators of a particular industry may increase their dependency on the "target population" for advice and technical support. Some employees of governmental regulatory agencies might perceive better employment prospects within the industry which they regulate and so become less stringent in their regulatory behaviour in order not to alienate prospective employers. Alternatively, a regulatory agency may be staffed with people who have previously worked in the regulated industry and who are thus likely to have a predisposed view about how and when to enforce the relevant laws. (The latter two examples are sometimes called "the revolving door phenomenon").[142] Whatever the cause, the theory is that a "captured" law enforcer will implement the law by reference to the dictates of the regulated industry rather than the intention of the law-makers.

One particular area of regulation where there is evidence of capture is the enforcement of occupational health and safety laws.[143] A specific example is the non-enforcement of safety standards in the mining industry. Non-enforcement by mine inspectors has been shown to take different forms;[144] in some cases inspections have been carried out so infrequently as to have no impact on hazardous work conditions. In addition, inspections can be rendered ineffective because inspectors give advance warning of their arrival, allowing mine operators

---

141 Amongst others, Tomasic identifies capture theory (discussed below), interest group theories (which "focus on the political aspects of the regulatory process"), and bureaucratic theories (which "have emphasized the dilemmas in administrative and regulatory action"): see n 53, 111-114.

142 Another cause of regulatory capture may occur in the "emergence stage" of the legislation, when powerful industry groups ensure that the agency will be given only limited powers or resources, thus ensuring its later reliance on those groups.

143 An observation made by Grabosky and Sutton, "Conclusion" in Grabosky and Sutton (eds), n 121, 243.

144 The following discussion relies on N Gunningham, "Negotiated Non-Compliance: A Case Study of Regulatory Failure" (1987) 9 *Law and Policy* 69.

to clean up (or, some would argue, cover up) any hazardous conditions. Finally, the response of the inspectors to any breaches of safety conditions may be inadequate. In their survey of Australian regulatory agencies, Grabosky and Braithwaite found that mining safety inspectorates had a particularly low level of prosecution activity, involving the imposition of very low fines on mine owners. One factor they singled out to explain this is that mining inspectors are usually recruited from the ranks of mine managers:

> Mine inspectors in all [Australian] states are required to have ... at least three years experience in mine management.... most states do not like to employ people who have not had at least ten years mining experience including experience as a mine manager.[145]

Whilst this undoubtedly has the advantage of ensuring that the inspectorate has a working knowledge of the mining industry, it also means that the inspectors will be the professional peers of those whose conduct is being regulated. As Grabosky and Braithwaite note, "with this familiarity comes the risk of capture".[146] As Gunningham found in his study of asbestos mining at Baryulgil in New South Wales, mine inspectors, confronted with powerful industrial interests, may tend to prefer an enforcement strategy that emphasises friendly persuasion, cooperation and conciliation, rather than accusation, confrontation and coercion.[147]

This is further illustrated in Hopkins' study of the 1979 explosion at the Appin coalmine in New South Wales which killed 14 miners. The explosion occurred during repairs to an exhaust fan when an electrical spark ignited a build up of methane gas in the mine shaft. At the time there were safety regulations in force which dealt with the ventilation of shafts, permitted levels of gas, and the procedures for making electrical repairs to the fans (so as to eliminate the risk of electrical sparks). As Hopkins found, however:

> When confronted with a problem such as excessive gas they [the inspectors] have a choice. One option is to stop the mining until the problem is rectified, with the consequent loss of thousands of dollars of company profit and the loss of workers' productivity bonuses. Such a choice would generally be opposed by management and workers alike. Alternatively they may request management to do something about the problem but allow mining to continue, knowing very well that the chances are minimal that any particular violation will lead to death or injury. The pressure to choose the latter course is overwhelming and since such situations arise routinely on mine inspections a pattern of non-enforcement develops.[148]

One way of explaining the non-enforcement of mining safety laws is to see it as the result of a continual process of political compromise between more or less equally powerful competing interests. Those interests could be listed as: the industry, represented by the mining companies, with a concern for profit maximisation; the workers, represented by trade unions, with a concern for safe and

---

145 P Grabosky and J Braithwaite, *Of Manners Gentle: Enforcement Strategies of Australian Business Regulatory Agencies*, Oxford UP, 1986, 62.

146 Ibid 198.

147 Gunningham, n 144.

148 A Hopkins, "Crime Without Punishment: The Appin Mine Disaster" in Grabosky and Sutton, n 121, 160 at 170. Hopkins describes this as a process of co-optation of the inspectors. It is arguable that capture and co-optation are not synonymous.

well-paid work; the government, with a concern for maintaining a certain level of economic activity; and, arguably, the general public.[149] This type of analysis would fall within a broadly pluralistic framework, but a more plausible account can be given by conflict theory. Here we begin with the reminder that regulatory bodies like the mining inspectorates are essentially agencies of the state.[150] Thus, rather than seeing the implementation of safety regulations in terms of interactions between a variety of equally powerful interest groups, a conflict analysis takes as its starting point the power differential between the state and the corporate capitalist class on the one hand, and the (sometimes poorly represented) workers on the other. Such an analysis then proceeds by pointing out that the state, via the inspectorates, cannot afford to pursue a vigorous enforcement strategy in the face of the possibility that industry might then withdraw or scale-down economically significant operations. Nevertheless:

> The existence of some protective legislation and a bureaucracy to administer it give the appearance that something is being done to prevent accidents and disease and that the interests of capital are not permitted to dominate those of labour. The state simultaneously maintains the appearance of neutrality and legitimacy.[151]

And for their part:

> Corporations depend on state regulatory agencies to stabilize the business environment. Health and safety legislation can assist the centralization of capital and expropriation of smaller capitalists when they cannot afford the capital expenditure required for safety technology.[152]

(iii)   Implementation, lawyers and the courts

Thus far we have concentrated on the role of law enforcers in the implementation process. Another important, and diverse, group are the rule interpreters, particularly legal practitioners and judges. In the previous chapter, we examined how lawyers play an active role in implementation, through the way that they "construct" or translate the demands of their clients into legal claims and defences. Lawyers, along with agencies like the police, operate as gatekeepers for the law. They can emphasise or suppress the significance of particular legal rules. New rules may create new rights of action or redress but yet not be used if lawyers do not bring them to the attention of clients (because of ignorance, misunderstanding or disapproval of the rule). A good illustration of this is provided in Stewart Macaulay's study of the impact of consumer protection legislation on lawyers in the United States.[153]

The legislation (known as the *Magnusson-Moss Warranty Act* of 1975) was introduced to help consumers in seeking compensation for faulty products, for example, by regulating the wording and public disclosure of warranties. In a

---

149 Gunningham, n 144, 87.

150 See, for example, Y De Michiel, "The Subjected Body: An Analysis of the Occupational Health and Safety Apparatus in New South Wales" (1983) 1 *Australian Journal of Law and Society* 5.

151 De Michiel, n 150, 22.

152 Ibid 22.

153   S Macaulay, "Lawyers and Consumer Protection Laws" (1979) 14 *Law and Society Review* 115.

survey of lawyers in Wisconsin, Macaulay found that those who were better informed about the contents of the Act were those who acted for business clients; this knowledge was necessary in order to ensure that their economically powerful clients would be seen to be complying with the Act's requirements. Macaulay also found that these lawyers tended to interpret those requirements in a way that minimised the burden on their clients. In contrast, those lawyers who were likely to act for individual consumers knew little if anything about the Act, and were thus unable to inform their clients (the consumers for whom the legislation had been enacted) of their legislative rights. Macaulay explains this by pointing out that these lawyers dealt with very few consumer matters, and those that they did deal with often resulted in relatively small fees for the lawyer. Consequently it was not in the lawyers' interests to put the considerable time and money required into learning and keeping up to date with new consumer protection laws. In short, Macaulay observes:

> The lawyers studied seem to be responding predictably to the social and economic structures in which the practice of law is embedded. Liberal reforms such as consumer protection laws create individual rights without providing the means to carry them out... . [I]n practice, justice is rationed by cost barriers and the lawyer's long-range interests.[154]

The role of judicial interpretation in determining the effect of legal rules is a much studied topic and it is beyond the scope of this chapter to canvass the arguments in detail. The debate stretches from the implausible claim of some formalists[155] that judges do not make law, they merely apply it, to the equally implausible argument that judicial decision-making is all a matter of subjective bias (sometimes satirised by realists as a claim that judicial decisions all depend on what the judge ate for breakfast). In between these extremes it has been argued that judges undoubtedly do have scope for exercising discretion in the interpretation and application of rules, but they are constrained in this by the conventions and practices of legal behaviour and legal institutions. Gerald Frug has put this argument in the following way:

> Legal decisionmakers operate within a legal system that they both inherit and construct. The fact that they inherit it means that their decisions cannot adequately be understood as subjective, and the fact that they construct it means that their decisions cannot adequately be understood as objective. The relationship between legal decisionmakers and the legal system is far too complex to be captured by either the concept of objectivity or subjectivity.[156]

(iv)   The police

An illustration of the power of both law enforcers and law interpreters in implementing legislation is found in numerous studies of the policing of domestic violence. Early research, in New South Wales, showed the police to be a powerful interest group both in enforcing and interpreting the law.[157]

---

154 Macaulay, n 153, 161.
155 See the discussion on formalism in Chapter 3.
156 G Frug, "A Critical Theory of Law" (1989) 1 *Legal Education Review* 43 at 52-53.
157 S Hatty, *Male Violence and the Police*, School of Social Work, University of New South Wales, 1988.

In the 1980s, a wide range of reforms was introduced in all Australian jurisdictions to address the perceived limitations in using the criminal law in response to domestic violence: police were given wider powers to enter private property to investigate domestic violence; and spouses could be made compellable witnesses in relation to domestic violence offences, thus preventing prosecutions being dropped when spouses refused to "press charges". Most significantly, the amendments also created a new civil restraining order that could be obtained following a complaint laid either by a victim of domestic violence or by the police before a magistrate.[158] Such orders (now generically called protection orders) operated prospectively to impose restrictions or prohibitions on the violent or potentially violent party regarding access to the victim and to specified premises. Breach of an order was made an offence, for which police were empowered to arrest without a warrant.

Hatty's study of the first six years of operation of these reforms in NSW revealed significant failures to enforce or implement the laws as enacted. Based on interviews with police and observation of domestic violence incidents, Hatty's conclusion was as follows:

> Whilst intervening in male violence constitutes a large proportion of police workload, this duty is being undertaken neither conscientiously through the application of the relevant legislation, nor effectively through a consideration of the needs of the victims of violence. Police are not implementing the Crimes (Domestic Violence) Amendment Act 1982 as intended.[159]

The study showed that arrests for violent spousal assault remained very low in the immediate period after the reforms.[160] This low arrest rate was not compensated by a high number of police applications for restraining orders (now called Apprehended Domestic Violence Orders). Surprisingly, the proportion of such applications actually fell from 7.3 per cent of cases in 1983 to 6 per cent in 1986.[161]

The findings in this study were attributed to a number of factors, including the fact that over one-third of police officers interviewed were ignorant of the new legislation.[162] The new laws, and the pro-enforcement policies adopted by senior NSW Police Management, were also found to contradict the advice contained in Police Handbooks that offered the traditional injunction to police not to interfere unnecessarily in family disputes unless there was serious violence or property damage.[163] This early study of domestic violence by Hatty not only revealed how police defined the operation of the new legislation; it also exposed their crucial role in influencing public perceptions of the very problem which the legislation was intended to address.

More than two decades since Hatty's study, this pattern of under-enforcement continues across Australia, notwithstanding further expansion of police powers, and even wider scope for seeking and granting protection orders. Indeed, there is

---

158 Bronitt and McSherry, n 6, 721-724.

159 Hatty, n 157, 182.

160 Ibid 68.

161 Ibid 19.

162 Ibid 20.

163 As Mark Finnane has pointed out, such instructions and policies formally persisted in some Australian States until the 1980s, and continue, informally, to reflect the attitudes of many police officers called to attend "domestics": M Finnane, *Police and Government*, Oxford UP, 1994, 104-110.

increasing scepticism that the protection order is an effective response,[164] and it may even have been counterproductive. A recent study in Queensland concluded that:

> [T]he effect of domestic violence legislation has been to separate "intimate partner" violence out from other forms of assault. The repositioning of violence between intimate partners within the civil, less publicly accountable, sphere has been to subtly construct it against the "more serious" categories of criminally vilified violence.[165]

This research was based on a five-month study of all domestic violence matters in Magistrates Courts in Brisbane and Ipswich. During this period only one male defendant appeared before the court charged with a violent offence against his spouse, though over this same period 694 domestic violence order applications were made. In relation to the domestic violence orders, less than half of all the applications were taken out by police, suggesting to the researchers that "the violence, or threat of violence, is often not perceived to be sufficiently 'serious' to warrant state intervention".[166] Despite the incidence of violence revealed in the study, few domestic violence applications resulted in criminal prosecution.

This chronic under-utilisation of the criminal law was not linked to the legislation or police policy, which imposed on Queensland police a mandatory duty to investigate domestic violence. Douglas and Godden identified the following reasons for the lack of criminal prosecutions:[167]

- women being unaware they have a right to make a criminal charge (despite police policy that police should actively canvass the possibility of criminal charges in conjunction with domestic violence orders);
- women believing that they must choose between making a criminal or civil response to domestic violence;
- women fearing their engagement with the criminal justice system would exacerbate current levels of violence; or
- a fear that a criminal record or incarceration of the offender would have a negative impact on the family in the longer term.

The above account reveals how the police function as "gatekeepers", defining whether or not the violence or threats amount to a legal wrong. Having decided that it is a legal matter, the police then have a discretion to decide which way to proceed: whether the matter should be prosecuted through ordinary criminal law or to assist the party to obtain a protection order. Alternatively, they may simply leave it to the aggrieved partner to pursue remedies of a civil nature on their own behalf.

From a liberal perspective, the story of domestic violence is viewed as a failure in legality: police discretion, unfettered by rules or principles, has fostered a police culture of non-compliance. From this perspective, the discretion of the

---

164 The increased reliance on civil protection orders to deal with domestic violence has been criticised in a recent empirical study of how domestic violence is treated in Queensland: H Douglas and L Godden, "The Decriminalisation of Domestic Violence: Examining the Interaction Between the Criminal Law and Domestic Violence" (2003) 27 *Criminal Law Journal* 32.

165 Ibid 42

166 Ibid 36.

167 Ibid 39-49.

officer on the ground must be constrained; if it cannot be eliminated, its exercise must be rendered transparent and accountable. Legislation mandating investigation of such cases has been introduced in some jurisdictions. Mandatory policing is a radical deviation from the doctrine of police independence, a common law doctrine in which the courts have generally declined to interfere in operational police decision-making.[168] In New South Wales and Queensland, for example, the legislature has enacted a statutory duty to investigate whether an act of domestic violence has been committed in cases where the police officer believes or suspects that domestic violence has been, is being or is likely to be committed.[169]

As we have seen, rule enforcers and rule interpreters can have an enormous impact on the implementation of legislation by the manner in which they process and modify legislative changes. Kidder has described them as "filtering agents"; that is, they can constrain, adapt or modify the intentions and policies that may have motivated the passage of legislation in the first place.[170] This is not an arbitrary process:

> [T]he routines which filter the impact of laws are not the result of impersonal, impartial, structural pressures, and their effects are not impartial. Rather they favour the wealthy, the powerful, because they are produced by pressures put on the law's interpretative institutions by those seeking to preserve and enhance their power and having the resources to do it.[171]

(h) Conclusion

In this chapter we have explored the relationship between power and law-making, exposing the wide array of interests that shape the formation, interpretation and enforcement of legal rules. What emerges is a more complex picture than the liberal image of law's role in society. Law may not conform to a perfect theoretical blueprint, but within systems that proclaim a commitment to liberal values, considerable emphasis is placed on ideas, or perhaps *ideals*, that seek to constrain power. These relate to the rule of law, discussed in Chapter 3, and the importance of protecting individual freedom and rights, equality before the law, access to justice and so on. The *extent* to which one's own picture of law departs from that liberal image may partly be determined by the view one takes of society generally. If society is conceived as held together by pure and unforced consensus, then the gap might be thought small. We have noted, however, that a considerable body of literature within modern sociology and political science casts doubt on such a consensus model; and emergence and implementation studies form part of the evidence. If, on the other hand, one sees society as racked with conflict, so that any semblance of order is maintained only by repression, then the gap between the liberal image of law and the reality of its operation is a huge one. The literature on the emergence and implementation of legislation certainly provides some support

---

168 Invoking the notion of constabulary independence, the courts have affirmed that police officers possess a wide discretion in exercising their duties that is *ordinarily* not reviewable: *R v Metropolitan Police Commissioner; Ex parte Blackburn* [1968] 2 QB 118.

169 *Crimes Act 1900* (NSW) s 562H; *Domestic and Family Violence Protection Act 1989* (Qld) s 67.

170 Kidder, n 138, 126. Within this description he also includes the population at whom the legislation is directed. This group has been the focus of many so-called "impact studies".

171 Ibid 136.

for such an analysis. But, whilst a pure conflict position might be applicable to conditions of extreme social upheaval, it is more difficult to maintain it as a description of the *norm* in western industrialised societies. Nor does the literature on legislation provide strong endorsement for it. More likely, one will concede a greater role for consent, but then focus on the degree to which that consent has been manipulated or manufactured by powerful groups. The better view, supported by many of the case studies in this chapter, is that the emergence of legislation can conform simultaneously to both consensus and conflict models. This hopefully should not present the student with too much unease – law, like many social practices, is messy, amenable to multiple and potentially contradictory interpretations!

In the space available, we have only been able to touch upon some of the case studies that bear on these major issues. We have certainly not been able to canvass every available position. We have, however, indicated the main lines of debate and some of the strengths and weaknesses in each kind of argument. Although the reader must form her or his own view of the size of the "gap" between ideal and reality, it seems undeniable that a better understanding of legislation cannot be divorced from an understanding of power in society.

Discussion Questions

1. Undertake an Internet-based search on the following topics. Identify the individuals (moral entrepreneurs) and group interests (represented by private and public associations etc) that are seeking to shape legislative responses to:
   - voluntary euthanasia,
   - the use of cannabis for medicinal purposes,
   - abortion,
   - damages claims for medical negligence.

   What are the conditions that explain the success (or otherwise) of individual or group efforts to enact legislation on the above topics? Do you think organised professional lobby groups are effective in Australia?

2. Over the past two decades, refugees have been presented variously through legislation as victims escaping persecution and human rights abuses; economic migrants seeking to "queue jump"; and, most recently, participants in an transnational organised crime network posing serious threats to national security. For a review of these stages of development, see S Pickering, *Refugees and State Crime*, Federation Press, 2005.

   What factors – economic, social and political – do you think explain these changes? What interests and individuals have played a role in constructing these distinct legislative phases? Compare the respective roles of NGOs, law enforcement and federal government?

3. What factors and interests – *not* considered in the above chapter – are shaping the direction of new laws in the 21st century? Who are the new moral entrepreneurs?

4. Understanding legislation, it has been suggested, is not simply a matter of consulting the relevant statutory provisions. If we accept this, how should law be redefined? What are the implications for legal education?

234

Chapter 8

Gender

(a)   Introduction

During the 1980s, the possibility of a specifically feminist jurisprudence was increasingly recognised within law schools, to the extent that virtually every law curriculum in Australia now includes a component where students are given the opportunity to reflect upon the relationship between law and gender.[1] There was considerable idealism that the core of the curriculum would become infused with gender perspective, and the Australian federal government funded a project to develop material specifically to be integrated into these courses in the mid-1990s.[2] While gender is taken more seriously, the anticipated changes have not eventuated: gender remains largely hidden from view in many law curricula.[3] If it is taken seriously, it is often addressed in special electives or in guest lectures by the faculty "feminist".

Feminists have been interested in law since feminism itself was identifiable in the early 19th century, although the term "feminism" itself did not come into usage until the late 19th century. Many campaigns have had the aim of bringing about legal change. Significant amongst these were campaigns for the vote, for reform of marriage laws in the 19th century and for laws prohibiting discrimination in employment in the 20th century. Indeed, the rights of women and formal equality between the sexes was championed by leading liberal philosophers of the time, including John Stuart Mill, whose views are further discussed below.

What has changed dramatically in recent years, however, is the attention now given to theories about *law itself*, not just the content of particular laws. The literature is voluminous. Since the first edition of this book in 1991, it has grown to the extent that it could not adequately be summarised in the space of one

---

1   This may be related to wider transformation of legal education. The Australian Law Reform Commission noted that legal education is less rigidly focused on case law, and the range of subjects now available for study in law schools has increased, especially in theoretical and critical studies: ALRC IP 21, *Review of the Adversarial System of Litigation – Rethinking Legal Education and Training* (1997) para. 5.12.

2   These materials, prepared by Reg Graycar and Jenny Morgan, are no longer easily accessible. They have been electronically archived on the National Library Archive, Pandora, *Work and Violence Themes: including Gender Issues in the Core Law Curriculum* (1996): <http://pandora. nla.gov.au/tep/10029>.

3   This suppression of gender in law and legal education is reflected in the title of the leading text on the subject: R Graycar and J Morgan, *The Hidden Gender of Law*, 2nd ed, Federation Press, 2002.

chapter.[4] The present discussion has two immediate purposes. The first is to introduce readers to some ways of classifying thinking within feminist juris-prudence and feminist thought more generally. The second is to take a specific area of feminist interest, such as anti-discrimination laws and affirmative action legislation,[5] and look at the debates surrounding it.

Our intention is to deepen the feminist perspectives introduced in Chapter 2 in the case study on the regulation of pornography. In this way, some of the themes of feminist theory can be seen in action. At the same time, our analysis of anti-discrimination measures does not amount to a test-case of any particular feminist theory. The literature and ideas are too complex to attempt such an exercise here. Some of the remarks we make about anti-discrimination measures in this chapter are also applicable to racial inequality. There are therefore clear con-nections between this Chapter and Chapter 9, which deals with race and multi-culturalism.

Aside from these two immediate purposes, our more general aim is to continue the theme of liberalism and the law. At least two strands of feminist literature on law are explicit rejections of liberalism as a guiding philosophical principle. Some of the writers have arrived at their position specifically through a scrutiny of the law. They have questioned how it is that gross inequality between the sexes can have co-existed with two centuries of laws which were supposedly based on values like individualism, equality before the law, justice and rationality. In seeking an answer, some feminists have concluded that the *liberal formulations* of these values are part of the problem. Liberalism, they say, is antithetical to feminism. No wonder, then, that liberalism implicit within law has done little to restrain male power, and moreover may have done much to sustain it.

Finally, we must make clear our belief that gender inequality continues to exist. It is certainly not the only kind of inequality in our society. It intersects with other inequalities based on class, race, sexuality and disability. But we have no doubt that, taken on its own, it amounts to a serious form of injustice. We adopt Tom Campbell's statement that:

> No feature of human societies is more evident than that men – as a result of humanly contrived cultural arrangements – have an easier, more varied and better rewarded life than women.[6]

There are still many within the world of legal practice, and some within the world of law teaching, who would not accept this claim.[7] Many also see no point in taking gender as a topic seriously, believing law is or should be "gender

---

4   See, in particular, N Naffine, *Law and the Sexes*, Allen and Unwin, 1990; Graycar and Morgan, n 3; N Lacey, *Unspeakable Subjects – Feminist Essays in Legal and Social Theory*, Hart Pub-lishing, 1998; N Naffine and R Owens (eds), *Sexing the Subject of Law*, LBC, 1997; P Easteal, *Less than Equal: Women and the Australian Legal System*, Butterworths, 2001; J Scutt, *Women and the Law*, Law Book Co, 1990. For a collection of representative articles, see F Olsen (ed), *Feminist Legal Theory* Vols I and II, Dartmouth, 1995. For an Australian collection specifically organised around questions of public and private, see M Thornton (ed) *Public and Private: Feminist Legal Debates*, Oxford UP, 1995.

5   Arguably, anti-discrimination and affirmative action legislation are discrete concerns. It is possible to approve of the former but not of the latter.

6   "Mistaking the Relevance of Gender" in S McLean and N Burrows (eds), *The Legal Relevance of Gender*, Macmillan, 1988.

7   Margaret Thornton has explored issues of gender bias and discrimination within the legal com-munity in *Dissonance and Distrust: Women in the Legal Profession*, Oxford UP, 1996.

neutral" so that courses and books on "law and gender" amount to incoherent collections of materials. Gender is not, it is said, a meaningful organising concept. Readers who share that position may find what follows uncongenial.

One brief note on terminology. There is an assumption in much of the literature that a gender analysis will be a feminist one. The "gender" referred to is female. One obvious reason for this is that most of the literature has been written from a feminist perspective. On the other hand, a theme in some scholarship is that both "man" and "woman" are socially constructed categories and that law plays a part in that process of construction.[8] The emphasis in gender analyses is on women because the sexes have been socially constructed as *unequal* and it is over-whelmingly women who are thought to have been disadvantaged.

(b) Feminist jurisprudence

It has been common to divide feminist theories into three or four categories; such as "liberal feminism", "radical feminism", "cultural feminism" and "socialist/ marxist feminism".

Liberal feminism argues that it is possible to have gender equality within a liberal society and that inequality in the past has been brought about solely through male prejudice.[9]

Radical feminism sees the political dominance by men over women ("patriarchy") as the fundamental division in societies and it is largely independent of the economic or social system.[10] Some radical feminists have identified the causes of this domination in the biological division of the sexes. Until reproductive technology is revolutionised so that women are freed from the burden of their biologically determined oppression then patriarchy will subsist.[11]

Cultural feminism is more difficult to define but it refers to work by writers like Carol Gilligan (discussed below) who argue that women have their own specific culture which has inherent value and that their distinctive voice or viewpoint must not be ignored or under-valued in the search for equality.[12]

Finally, *Marxist/socialist feminism* seeks to reconcile a traditional marxist analysis, which takes society as comprising antagonistic social classes, with a feminist analysis. The effect is that gender rather than class is viewed as the primary division in society. In Michele Barrett's words, the object of Marxist

---

8   See R Collier, *Masculinity, Law and the Family*, Routledge, 1995. Indeed, the position of transsexual or transgendered persons reveals this construction clearly, revealing the difficulties in maintaining a strict binary conception of gender. From a legal perspective, notwithstanding gender-neutral laws, these individuals often experience difficulties asserting rights or claiming protection under the law. For a review of the problems invoking the criminal law to deal with the sexual abuse of transsexuals, see A Sharpe, "The Precarious Position of the Transsexual Rape Victim" (1994) 6(2) *Current Issues in Criminal Justice* 303; A Sharpe, "Attempting the 'Impossible': The Case of Transsexual Rape" (1997) 21 *Criminal Law Journal* 23.

9   For a clear discussion, designed for new law students, see M Davies, *Asking the Law Question*, 2nd ed, Lawbook Co, 2002, 209-220.

10   See, for example, Kate Millett, *Sexual Politics*, Virago, 1977.

11   See S Firestone, *The Dialectic of Sex*, W Morrow, 1970. Radical feminism is, however, increasingly diverse, particularly amongst legal scholars; see Davies, n 9, 193.

12   C Gilligan, *In a Different Voice*, Harvard UP, 1982. For a general discussion, see G Simpson and H Charlesworth, "Objecting to objectivity: the radical challenge to legal liberalism" in *Thinking About Law*, Allen and Unwin, 1995, 86 at 113.

feminism is "to identify the operation of gender relations as and where they may be distinct from, or connected with, the processes of production and reproduction understood by historical materialism".[13]

More recent feminist study has doubted the benefits that can be derived from these labels. As Carol Smart has said:

> We need ... to transcend the all too familiar practice of categorizing feminism into radical, socialist, cultural and liberal feminisms because these conceptual straitjackets now conceal more than they reveal.[14]

In the first reading extracted below, Ngaire Naffine describes feminism under different headings. She refers to three phases of feminist thought on law. The phases roughly correspond to chronological development, but literature from all three phases is still being written. Furthermore, there is a certain amount of overlap and intersection between the three kinds of writing. In a loose way, however, first phase can be identified with liberal feminism, second phase with radical and cultural feminisms and third phase with socialist and marxist feminism. These are by no means exact fits but there are broad alignments.

First phase feminist writing on law concerns the pursuit of formal equality, particularly in the public sphere. The assumption is that law has been biased in favour of men and has helped to preserve male monopolies. It argues for legal change but does not challenge the *idea* of law. Second phase feminism argues that male bias extends to virtually *all aspects of law*. There is a fundamental maleness about law and legal process and so an alternative, feminist, jurisprudence must be constructed. Unlike first phase feminism, therefore, it refuses to accept law on its own terms or to argue merely for isolated reforms. Third phase feminism builds upon the second phase analysis but suggests a more complex picture. This might be termed the postmodern feminist phase. Whilst law is undoubtedly connected with the values of a male-dominated society, this approach exposes the contradictions within it. Some aspects of law can favour women and the postmodern feminist task is to take conventional liberal values – such as equality, privacy, autonomy and rights – and to redefine them in a way that addresses the subordination of women.

The extract below provides a general review of literature from all phases. It is followed by some of our own discussion of particular issues.

Ngaire Naffine, *Law and the Sexes*
(1990, some references have been omitted; others have been placed in footnotes)

First-phase feminism: the male monopoly
The largest body of feminist work on law is about the pursuit of formal equality for women: from the acquisition of citizenship to the introduction of anti-discrimination legislation. It describes a male monopoly in the public sphere

---

13   M Barrett, *Women's Oppression Today*, Verso, 1980 9. "Historical materialism", as we saw in Chapter 7, pp 204-205, is the methodology which Marxists use to explain social change. For a discussion of Marxist-feminism in the context of social security, see S Shaver, "Gender, Class and the Welfare State: The Case of Income Security in Australia" (1989) *Feminist Review* 90.

14   C Smart, "Law's Power, the Sexed Body, and Feminist Discourse" (1990) 16 *Journal of Law and Society* 194.

which a male-controlled law has supported systematically. Its goal has been the removal of legal constraints on women and the acquisition of equal civil rights designed to allow women to compete freely with men in the marketplace.

This first phase of writing contends that legal men have used their position of dominance to keep the public sphere a male preserve. In the courts and in the parliaments, men have actively sought to exclude women from positions of influence. The aim of feminists is thus to have women placed fully on the legal agenda, to have full legal rights extended to women.

A distinguishing feature of the first phase is its tendency to accept, and approve, law's own account of itself when it is not dealing with women. Law is seen therefore to be essentially a rational and fair institution concerned with the arbitration of conflicting rights between citizens. The problem with law is that it has not yet developed full and effective public rights for women. It was once overtly discriminatory. Today it indirectly denies women rights by constituting a subordinate, domestic role for them in the private sphere.

In the first-phase analysis, the present character and outlook of law are largely left intact. The prevailing idea is accepted that law should be (and can be) impartial and reasoned. The objection is to the failure of law to adhere to its own professed standards when it invokes discriminatory laws and practices. That is, the objection is to bad law.

Two books figure prominently in the writing of first-phase feminism. Both are substantial works which endeavour to treat in a comprehensive fashion the problem of legal sexism. In *Sexism and the Law*, Albie Sachs and Joan Hoff Wilson (1978) examine male bias in legal thinking in Britain and America in the nineteenth and twentieth century. *Women and the Law*, by Susan Atkins and Brenda Hoggett (1984), is principally about the legal treatment and construction of British women today.

To Sachs and Wilson, what is wrong with law, from the point of view of women, is that it constitutes a male monopoly. Far from being the agents of social change, legal men have determinedly fought women in their bid to enter the professions and public life. Sachs and Wilson see this as an effort by men to protect male interests: to preserve jobs for the boys and to keep women in the home performing their domestic labours. In the nineteenth century, male control of the Bench and the Bar was perfect and so the traditional male view of women as dependent homemakers prevailed. In the face of massive resistance from the legal profession (we are told that judges were "enthusiasts for inequality"), women struggled valiantly to be treated as equals, both as citizens and spouses. We sought even to find a place alongside men at the Bar. Though we have made substantial gains, men still dominate the legal profession and, at best, "manifest a grudging tolerance rather than facilitative welcome to women entrants".[15]

Sachs and Wilson have been criticised for restricting their analysis to sexism in legal attitudes, as if this were a sufficient explanation of the law's oppression of women. More particularly, there have been objections to their failure to examine critically the character and ideology of law. Implicit in their writing, it is said, is an uncritical acceptance of law's own view of the social world (as a community of competing and self-interested strangers). Dissatisfaction has been expressed also over the failure of Sachs and Wilson to raise questions about the possible sexism of law's method: how it endeavours to resolve social conflict through a competitive and aggressive adversarial system. Instead, they seem to display a tacit faith in much of the legal system, wishing only "to see the law

---

15   A Sachs and J H Wilson, *Sexism and the Law*, Martin Robertson, 1978, 226.

functioning as a better instrument for serving the community".[16] As we will see in the work of second- and third-phase writers, each of these aspects of law has since been subjected to feminist scrutiny. ...

The other example of feminist analysis of the first phase is Atkins and Hoggett's *Women and the Law*. In this volume, the authors operate as conventional lawyers within the given framework and categories of law, the format of their book reflecting the traditional divisions. Hence there are chapters on the law's sexist treatment of women within the "public" sphere of work and others on the law's approach to women within the "private" sphere of marriage, sexuality and violence in the home. And yet their volume is more than just an atheoretical compendium of laws affecting women. Atkins and Hoggett attempt to theorise the sexism of law by drawing connections between different discriminatory legal practices and identifying a number of sexist themes running through the law. They show, for example, how the law has consistently viewed women as less responsible than men. They also note the uniform legal construction of women across the different areas of law as primarily wives and mothers. Consistently, the law has imposed on women the roles of child-bearer, child-rearer and domestic servant. The central organising idea, however, is of a male monopoly of law. It is the proposition that men, who dominate the legal system, have used it for their own devices – to preserve a powerful public role for themselves and to cast women in a less desirable, subordinate domestic role.

Notwithstanding subsequent developments in feminist legal thinking which (as we will see) have greatly extended the challenge of the first-phase theorists, it would be wrong to see this early work as fatally flawed by the limitations of its vision, as too short-sighted in its focus on the male personnel of law. The contribution of the first phase to women's struggle for legal change has been considerable. Not only does it represent the first feminist excavation into the male foundations of law, the first archeological dig, but its challenge to male dominance of legal institutions and to discriminatory legislation has been instrumental in reshaping and reforming much of the law for women. Indeed one writer goes so far as to say that it represents "the single most important feminist legal strategy ... the theoretical underpinning of the entire women's rights movement in law".[17] By demonstrating how laws which constrain only one of the sexes, and seem to work for the benefit of the other, fail to meet law's own self-professed standards (of fairness, rationality and impartiality), it has indicted law on its own terms and supplied the intellectual framework for women's demands for equal treatment. Its sustained attacks on legal sexism have also come close to winning for women formal equality within the substantive law.

Second-phase feminism: the male culture of law

Feminists of the first phase, such as Sachs and Wilson, appear to believe that law could operate fairly and for the common good if only it would recognise the equal rights of women. The second-phase feminists are more swingeing in their critique of law's claim to impartiality and justice for all. These are merely high-minded principles which legal men have employed as protective cover. They obscure law's actual partiality: its preference for men and their view of the world. The truth is that men have fashioned a legal system in their own image. They have developed a harsh, uncaring, combative, adversarial style of justice which essentially reflects their own way of doing things and therefore quite naturally

---

16 Ibid 13.
17 F Olsen, "The Sex of Law", transcript of a speech given at UCLA Law School, 1984, 12.

advantages the male litigant. Law treats people as unfeeling automatons, as selfish individuals who care only for their own rights and who feel constantly under threat from other equally self-absorbed holders of rights. This is a male view of society, they say, which ignores and devalues the priorities of women – those of human interdependence, human compassion and human need.

Second-phase feminists also take issue with law's conception of its own objectivity. This is a highly suspect notion, they say, not just because it has been used as a smokescreen to conceal male bias but because it invokes a particular approach to the social world with which many feminists take issue. Law's objectivity, they say, seeks to invoke a detached, dispassionate approach to social conflict. In the rhetoric of law, impartiality is secured by the maintenance of a healthy distance between the "fact-finder" and the subjects of the dispute. This is the means by which judges maintain their closely guarded neutrality and hence their objectivity. To second-phase feminists, detachment may not be the best approach to resolving disputes: involvement and close proximity to the subject may be better.

The belief that because men have the numbers in the legal system they make sure it represents their interests is merely the starting point of the second-phase feminist criticism of law. At this point it could be described as a variety of male monopoly theory reminiscent of the work of Sachs and Wilson. Thus: "The judiciary remains overwhelming male. Judges have grown up in a patriarchal culture; their attitudes are inevitably shaped by their life experiences and by their position as the beneficiaries of male supremacy".[18] But the theory then is taken to its logical extreme. Law is deemed to be essentially an expression of masculinity, not only in its content but also in its modus operandi: "The whole structure of law – its hierarchical organisation; its combative, adversarial format; and its undeviating bias in favour of rationality over all other values – defines it as a fundamentally patriarchal institution".[19]

The proposition that law is imbued with the culture of men moves beyond the claim that law is made by men and therefore tends to entrench their position and dominance. The indictment is more far-reaching. Law, it is said, is conceived through the male eye; it represents the male perspective. It starts from the male experience and fails to recognise the female view. To Janet Rifkin, for example, law is "a paradigm of maleness", a "symbol and a vehicle of male authority".[20] Law treats as axiomatic the subordination of women to men: it is culturally a male institution which serves to ensure that men remain the dominant sex. ...

The most prolific and widely quoted writer of the second phase is the American feminist Catharine MacKinnon. Consistently, her central argument has taken the form of a dispute with other feminist writers on the nature of the "woman question". MacKinnon maintains that it has been fundamentally misconceived. For too long, feminists have interpreted the problem of women's oppression in terms of women's differences from men; women's inferior position has been explained in terms of their failure to achieve the standards of men. Consequently some feminists have striven to advance the position of women so that they can be as good as men and therefore justify equal and like treatment. Where women have displayed distinctive "weaknesses" (such as pregnancy) some feminists

---

18   D Polan, "Toward a Theory of Law and Patriarchy" in D Kairys (ed), *Law and Power*, Pantheon, 1982, 302.

19   Ibid 303.

20   J Rifkin, "Toward a Theory of Law and Patriarchy" (1980) 3 *Harvard Women's Law Journal* 83 at 84.

have sought to have such female differences recognised as legitimate reasons for the special protection of women.

Feminists have misread the problem, according to MacKinnon. Both strategies (that is, "like" and "special" treatment) try to fit women to an existing system instead of asking what the system would be like if women, not men, were its starting point. She explains: "If you see gender as hierarchy – in which some people have power and some people are powerless – you realise that the oppositions of either being the same as men or being different from men are just two ways of having men as your standard".[21] To MacKinnon, gender is not a question of difference but a question of dominance. The central issue for feminists is to address the fact that the sexes are not equal. Instead, men have the power to dominate and to oppress women and they do so by controlling our language, our culture, our social and legal institutions, and thus, most importantly, our bodies. ...

In her later writing, MacKinnon extends her criticism to the law and the state, in toto, maintaining that both are fully implicated in the sexual oppression of women. MacKinnon pulls no punches. Her work is full of strong statements about the sexism of law and its institutions. Developing the notion that "sexuality is the linchpin of gender inequality",[22] that men's nearly total power over women resides in their ability to reduce women to "walking embodiments" of men's sexual needs,[23] MacKinnon charges the law with endorsing and entrenching this state of affairs, rather than supplying solutions to women.

MacKinnon's indictment of law is thorough: "The law sees and treats women the way men see and treat women".[24] At every level, the law reproduces sexual experience from the perspective of the male, not the female, and thereby ensures male control over the bodies of women. ...

The maleness of law, however, goes beyond its practice of preserving male sexual interests in women. To MacKinnon, law's maleness is not limited to the substance of any individual law but extends to law's very style, its form, and its view of the world. In other words, "law not only reflects a society in which men rule women [but] it rules in a male way". When law professes to be neutral and value-free, it calls itself objective. Through a leviathan structure of rules, regulations and ritual language, it endeavours to present itself as "dispassionate", "impersonal" and "disinterested" and to conceal its real interests. The reality is that law is not impartial; it is equated with the male viewpoint, and detachment and disinterest are qualities, valued by men, specifically invoked to obscure the masculinity of law's bias. ...

Catharine MacKinnon has had a considerable impact on feminist thinking about law, particularly among American theorists. Her protagonists accept that the culture of law is male, that legal institutions and legal methods display an essential masculinity. David Cole, for instance, describes law as operating "like a man's mind". Law, he declares, "is identifiably male, in its implicit substantive norms, its adversarial operation, and its paternalistic remedies. The law reflects male 'value judgements' so deeply and pervasively that male values begin to look

---

21   C MacKinnon, "Feminist Discourse, Moral Values and the Law – A Conversation" (1985) 34 *Buffalo LR* 21.

22   C MacKinnon, "Feminism, Marxism, Method and the State: An Agenda for Theory" (1982) 7 *Signs* 533.

23   Ibid 534.

24   C MacKinnon, "Feminism, Marxism, Method and the State: Towards a Feminist Jurisprudence" (1983) 8 *Signs* 644.

like neutral normative standards. The feminist perspective exposes the substance and procedure of law as inherently male-biased".[25] ...

Implicit in this argument is a suggestion that women would do things better. It is assumed that "women's subjugated position provides the possibility of more complete and less perverse understandings".[26] Feminism, it is claimed, offers to law the insights of the second sex, "a new vision of the world from the perspective of women".[27] According to a number of writers of this school, women possess particular qualities which could form the basis of a more desirable legal system.

Ann Scales, another exponent of MacKinnon's thesis, has considered what a legal system might look like if it were moulded in the image of women, not men. Her starting premise is that there is such a thing as a male and female legal or ethical style: that justice means different things to men and women. Drawing on the work of psychologist Carol Gilligan, Scales contends that boys and girls are brought up to see the social world in different ways and so develop opposing styles of moral reasoning. Boys, who are encouraged to detach themselves from their mothers and flourish as independent beings, develop an "ethic of rights". Their priority becomes the preservation of the autonomy of individuals against the claims of others. By contrast, girls are allowed to stay close to their mothers (because they are the same sex and will one day be mothers themselves) and so come to value relationships. Their style of justice is an "ethic of care". It gives priority to responsibility for others, to loving and preventing harm. (Though feminists, such as Scales, have absorbed the ideas of both MacKinnon and Gilligan, one must not conflate the two approaches. MacKinnon disputes the idea of a female ethical style which she sees as the convenient artifact of men. And yet we may still observe a good deal of common ground: both women indict the maleness of the prevailing legal ethic.)

Scales deplores the existing male style of law. She objects to its rigid focus on the rights of disconnected individuals. This is an uncaring law whose sole concern is getting right abstract principles without reference to the particular human beings involved. In it, competing claims between individuals are settled bloodlessly, according to standards of supposed fairness and impartiality. People must be treated alike whatever the individual need, whatever the social context and whatever the unfortunate consequences for nearest and dearest. The alternative female mode, she speculates, "expand[s] the available universe of facts, rules, and relationships to find a unique solution to each unique problem".[28] ...

The theories of Carol Gilligan have influenced the thinking of a number of other legal critics who equate law with the culture of men and who advocate a new female style of justice to supplant the present one. To such feminists, women have special virtues: in particular, they share a greater sense of responsibility for others and accord priority to the virtue of caring. A female style of justice, it is claimed, would focus on conciliation as opposed to the more combative male ego style, which stresses, selfishly, the need to preserve the unimpeded rights of individuals to pursue their own ends. Thus one legal writer demands that we "build on broader feminist values that transcend the legal individualist legacy" –

---

25 D Cole, "Strategies of Difference: Litigating for Women's Rights in a Man's World" (1984) 2 *Law and Inequality* 33 at 51.

26 S Harding, *The Science Question in Woman*, Cornell UP, 1986, 26.

27 M Thornton , "Feminist Jurisprudence: Illusion or Reality?" (1986) 3 *Australian Journal of Law and Society* 5 at 22.

28 A Scales, "The Emergence of Feminist Jurisprudence: An Essay" (1986) 95 *Yale Law Journal* 1373 at 1381.

a legacy which conceives us as all discrete and detached individual units, always potentially in conflict, never benefiting from the good offices of others. To another what is needed is an "ideology of solidarity and collective decision-making characteristic of much ... feminist thinking".[29] Still other writers talk in terms of a new female language of responsibility in law, one which will supplant law's current concern with the rights of the individual to remain free from the hostile interventions of others.

Implicit in all these statements is the second-phase feminist argument that law has a male character: it embodies a male norm and is thus an expression of masculinity. The feminist project is to expose the maleness of law and, for some, it is to devise a new legal approach which is more in harmony with the lives and thus the culture of women. It is on both of these points that the feminists of the second phase can be distinguished from the writers of the third phase.

Third-phase feminism: legal rhetoric and the patriarchal social order

Third-phase feminist theory concedes that law is both male-dominated and full of biases, one of which pertains to the sex of the litigant. However, it resists the notion that law represents male interests in anything like a coordinated or uniform fashion. The reason is that law is not the coherent, logical, internally consistent and rational body of doctrine it professes to be. Part of the feminist challenge here is to the very concepts law has employed to represent itself as a fair and impartial institution. Law, they say, is not to be regarded – as it has traditionally – as a neutral and dispassionate institution which accordingly resolves disputes and organises social relations justly. The various epithets conventionally used to describe law, such as "rational", "autonomous" and "principled", are in fact male legal ideals. They describe a set of qualities to which men might aspire but they are not, and could not be, the truth of law because nothing in life is ever organised in this way. Vital dimensions of human existence, dimensions conventionally associated with women, are missing from law's depiction of itself. The reality of law is that it is "as irrational, subjective, concrete and contextualised as it is rational, objective, abstract and principled".[30]

Another concern of the third-phase feminists is to show that while law presents itself as autonomous and value-neutral, the truth is that law reflects the priorities of the dominant patriarchal social order, priorities which are themselves not always coherent or consistent but which generally constitute women as the subordinate sex. Also central to third-phase feminism is an explicit rejection of grand theory and a commitment to the study of particular instances of law's oppression of women.

Two writers dominate the literature of the third phase. Though one addresses the sexism of English law, the other the implications of American justice for women, they have arrived at remarkably similar conclusions. Both agree that law should not be regarded as a unity, as a single set of cultural values. Law, they say, is as complex and contradictory as the dominant social order it reflects. Though it lays claims to rationality, consistency and uniformity in its approach to the social world, in fact it has no one colour, no essence. Though it professes to be independent of the values of the society it serves, in fact it is intimately linked to those values, which are themselves mixed and contradictory. ...

The British author Carol Smart has been writing about the problems of law for women for well over a decade. Her earliest work criticised the processes of

---

29   E Kingdom, "Legal Recognition of a Woman's Right to Choose" in J Brophy and C Smart (eds), *Women in Law*, RKP, 1985, 154.

30   Olsen, n 17, 16.

criminal justice from a feminist perspective. Since the early 1980s, she has concentrated mainly on family law and its implications for women. In the course of her writing she has advanced and maintained a consistent position on the nature of the law as a whole: both as a system and as a body of doctrine.

The large degree to which family law intrudes on the lives of women is the reason why Smart selects it as the focus of her analysis. This category of law, she tells us, has determined the structure of the family, and it is the family which constitutes the major site of women's oppression. It is therefore legitimate to generate a feminist account of law's relation to women from the study of just one of its many branches. ...

Smart is at pains to distance her view of law from any form of conspiracy theory. Thus she distinguishes her work from that of the first-phase writers Sachs and Wilson who identified the law as a whole with the interests of the men running the system. The fact that one can find moments in legal history when the law has positively benefited women (she cites the legal requirement that men pay maintenance) is taken by her as evidence of the uneven nature of law: male interests are not inevitably given legal priority. Moreover, it is often far from clear what those male interests might be, were they always to be represented, or just how they might best be served. What is more, the male conspiracy theory tends to leave out the dimension of class. If the law favours men, it often does so selectively, to the disadvantage of working-class males. ...

Though Smart makes a number of far-reaching claims about the oppressive nature of both law and legal practice for women, she denies that her purpose is "to produce the definitive grand theory on Law and Patriarchy". She is more interested in explaining "the specificity of women's oppression" by observing the operation of a single area of law which looms large in the lives of many women. Smart chides those who would seek to develop general feminist theories of law, describing such efforts as "misguided". She wishes "to deconstruct ideas about law as a monolithic, homogeneous power which controls women and is exercised by men".[31] Consistent with this aim, her concluding statement in *The Ties that Bind* stresses the uneven development of law on the family. Thus , "I do not see the law simply as a conservative force which intransigently resists change ... On the contrary, law itself is seen as a multifaceted system of regulation, containing its own contradictions and not just negative restraint".[32] ...

A further demonstration of Smart's theory of the uneven nature of law is provided by domestic violence legislation. In the 1970s, the British government introduced laws designed to provide remedies for battered wives. Though these reforms might have been more extensive, they represented nevertheless a real gain for women, at least in theory. In practice, however, there was little change in the position of battered women for the simple reason that law-enforcers did not like the law. Non-compliant police made it difficult for women to proceed against violent husbands; a conservative judiciary imposed restrictive interpretations on the legislation, further limiting its value. Domestic violence laws therefore fell prey to the problem of even development. "Law-as-legislation [was] undermined by law-in-practice".[33] [The experience in Australia is similar, as discussed in Chapter 7 of this book].

---

31   C Smart, *The Ties that Bind*, RKP, 1984, xii.

32   Ibid 221.

33   C Smart, "Feminism and Law: Some Problems of Analysis and Strategy" (1986) 14 *Int Jnl of Sociology of Law* 109 at 119.

In a similar vein, the American legal critic Frances Olsen believes that it is wrong to attribute to law a male essence or an "immutable nature". Feminists have found too much consistency of style and character in law, says Olsen, when in fact law has no clear line, no identifiable persona. It is neither all male nor consistently anti-female. Also in tune with the thinking of Smart is Olsen's claim that there is much that is good for women in law. It does not simply represent the interests of men, as the second-phase writers suggest. Feminist struggles have won for women real reforms which should not be discounted in the rush to condemn law as sexist. ...

According to Olsen, our male-oriented law presents a view of social organisation which is positively damaging to all women. Law splits the world into public and private, and into male and female, and then identifies itself with the male and public world, and purports to confine its activities to this sphere. Meanwhile, the private sphere is in certain respects left unregulated and the women who are consigned to the domestic realm are deprived of legal redress. Women are left in the home tending children, without a wage, and without the protections that law offers to public individuals – such as the right to sue for payment for services provided or (until recently) the right to seek remedies for physical or sexual abuse. By deeming the home to be beyond its sphere of influence, the law ratifies the unequal private roles of men and women.

Notwithstanding its rhetoric of non-intervention in the home, ... in other ways law has gone to considerable efforts to define and construct a role for women in the private sphere (Olsen, 1985). Along the same lines as Smart, Olsen maintains that law has played an active role in the reproduction of the dominant patriarchal social order and usually in the name of the sanctity of the home. She draws our attention to a series of laws operating last century ... which assumed that the natural place of women was in the home as economic and social dependants of their husbands. For example, the husband possessed the legal right to choose the family domicile and the wife was obliged to live there. He was also "the juridical head of the family" in that he was entitled to control and admonish his wife and children and to act on their behalf as the financial head. Thus law reinforced the power of husbands over wives within the home, a form of domination which was taken to be part of the natural sexual order, though it clearly needed the law's intervention to secure the "natural" sexual hierarchy.[34]

We saw in the above extract that the work of first phase feminists like Sachs and Wilson has been criticised for failing to examine critically the character and ideology of law. Nevertheless, the account they give of women using law in their struggle to enter into the public world of men is a powerful one which broke new ground at the time and their treatment of the so-called "person's cases" is worth stressing here. Although Sachs and Wilson were referring to cases in England and Scotland, much the same kind of litigation occurred in the Australian colonies in the early years after Federation.[35]

---

34 Naffine, n 4, 3-19.

35 The Scottish experience in excluding women from the legal profession was reviewed by Sachs and Wilson, n 15, 22-33, focusing on the decision of *Hall v Incorporated Society of Law Agents* (1901) which held that the statutory word "person" was ambiguous and thus should be interpreted in the light of inveterate usage. An account of Australian legal history can be found in Jocelynne Scutt, n 4, Ch 1; J Allen, "Breaking into the Public Sphere: The Struggle for Women's Citizenship in NSW 1890-1920" in J Mackinolty and H Radi (eds), *In Pursuit of Justice: Australian Women and the Law 1788-1979*, Hale and Ironmonger, 1979.

Women struggled both in the United Kingdom and the colonies to gain law degrees and to be recognised as "persons" qualified for admission to practice. In Australia, as Margaret Thornton notes, the first woman to graduate with an LLB was Ada Evans in 1902.[36] Although the *Legal Practitioners Act 1898* (NSW) used the gender-neutral term "person", the Supreme Court of New South Wales advised Ada that admission would require legislative change. This situation continued until the enactment of the *Women's Legal Status Act 1918* (NSW). As Thornton notes, the pattern was similar throughout Australia. She argues that although formal legal barriers to admission of women could be overcome, legal culture continued to view women lawyers as a threat to male power: "The discourse not only ensured the continuance of the hegemony of masculinity in law and legality, it also ensured the containment of the feminine so that the women who were 'let in' had to accept homologisation with benchmark men".[37]

Even when questions about women's entry into the public sphere did not concern a matter of statutory interpretation, vague notions of policy or "human nature" have been invoked by the courts to preserve male privileges. In these cases the judges were forced to express openly the kinds of thinking that were covertly being applied in the "persons" cases. Take, for example, the reasons given by the Supreme Court of Wisconsin in 1875 for refusing to admit a woman to the Bar.

Re Goodell
(1875) 39 Wisc 232

RYAN CJ: This is the first application for admission of a female to the bar of this court. And it is just matter for congratulation that it is made in favour of a lady whose character raises no personal objections: something perhaps not always to be looked for in women who forsake the ways of their sex for the ways of ours.... . [But] we find no statutory authority for the admission of females to the bar of any court of this state. And, with all the respect and sympathy for this lady which all men owe to all good women, we cannot regret that we do not. We cannot but think the common law wise in excluding women from the profession of the law. The profession enters largely into the well-being of society; and, to be honourably filled and safely to society, exacts the devotion of life. The law of nature destines and qualifies the female sex for the bearing and nurture of the children of our race and for the custody of the homes of the world and their maintenance in love and honour. And all life-long callings of women, inconsistent with these radical and sacred duties of their sex, as is the profession of the law, are departures from the order of nature; and, when voluntary, treason against it. The cruel chances of life sometimes baffles both sexes, and may leave women free from the peculiar duties of their sex. These may need employment, and should be welcome to any not derogatory to their sex and its proprieties, or inconsistent with the good order of society. But it is public policy to provide for the sex, and not for its superfluous members: and not to tempt women from the proper duties of their sex by opening to them duties peculiar to ours.

---

36   M Thornton, "Women as Fringe-Dwellers of the Jurisprudential Community" in D Kirkby (ed), *Sex, Power and Justice: Historical Perspectives of Law in Australia*, Oxford UP, 1995.

37   Thornton, n 36, 201.

There are many employments in life not unfit for female characters. The profession of the law is surely not one of these. The peculiar qualities of woman-hood, its gentle graces, its quick sensibility, its tender susceptibility, its purity, its delicacy, its emotional impulses, its subordination of hard reason to sympathetic feeling, are surely not qualifications for forensic strife. Nature has tempered woman as little for the judicial conflicts of the court room as for the physical conflicts of the battlefield. Womanhood is moulded for gentler and better things, and it is not the saints of the world who chiefly give employment to our profes-sion. It has essentially and habitually to do with all that is selfish and malicious, knavish and criminal, coarse and brutal, repulsive and obscene, in human life. It would be revolting to all female sense of the innocence and sanctity of their sex, shocking to man's reverence for womanhood and faith in woman, on which hinge all the better affections and humanities of life, that woman should be permitted to mix professionally in all the nastiness of the world which finds its way into courts of justice. All the unclear issues, all the collateral questions of sodomy, incest, rape, seduction, fornication, adultery, pregnancy, bastardy, legitimacy, prostitu-tion, lascivious cohabitation, abortion, infanticide, obscene publications, libel and slander of sex, impotence, divorce, all the nameless catalogue of indecencies, la chronique scandaleuse of all the vices and all the infirmities of all society with which this profession has to deal... . This is bad enough for men. We hold in too high reverence the sex without which, as it is truly and beautifully written, le commencement de la vie est sans secours, le milieu sans plaisir, et le fin sans consolation, voluntarily to commit it to such studies and such occupations.

Margaret Thornton's survey of Australian cases dealing with admission to univer-sity and the legal profession in the late 19th century highlights similar sentiments from judges, academics and senior members of the legal profession: these "crystallise into two main strands revolving around women's averred intellectual inferiority and female sexuality both of which possessed the potential to corrode the sphere of rationality".[38]

In first phase feminism, as Naffine says, the character and outlook of law are largely left intact. The only objection is that law fails, or has in the past failed, to live up to its own ideals by being discriminatory. Second phase feminism, in contrast, is a swingeing critique of liberal law generally. Law is said to embody a male culture and as a result it inevitably favours men. Two names which figure prominently, although for different reasons, are Carol Gilligan and Catharine MacKinnon.

Gilligan is a psychologist who carried out research on how children and young adults approach ethical questions. Her results were published in 1982 in a book called *In a Different Voice*.[39] The most celebrated part concerns two 11-year olds, Jake and Amy, who were confronted with a moral dilemma. A man's wife is dying of cancer but her death could be prevented by a drug available from a nearby pharmacist. The man cannot afford the drug. The question was: should the man steal the drug?

According to Gilligan, Jake said the man should steal the drug because life is more important than property. He used abstract reasoning. In other words, he

---

38 Ibid 189.

39 Gilligan, n 12. A good discussion of the Jake and Amy story can be found in Graycar and Morgan, n 3, and K Daly, "Criminal Justice Ideologies and Practices in Different Voices: Some Feminist Questions about Justice" in N Lacey (ed), *Criminal Justice*, Oxford UP, 1994.

converted the facts into general categories, the importance of life as against the importance of property, and resolved the dilemma by establishing priorities between the categories. Amy, on the other hand, was more hesitant. She suggested that the man should talk it over with the pharmacist in an attempt to make the pharmacist see the problem from the man's point of view.

Gilligan's conclusions were that the boy used the "logic of justice" whereas the girl used "the ethic of care". Jake saw the issue in terms of separateness, the man versus the pharmacist, whereas Amy saw it in terms of connectedness. The boy looked at the situation as a conflict of rules whilst the girl saw it as a ruptured relationship between people, a relationship that needed attention.

Gilligan did not claim there was anything biological or genetic about this, although there are hints of some "essentialism" in her book. Amy's "different voice" is simply the voice that, through socialisation, women use more than men in our society at present.

The analysis is, however, potentially attractive for some feminist lawyers, as we have seen. They regard the legal system, with its abstract rules and separated individuals, as embodying a male view of the world, as we noted in Chapter 6. The law pays little attention to the long-term relationship between the parties, nor to compromise. What emerges from this is a distinct feminist perspective on dispute resolution, which is contrasted with the masculine construction of "justice" in terms of rights, autonomy and impartiality. This has led many feminists to embrace Alternative Dispute Resolution (ADR). As we saw in Chapter 4, however, while ADR offers advantages in contextualising disputes and producing consensual outcomes for the parties, it also poses the risk (especially vivid in the criminal justice context) that legal wrongs against women are concealed from public scrutiny. As Rosemary Hunter and Kathy Mack point out: "The emphasis on privacy and confidentiality [in mediation] can reinforce the law's construction of sexed harms to women as not suitable for consideration or remedy by formal legal processes".[40] This has spilled over into a debate about the desirability of using conferencing and the idea of restorative justice to deal with domestic violence.[41] A number of feminists have argued that the gendered dynamics of family violence are inconsistent with a restorative justice approach; that it poses a risk to the victim's safety; and perpetuates the privatisation of family violence.[42] Notwithstanding these concerns, some jurisdictions have extended restorative justice conferences to domestic violence offences: for example, the *Crimes (Restorative Justice) Act 2004* (ACT) s 16.

---

40 "Exclusion and Silence: Procedure and Evidence" in Naffine and Owens (eds), *Sexing the Subject of Law*, n 4. Kathy Daly has pointed out that the common feminist accusation of "justice" as being masculine and therefore incapable of feminine "care" is an oversimplified representation of existing criminal processes. In many areas, such as the discretion to prosecute and the sentencing stage, considerations of "care" do intrude, taking into account the potential negative impact of prosecution or imprisonment on dependent family members: "Criminal Justice Ideologies and Practices in Different Voices: Some Feminist Questions about Justice" in Lacey, n 39, 238.

41 At the heart of the restorative justice ideal is the idea that offenders who accept responsibility for their actions are diverted into a conference which brings them together with the victims of their crime, usually with their respective families and a facilitator, in order to discuss the impact of their actions on the victim and the community, and the ways that they can repair the harm done.

42 Julie Stubbs, "Domestic Violence and Women's Safety: Feminist Challenges to Restorative Justice" in H Strang and J Braithwaite (eds), *Restorative Justice and Family Violence*, Cambridge UP, 2002.

The other writer whom Naffine regards as an important second phase feminist is Catharine MacKinnon. MacKinnon actually criticises Gilligan for arguing that the woman's voice should be affirmed. She says that women speak in the voice that men provide for them. They do not so much speak in a different voice as in a higher register. She is referring here to the way that femininity is constructed to suit the interests of men. The extract from *Re Goodell*, above, where the Wisconsin Supreme Court referred to the "peculiar qualities of womanhood, its gentle graces, its quick sensibility, its tender susceptibility, its purity, its delicacy, its emotional impulses" and so on can be seen as part of this process whereby femininity is constructed.

Despite the major differences between Gilligan and MacKinnon they have one important thing in common for our purposes. This is that law, legal language and the legal system encode a male view of justice masquerading as a universal view.[43] It is important to see how this differs from the first phase approach. First phase writers claim that law is not as neutral or objective as it purports to be because women are discriminated against in certain areas. The second phase is a much more general critique of law which claims that law is imbued with maleness. It is a critique of the content and processes of law[44] and also of legal education.[45]

We saw in the extract from Ngaire Naffine that third phase feminism resists the notion that law represents male interests in anything like a coordinated or uniform fashion. It accepts that law is male-dominated and full of biases. On the other hand, law is also full of contradictions. Men might *want* law to be rational, objective and principled but it does not work out that way. Third phase feminism therefore absorbs ideas from the Law and Society and Critical Legal Studies movements. It pays attention to the apparent realities of legal process[46] and also to the implausibility of legal reasoning ever taking place in the way that formalists claim. Yet third phase feminism differs from those movements, in emphasis and perhaps in substance, to the extent that it is desirable, or indeed possible, to propose any grand theory of law: that is, a theory that can explain it all. In the following extract Carol Smart reviews the work of Gilligan and MacKinnon and suggests its strengths and weaknesses.

Carol Smart, *Feminism and the Power of Law*
(1990, references omitted)

Both Carol Gilligan and Catharine MacKinnon have made a deep impact on feminist work on law. MacKinnon most especially has dragged North American feminist lawyers and academics out of the trough of liberalism, which has tended to be the downfall of feminist thought and policy programmes. She has constructed a radical feminist discourse which resists assimilation and is a productive counterpoint which generates further feminist discourses. In this sense her work

---

43   See generally L Finlay, "Breaking Women's Silence in Law: The Dilemma of the Gendered Nature of Legal Reasoning" (1989) 64 *Notre Dame Law Review* 886.

44   See in particular *Feminism Unmodified*, Harvard UP, 1987 and *Toward a Feminist Theory of the State*, Harvard UP, 1989.

45   A brief but clear example of MacKinnon's thought which reviews the curriculum and teaching style of much legal education and which is directed at an Australian audience is "Feminism in Legal Education" (1989) 1 *Legal Education Review* 85.

46   See back to the extracts from Sarat and Felstiner in Chapter 6.

is an exercise of power (in particular the power of redefinition or assertion of an unvalidated discourse) from which all feminists can learn. But just as all power produces resistance, so it is necessary to resist the certainties, the dogma, the programme of action, the hierarchy of truth explicit in her work. Gilligan's work is not constructed in the oppositional way that MacKinnon's is. However, its impact has been felt very widely inside and outside the USA because of its power to validate the "feminine" and to give meaning to that which is constantly dismissed as irrational, illogical, and inconsistent... .

It is important to consider the criticism levelled at Gilligan by MacKinnon. Her dismissal of the politics of affirming difference is total.

> [Gilligan] achieves for moral reasoning what the special protection rule achieves in law: the affirmative rather than the negative valuation of that which has accurately distinguished women from men, by making it seem as though these attributes, with their consequences, really are somehow ours, rather than what male supremacy has attributed to us for its own use. For women to affirm difference, when difference means dominance, as it does with gender, means to affirm the qualities and characteristics of power-lessness... . I do not think that the way women reason morally is morality "in a different voice". I think it is morality in a higher register, in the feminine voice.

In this passage MacKinnon's position is very clear. She adopts the view that men's voices speak from women's bodies, that what we know as feminine is what men have constructed as the female that suits their interests. She avoids completely the assimilation by the status quo that Gilligan's work begs, but she does so at the cost of negating not only femininity but also women. For MacKinnon women appear as constructed by men, the question that this then provokes is whether we can ever avoid the omnipotent grip of the patriarch who is in our hearts, bodies, and minds... .

I would like to acknowledge her major contribution to this area of work. First, she has attempted to provide a way out of the engulfing embrace of liberalism which, in the form of law reform, has done so little to emancipate women. She has also drawn sharp attention to the failure of socialist programmes for challenging women's oppression. In doing this she has challenged the orthodoxy of legal discourse to represent the interests of women as well as men. Finally she has achieved the "praxis" which so many feminists seek, namely a theory from which action flows, but which has been built on a methodology which reveals the truth of women's experience. Unfortunately, if one cannot accept the notion of the truth, let alone the ideas of a scientific method to uncover the truth or the idea that the theory leads to correct action, then MacKinnon's work leads one up a cul-de-sac... .

Where MacKinnon is most persuasive in her work on feminist jurisprudence is in her critique of law as a universal, objective system of adjudication. It is here that she comes closest to Gilligan in the recognition that law's neutrality is in fact the expression of gendered interests. She argues,

> I propose that the state is male in the feminist sense. The law sees and treats women the way men see and treat women.
>
> When [the state] is most ruthlessly neutral, it will be most male; when it is most sex blind, it will be most blind to the sex of the standard being applied... . Once masculinity appears as a specific position, not just the way things are, its judgments will be revealed in process and procedure, as well as adjudication and legislation... . However autonomous of class the liberal state may appear, it is not autonomous of sex.

The basic insight of these passages lies in the argument that all social relationships are gendered. There is no neutral terrain, and law least of all can be said to occupy that mythical space. This may seem self-evident to feminists, but it remains a heresy to traditional lawyers. But MacKinnon goes beyond this to argue that the gender order is one of domination, in fact one of totalitarianism. I would agree that the gender order is indeed a site of power and resistance, but I am less certain that women are so powerless in a general sense. The problem is that MacKinnon sees no division between law, the state, and society. For her these are virtually interchangeable concepts – they are all manifestations of male power. I would argue that the law occupies a specific place in the politics of gender ... which ensures that law is exceptionally powerful and oppressive of women, but I would not generalize from this in a blanket fashion as if law were the barometer of the social world. In doing this MacKinnon gives too much authority to law, it becomes the central plank to her political analysis and strategy even against her wishes. ...[47]

The third phase analysis of law, then, doubts whether law is always as powerful and male-biased as second phase writers have argued. It accepts that some areas of law actually protect and benefit women. At the same time, however, it insists that law operates *by and large* to reproduce patriarchy: a society run by and for men.

Ngaire Naffine's own thesis is more closely associated with third phase writing but incorporates elements of the first and second phases.[48] Drawing on sociological research into legal process, she argues that those who interpret and administer the law do not always treat people who come before them in an equal and dispassionate manner, despite their protestations of value-neutrality. Nevertheless, an important organising concept in law is the idea of an abstract individual, embodied classically in legal doctrine as the "reasonable man". The law invokes and serves a sort of universal "man" when it lays down standards of responsibility and makes assumptions about human rationality. The reasonable man in tort and criminal law is an obvious example. This hypothetical individual is devoid of cultural and socio-economic background, and even in the modern context has been re-invented as the genderless "reasonable person". Upon closer scrutiny, however, critical and feminist scholars have revealed that the norm against which real people are judged is Anglo-Celtic, middle class, as well as male. To Naffine, he is "assertive, articulate, independent, calculating, competitive and competent".[49] He flourishes in, and dominates, the type of society conceived by law. Although all men might be said to derive benefits from this kind of society, some men – those who fail the tests of middle-class masculinity – do less well. Naffine's thesis thus draws on first phase feminism, insofar as it shows how law actually impacts unequally on men and women, second phase feminism, insofar as law is said to be imbued with a particular conception of maleness, and third phase feminism insofar as it suggests a complex picture where the advantages of law are shared unevenly between classes and ethnic groups.

---

47   C Smart, *Feminism and the Power of Law*, Routledge, 1990, 72-82.

48   This summary is taken from Naffine, n 4, 21-23.

49   Naffine, n 4, 22.

(c)   Feminist perspectives on the public-private divide

A critical aspect of the liberal philosophical blueprint described in Chapters 2 and 3 is the division of our social world into public and private spheres. This zone of privacy, in which individual interests are protected from unnecessary interference by the state or third parties, has been elevated to a legal right. The "right to privacy" is a relatively recent innovation, emerging as being distinct from rights to property in the late 19th century.[50] This period of legal development witnessed a significant shift in focus from the protection of physical interests (such as property) to less tangible, psychological interests (such as privacy).[51]

The consequence of the classic liberal split is that politics and public life are viewed as spheres of influence exclusively suitable for men. The family, regarded as the proper sphere for women, is no business of the state. The legal inviolability of relationships within the family may also be viewed as an extension of the legal protection conferred upon property rights, which husbands could invoke in relation to their spouses. Indeed, married women, until the late 19th century, had limited legal personality distinct from their husbands, unable to hold property or enter into commercial arrangements in their own right. Not all liberal theorists accepted this view. Indeed, a liberal commitment to equality before the law would rule out such discrimination. John Stuart Mill, although adamant about the need for a sphere of privacy immune from state intervention, argued in his feminist essay *The Subjection of Women* (1869)[52] that the legal subordination of women to men was wrong in principle and should be replaced with complete formal equality. But in arguing for equality within marriage, he nevertheless accepted a division of labour between the sexes along traditional lines, albeit one not entrenched in law.[53]

Women now hold the vote, women can own property in their own right and participate freely in many areas of public life. But this division between the public and the private is not merely of historical interest. Modern feminists continue to focus on the legal division between the public and private spheres, exposing the ways in which it continues to play a significant role in concealing and legitimating the subordination of certain groups in society. The private sphere of the "family" remains the site for female subordination. The placement of "domestic" violence and "marital" rape within the private sphere relegates this type of violence outside the sphere of state responsibility. The challenge for feminists has been to render these gendered harms visible and relocate them to public domain, where they can be more effectively policed and prosecuted. But, as we saw in Chapter 7, reforms to the law that aim to render these gendered harms amenable to the law do not always deliver the change that feminists want. Although the spousal defences for assault and rape have been removed from the substantive law, even today,

---

50   The legal conception of privacy is traced to a famous article in the *Harvard Law Review* in 1890 by Warren and Brandeis (both subsequently United States Supreme Court Justices). Drawing analogies from a range of civil law remedies, the authors rationalised the right to privacy as "the right to be let alone": S Warren and L Brandeis, "The Right to Privacy" (1890) 4 *Harvard Law Rev* 193 at 193.

51   P Alldridge, *Relocating Criminal Law*, Ashgate, 2000, 107-108.

52   See JS Mill, *Three Essays*, Oxford UP, 1975, 427.

53   See the discussion in K O'Donovan, *Sexual Divisions in Law*, Weidenfeld and Nicolson, 1985, 8-9.

authorities are often slow to intervene against violence that occurs within the family.

From a feminist perspective, the public sphere continues to be constructed around male interests. Carole Pateman has argued that the distinction between public and private spheres is a gendered distinction, not a neutral one.[54] The following passage from Carole Pateman sets out clearly the role of the public/private dichotomy in feminist thought and also deals briefly with the question of whether liberalism and feminism are compatible.

> The dichotomy between the private and the public is central to almost two centuries of feminist writing and political struggle; it is, ultimately, what the feminist movement is about. Although some feminists treat the dichotomy as a universal, trans-historical and trans-cultural feature of human existence, feminist criticism is primarily directed at the separation and opposition between the public and private spheres in liberal theory and practice.
>
> The relationship between feminism and liberalism is extremely close but also exceedingly complex. The roots of both doctrines lie in the emergence of individualism as a general theory of social life; neither liberalism nor feminism is conceivable without some conception of individuals as free and equal beings, emancipated from the ascribed, hierarchical bonds of traditional society. But if liberalism and feminism share a common origin, their adherents have often been opposed over the past two hundred years. The direction and scope of feminist criticism of liberal conceptions of the public and the private have varied greatly in different phases of the feminist movement. An analysis of this criticism is made more complicated because liberalism is inherently ambiguous about the "public" and the "private", and feminists and liberals disagree about where and why the dividing line is to be drawn between the two spheres, or, according to certain contemporary feminist arguments, whether it should be drawn at all.
>
> Feminism is often seen as nothing more than the completion of the liberal or bourgeois revolution, as an extension of liberal principles and rights to women as well as men. The demand for equal rights has, of course, always been an important part of feminism. However, the attempt to universalise liberalism has more far-reaching consequences than is often appreciated because, in the end, it inevitably challenges liberalism itself. Liberal feminism has radical implications, not least in challenging the separation and opposition between the private and public spheres that is fundamental to liberal theory and practice. The liberal contrast between private and public is more than a distinction between two kinds of social activities. The public sphere, and the principles that govern it, are seen as separate from, or independent of, the relationships in the private sphere. A familiar illustration of this claim is the long controversy between liberal and radical political scientists about participation, the radicals denying the liberal claim that the social inequalities of the private sphere are irrelevant to questions about the political equality, universal suffrage and associated civil liberties of the public realm.
>
> Not all feminists, however, are liberals; "feminism" goes far beyond liberal-feminism. Other feminists explicitly reject liberal conceptions of the private and public and see the social structure of liberalism as the political problem, not a starting point from which equal rights can be claimed.[55]

54   See C Pateman, *The Sexual Contract*, Polity, 1988.
55   C Pateman, "Feminist Critiques of the Public/Private Dichotomy" in SI Benn and GF Gaus (eds), *Public and Private in Social Life*, Croom Helm, 1983, 281-282.

Pateman concludes her critique of the public/private dichotomy as follows:

> While women are identified with this "private" work, their public status is always undermined. This conclusion does not, as is often alleged, deny the natural biological fact that women not men *bear* children; it does deny the patriarchal assumption that only women can *rear* children. Equal parenting and equal participation in the other activities of domestic life presuppose some radical changes in the public sphere, in the organisation of production, in what we mean by "work" and the practice of citizenship.[56]

Pateman's reference to women being "identified" with private work brings in the related idea that men and women should operate in *separate* spheres. Taken literally, the ideology of privacy does not require *women* to be located within the home and domesticity. It simply requires that the home and domesticity be treated differently from work and public life. This is actually the position of some liberal feminists who believe that gender equality, inside and outside the home, can be achieved without destroying the idea of family privacy.

The response of most feminists, however, is that the public/private dichotomy is *in fact* linked with the separate spheres idea so that the ideas of "private" and "woman", and "public" and "man", are bonded together. A clear illustration of this is found in a book written by Lord Denning in the late 1970s, which purports to tell the story "by which women have become equal".[57] The remarks set out below are of particular interest because Lord Denning is often credited with being the architect of modern English family law through his landmark decisions concerning married women's property and de facto relationships.

> No matter how you may dispute and argue, you cannot alter the fact that women are different from men. The principal task in life of women is to bear and rear children: and it is a task which occupies the best years of their lives. The man's part in bringing up the children is no doubt as important as hers, but of necessity he cannot devote so much time to it. He is physically the stronger and she the weaker. He is temperamentally the more aggressive and she the more submissive. It is he who takes the initiative and she who responds. These diversities of function and temperament lead to differences of outlook which cannot be ignored. But they are, none of them, any reason for putting women under the subjection of men. A woman feels as keenly, thinks as clearly, as a man. She in her sphere does work as useful as man does in his. She has as much right to her freedom – to develop her personality to the full – as a man. When she marries, she does not become the husband's servant but his equal partner. If his work is more important in the life of the community, hers is more important in the life of the family. Neither can do without the other. Neither is above the other or under the other. They are equals.
>
> Few will dispute the justice of woman's claim to equality: but it is only in recent years that it has been realised. This is one of the most significant revolutions of our time. It has tremendous potentialities for our civilisation.[58]

The reference to a woman "in her sphere" ties in well with the standard liberal idea of society being divided into public and private spheres. Moreover, the "separate but equal" notion seems to be a modern method of legitimating the

---

56   Pateman, n 55, 299 (original emphasis).
57   Lord Denning MR, *The Due Process of Law*, Butterworths, 1980, 193.
58   Ibid 194-195.

reality that women do the majority of domestic labour in our society.[59] Note the following passage from Lord Denning which is taken from the same chapter as the previous quotation:

> This freedom which women have achieved carries with it equal responsibilities. If they live up to their responsibilities, their equality is not only a matter of absolute justice, but is also capable of great benefits to the human race: and of all their responsibilities, the chief is to maintain a sound and healthy family life in the land. To this chief responsibility all other interests must be subordinated.[60]

This kind of attitude has been ridiculed by feminists. Janet Radcliffe Richards, for example, has said:

> Scratch the egalitarian veneer even slightly, and all the differences of role between the sexes seem to depend on women's being *less* strong, *less* rational, and *less* just about everything else worth while than men, which supposed deficiencies have traditionally been the excuse for excluding women from everything men have been inclined to keep for themselves.[61]

Liberal rights to equality and privacy can be hard to reconcile.[62] The challenge for some feminists is not to prioritise one over the other, to abandon privacy in favour of equality, but rather to reconceptualise both concepts.

In relation to privacy, it has been suggested that the right to respect for private life could be reconceptualised. The boundaries between the spheres of public and private are neither immutable nor universal. As Margaret Thornton observes, "the public/private dichotomy of liberal thought, far from constituting two analytically discrete realms, is a malleable creation of the public realm".[63] Working within this traditional framework, it is possible to reconstruct privacy in ways that provide individuals with greater freedom to express and fulfil their emotional needs. Privacy may be viewed not merely as a shield, but as a positive basis for the recognition of personal needs and aspirations. The European Commission has observed that the right to privacy protected under the European Convention on Human Rights includes "to a certain extent, the right to establish and to develop relationships with other human beings, especially in the emotional field for the development and fulfilment of one's own personality".[64] This approach expands the *negative* conception of privacy as freedom from unwarranted state intrusion into one's private life, to include the *positive* right to establish, develop and fulfil

---

59   P Parkinson and J Behrens, *Australian Family Law in Context*, 3rd ed, LBC, 2004, 90-101.

60   Denning, n 57, 201.

61   JR Richards, "Separate Spheres" in P Singer (ed), *Applied Ethics*, Oxford UP, 1986 185, 186.

62   As we shall see below, a key disagreement in the Australian Law Reform Commission's Report on *Equality Before the Law* (1994) was whether or not the proposed Equality Act should extend from the public to the private sphere.

63   M Thornton, "The Public/Private Dichotomy: Gendered and Discriminatory" (1991) 18 *Journal of Law and Society* 448 at 459. See generally M Thornton (ed), *Public and Private: Feminist Legal Debates*, Oxford UP, 1995.

64   App No 6825/74, 5 Eur Com HR Dec & Rep 86 at 87. This broader conception of privacy is reflected in *Dudgeon v United Kingdom*, 45 Eur Ct HR (ser A) (1981); 4 Eur HR Rep 149 (1982). It has been suggested that the state should assume a greater role in *promoting*, rather than simply protecting, the right to respect for private life under Art 8.

one's own emotional needs.[65] Alldridge sums this up by talking of "privacy as autonomy".[66]

From privacy, we now turn to equality, examining from feminist perspectives how various liberal constructions of equality – such as equal treatment and equal opportunity – serve as a legal basis for anti-discrimination laws. We also explore the difficulties, within a liberal framework, of adopting special measures, such as affirmative action, to tackle structural disadvantage that impede integration and participation of women in the workforce.

(d) Equality rights: anti-discrimination and affirmative action laws

Legislation designed to outlaw discrimination against women is often claimed to be one of the most direct and efficient[67] ways in which the law can be used to challenge male power. If this legislation extends to offering women *advantages* in areas where they have hitherto been disadvantaged – affirmative action or "positive discrimination" laws – then gender equality should be secured all the quicker. With differing degrees of enthusiasm, qualification and optimism, anti-discrimination measures are approved of by most feminists. They are joined in this approval by some who would describe themselves primarily as liberals rather than feminists. In Chapter 2 we saw that liberal theorists like Ronald Dworkin employ a stronger conception of equality than the formal idea common in 19th century liberalism; a conception which permits greater interference with individual liberty for the purpose of achieving substantive equality.[68]

There is, however, considerable potential for both kinds of legislation (anti-discrimination and affirmative action) to *offend* against particular formulations of liberalism. It is still a conventional liberal position that the state has no business interfering with the individual's choice as to whom to employ or supply with services – this is fundamentally connected to the principle of liberty, privacy and individual autonomy. If an employer or supplier decides not to deal with a woman, or to deal with her on terms less favourable than a man, then that is an exercise of the employer's or seller's liberty. It may be reprehensible conduct, but that is not a sufficient ground for attaching legal sanctions. Though this offends the idea of equality – because it treats men and women similarly situated in a different fashion – some liberals seek to justify this unequal treatment. Those on the conservative end of the spectrum frequently argue that the institution of the family and the traditional division of labour between the sexes is vital for "social stability". This can lead them to oppose legislation which might erode the idea that women

---

65   AM Connelly, "Problems of Interpretation of Article 8 of the *European Convention on Human Rights*" (1986) 35 *International and Comparative Law Quarterly* 567 at 574-575.

66   Peter Alldridge, *Relocating Criminal Law*, Ashgate, 2000, 114.

67   Efficient in the sense that anti-discrimination legislation can encompass a *range* of circumstances in which women are discriminated against. This avoids the need for the kind of piecemeal reform of the 19th and early 20th centuries when individual pieces of legislation were passed to permit women to enter the professions, sit on juries, become postmistresses etc. See Scutt, n 4, 41.

68   See R Dworkin, "Why Bakke has no Case" *New York Review of Books*, November 1977 and *Taking Rights Seriously*, Duckworth, 1977. Dworkin's position is discussed and criticised by M Sandel in *Liberalism and the Limits of Justice*, Cambridge UP, 1982, 135-137.

are different from men and each has their proper place.[69] And then, of course, there is simple unreasoning sexism.

These introductory remarks lead one to suspect that measures designed to overcome male prejudice, and in particular those which might put women ahead of men in certain kinds of competition, will be contentious. We might also suspect that their advocates will be pressed to make compromises about the form that the laws should take and the manner in which they are to be enforced. By exploring the nature of this pressure we are taken further in our inquiry about the limits of liberalism and the extent to which it can be compatible with feminism. This in turn helps us form a view about how safely one can pin hopes on law reform as a strategy for challenging male power.

What follows is not intended as a comprehensive account of the relevant legislation nor the practical obstacles to a successful complaint. Instead, our purpose is to draw out some general themes which add to our understanding of the context of law and its relationship with social power. To do this, however, we need to know the meaning of some key terms. We need to know the meaning of "discrimination", the differences between conscious and unconscious discrimination and the differences between direct and indirect discrimination. In one form or another the ideas underlying these terms, if not the actual words, are used in most legislation.

Applied to the context of gender, race, religion, disability and some other bases for dividing up people, discrimination is deemed to be unlawful. In modern usage at least two separate elements of discrimination can be identified:

(i)   the unreasonable disadvantaging of a person or group;

(ii) on grounds which are irrelevant to the matter in hand.

It is important to note that distinguishing between different kinds of people need not amount to unlawful discrimination. Literally, of course, to discriminate is simply to distinguish between people or things. It might be that certain tasks can only be carried out by people with particular attributes. In a genuine case, therefore, one could refuse to employ a person who is unable to carry them out. The disadvantaging of the person would not be unreasonable in (i), nor would it be on irrelevant grounds in (ii). Much turns on whether those differences are genuine, based on "relevant" considerations, rather than simply contrived justifications that cloak negative attitudes to women undertaking activity that has been conventionally undertaken by men.

A further consequence of this definition is that discrimination relates in some way to the victim's membership of a group. For example, X might choose not to do business with Y because X has had difficulties with Y in the past and does not trust Y. This may well not amount to discrimination. If, on the other hand, X is a man who refuses to do business with Y because she is a woman and he has a "policy" of never doing business with women then his refusal is discriminatory.

From what we have said so far it should be clear that discrimination suggests prejudice, in the sense of pre-judgement. Furthermore, that pre-judgement is an insulting one. It denigrates a person without reference to her specific qualities. On

---

69   Even in Sweden, which has a long tradition of proclaiming egalitarianism, the Conservatives have emphasised the role of the family; see D Bradley, "Sexual Equality in Sweden" (1990) 53 *Modern Law Review* 283 at 286.

the other hand, it is now generally recognised that one can discriminate without actually *intending* any insult. Culture and upbringing might make one's views feel natural. Discrimination can be a genuine reflection of one's views on life, of one's total ideology. Nevertheless it can be judged as discrimination because the perpetuation of stereotypes is the basis for the perpetuation of group inequality.

In addition to this distinction between conscious and unconscious discrimination there is a distinction between *direct* and *indirect* discrimination. An example of direct discrimination might be a rule which precludes women from holding a certain job. Ansett Airlines in the 1970s was a clear case in point. As the General Manager said in a letter to the Women's Electoral Lobby in February 1979:

> We have a good record of employing females in a wide range of positions within our organisation but have adopted a policy of only employing men as pilots. This does not mean that women cannot be good pilots, but we are concerned with the provision of the safest and most efficient air service possible. In this regard we feel that an all male pilot crew is safer than one in which the sexes are mixed.[70]

Ansett were subsequently found by the Equal Opportunity Board in Victoria to have discriminated against a female applicant whose average assessment score was higher than seven of the 14 successful candidates.[71]

Indirect discrimination can stem from rules which seem neutral on their face but which unreasonably define a job in such a way that women are disproportionately excluded. For example, weight or height requirements which disproportionately exclude women may be indirectly discriminatory if people under the set weight or height are capable of doing the job. Another example are employment policies related to pregnancy that restrict or limit participation in the workforce, a source of discrimination which is explored in Lacey's extract below.

Indirect discrimination can also be conscious or unconscious. For example, recruitment or promotion policies are sometimes devised for the purpose of excluding women even though women are not expressly mentioned in those policies. One common motive for employers is the avoidance of alleged disruption to work routines in the event of maternity. That is clearly capable of being conscious, indirect discrimination. On the other hand, recruitment or promotion decisions might unconsciously be guided by stereotypes; for example, a woman refused promotion due to an allegedly aggressive personality. This might, in the circumstances, be unconscious, indirect discrimination if a man would not have been refused promotion on these grounds. Quite possibly, as Gaze and Jones say, the woman is paying the price for not conforming to expectations of feminine gentleness and passivity.[72] Another example of unintentional indirect discrimination might be the withholding of benefits, such as superannuation schemes, from part-time workers. Because women form the majority of part-time workers, this practice might be indirectly discriminatory, even though unintentional.[73]

---

70   Quoted in Scutt, n 4, 45.

71   *Wardley v Ansett Transport Industries* (1984) EOC ¶92-002.

72   See B Gaze and M Jones, *Law, Liberty and Australian Democracy*, Lawbook Co, 1990, 414. See also the account of *Harrison v Department of Technical and Further Education* in Scutt, n 4, 58.

73   A leading Australian case is *Australian Iron and Steel Ltd v Banovic* (1990) 89 ALR 1. Here a last-on, first-off policy for retrenchments was held by the majority of the High Court to be indirectly discriminatory because women had been required to wait longer than men on a waiting list before being employed. They were therefore more likely to be "last on" and so disproportionately affected by the retrenchment policy which made them "first off".

Having identified some of the key terms in debates about discrimination legislation we need to do one more piece of scene-setting before we can look directly at some examples of anti-discrimination and affirmative action laws. We need to elaborate further the ideology of privacy which many feminists argue is a serious obstacle to the successful use of law as a means of attaining equality.

In the section above we referred to the tendency in liberal thought to divide social life into public and private spheres. The standard reason given for this is that it is a device for containing the power of the state. An ideology of privacy serves as an important reminder that some activities ought to be beyond government or state control. Feminists have drawn different inferences from the public/private dichotomy, and in the context of anti-discrimination laws we see how the concept, once more, may be invoked to limit the scope of the right to equality being offered to women

Since the 1970s, a number of statutes have been passed to deal with discrimination on the grounds of sex. There is general Commonwealth legislation, the *Sex Discrimination Act 1984*, to cover some matters within federal jurisdiction, and there is also general legislation in States and Territories. Apart from general measures which outlaw[74] different forms of discrimination on stated grounds in broad kinds of circumstance, other statutes have been amended to prohibit discrimination in particular instances with which the legislation is concerned. Obvious examples are Public Service Acts which deal only with the employment of public servants.

When the Commonwealth Sex Discrimination Bill was introduced in 1983 there was, in Chris Ronalds' words, "a public furore".[75] The leader of the National Party, Doug Anthony, claimed that such a law would "open the way to a further weakening of the basic unit of our society – the family".[76] Mr Anthony argued that the Bill would make mothers and housewives feel inadequate and this would encourage the breakdown of the family unit. Peter Bailey summarises the opposition in this way:

> Churches voiced their protest about reductions in their freedom to select suitable staff; there were fears that employers would not be able to select suitable people for vacant positions; there were suggestions that the Bill was designed to break up the traditional family structure by forcing women out to work; it was alleged that its purpose was to assist lesbians; and there was criticism that the common law right to legal representation was being denied.[77]

Whilst protests like these can be dismissed as mere unsubstantiated dogma, they do reveal the sense of threat that even modest proposals can provoke in a gendered society. In the event, after the government had agreed to certain amendments designed to reduce some of these alleged public fears, the Act was passed and came into effect on 1 August 1984.

The Act makes unlawful acts of discrimination in particular areas of activity. "Unlawful" does not mean that the acts are criminal, nor are they actionable at

---

74   None of the sex discrimination legislation makes discrimination a criminal offence. Powers exist to award damages, to order reinstatement and to order alteration to practices.

75   C Ronalds, *Affirmative Action and Sex Discrimination*, Pluto Press, 2nd ed, 1991, 14. See also P Bailey, *Human Rights*, Butterworths, 1990, 151-159.

76   *Sydney Morning Herald*, 30 September 1983.

77   Bailey, n 75, 151.

civil law in the normal sense of giving rise to an immediate action for damages. Instead, the aggrieved person complains to the Human Rights and Equal Opportunity Commission (HREOC) and the complaint is channelled down a path of conciliation.

In summary, to be unlawful the act complained of must, first, have been carried out on the grounds of sex, marital status, pregnancy or potential pregnancy, or family responsibilities (sexual harassment is made a special form of discrimination under s 28A of the Act) and, secondly, have taken place in one of the areas specified in the Act. These areas are employment and superannuation, education, accommodation, clubs, the provision of goods, services or facilities, the disposal of an interest in land, requests for the provision of information, and the implementation of Commonwealth laws or programs. Although complaints have been made to the Commission on all of the grounds, we concentrate here on the ground of sex.

Section 5 of the Act deals with direct and indirect discrimination in separate subsections as follows:

> 5. (1) For the purposes of this Act, a person (in this subsection referred to as the *discriminator*) discriminates against another person (in this subsection referred to as the *aggrieved person*) on the ground of the sex of the aggrieved person if, by reason of:
> (a) the sex of the aggrieved person;
> (b) a characteristic that appertains generally to persons of the sex of the aggrieved person; or
> (c) a characteristic that is generally imputed to persons of the sex of the aggrieved person;
> the discriminator treats the aggrieved person less favourably than, in circumstances that are the same or are not materially different, the discriminator treats or would treat a person of the opposite sex.
> (1A) ...
> (2) For the purposes of this Act, a person (the *discriminator*) discriminates against another person (the *aggrieved person*) on the ground of the sex of the aggrieved person if the discriminator imposes, or proposes to impose, a condition, requirement or practice that has, or is likely to have, the effect of disadvantaging persons of the same sex as the aggrieved person.

Indirect discrimination is not caught by s 5(2) if it is reasonable in the circumstances, having regard to matters such as the nature and extent of the disadvantage resulting from the imposition of the condition, requirement or practice, the feasibility of overcoming or mitigating the disadvantage, and whether the disadvantage is proportionate to the result sought (s 7B).

Clearly, this legislation is potentially very useful, particularly in the context of indirect employment discrimination. It attacks unreasonable job requirements and practices which disproportionately disadvantage women. On the other hand, feminists have pointed out some weaknesses or problems in this kind of measure, of a conceptual, as well as practical, nature.

First, the legislation covers only "public" areas of life. There is no attempt, for example, to give wives rights to equal treatment in the home. If legislation were proposed which required domestic labour and child-rearing to be shared equally between men and women there would probably be an enormous outcry (from men, at any rate) about the government exceeding its bounds. The legislation would also be characterised as hopelessly impractical because of the difficulties of enforcing it. This opposition might overlook the difficulties there already are in enforcing anti-discrimination legislation in areas where it is less controversial. And it would also overlook the important symbolic functions that measures like this could have. On the other hand, the opposition would be testimony to the strength of the presumption that the home is private. Perhaps, as Margaret Thornton has said, the unenviable task of the liberal state in having to mediate between irreconcilable forces (such as patriarchy versus feminism) is made easier if there are some areas conceptualised as so private that it does not have to grapple with them.[78]

Secondly, there is the question of procedure. The main method of dealing with complaints under anti-discrimination legislation is by conciliation rather than traditional litigation. In the passage below, Margaret Thornton expresses concerns about conciliation (although, as she admits, the traditional adversary process also lacks appeal to feminists) and she links these concerns with the public/private dichotomy.

Margaret Thornton, *The Public/Private Dichotomy: Gendered and Discriminatory*
(1990, footnotes omitted)

Procedure

No less a dramatic manifestation of the way in which the public/private web is woven into discrimination law occurs in the actual mode of dispute resolution, as anti-discrimination legislation sets out to resolve the preponderance of disputes within the privatised setting of conciliation, preferably without the aid of lawyers. Conciliation involves a range of interventions by a conciliation officer; it does not necessarily involve a round-table conference. It may be undesirable for the disputants to face each other and a settlement can be effected by whatever means is thought to be appropriate, including telephone calls, letters and informal overtures. Of course, a conference may be the most appropriate way of resolving a dispute and some legislation makes provision for a compulsory conference to be called if a voluntary conference cannot be effected. Less than two per cent of complaints proceed to a formal inquiry within a public setting.

One inference to be drawn from this emphasis on conciliation is that discrimination in social life is a private matter which should not occupy public adjudicative space as is the case with other social harms. Furthermore, the fact that the process cannot be scrutinised renders it immune from public accountability. Potential complainants are also ignorant as to what occurs behind closed doors. They are thereby denied the empowering outcome of any success. The flexibility and informality of conciliation mean that the process is not systematised and governed by the rules of precedent as with a formal judicial hearing.

It is this very absence of formalism, however, which constitutes the strength of conciliation because women and minority groups who have felt disempowered within the alienating, adversarial adjudicative system, dominated by white male

---

78   M Thornton, "The Public/Private Dichotomy: Gendered and Discriminatory", paper presented to the Australasian Law Teachers' Association Annual Conference, 27-30 September 1990, The Australian National University, 4. See generally, M Thornton, *The Liberal Promise: Anti-Discrimination Legislation in Australia*, Oxford UP, 1990.

authority figures, are permitted a space within a conciliation conference in which to express themselves. Silbey and Merry have described the therapeutic style of conciliation as one in which the disputants work through their emotions. Thus, in contradistinction to the coldness and abstraction of adversarialism, there is space for the affective in which the disputants may tell their stories unimpeded by the inhibitions of the judicial arena.

Instead of the individualised *lis inter partes* of a formal mode of adjudication, conciliation represents a step towards a caring, communal and co-operative form of dispute resolution reminiscent of a past age, hailed as a welcome move in light of the anomie and alienation generated by the combative litigation of contemporary capitalist society: "Litigation expresses a chilling, Hobbesian vision of human nature". Feminist scholars, in particular, have stressed the sense of interconnectedness emanating from women's lives; the autonomous individual of classical liberalism is paradigmatically male. Thus, a growing communitarian consciousness has heightened the idea that there might be an homology between women and conciliation, on the one hand, and between men and the aggressive, competitive, Anglo-Australian style of adjudication, on the other hand.

However, just as some feminist scholars have responded positively to the concept of conciliation and seen it as dispute resolution in a female voice, others have warned against the dangers of a privatised procedure. Since the domestic sphere has been the locus of exploitation and domination for women, immunised by the rubric of "private" and the rhetoric of love and caring, the concern is that the privatised carapace and the ethic of care associated with conciliation may have similarly served to obscure its exploitative underside. Critics of conciliation have been most vociferous in their denunciation of the procedure because it denies formal protection to the party who is in a weaker bargaining position. As I have argued elsewhere, however, the belief that formal equality before the law can be effective in securing substantive justice is misconceived. No forum, public or private, can overcome the advantage of power:

> Experience shows that, regardless of the form of dispute resolution or the nature of the dispute, any outcome will disproportionately benefit the party which has the benefit of power.

The formal arena can give only the appearance of equality through representation and a myriad of formal procedures. It is a fundamental myth of liberal legalism that the formal process of adjudication necessarily guarantees a just outcome. Like equality, justice is a facet of legality which can hardly be imagined, let alone realised, in a private informal context. ...

While the process of conciliation ostensibly possesses all the hallmarks of an alternative and independent mode of dispute resolution, it is closely linked to the state. Indeed, Hofrichter argues that informal dispute resolution is an agency of the capitalist state and that what we see happening is the state extending further into civil society in its new guise of "non-state". With its emphasis on co-operation and consensus, conciliation operates as a seductive mechanism for reasserting the threatened hegemony of the state.

While this analysis is compelling at one level, conciliation is an empowering mechanism which affords individual women and minorities a space which would not be available to them within judicial formalism. The private sphere values of caring and affectivity, which are alien to public adjudication, render conciliation an attractive prospect for women alleging sex discrimination. Indeed, the very idea of recognising the value of the caring voice in dispute resolution corrodes the abstract formalism of legality. The ambiguities in this area of law beset us from every direction and reflect the inherent ambiguities of the public/private dichotomy.[79]

This resonates with the concerns, noted above, about diverting family violence to restorative justice "conferences".

A third problem that some feminists have identified in anti-discrimination legislation lies in the elusive nature of the definition of equality which underpins it. The extract from Nicola Lacey below discusses the UK *Sex Discrimination Act 1975* which, in material respects, is similar to the Commonwealth legislation here.[80]

Nicola Lacey, *Legislation Against Sex Discrimination: Questions from a Feminist Perspective*
(1987)

1. The Ideal of Equality

Starting at the most fundamental level, one obvious set of questions has to do with just what the *Sex Discrimination Act 1975* sets out to achieve and the nature of the political commitment from which it proceeded. One way of looking at this question is to understand anti-discrimination law as proceeding from a commitment to the value of equality, which rules out discrimination on certain grounds. Equality, however, is a deeply-contested notion, and several conceptions of equality present themselves as possible candidates to be bases for anti-discrimination law. Perhaps most obviously there is the ideal of formal equality; after all, equality before the law and equal rights – particularly in terms of women's position in the public sphere of paid employment, market transactions, and education – have long been cherished goals of liberal feminism. But the limitations of formal equality as a feminist goal are now widely recognised: it has little bite in view of the disadvantages which women suffer in "private" areas such as family life, untouched by the sex discrimination legislation. No concept of discrimination which is based exclusively on formal equality can take proper account of aspects of women's different position resulting from prior discrimination and disadvantage in spheres which fall outside the relatively limited ambit of the legislation. Similar limitations surround a second candidate: equality of treatment exclusively on the basis of "relevant" reasons. Given the history and structure of sex discrimination, merely ruling out sex as a relevant reason for action in certain areas promises little progress in terms of dismantling women's disadvantage. It may even be counter-productive in ruling out sex as a remedially relevant reason in the context, for example, of affirmative action programmes.

It is clear from the content of the *Sex Discrimination Act 1975* that neither formal nor relevant reasons for equality formed its exclusive underlying ideal. The concept of indirect discrimination takes on board the idea that women's disadvantage is not solely or even principally the result of individual acts of prejudiced discrimination but of structural discrimination embedded in the practices of social institutions. Practical problems still arise, in that the operation

---

79 Thornton, n 78, 15-21. The quotation in the fourth paragraph of the extract is from J Auerbach, "Justice without Law" in LL Riskin and JE Westbrook (eds), *Dispute Resolution and Lawyers*, West Publishing, 1987, 47.

80 All Australian anti-discrimination legislation is modelled on the British legislation to do with race and sex discrimination; see C Ronalds, "To Right a Few Wrongs" in Mackinolty and Radi, n 35, 199.

of the test of what prima facie indirect discrimination is justifiable is inherently vulnerable to the prejudices of the tribunal and the (often low) importance it gives to sexual equality as a social goal. But it is clear that indirect discrimination moves beyond formal or "relevant reasons" equality. It aspires towards a more programmatic vision of equality of opportunity – an ideal which is stated in the preamble to the 1975 Act and reflected in the name of the administrative agency which it set up. In effect, the Act uses inequalities of results in certain circumstances as raising prima facie cases of unjust inequality of opportunity, which then have to be justified by the defendant. But what exactly does equality of opportunity mean, how thoroughly is it embedded as the organising principle of the legislation, and does it offer an acceptable goal for feminism?

2. Equality of Opportunity

Equality of opportunity represents only one among many of the more programmatic conceptions of equality described and defended in modern political theory. Equality of welfare, results, resources, and consideration of interests, to name but a few, have been energetically and ably defended. Any of these conceptions might be easier to extend beyond a liberal world-view or more susceptible of being given a distinctively feminist content than is equality of opportunity. But it is important to analyse the idea of equality of opportunity and to reflect on its status as the chosen stated ideal for current anti-discrimination legislation. And what emerges from such reflection is the clear fact that the idea provided a crucially important campaigning slogan for the legislation, but that, by the same token, it was not discussed or analysed in any open or rigorous way. Had it been, it seems likely that both its ambiguity and its potentially radical implications would have come to the surface and it would have lost its capacity to unite diverse political groups. How many liberal supporters of the current legislation, for example, would have been content to reflect on the implications of a thorough-going commitment to equality of opportunity in terms of socialisation of child-rearing or even genetic engineering? Thus, we should not expect to find that the legislation conforms to a coherent or unitary ideal of equality. We should rather recognise equality of opportunity as a crucial piece of political rhetoric which also provides guiding and limiting principles. These combine in the legislation with an underlying commitment to formal and "relevant reasons" equality within the public spheres of community activity which form the appropriate focus for political intervention according to liberal theory.

But does equality of opportunity represent an attractive organising ideal for feminists concerned to argue for the reform of anti-discrimination legislation? As we have seen, indirect discrimination uses inequality of impact in certain very limited circumstances as a test of prima facie inequality of opportunity. This, of course, implies that in other spheres inequality of impact is not an instance of unjust inequality. This is consistent with an equal-opportunity world-view, because the discourse of equality of opportunity presupposes a world inhabited by autonomous individuals making choices. These choices may differ along gender lines, resulting in a very different distribution of jobs or other goods as between women and men. At this point the critical edge of the ideal of equal opportunity is, quite simply, blunt. An equal opportunity principle is inadequate to criticise and transform a world in which the distribution of goods is structured along gender lines. And this relates back to practical problems faced by litigants. Differential treatment and unequal impact, even within the ambit of prima facie discrimination, may be legitimated subconsciously by industrial tribunal members who believe women and men just do typically make different choices.

265

Different finishing points are not seen as problematic. In this way the very stereotypes which the legislation is presumably meant to undermine inevitably and invisibly affect the tribunal's reading of legal issues, such as what counts as less favourable or detrimental treatment, or justifiable requirements or conditions.

These difficulties with the ideology underlying the legislation are compounded by its limited scope. Prohibition of differential treatment and unequal impact in a small selection of spheres, all of them within the "public realm", is unlikely to have any real effect on women's oppression. Attempts to extend the formal market conditions for equal competition between the sexes within an ideology of equal opportunity hardly seems an adequate goal for any really critical feminism. Rather, we must look for a normative basis which provides a real cutting edge against the widespread inequality and injustice which flows from action based on stereotyped assumptions and from the genuinely different socialisation and expectations which still exist between the sexes. For however deplorable we find the fact that gender is still an important factor in the creation and structure of social practices, we cannot ignore it if we are to secure real progress for women.

3. The symmetry of equality principles.

The logic of the ideal of equal treatment and formal equality which underlies much of the legislation creates another difficulty. Part of this logic is a symmetry – a conception of sex discrimination which encompasses treatment of both men and women – which clearly does not match the nature of the social problem to which, from a feminist perspective, sex discrimination legislation should be addressed. This is the problem of discrimination against and disadvantage of women. ... [T]he result of the compelling logic of the symmetrical principle proscribing direct discrimination is to outlaw any form of reverse discrimination or affirmative action. Even the very moderate practice of choosing the women from a number of equally suitable applicants would be ruled out on a strict approach. Thus, the possibility of determinate, concrete practices designed to secure tangible advances for at least some women are ruled out in favour of an unhappy combination of commitments to rigid equal treatment in a limited sphere and the fluid and intangible goal of equal opportunity. And this ideological framework also renders problematic the accommodation of even the limited provisions which we may currently want to make in recognition of gender difference. For even though issues such as protective legislation of various kinds are recognised as very difficult by feminists and anti-feminists alike, debates about issues such as whether pre-menstrual tension should act as a mitigating principle in criminal law are rendered much more dangerous to women's interests within the context of subscription to an ideal of formal equality because any accommodation of difference can be represented as "special pleading". Such accommodations tend to be seen as acknowledgments of women's special needs and weaknesses, represented principally as questions of sex as a biological category rather than as questions of the socially constructed, mutable category of gender. Such dangers are well illustrated by the fact that "special features" such as child-bearing capacity have on occasion been used to deny women even their formal rights under the Sex Discrimination Act.

4. The comparative aspect.

Further problems from a feminist perspective arise from the fact that the concept of discrimination imports the notion of comparison – of less favourable treatment as opposed to purely unfavourable treatment. Perhaps the most spectacular example of such problems is the history of cases about discrimination on grounds of pregnancy under the British legislation. [Lacey then reviewed the early cases on pregnancy discrimination where the courts found dismissal because of pregnancy was not gender discrimination because there was no male comparator who was being treated differently, and subsequent cases that held that such treatment was not different to action taken against men suffering 'ill health'] ...

But a deeper problem with the comparative approach underlies these obvious examples. This is that it presupposes (yet suppresses) the idea of a norm with which the scrutinised behaviour is compared. In the case of claims brought by women, that norm is the treatment usually accorded to men: thus, in so far as the sex discrimination legislation prescribes equality, it is equality in terms of a norm set by and for men – the logic of discrimination allows no challenge to the general practices in any area. By definition, sex discrimination cases do not provide a jumping-off point for criticism of general social practices or real debate about what kind of equality is worth having, and with whom. At best, the legislation promises some dismantling of practices restrictive of access to goods and resources which present (that is, male-dominated) culture has determined as valuable. It may go some way towards reducing the overt significance of sex in the allocation of certain goods, but it has no cutting edge against the significance of gender in setting them up as goods in the first place.[81]

The problem here is that inequality is approached from the liberal (and invariably legal) standpoint of individualism. By conceiving discrimination as the different treatment of individuals on specified grounds such as gender or race, there is only limited scope for addressing and remedying group-based disadvantage. It also adopts a normative standard that is male, as Lacey eloquently observes:

> In the case of equality, it has been argued that liberal notions of equality are fundamentally premised on the idea of sameness: equal treatment is due to all who are similarly situated to the full liberal subject. Hence, if the subject is implicitly marked as masculine – is understood in terms of bodily and psychic characteristics which have been culturally understood to be associated with men – then the strategy of equality amounts to the assimilation of women to a *norm set by and for men*.[82]

Lacey is by no means the only feminist to be troubled by the conceptions of equality that underpin modern anti-discrimination legislation. Carol Smart has described the equal treatment versus different treatment debate as an "exquisite trap" because of its "either/or" nature. To promote one means that we inevitably undermine the other. The weakness with gender discrimination laws based on either equality or difference is the presumption that men are the norm against which women are measured.[83]

An influential attempt to escape the equality/difference framework of analysis emerged in the writings of feminist legal theorist, Catharine MacKinnon. MacKinnon, whose work we discussed under the label of second phase feminism, argued that anti-discrimination legislation is merely about allowing women to be equal with men in particular instances. Men are the measuring rod of equality. Sex

---

81   N Lacey, "Legislation Against Sex Discrimination: Questions from a Feminist Perspective" (1987) 14 *Journal of Law and Society* 411 at 413-417.

82   Lacey, n 4, 240 (emphasis added).

83   For an excellent review of the equal treatment/special treatment debate, examining both US and European approaches, see J Sohrab, "Avoiding the 'Exquisite Trap': A Critical Look at the Equal Treatment/Special Treatment Debate in Law" (1993) 1 *Feminist Legal Studies* 141.

discrimination law, drawing on liberal theory, is based on issues of sameness and difference. In some instances women are the same as men and should be treated like them. In other instances they are different from men and should be treated unlike them. The sameness/difference duality precludes more fundamental questions about the appropriateness of the male yardstick in the first place.

Catharine MacKinnon, *Toward a Feminist Theory of the State*
(1989)

The philosophy underlying the sameness/difference approach applies liberalism to women. Sex is a natural difference, a division, a distinction, beneath which lies a stratum of human commonality, sameness. The moral thrust of the sameness branch of the doctrine conforms normative rules to empirical reality by granting women access to what men have: to the extent women are no different from men, women deserve what men have. The differences branch, which is generally regarded as patronizing and unprincipled but necessary to avoid absurdity, exists to value or compensate women for what they are or have become distinctively as women – by which is meant, unlike men, or to leave women as "different" as equality law finds them.

Most scholarship on sex discrimination law concerns which of these paths to sex equality is preferable in the long run or more appropriate to any particular issue, as if they were all there is. As a prior matter, however, treating issues of sex equality as issues of sameness and difference is to take a particular approach. This approach is here termed the sameness/difference approach because it is obsessed with the sex difference. Its main theme is: "we're the same, we're the same, we're the same". Its counterpoint theme (in a higher register) goes: "but we're different, but we're different, but we're different". Its story is: on the first day, difference was; on the second day, a division was created upon it; on the third day, occasional dominance arose. Division may be rational or irrational. Dominance either seems or is justified or unjustified. Difference is.

Concealed is the substantive way in which man has become the measure of all things. Under the sameness rubric, women are measured according to correspondence with man, their equality judged by proximity to his measure. Under the difference rubric, women are measured according to their lack of correspondence from man, their womanhood judged by their distance from his measure. Gender neutrality is the male standard. The special protection rule is the female standard. Masculinity or maleness is the referent for both. Approaching sex discrimination in this way, as if sex questions were difference questions and equality questions were sameness questions, merely provides two ways for the law to hold women to a male standard and to call that sex equality.[84]

It follows from MacKinnon's analysis that a subordination or dominance approach views inequality not as an issue of whether women are the same as men or different from men, but as the consequence of the relative distribution of power between women and men. It examines laws, policies and practices to determine whether they operate to maintain women in a subordinate position. This approach can lead to significant remodelling of existing legal strategies (see, for example, the case study in Chapter 2 on how MacKinnon and Andrea Dworkin reconcep-

---

84   C MacKinnon, "Sex Equality: On Difference and Dominance" in *Toward A Feminist Theory of the State*, Harvard UP, 1989, Ch 12, 220-221.

tualised legislative approaches to pornography). In the next section, we explore the Australian Law Reform Commission's contentious proposals, not yet implemented, to entrench a right to equality based on the concept of subordination.

Legislating for gender equality is seen as bringing about important improvements on the previous position of women, but from the perspective of some feminists, law is unable to bring about the kind of fundamental change that they consider necessary. The laws discussed above are shaped by the ideology of privacy and individualism, and do not purport to challenge domestic structural inequality. But anti-discrimination legislation is not the whole picture. It can be supplemented by affirmative action programs. Intuitively, at least, these are more likely to be appealing to many feminists, even if they offend the central ideals of liberalism and would be abhorrent to many liberals.

Affirmative action is usually taken to involve a positive program of giving an advantage to people in certain groups because they have been discriminated against in the past. It is also often referred to as "positive discrimination" or "reverse discrimination". The passage from Bailey describes briefly the affirmative action programs in Commonwealth legislation and some of the arguments for its introduction.

> Legislation to introduce some form of affirmative action program is complementary to anti-discrimination legislation. The purpose of affirmative action (reverse discrimination) is to ensure that those operating the program plan in such a way as to eliminate what has normally been a long-term pattern of disadvantage or discrimination by attempting to remove the underlying causes, for example by a training program. In most cases, affirmative action programs are designed to apply to employment. In Australia, the Commonwealth has enacted two pieces of legislation, the *Affirmative Action (Equal Employment Opportunity for Women) Act 1986* and the *Equal Employment Opportunity (Commonwealth Authorities) Act 1987*. Between them, these two Acts introduce requirements for the progressive development of affirmative action programs for women in all businesses employing more than 100 persons, all universities and colleges of advanced education and virtually all Commonwealth authorities (the main – and regrettable – exception being statutory marketing authorities). New South Wales, Victoria and Western Australia have also included in their equal opportunity legislation provisions to cover State employees (but not employees in the private sector). The main reasons why affirmative action programs for women have been felt to be necessary in Australia arise from the disadvantages they have suffered in the employment field. Thus women are concentrated in a narrow range of occupations and industries – 64 per cent of women workers being employed in clerical, sales, or service, sport and recreation positions in 1984. Women were under-represented in most other areas. Even where women are employed in significant numbers, their status is often at the lower end of the hierarchy and they are often denied benefits such as superannuation. Unemployment amongst women is higher than for men and women engage much more in part-time employment. Further, women are often less able to receive assistance through training programs than are men.[85]

---

85   Bailey, n 75, 164-165. For a fuller account of the history, especially in the US, and the range of special measures adopted in Australia, see N O'Neill, S Rice, and R Douglas, *Retreat from Injustice – Human Rights Law in Australia*, 2nd ed, Federation Press, 2004, 548-556.

The 1986 Act has since been renamed the *Equal Opportunity for Women in the Workplace Act 1999* (Cth). Banishing the language of affirmative action is highly symbolic, reflecting the political unease over the "reverse discrimination" inherent in these programs. The name change also locates gender-based disadvantage with the opportunities available to *individuals* rather than wider structural or group based disadvantage. It also conceptualises the problem of discrimination in gender-neutral terms. As the website of the Equal Opportunity Workplace Agency (EOWA), which was created by the 1999 Act, explains "equal opportunity means that all employees have equal access to the opportunities that are available at work. This means all employees are treated with fairness and respect in that they are not subject to discrimination or harassment in the workplace".[86]

Under the 1999 Act, employers are required to implement "equal opportunity for women in the workplace" programs. The employers are required to report annually on their actions and programs, submitting these to the EOWA, which assumed the role previously performed by the Director of Affirmative Action under the 1986 Act. Like the earlier scheme, the new agency has no recourse to legal sanctions in the event of non-compliance. The principal sanction is the risk of a report by the agency.

Many objections have been made about the very concept of affirmative action, although these may have been based more on the experience of the United States, which Australia has been anxious to avoid. In particular, the use of minimum quotas of disadvantaged groups in employment and higher education has given rise to political and legal controversy in the US. One specific objection to US affirmative action programs is that they fail to reward the merit of those excluded and they are therefore unjust.[87] Indeed, addressing this specific concern, s 3(4) of the 1999 Act places limits on how far special measures can go in advancing the interests of women:

> Nothing in this Act shall be taken to require a relevant employer to take any action incompatible with the principle that employment matters should be dealt with on the basis of merit.

Because this argument is raised frequently by many liberals when affirmative action is proposed, it is worth analysing in a little detail.

Tom Campbell has suggested that affirmative action is not discrimination in the sense we are using it here.[88] The reasons for distinguishing between people *are* relevant to the matter in hand; namely, the redistribution of benefits to make up for past improper distributions. Furthermore, there is no element of insult to the group now being disfavoured. As for the claim of injustice, Campbell says that if one takes an individualist meritorian view of justice then the objections to affirmative action do seem strong. In other words, if benefits ought to go to those who have voluntarily carried out morally praiseworthy acts then affirmative action in favour of some groups seems potentially unjust to others. On the other hand, there are real limits to that theory of justice in the first place. Moral qualities are only one component of success. Others may be basic intelligence, personality, educational opportunity and social background. The individual can take little

---

86   The functions, remit and activities of the agency can be found on its website: <http://www.eowa. gov.au>.

87   See Chapter 2 for a brief discussion of theories of justice, p36ff.

88   T Campbell, *Justice*, 2nd ed, Macmillan, 2001, 85-88, 214-218.

GENDER

credit for these. So, if one really presses the meritorian argument, nearly all allocations of benefits in liberal societies seem unjust.

Criticism of affirmative action comes not only from within liberalism. The feminist concerns about anti-discrimination legislation that we have already mentioned are also applicable to affirmative action legislation.[89] These concerns include the wide areas in which such schemes do not apply, the weak or non-existent enforcement mechanisms, and the underlying liberal/male conception of equality and equal opportunity that is being promoted. In particular, Australian enforcement procedures, being basically limited to public naming (from which a sense of shame and contrition is presumed to follow), are weak. Furthermore, progress is continually at risk of being undermined by other processes. Jocelynne Scutt has described the "tipping effect" whereby formerly male jobs become less well paid when men move out:

> Achieving, through legal processes, equal access for women to well paid jobs is not easy. There seems to be little point in encouraging women to enter non-traditional spheres if what in the United States of America has been dubbed "the tipping effect" occurs: that is, women move in, men move out, and formerly well paid jobs become moderately well, or low, paid. The real estate industry in the United States has suffered the tipping effect; in Australia, teaching and secretarial work suffered it decades ago, and more recently bank telling. It is also doubtful whether the problems will be overcome simply by women moving into non-traditional fields which remain dominated by men. Women may be lawyers and doctors, but are clustered in certain areas of each profession. Men become surgeons: highly prestigious and lucrative jobs. Women are general practitioners: with less status and (relatively) modest incomes. Women (it is said, though it is slowly changing) practice mainly in family law and criminal law, because so much is done by way of legal aid, with fees in the lower realms and unattractive to men. Male lawyers predominate in corporate and taxation law.
>
> It remains insufficient to encourage women and girls into other fields, or to require employers to be mindful of the talents and capabilities of women for jobs previously considered to be "unsuitable". Sexual harassment, particularly, remains a major problem (as it does in traditional fields). When women move into male dominated areas "sexist harassment" emerges in the form of slights, interference or aggression directed at women by male co-workers or subordinates, unable to cope with women as equals or as supervisors or employers. That girls wishing to enter plumbing and electrical apprenticeships are enabled to do so is positive. Yet merely counting the numbers and failing to recognise the culture into which the young women go is neglect. The need to establish and maintain strong, effective support groups is essential.[90]

To continue on this pessimistic note, Jeanne Gregory has suggested affirmative action legislation can actually be dangerous in the longer term if it "co-opts" sufficient numbers of the disadvantaged and leads to a loss of pressure for change:

> [Affirmative] action measures are an important step on the road to justice, but they will not by themselves guarantee the production of a just society. The commitment must be sustained and total, otherwise there is the danger that a few

---

89 See H Eisenstein, "The Gender of Bureaucracy: Reflections on Feminism and the State" in J Goodnow and C Pateman (eds), *Women, Social Science and Public Policy*, Allen and Unwin, 1985.

90 Scutt, n 4, 125.

"token" individuals, the least disadvantaged members of the disadvantaged group, will be co-opted into the ranks of the privileged, merely increasing the despair of those left behind. Positive action may help us to integrate a larger number of women and black people into existing structures, but unless that is seen as the first step in a fundamental re-shaping of the structures themselves, then those people will simply be replaced by yet another disadvantaged group.[91]

Notwithstanding these powerful feminist critiques, the idea of equality continues to dominate our legal strategies to tackle discrimination against women. The Report by the Australian Law Reform Commission, ALRC 69, *Equality Before the Law: Justice for Women* (1994), provided a glimmer of hope that a new conception of equality, breaking free from the shackles of liberal individualism, might be entrenched into Australian law.[92] Following the ALRC's critical examination of how the legal system and law discriminates against women, Part II of the Report, subtitled "Women's Equality", embraced a radically new approach to equality based on subordination':

> To achieve equality for women the law must be capable of responding to the situation and experiences of women. This requires the starting point to be the effects of a law, policy or program and its social context. For that legal analysis must move away from principles that require a superficial comparison with men to a more substantive understanding of equality as a response to economic, social and political disadvantage of women. The next chapter discusses how the law can provide a more comprehensive response to women's inequality based upon the subordination approach.[93]

Critical to this approach was the proposal to enshrining the legal protection into a federal Equality Act. However, the Commission divided over how the law should frame that equality guarantee, and whether or not that guarantee should extend into the private as well as public spheres. The majority of Commissioners took the view that although the Equality Act should be *primarily* addressed to the needs of women, men should not be denied access to the rights under the Act:

> **An issue for women and men.** The equality of all persons is a fundamental ethical and legal principle. It is applicable to all and cannot logically be confined to any one group. Equality should be able to take into account measures that assist both women and men.[94]

The minority view was led by three leading feminist legal scholars, Hilary Charlesworth, Regina Graycar and Jenny Morgan. While welcoming the majority's adoption of a more contextual approach to discrimination, the minority disagreed with the idea of an equality guarantee, limited to the public sphere, that did not focus on women's disadvantage *exclusively*:

> **The equality guarantee.** ... Legislation that is separate from anti-discrimination legislation, dealing more fundamentally with equality in law, could be a powerful

---

91 J Gregory, *Sex, Race and the Law*, Sage, 1987, 66.
92 ALRC 69 undertook a wide-ranging examination of how the law and legal system discriminates against women, addressing procedural and substantive issues. After reading this two-volume report, the reader may be left with the feeling that, notwithstanding the large body of feminist critique, feminist activism and more than 25 years of anti-discrimination legislation, little has been achieved to advance the interests of women.
93 ALRC 69, *Equality Before the Law*, Part II, 1994 at para 3.29.
94 Ibid para 4.26.

force to advance women's equality. We also agree generally with the recommendations as to how it would operate, although, unlike the majority, we think the equality guarantee should extend in full to actions in the so-called private sphere (discussed further below). We endorse, in particular, that part of the majority's definition of equality which insists on turning to the context of a law or practice to decide whether there is a real or practical inequality.

The basic disagreement between us and the majority of the Commissioners is whether the guarantee of equality should apply "for the benefit of both women and men" or for the benefit of women only. In our view, an equality guarantee should apply only for the benefit of women. Hence our preferred starting point is an Act, a Status of Women Act which states that

Every woman has the right to equality in law.[95]

A decade on, neither the recommendations of the majority nor the minority have been implemented by the federal government. The areas of consensus and conflict within ALRC Report No 69 mirror the theoretical divisions between liberal and cultural feminists, as well traversing critical and postmodern perspectives on the issue of discrimination.

Most feminists today have abandoned the utopian idea that discrimination can be addressed simply by "consciousness raising" – indeed, the inescapable political and juridical power of equality has led some feminists to a more realistic position of working within existing frameworks. Indeed, several feminists have begun the task of "normative reconstruction", sketching out a new legal vision of equality in wider terms such as "equality as acceptance" or "equality as respect for difference".[96]

(d) Conclusion

It is undeniable that there have been some significant legal reforms aimed at improving the treatment of women by the legal system. In the criminal context Celia Wells, a leading feminist scholar, has concluded: "Viewing criminal law and justice through a feminist lens has revealed both profound transformations and 'business as usual'".[97] Profound transformations take the form of changes to the statute book – for example, rules of evidence and procedure that discriminate against women who allege sexual abuse have been removed or significantly modified. Yet, changes to the statute book do not, as we emphasised throughout this book, always have the desired impact. Empirical studies have demonstrated that, notwithstanding significant reforms to the law, it remains "business as usual". In the field of rape law, in particular, empirical studies cast doubt on the view that law reform has produced significant improvements to the treatment of victims by the legal process.[98] In relation to judicial development of the common law, it is

---

95 Ibid paras 16.19, 16.22.

96 Lacey, n 4, 239-241, discussing the work of feminist theorists, Drucilla Cornell and Luce Irigaray.

97 C Wells, "The Impact of Feminist Thinking on Criminal Law and Justice: Contradiction, Complexity, Conviction and Connection" [2004] *Crim Law Review* 503 at 515.

98 See Department of Women (NSW), *Heroines of Fortitude* (1996); Department of Justice (Vic), *Rape Law Reform Evaluation Project – The Crimes (Rape) Act 1991* (1997). See generally G Mason, "Reforming the Law of Rape" in Kirkby, n 36, Ch 4. For a useful collection of essays exploring these reforms and empirical research, see P Easteal (ed), *Balancing the Scales: Rape, Law Reform and Australian Culture*, Federation Press, 1998; G Mason, "Reforming the Law of Rape" in Kirkby, n 36, Ch 4.

also possible to point to a number of cases where the judiciary sought to rectify discriminatory aspects of the criminal law (such as abolishing the marital rape immunity and widening the basis for the defence of provocation and self-defence for women who kill their abusive partners). However, these landmark decisions cannot really be heralded as evidence of feminism's success, since few of them made use of the significant feminist literature or campaigns by feminists on these topics.[99]

Feminist inspired reforms have failed to deliver on their promises, due to a range of legal and non-legal reasons. Law has limited capacity to produce major transformations in social relations, especially in areas that lie beyond the public sphere. The example of marital or spousal rape is illustrative. While the legal hurdles to prosecuting this type of rape have been largely removed, discriminatory attitudes of police, prosecutors and judges during investigation, trial and sentencing continue to downgrade the seriousness of non-stranger rape (rape by a spouse, partner or acquaintance).[100] As Lacey concludes, the law has only limited potential to achieve sexual equality in some fields, such as marriage, "because of all sorts of other flows of power – economic power being significant among them – which cannot be affected except by very radical social change which cannot be engendered directly by legal means".[101]

The chapter has explored the various strands of feminism and feminist critique of law, providing a thumbnail sketch of the evolution of feminist legal theory. The feminist enterprise has had a number of objectives – to challenge the way in which justice and law's truth is understood, and how liberal legal values such as autonomy, privacy and equality, have failed in large measure to deliver justice for women. Some feminists doubt the value and effectiveness of addressing discrimination through liberal ideas such as equality: an idea that requires women to be treated like men, with an implicit normative standard of comparison structured around male needs and interests. Equality of opportunity, and affirmative action, repackage those concepts, but are susceptible to the same criticisms. That said, engagement with liberalism and its arguments seems unavoidable for feminism – as we have demonstrated in this chapter, it remains the dominant legal philosophical paradigm within which much feminist law reform is debated.

Questions

1. Consider the following statements:

   When carefully scrutinised, legal doctrines do not 'embody' male values. Rather law tends to be imprinted with a liberal (rather than inherently male) set of values or attributes, in particular those of individual autonomy, rationality and impartiality etc. These values or attributes are no more or less male or female.

   Simply broadening the 'reasonable man' standard to include the 'reasonable women' or 'reasonable person' does not change the fundamental liberal character of the legal subject.

   Discuss in light of the readings and research reviewed in this chapter.

---

99   Wells, n 97, 508, 515.

100   Ibid 515.

101   Lacey, n 4, 241.

2.   The dissenting Law Commissioners in ALRC 69 *Equality Before the Law: Justice for Women* were concerned that legislating for equality between the sexes often backfires on women, and does little to remedy the disadvantage faced by women especially in the private sphere. Do you agree with the minority's approach that the proposed Equality Act should confer the right of equality on women *only*. Would this approach work? How should the concept of equality be understood when the critical point of comparison (male) is removed from the guarantee? Would this approach be more effective in remedying the disadvantages that women face than our existing approaches to and conceptions of equality?

3.   Review the policies, terms and conditions governing any aspect of your current employment, university enrolment or club/association membership. Are there any aspects of these which you consider to be either directly or indirectly discriminatory on the grounds of gender? If there is different treatment, is it justifiable? Are there any special provisions dealing with pregnancy/parenting etc, and do you think these are discriminatory? What anti-discrimination laws (at State, Territory and Commonwealth level) apply? Do you think that these available laws and remedies are effective?

4.   Divide the class into groups. Each group should identify one case that you have studied in an introductory course (eg torts, contracts, corporations law or criminal law) where the issue of gender, expressly or impliedly, has influenced the outcome of the decision or prompted law reform. The groups should discuss the significance of their selected case and need for reform in light of the themes and ideas raised in this chapter.

Chapter 9

Race and Multiculturalism

(a)   Introduction

> The issue of race is culturally and socially constructed and structured, directly or indirectly, by relations of power.[1]

The concept of race is often used to distinguish between different groups in a society. Fundamentally, as the above quote states, race is a social, political and cultural construct. While we may describe ourselves as Aboriginal, Anglo-Saxon-Celtic, Asian or even European in background these apparently stable cultural constructions contain elements of unity and disunity. Lumping people who descend from Celts in with Anglo-Saxons, a common tendency in Australia, may provoke a fierce reaction from those of Irish and Scottish descent![2] The point here is that race is a construct that is malleable as well as historically contingent. Attempts to impose scientific classification on race – a large focus of the disciplinary efforts of 19th century biological and social sciences such as anthropology – often concealed a political mission to discover, distinguish and contain the perceived threats from "inferior races". Much of the scientific work in the 19th century provided the basis for the new science of eugenics, and ultimately the manifesto for genocide in many parts of the world. As we shall see below, the law's approach to race has simply reflected and responded to the rival disciplinary discourses that have attempted to classify, systematise and ultimately regulate the human condition.

In this chapter, the position of Indigenous peoples in Australia is given prominence. For them, race has been encoded into law and justice, either expressly or implicitly, since their first contact with "Europeans". Today, race-based legislation has been expunged from Australia's statute books. As we shall see below, race as a formal legal category exists only in legislative provisions that outlaw race discrimination and racial vilification at federal, State and Territory

---

1   B Morris, "Racism, egalitarianism and aborigines" (1990) 3 *Jnl Social Justice Studies* 61 at 63.

2   In the High Court decision of *Masciantonio v The Queen* (1995) 183 CLR 58, McHugh J rejected the objective standard of self-control in the provocation defence on the grounds that the juries would judge the accused by "the standard of self-control attributed to a middle class Australian of Anglo-Saxon-Celtic heritage, that being the stereotype of the ordinary person with which the jurors are most familiar": at 73. Although the labels "Anglo-Celtic" and "Anglo-Saxon-Celtic" are commonly used in Australia, implying an inappropriate homogeneity between the English and the Celts, there are strong claims that the Celts themselves (the Scots and Welsh, as well as the Irish) have suffered from colonialism at the hands of the English. See M Hechter, *Internal Colonialism*, Routledge and Kegan Paul, 1975, and T Nairn, *The Break-Up of Britain*, New Left Books, 1977.

levels. Notwithstanding reforms of the "law in the books", we shall see that the "law in action" continues to be a site of oppression for many minorities.

Legal discussion about race often tends to focus on "difference" in negative terms as discrimination against individuals and groups. Departing from the approach adopted in previous editions, we will also focus on difference in positive terms as the challenge to promote multiculturalism within Australian law. The legal issues raised by Aboriginal rights and multiculturalism are often considered separately. The Australian Law Reform Commission adopted this approach when examining multiculturalism in the 1990s.[3] While some of the arguments about the failure of Australian law to recognise Aboriginal culture can certainly be applied with equal force to other groups who do not come from Anglo-Saxon-Celtic backgrounds, there are significant differences. Indeed, the status and recognition of Aboriginal laws, often called "customary laws", within our legal system raises particular questions more closely related to sovereignty and self-determination than the cultural sensitivity of Australian law. Moreover, the treatment of Aboriginal peoples has been, and continues to be, so markedly unjust that it warrants treatment on its own. As Murphy J once noted:

> The history of the Aboriginal people of Australia since European settlement is that they have been the subject of unprovoked aggression, conquest, pillage, rape brutalization, attempted genocide and systematic and unsystematic destruction of their culture.[4]

This distinctive history leads some people to support an idea of multiculturalism in Australia that does not actually include Aboriginal peoples.[5] This chapter adopts a more pluralist approach to culture, though paying special attention to how Aboriginal people, their culture and laws are disadvantaged, both historically and currently, under the Australian legal system.

(b)   The legal construction of race and multiculturalism

A central concern related to both issues of race and multiculturalism is discrimination. Australian anti-discrimination legislation largely owes its existence to international human rights treaties which prohibit discrimination on the grounds of race, as well as other characteristics.[6] The key federal provision is the *Racial Discrimination Act 1975* (Cth) which was adopted following Australia's ratification of the International Convention for the Elimination of All Forms of Racial

---

3   ALRC Report No 31, *The Recognition of Aboriginal Customary Laws*, AGPS, 1988; ALRC Report No 57, *Multiculturalism and the Law*, AGPS, 1992.

4   *Commonwealth v Tasmania* (1983) 158 CLR 1 at 180.

5   The Social Justice Collective, *Inequality in Australia*, Heinemann, 1991, 194.

6   *Discrimination Act 1991* (ACT); *Anti-Discrimination Act 1977* (NSW); *Anti-Discrimination Act 1992* (NT); *Anti-Discrimination Act 1991* (Qld); *Equal Opportunity Act 1984* (SA) and the *Racial Vilification Act 1996* (SA); *Anti-Discrimination Act 1998* (Tas); *Equal Opportunity Act 1995* (Vic) and the *Racial and Religious Tolerance Act 2001* (Vic); *Equal Opportunity Act 1984* (WA). See N O'Neill, S Rice and R Douglas, *Retreat from Injustice: Human Rights in Australia*, 2nd ed, Federation Press, 2004. The International Covenant on Civil and Political Rights contains a similar provision in Art 26, which states that "the law shall prohibit any discrimination and guarantee to all persons equal and effective protection against discrimination on any ground such as race, colour, sex, language, religion, political or other opinion, national or social origin, property, birth or other status".

Discrimination (CERD). Yet the *Racial Discrimination Act* has no statutory definition of race, leaving the High Court to define the concept in specific contexts. By contrast, anti-discrimination legislation at State and Territory level has included statutory definitions. For example, "race" is broadly defined in the New South Wales anti-discrimination legislation as including physical or cultural criteria such as colour, nationality, descent, national origin, ethnicity and ethno-religious identity.[7] The Australian Capital Territory has recently adopted the first Bill of Rights in Australia. The *Human Rights Act 2004* (ACT), following the approach in the International Covenant on Civil and Political Rights (ICCPR), has recognised a right to equality before the law and equal protection of the law without discrimination (s 8). "Race" is included as one of the examples of discrimination along with colour, sex, gender etc. The Act also protects the rights of minorities, specifically the right of individuals from ethnic, religious and linguistic minorities, with other members of the minority, to enjoy their culture, declare and practise their religion or use language (s 27). These provisions raise questions about the scope and limits of legal definitions of race.

In the specific context of laws dealing with Aboriginal people, Australian law has a long history of attempting to define and categorise Aboriginality. "Protection" statutes enacted in the colonial period contained elaborate pseudo-scientific classifications based on *degrees* of Aboriginality. Peggy Brock has noted that 67 distinct legal classifications of race have been identified in Australian colonial legislation:

> These classifications defined Aboriginal people, but not other groups in Austra-lia, in racial terms. This contrasts with apartheid policies in South Africa where everyone was defined in terms of fixed racial categories and relations between these categories were stringently controlled by law. Nevertheless, a caste system was constructed under Australian law, but only for people of Aboriginal descent. There were "full bloods", "three quarter castes", "half castes", "quarter castes" (also referred to as "quadroons") and "octoroons". These people were all defined as Aboriginal despite their European-Australian (or Chinese-Australian etc) descent.[8]

From a modern perspective, classifications based on the "quantum of blood" are offensive and discriminatory and have been removed entirely from the statute books. That said, the law continues to grapple with defining the contours and limits of the concept of "race" in the context of anti-discrimination laws, since discrimination on the grounds of race or racial characteristics is one of the pro-scribed grounds.

Also in the field of constitutional law, the High Court has had to consider the meaning and scope of the "race" power under s 51 of the Constitution. Section 51(xxvi) states that the Commonwealth Parliament may make laws with respect to: "The people of any race for whom it is deemed necessary to make special laws". Section 51(xxvi) was initially drafted as empowering the Commonwealth to make laws with respect to "The people of any race, *other than the aboriginal race*

---

7   Section 4 of the *Anti-Discrimination Act 1977* (NSW); see also *Discrimination Act 1991* (ACT) Dictionary; *Racial and Religious Tolerance Act 2001* (Vic) s 3.

8   "Aboriginal families and the law in the era of segregation and assimilation, 1890s-1950s" in D Kirkby (ed), *Sex Power and Justice: Historical Perspectives on Law in Australia*, Oxford UP, 1995, 134.

in any State, for whom it is deemed necessary to make special laws" (emphasis added). The provision was supplemented by s 127, a provision titled "Aborigines not to be counted in reckoning population", that stated that "In reckoning the numbers of people of the Commonwealth, or of a State or any other part of the Commonwealth, aboriginal natives shall not be counted". Section 127 and the italicised part of s 51(xxvi) were deleted from the Constitution following a referendum in 1967.

The origins of the race power lie in an initial desire to limit the movement within Australia of certain races; consequently s 51(xxvi) was included in the Constitution to ensure that the Commonwealth would have the power to legislate over ethnic minorities.[9] A majority of founders stated that they wanted the ability to discriminate and maintain the power to impose racially discriminatory laws, including the ability to exclude certain racial groups from entering and remaining in Australia. Brennan quotes Sir John Forrest's speech to the Convention, "It is of no use for us to shut our eyes to the fact that there is a great feeling all over Australia against the introduction of coloured persons. It goes without saying that we do not like to talk about it, but it is still so", suggesting that one motivation was to limit the movement of the Chinese.[10] Blackshield and Williams note the speech of Sir Edmund Barton at the 1898 Convention in Melbourne, arguing that the power was necessary to "regulate the affairs of the people of coloured or inferior races who are in the Commonwealth".[11] This view was dominant but not exclusive. Blackshield and Williams also make note of some who spoke against the race power such as Josiah Symon QC who stated: "It is monstrous to put a brand on these people when you admit them. It is degrading to us and our citizenship to do such a thing. If we say they are fit to be admitted amongst us, we ought not to degrade them by putting on them a brand of inferiority".[12]

The history of s 51(xxvi) and the High Court's approach to its interpretation reflects the wider concern about rigidity of classifying and delimiting race in scientific or quasi-scientific terms. The High Court upheld a law protecting Aboriginal artefacts and relics under the races power in the *Commonwealth v Tasmania* ("*Tasmanian Dam Case*"). In this case the High Court held that

---

9   T Blackshield and G Williams, *Australian Constitutional Law and Theory: Commentary and Materials*, 4th ed, Federation Press, 2006, 987.

10 F Brennan, "Race, the Constitution and reconciliation" *Strategies Against Racism Forum*, Ethnic Communities Council of New South Wales, 16 June 1997. At beginning of the 20th century, the newly federated colonies strived to promote Australia as a British society. Race had become a pressing political concern through the 19th century with Chinese migration targeted as a source of cheap labour and "cultural contamination". As well as imposing limits on Chinese migration, laws were adopted to regulate the "Chinese vices" including opium smoking. The racial aspects of new drug legislation were apparent at their inception. The *Sale and Use of Poisons Act 1891* (Qld) prohibited the supply of "any opium to aboriginal natives of Australia or half caste of that race except for medicinal purposes". While formally neutral, this Act was in fact directed against the Chinese customary usage of opium as a means of barter and exchange. The first drug laws in Australia were the products of xenophobia, economic protectionism and paternalism toward Aboriginal people. It is important to appreciate that the restrictions on dealing in opiates were directed only to opium suitable for smoking and did not restrict its widespread medicinal use. These issues are explored in D Manderson, *From Mr Sin to Mr Big – A History of Australian Drug Laws*, Oxford UP, 1993.

11 *Official Record of the Debates of the Australasian Federal Convention* (1891-1898), reprinted Legal Books 1986), Vol 4, Melbourne 1898; excerpted from Blackshield and Williams, n 9, 987.

12 Ibid.

Tasmanian Aboriginals fell within the race power, with Brennan J promoting a broad definition of race:

> Though the biological element is … an essential element of membership of a race, it does not ordinarily exhaust the characteristics of a racial group. Physical similarities, and a common history, a common religion or spiritual beliefs and a common culture are factors that tend to create a sense of identity among members of a race and to which others have regard in identifying people as members of a race. As the people of a group identify themselves and are identified by others as a race by reference to their common history, religion, spiritual beliefs or culture as well as by reference to their biological origins and physical similarities, an indication is given of the scope and purpose of the power granted by para (xxvi). The kinds of benefits that laws might properly confer upon people as members of a race are benefits which tend to protect or foster their common intangible heritage or their common sense of identity. Their genetic inheritance is fixed at birth; the historic, religious, spiritual and cultural heritage are acquired and are susceptible to influences for which a law may provide. The advancement of the people of any race in any of these aspects of their group life falls within the power.[13]

The court, perhaps mindful of avoiding criticism about cultural essentialism, added no further indicators of Aboriginality. Indeed, this definitional approach was endorsed by the Australian Law Reform Commission in ALRC Report No 31, *The Recognition of Aboriginal Customary Laws* (1986):

> **95. The Commission's View**
>
> Experience under Commonwealth and State legislation suggests that it is not necessary to spell out a detailed definition of who is an Aborigine, and that there are distinct advantages in leaving the application of the definition to be worked out, so far as is necessary, on a case by case basis. Constitutionally this presents no difficulties, as the High Court's decision is *Commonwealth v Tasmania* show. On the other hand, it has sometimes been suggested that a special and more restrictive definition of "traditional Aborigine" should be adopted for the purposes of this Report and its implementation. There are several reasons why such a special definition is both unnecessary and undesirable. Restrictive definitions of this kind have not been adopted in other related contexts. Experience so far does not suggest a need for more stringent definitions. The application of the Commission's recommendations in appropriate cases is to be achieved by the substantive requirements of the provision in question, and by related evidentiary requirements. Indeed, there may be cases where it is appropriate that provisions for the recognition of Aboriginal customary laws should apply to persons who are not Aborigines. These questions have to be considered on their merits, and cannot be resolved through the adoption of any more-or-less restrictive definition of "traditional Aborigine". (footnotes omitted).

Ultimately it is important to recognise the political context of law's attempt to construct "identity". For example, the following passage puts forcefully the claim that Aboriginality and powerlessness are closely related:

> Powerlessness means, among other things, having others say who you are, with the naming usually counting against you. Aborigines have been rendered largely invisible and Aboriginal rights have been effectively denied throughout much of

---

13   (1983) 158 CLR 1 at 244.

white Australian history. Who is "really" Aboriginal, and what flows from that, has been laid down by governments, policemen, local officials and, more recently, anthropologists. Many Australians still make a distinction between "real" Aborigines (usually presumed tribal/traditional/"full-blood") and "part" and/or urban Aborigines – despite the discrediting of genetic determinism, and the fact that many "urban" Aborigines know and have close links with country and kin. Such distinctions are not only personally and socially offensive and hurtful; they also have powerful political functions in challenging many Aborigines' right to speak for, or even about, Aboriginal claims.[14]

Multiculturalism emerges in the late 20th century as the obverse of ethnocentric mono-culturalism, demanding that the state and society more generally must respect, protect and celebrate the cultural and ethnic differences of individuals. The idea of "culture" comes to displace "race" as the critical identity being protected. In the Australian context, the key policy framework for multiculturalism was adopted in 1989, when the federal government published *A National Agenda for a Multicultural Australia*. This document promoted the value of cultural and social diversity, though its rationale was fundamentally related to protecting core liberal values and rights of individuals, especially the right not to be discriminated against on the basis of race, religion or culture. The centrality of equality to the idea of multiculturalism resonates strongly with the liberal philosophical foundations of law, explored in Chapter 2. As the National Agenda concluded:

> Fundamentally, multiculturalism is about the rights of the individual – the right to equality of treatment; to be able to express one's identity; to be accepted as an Australian without having to assimilate to some stereotyped model of behaviour.[15]

In legal terms, multiculturalism in Australia is viewed as a manifestation of the *individual* right to equality, rather than a *communal* right to enjoy their culture, religion or language.

As a result of this political initiative in 1989, multiculturalism was placed on the national law reform agenda. The Australian Law Reform Commission was asked to undertake a major review of family law, civil and criminal law to determine whether the underlying principles of law and dispute resolution methods "take adequate account of the cultural diversity present in the Australian community".[16] The challenge, as we shall explore below, is whether the liberal promise of equality before the law can in fact respect and protect cultural and group-based difference. In Chapter 8 we examined how feminism continues to struggle with equality, with many scholars expressing concern that this universal and fundamental value has only limited capacity to tackle structural disadvantage and remedy the continuing subordination of women. The feminist debates about equality and difference resonate in the field of race and multiculturalism.

---

14 J Pettman, "Learning about power and powerlessness: Aborigines and white Australia's bicentenary" (1988) 29(20) *Race and Class* 69 at 75-76.

15 Commonwealth of Australia, Office of Multicultural Affairs, *National Agenda for a Multicultural Australia*, AGPS, 1989; discussed in L McNamara, "Regulating racism: racial vilification laws in Australia", Institute of Criminology, University of Sydney Law School, 2002.

16 ALRC Report No 57, n 3, Terms of Reference.

This chapter is a selective overview of the legal debates about race and multiculturalism. Our aim is not to construct the "whole story" of oppression and discrimination of Aboriginal peoples, and other disadvantaged ethnic and cultural minorities. Rather the aim is to examine how liberalism and the rule of law – embodied in principles like equality before the law – struggle to accommodate different systems of law (that is legal pluralism) as well as cultural difference. We encourage readers to pursue further these topics through the specialised texts on racial discrimination included in the footnotes.

(c) Rethinking Aboriginal (in)justice: the recognition of Aboriginal law

An essential element of liberalism and the rule of law is the ideal that all persons stand equal before the law. As noted in Chapter 2, these claims to equality are powerful legitimating forces in legal culture. Yet it is clear that the law has not been able to eradicate inequalities based upon social class, gender and race – the law and legal arena is not able to remedy many (if any) of the structural causes of disadvantage.

Part of law's failure to live up to its liberal promise lies in the contested definitions of equality. In Chapter 8 we explored from the perspective of gender the logic of equality and the limitations which affect its various manifestations, including formal and substantive equality and remedial concepts such as equality of opportunity. As we shall explore below, in relation to treatment of Aboriginal people, in both earlier colonial and modern times, the law does not always deliver on its promise of equality. Contemporary criminal justice policies such as "zero tolerance" and mandatory sentencing are often justified by reference to equality before the law; however, there is mounting evidence suggesting that these policies of treating "all persons the same" may in fact compound the suffering of disadvantaged groups.[17]

(i) Our colonial legacy: terra nullius and legal fictions?

At a fundamental level, law seems to espouse a commitment to "one law for all". During the colonial period, however, Aboriginal people were not generally recognised as rights holders especially in relation to land. On one view, Aboriginal persons should have been regarded as British subjects from the outset benefiting from the protection of the received English common law and statutes. Although silent on the precise legal status of "natives" and their laws, Governor Phillip's Instructions suggest that Aboriginal people were to be protected by English law against predation by the British colonists:

---

17 Mandatory sentencing policies were adopted in Australia during the mid-1990s, modelled on the United States federal policy of "Three Strikes and You're Out": see *Criminal Code* (WA) s 401 (adults and juveniles); *Sentencing Act 1995* (NT) s 78A (adults); *Juvenile Justice Act 1996* (NT) s 53(1) (juveniles). Responding to community concern about inconsistent sentencing and excessive lenient sentences for some minority groups, these reforms limited judicial discretion. They have been trenchantly criticised by researchers and judges, as well as the United Nations Human Rights Committee: see S Bronitt and B McSherry, *Principles of Criminal Law*, 2nd ed, Lawbook Co, 2005, 138ff. The Northern Territory provisions were repealed in 2001 following a change of government.

You are to endeavour, by every possible means to open an intercourse with the natives, and to conciliate their affections, enjoining all our subjects to live in amity and kindness with them. And if any of our subjects shall wantonly destroy them, or give them any unnecessary interruptions in the exercise of their several occupations, it is our will and pleasure that you do cause such offenders to be brought to punishment according to the degree of the offence.[18]

While Aborigines were supposed to enjoy the legal protection due to them as British subjects, in fact, their status remained ambiguous. In David Neal's terms, Aboriginal people were "some hybrid of outlaw, foreign enemy and protected race [to whom] the rule of law provided cold comfort".[19]

It would be wrong to assume that this colonial legal blind spot was solely related to the impoverished state of civil society in a penal settlement comprised largely of felons and military officers. From early colonial court records, it is clear that the many of the key ideas behind the rule of law, particularly legality and procedural justice, were not ignored. Rather, these ideas of justice played a critical role in legitimising and limiting the powers of government during the colonial period. In an era before the establishment of responsible government in the Australian colonies, the courts provided the only forum for challenging the absolute powers of the Governor. The idea of legality and equality before the law meant that Governors and their officials were "not above the law". As the early colonial litigation records reveal, convicts routinely were able to challenge abuses of power by public officials, justices of the peace and landowners before the courts, and also to recover substantial damages.[20]

Convicts had rights to sue particularly in relation to property that simply would have been denied them following their conviction in England through the doctrine of attainder.[21] Why then were the legal rights of Aboriginal people (who had not been subject to the legal disability of the convict's taint) overlooked? There are competing theories as to why Governor Phillip had no instructions from the Imperial government as to the status of Aboriginal rights when he arrived with the First Fleet in 1788. Perhaps it was because the British believed that Australia was virtually uninhabited or *terra nullius* – a legal concept explored further below. Or perhaps it was a result of a view by European colonial powers that Aboriginal inhabitants were too "primitive" to negotiate a Treaty or that their nomadic way of life precluded them from any legitimate claim to the land as had happened with the Maori in New Zealand and some First Nations peoples of Canada. Through a combination of these beliefs, and the practical difficulties of accessing courts of justice, Aboriginal people figuratively and legally speaking were rendered outlaws. Conversely, the convicts, the true outlaws, were able to access a legal system that recognised and vindicated their rights and interests.[22]

---

18   Barton, "Phillip's Instructions" (1889), 481, 483, 485, 486 excerpted from H McRae, G Nettheim, L Beacroft, *Indigenous Legal Issues: Commentary and Materials*, 2nd ed, Law Book Co, 1997, 33.

19   D Neal, *The Rule of Law in a Penal Colony*, Cambridge UP, 1991, 78, 151.

20   Ibid 67. See also Bruce Kercher, *The Unruly Child: A History of Law in Australia*, Allen and Unwin, 1995.

21   The doctrine of attainder stripped convicted felons of all civil rights, including the right to hold property and institute legal proceedings: Bronitt and McSherry, n 17, 96ff.

22   John Braithwaite has suggested that the role of procedural justice for convicts in the 18th and 19th centuries was crucial in promoting reintegration, rehabilitation and the transformation of Australia to a low crime society: "Crime in a Convict Republic" (2001) 64(1) *Modern Law Review* 11.

Terra nullius, an undoubted legal fiction, survived as the accepted legal basis of Australia's colonisation until the High Court decision in *Mabo* in 1992.[23] Before *Mabo*, the conventional legal view was that the continent of Australia was *terra nullius*: a land belonging to no one.[24] As a "settled" territory, there was no scope to recognise Aboriginal laws. Until this legal fiction was ousted by *Mabo*, the law did not recognise native land rights unless these rights were created by legislation.[25] Notwithstanding 40,000 years of inhabitation by Indigenous peoples, it was only in 1982, when Eddie Koiki Mabo and his fellow claimants commenced proceedings against Queensland and the Commonwealth, that Australian courts were presented with the critical legal issue of whether the existence of customs and traditions incorporating traditional rights and interests to land delivered enforceable property rights to Indigenous people known to the common law.

The claimants in *Mabo*, all members of the Meriam people, brought proceedings in the original jurisdiction of the High Court seeking declarations that they held traditional native title to lands and waters in the Murray Islands of the Torres Strait which had not been extinguished by colonisation or subsequent government legislative action. The *Mabo* litigation lasted for 10 years and resulted in two separate Full Court decisions of the High Court. In the final decision, handed down on 3 June 1992, the Court held by a 6:1 majority that the Australian common law did recognise the pre-existing land rights of Indigenous peoples. As a result they found that the Meriam people were entitled against the whole world to the possession, occupation, use and enjoyment of the Murray Islands.

The decision involved a re-examination of the classification of Australia as *terra nullius*, which was the basis for the acquisition of sovereignty over uninhabited lands by colonising nations. Brennan J described the application of such a notion to the continent of Australia as "false in fact"[26] and the High Court found that native title to land survived the Crown's acquisition of sovereignty and radical title. As we shall see in the next section, the decision has had profound impact upon Aboriginal peoples, most significantly, empowering them, beyond the arena of land rights, with a new legal vocabulary in which Aboriginal rights, customs and laws can be expressed and potentially recognised under Australian law. The decision in *Mabo* left the doctrine of settlement undisturbed, though it did open a basis for argument, by analogy with native title, that Aboriginal

---

23   *Mabo v Queensland (No 2)* (1992) 175 CLR 1 (*"Mabo"*).

24   A key decision affirming this was the Privy Council ruling in *Cooper v Stuart* (1889) 14 App Cas 286 that the colony of New South Wales was "peacefully annexed" rather than conquered, because, at the time, it "consisted of a tract of territory practically unoccupied": at 291. Until 1992, the High Court accepted this view, with some significant dissent from Murphy J who described it as a "convenient falsehood": *Coe v Commonwealth* (1979) 24 ALR 118 at 138. Gibbs J, for the majority in this case, continued to affirm the view that "settled colony" theory was "fundamental": at 129.

25   The first piece of legislation to do so was the *Aboriginal Land Rights (Northern Territory) Act 1976* (Cth). The Act established a legislative regime of land rights in the Northern Territory under which traditional owners could make land claims over various areas of land listed as available for claim. It was enacted following the findings and recommendations of the Woodward inquiry into Aboriginal land rights in 1974: Commonwealth of Australia, *Commissions of Inquiry: Aboriginal Land Rights Commission*, AE Woodward, 8 February 1973–17 July 1974. The inquiry was established by the federal government in response to the decision of Blackburn J in *Milirrpum v Nabalco Pty Ltd* (*Gove Land Rights Case*) (1971) 17 FLR 141.

26   *Mabo v Queensland (No 2)* (1992) 175 CLR 1 at 40 per Brennan J.

criminal laws (including customary defences) may have survived British occupation. As Deane and Gaudron JJ observed in *Mabo*:

> The common law so introduced was adjusted in accordance with the principle that, in settled colonies, only so much of it was introduced as was "reasonably applicable to the circumstances of the colony". This left room for the continued operation of some local laws or customs among the native people and even the incorporation of some of those laws and customs as part of the common law.[27]

This issue of recognition of Aboriginal law is often represented politically as a question of Aboriginal sovereignty or self-determination. Although Aboriginal sovereignty is sometimes invoked in political debate, most representatives of Aboriginal groups in Australia conceptualise the issue of governance in terms of a right to self-determination.[28] Drawn from the international human rights treaties, the "right to self-determination" suggests that colonised peoples are entitled to autonomy in a wide range of domains, and ultimately a right to liberation and independence. In the Australian context, Aboriginal claims of self-determination are not liberationist, but seek to use the language to self-determination to project human rights claims and some degree of autonomy in governance of their own communities. As Mick Dodson pointed out, in his role as the federal Aboriginal and Torres Strait Islander Social Justice Commissioner, "self determination is the river in which all other rights swim".[29]

The impact of *Mabo* on the domestic legal system was profound, raising some concern that federal, State and Territory law, in specific areas, could be ousted by "native jurisdiction". Shortly after *Mabo*, Professor Stanley Yeo, a leading criminal lawyer, wrote an article in which he suggested, by analogy with native title, that Aboriginal criminal jurisdiction survived unless it was expressly abrogated by parliament or executive action.[30] Yeo suggested that even if Aboriginal criminal jurisdiction was held to have been abrogated by the enactment of comprehensive criminal codes or legislation, *Mabo* provided a moral basis for its reinstatement as a gesture of reconciliation consistent with the trend toward recognition of Indigenous rights to self-determination or self-management.[31] This argument is an example of how debate about recognition of Aboriginal laws *within* the framework of Australian law slips into a wider discussion of self-determination.

The difficulty of reconciling different systems of law within the Australian legal system is apparent in the High Court's decision in *Walker v New South*

---

27   Ibid 79 per Deane and Gaudron JJ.

28   For a recent book exploring the concept and its implications for Australia, see B Hocking, *Unfinished Constitutional Business? Rethinking Indigenous Self Determination*, Aboriginal Studies Press, 2005. See also S Brennan, L Behrendt, L Strelein and G Williams, *Treaty*, Federation Press, 2005, which examines the processes of treaties in the United States, Canada and New Zealand, raising the question whether Australia too should go down the treaty path.

29   Quoted in C Cunneen, *Conflict, Politics and Crime – Aboriginal Communities and the Police*, Allen and Unwin, 2001, 240. As Cunneen notes, the Howard government abandoned the language of self-determination in favour of a diluted administrative concept of self-management and self-empowerment: at 242.

30   S Yeo, "Native criminal jurisdiction after Mabo" (1994) 6 *Current Issues in Criminal Justice* 9; S Yeo, "Editorial – recognition of aboriginal criminal jurisdiction" (1994) 18 *Criminal Law Journal* 193.

31   Yeo, "Editorial – recognition of aboriginal criminal jurisdiction", ibid, 196.

Wales.[32] This case concerned an attempt to claim, through the civil courts, that the Commonwealth and State parliaments lacked the power to legislate over Aboriginal people without their consent. During the course of oral argument, the plaintiff introduced a further argument that Aboriginal criminal customary law had not been extinguished by British settlement. Refusing leave to appeal, Mason CJ noted that an argument framed in terms of Indigenous sovereignty and rights of self-determination was doomed to failure, as it had been in *Mabo*. The second argument also failed on the ground that the proposed recognition of two concurrent, potentially overlapping, systems of criminal law was not only confusing to citizens – more fundamentally, it contradicted the principle of equality before the law:

> It is a basic principle that all people should stand equal before the law. A construction which results in different criminal sanctions applying to different persons for the same conduct offends that basic principle. The general rule is that an enactment applies to all persons and matters within the territory to which it extends, but not to any other persons and matters.... The presumption applies with added force in the case of the criminal law, which is inherently universal in its operation, and whose aims would otherwise be frustrated.[33]

Jennifer Nielsen and Gary Martin were highly critical of this passage in *Walker* and the use of equality to close down legal argument about the recognition of native criminal jurisdiction: "[T]his formal reading of the notion of equality is out of kilter with international jurisprudence, and so the continued denial of the Indigenous criminal justice system contravenes the cultural rights of Indigenous Australians".[34]

Even if some elements of the customary criminal law of Aboriginal peoples had survived settlement Mason CJ took the view that it had been subsequently extinguished by the passage of criminal statutes of general application, specifically in this context, the *Crimes Act 1900* (NSW).[35] In his view, no analogy could be drawn with native title:

> English criminal law did not, and Australian criminal law does not, accommodate an alternative body of law operating alongside it. There is nothing in *Mabo (No 2)* to provide any support at all for the proposition that criminal laws of general application do not apply to Aboriginal people.[36]

Walker seems to have laid to rest arguments about recognition of Aboriginal law through the development of common law doctrine, though the decision continues to raise the following questions:

- Is Mason CJ correct to claim that English and now Australian criminal law did not (and implicitly should not) recognise Aboriginal law?
- Does "equality before the law" preclude recognition of another system of law within our legal system?
- If not, what model(s) of parallel Aboriginal justice should we consider adopting in Australia?

---

32 (1994) 182 CLR 45.
33 *Walker v New South Wales* (1994) 182 CLR 45 at 49-50.
34 J Nielsen and G Martin, "Indigenous Australian peoples and human rights" in D Kinley (ed), *Human Rights in Australian Law*, Federation Press, 1998, 111. See further G Bird, G Martin and J Nielsen, *Majah: Indigenous Peoples and the Law*, Federation Press, 1996.
35 (1994) 182 CLR 45 at 50.
36 Ibid.

(ii)   Recognition of Aboriginal law: historical and comparative perspectives

By adopting a stronger historical and comparative approach, different perspectives on the interaction between Aboriginal systems of justice and the English common law can emerge. In the 18th century, *Blackstone's Commentaries*, reflecting the position under international law, summarised the various approaches to acquisition of territory, distinguishing between settled, ceded and conquered territories in the following terms:

> [I]f an uninhabited country by discovered and planted by English subjects, all the English laws are immediately there in force. For as the law is the birthright of every subject, so wherever they go they carry their laws with them. But in conquered or ceded countries, that have already laws of their own, the king may indeed alter and change those laws; but, till he does actually change them, the ancient laws of the country remain, unless such as are against the law of God, as in the case of an infidel country.[37]

These basic categories still apply, as Blackburn J in *Milirrpum v Nabalco Pty*[38] summarised:

> There is a distinction between settled colonies, where the land, being desert and uncultivated, is claimed by right of occupancy, and conquered or ceded colonies.... The difference between the laws of the two kinds of colony is that in those of the former kind all the English laws which are applicable to the colony are immediately in force there upon its foundation. In those of the latter kind, the colony already having law of its own, that law remains in force until altered.

As noted above, under the theory of "settled colonies" only so much English law (common law and statute) as appropriate to local conditions is received into the colonial legal system. It is sometimes claimed that, upon arrival of European settlers, the laws of England applied automatically to the whole continent to the exclusion of Aboriginal laws. The first edition of this book stated the formal legal position of Aborigines in these terms: "as a consequence of British settlement Aborigines became subject to British, and later Australian, law. Any rights which they may have had arising from their own system of law were extinguished by that very act of settlement".[39] But closer scrutiny of surviving historical material, some of it only recently uncovered through the research efforts of Bruce Kercher, reveals that the common law as received and applied in the early colonial period, consistent with practices in other British colonies, was far more pluralistic and fractured than conventional legal wisdom would have it.[40] Colonial law was a highly adaptive system of law, selectively importing (and ignoring) English legal rules on the grounds of their perceived suitability to local conditions.

It should be noted that this legal pluralism was not some colonial deviation. The English legal system was highly pluralistic, recognising multiple jurisdictions

---

37   *Blackstone's Commentaries*, 17th ed, 1830, Vol 1, 104-105.

38   *Milirrpum v Nabalco Pty Ltd (Gove Land Rights Case)* (1971) 17 FLR 141 at 201 per Blackburn J.

39   S Bottomley, N Gunningham and S Parker, *Law in Context*, 1st ed, Federation Press, 1991, 287 (footnotes omitted).

40   B Kercher, "Recognition of Indigenous Legal Autonomy in Nineteenth Century New South Wales" (1998) 4 *Indigenous Law Bulletin* 7. See B Kercher, "Publication of Forgotten Case Law of the New South Wales Supreme Court" (1998) 72 *Australian Law Journal* 876.

and bodies of law. Far from being a unitary and coherent system of law, the English legal system of the 18th and 19th centuries was jurisdictionally complex, with many competing and overlapping systems of legal norms. At its heart was the common law, administered centrally through the Royal Courts of Justice in London. However, the common law was supplemented by and competed with specialised and local courts applying their own legal rules (such as equity, maritime and ecclesiastical law). Courts competed for litigants' business and inevitably this generated jurisdictional conflict, the most famous being the historic struggle between the common law courts and courts of equity which was only resolved by the "fusion" of common law and equitable jurisdictions by legislation in the 19th century.[41] There were also many localised variations. Different localities within England developed their own customary rights and practices, particularly in relation to land. These were confined to specific regions, recognised both in local courts and also within the common law. By the 19th century, this complexity had became untenable, conflicting with the universalising tendency of the common law and parliament's efforts to eradicate local customs through the enactment of general statutes.[42]

This historical digression reveals that legal pluralism is not something alien to the traditions of English law. In fact, it is quite the reverse. No doubt familiar with this legal and jurisdictional complexity, early judges of the Australian colonies were initially prepared to accept that English law did not apply to "native tribes" particularly in relation to resolving disputes among themselves. This is clear from the case of *R v Ballard*.[43] In this recently uncovered case, the New South Wales Supreme Court, led by Forbes CJ, held that in the absence of legal authority to the contrary and consistent with practices of the North American colonies, English law had no application to crimes committed between Aborigines. In Forbes CJ's view, it was improper to interfere with the institutions of natural justice in which Aborigines redressed their wrongs by retaliation rather than through the courts.

What is interesting is that cases like *Ballard* have been largely forgotten in contemporary debate about the recognition of Aboriginal law.[44] The decision has been overshadowed by later cases such as *R v Jack Congo Murrell*[45] in which the New South Wales Supreme Court held that Aborigines were amenable to English law for offences committed against one another. Forbes CJ sat on both decisions, careful to distinguish the earlier decision of *Ballard* on the facts. However, the latter case is taken as effectively reversing the earlier decision. *Murrell* today is cited as legal authority for the point that Aboriginal customary law did not survive settlement – that the English common law applied to Aboriginal people even in relation to crimes committed amongst themselves As Kercher notes, interpreted in

---

41   P Parkinson, *Tradition and Change in Australian Law*, 3rd ed, Lawbook Co, 2005, 76ff. Interestingly, this fusion was delayed in the colonies, with New South Wales maintaining separation divisions of the Supreme Court until 1972: s 57 of the *Supreme Court Act 1970* (NSW).

42   19th century England witnessed much political and legal conflict over the enclosure of the "commons", a process which sought to displace or abolish customary rights in relation to land, especially those rights held communally rather than individually: see EP Thompson, *Customs in Common*, New Press, 1991.

43   [1829] NSWSC 26.

44   A point made by B Kercher in "*R v Ballard, R v Murrell* and *R v Bonjon*" (1998) 3(3) *Australian Indigenous Law Reporter* 410 at 412.

45   (1836) Legge 72.

this way, "[*Murrell*] has the dubious reputation of being the founding case for the application of the *terra nullius* doctrine in Australia".[46]

The point to draw from this discussion is that the theory of Australia as *terra nullius* and a "settled colony" did not necessarily deny a space for Aboriginal laws and systems of justice.[47] For nearly 50 years after 1788, Aboriginal and English systems of justice did co-exist, albeit uneasily, in defined spheres applying their own laws, systems of dispute resolution and punishments. As Kercher concludes this period of legal "first contact", manifested in cases like *Ballard*, is worthy of further critical attention:

> Not least because they are more consistent with the writings of Vattel [a distinguished international law scholar of the period] on the rights of nomadic peoples and … because they are more consistent with the rights of native peoples in other jurisdictions.[48]

This (re)reading of historical sources suggests that the denial of Aboriginal law and jurisdiction was not inevitable. However, as the 19th century proceeded, the spreading fiction of *terra nullius* and the arrival of more European "settlors" greedy to take land for cultivation, made it difficult, if not impossible, to preserve legal space in Australia for Aboriginal ways of doing justice.

From a comparative perspective we see a dramatically different approach to the legal recognition of the rights of Indigenous peoples especially in relation to land rights.[49] In the colonisation of New Zealand, a very different approach was taken. The Treaty of Waitangi (1840) ceded sovereignty to the British, while preserving a wide range of Maori rights. The significance of this development for the Maori is apparent today, with the Treaty occupying a central place in public debate. This is not to suggest that recognition of Indigenous law and rights was always benign or indeed beneficial to Indigenous peoples. There were clearly assimilationist tendencies in these colonial processes of recognising Indigenous practices as "rights". As English historian EP Thompson points out, in New Zealand, through the process of managing native title, the law radically redefined "communal" landholding:

> The Native Land Act of 1865 whose aim was to assimilate native rights to land "as nearly as possible to the ownership of land according to British law". Since British law could never recognise a communist legal personality, section 23 of the Act ordered that communal rights could not be vested in more than ten persons.[50]

---

46   Kercher, n 44, 410. Historical research has pointed out that while the courts took this formal position that Aboriginals were both subject to and protected by colonial law, "[n]ineteenth century colonial practice was quite capable of staying at a distance from indigenous law … there appears to have been a general reluctance to prosecute Aborigines for deaths arising within their own communities": see M Finnane, " 'Payback', Customary Law and Criminal Law in Colonised Australia" (2001) 29 *International Journal of the Sociology of Law* 293, 303.

47   See further B Kercher, "Native Title in the Shadows: the Origins of the Myth of *Terra Nullius* in Early New South Wales Courts" in G Blue, M Bunton, and R Crozier (eds), *Colonialism and the Modern World Order: Selected Studies*, ME Sharpe, 2002; B Kercher, "The recognition of aboriginal status and laws in the Supreme Court of New South Wales under Forbes CJ, 1824-1836" in A Buck, J McLaren and N Wright (eds), *Land and Freedom: Law, Property Rights and the British Diaspora*, Ashgate, 2001.

48   Kercher, n 44.

49   Thompson, n 42, 165-166, for a discussion of these various colonial approaches.

50   Ibid 166-167.

Historical and comparative perspectives provide powerful antidotes to legal and factual fictions such as *terra nullius*. The claim that English and Australian law never recognised parallel systems of Indigenous law and justice is not beyond challenge. Recognition could and did occur, with some courts recognising the legitimacy of Aboriginal laws albeit in defined spheres. The modern day denial of Aboriginal law is justified, according to Mason CJ in *Walker*, by reference to the fundamental principle of equality before the law, an idea which is rooted deeply in liberalism. It is the power of this principle and liberal theory more generally that continues to deny Indigenous claims for greater legal pluralism. Legal history and comparative legal analysis suggest otherwise. As we have demonstrated here, the historical denial of Aboriginal law and jurisdiction within our own system was neither inevitable nor followed in comparable colonial societies. We now turn our attention theoretically to whether the recognition of Aboriginal systems of law is compatible with liberal legal values such as legal certainty and equality before the law.

(iii) Recognition of Aboriginal law: liberal objections

Liberal philosophy embodies a number of core elements. As noted in Chapter 2, central to the idea of law's ability to protect liberty is the idea that laws must be clear and certain in their form and application. This permits individuals to know the law, and to regulate their conduct accordingly. A commonly heard objection to the recognition of Aboriginal laws (or indeed any other system of law such as Islamic law) is that these norms are "customary": that is, they are unwritten, "informal" and thus not easily accessible to individuals. It is claimed that it is difficult to obtain accurate information about what these customary laws are. These laws are not written down or codified, and significantly vary from one Aboriginal group to another.

The Australian Law Reform Commission (ALRC) in its Report on the *Recognition of Aboriginal Customary Laws*[51] noted how the characteristics of Aboriginal customary law, particularly the relative lack of visibility and failure to promulgate laws in advance, presented challenging obstacles for recognition within the Australian legal system. Indeed, as the ALRC noted, disclosure and publicity of Aboriginal laws could be criminal in some contexts: "some aspects of Aboriginal customary laws, especially concerning certain sacred and ritual matters, are secret, and disclosure to unqualified persons is a serious offence".[52] Underlying these concerns is a view that recognising such legal pluralism "is divisive and violates the principle of the unity of the law".[53] This argument, which some have termed "legal centralism" in opposition to legal pluralism, is that there should be one law for all and "that should be the law of the state, uniform for all persons, exclusive of all other law, and administered by a single set of state institutions".[54]

Another objection to legal pluralism is that, unless confined to a particular geographical territory, jurisdiction in relation to Aboriginal law would be deter-

---

51   ALRC Report No 31, n 3.
52   Ibid para 115.
53   Ibid para 166.
54   J Griffiths, "What is legal pluralism?" (1986) 24 *Jnl of Legal Pluralism* 1 at 3.

mined on the basis of one's *status* as a member of a particular race. Reading all of these objections together gives us a clear impression of the powerful hold that liberal values exert on the recognition debate. The objections invoke most of the rule of law ideals discussed in Chapter 3, most prominently, that laws should be promulgated in advance, as well as being certain and general in their application.

These objections to the recognition of Aboriginal law are not, however, irrefutable. A concern that Aboriginal law resides in the hands of an unelected caste of knowledgeable elders seems to be one that may equally be levelled at the Australian legal system: appointed judges are tasked with adjudication of disputes applying and in some cases developing the law from the particular context of the disputes presented to them.[55] The structural difference between Aboriginal "customary" law and Australian common law is less stark if we reject the positivist "rule book" concept of law, a model which, as we explored in Chapter 3, is descriptively and normatively contestable.

Lack of legal certainty presents problems, but it should not be overstated. Definition in law is often left hazy by the legislature and the courts. Legal scholars and senior judges can fashion careers pursuing the elusive task of promoting legal certainty. Notwithstanding these levels of uncertainty, the current system of law continues to work tolerably well. As we have noted in Chapter 5, in the context of litigation, the indeterminacy of legal rules will be negotiated by the parties without even recourse to the courts. Indeed, many disputes over native title are resolved, to the satisfaction of the parties, without necessarily resorting to a judicial hearing to determine the validity of those claims.[56]

Another objection is that recognition of Aboriginal law would promote and multiply conflicts between overlapping and potentially contradictory systems of law. In federal systems, which confront this type of "conflict of laws" problem every day, such an objection is hardly persuasive. As Jennifer Nielsen and Gary Martin pointed out, the rejection of Indigenous criminal law by the High Court in *Walker* ignored "the pluralism already inherent within the Australian federation, which is comprised of three tiers of law-making authority, each of which is supposed to complement the others".[57] Law within Australia is already fragmented, divided between the nine jurisdictions of the Commonwealth, States and Territories, not to mention the various external territories. It is also further overlaid by the military criminal jurisdiction, which is the example *par excellence* of using "status" of the parties to determine jurisdiction (in this case status is determined by membership of the Australian Defence Force). Moreover, the application of Australia's military laws, including criminal offences, is not confined to Australia's territorial borders.[58] With such complexity, legal and administrative mechanisms are developed to "share" jurisdiction and to resolve

---

55   It must be recalled that official law reporting is a 19th century development, and that much early law survives through the private reporting of cases, by lawyers and court reporters. Indeed, only in the late 20th century, with the advent of <www.austlii.edu.au> in the 1990s and other searchable databases, have unreported decisions become generally accessible.

56   See R Bartlett, *Native Title in Australia*, 2004, LexisNexis Butterworths, 198.

57   Nielsen and Martin, n 34, 111.

58   See, for example, *Re Colonel Aird; Ex parte Alpert* [2004] HCA 44, where the majority of the High Court upheld the validity of the powers under the *Defence Force Discipline Act 1982* (Cth) that permitted an Australian soldier serving in Malaysia to be subject to a court martial for an alleged rape committed on a young British backpacker while on recreational leave in Thailand.

potential conflicts. In some spheres, federal law will have an overriding effect: State and Territory offences may be subject to challenge under s 109 of the Constitution that they are inoperative to the extent of their inconsistency with federal legislation.

Turning from this inherent pluralism of Australia's legal system to the question of the recognition of Aboriginal law, State and Territory legislation could be developed to address the conflict of laws problems. Indeed, the federal race power could provide a constitutional basis for the recognition of key Aboriginal laws, selected on a case-by-case basis, including specific cultural defences. In this way, the potential conflict between Indigenous and non-Indigenous systems would be addressed and resolved through legislation. Such legislation may clarify the scope and limits of Indigenous law, including determining how customary laws and practices are to be established in the courts, as in the case of native title claims.

An objection to such initiatives remains their compatibility with the principle of equality before the law. But must equality before the law be conceived in terms which deny a place for Aboriginal law and justice? The continuing challenge in debates about the recognition of Aboriginal law is whether equality before the law can be reconceptualised as respect for difference. The proposed "difference" approach resonates with the feminist critique of equality discussed in Chapter 8, and supports rather than denies systems of parallel justice.

The Australian Law Reform Commission did address the equality arguments in its report on *The Recognition of Aboriginal Customary Laws*. The ALRC took the view that any "special" measures for the recognition of Aboriginal customary laws had to comply with the principle of equality before law. In its view, the principle of equality did not rule out different treatment for Indigenous people provided that the measures:

- are reasonable responses to the special needs of Aboriginal people affected by the proposals;
- are generally accepted by them;
- do not deprive individual Aborigines of basic human rights, or access to the general legal system and its institutions.[59]

Applied to the criminal law context, the ALRC was generally reluctant to propose the adoption of special offences and a general cultural defence. Its preferred strategy was to recommend that the issue of Aboriginality and Aboriginal customary law should be addressed, with adaptation where necessary, within the administration of *existing* substantive and procedural laws. Under this approach, the cultural dimensions of offending are pushed to the margins of law, relevant only to guiding the discretion exercised by the police, prosecutors and judges in relation to charging or sentencing offenders.

The ALRC unsurprisingly adopted a similar approach to the recognition of broader cultural defences in its report *Multiculturalism and the Law*, specifically rejecting a general cultural defence that would involve modification to the general rule of the criminal law that "ignorance of the law is no excuse".[60] Although recognising that this rule has the potential to operate harshly in a multicultural society, the ALRC nevertheless concluded:

---

59   ALRC Report No 31, n 3, para 166.
60   ALRC Report No 57, n 3, para 2.12.

The basic principle of imposing responsibility on all members of the community to know what is and is not allowed should not be disturbed merely because it is difficult for some people to know what the law is. Instead, governments and responsible agencies should improve their efforts to communicate the substance of legal restrictions to those likely to be affected by them.[61]

The ALRC's approach to cultural defences views legal policy as a choice between "equal versus special treatment" (with the latter permissible only where there is "exceptional" justification). In Canada, a more progressive approach to the interpretation of equality has emerged. In reviewing the argument for and against the recognition of Aboriginal law in the criminal justice system, the Law Reform Commission of Canada recognised the limits of existing equality jurisprudence. Rather than limit equality simply to equal or same treatment, the Commission proposed the higher goal of "ensuring equal access to justice, equitable treatment and respect" for Aboriginal peoples within the criminal justice system.[62]

The different approach to equality in Canada has manifested itself in a number of ways. There have been significant steps towards recognising and legitimating the role of Indigenous law and systems of justice through the involvement of Aboriginal communities in "Circle Sentencing" courts which have been established in Canada since 1992. As we see below, circle sentencing has provided a template for many new initiatives in Australia. Building on these Indigenous justice experiments, the Canadian federal parliament took another significant step for the greater recognition of Aboriginal law by creating a self-governing region in northern Canada called the Nunavut. The creation of Nunavut has granted a large measure of legal and political autonomy to the Inuit, the First Nations People who compromise 85 per cent of the population living within the territory.[63]

Compared with Canada, the movement in Australia towards greater recognition of systems of Aboriginal justice has been much slower. In the absence of any federal role in implementing the ALRC's recommendations in relation to recognition of Aboriginal law, the States and Territories have adopted their own ad hoc approach. The Northern Territory Law Reform Committee recently proposed that recognition of Aboriginal laws should be permitted at community level subject to the following qualifications:

> That upon application to the Attorney-General an Aboriginal community may apply for recognition, within the community, and by those who consent to it, of such Aboriginal customs and traditions as the community sees fit and which shall therefore be recognised as lawful and binding upon those who accept it, provided that such customs and traditions do not transgress the general laws of the Northern Territory or universal human rights and fundamental freedoms.[64]

Under this proposed model, the recognition of Aboriginal law is conditional, subject to the consent of the communities, and as well ensuring that Aboriginal laws conform both with the general laws of the Northern Territory and international human rights law. The concern about possible human rights violations

---

61   Ibid para 8.24.
62   Law Reform Commission of Canada, *Report on Aboriginal Peoples and Criminal Justice: Equality, Respect and Search for Justice*, Report No 34, 1991, Ch 3.
63   The Nunavut was created as a self-governing territory in 1999: see <http://www.gov.nu.ca/>.
64   Northern Territory Law Reform Committee, *Report on Aboriginal Customary Law*, 2003, 19; available at <http://www.nt.gov.au/justice/docs/lawmake/ntlrc_final_report.pdf>.

stems from the controversies surrounding some indigenous punishment practices. The Aboriginal practice of payback[65] continues to vex Australian courts, raising concern about the legality of practices such as thigh-spearing under domestic and international human rights law.[66] Indeed, the Northern Territory proposal reflects the earlier ALRC recommendation that recognition of Aboriginal customary punishment is problematic where the proposed sentencing orders would involve a breach of the general law or breach fundamental human rights.[67]

Less contentious initiatives being trialled in Australia have grafted Indigenous justice practices onto existing legal structures.[68] Aware that the existing criminal justice system has failed to deliver justice to Aboriginal communities, a number of jurisdictions in Australia have been experimenting with incorporating Indigenous justice institutions into their legal systems. As Robyn Lincoln and Paul Wilson note, of particular importance are the Indigenous courts:

> which vary enormously across jurisdictions from the Murri courts in Queensland to Nunga ones in South Australia to the Koori sentencing circles in New South Wales – but all designed to give Indigenous people more of a voice. While these courts often take place in existing Magistrates' Court rooms there is some rearrangement of the furniture and traditional paintings can adorn the walls. They involve a relaxing of the rules and most generally the inclusion of local elders. It has been shown that Indigenous offenders are more likely to show up and thereby the number of sanctions for justice breaches is reduced. They have also encouraged the development of greater levels of trust between Indigenous communities and justice systems. Of course, more focused evaluations of these Indigenous courts are required, a cautious approach would be sensible to guard against acceptance of practices that may well be tokenistic or paternalistic.[69]

While sharing some of the structural features and objectives of restorative justice,[70] which has been reviewed in Chapters 2 and 8, Indigenous courts and justice practices have distinctive characteristics. Drawing on empirical fieldwork from around Australia, Elena Marchetti and Kathleen Daly argue that these recent developments should be viewed as *sui generis*, that is, in a category of their own,

---

65 Payback is an Aboriginal-English term used to describe the wide range of methods used to punish wrongdoers and to appease victims within some Indigenous communities. It is not a form of revenge, but constitutes an admission of responsibility, typically involving some form of restitution or gift to the victim, or acceptance of punishment by the wrongdoer. Forms of payback vary widely, ranging from death, spearing and duelling, through to shaming, education, compensation or exclusion. In areas with large Aboriginal populations, there is a long history of courts considering local customary laws and practices in decision-making process: Finnane, n 46, and H Douglas, "Customary Law, Sentencing and the Limits of the State" (2005) 20(1) *Canadian Journal of Law and Society* 141.

66 *Jadurin v The Queen* (1982) 44 ALR 424 at 427-428 contains a vivid description of a payback ceremony and its consequences for those involved. The legal controversy and arguments for and against recognition of payback is discussed in Bronitt and McSherry, n 17, 135ff.

67 ALRC Report No 31, n 3, paras 502ff.

68 E Marchetti and K Daly, "Indigenous courts and justice practices in Australia" in *Trends & Issues in Crime and Criminal Justice No 277*, Australian Institute of Criminology, 2004.

69 R Lincoln and P Wilson, "The Aboriginal crime and justice landscape: Time for a rethink" in D Chappell and P Wilson (eds), *Issues in Australian Crime and Criminal Justice*, LexisNexis Butts, 2005, 226.

70 Indigenous justice institutions are commonly viewed as exemplifying therapeutic or restorative justice: A Freiberg, "Problem-oriented courts: Innovative solutions to intractable problems?" (2001) 11(1) *Journal of Judicial Administration* 7 and Finnane, n 46.

rather than as a subset of restorative justice. The distinctiveness of such initiatives lies in the key role that Indigenous communities themselves play in "correcting and modifying established criminal processes in ways that are less apparent to relevant 'communities' in other specialized courts".[71] The survey by Marchetti and Daly further concludes that these developments have something to offer the wider system of criminal justice:

> The core element of animating these courts – improved communication, citizen knowledge/control and appropriate penalties – could be applied to all court processes and all defendants.[72]

Although restorative justice has been embraced around Australia, it has largely overlooked the potential of local Aboriginal dispute resolution processes to reshape the wider non-Indigenous legal system.[73]

The spread of restorative justice and its institutions offers the prospect of securing just and effective outcomes for offenders, victims and their communities. Beyond the Aboriginal context, the concepts and institutions of restorative justice have the potential to reveal the wider cultural context of offending, to harness reintegrative rather than stigmatic shaming and to develop community-based punishment that is sensitive to cultural issues and traditions of those involved. That said, there is concern that these initiatives are tokenistic and simply tinker at the edges. After reviewing the state of Aboriginal crime and justice Lincoln and Wilson conclude that a more radical rethink is needed:

> For the future, the simple retort will not be to invoke "self-determination" for that has been tried and, given the demise of ATSIC, is seen as a failure. Thus the future must involve a totally separate system. While many commentators appear to suggest that cultural accommodation is inevitable (especially where one culture is a powerful majority), it seems inescapable that an Aboriginal criminal justice system is needed if inroads into the appalling rates of criminalisation of Indigenous Australia are to be made ...
>
> The way forward, while not easy, clearly has to involve a radical rethink. The ALRC recommended the adoption (albeit not wholesale) of Aboriginal customary law back in the early 1980s and not much has advanced on that major transformative suggestion. It is hoped that action will be taken with this recommendation for an Aboriginal criminal justice system. How this is put in place is for Indigenous peoples and their local communities to decide. By virtue of the definition of the kind of self-determination proposed here this is the only way forward for such a radical rethink – on Aboriginal terms.[74]

In conclusion, there is emerging in some parts of Australia a form of "soft" legal pluralism which recognises some legal space for Aboriginal customary law.[75] While such developments offer the potential to restore peace within Aboriginal communities, Heather Douglas concludes that limiting the recognition of Aboriginal customary law to the margins of sentencing is "a kind of weak legal

---

71 Marchetti and Daly, n 68, 4.

72 Ibid.

73 Paradoxically, restorative justice in Australia draws its inspiration from the community-based systems developed to advance justice within Maori communities in New Zealand: Finnane, n 46, 308.

74 Lincoln and Wilson, n 69, 230-231.

75 Douglas, n 65, 141.

pluralism. 'Weak' because there is informal recognition of Aboriginal customary law which gives some small space for an alternative legal authority to operate albeit under conditions purported to be scrutinised by the white legal authority".[76] Much more needs to be done in Australia, both legislatively and constitutionally, to recognise the inherent legitimacy, autonomy and authority of indigenous justice institutions and laws within Aboriginal communities.

(d) Rethinking Aboriginal crime: offensive behaviour or offensive policing?

The criminal justice system is not an equal opportunity phenomenon. There is no shortage of research demonstrating that at every stage of the legal system – from encounters with police on the street, through to arrest, charge, bail, prosecution and imprisonment – Aboriginal people are significantly over-represented compared with non-Indigenous people. How is it that over one-fifth of all prison inmates are Indigenous, translating as a over-representation factor of 16 times?[77] Of greater concern perhaps is that this rate is only a marginal improvement on the rate of over-representation exposed by the Royal Commission into Aboriginal Deaths in Custody in 1991.

What are the causes of this over-representation? Lincoln and Wilson have offered four structural explanations:

- racism and discrimination;
- history of colonisation and oppression;
- crime-as-resistance; and
- cultural differences.[78]

Racism and discrimination can be overt, and there is no shortage of evidence that Aboriginal people suffer racist violence from within and outside the legal system.[79] But racism and discrimination may also be indirect, manifesting in how particular crimes are legally defined and enforced by police and prosecutors. It is not drug offences and murder that feature most in the criminal histories of Aboriginal offenders, but rather minor property and public order crimes.[80] Research has revealed that these minor summary offences, particularly offensive conduct, are disproportionately enforced against Aboriginal people and juveniles. This raises the question about "over-criminalisation" and what precisely can be inferred from findings that minorities are over-represented in criminal statistics.

Is it not possible that the disproportionate use of minor summary offences against Aboriginal people and other minority groups simply reflects the fact that some communities have more disorder and crime problems than others? Janet Chan has rejected this suggestion, pointing out that the patterns of public order policing and the heavy-handed tactics used against Aboriginal people cannot be interpreted as simply "reactive policing".[81] It is important to consider critical what

---

76   Ibid 156.
77   Lincoln and Wilson, n 69, 222.
78   Ibid 227.
79   Human Rights and Equal Opportunity Commission, *Racist Violence*, AGPS, 1991.
80   Lincoln and Wilson, n 69, 225.
81   J Chan, *Changing Police Culture: Policing in A Multicultural Society*, Cambridge UP, 1997.

types of behaviours are receiving high levels of police attention, and what impact these law enforcement strategies have on police-community relations.

What constitutes "offensive behaviour" has an obvious cultural dimension, with intoxication and swearing in public featuring largely as the basis for police intrusion into the lives of Aboriginal people. As we shall see below, such intervention invariably escalates tension producing more serious charges of "assault police" and "resist arrest", which compound the underlying minor crime of "offensive behaviour or language". This cyclical pattern and common trilogy of charges is known as the "trifecta" in Australia.[82] It has a particularly harsh impact on Aboriginal people, with available data suggesting that an initial arrest for an offensive language charge dramatically increases the risk of subsequent re-arrest.[83] While this pattern of Aboriginal offending might be described as "crime-as-resistance", it would be wrong to view all crime within Aboriginal communities as simply political acts of resistance against harsh and discriminatory policing. Within these disadvantaged communities there are also high levels of intra-communal and domestic violence.[84]

(i)   Policing Aboriginal communities: from protection to criminalisation

As noted above, it is important to place Aboriginal crime within the history of colonisation and oppression. The present pattern of social control over Aboriginal people forms part of a longer historical narrative. In the 19th and early 20th centuries, the police in Australia performed a wide range of welfare functions in Aboriginal communities, culminating in their complicity in the forcible removal of children in the 1950s under protectionist policies.[85] In the latter half of the 20th century, these overtly paternalist policies and protection laws were abandoned, though, as Chris Cunneen has pointed out, the traditional policing role did not significantly change:

> Policing acts as a "normalising" force which imposes the standards of sections of the non-Indigenous society as a universal norm. Excluded from the private venues of non-Aboriginal Australia, Indigenous social life become subject to regulation – not under the "special" legislation of the protection era, but under the general criminal law covering alcohol consumption, language and other aspects of public behaviour.[86]

Cunneen concludes that police intervention in the lives of Aboriginal young people has "shifted from one of government-authorised removal policies to increasing criminalisation".[87] Liberalism may preclude race-based laws and policing powers, though discrimination continues to occur *indirectly* through discriminatory practices and cultures within law enforcement.

---

82   Trifecta is a gambling term used to describe a bet that predicts the first three places in a race.

83   This appears to be because an arrest record labels the person as "known to police" and therefore within the scope of legitimate police work: Cunneen, n 29, 133.

84   Ibid 225.

85   The Stolen Generation Report can be accessed at: <http://www.austlii.edu.au/au/special/rsjproject/rsjlibrary/hreoc/stolen/>.

86   Cunneen, n 29, 92.

87   Ibid 154.

The laws relating to public intoxication are a good example of how formal changes to the statute book do not necessarily lead to a change in police functions over Aboriginal communities. There is no doubt that alcohol abuse is a significant problem affecting many communities and individuals in Australia, and its impact has been particularly heavy on socio-economically disadvantaged groups. Historically, police in Australia had extensive legal powers to lock up and charge individuals with being drunk and disorderly in public places.[88] While these drunkenness offences have been repealed in all jurisdictions, in practice the police continue to use general public order offences and powers, supplemented by civil powers, to control and remove intoxicated individuals from public places. Indeed "street offences" which prohibit offensive behaviour or language and "move on powers" now provide the legal basis for responding to individuals who have been drinking in public places. There is no doubt that such laws, while formally neutral and imposing the same restrictions on people regardless of their cultural background, are disproportionately used against young people, Aboriginals and minorities.[89]

More than decade ago, the Royal Commission into Aboriginal Deaths in Custody (RCADIC) identified the problem of overuse of minor public order offences in the following terms:

> Charges about language just become part of an oppressive mechanism of control of Aboriginals. Too often the attempt to arrest or charge an Aboriginal for offensive language sets in train a sequence of offences by that person and others – resisting arrest, assaulting police, hindering police and so on, none of which would have occurred if police were not so easily "offended". It particularly brings the law into disrepute when police use similar language, often with racist overtones, to Aboriginals.[90]

Notwithstanding these publicised abuses of the misuse of offensive language charges, the Royal Commission did not go so far as to recommend the abolition of the offence, rather it recommended restraint in the use of offensive language charges.[91] Such restraint is not apparent from a review of the criminal statistics in the past 15 years. Aboriginal and young people from ethnic minorities continue to be over-represented in the charging statistics.[92] One study in New South Wales

---

88   Public drunkenness was the most commonly prosecuted public order offence in the 20th century: D Brown, D Farrier, S Egger and L McNamara, *Brown Farrier Neal and Weisbrot's Criminal Laws*, 4th ed, Federation Press, 2006, 843. Arrest and prosecution for public drunkenness were no longer available, though intoxicated persons could be detained until they become sober: *Intoxicated Persons Act 1979* (NSW) s 5(6)(f).

89   C Cunneen, "Enforcing genocide? Aboriginal young people and the police" in R White and C Alder (eds), *The Police and Young People in Australia*, Cambridge UP, 1994, Ch 6.

90   RCADIC, Regional Report NSW, Vic and Tas (1991), observed, 145. This depressing pattern of policing was revealed in the television documentary "Cop it Sweet" (1992), which involved a TV crew following a group of new police recruits being inducted into beat policing in Redfern, Sydney.

91   Ibid Recommendation 86.

92   See R Jochelson, "Aborigines and public order legislation in New South Wales" *Crime and Justice Bulletin No 34*, BOCSAR, 1997. See also S Egger and M Findlay, "The politics of police discretion" in M Findlay and R Hogg (eds), *Understanding Crime and Criminal Justice*, LBC, 1988, 218. For a broader discussion of arrest rates in Aboriginal communities, see B Hunter, *Indigenous Australian Arrest Rates: Economic and Social Factors Underlying the Incidence and Number of Arrests*, Centre for Aboriginal Economic Police Research, Australian National University, 2001.

suggests that Aboriginal persons continue to be grossly over-represented among arrests for offensive language and conduct offences, and that moreover there was a positive and statistically significant correlation between areas with higher proportions of Aboriginal residents and areas with higher court appearance rates for offensive conduct and language.[93] A report by the New South Wales Aboriginal Justice Advisory Committee in 2000 found that, on average, Aboriginal people were 15 times more likely to be prosecuted than non-Aboriginal people for offensive language or conduct.[94] In some places, this figure skyrocketed to around 80 times the State average.

Offensive language crimes have been an instrument of oppression against Aboriginal people. Although these summary offences *could* be used to criminalise public acts of racial vilification and racist insults, empirical evidence has revealed that these laws are enforced against minorities. The verbal hurtful victimisation of Aboriginal people at the hands of racists is simply not considered legally actionable under these laws. As legal theorist Wojciech Sadurski points out, the present pattern of law enforcement in Australia "over-emphasises the seriousness of insults against majority (in particular, against enforcement agents themselves) and undervalues insults against disadvantaged minorities".[95]

This led to the wider question of whether racial vilification should be a distinct offence.[96] This is highly contentious in Australia.[97] At the federal level, racial vilification was not made an offence under the *Racial Discrimination Act 1975* (Cth), which implemented Australia's obligations under the International Convention for the Elimination of All Forms of Racial Discrimination (CERD). Rather the federal Act was amended in 1995 to make it "unlawful" (in the civil rather than criminal sense) to engage, otherwise than in private, in offensive conduct because of race, colour or national or ethnic origin.[98] Racial vilification provided a ground for making a complaint to the Human Rights and Equal Opportunity Commission (HREOC) for conciliation and referral of the complaint to the Federal Magistrates Court for adjudication.

Racist threats and incitement to violence could be prosecuted under the general criminal law. The problem is that the racial motivation behind such conduct would be deemed legally irrelevant by the court or, worse still, may lead to more lenient treatment by police and prosecutors, operating as a mitigating rather than aggravating factor.[99] Racial vilification offences, by contrast, direct legal attention towards the motives of the accused.

---

93   Jochelson, ibid.

94   B Thomas, *Policing Public Order: Offensive Language and Conduct, the Impact on Aboriginal People*, Aboriginal Justice and Advisory Committee, Sydney, 2000, 1.

95   W Sadurski "Racial vilification, psychic harm and affirmative action" in T Campbell and W Sadurski (eds), *Freedom of Communication*, Dartmouth, 1994, 90.

96   Racial vilification offences perform an important symbolic role in outlawing racist violence. However, there is a contrary argument that it would be far better, symbolically and practically, to promote the rigorous enforcement of the existing offences (of which there are no shortage) and forthright punishment of such conduct: P Gordon, "Racist harassment and violence" in E Stanko (ed), *Perspectives on Violence*, Quartet Books, 1994, 51.

97   See, generally, McNamara, n 15.

98   *Racial Discrimination Act 1975* (Cth) s 18C.

99   HREOC, n 79, 277.

In 1991, HREOC recommended that specific federal offences should be enacted proscribing (1) racist violence and intimidation; and (2) incitement to racial violence.[100] These recommendations have been implemented in most Australian States and Territories, but not at the federal level.[101] Racial vilification offences in these terms have been adopted in other common law jurisdictions including Canada, New Zealand, the United States and the United Kingdom.[102] The reluctance to enact similar offences at the federal level relates to the concern that they may violate the implied freedom of political discussion under the Commonwealth Constitution, discussed further in Chapter 14.[103]

The current civil regime for racial vilification under federal law expressly preserves the operation of State and Territory racial vilification offences. A typical offence is s 4 of the *Racial Vilification Act 1996* (SA), which provides:

> A person must not, by a public act, incite hatred towards, serious contempt for, or severe ridicule of, a person or group of persons on the ground of their race by –
>
> (a) threatening physical harm to the person, or members of the group, or to property of the person or members of the group; or
>
> (b) inciting others to threaten physical harm to the person, or members of the group, or to property of the person or members of the group.
>
> Maximum penalty –
> If the offender is a body corporate – $25 000.
> If the offender is a natural person – $5 000, or imprisonment for 3 years, or both.

In New South Wales, the offence is framed as one of "serious racial vilification" under the *Anti-Discrimination Act 1977* (NSW).[104] The vilification must manifest itself by a "public act";[105] and occur by means which include threats of physical harm towards persons or groups of persons or property or inciting others to perpetrate such threats.[106]

(ii)   Zero tolerance and Aboriginal crime: the future of law and order

The prosecution of minor public order offences is becoming more prevalent in many parts of Australia. Over-representation of Aboriginal people cannot be attributed solely to racism within law enforcement, but must be seen within the context of broader "law and order" campaigns within Australia.[107] In the present

---

100 Ibid 296-302.

101 *Anti-Discrimination Act 1977* (NSW) Div 3A; *Anti-Discrimination Act 1991* (Qld) Part 4; *Racial Vilification Act 1996* (SA); *Anti-Discrimination Act 1998* (Tas) ss 19, 20; *Racial and Religious Tolerance Act 2001* (Vic); *Criminal Code* (WA) Chapter XI; *Discrimination Act 1991* (ACT) Part 6. The Northern Territory has no specific provisions dealing with racist violence and intimidation or incitement.

102 See, generally, HREOC, n 79, Ch 11.

103 It has been suggested that these constitutional concerns are overstated since "there is no basis for concluding that racial vilification is 'political speech' in terms relevant to the implied constitutional freedom recognised by the High Court": L McNamara and T Solomon, "The Commonwealth *Racial Hatred Act* 1995: Achievement or Disappointment?" (1996) 18(2) *Adelaide Law Review* 259 at 281. See, further, McNamara, n 15.

104 Section 20D.

105 Section 20B.

106 Section 20D.

107 R Hogg and K Carrington, "Crime, rurality and community" (1998) 31 *Australian and New Zealand Journal of Criminology* 160. See generally R Hogg and D Brown, *Rethinking Law and Order*, Pluto Press, 1998.

climate of "law and order" politics, politicians and the media clamour for more police on the streets, with wider powers to deal with the problems of "youth crime" and "street gangs". New South Wales in 1998 enacted broad powers to "stop and search" and "move on" individuals who engage in antisocial conduct falling short of a criminal offence.[108]

The politics of "law and order" in Australia promoted a style of law enforcement more consistent with "zero tolerance" policing than community policing. It has been suggested that there are three elements to zero tolerance policing:

1. being "tough on crime", including the enforcement of all applicable laws;
2. strict, non-discretionary law enforcement;
3. police action against minor offences and disorder.[109]

This strategy of policing, developed in the United States in the 1990s, has high levels of political appeal. Although zero tolerance is not the official policy of any police force in Australia, there is no doubt that aspects of the strategy have been deployed at both State and local command level across Australia.[110] Zero tolerance policing promises significant reductions in levels of crime, though it must be said that these claims have rarely been empirically tested and, indeed, have been vigorously rejected in the United States.[111]

Zero tolerance implies the *full enforcement* of applicable laws, which is consistent with the rule of law, in particular the principle of equality before the law. The idea that offenders will be subjected to the same impartial treatment under the same laws by the police is a powerful claim of neutrality for law enforcement. However, it ignores the fact that the police have a wide leeway in relation to the *choice* of laws to be subjected to full enforcement. Under present policies, zero tolerance is applied most vigorously to the crimes of the powerless, rather than the crimes of the powerful.[112] As Chris Cunneen has pointed out:

> Zero tolerance policing rests on a spurious assumption that the law is neutral and can be enforced in all situations – that complete enforcement is a possibility. However, public order and the actions which constitute disorder are broadly defined and open to constant interpretation and discretionary decisions by police.

---

108 The recent reforms to public order powers, including the statutory power to "move on" persons who may not have committed any offence, are discussed in Bronitt and McSherry, n 17, Ch 13, 741ff.

109 J Marshall, "Zero tolerance policing", *Information Bulletin*, Issue No 9, SA Office of Crime Statistics, 1999; and P Grabosky, "Zero tolerance policing" *Australian Institute of Criminology Trends and Issues in Crime and Criminal Justice*, Issue No 102, Australian Institute of Criminology, 1999.

110 For further discussion of zero tolerance in the Australian context, see Bronitt and McSherry, n 17, Ch 13, 745ff.

111 As Bernard Harcourt notes: "The basic plot is simple: fighting minor disorder deters serious crime": *Illusion of Order: The False Promise of Broken Windows Policing*, Harvard UP, 2001, 27. While widely credited by politicians, media and some academics for solving crime problems in large cities including New York and Chicago, Harcourt and others note that there is a pervasive lack of empirical data to support this hypothesis: at 8.

112 A class-based conspiracy is not the most persuasive explanatory of this differential pattern of enforcement. Crimes of the powerful (such as financial and tax crimes) are often more complex and difficult to detect, requiring significantly more resources in investigation and enforcement. On the different approaches to the criminalisation of tax and welfare cheats, see Bronitt and McSherry, n 17, 638-640.

By pretending that zero tolerance is possible, the more important question of who gets arrested is obscured.[113]

The rhetoric of zero tolerance also suppresses and de-legitimises the significance of discretion to policing, which is universally recognised by scholars and police themselves as an unavoidable and legitimate aspect of police work.[114] Increased police attention on minor "street offences" may have a number of unintended consequences including: damaging the trust and perceived legitimacy of police within disadvantaged communities; and exacerbating levels of over-representation of minorities in the criminal justice system. As Chris Cunneen has concluded, the adoption of zero-tolerance policing significantly increases the level of criminalisation for Aboriginal people, and would be incompatible with the recommendations of the Royal Commission into Aboriginal Deaths in Custody (1991).

More than 20 years ago, Colin Tatz summed up the position of Aboriginal people in the Australian legal system as follows:

> Many laws omit reference to Aborigines, but are applied to them with excessive vigour by police and lower courts: being drunk and disorderly, using unseemly words, and vagrancy in particular. The working of the bail and remand system, the warehousing of Aborigines in inner cells and in country lockups, the absence of legal aid until recently, the structural inequality of the laws of landlord and tenant and of hire-purchase are examples of how to keep people in a position of inferiority by attitudes, actions and structures which don't use colour directly as the subordinating mechanism.[115]

In the intervening period there has been a Royal Commission into Aboriginal Deaths in Custody (RCADIC), and extensive political and public policy attention to crime and justice within Aboriginal communities. Yet a recent assessment of progress to date suggests that "little has changed despite this sustained interest".[116] Offensive language charges and the trifecta remain continuing sources of conflict between police and Aboriginal communities, contributing to disproportionate levels of criminalisation and rates of imprisonment. In many respects, the patterns of overpolicing have intensified under the rubric of zero tolerance policing and tougher political "law and order" agendas. There have been some improvements in the formal legal position of Indigenous people since Tatz's assessment in 1984. Formal inequalities embedded in the law have been eradicated: protectionist laws have been repealed (including the power to detain for drunkenness). As Chapter 4 has explored, when Aboriginal offenders are prosecuted there is better provision for legal representation through legal aid. The challenge for the future lies in the recognition that Aboriginal communities *themselves* must play a critical role in finding the solutions for restoring peace, and delivering justice for both offenders and victims within their communities. With the advent of Indigenous courts and justice practices, Aboriginal people, their customs and laws, now have a platform

---

113 Aboriginal and Torres Strait Islander Commission, *Law and Justice Issues: Zero Tolerance Policing* 1999, Executive Summary, <http://www.atsic.gov.au/issues/law_and_justice/zero_tolerance_policing/Report/>.

114 A Goldsmith, M Israel and K Daly (eds), *Crime and Justice: An Australian Textbook in Criminology*, 2nd ed, Law Book Co, 2003.

115 C Tatz, "Aborigines and civil law" in P Hanks and B Keon-Cohen (eds), *Aborigines and the Law*, Allen and Unwin 1984, 103 at 110 (emphasis in original).

116 Lincoln and Wilson, n 69, 220.

within the Australian legal system. This may provide the first steps towards the recognition of Aboriginal justice systems that complement rather than compete with the other legal systems in Australia.

(e) "One law for all": multicultural blindness and the reasonable person

In many areas of law, both civil and criminal, the courts resort to objective standards against which behaviour is judged. Perhaps the best known form of these standards is the hypothetical "reasonable man", who emerged in the 19th century and remains the paradigm legal construct used in torts and criminal law for determining the boundaries of appropriate behaviour. This legal icon has been reconfigured in the late 20th century as the gender-neutral "reasonable person".[117] However, as noted in Chapter 8, critical and feminist scholars have pointed out that the norm against which real people are judged is that of an Anglo-Saxon-Celtic, middle class male. In this section we explore how the adoption of purportedly objective standards – which deem irrelevant individual and group-based difference – may contribute to discrimination and injustice for ethnic and cultural minorities.

Legal standards are constructed by legislators, judges and juries according to their own standards of reasonableness. Where minorities are not adequately represented among law-makers, judges and juries, there is a danger that objective standards will be determined exclusively by the values of the dominant Anglo-Saxon-Celtic culture.[118] Rather than delivering on its promise of consistency and neutrality, the objective standard in fact produces highly subjective forms of regulation. In the context of criminal law, it has been suggested that:

> The operation of "objective" tests in fact results in highly discretionary regulation. The tribunal here is effectively constructing the standard against which the defendant is judged: the legal process goes on to legitimise that standard as "objective" and neutral.[119]

The objective standard has been a feature of our legal system since the 19th century, though it has not stood without challenge from both judges and legal scholars. In *Moffa v The Queen*,[120] Murphy J took the view that the defence of provocation (which reduces murder to manslaughter) required significant reform. At its core, lay an objective test based on the reasonable/ordinary person against which the subjective reactions of the accused had to be judged. In his view:

---

117 The "reasonable man" test emerged in the provocation defence in *R v Welsh* (1869) 11 Cox 336. In the law of negligence the concept of the "reasonable man" was originally encapsulated by the phrase "the man on the Clapham omnibus", a term attributed to Lord Justice Bowen and brought to prominence in the case of *McQuire v Western Morning News Co Ltd* [1903] 2 KB 100 (CA) at 109 per Collins MR. In Australia the phrase was transmogrified in Australia into "the hypothetical person on a hypothetical Bondi tram" by Deane J in *Papatonakis v Australian Telecommunications Commission* (1985) 156 CLR 7 at 36.

118 ALRC Report No 57, n 3, paras 8.31-8.34. See also K Amirthalingam and S Bronitt, "Cultural blindness – criminal law in multicultural Australia" (1996) 21(2) *Alternative Law Journal* 58 at 60.

119 N Lacey, C Wells and O Quick, *Reconstructing Criminal Law*, 3rd ed, Butterworths, 2003, 56.

120 (1977) 138 CLR 601.

The objective test is not suitable even for a superficially homogeneous society, and the more heterogeneous our society becomes, the more inappropriate the test is. Behaviour is influenced by age, sex, ethnic origin, climatic and other living conditions, biorhythms, education, occupation and, above all, individual differences. It is impossible to construct a model of a reasonable or ordinary South Australian for the purpose of assessing emotional flashpoint, loss of self-control and capacity to kill under particular circumstances ... The same considerations apply to cultural sub-groups such as migrants. The objective test should not be modified by establishing different standards for different groups in society. This would result in unequal treatment ... The objective test should be discarded. It has no place in rational criminal jurisprudence.[121]

Murphy J's dissent went unheeded. The reasonable/ordinary person test continues to govern the operation of defences such as provocation and self-defence in jurisdictions in Australia.[122]

Rather than abandon objective standards entirely, the modern approach in Australia has been to adapt or modify the reasonable/ordinary person standard. In the context of provocation, the courts were prepared to attribute to the hypothetical legal person the particular cultural background of the accused in order to assess the gravity of the provocation. In the Northern Territory, the courts went further, attributing to the reasonable or ordinary person the accused's Aboriginal background for the purpose of determining both the gravity of provocation and the standard of self-control.[123] Stanley Yeo has criticised the approach taken in the Northern Territory, pointing to the danger that this approach may condone offensive and negative stereotypes that Aboriginal people have less self-control than other groups:

> Doubtless, the judges who delivered these decisions had fairness and justice as their paramount aims. However, their decisions had the effect of promoting a great evil, namely, a negative stereotype of Aborigines being at a lower order of the evolutionary scale than other ethnic groups.[124]

The current approach adopted by the High Court could be described as a compromise. In a series of cases since the 1990s, the Court has held that the cultural background of the accused is relevant to provocation though only in the limited sense of determining the gravity of the provocation. In other words, cultural background can be used to contextualise the insults or threats that provoked the accused to violence. However, the standard of self-control expected of the accused and against which he or she is judged must be that of an ordinary person devoid of the accused's particular culture or background. The rationale for law's "cultural blindness", according to the majority of the High Court in *Stingel*, was the importance attached to the principle of equality before the law:

> No doubt, there are classes or groups within the community whose average powers of self-control may be higher or lower than the community average.

---

121 Ibid 625-626 per Murphy J.

122 Bronitt and McSherry, n 17, Ch 5.

123 *R v Patipatu* [1951-1976] NTJ 18; *R v MacDonald* [1951-1976] NTJ 186; *R v Muddarubba* [1951-1976] NTJ 317; *R v Jimmy BalirBalir* [1951-1976] NTJ 633; *R v Nelson* [1951-1976] NTJ 327; *Jabarula v Poore* (1989) 42 A Crim R 479. *Mungatopi v The Queen* (1992) 2 NTR 1.

124 S Yeo, "Sex, ethnicity, power of self-control and provocation" (1996) 18 *Sydney Law Review* 304 at 316.

Indeed, it may be that the average power of self-control of the members of one sex is higher or lower than the average power of self-control of members of the other sex. The principle of equality before the law requires, however, that the differences between different classes or groups be reflected only in the limits within which a particular level of self-control can be characterized as ordinary.[125]

Liberalism demands that cultural difference must be suppressed or disregarded with the consequent danger that, by excluding *salient* difference, tribunals will simply apply the dominant values and culture (typically Anglo-Saxon-Celtic) to construct the relevant objective standard. McHugh J had subscribed to this position in *Stingel*, though subsequently recanted in a later decision, *Masciantonio v The Queen*:[126]

> I was a party to the joint judgment of the Court in *Stingel*. At the time, I thought that the principle of equality before the law, which is the rationale of the objective standard, justified rejecting any attribute of the accused to the "ordinary person" except that of age. But after reading Mr Stanley Yeo's criticism of this aspect of *Stingel* and further reflection on the matter, I have concluded that, unless the ethnic or cultural background of the accused is attributed to the ordinary person, the objective test of self-control results in inequality before the law. Real equality before the law cannot exist when ethnic or cultural minorities are convicted or acquitted of murder according to a standard that reflects the values of the dominant class but does not reflect the values of those minorities.
>
> If it is objected that this will result in one law of provocation for one class of persons and another law for a different class, I would answer that that must be the natural consequence of true equality before the law in a multicultural society when the criterion of criminal liability is made to depend upon objective standards of personhood. ... In any event, it would be much better to abolish the objective test of self-control in the law of provocation than to perpetuate the injustice of an "ordinary person" test that did not take into account the ethnic or cultural background of the accused.

Significantly, Yeo subsequently reassessed his own critique of objective standards. Persuaded by the work of another legal scholar,[127] Yeo recanted his earlier views, concluding that constructing the ordinary person using the accused's ethnic or cultural background may give rise to essentialist views of various cultures and lead to racism.[128] Recognising the difficulties of accommodating cultural background in the defence of provocation, many scholars have called for the abolition of the defence.[129] Thus far, only Tasmania has taken this approach in Australia, influenced in part by feminist critique that the defence is gender biased

---

125 *Stingel v The Queen* (1990) 171 CLR 312 at 329 per Mason CJ, Brennan, Deane, Dawson, Toohey, Gaudron and McHugh JJ.

126 *Masciantonio* (1995) 183 CLR 58 at 74 per McHugh J.

127 I Leader-Elliott, "Sex, race and provocation: In defence of *Stingel*" (1996) 20 *Criminal Law Journal* 72.

128 Yeo, n 124.

129 There is now a wealth of academic literature supporting the abolition of the defence of provocation: J Horder, *Provocation and Responsibility*, Clarendon Press, 1992; A Howe, "The provocation defence: Finally provoking its own demise?" (1998) 22 *Melbourne University Law Review* 466; A Howe, "Reforming provocation (more or less)" (1999) 12 *Australian Feminist Law Journal* 127; C Wells, "Provocation: The case for abolition" in A Ashworth and B Mitchell (eds), *Rethinking English Homicide Law*, Oxford UP, 2000; L Neal and M Bagaric, "Provocation: The ongoing subservience of principle to tradition" (2003) 67 *Journal of Criminal Law* 237.

and subject to abuse, and the belief that provocation can be considered at the sentencing phase.[130] The consideration of race and culture in the construction of standards of legal responsibility is clearly controversial. However, abolition of the defence would simply mean that these issues would have to be considered at prosecution and/or sentencing stage, which only relocates the discussion about equality to the highly discretionary and less visible domain. It also becomes an issue for the professional lawyer and judge, rather than the lay jury.

What does this discussion of race, culture, and legal objectivity reveal? Legal doctrine continues to struggle with competing and conflicting conceptions of equality. On the one hand, formal equality demands that all people, regardless of their sex and gender, should be treated the same. On the other hand, to be treated *as an equal* the accused's cultural background seems critical to contextualising behaviour and setting standards of appropriate behaviour, particularly in relation to determining the availability of defences such as provocation and self-defence. An equality standard that ruled out the relevance of salient group-based difference and disadvantage would, as McHugh J pointed out, simply perpetuate further injustice. The current law with its two-stage test, which is both subjective and objective, embodies this tension over the competing conceptions of equality.

A better approach, which avoids the inherent dangers of essentialising and negatively stereotyping persons from different cultures, is to develop a broader multicultural reference standard for the reasonable/ordinary person. More is required than just embodying this new multicultural standard in legal tests or definitions: the repackaging of the reasonable person as a person with a multi-cultural background would probably be unhelpful and perceived to be tokenistic. A better strategy is to explore how *specific* legal rules (defences and offences) discriminate against particularly cultural beliefs, and what reforms are needed to maintain respect for cultural differences. Clearly the law should also mandate further cross-cultural training for judges and lawyers, and ensure better repre-sentation of minorities on juries, as well as allowing a wider range of expert evidence to be admitted in appropriate cases to educate tribunals and juries.

There will be cases where the law's commitment to respecting cultural difference collides with feminist claims to equality (see discussion in Chapter 8). To what extent should the law accommodate cultural practices which the dominant culture regards as harmful such as "female genital mutilation" or admit the defence of provocation where the defendant acted violently on culturally endorsed beliefs that are misogynist and discriminatory? Concerned that "culture" can become an excuse for tolerating violence against women, the United Nations in 1993 adopted the *Declaration on the Elimination of Violence Against Women* (DEVAW), specifically noting that "States should condemn violence against women and should not invoke any custom, tradition or religious consideration to avoid their obligations with respect to its elimination".[131]

---

130 *Criminal Code Amendment (Abolition of Defence of Provocation) Act 2003* (Tas). See R Bradfield, "The demise of provocation in Tasmania" (2003) 27 *Criminal Law Journal* 322. The arguments for an against abolition are discussed in Bronitt and McSherry, n 17, Ch 5.

131 Article 4, GA res 48/104, 48 UN GAOR Supp (No 49) at 217, UN Doc A/48/49 (1993). For an article that explores the legal and human rights issues around "culture" and "violence" against women, see K Amirthalingam, "Women's rights, international norms, and domestic violence: Asian perspectives" (2005) 27(2) *Human Rights Quarterly* 683.

Is it possible for law to achieve a balance between feminist and cultural imperatives? Such cases raise an irreconcilable conflict between these imperatives, leading some to suggest that the choice is a political one, and the determination of which interest should prevail in any particular context should be a matter for the legislature rather than the courts.[132]

(f) Conclusion

This chapter has explored the connections between race, culture and law. Discrimination based on race, colour, religion and culture is proscribed under both domestic and international law. The various sections revealed how legal efforts to address cultural difference struggle with the law's liberal commitment to the principle of equality before the law. As in the case of affirmative action in relation to gender discrimination (see Chapter 8), special laws and different treatment of minorities provoke accusations that they are inconsistent with the principle of equality before the law. For this reason perhaps, the federal government has rarely used its power under s 51(xxvi) of the Commonwealth Constitution to make "special laws" for people of any race.

In some ways this chapter offers a parallel thesis to the one developed for the gender chapter. Equality is a powerful political and legal ideal that requires disadvantaged minorities to be treated the same as others. However, its limitation is that the implicit normative standard for comparison remains structured around needs and interests of individuals from the dominant culture. Shortly before the High Court handed down its decision in *Mabo*, the limitations of equality rhetoric as the foundation for anti-discrimination laws and policies were identified by two leading legal scholars, Frank Brennan and James Crawford:

> In a subtle but very significant way the notion of "equality" has been an obstacle to developments in Aboriginal affairs. To treat Aborigines as such is seen as "patronising": thus the decision-makers have been able to rely on an unstated ideology of sameness which avoids by definitional means the issue which Aboriginality raises. For example, it is argued against legislative, and even administrative, recognition of Aboriginal rights or traditions that this would be discriminatory or unequal, or would violate the principle that all persons in a democratic society should be subject to "one law".[133]

Equality of opportunity and affirmative action attempt to repackage the concept to address these limitations, though they are susceptible to the same criticisms.

With its commitment to individualism, liberalism and the principle of equality before the law seems unable to remedy the underlying structural causes of discrimination faced by minorities. Indeed the law's commitment to formal neutrality between different groups and cultures often masks the inherent privileging of dominant groups at the expense of others. Liberalism depicts the law as neutral and innocent, with the racial identity of individuals and groups denied any legal salience.[134] Legal standards applied in the civil and criminal law are based on the "reasonable or ordinary person". While represented as culturally neutral or

---

132 Amirthalingam and Bronitt, n 118 60.

133 F Brennan and J Crawford, "Aboriginality, recognition and Australian law: Where to from here?" (1990) 1 *Public LR* 53 at 64.

134 P Fitzpatrick, "Racism and the innocence of law" (1987) 14 *Journal of Law and Society* 119.

indeterminate, the reasonable person is a normative standard created by lawyers, reflecting the values both of liberalism and the dominant Anglo-Saxon-Celtic culture. This is not a conspiracy against minorities, but simply a reflection that the law-makers, tribunals and juries construct their standards of judgment about "reasonableness" according to their own values and experience – with limited participation of ethnic and cultural minorities in our institutions of justice, except when appearing as defendants or victims, there is little chance that the denial of the significance of culture in the process of adjudication can be effectively addressed. While this type of critical scholarship can offer diagnosis of liberalism's deficiencies, engagement with equality arguments seems to be politically unavoidable – it remains the dominant legal philosophical paradigm within which anti-discrimination laws and multiculturalism policies are debated.

An underlying theme in this chapter has been the extent to which the Australian legal system could do more to accommodate "legal pluralism". Legal pluralism admits the possibility of co-existence within the one state of different bodies of law for different ethnic and cultural groups. With issues relating to self-determination unresolved, the position of Indigenous Australians must be distinguished from treatment of other minorities. Drawing on the Canadian model of the Nunavut, Australia could further consider the prospect of creating self-governing territories in some areas. Prospects seem remote in Australia, with the recent abolition of ATSIC in 2004. The current federal government abandonment of self-determination (symbolised by the abolition of ATSIC) has produced a diluted administrative concept of "mainstreaming", self-management and self-empowerment.[135] The success of this model remains to be seen. However, under the rubric of self-management and self-empowerment, there are ways in which Aboriginal law and justice systems can be further recognised within Australian jurisdictions. We have examined how the criminal justice system can graft onto customary dispute resolution methods involving elders, as well as providing tribunals with more cultural experts who can contextualise offending and to develop appropriate punishments. The development of Indigenous courts and justice institutions in the criminal justice system is an exciting initiative offering the prospect of delivering justice and restoring peace within Indigenous communities. Aligned with restorative justice institutions, these developments demonstrate, notwithstanding the history of chronic "cultural blindness" in Australian law,[136] that the system has the potential to accommodate further legal pluralism and to develop practical solutions to the issues of disadvantage facing many ethnic and cultural minorities today.

Questions

1. Imagine that you are employed by the Aboriginal Legal Service as a research officer. To minimise discriminatory patterns of policing within the local Aboriginal community, you have been asked to develop guidelines on the police use of public order laws, with specific attention to the use of offensive behaviour charges.

---

135 Lincoln and Wilson, n 69, 228-229.
136 Amirthalingam and Bronitt, n 118.

2. Should racial vilification be a federal offence? What are the arguments for and against criminalisation?

3. "The 'reasonable person' is not the embodiment of Australian Anglo-Celtic values. Rather it is a normative standard set by lawyers and judges, embodying the liberal values of individualism, autonomy, rationality and free choice etc. The challenge is not to transform the reasonable person into the multicultural person, another potentially confusing legal fiction. Rather it is to confront and reshape key liberal values in ways that are more inclusive, pluralistic and less discriminatory." Discuss.

4. The principle of equality before the law is central to sentencing law. An offender's racial or ethnic background cannot provide a basis for harsher or more lenient punishment. That said, courts are prepared to consider *the effects* that flow from the offender's membership of a particular ethnic group. Aboriginality does not generate a sentencing discount, though courts may consider as mitigating factors alcohol abuse and socio-economic deprivation that affect the offender's community. As Brennan J observed in *Neal v The Queen* (1982) 149 CLR 305 at 326:

   > The same sentencing principles are to be applied, of course, in every case, irrespective of the identity of a particular offender or his membership of an ethnic or other group. But in imposing sentences courts are bound to take into account, in accordance with those principles, all material facts including those facts which exist only by reason of the offender's membership of an ethnic or other group. So much is essential to the even administration of criminal justice.

   Ethnic identity is formally irrelevant. Is this exclusion of race and ethnic background justified? Why does Brennan J draw this subtle distinction?

   Rather than equality, what alternate principle should be used to guide the exercise of sentencing discretion? See further J Nicholson, "The sentencing of aboriginal offenders" (1999) 23 *Criminal Law Journal* 85.

5. In 2005, France enacted a new law banning religious symbols from public schools as part of its policy of secularisation and reflecting the Republic's constitutional separation of state and religion: LOI n0 2004-228 du 15 mars 2004 (French Text: <http://www.legifrance.gouv.fr/html/actualite/actualite_legislative/2004-228/laicite.htm>) The new law applied to all religious symbols, singling out no specific religion. However, most community concern and enforcement of this rule has been directed towards Muslim female students wearing the hijab (a headscarf). The concerns range from the belief that the hijab is a challenge to Western gender equity or a sign of fundamentalist extremism. The issue has reached Australia, with Liberal backbencher Bronwyn Bishop proposing a similar ban on Muslim girls wearing the headscarf, or hijab, at public schools.

   France is party to the European Convention on Human Rights which protects freedom of religion in the following terms.

   ARTICLE 9
   Everyone has the right to freedom of thought, conscience and religion; this right includes freedom to change his religion or belief, and freedom, either alone or in community with others and in public or private, to manifest his religion or belief, in worship, teaching, practice and observance.

Freedom to manifest one's religion or beliefs shall be subject only to such limitations as are prescribed by law and are necessary in a democratic society in the interests of public safety, for the protection of public order, health or morals, or the protection of the rights and freedoms of others.

Article 9 is similar to Art 18 of the International Covenant on Civil and Political Rights (ICCPR) to which Australia is a party.

Divide the class into two groups. Group 1 should develop arguments related to the freedom of religion. Group 2 should develop arguments related to the limitations promoting public safety, for the protection of public order, health or morals, or the protection of the rights and freedoms of others.

After this class discussion, review your arguments in light of the recent decisions of the European Court of Human Rights and the English Court of Appeal concerning the banning of hijabs in public schools and universities:

- *Case of Leyla Sahin v Turkey* (Application no 44774/98) (19 June 2004)

- *SB, R (on the application of) v Denbigh High School* [2005] EWCA Civ 199.

6. Drawing from any area of law that you have studied, identify a legal rule that purports to apply equally to everyone, though in its impact, directly or indirectly, discriminates against people from distinct cultural or ethnic backgrounds.

PART C

Law and Regulation

Chapter 10

Law and Regulation

(a) Introduction

In Part B of the book, we looked at the ideas of justice and inequality as themes that can be used to assess law and the legal system. In Part C we shift our attention to the role of law in regulating the actions of individuals, groups and corporations. We do this in two ways. First, in this chapter, we examine the idea of regulation and its relationship to law. Secondly, in the next three chapters, we look at the economic analysis of law, a field of inquiry that has had a lot to say about the purposes and goals which should be served by the legal system.

In this chapter we present an introductory overview of the relationship between law and regulation. As will be seen, there has been considerable research on this topic and, consequently, there are many different perspectives and ways of conceptualising the relationship. We do not pretend to offer a way of unifying these various ideas. Instead, our purpose is to introduce the first-time reader to conceptual richness that can be found in this emerging area of contextual legal inquiry.

(b) Law and regulation

It is surprisingly difficult to define the term "regulation". It is surprising because lawyers are used to thinking of law – especially legislation – as a means of regulating social or economic conduct. There is a large literature that examines the idea of regulation from a legal perspective, asking why some rules are effective while others seem to have little impact on social or economic behaviour. We have examined some of this literature in Chapter 7 when we looked at the emergence and impact of legislation. But, as we will see in this present chapter, regulation does not always involve the enforcement of legal rules and it does not always require direct intentional action by the state. It is when we move beyond an exclusively governmental/legal focus that the difficulty in producing a comprehensive definition of the term becomes apparent.

One reason for the variety of definitions is the different disciplinary perspectives from which the topic of regulation is studied. Economists and sociologists, for example, define the area of study according to their own particular disciplinary assumptions and methodologies. Economic research on regulation examines the political origins of regulatory regimes – the politics of regulation. We look at this in more detail in Chapter 13. Thus Ogus, writing from an economic perspective, defines regulation as "fundamentally a politico-economic concept ... [that] can best be understood by reference to different systems of economic organization and the legal forms which maintain them".[1] Sociological approaches look at "the diverse interactions of people (individual and socially), perceptions (of themselves, their tasks and others) and processes (legal, interpretive, and informal)".[2] Because subsequent chapters focus on economic perspectives, in this chapter we concentrate more on this sociological literature.

Julia Black identifies three standard "textbook" definitions of regulation. The first defines regulation as "the promulgation of rules accompanied by mechanisms for monitoring and enforcement", with all three functions being carried out by government. Secondly, regulation can be defined a little more broadly to include all forms of direct and intentional intervention by the state. The second definition would include the imposition of taxes and levies to control economic behaviour, for example. The third definition is the broadest, defining regulation as "all mechanisms of social control or influence affecting behaviour from whatever source, whether intentional or not".[3]

One response to this definitional difficulty is to accept that a single definition may be unhelpful and that:

> [T]here is merit in defining regulation in different ways – excluding or including regulation by non-government actors, excluding or including governance without rules, including only intentional attempts to influence behaviour, or including all actions that have regulatory effects.[4]

Already in this chapter we see hints that the relationship between law and regulation is not as straightforward as a first glance might suggest. A particular aspect of this relationship concerns the implications for the idea of the rule of law. We examined the rule of law idea in Chapter 3, where we saw that it entails certain ideals, such as the need for laws to be general in application, to be public, clearly expressed and stable. There is the potential for some approaches to regulation to clash with ideas about the rule of law. To understand how this might occur we first need to know more about the idea of regulation, so we postpone our discussion of a potential clash of ideas until later in this chapter.

(c)   Forms of regulation

When lawyers think about regulation they are likely to think of the application of rules made by governments or courts to control the behaviour of citizens and other social actors (eg, companies). This is the standard image of regulation: it takes a "top-down" or "command and control" perspective, in which rules are made by higher authorities and imposed on the conduct of social and economic actors. This was the focal point of regulatory research during the 1980s in which:

1   A Ogus, *Regulation: Legal Form and Economic Theory*, Oxford UP, 1994, 1, cited in J Black, "Decentring Regulation: Understanding the Role of Regulation and Self-Regulation in a Post-Regulatory' World" [2001] *Current Legal Problems* 103 at 131.

2   H Bird, D Chow, J Lenne, I Ramsay, *ASIC Enforcement Patterns*, Centre for Corporate Law and Securities Regulation, University of Melbourne, 2003, 6.

3   Black, n 1, 129, referring to R Baldwin, C Scott, and C Hood, *A Reader on Regulation*, Oxford UP, 1998; R Baldwin and M Cave, *Understanding Regulation*, Oxford UP, 1999.

4   C Parker, C Scott, N Lacey and J Braithwaite, "Introduction" in C Parker et al (eds), *Regulating Law*, Oxford UP, 2004, 1.

The major focus was on the ability of the political process and agencies of the state to deliver appropriately democratic regulation, regulatory decisions that reflected the will of the people, not capture by interest groups.[5]

Undoubtedly, this standard view is still an accurate description of some aspects of modern regulation but it is only a partial picture and, increasingly, other parts of the regulatory picture are gaining importance. One way of describing this diversity is to distinguish between different forms of regulation; that is, we can distinguish between self-regulation, quasi-regulation, co-regulation, and (the standard image) government regulation.[6] In some analyses, these different forms of regulation are lined up along a continuum from self-regulation at one end to government regulation at the other. As we will see, however, there can be considerable overlap, such that different forms co-exist, working in tandem.

Below we describe each of these four forms of regulation in a little more detail. We also add two further sub-headings to this categorisation: regulation without rules, and meta-regulation.

(i)   Self-regulation

On one view, self-regulation describes the situation where an industry, profession or other area of practice is solely responsible for establishing and enforcing standards or rules of conduct that apply to members of that industry or profession.[7] This might be done through codes of practice or conduct. An often-cited example, which we looked at in Chapter 6, is the rules of professional conduct promulgated by law societies and bar associations that govern the actions of lawyers in their dealings with each other and with clients. The key feature here is that there is no government involvement, either in prompting or in conducting the regulation.

The advantages claimed for self-regulation are that it is more responsive to the concerns and interests of those in the particular industry; the rules are made by those with experience and expertise in the field; compliance with the rules is therefore more likely; and the rules can be changed and updated more easily than is the case with government regulation. The disadvantages can readily be seen in our discussion in Chapter 6 of legal professional rules. There is the prospect that:

- industry or professional rules will be self-serving, establishing only minimal standards of conduct;

- self-regulatory standards may be enforced inadequately, either due to a lack of legal power or because of reluctance;

- self-regulation may be used as a means of screening members from effective public scrutiny; and

- by excluding or limiting entrants into an area of practice, self-regulation may create unfair commercial advantage or limit effective competition.

---

5   C Parker and J Braithwaite, "Regulation" in P Cane and M Tushnet (eds), *The Oxford Handbook of Legal Studies*, Oxford UP, 2003, 119, 127.

6   This categorisation is taken from Office of Regulation Review, *A Guide to Regulation*, 2nd ed, 1998, Cth of Australia.

7   Just like the term "regulation", there are different ways of defining "self-regulation": see Black, n 1, 114-122.

(ii)   Quasi-regulation

As described by the Federal Government's Office of Regulation Review:[8]

> Quasi-regulation refers to the range of rules, instruments and standards whereby government influences business to comply, but which do not form part of explicit government regulation. Some examples of quasi-regulation include government endorsed industry codes of practice or standards, government agency guidance notes, industry-government agreements and national accreditation schemes.[9]

One example is the Electronic Funds Transfer Code of Conduct which sets out rules governing the operation of electronic funds transfers via ATMs, EFTPOS, telephone and computer internet banking and similar facilities. The Code specifies things such as the content, form and timing of information that must be provided to customers, liability for unauthorised transactions on a customer's account, and procedures for making complaints. The Code has been developed by a working group convened by the Australian Securities and Investments Commission (which also monitors compliance with the Code), with representatives from the banking and telecommunications industries, consumer organisations and relevant government departments. Adoption of the Code by financial institutions is voluntary, with over 200 institutions doing so as at March 2003.

(iii)   Co-regulation

A co-regulatory system has elements of industry and government regulation. For example, industry or professional codes may be given legislative backing. Legislation may set out certain mandatory standards that will apply in the event that the relevant industry does not develop standards of its own, or legislation may delegate to industry the power to enforce codes. An example of co-regulation is found in the Australian Stock Exchange Ltd, a private company the rules of which govern public companies that wish to have their shares traded on the exchange. These rules are given legislative recognition by the *Corporations Act 2001* (Cth).[10]

A particular feature of co-regulation and quasi-regulation, then, is that they each combine aspects of private and public regulation. That is, they remind us that modern regulatory systems cannot be understood as "either/or" choice between government regulation and self-regulation.

(iv)   Government regulation

As indicated above, this is usually what is thought of when people first begin to think about regulation. This is usually the preferred form of regulation for dealing with "high risk, high impact public issues".[11] It usually involves the promulgation of detailed rules by government to control or direct a defined area of behaviour, whether it be driving on the road, offering investment products or running a

---

8   The Office of Regulation Review (ORR) is part of the Productivity Commission, an independent statutory agency that advises the Federal Government on microeconomic policy and regulation. The ORR advise the government and its departments, regulatory agencies and statutory authorities on the development of regulatory proposals and the review of existing regulations.

9   Office of Regulation Review, n 6, Appendix E, 9.

10   Sections 793A-793D.

11   Office of Regulation Review, n 6, Appendix E, 14.

private health facility. Typically, government regulation relies on systems of monitoring, inspection or policing to ensure compliance with the rules. The consequences of non-compliance usually involve punishment in the form of licence revocation, fines or incarceration.

But even here the government is not the only player. As Black points out, "government does not have a monopoly on the exercise of power and control, rather that is fragmented between social actors and between actors and the state".[12] This dispersal of power and control gives rise to complex interactions between various actors, interactions which vary across different regulatory settings (we could expect to find different patterns, for example, in environmental regulation compared with the regulation of airline safety).

The perceived disadvantages of government regulation include the following problems:

- inflexible and "one-size-fits-all" regulations that do not respond sufficiently to the diverse circumstances of those being regulated;

- problems of complexity as drafters attempt to write rules that will "cover the field" comprehensively;

- problems of creative compliance,[13] as those who are subject to the rules seek to exploit loopholes and ambiguities in rules that are imposed "from above"; and

- high costs incurred in maintaining an adequate system of compliance monitoring and enforcement.

(v) Regulation without rules

While identifying the different forms of regulation in this way opens up our understanding of regulation, the four-fold classification described above still does not provide a complete picture of the regulatory landscape. One of the limitations in this categorisation is that each form of regulation focuses on the direct use of rules, whether they are located in industry codes of practice, in government legislation or in some combination of both.

Regulation need not involve the direct or instrumental use of rules. As Parker and Braithwaite observe, "much regulation is accomplished without recourse to rules of any kind".[14] For example, instead of prescribing standards of conduct, one way of regulating undesirable practices by suppliers of goods or services might be through a program of educating consumers about their rights and providing information about those practices. Taxes, subsidies, fees and charges represent another regulatory option, attaching economic incentives (or disincentives) to particular behaviour. Thus, a government might seek to regulate domestic water consumption by imposing charges on usage (perhaps in addition to educating householders about good water use practices and offering tax advantages or rebates for adopting certain water-saving practices). Yet another regulatory option, described by the Office of Regulation Review, is the use of tradeable property rights:

---

12   Black, n 1, 108.

13   See, for example, D McBarnet and C Whelan, "Creative Compliance and the Defeat of Legal Control: The Magic of the Orphan Subsidiary" in K Hawkins (ed), *The Human Face of Law*, Clarendon Press, 1997.

14   Parker and Braithwaite, n 5, 119.

Examples of tradeable permits are water or air pollutant permits. As pollution cannot be reduced to zero because it would be too costly in terms of production and employment lost, a desired total level of a particular pollutant needs to be set as a ceiling. Once this level is defined, permits are issued which allow the holder to produce a certain share of the total.

By allowing a trade in permits, those firms that find it easiest or least costly to reduce pollutants can do so and sell their excess permits to other firms that are unable to reduce emissions, except at relatively high costs.

This type of system achieves the desired reduction in overall pollution in a more cost effective way than would a set reduction in pollutants for each firm in the sector.[15]

Publicly identifying businesses that do not meet acceptable standards (a practice known in the regulatory literature as "shaming") can also persuade other businesses to adjust their practices. Fisse and Braithwaite found that companies are sensitive about their public image and consequently the threat of adverse publicity can achieve a measure of control over corporate misconduct.[16]

The architecture of buildings and spaces can also be used to regulate behaviour. A classic example is the 18th century utilitarian philosopher Jeremy Bentham's plan for a prison, known as the Panopticon.[17] This was designed as multi-story ring-shaped building, divided into cells, each cell having a window facing the inside of the ring. The centre of the ring was occupied by an observation tower from which guards could watch the prisoners in their cells. The key part of the design was that the observers in the central tower would not be visible from the cells. Consequently prisoners, not knowing if they were being watched at any particular time, would have to assume that they were being observed and behave accordingly. In this way the building's architecture thus regulated behaviour by imposing a form of self-discipline on the prisoners. Taking another example, Shearing and Stenning describe the more subtle regulatory effect of architecture and design in Disney theme parks, where "virtually every pool, fountain, and flower bed serves both as an aesthetic object and to direct visitors away from, or towards, particular locations", where many exhibits are accessible only via special vehicles, and where "opportunities for disorder are minimized by constant instruction, [and] by physical barriers which severely limit the choice of action available".[18]

(vi) Meta-regulation

Regulatory theorists have coined the term "meta-regulation" to describe what they see occurring in the complex regulatory picture that we have described above.

One idea here is that government today does less direct regulating, leaving this to industries, professions, companies and so on. Instead, the role of government is to regulate the regulators. The work of the Office of Regulation Review,

---

15   Office of Regulation Review, n 6, Appendix E, 19.

16   B Fisse and J Braithwaite, *The Impact of Publicity on Corporate Offenders*, State University of New York Press, 1983.

17   We also refer to the Panopticon in Chapter 7, p 194.

18   C Shearing and P Stenning, "Say Cheese!': The Disney Order that is Not So Mickey Mouse" in C Shearing and P Stenning (eds), *Private Policing*, Sage, 1987, 317, 319.

described earlier, is an example.[19] Although meta-regulation is sometimes described as "the regulation of self-regulation", the idea is not limited to the relationship between government and self-regulators. Indeed it encompasses the relationship between all regulators. It describes a model in which there are "various layers of regulation each doing their own regulating. At the same time, each layer regulates the regulation of each other in various combinations of horizontal and vertical influence".[20] Furthermore, these "combinations of influence" operate in both directions. So, an example of vertical influence from the top-down is found in the role of constitutional law (and, indeed, international law) in regulating the regulatory behaviour of state agencies and legislators.[21] An example of bottom-up influence occurs when powerful multinational corporations are able to determine the content of regulatory standards; for example, Braithwaite and Drahos note that "for years some of Australia's air safety standards have been written by the Boeing Corporation in Seattle".[22]

(d)   Problems in regulation

Parker and Braithwaite borrow Teubner's idea of a "regulatory trilemma" to describe the problems that confront any attempt to influence social institutions or social practices by regulation.[23] The three components of the trilemma are the problems of effectiveness, responsiveness and coherence.

First, regulation, whatever form it takes, may fail to be effective in shaping institutions or determining social or economic practices. This may be due to poorly designed rules (eg, rules that are unclear, too complex, or too generalised); inappropriate regulatory strategies (eg, over-reliance on prosecution or, conversely, on out-of-court settlements); or inadequate enforcement (perhaps because of inadequate resources). There is a considerable literature that examines why people do – or do not – comply with regulation.[24]

Even where regulation *is* effective this may lead to the second problem of responsiveness. As Parker and Braithwaite describe it, the problem here is that "regulation may be so effective that it subverts and destroys otherwise desirable social practices". Regulation and regulatory institutions must be responsive to:

> [T]he practices and norms of the targets of regulation, including issues of efficiency and practicality of compliance and the extent to which the values represented in regulation and the techniques used to monitor and enforce

---

19   See n 8.

20   Parker, Scott, Lacey and Braithwaite, n 4, 6.

21   These examples are derived from J Braithwaite and C Parker, "Conclusion" in Parker et al, n 4, 284.

22   J Braithwaite and P Drahos, *Global Business Regulation*, Cambridge UP, 2000, 3.

23   Parker and Braithwaite, n 5, 127-129, referring to G Teubner, "Juridification: Concepts, Aspects, Limits, Solutions" in G Teubner (ed), *Juridification of Social Spheres: A Comparative Analysis of the Areas of Labor, Corporate, Antitrust, and Social Welfare Law*, Walter de Gruyter, 1987, 3.

24   See, for example, B Hutter, *Compliance: Regulation and Environment*, Clarendon Press, 1997; B Hutter, *Regulation and Risk: Occupational Health and Safety on the Railways*, Oxford UP, 2001; Tom Tyler, *Why People Obey the Law*, Yale UP, 1990; F Pearce and S Tombs, *Toxic Capitalism: Corporate Crime and the Chemical Industry*, Ashgate, 1998.

compliance with regulatory standards fit with pre-existing norms and social ordering in the target population.[25]

The third problem is that regulation may be *too* responsive to the concerns of those being regulated. As a consequence the regulatory effort may not be coherent with underlying values of the legal system, such as fairness, accountability, consistency and predictability.[26] Alternatively, regulation that over-emphasises the goal of effectiveness may undermine the coherence of the legal system. For example, over-use of the criminal law as a regulatory tool may undermine the "special nature of the criminal law as being reserved for behaviour deserving of moral opprobrium".[27]

(e) Models of regulation

We have seen that the relationship between law and regulation can be studied by looking at different forms of regulation. Another way of studying this relationship, which cuts across the discussion of different forms, is to examine different models of regulation. Below we examine two models that have dominated the analysis of regulation in recent years. As with the discussion on regulatory forms, while it is helpful to identify particular models so as to highlight particular issues, in practice these will rarely exist as distinct "either/or" categories.

(i) Deterrence

The standard image of regulation assumes that regulation works by deterrence. That is, rules are made to proscribe or control certain conduct, and compliance with those rules is monitored by state agencies, and instances of non-compliance are met with punitive sanctions. Deterrence is said to work either *specifically*, where legal action is brought against a person for actual instances of wrongdoing, or *generally*, where the prospect or possibility of legal action against one person deters other people from misconduct. Either form of deterrence requires that those who are subject to the rules should be monitored so that regulators will know when to take action. Moreover, the regulatees must know they are being monitored so that they are aware of the risk of action being taken.

This deterrence model (sometimes called the "command-and-control" model) of regulation makes a number of assumptions about the enforcement and compliance process. First, it assumes that regulation is about prevention and control:

> Regulation is often thought of as an activity that restricts behaviour and prevents the occurrence of certain undesirable activities (a "red light" concept) but the influence of regulation may also be *enabling* or *facilitative* ("green light") as, for example, where the airwaves are regulated so as to allow broadcasting operations to be conducted in an ordered fashion rather than left to the potential chaos of uncontrolled market.[28]

---

25   Parker and Braithwaite, n 5, 128.

26   See the discussion in Chapter 2 of this book.

27   Australian Law Reform Commission, *Principled Regulation: Federal Civil and Administrative Penalties in Australia*, Report 95, 2002, 112-113.

28   Baldwin and Cave, n 3, 2.

There is also a paradox evident when regulation occurs by way of criminal laws. As Bronitt and McSherry observe:

> To criminalise conduct places the subject and conduct practically and symbolically beyond the boundaries of legality and civil society. The criminal is literally and legally rendered outlaw. This is the paradox of criminalisation. The process of criminalisation, while potently symbolic, weakens the instrumental capacity of law to regulate the prohibited conduct. For example, where there exists a continuing market for goods or services that have been prohibited, such as illicit drugs or prostitution, the regulatory impact of the criminal law may be marginal or even counterproductive. Criminalisation may simply serve to stimulate the illegal market by increasing the profit to be gained from the delivery of illicit goods and services. It may also undermine law enforcement more generally by increasing the likelihood of police corruption and weakening public confidence in the administration of justice.[29]

Secondly, the deterrence model assumes that the state is *the* source of regulatory power. As Black points out, however, self-regulation can just as easily involve the use of "command and control" styles of regulation.[30] Thirdly, it is assumed that there is a straightforward connection between the making of rules and their enforcement. Furthermore, the deterrence model "assumes an essentially adversarial and antagonistic relationship between regulators and regulatees".[31] That is, those who are being regulated are assumed to be resistant to regulation, choosing to comply only to the minimum extent that is consistent with their own self-interests. Another aspect of this assumption is that regulators are able to obtain compliance ultimately through the threat of punishment.

For reasons that we have already encountered in this chapter, it is difficult to find examples of the simple deterrence model working in practice.[32] For example, regulatory agencies often find that they are unable effectively to monitor and enforce the rules due to inadequate resources, uncertainties about the application of the rules,[33] or inadequate rules. Additionally, those who are subjected to regulation may simply calculate that the risk of non-compliant behaviour being detected is too slight to warrant a change in their behaviour. Another problem can be found in the level of sanctions that are prescribed for non-compliance. Penalties may be too low, with the result that regulatees prefer to pay the fine rather than incur the higher costs of compliance, treating the penalty as a "cost of doing business". Alternatively, fines may be so high that they are beyond the capacity of regulatees to pay. In this instance, the deterrent effect of the penalty will disappear.[34]

To sum up, there is more to the ideas of enforcement and compliance than the simple deterrence model allows for. Enforcement is not simply a matter of

---

29   S Bronitt and B McSherry, *Principles of Criminal Law*, Lawbook Co, 2nd ed, 2005, 12.

30   Black, n 1, 123.

31   Parker and Braithwaite, n 5, 129.

32   Another reason, as Julia Black points out, is that as it is usually depicted, the command and control model is "more a caricature than an accurate description of the operation of any particular regulatory system": Black, n 1, 105.

33   The enforcement of laws against insider trading in Australia is an example. See V Goldwasser, "The Enforcement Dilemma in Australian Securities Regulation" (1999) 27 *Australian Business Law Review* 482.

34   See J Coffee, "No Soul to Damn: No Body to Kick'; An Unscandalized Inquiry Into the Problem of Corporate Punishment" (1981) 79 *Michigan Law Review* 386.

prosecution or court-action. Depending on the legal setting and the particular situation, it may involve negotiated agreements,[35] enforceable undertakings,[36] audits[37] or a range of other mechanisms. Compliance with regulation is rarely the product of regulatees making simple rational calculations about the economic cost of getting caught. Research shows that many other factors come into play, including social and cultural mores, concern about reputation and maintaining legitimacy "in the eyes of government, industry peers, and the public".[38]

(ii) Responsive regulation

A key problem with the simple deterrence model is that it does not take account of the variety of available regulatory methods, such as those identified earlier in this chapter. The "responsive regulation" model developed by Ayres and Braithwaite seeks to address this shortcoming. As they describe it:

> We suggest that regulation be responsive to industry structure in that different structures will be conducive to different degrees and forms of regulation. Government should also be attuned to differing motivations of regulated actors. Efficacious regulation should speak to the diverse objectives of regulated firms, industry associations, and individuals within them. Regulations can affect structure (eg, the number of firms in the industry) and can affect motivations of the regulated.
>
> We also conceive that regulation should respond to industry conduct, to how effectively industry is making private regulation work. The very behaviour of an industry or the firms therein should channel the regulatory strategy to greater or lesser degrees of government intervention.[39]

Ayres and Braithwaite explain their model in terms of an "enforcement pyramid". The pyramid is divided into layers, with non-punitive, less interventionist strategies (such as persuasion by regulatory inspectors) at the base, and punitive or coercive sanctions (such as imprisonment or licence revocation) at the top. The intermediate layers represent regulatory responses of increasing severity, escalating from civil monetary penalties to agreed undertakings through to community service orders or fines.[40] A "standard" version of the pyramid looks like this:

---

35 During the late 1980s the National Companies and Securities Commission (Australia's first national companies regulator; see now the Australian Securities and Investments Commission) had a policy of seeking compliance by informal negotiations with company personnel, rather than using court processes: R Tomasic and S Bottomley, *Directing the Top 500: Corporate Governance and Accountability in Australian Companies*, Allen and Unwin, 1993, 129. See also Ogus, n 1, 97 discussing "negotiated compliance".

36 An enforceable undertaking is a promise made by a regulatee to a regulator that is enforceable in court. This allows a regulator to tailor the enforcement process to the particular circumstances. They are found in the *Australian Securities and Investments Commission Act 2001* (Cth) and the *Trade Practices Act 1974* (Cth). On the latter, see C Parker, "Restorative Justice in Business Regulation? The Australian Competition and Consumer Commission's Use of Enforceable Undertakings" (2004) 67 *Modern Law Review* 209.

37 See, for example, C Parker, "Regulator-Required Corporate Compliance Program Audits" (2003) 25 *Law and Policy* 221.

38 Parker and Braithwaite, n 5, 131.

39 I Ayres and J Braithwaite, *Responsive Regulation: Transcending the Deregulation Debate*, Oxford UP, 1992, 4.

40 The pyramid first appeared in Ayres and Braithwaite, n 39. This version appears in J Braithwaite, "Inequality and Republican Criminology" in J Hagan and R Peterson (eds), *Crime and Inequality*, Stanford UP, 1995, 299.

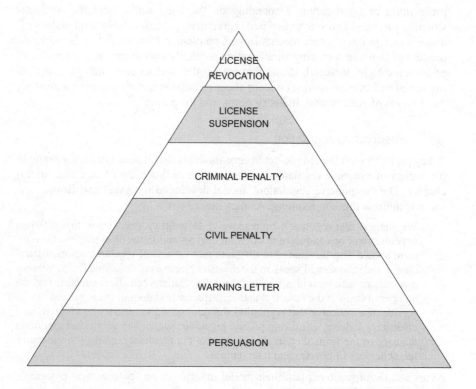

Different versions of the enforcement pyramid can be applied to different regulatory settings so that, for example, there can be a domestic violence enforcement pyramid,[41] a corporate accountability pyramid, and so on. In each setting, the particular strategies at each level will vary, but the overall structure is the same: less interventionist, informal, self-regulatory mechanisms occupy the base of the pyramid, escalating towards highly interventionist, formal sanctions at the top.

As Ayres and Braithwaite conceive it, most regulatory action will occur at the bottom of the pyramid, where the initial response of regulators is to educate and persuade regulated actors to comply. In the event of non-compliance, regulatory responses can then escalate to the next level. At the lower levels of the pyramid the idea is that individuals should take responsibility for compliance, but the possibility of external sanctions remains. The underlying idea is that "actors, individual or corporate, are most likely to comply if they know that enforcement is backed by sanctions which can be escalated in response to any given level of non-compliance, whether minor or egregious".[42] In a sense the enforcement period is another example of the idea – discussed in Chapter 5 – of actors "bargaining in the shadow of the law".

---

41 See Bronitt and McSherry, n 29, 725.
42 B Fisse and J Braithwaite, *Corporations, Crime and Accountability*, Cambridge UP, 1993, 143.

(f) Regulation and the rule of law

Earlier in this chapter we noted the possibility of a clash between ideas about regulation and the ideals associated with the rule of law. Now that we have investigated the scope of regulatory thinking and its recommendations for what constitutes "good" regulation, we return to examine this potential conflict in this concluding section of the chapter.

Recalling what was said in Chapter 3, the rule of law[43] embodies the idea of constitutionality (that government should occur *through* laws, but government itself should also be *subject to* laws); the idea of formal legality (that laws should be general, promulgated, clear, specific, prospective, practicable and stable); and the idea of procedural legality (that disputes about the application of laws should be decided by unbiased and disinterested bodies that hear both sides of the case and are exposed to public scrutiny).

A model of regulation that complies with these ideas would be state-centred, law-based, and government-enforced. It would, in other words, have the attributes associated with the deterrence or command-and-control model described earlier. As we have seen, however, many regulatory theorists point out that in practice modern regulation involves significant non-state and non-law elements. They also argue that a "responsive" use of these elements can produce good regulatory outcomes. This suggests that there may be a tension between the rule of law and modern regulatory thinking.[44] Does this mean that "the rule of law is out of step with the realities of how social and economic life is regulated"?[45] Or, conversely, does it mean that many forms of regulation "violate the rule of law precept"?[46] Are we faced with an either/or choice between the relevance of the rule of law and the validity of modern regulation?

There are reasons to think that this dilemma can be resolved and, indeed, that it may be less of a problem than it first appears to be. Leighton McDonald argues, for example, that "there is no necessary reason why many features of flexible and collaborative regulatory regimes, such as various forms of self-regulation, detract from the rule of law". What is needed, he suggests, is "a conception of the rule of law which accepts that the existence of rules is only one legal device for the prevention of regulatory arbitrariness".[47] For example, rules that are generated within a particular industry to regulate the conduct of industry participants can meet the rule of law attributes (clarity, non-retrospectivity and so on) and their validity can be assessed on that basis. Further, as McDonald says, "there is no reason why a principled use of, for example, an "enforcement pyramid" would undermine rule of law values".[48]

In other words, and this serves as an appropriate conclusion to this chapter, just as the study of regulation can give us a better understanding of the role and impact of law on social and economic behaviour, it can also be a useful way of

---

43 As we noted in Chapter 3, there is debate about the rule of law concept – what it means and which concepts it embodies.

44 See L McDonald, "The Rule of Law in The New Regulatory State'" (2004) 33 *Common Law World Review* 197 for a succinct analysis of this tension.

45 Ibid 197.

46 Ibid 217.

47 Ibid 215 and 219.

48 Ibid 262 (footnote, references to Ayres and Braithwaite omitted).

looking at, and seeking to conceptualise, law. In this chapter, therefore, we have moved, in effect, from looking at regulation through a legal lens to looking at law through a regulatory lens.

Chapter 11

Foundations of Economic Analysis

(a) Introduction

During the past 40 years or so, the economic analysis of law has established itself as one of the most influential intellectual movements within legal scholarship and teaching. When we wrote about law and economics in the first edition of this book we did so in the expectation that it would take hold in Australian law schools and law curricula in the same way as it has in the United States.[1] By the time of the second edition there was some reason to think that the impact of law and economics in Australian legal circles was not as strong as in the United States. At the time of this third edition the picture is much more clear. In Australia law and economics has a significant influence on the contextual study of law, but its main impact tends to be confined to particular areas of law, predominantly those dealing with business and market transactions. Significantly, in the United States there are also signs that the impact law and economics may have reached its zenith (although commentators have been mis-predicting its demise for many years).[2]

The literature on law and economics has proliferated rapidly from about 1960. Whereas the use of economic approaches was initially applied to areas of law with an obvious economic content (eg, trade practices and regulation of industry), today economists expanded their techniques of analysis across the board to explain family law, crime, torts, contracts,[3] property, legislation, remedies, sanctions, and legal institutions and procedures. Economics has supplied an account of everything from suicide[4] to whether there should be a free market in adopted babies.[5] As Swan remarks, "if economics can have something to say

1   For discussion of these developments in the late 1980s, see A Duggan, "Law and Economics in Australia" (1989) 1 *Legal Education Review* 37.

2   A Bernstein, "Whatever Happened to Law and Economics?" (2005) 64 *Maryland Law Review* 101.

3   See, for example, NC Seddon and MP Ellinghaus *Cheshire & Fifoot's Law of Contract*, 8th Aus ed, Butterworths, 2002, paras 28.11–28.21.

4   ADS Hermermesh and NM Soss, "An Economic Theory of Suicide" (1974) 82 *Journal of Political Economy* 83.

5   EM Landes and R Posner, "The Economics of the Baby Shortage" (1978) 7 *Journal of Legal Studies* 323.

about … brushing one's teeth and extra-marital affairs, it certainly has something to say about law".[6]

There is no single coherent explanatory theory of law and economics. Rather, different (and sometimes conflicting) schools of thought have developed. Malloy,[7] for example, identifies conservative law and economics, liberal perspectives on law and economics, critical and Marxist approaches, and the libertarian conception of law and economics, amongst others.[8] As Richardson observes, there is now a market in law and economics approaches.[9]

Within the confines of an introductory text, it is not possible to address all the different dimensions of law and economics. Instead, we take a more selective approach. Our principal focus is on the "neo-classical"[10] economic analysis of law and, in particular, on the contribution of the "Chicago school" approach. The Chicago school is a group of economists (initially associated with the Economics Faculty of the University of Chicago), with a strong commitment to free market ideology and the belief that simple market economics has extraordinary explanatory power in all fields of human and institutional activity.[11] We explain the contribution of the Chicago school to the economic analysis of law, but we also explore the methodological shortcomings of that approach, its ideological underpinnings and its inherent limitations.

---

6   P Swan, "The Economics of Law: Economic Imperialism and Negligence Law" (1986) 3 *Aust Economic Review* 92. Ronald Coase, regarded by some as the founder of modern law and economics, has commented sceptically that "[t]he reason for this movement of economists into neighbouring fields is certainly not that we have solved the problems of the economic system; it would perhaps be more plausible to argue that economists are looking for fields in which they can have some success": "Economics and Contiguous Disciplines" (1978) 7 *Journal of Legal Studies* 201 at 203.

7   RP Malloy, *Law and Economics: A Comparative Approach to Theory and Practice*, West Publishing Co, 1990, Part 2. See also N Mercuro and TP Ryan, *Law, Economics and Public Policy*, 1984, JAI Press, 1, for a further description of different approaches.

8   The conservative approach is identified with the work of Richard Posner, to which we refer extensively in the following chapters, especially *The Economic Analysis of Law*, 5th ed, Little Brown, 1998. For examples of a liberal perspective, see B Ackerman, *Social Justice in the Liberal State*, Yale UP, 1980, and "Law, Economics, and the Problem of Legal Culture" [1986] *Duke Law Jnl* 929. For examples of a critical approach to economic analysis, see M Kelman, "Misunderstanding Social Life: A Critique of the Core Premises of Law and Economics" (1983) 33 *Journal of Legal Education* 274; D Kennedy, "Cost-Benefit Analysis of Entitlement Problems: A Critique" (1981) 33 *Stanford Law Review* 387; and W Wiegers, "Economic Analysis of Law and Private Ordering': A Feminist Critique" (1992) 42 *University of Toronto Law Journal* 170. The libertarian approach is demonstrated in Richard Epstein's work, including *Takings: Private Property and the Power of Eminent Domain*, Harvard UP, 1985. Malloy has also produced a critique of traditional law and economics, which he calls "law and market economy", that focuses on the social, political, and cultural context of exchange relations: R Malloy, *Law and Market Economy*, Cambridge UP, 2000. For a bibliographical survey of the diversity of analyses in the economic analysis of law, see AM Polinsky, *An Introduction to Law and Economics*, 3rd ed, Little Brown, 2003.

9   M Richardson, "The Second Wave in Context" in M Richardson and G Hadfield (eds), *The Second Wave of Law and Economics*, Federation Press, 1999, 2.

10   Neo-classical economics dates from the 1870s. It is based on the idea of allowing the forces of supply and demand to reach equilibrium in a competitive market.

11   See, for example, M Friedman, *Capitalism and Freedom*, U of Chicago Press, 1962. The school "applies the simple tenets of rational maximising behaviour to all walks of life to elicit testable propositions about the way people and institutions will react to changes in their environment, and to construct proposals for legal reform based on the criterion of economic efficiency": C Veljanovski, *The Economics of Law*, Hobart Paper, Institute of Economic Affairs, 1990, 19.

The influence of the Chicago school was particularly noticeable after the 1980s as a result of a convergence of its own ideology with that of conservative political administrations in the United States, United Kingdom, New Zaland and Australia. As a result law and economics became almost synonymous with the Chicago school version.[12] This impression is encouraged by its proponents, who commonly write as if they represent economists as a whole.[13] Clearly they do not, and so we also endeavour to cover some of the alternative analyses that have developed.[14]

(b) The claims of economic analysis

Economists claim that economics has considerable predictive power and that it achieves a degree of precision in analysis which is often lacking in other social sciences. The claimed predictive power comes about because of the simplifying assumptions which economists make about human behaviour. We examine some of these assumptions later in this chapter.

Economics claims analytical precision through its reliance on the "measuring rod of money" as a central means of analysis.[15] As Ronald Coase, a pivotal figure in the law and economics movement, argues:

> [S]ince what is measured by money are important determinants of human behaviour in the economic system, the analysis has considerable explanatory power.[16]

For example,[17] consider this question: if liability is imposed on a manufacturer for damages resulting from a defective product, how will this affect the product's

---

12 Richardson and Hadfield argue that the Chicago school represents the "first wave" of law and economics which has since been superseded by a "second wave" (eg, M Trebilcock, *The Limits of Freedom of Contract*, Harvard UP, 1993) that is more sceptical of the grand claims made by "first wave" writers: Richardson and Hadfield, n 9. They point out, nevertheless, that the second wave relies on core concepts such as efficiency and rational choice that, as will be seen, are central to the still-influential Chicago school.

13 This has prompted some commentators to ask whether there is *any* dissenting tradition in law and economics. N Duxbury, "Is there a Dissenting Tradition in Law and Economics?" (1991) 54 *Modern Law Review* 300. Similarly, Susan Rose-Ackerman has argued for the development of a credible *progressive* law and economics, suggesting that there is no inherent reason why law and economics *should* be associated with conservative ideologies such as that of the Chicago school: S Rose-Ackerman, "Progressive Law and Economics – And the New Administrative Law" (1988) 98 *Yale Law Journal* 294.

14 For example, we explore the neo-institutional approach and the "Yale Realist" approach of Calabresi in Chapter 12, and the Public Choice analysis of the "Virginia School" in Chapter 13.

15 As Veljanovski, n 11, 41, points out, "in order to evaluate an activity which produces a variety of benefits we must have a common measuring rod. Economists use money ... The willingness-to-pay measure seeks to provide a quantitative indication of an individual's *intensity* of preferences".

16 Coase, n 6, 209. Coase further argues, at 209-210, that:
     The success of economists in moving into the other social sciences is a sign that they possess certain advantages in handling the problems of those disciplines. One is, I believe, that they study the economic system as a unified interdependent system and, therefore, are more likely to uncover the basic interrelationships within a social system than is someone less accustomed to looking at the working of a system as a whole. Another is that a study of economics makes it difficult to ignore factors which are clearly important and which play a part in all social systems. The economist's analysis may fail to touch some of the problems found in the other social systems, but often the analysis can be brought to bear. And the economist will take full advantage of those opportunities which occur when the "measuring rod of money" can be used.

17 This example is taken from R Cooter, "Law and Unified Social Theory" (1995) 22 *Journal of Law and Society* 50 at 51-52.

future safety and price? Economists answer the question by regarding legal liability in terms of costs and prices. They can then make predictions about how a rational manufacturer will balance the cost of safety with the price of injuries to consumers. So, economics claims to provide a set of tools which can be used to illuminate a wide range of legal problems and to generate a deeper understanding of the way in which law affects, and is affected by, the economic environment.

Students studying a law subject for the first time are often struck by a sense of incoherence, the lack of any apparent rationale to link the numerous legal authorities which they are asked to come to terms with. That coherence does not always seem to be provided by the internal logic of the law. Economics, however, claims that there is an *external* logic, one which is to be found not in law itself, but in the concept of "economic efficiency". For example, contract law might be seen as striving to achieve efficiency in individual exchange relationships. Not only (some economists say) is this what it does do but also, this is what it *should* do.[18] In other words, the claims of the law and economics movement have a descriptive and a normative aspect. Economics promises to provide a framework (a "glue" or logic) which enables law students to make sense of cases which otherwise might seem to be unconnected.

The economic analysis of law claims practical and policy advantages for lawyers in providing advice and services to their clients, for courts in reaching their decisions and for those who contribute to policy formation and the debate on law reform. It is essential in carrying out all those tasks to have an understanding of the nature of legal institutions and how they behave. Economic analysis claims to illuminate two fundamental questions: what effects do rules have on society, and how do social forces shape and determine the law?

There are three roles economists might play in the analysis of law.[19] First, the economist may act as technician, taking the problem facing a legal decision-maker and bringing her expertise to bear in dealing with a specific aspect of a case. For example, even where the overall question raised by a case is not economic in nature:

> [A]t some point an understanding of how markets work, how markets value commodities, services, and assets, and how individuals interact in their economic roles may become critical in deciding the ultimate disposition of the case.[20]

Aspects of damages calculations, and estimating the market share of an alleged monopoly, would be examples of this first contribution of economics to law.

A second role an economist can play is what Klevorick describes as the "supertechnician". Again, the economist takes the problem as posed by the legal decision-maker:

> [B]ut in this instance the entire structure of the problem area has economic roots. The objectives and design of the institutions and doctrine are explicitly stated in economic terms, and the economist is called upon to evaluate and give advice about the best ways to achieve the specified objective(s).[21]

---

18 These issues are developed further in this chapter and Chapter 12.
19 A Klevorick, "Law and Economic Theory: An Economist's View" (1975) 65 *American Economic Review* 237 at 237-241.
20 Ibid 237.
21 Ibid 239.

For example, in areas such as trade practices law and labour law, the central questions include how an industry or sector may be structured in the most efficient manner. Here the economist can provide an evaluation of the relative advantages and disadvantages of alternative approaches to regulation, of the indirect as well as the direct effects which a particular measure may have on the industry and its consumers, or on the economy generally, and on its income or wealth distributional implications. Most important, the economist can assist in designing the particular legal structure that is eventually chosen to cope with the given legal problem.

The third role – what we might call "the economist as a conceptualist" – has become the central one in the economic analysis of law. Principally, it is this role which is explored in this part of the book. It arises where the economist

> takes the general problem area with which the lawyer is concerned – say, torts, or property, or procedure – and poses in his own terms – that is, in economic terms – the problem he sees the legal structure or legal doctrine confronting. He provides, thereby, a different way of looking at the legal issue which yields alternative explanations of how current law came to be what it is and new proposals for new law.
>
> In the area of torts, for example, some economic theorists have posed the problem facing society as minimization of the expected social costs of accidents, taking account of: the costs incurred when accidents occur and the probabilities that such accidents will occur; the relationship between those accident costs and probabilities and the steps people take to avoid accidents; the costs of the resources devoted to avoiding accidents and the costs any administrative structure used to make decisions about the optimal level and allocation of these several kinds of costs among members of society. Economic theorists have used this type of framework to discuss and evaluate the traditional negligence rules, to provide a critique of the fault system of accident law, and to evaluate new proposals for automobile accident law, for example, no-fault plans.[22]

(c) Methodology, assumptions and concepts in economic analysis

Neo-classical economic analysis is founded on a number of basic assumptions and it uses some distinctive concepts. We describe these in the remainder of this chapter. In the two subsequent chapters these assumptions and concepts are applied in a variety of legal contexts. But before going into the descriptions it is important to make some points about the role of assumptions and the development of models in economic analysis. That is, we need to understand the basic methodology of economic analysis.

In studying any form of behaviour, economists make a number of assumptions. They make them for much the same reasons that lawyers and others do: the world is too complicated to understand without some degree of abstraction. However, what distinguishes economics is not only the nature of its core assumptions, but also that those assumptions are made for the specific purpose of developing various theoretical models of behaviour.

It is crucial to grasp the centrality of model-building to the economics enterprise. As Veljanovski puts it:

---

22   Ibid 240-241.

Models simplify in order to enable a better understanding of the real world. Because legal and economic processes are complex, a thorough understanding of the underlying forces and interrelationships is generally impossible. Models break up phenomena into more manageable portions by abstracting those variables that are believed to be a significant influence on choice and subjecting them to deductive reasoning based on a set of accepted axioms. Logical conclusions are then derived which must be translated into propositions about the real world. These propositions or predictions must then be compared to actual behaviour and experience, either by observation or statistical methods.[23]

The economist will generally begin with the simplest possible model, one which isolates one or two key variables while making simplifying and often unrealistic assumptions to eliminate the others. In this respect, the economist's methodology is similar to that of a natural scientist. As Posner has pointed out:

> Newton's law of falling bodies, for example, is unrealistic in its basic assumption that bodies fall in a vacuum, but it is still a useful theory because it predicts with sufficient though not complete accuracy the behaviour of a wide variety of falling bodies in the real world.[24]

Having analysed the simplest model, the economic theorist can then relax some of the unrealistic assumptions in order to develop a more complex model which more closely approximates behaviour in the real world. In this way, the economist develops generalisations which partially, if not completely, explain the behaviour examined.

With this methodology in mind, we move on to examine some of the core assumptions and concepts in the economic analysis of law.[25]

(i)   Rational choice

Neo-classical economics treats the individual as the basic unit of analysis. It assumes that individuals are the best judges of their own welfare, and that individuals act rationally[26] to maximise their own self-interest.[27] In economic terms, individuals are assumed to make choices so as to maximise their "utility".[28]

---

23   C Veljanovski, *The New Law and Economics*, Oxford, 1982, 19-20.

24   Posner, n 8, 18.

25   The following list is not exhaustive. For example, Cooter sees maximisation and equilibrium as core concepts of economic analysis: n 17, 54-57.

26   Compare the liberal assumption of rationality, discussed in Chapter 2.

27   Posner, n 8, 4, points out that one should not equate self-interest with selfishness. The happiness (or misery) of other people may be part of one's satisfactions. It can be argued that the "rational" person, in seeking her or his self-interest, takes into consideration the effect of her or his decision on others.

28   As E Gellhorn and GO Robinson, "The Role of Economic Analysis in Legal Education" (1983) 33 *Journal of Legal Education* 247 at 249 point out:

It is common among critical noneconomists, and even some economists, to describe this assumption as an empty abstraction or a mere tautology (whatever people are perceived to seek must be, *ipso facto*, their "utility"). But however general and protean the concept of utility-enhancing behaviour, it is not a useless tautology. In simple essence it is an assumption of human purposiveness that postulates behaviour can be explained by assuming that people generally act rationally to fulfil personal objectives – on the basis of the information available to them. This does not seem to us to be a very bold hypothesis. Indeed, we wonder why it should be thought to be a special insight of economists. Yet it is a premise that many non-economists hesitate to embrace.

In relation to behaviour in the marketplace, the implications of this assumption are fairly clear. For example, there will usually be an inverse relation between the price charged for a product, and the quantity of the product demanded. Although this model of behaviour would only appear to have implications for relatively specialised areas of law to which market behaviour is central, economists have extended their analysis to what non-economists would regard as decisions made outside any market. For example, it is assumed that people equally act as rational maximisers in making decisions about whether to marry or divorce, commit or refrain from committing crimes, make an arrest, litigate or settle a lawsuit, drive a car carefully or carelessly, pollute, refuse to associate with people of a different race, and fix a mandatory retirement age for employees.[29]

The assumption of rational choice is central to all economic analysis, including the economic analysis of law, but it is easily misunderstood. It is not meant to imply that people *actually* behave like computers, or that they are concerned only with money. Instead, economic theory argues that people's behaviour can be explained *as if* they were rational maximisers of their welfare.[30] As Posner points out: "The concept of man as a rational maximiser of his self-interest implies that people respond to incentives".[31]

Economists acknowledge that "people are not perfect utility maximisers":[32]

> In pursuing these ends, they are short of time, intelligence and information. This shortage is part of rationality and constraint. Rationality does not imply constant calculation and deliberation; we rationally form habits and acquire predispositions that release time for other endeavours. Knowledge is scarce; time itself is the commodity we cannot get more of. Economic study takes these scarcities into account; one may (and should) study them as any other scarcity. Rationality implies no more than a good fit between means and ends. ...
>
> There are limits, of course. Some people will misunderstand all things; most people will misunderstand some things, especially the probabilities and consequences of rare events such as floods. But when decisions are made repeatedly, either people learn from experience or those who do learn drive out those who do not. The (relatively) rational calculators will set the standard (an economist would call it the price) to which the group conforms. The stock market is a good example. Those who cannot deal astutely with uncertainty and discount future events, soon lose their money to those who can; the market as a whole then behaves as a compound of the canniest predictors and evaluators.[33]

Nevertheless, critics have pointed to the sharp divide between the model of the rational actor and behaviour of "real people in the real world". This has led to the emergence of a new movement, behavioural law and economics, which seeks to integrate knowledge from the behavioural sciences into the assumptions of law and economics.[34]

---

29   These examples are taken from R Posner, "The Law and Economics Movement" *AEA Papers and Proceedings* (1987) Vol 77, No 2, 5.

30   Veljanovski, n 23, 27.

31   Posner, n 8, 4.

32   T Rostain, "Educating Homo Economicus: Cautionary Notes on the New Behavioural Law and Economics Movement" (2000) 34 *Law and Society Rev* 973 at 979.

33   F Easterbrook, "The Inevitability of Law and Economics" (1989) 1 *Legal Education Review* 3 at 5-6.

34   See, for example, C Jolls, C Sunstein and R Thaler, "A Behavioural Approach to Law and Economics" (1998) 50 *Stanford Law Review* 1471.

(ii) Law as a system of constraints and rewards

The next assumption draws upon the economist's concern with markets and prices. As Veljanovski points out:

> The concepts of a market and price play key roles in economics. Even in areas where there is not an explicit market, the economic approach will often analyse the subject by analogy with the market concepts of supply, demand and price. A market is simply a decentralized mechanism for allocating resources.[35]

Economists assume that rules of law operate to impose prices on (or sometimes subsidise) activities and that individuals (acting rationally) adjust their activities to avoid the costs of laws or to obtain the benefits. Thus economists perceive law as being very much like a giant pricing machine, a "framework of duties, rights and obligations [which] creates a system of constraints and penalties which alter the net benefits of different courses of action. In a crude way, the law prices and taxes individual human behaviour and therefore influences that behaviour".[36]

Accordingly, changes in the rules are likely to alter the amount or the character of the activity in question. Thus, the law is conceived as a system of constraints and rewards interacting with individuals. A central objective of law and economics is to analyse this interaction in terms of its effects on behaviour, usually with a view to pushing that behaviour in the desired direction. Chicago school economics has expressed a strong preference for the market mechanism (especially freedom of contract) over state intervention and, where the market malfunctions, for common law (which "mimics" the market) over statute law.

(iii) Costs

Economists analyse laws in terms of their effects on the costs incurred by individuals in choosing one course of action over another. There is more to the idea of "cost" than what the individual pays "up front" for goods or services. This is made clear if we consider the economic concepts of opportunity cost and transaction costs.

The concept of opportunity cost involves the valuation of alternatives. The opportunity cost of a resource is its value in its next best use. As Veljanovski puts it, for an economist:

> The economic value of a good, service or activity is measured by the individual's willingness to pay, either in money or in kind, to acquire it. Value in economics is exchange or scarcity value – that is, preferences backed by willingness to pay by giving up alternative choices. The economic cost of a resource used for any purpose is equal to its value in the next best alternative use; its *opportunity cost*.[37]

For example, suppose Mrs Brown owns a paddock which she inherited and on which she therefore pays no rent. She grazes two cows on it and sells the milk for $200 pa. Feeding the cows costs her $150 pa in feed. It might be thought that she is making a profit of $50 pa. However, if she could rent the paddock out to a neighbour for $100 pa, an economist would say that the "opportunity costs" of the paddock is $100 a year. That is, she is not currently making the best economic

---

35   Veljanovski, n 23, 31

36   Veljanovski, n 11, 88.

37   Veljanovski, n 23, 29-30.

value of her asset, and in that sense she is making a loss of $50, rather than a profit of $50.[38]

In the real world individuals who transact with each other incur a variety of costs. These include the cost of locating each other, assessing the quality of the goods or services being exchanged, negotiating the terms of the transaction, drawing up any necessary documents, and then monitoring and enforcing those terms. All of these "transaction costs" contribute to the overall cost of the exchange. Obviously, transaction costs will vary depending upon the type of transaction (remembering that for the economist, the idea of a transaction is not restricted to contractual or market-based relations), the number of parties, their geographical distribution, and so on. In some instances the transaction costs will be so high that bargaining between the parties is not possible. For example, it is generally not feasible for motorists and pedestrians to negotiate with each other in advance about their respective positions. This has implications for the construction of liability rules. We look at this example more closely in a later chapter. We will also see that the idea of transaction costs forms the basis of a distinct school of law and economic theory that complements the Chicago school approach.

(iv) Efficiency

Another distinguishing feature of the economic analysis of law is its focus on the organising principle of efficiency. Lawyers may commonly debate the value of legal rules in terms of concepts of justice or fairness. Economists ask a different question: are the rules efficient? As McEwin puts it: "Rules are explained in terms of their economic efficiency in the same way as feminists explain the world in terms of gender or Marxists in terms of class".[39]

In broad terms, efficiency refers to the relationship between the aggregate benefit of a situation and the aggregate costs of the situation.[40] To take a simple example, lawyers may concern themselves with how to achieve the fairest distribution of a limited legal aid budget, debating the justice issues of giving priority to criminal cases over family law cases. In contrast economists, concerned with the efficient use of resources, focus on how to maximise the overall legal aid budget given those resources. The analogy here is the difference between, on the one hand, deciding how a pie of a given size should be divided and, on the other hand, trying to produce the biggest pie possible given the available resources.[41]

Chicago school economists use the concept of efficiency in a more defined way than this simple example suggests. They are principally concerned with *allocative* efficiency: that is, they seek to develop a criterion for determining whether a shift from one allocation of resources to another is efficient. There are two main economic theories of allocative efficiency, one devised in 1927 by the Italian sociologist Vilfredo Pareto and the other authored by two economists in England, Nicholas Kaldor and John R Hicks in 1939.

---

38   This example is based on FH Stephen, *The Economics of the Law*, Wheatsheaf, 1988, 46-47.

39   I McEwin, "Liberty, Law and Economics" in S Ratnapala and G Moens (eds), *Jurisprudence of Liberty*, Butterworths, 1996, 165, 172.

40   See further Polinsky, n 8, 7.

41   The potential conflict between equity and efficiency is addressed in Chapter 12 below.

Pareto efficiency is achieved when, in a given situation, it is not possible to improve the welfare of one person (as he or she perceives it) without reducing the welfare of another. The Pareto criterion for efficiency tends to preserve the status quo. This is because most reallocations of resources will make at least one person worse off (in their own view), and thus would not be a Pareto improvement. This is a problem that the idea of Kaldor-Hicks efficiency seeks to overcome. On this criterion if those who benefit from a particular policy or change in the law can compensate those whose welfare is reduced, then the policy or change is efficient and should be pursued. One problem with this test of efficiency is that it does not require actual compensation – the test is satisfied if *in theory* the "winners" can compensate the "losers".

The following example[42] gives a simple illustration of the difference between a Pareto approach and a Kaldor-Hicks approach. Imagine that a person owns and runs a business from an office building in downtown Sydney. The market value of the building, given its current use, is $1 million. The city council would like to see the site redeveloped by the construction of a large hotel. A hotel chain proposes a plan for a hotel that would provide the community with $2 million worth of value. The current owner does not want to sell; she places a higher value on continuing her current business than with obtaining the market value of $1 million. Under a Pareto approach, it would not be efficient for the council to compulsorily acquire the property (assuming it has the legal power to do this), since the current owner would have less utility and as a result would be worse off. Under the Kaldor-Hicks approach the council should acquire the property and transfer it to the hotel chain, because in theory the increase in value to the community is sufficient to compensate the current owner for her loss.

Again, it is important to be clear about the difference between the efficiency of a particular allocation of resources and the fairness or justice of the resulting distribution of resources. Allocative efficiency, especially in its Kaldor-Hicks form, is concerned with the cumulative effect of resource allocation, not with its distributive consequences. This distinction is discussed in the following extract by Veljanovski.

C Veljanovski, *The New Law and Economics*
(1982)

Each allocative change not only alters total wealth but distributes it in different proportions among individuals. The latter is also an economic problem, one that economists have had little success in modelling. Even if one is not principally concerned with the distribution of wealth, it is necessary to recognize that efficiency and the economic value of goods and services cannot be separated from distributional questions.

The distribution of wealth (or entitlements which confer legal rights to wealth) determine in part both the economic value and optimal allocation of resources in an economy. To say that a situation is allocatively efficient is to say only that all the (potential or actual) gains from trade have been exhausted, given the initial distribution of wealth among individuals. If the wealth in society were redistributed then there would be a different efficient allocation of resources. To

---

42   This example is based on Malloy, n 7, 41-42.

take a rather extreme example, if wealth is concentrated in the hands of a few rich landowners who buy Rolls Royces and caviar, then allocative efficiency will be consistent with the poor starving and the economy's productive activity chan- nelled into the manufacture of these luxury items. If wealth were to be distributed more equitably, less Rolls Royces and caviar and more of the necessities of life would be produced.

Thus each different distribution of wealth generates a different pattern of demand, a different set of prices and different production decisions. Economic value and the efficient allocation of resources are both intractably related and vary according to the distribution of wealth in society. There thus exists literally an infinite number of allocatively efficient outcomes that differ only with respect to the distribution of welfare among individuals in society. Efficiency is therefore little more than a technocratic principle of unimprovability; there is no rearrangement of society's productive activity or allocation of goods and services that will improve the economic welfare of society given the distribution of wealth upon which market transactions are based.

Allocative efficiency is a necessary but not sufficient condition for the maximization of a social welfare function that incorporates a value judgement regarding the ethical deserts of various members of society. The orthodox view is that the desirability of a given income distribution is not a question of efficiency. The attainment of an optimum that maximizes social welfare is seen as involving state intervention to rectify the initial distribution of resources so as to make each consumer dollar voting in the market of equal social deserts.

The recognition of the inseparable relationship between the distribution of wealth and efficiency gives rise to certain propositions that have not been sufficiently emphasized in the literature:

1. the only Pareto efficient outcome that is socially desirable is that based on a just distribution of income and property rights and;
2. inefficiency may be acceptable in practice if it leads to a more desirable or ethically attractive distribution of wealth.

Thus it is apparent that normative economics needs a theory of distributive justice that will enable the analyst to rank efficient outcomes in terms of their ethical attractiveness. Economists have shied away from this task largely because of a widely held professional view that distributive justice is a nebulous concept that defies scientific evaluation and the obvious difficulties of defining and enforcing a social welfare function which would at the same time be consistent with the paretian assumptions.[43]

As we shall see later, Posner, invoking a variant of the Kaldor-Hicks criteria which he calls the "wealth maximization principle", *does* claim to provide an ethically attractive theory of distributive justice. Whether he succeeds in this enterprise is far from clear. In Chapter 12 we examine these claims further. In particular, we explore the conflict between equity and efficiency, whether "wealth maximisation" can provide an adequate concept of justice and the serious criticisms that have been levelled at the normative approach, and Posner's work in particular.

---

43   Veljanovski, n 23, 31-44 (with omissions).

(v)   Marginal effects

Economic analysis is concerned with *marginal* rather than with average or gross effects. Accordingly, what is important to an economist is not that all people behave in a particular way in response to a change in the law, but rather that *some* people ("those at the margin") do so. Easterbrook elaborates on this point:

> If we wish to know the effects of rules and decisions, where shall we look, and for what? Economists say, look at the margin. This means incremental effects. To know whether the death penalty is a useful punishment, look at the change in the volume of murders that accompanies a change in punishment, not at whether there is "a lot" of murder with or without capital punishment. It is common to say, "criminal law does not deter; look at all the crimes". This is like saying that a higher price does not discourage the sale of cigarettes; they are addictive, and look at all the sales. Rates of change are more important. It turns out, much to most people's surprise, that the sales of cigarettes and liquor fall off faster when prices rise than do sales of yams or automobiles. People substitute from cigarettes to chocolate faster, when the price of cigarettes rises relative to chocolate, than they substitute from soda pop to chocolate. Even though it is hard to give up cigarettes, it turns out to be relatively easy to cut back on smoking; and for some persons a change in price makes it worthwhile to give up altogether. The sales of cigarettes are high, and nicotine is habit forming; but it would be a grievous mistake to assume that law has a limited influence over such things just because, on average, it is hard for a given person to kick the habit. That is a lesson with general application.[44]

(vi)   Ex ante effects

The lawyer, analysing a particular event, favours an *ex-post* approach; that is, the law is seen as a way of remedying a problem *after* the event. An accident has occurred, a contract has been broken; how should the innocent party be compensated? The courts look at past events and actual cases. While they may be conscious that the precedent or principle that emerges will have an impact on other persons in similar future circumstances, their main focus is on the parties to the particular case. In contrast, the economist views the law as an incentive system affecting *future* actions, and for this reason favours an *ex-ante* approach. In Veljanovski's words:

> [The economic approach] focuses on the incentives and implications for prospective behaviour that changes in variables or policy may have ... Thus the economic analysis of tort law would examine the effects that different liability rules have on investment in [future] safety rather than their adequacy in resolving a dispute or redressing the violation of individual rights.[45]

The economist's case in favour of an *ex-ante* approach has been put strongly by Easterbrook. He maintains that legal rules are about deterrence and that to look backwards, viewing the law as mainly concerned with achieving a fair division of the stakes, is to miss its most important effects:

> Judges who disregard future effects may well come to the right conclusion, but their work will be less stable, because it can easily be attacked by analysis

---

44   Easterbrook, n 33, 15-16.
45   Veljanovski, n 23, 30.

appealing to "fairness" and similar ex post contentions. I offer as an illustration the decision of the High Court in Australia in *Breavington v Godleman*.[46] The High Court considered whether to replace Australia's prevailing rule that the law of the state in which the suit was filed applied to torts, no matter where they took place. The Northern Territory adopted a no-fault motor vehicle insurance scheme, under which recovery for injuries is certain but limited; Victoria uses a negligence system, under which recovery is less likely but more generous. Breavington filed suit in Victoria to recover for an accident that occurred in the Northern Territory. All seven Justices held, in six judgments, that the law of the place of the accident must be applied, discarding the former law in Australia.

Lex loci delicti is a plausible rule. It may serve many functions. It enables persons to know with greater certainty the consequences of their acts, and thus to plan intelligently – something especially important in designing and manufacturing products and drugs. Those who know rules also can take precautions such as obtaining insurance; and insurers will sell the product at lower cost if they, too, can assess their exposure. It cuts down on litigation about choice of law. It enables states to tailor their rules to achieve optimal deterrence and compensation. Both a high probability of a modest award (as under no-fault systems) and a lower probability of a higher award (as under negligence systems) may have the same expected value; but if the injured party with the best case can choose to sue in the state using a negligence rule (obtaining the higher award), while the party with a low chance of showing negligence can collect under the no-fault system, then net recoveries will be higher than either state envisages – a result that may discourage driving (and other risky activities) without making drivers more careful. These and other economic functions of the tort system could have led to a well-supported decision to favour the law where the accident occurred.

Not one Justice of the High Court mentioned any of this. Several, however, spoke of the evils of "forum shopping" without explaining what these were. Perhaps an objection to forum shopping is shorthand notation for these kinds of considerations, but perhaps not. Who could tell? Maybe an objection to forum shopping is only an instinct for what is "fair" to defendants. But why is it the purpose of tort law to be fair to tortfeasors? Why not be fair to victims? Since fairness to victims often seems to mean higher recoveries, what is wrong with forum shopping? Sometimes forum shopping appears inevitable. Think of an injury caused by a product designed in [s]tate A, manufactured in State B, sold in State C to a resident in State D, repaired in State E, which breaks in State F gravely injuring a resident in State G, who later moves to State H, which affords him medical care at public expense. What is fair about applying State F's law to this tort? A court that lacks a theory – as opposed to a slogan – about why one choice of law rule is preferable to another will not be able to cope with this kind of case, which presents the pressures for ex post analysis that recur in the law.

It is not my purpose to criticise the High Court, for *Breavington* is not inferior in any way to the analysis which courts in the United States apply to questions of this sort. Indeed, I rather prefer *Breavington* to American cases, for a majority of the states in the United States has abandoned the *lex loci* rule in favour of the "choice-influencing considerations" approach sketched by the American Law Institute. The development of American conflicts law has been driven by consistent yielding to the siren of "fairness" – at each turn choosing the rule that maximises plaintiffs' recovery, in large part because courts lack a theory

---

46   (1988) 80 ALR 362.

about choice of law and the consequences of tort doctrines. The upshot includes products that are uninsurable (and hence not made), even though they have substantial benefits. This "modern" approach has come under increasing criticism by commentators who point out economic (and other) adverse consequences of an approach so foggy that it is no rule at all. A court without a theory of consequences is a court without a stable law. If Australia is to follow in the path of American choice of law decisions, it ought to have a clear view of what it is getting.[47]

(d) Applying economic theory to law

Having examined some of the core assumptions, concepts and perspectives that are used in the economic analysis of law, it is useful to return to an examination of the role which economics claims to play in analysing the law. Self-evidently, all these central aspects of the economic analysis of law are intimately connected with the core liberal values of individualism, autonomy, liberty, limited government and formal equality, which we examined in Chapter 2.

There are essentially three different but related applications of economics to the law. The first approach uses economics to discover the *effect* of laws (in economic jargon: positive or predictive economics); the second applies economics to *explain* the legal system as it is (descriptive economics); and the third uses it to recommend changes that might improve the law (normative or prescriptive economics).

The first enterprise involves an analysis of how legal rules affect human behaviour, particularly resource use. This approach is essentially predictive and empirical. It postulates (relying on the core economic assumptions) that people act as rational maximisers of their self-interest, basing their choices on relatively constant preferences or desires. This hypothesis is then used to generate testable (ie refutable) predictions concerning the effects of legal measures on behaviour.

A predictive theory must be judged in terms of how closely its predictions correspond to the "facts". For example, does the adoption of negligence rather than no-fault liability affect the level of motor accidents in the direction predicted? If the theory predicts more accurately than any competing theory, then it is useful, irrespective of whether its underlying assumptions are realistic or descriptively accurate.[48]

However, because they are based on simplified assumptions, the predictions of positive economic models must be treated with care.[49] Some critics argue that the predictive power of the economic analysis of law is limited to predicting outcomes after events have occurred rather than forecasting future events.[50]

The second enterprise of law and economics involves descriptive theories. These seek to explain *why* the laws are the way they are. They focus on the

---

47   Easterbrook, n 33, 8-15 (with omissions). Note that since this article was written, a differently constituted High Court affirmed its approach in *Breavington v Godleman*: see *John Pfeiffer Pty Ltd v Rogerson* (2000) 172 ALR 625.

48   For example, the assumption of utility-maximising behaviour has been described by P Burrows and C Veljanovski, *The Economic Approach to Law*, Butterworths, 1981, 3 simply as "a fiction, but one that has proved extremely useful in analysing the behaviour of groups".

49   Veljanovski, n 23, 21-22. See also McEwin, n 39, 169-170.

50   Bernstein, n 2, 116-117.

evolution of legal form, and the structure of the legal system itself. The most well-known application of the descriptive approach is Posner's *Economic Analysis of Law*, in which he argues that common law rules are often best explained as efforts (whether deliberate or not) to bring about an efficient allocation of resources. We examine Posner's arguments in detail in Chapter 12. His views are highly contentious and particularly difficult to evaluate and test, given that judges (at least until recently) have rarely couched their judgments explicitly in economic or policy terms.[51]

The third enterprise involves normative theories. These embody value judgments as to what the law *ought* to be. The most common value judgment underpinning normative analysis is that rules should seek to maximise social welfare, and that to achieve this (as we have seen), rules should be evaluated primarily in terms of their allocative efficiency. Posner and some of his Chicago school colleagues are among the most vocal adherents of this approach. The central question such economists ask is: does a particular rule or legal institution generate a socially efficient allocation of resources? If it does not, they argue that the rules should be changed in order to achieve such an outcome.

Ultimately, economics is valuable to the extent that it provides a useful mechanism for making sense of complex legal phenomena. It provides tools which enable us to handle any legal problem in the most cost-effective way. This in itself is a substantial contribution. Lawyers too frequently forget that "every law involves a choice, entails a trade off and hence gives rise to a cost".[52] Economics tries to reveal what those costs are (whether in time, money or energy) and it makes explicit the choices that are inevitable in conditions of scarcity.

Used carefully, with awareness of the limitations of its assumptions and its ideology, economic analysis of law provides useful insights into the complexities of law in modern society; the effects of law on the economy; the costs and benefits of the law; the political decision-making and regulatory processes;[53] and crucially "the study of rational behaviour in the face of scarcity".[54] As even one of its fiercest critics recognises:

> While one may find the underlying values of law and economics distasteful, disagree with its underlying assumptions or empirical assertions, retain a skepticism as to the use of efficiency as a judicial decisional rule, and reject its political orientation, it is difficult to ignore the realism of an approach which reminds us that in a world of scarcity, tradeoffs are inevitable and that "[g]iven scarcity, judicial decisions ... create, transfer, or destroy valuable things and affect people's decisions".[55]

---

51 While the weakness of underlying assumptions is not crucial in predictive economics (which can be tested by results), it is central to approaches which purport to describe the existing system of law and influences upon it. (See further B Caldwell, *Beyond Positive Economics*, Allen and Unwin, 1983.) Yet such approaches are rarely capable of rigorous empirical testing, and so their contentious claims are rarely refutable. See Veljanovski, n 23, 26 who adds: "The difficulty of testing the theories strengthens the need for descriptive accuracy, otherwise neither assumptions nor conclusions will be subject to verification".

52 Veljanovski, n 11, 36.

53 See Chapter 13 below.

54 Easterbrook, n 33.

55 G Minda, "The Law and Economics and Critical Legal Studies Movements in American Law" in N Mercuro (ed), *Law and Economics*, Kluwer, 1980, 104.

It is interesting to conclude this chapter with the observations of Arthur Leff who, whilst he is no friend of law and economics, nevertheless acknowledges that it has some fundamentally important things to say about law.

Arthur Leff, *Economic Analysis of Law: Some Realism about Nominalism*
(1974)

The central tenet and most important operative principle of economic analysis is to ask, of every move (1) how much it will cost; (2) who pays; and (3) who ought to decide both questions.

That might seem obvious. In fact, it is not. It is a most common experience in law schools to have someone say, of some action or state of events, "how awful", with the clear implication that reversing it will de-awfulize the world to the full extent of the initial awfulness. But the true situation, of course, is that eliminating the "bad" state of affairs will not lead to the opposite of that bad state, but to a third state, neither the bad one nor its opposite. That is, before agreeing with any "how awful" critic, one must always ask him the really nasty question, "compared to what?" Moreover, it should be, but often is not, apparent to everyone that the process of moving the world from one state to another is itself costly. If one were not doing *that* with those resources (money, energy, attention), one could be doing something else, perhaps righting a few different wrongs, a separate pile of "how ghastly's".

One can illustrate this basic kind of economic analysis by working with quite simple fact situations. There is this old widow, see, with six children. It is December and the weather is rotten. She defaults on the mortgage on her (and her babies') family home. The mortgagee, twirling his black moustache, takes the requisite legal steps to foreclose the mortgage and throw them all out into the cold. She pleads her total poverty to the judge. Rising behind the bench, the judge points her and her brood out into the swirling blizzard. "Go", he says. "Your plight moves me not". "How awful", you say?

"Nonsense", says the economic analyst. If the old lady and kids slip out into the storm, they most likely won't die. There are people a large part of whose satisfactions come from relieving the distress of others, who have, that is, high utilities for beneficence and gratitude. So the costs to the widow are unlikely to be infinite. Moreover, look at the other side of the (you should pardon the expression) coin. What would happen if the judge let the old lady stay on just because she was out of money? First of all, lenders would in the future be loathe to lend to old widows with children. I don't say that they wouldn't lend at all; they'd just be more careful about marginal cases, and raise the price of credit for the less marginal cases. The aggregate cost to the class of old ladies with homesteads would most likely rise much more than the cost imposed on this particular widow. That is, the aggregate value of all their homes (also known as their wealth) would fall, and they'd all be worse off.

More than that, look at what such a decision would do to the motivation of old widows. Knowing that their failure to pay their debts would not be visited with swift retribution, they would have less incentive to prevent defaults. They might start giving an occasional piece of chicken to the kids, or even work up to a fragment of beef from time to time. Profligacy like that would lead to even less credit-worthiness as their default rates climbed. More and more of them would be priced out of the money market until no widow could ever *decide for herself* to mortgage her house to get the capital necessary to start a seamstress business to pull herself (and her infants) out of poverty. What do you mean, "awful"? What have you got against widows and orphans?[56]

Discussion Questions

1. Identify some of the simplifying assumptions which lawyers make in the areas of contract and tort law. How do these assumptions compare with the economic assumptions discussed in this chapter?

2. Can the idea of efficiency be reconciled with the ideas of justice and fairness? Which is fairer – the Pareto or the Kaldor-Hicks criterion of economic efficiency?

3. Compare and contrast the assumptions about rationality which are made by economists (see earlier in this chapter) and by liberal theorists (see Chapter 2).

4. Consider Easterbrook's arguments in support of the decision in *Breavington v Godleman* (see p 337). Do you agree? Consider the following:

   The plaintiff, a resident of NSW, is injured in South Australia during the course of her employment. Five years later she commences proceedings in NSW for damages. The defendant, a resident of South Australia, points to a South Australian statute which sets a limitation period of three years on the commencement of such an action. There is no such limitation in NSW. Which law should apply?

---

56   A Leff, "Economic Analysis of Law: Some Realism about Nominalism" (1974) 60 *Virginia Law Review* 451 at 460-461.

Chapter 12

Economics and the Common Law

In this chapter we investigate the contribution that economics has made to an understanding of the role of the common law. We do this in two ways. First, we look at two specific areas of common law doctrine: contracts and torts. Within these two subject areas, we take a number of examples which demonstrate how economics can contribute to legal and policy analysis. These examples are also useful in demonstrating both the strengths and limitations of economic analysis in its practical application to law. In fact we examine different types of economic analysis and find that each has different strengths and limitations.[1] Secondly, we take a step back and look at economic claims about the common law in general.[2] We investigate the claim that the common law does – and should – promote efficiency.

(a)   Contracts, torts and the Coase theorem

Given the economist's concern with questions of allocative efficiency in the market place, it is perhaps not surprising that these areas have come in for economic attention. From an economic perspective both contract and tort law are concerned with property rights. The law of contract is primarily concerned with providing for the transferability of property rights, while one of the functions of the law of torts is the protection property rights (through laws relating to trespass, conversion, detinue and nuisance).[3]

The economic analysis of contracts and torts begins with the Coase theorem, undoubtedly the single most important development in the economic analysis of law. Indeed, the present law and economics movement could never have developed the way it has without the benefit of the insights which Ronald Coase generated.[4]

---

1   Useful introductions to the economic analysis of contract law and tort law can be found in R Craswell and A Schwartz, *Foundations of Contract Law*, Oxford UP, 1994; and S Levmore, *Foundations of Tort Law*, Oxford UP, 1994.

2   For these purposes, "common law" means those areas of law which are created mainly by judicial decision rather than by legislative enactment. We examine the economic analysis of legislation in Chapter 13.

3   M Trebilcock, *The Limits of Freedom of Contract*, Harvard UP, 1993, 9.

4   RH Coase, "The Problem of Social Cost" (1960) 3 *Journal of Law and Economics* 1. Although this paper is the source of the Coase theorem, it is not set out as such in the paper. Coase credits another economist, George Stigler, with coining the term "Coase theorem", and with its popular formulation.

At its simplest, the Coase theorem maintains that, in the absence of transaction costs, an efficient allocation of resources will result, irrespective of legal rules; that is, irrespective of which party is assigned the property right in a situation of conflicting uses. The theorem, and its broader implications, are best described by example. Polinsky, in the passage extracted below, provides a particularly clear exposition of the theorem, drawing from the classic parable of the factory which emits smoke and thus dirties neighbours' laundered clothes.

AM Polinsky, *The Coase Theorem*
(1989)

Consider a factory whose smoke causes damage to the laundry hung outdoors by five nearby residents. In the absence of any corrective action each resident would suffer $75 in damages, a total of $375. The smoke damage can be eliminated by either of two ways: A smokescreen can be installed on the factory's chimney, at a cost of $150, or each resident can be provided with an electric dryer, at a cost of $50 per resident. The efficient solution is clearly to install the smokescreen because it eliminates total damages of $375 for an outlay of only $150, and it is cheaper than purchasing five dryers for $250.

Zero Transaction Costs

The question asked by Coase was whether the efficient outcome would result if the right to clean air is assigned to the residents or if the right to pollute is given to the factory. If there is a right to clean air, then the factory has three choices: pollute and pay $375 in damages, install a smokescreen for $150, or purchase five dryers for the residents at a total cost of $250. Clearly, the factory would install the smokescreen, the efficient solution. If there is a right to pollute, then the residents face three choices: suffer their collective damages of $375, purchase five dryers for $250, or buy a smokescreen for the factory for $150. The residents also would purchase the smokescreen. In other words, the efficient outcome will be achieved regardless of the assignment of the legal right.

It was implicitly assumed in this example that the residents could costlessly get together and negotiate with the factory. In Coase's language, this is referred to as the assumption of **zero transaction costs**. In general, transaction costs include the costs of identifying the parties with whom one has to bargain, the costs of getting together with them, the costs of the bargaining process itself, and the costs of enforcing any bargain reached. With this general definition of transaction costs in mind, we can now state the simple version of the Coase Theorem: If there are zero transaction costs, the efficient outcome will occur regardless of the choice of legal rule.

Note that, although the choice of the legal rule does not affect the attainment of the efficient solution when there are zero transaction costs, it does affect the distribution of income. If the residents have the right to clean air, the factory pays $150 for the smokescreen, whereas if the factory has the right to pollute, the residents pay for the smokescreen. Thus, the choice of the legal rule redistributes income by the amount of the least-cost solution to the conflict. Because it is assumed for now that income can be costlessly redistributed, this distributional effect is of no consequence – if it is not desired, it can be easily corrected.

Positive Transaction Costs

The assumption of zero transaction costs obviously is unrealistic in many conflict situations. At the very least, the disputing parties usually would have to spend time and/or money to get together to discuss the dispute. To see the consequences of positive transaction costs, suppose in the example that it costs each resident $60 to get together with the others (due, say, to transportation costs and the value attached to time). If the residents have a right to clean air, the factory again faces the choice of paying damages, buying a smokescreen, or buying five dryers. The factory again would purchase the smokescreen, the efficient solution. If the factory has a right to pollute, each resident now has to decide whether to bear the losses of $75, buy a dryer for $50, or get together with the other residents for $60 to collectively buy a smokescreen for $150. Clearly, each resident will choose to purchase a dryer, an inefficient outcome. Thus given the transaction costs described, the right to clean air is efficient, but the right to pollute is not.

Note that in the example the preferred legal rule minimized the effects of transaction costs in the following sense. Under the right to clean air, the factory had to decide whether to pay damages, install a smokescreen, or buy five dryers. Because it was not necessary for the factory to get together with the residents to decide what to do, the transaction costs – the costs of the residents to get together – did not have any effect. Under the right to pollute, the residents had to decide what to do. Because the residents were induced to choose an inefficient solution in order to avoid the cost of getting together, the transaction costs did have an effect. Thus, even though no transaction costs were actually incurred under the right to pollute because the residents did not get together, the effects of transaction costs were greater under that rule.

We can now state the more complicated version of the Coase Theorem: If there are positive transaction costs, the efficient outcome may not occur under every legal rule. In these circumstances, the preferred legal rule is the rule that minimizes the effects of transaction costs. These effects include actually incurring transaction costs as well as the inefficient choices induced by a desire to avoid transaction costs.[5]

In the first part of this chapter we explore particular applications of the Coase theorem to contracts and torts.

(b) Contract law

(i) Introduction

Contract law has an obvious relevance to economic analysis because it governs individual exchange relations. Within the economic literature on contract, two models have developed; the market-based (or neo-classical) model and the transaction cost model. These models offer different insights into contract law. The market-based model is concerned primarily with how contract law can make exchange transactions efficient. The transaction cost model seeks to demonstrate that often the market and contract law may not provide the most efficient outcome, and that other forms of exchange relations may be preferred. Both models are concerned, in different ways, with the regulation of exchange relations. We examine these models in more detail under the following two sub-headings.

---

5   AM Polinsky, *An Introduction to Law and Economics*, 2nd ed, Little Brown, 1989, 11-14. As Polinsky notes: The distributional consequences of legal rules are somewhat more complicated when there are transaction costs. It is no longer true, as it was when there were zero transaction costs, that the choice of the rule redistributes income by the amount of the least-cost solution. In the example, if the residents have the right to clean air, the factory pays $150 for the smokescreen, whereas if the factory has the right to pollute, the residents pay $250 for five dryers.

(ii)   The market-based (or neo-classical) model

The market-based model is strongly influenced by the Coase theorem. It assumes that bargaining takes place between a small number of individuals. According to Coase, if there are no transaction costs, an efficient outcome will be achieved in the marketplace irrespective of the legal rules. However, in the real world it is inevitable that there *will* be substantial transaction costs. These include limited information, the cost of locating an appropriate person to bargain with, the cost of getting together, the cost of negotiating, the cost of recording the terms of the agreement, the temptation to renege on agreements, and other impediments to bargaining, such as uncertainty. According to proponents of the market model, the law should be structured so as to maximise the joint value or minimise the joint costs involved in the interaction of buyer and seller, thereby making the market solution more likely, and thus maximising efficiency.

On this view, many existing rules of contract law are already structured with the efficiency objective in mind. As Veljanovski points out, contract law has three main efficiency-related purposes.[6] First, it provides for remedies that will discourage inefficient breaches of contract. Some economists make the same point by arguing that the law should encourage optimal breaches. How does contract law discourage inefficient breaches? At its starkest:

> [It] provide[s] a sanction for reneging, which, in the absence of sanctions, is sometimes tempting where the parties' performance is not simultaneous. During the process of an extended exchange, a point may be reached where it is in the interest (though perhaps only the very narrow, short-run interest) of one of the parties to terminate performance. If A agrees to build a house for B and B pays him in advance, A can make himself better off, at least if loss of reputation (which, depending on A's particular situation, may be unimportant to him) is ignored, by pocketing B's money and not building the house. The problem arises because the non-simultaneous character of the exchange offers one of the parties a strategic advantage which he can use to obtain a transfer payment that utterly vitiates the advantages of the contract to the other party. Clearly, if such conduct were permitted, people would be reluctant to enter into contracts and the process of economic exchange would be retarded.[7]

As Veljanovski shows, there are also more subtle ways in which contract law discourages inefficient breaches:

> [I]f the breach is avoidable, the breaching party should make good the other's loss thereby providing a test of the breach's efficiency. If in anticipation of paying the victim's loss the breaching party still decides to breach, the implication is that the resources thereby released are being allocated to more efficient uses. Where the breach is due to mistake or is unavoidable because of events beyond the control of the parties to the contract, the loss should be imposed on the superior information-producer in the former case and on the superior risk-bearer in the latter case.[8]

The notion of efficient and inefficient breaches of contract will surprise many students of contract law. Surely all breaches should be discouraged and parties

---

6   C Veljanovski, *The New Law and Economics*, Oxford, 1982, 77-78.
7   A Kronman and R Posner, *The Economics of Contract Law*, Little Brown, 1979, 4.
8   Veljanovski, n 6, 77.

held to their promises? It is important to remember that under the criterion of efficiency the economist sees contractual obligations in instrumental, rather than moral, terms.[9]

The second efficiency-related purpose of contract law is that it reduces the costs of the exchange process and thereby generates efficiency by implying a set of standard terms into each contract. Such terms are desirable because it is costly to negotiate and draft a contract which anticipates and addresses every possible contingency. Accordingly, as Polinsky indicates:

> Contract law can be viewed as filling in these "gaps" in the contract – attempting to reproduce what the parties would have agreed to if they could have costlessly planned for the event initially. Since the parties would have included contract terms that maximise their joint benefits net of their joint costs – both parties can thereby be made better off – this approach is equivalent to designing contract law according to the efficiency criterion.[10]

In other words, standard implied terms serve to minimise transactions costs, reducing uncertainty and the costs of explicit negotiation over a wide range of issues, and thereby encouraging bargaining.

Thirdly, "contract law provides a framework for the regulation of abuses in the contracting process such as fraud, misrepresentation and duress that impede or are poorly controlled by market forces".[11] Similarly, the law of contracts imposes costs on, and thereby discourages, careless behaviour in the contracting process, behaviour which unnecessarily increases the costs of the process itself. Kronman and Posner provide an example:

> Suppose A promises to give B a boat if B stops smoking, B complies with this condition (at some cost to himself), but A refuses to give him the boat. A proves that B misunderstood him – he never meant to promise him a boat. B in turn proves that he was reasonably induced by A's words and conduct to believe that A had indeed promised him the boat. If we believe that A did not in fact intend such a promise, then enforcement of the promise cannot be justified as necessary to prevent frustration of a value-maximizing exchange; there is no basis for presuming that an exchange will make the parties better off if one of them never intended to make it. But we may still want to enforce the contract in order to give people in A's position an incentive to avoid carelessly inducing others to incur costs in reliance on the existence of a contract. This problem may seem to belong to the law of torts rather than contracts, since enforcement serves not to promote a mutually beneficial exchange but instead to deter careless behaviour. But enforcement does promote the contractual process by discouraging a costly form of carelessness that would tend to impede it.[12]

One further and more complex example of the neo-classical approach is provided by Posner's analysis of principles of contract damages.

---

9   See further A Duggan, M Bryan, F Hanks, *Contractual Non-Disclosure*, Longman, 1994, 205-207.

10   Polinsky, n 5, 27.

11   Ibid 78.

12   Kronman and Posner, n 7, 5.

RA Posner, *Economic Analysis of Law*
(1977)

When a breach of contract is established, the issue becomes one of the proper remedy. A starting point for analysis is Holmes's view that it is not the policy of the law to compel adherence to contracts but only to require each party to choose between performing in accordance with the contract and compensating the other party for any injury resulting from a failure to perform. This view contains an important economic insight. In many cases it is uneconomical to induce the completion of a contract after it has been breached. I agree to purchase 100,000 widgets custom-ground for use as components in a machine that I manufacture. After I have taken delivery of 10,000, the market for my machine collapses. I promptly notify my supplier that I am terminating the contract, and admit that my termination is a breach of the contract. When notified of the termination he has not yet begun the custom grinding of the other 90,000 widgets, but he informs me that he intends to complete his performance under the contract and bill me accordingly. The custom-ground widgets have no use other than in my machine, and a negligible scrap value. Plainly, to grant the supplier any remedy that induced him to complete the contract after the breach would result in a waste of resources. The law is alert to this danger and, under the doctrine of mitigation of damages, would refuse to permit the supplier to recover any costs he incurred in continuing production after my notice of termination.

Let us change the facts. I need 100,000 custom-ground widgets for my machine but the supplier, after producing 50,000, is forced to suspend production because of a mechanical failure. Other suppliers are in a position to supply the remaining widgets that I need, but I insist that the original supplier complete his performance of the contract. If the law compels completion, the supplier will probably have to make arrangements with other widget producers to complete his contract with me. But it may be more costly to him to procure an alternative supplier than for me to do so directly; indeed, were it cheaper for him than for me, he would do it voluntarily in order to minimize his liability for breach of contract. To compel completion of the contract would again result in a waste of resources and again the law does not compel completion but remits the victim to a simple damages remedy.

The problem exposed in the foregoing example is a quite general one. It results from the fact, remarked earlier, that contract remedies are frequently invoked in cases where there is no presumption that an exchange pursuant to the (defective) contract would in fact increase value (for example, cases of defective communication). Here we clearly do not want a remedy that will induce the party made liable to complete the exchange.

The objective of giving the party to a contract an incentive to fulfil his promise unless the result would be an inefficient use of resources (the production of the unwanted widgets in the first example, the round-about procurement of a substitute supplier in the second) can usually be achieved by allowing the victim of a breach to recover his expected profit on the transaction. If the supplier in the first example receives his expected profit from completing the 10,000 widgets, he will have no incentive to produce the remaining 90,000. We do not want him to produce them; no one wants them. In the second example, if I receive my expected profit from dealing with the original supplier, I become indifferent to whether he completes his performance.

In these examples the breach was in a sense involuntary. It was committed only to avert a larger loss. The breaching party would have been happier had there been no occasion to commit a breach. But in some cases a party would be tempted to breach the contract simply because his profit from breach would exceed his expected profit from completion of the contract. If his profit from breach would also exceed the expected profit to the other party from completion of the contract, and if damages are limited to loss of expected profit, there will be an incentive to commit a breach. There should be. The opportunity cost of completion to the breaching party is the profit that he would make from a breach, and if it is greater than his profit from completion, then completion will involve a loss to him. If that loss is greater than the gain to the other party from completion, breach would be value-maximizing and should be encouraged. And because the victim of the breach is made whole for his loss, he is indifferent; hence encouraging breaches in these circumstances will not deter people from entering into contracts in the future ...

Thus far the emphasis has been on the economic importance of not awarding damages in excess of the lost expectation. It is equally important, however, not to award less than the expectation loss. Suppose A contracts to sell B for $100,000 a machine that is worth $110,000 to B, ie, that would yield him a profit of $10,000. Before delivery C comes to A and offers him $109,000 for the machine promised B. A would be tempted to breach were he not liable to B for B's loss of expected profit. Given that measure of damages, C will not be able to induce a breach of A's contract with B unless he offers B more than $110,000, thereby indicating that the machine really is worth more to him than to B. The expectation rule thus assures that the machine ends up where is it most valuable ...

One superficially attractive alternative to measuring contract damages by loss of expectation (ie, lost profits) is to measure them by the reliance loss, especially in cases where liability is imposed not to induce performance but to penalize careless behavior. And even in the case where the breach is deliberate, it is arguable that expectation damages may overcompensate the victim of the breach. Suppose I sign a contract to deliver 10,000 widgets in six months, and the day after the contract is signed I default. The buyer's reliance loss – the sum of the costs he has irretrievably incurred as a result of the contract – is, let us say, zero, but his lost profit $1000. Why should he be allowed to reap a windfall gain by the use of a measure of damages that does not correspond to any actual social cost?

One answer has already been given: the lost-profit measure is necessary to assure that the only breaches made are those that promote efficiency. But there is another answer: that on average, though not in every case, the lost-profit method will give a better approximation than the reliance measure to the actual social costs of contract breach. In long-run competitive equilibrium, the total revenues of the sellers in a market are just equal to their total costs; there are no "profits" in the economic sense. What law and accounting call profits are frequently not profits in that sense at all, but rather reimbursements of the costs of capital, of entrepreneurial effort, and of other inputs. These items of cost are excluded by the reliance measure of damages, which will therefore tend to understate the true social costs of breach.[13]

Similar market-based analyses have been applied to many other core areas of contract law, such as consideration and mistake.

---

[13] RA Posner, *Economic Analysis of Law*, 2nd ed, Little Brown, 1977, 88-92, with omissions. This extract was preferred to the more detailed analysis contained in more recent editions of Posner's book.

(iii)   The transaction cost model

Proponents of the market-based model would acknowledge that free exchange only results in an efficient outcome provided that certain assumptions are satisfied (for example: adequate information, the ability to monitor the behaviour of the other party to the contract). This recognition has led to the development of a second economic approach to contract, known as the "transaction cost" or "neo-institutional" model. A further approach, which can be regarded as a sub-category, is the "relational contracting" model. For the sake of this introductory treatment, we deal with these models under the one heading.

It is easiest to begin by examining the idea of relational contracting. The relational approach begins by highlighting some limitations in the market-based model. In particular, the market model is based on a timeless model of contract,[14] and takes as its paradigm case the sale of goods (or "spot") contract. That is, its typical case is a form of contract where one contracts now for performance in the future.

But this is not representative of the many contracts that people and business entities enter into. Those adopting the "relational perspective", particularly Ian MacNeil and Victor Goldberg, characterise the market-based approach as primarily addressing discrete (as contrasted with relational) transactions. Discrete transactions, as MacNeil describes them,

> are contracts of short duration, with limited personal interactions, and with precise party measurements of easily measured objects of exchange, for example money and grain. They are transactions requiring a minimum of future cooperative behaviour between the parties and not requiring a sharing of benefits or burdens. They bind the two parties tightly and precisely. The parties view such transactions as deals free of entangling strings, and they certainly expect no altruism. The parties see virtually everything connected with such transactions as clearly defined and presented. If trouble is anticipated at all, it is anticipated only if someone or something turns out unexpectedly badly.[15]

In this type of anonymous exchange, "no duties exist between the parties prior to the contract formation and ... the duties of the parties are determined at the formation stage".[16] This type of transaction, MacNeil points out, "could occur, if at all, only between total strangers brought together by chance".[17]

Most contracts, relational theorists argue, are not like this. Rather, they involve parties who have had relationships in the past and are likely to have further relations in the future. The significance of this is borne out by Macaulay's empirical work on relations between business people, referred to in Chapter 4. These relational transactions have the following features:

---

14   That is, it assumes that people make a single unchanging decision in a fixed and static world.

15   IR MacNeil, "A Primer of Contract Planning" (1975) 48 *Southern California Law Review* 627 at 632-633. See generally VP Goldberg (ed), *Readings in the Economics of Contract Law*, Cambridge UP, 1989.

16   VP Goldberg, "Toward an Expanded Economic Theory of Contract" (1976) 10 *Journal of Economic Issues* 45 at 49.

17   IR MacNeil, "Contracts: Adjustments of Long-Term Economic Relations under Classical, Neo-classical and Relational Contract Law" (1977-78) 72 *Northwestern University Law Review* 854 at 856.

The relations are of significant duration (for example, franchising). Close whole person relations form an integral aspect of the relation (employment). The object of exchange typically includes both easily measured quantities (wages) and quantities not easily measured (the projection of personality by an airline stewardess). Many individuals with individual and collective poles of interest are involved in the relation (industrial relations). Future cooperative behavior is anticipated (the players and management of the Oakland Raiders). The benefits and burdens of the relation are to be shared rather than divided and allocated (a law partnership). The bindingness of the relation is limited (again a law partnership in which in theory each member is free to quit almost at will). The entangling strings of friendship, reputation, interdependence, morality, and altruistic desires are integral parts of the relation (a theatrical agent and his clients). Trouble is expected as a matter of course (a collective bargaining agreement). Finally, the participants never intend or expect to see the whole future of the relation as presented at any single time, but view the relation as an ongoing integration of behavior which will grow and vary with events in a largely unforeseeable future (a marriage; and a family business).[18]

Relational arrangements involve very different types of contractual factors from discrete transactions. As Goldberg points out:

> The longer the anticipated relation and more complexity and uncertainty entailed in that relation, the less significance will be placed upon the price and quantity variables at the formation stage. The emphasis instead will be upon establishing (explicitly or by the incorporation of tacit assumption), rules to govern the relationship: rules determining the adjustment to factors that will rise in the course of the relationship and rules concerning termination of that relationship.[19]

When one is dealing with non-market relational contracts, then the market-based approach misses much that is important. Market theorists, in seeking to generalise from this limited type of transaction, may be making exaggerated claims as to the applicability of their particular framework of analysis.

The transaction cost model builds upon the insights of the relational contracting model. Recall that the market-based approach assumes that exchange relations typically take the form of one-off transactions between autonomous parties. This is the realm of classical contract law. The transaction cost model begins by noting that many transactions do not occur in the market. In some cases transactions take place in the context of long-term contractual relations (as the relational model points out), while in other cases transactions between parties occur within a single enterprise (a firm).

To use a simple example, assume that a car manufacturing firm has a need for certain car parts. In theory the firm could enter into a series of one-off contracts every time it needs new parts. This is the picture assumed by the market-based model, where each contract is considered in isolation. Alternatively, the manufacturing firm could enter into a long-term supply relationship with another firm which manufactured parts. In time, these two firms might merge into one firm, thus bringing their exchange relationship under one new organisational umbrella. What will cause any of these types of exchange relationship to be preferred? Why

---

18   MacNeil, n 15, 633-634.
19   Goldberg, n 16, 49-50.

is it that discrete market-based contracts will not always be the preferred method of organising exchange relations?

One answer is that differences in transaction costs are the crucial determinant – hence the name: "transaction cost model". In other words, the costs of repeatedly negotiating, entering into, and then monitoring, new supply contracts can be reduced by a long-term, or a firm-based, arrangement. So, the transaction cost model alerts us to the existence of different forms of economic governance structures, and helps us understand how they come about

> by placing heavier emphasis on the frictions and uncertainties associated with contractual activity; by confronting more squarely the difficulty and comparative cost of planning, adapting and monitoring contractual performance under alternative governance modes (the market, law, arbitration, contract renegotiation).[20]

If contract often turns out to be a defective tool for co-ordination, then transaction cost analysis argues that other (non-contractual) legal forms may better enable people to overcome the frictions and limitations of the contract setting.

The leading exponent of this approach is Oliver Williamson. Williamson's approach has been summarised by Frank Stephen.

Frank H Stephen, *The Economics of the Law*
(1989)

Williamson (1975; 1979; 1985) argues that two sets of factors are important in determining transaction costs: (i) human characteristics, and (ii) environmental characteristics. The first human characteristic is *bounded rationality*. Human behaviour is "intendedly rational but only limitedly so", to use Simon's phrase. Much economic theory treats human beings as hyper-rational. Bounds are set on our rationality by the computational (neurophysiological) limits of our brains and by language limitations – our inability to convey completely our thoughts to others. The second human characteristic is *opportunism*. Economists usually analyse behaviour on the assumption that humans are self-interested – they maximise utility. Opportunism extends this to self-seeking with *guile...*. Williamson does not suggest that all economic agents behave opportunistically only that some do, but it is costly to sort out who are who in advance.

These human characteristics are not sufficient on their own to generate transaction costs. It is only when they are paired with certain environmental characteristics that they do. The first environmental characteristic is *uncertainty/complexity*. Bounded rationality is not a problem with simple situations or determinate situations. If all possible outcomes are known with certainty and there are not many it may be easy to draw up a fully comprehensive *contingent claims contract* – one that says what the obligations of the parties will be in all possible states. Very often, however, even if a problem is determinate it is complex (eg chess). Most importantly for contractual relations, the world is uncertain. We cannot predict all contingencies. Thus the pairing of bounded rationality with complexity/uncertainty can generate transaction costs – difficulties in drawing up a contingent claims contract.

However, the pairing of bounded rationality with uncertainty/complexity would not be a problem but for *opportunism*. In the absence of opportunism all contracts could include a clause by which each party undertook to act in all

---

20   Veljanovski, n 6, 78.

circumstances in the best interests of the parties jointly. Thus gaps in the contract would not be exploited to the advantage of one party and the detriment of the other. No party would exploit any asymmetric knowledge which was available on the true state of the contract (no information impactedness).

The second environmental characteristic of relevance is what Williamson calls the *small numbers condition*. Opportunism is not really a problem where a transaction (or contract) is of a recurring nature: if a party behaves opportunistically on one occasion he is unlikely to be awarded the contract on an other occasion. Thus frequency of transaction is of importance. A second dimension of the small numbers condition is the number of potential suppliers (or customers). The larger this number the more competitive will be the process by which contract terms are arrived at. Part of the competitive process will be the willingness of parties to reveal information to which the other party does not have access. Thus the larger the number of potential suppliers the less likely *ex ante* opportunistic behaviour will be to arise.

Opportunistic behaviour might still arise *ex post* due to information impactedness or to *first mover advantage* – the fact that the party successful on the first round may have a strategic advantage in negotiations for subsequent contracts. A large numbers situation is effectively converted into a small numbers situation in subsequent rounds (eg local TV and radio franchises).

The pairing of the small numbers condition with opportunism gives rise to transactions costs. The pairings of human characteristics and environmental conditions can be shown schematically thus:

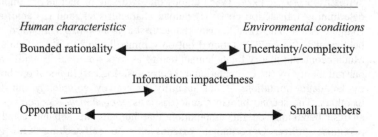

Human characteristics   *Environmental conditions*

Bounded rationality ◄─────────────────► Uncertainty/complexity

Information impactedness

Opportunism ◄─────────────────► Small numbers

... Much of Williamson's work has focused on the *small numbers condition*. Notice that the human characteristics of bounded rationality and opportunism are always potentially present. Simple environments pose little problem whilst uncertainty is almost always with us. We have seen that the small numbers condition involves both the frequency with which the transaction is likely to occur and the number of potential contractors. The latter is likely to be related to how specialised the transaction is: are there costs that must be incurred to support the transaction but which cannot be covered if the transaction falls through? Such costs Williamson calls *transaction-specific investment*. They are investments because they are incurred now on the expectation that they will generate benefits in the future (ie the benefits of the transaction). But the investment is specific to the transaction. Williamson refers to such a situation as *idiosyncratic exchange*. However, it is likely that the situation will not be black-and-white. There may be degrees of specificity of investment supporting the transaction. It may have a limited number of alternative uses rather than none.

It might be helpful in elucidating these concepts if we take a specific example. Consider a firm deciding to set up a car assembly plant in a country where there have been no locally-produced cars. Amongst other things the firm will need a supply of body shells and panels. These are produced by stamping them out of metal sheets using huge presses with dies of the appropriate shape. Note that since car shapes are distinctive these dies are unique to a particular model or model range so that the cost of producing them is a highly transaction-specific investment. Furthermore, car bodies are bulky relative to their value and therefore are costly to transport. The firm will want to minimise transport costs by having the bodies manufactured close to the assembly plant. Thus there will be locational specificity.

The dies themselves are expensive to produce: holding duplicates would raise costs unacceptably. The effect of all this is that the cheapest way of providing the body pressings for the car plant is to have the two sited together and for the two plants to be tied and dependent on each other. Having chosen the site for the assembly plant, the pressings manufacturer will have to engage in highly transaction-specific investment.

The contract between the two firms is unlikely to be able to cover all contingencies because the environment is complex and uncertain and therefore the bounds of rationality will be reached. Since by definition we are *ex post* in a small numbers relation (bilateral monopoly) there is scope for opportunism on both sides. Either party could extort some of the other's profits by threatening to pull out on the grounds of some contingency not covered in the contract.

A straightforward market relationship between two firms would seem to be out of the question here. What alternatives are there: (a) vertical integration (ie the assembly pressings plant is owned and operated as an integrated whole by the assembler); (b) two companies (assembler, pressings manufacturer) set up a joint venture (only makes sense if one party does not have the know-how to operate the other's plant); (c) some sort of arrangement whereby each party makes a bonding payment to the other. This would mean that if one party "ratted" it would be inflicting a loss on itself, eg assembler pays for the dies so that if it pulls out it suffers a loss.

Williamson argues that which form is chosen will depend on the degree of transaction-specific investment and the frequency of the transaction (in terms of our example, frequency relates to the sale of car bodies). This may be shown schematically by Figure 2.2 from Williamson (1979), which is reproduced here as Figure 8.2.

	Investment characteristics		
Frequency characteristics	Non-specific	Mixed	Idiosyncratic
Infrequent	Market	Trilateral	
Frequent	Market governance	Bilateral governance	Unified governance

Figure 8.2

Where a transaction does not involve transaction-specific investment frequency of the transaction does not affect its governance structure and the market is suitable. This is because the non-specificity means that the investment associated with the transaction has alternative uses (or alternative outlets). Thus it is not a small numbers situation: if one party to the contract pulls out a substitute can easily be found; the subject of the transaction in this case is likely to be highly standardised.

In this mode the identity of the parties is not of much relevance and it is really the existence of alternatives in the market that disciplines the parties. The law is only used to settle claims not to deter. Williamson says that this situation corresponds to what MacNeil (1978) called classical contract law which sought to emphasise discreteness and presentation. Formal matters were of principal importance.

Where a transaction's frequency is only occasional and investment in it is of a mixed or idiosyncratic character recourse to alternative parties in the event of a contractual breakdown is not so readily possible. The degree of specificity of the investment reduces its alternative uses and in the extremity they are zero. The costs of finding an alternative supplier will also be large. The parties are in a sense locked into the contract.

The parties have an interest in these circumstances in maintaining the contractual relationship. "Going to law" to resolve a dispute is unlikely to maintain the contractual relationship. In this circumstance both parties will (*ex ante*) have an interest in building into their contract a mechanism for resolving disputes. This will usually involve bringing in a third party to adjudicate or arbitrate such disputes. Thus Williamson refers to the mode of governance here as *trilateral* (it involves three parties). Thus for example, civil engineering contracts usually provide for the resolution of disputes by a consulting engineer or a professional arbitrator. This corresponds to what MacNeil has called neoclassical contracting – long-term contracts with gaps which are filled at the time they arise with third party assistance.

When a transaction occurs frequently the costs of a transaction-specific governance structure become more acceptable – they are spread over many more transactions. Take our problem of supplying car bodies to an assembler. There is a high degree of transaction-specific investment (dies, location) but if there are large numbers of car bodies involved it is likely to be worthwhile for the assembler to undertake the production of pressings himself – vertical integration (unified governance).

With unified governance unforeseen contingencies are not a problem. They can be handled by "adaptive sequential decision-making". Even in cases of low frequency transactions it may well be worthwhile integrating if the transaction-specific investment is highly idiosyncratic because then there are no economies of scale to be lost by self-production.

Where the transaction-specific investment lies between the non-specific and the idiosyncratic (what Williamson calls mixed) there may be benefits from outside procurement due to limited scale economies and the market nature of the transaction may help to reduce costs. However there is the problem of dealing with contingencies. Both parties have a stake in maintaining the relationship because of the transaction-specific investment and this leads to what Williamson calls "mutual follow-on agreements".

Williamson points out that quantity adjustments are likely to be less opportunistic than price adjustments. Price adjustments are zero sum and look like the reallocation of profits. Quantity adjustments (including time) may be seen to be more likely to arise from exogenous events. This is all the more so given that the assets involved are of mixed specificity. Thus it is argued that a bilateral governance structure will evolve which allows routine quantity adjustments.

Williamson identified both unified and bilateral governance with what MacNeil calls *relational contracting* [see above] in which he described the reference point as not being the original contract but "the entire relation as it has developed … [through] time. This may or may not include the original agreement'; and if it does, may or may not result in great deference being given to it".

What is the difference between the [market] approach to contract law … and the neo-institutional approach? The former is efficiency-based, therefore it sees the law of contract as providing rules and implicit contract terms which will result in efficient resource allocation. These are designed to discourage inefficient breach and where breach is unavoidable to impose the burden on the party best positioned to bear the cost (best information producer; best risk-bearer). Efficiency is also encouraged by reducing transaction costs and uncertainty (by supplying standard terms). It also provides a framework for regulating abuses that impede or are poorly controlled by market forces. The neo-institutional approach may be seen as superior because it gives greater recognition to the temporal nature of contract and the uncertainty that arises. It sees a crucial role being played by transaction costs. Most of all it sees that contracts involve relations between the parties which differ from those of a sale of goods contract (which might be seen as the paradigm case of the market approach). The neo-institutional approach is also efficiency-oriented but it is more concerned with *procedural* efficiency than *allocative* efficiency.[21]

For present purposes, the most important contribution of the transaction approach is its implicit critique of the neo-classical (or market-based) model. Specifically, that model works best in respect of certain types of contract (the sale of goods, "spot" contract). It is only by focusing so heavily on this type of contract that market theorists, and the Chicago school in particular, are able to portray contract law as efficient "across the board". Williamson, in particular, shows the selective nature of this paradigm and how, in respect of certain other types of contract, the market and contract law may not provide the most efficient outcome. This is why they are commonly by-passed in favour of vertical integration and other measures.

(c) Tort Law

(i) Introduction

Chicago school economists and others who begin with the competitive-market paradigm as their theoretical starting point view the law's purpose as primarily to promote efficiency in resource use. In the context of tort law, this perspective works in the following way. The harm caused by tortious conduct imposes costs on the tort victim. Equally, the potential tortfeasor may incur costs by initiating precautionary and preventive measures. In economic terms, the role of tort law is to minimise the sum of these two sets of costs.

We explore these issues using unintended torts (accidents) as our main focus. In the case of unintended torts, economists regard the law's principal role as being

---

21   F Stephen, *The Economics of the Law*, Wheatsheaf, 1988, 185-193 (with omissions). References in this article are: MacNeil, n 17; OE Williamson, *Markets and Hierarchies: Analysis and Antitrust Implications*, Free Press, 1975; "Transaction Cost Economics: The Governance of Contractual Relations" (1979) 22 *Journal of Law and Economics* 233-261; *The Economic Institutions of Capitalism*, Free Press, 1975. See also OE Williamson, *The Mechanisms of Governance*, Oxford UP, 1996.

to provide the "optimum" degree of deterrence, rather than to provide just or timely compensation. This reflects the *ex ante* perspective that we described in Chapter 11. That is, their concern is with how the law might reduce the amount of harm to an "efficient" level. The question of achieving an equitable redistribution of income after the harm has occurred is regarded as a secondary issue.[22]

Note that the assumption in this approach is that we do not want to avoid accidents "at all costs". This is because there is a point at which the cost of additional precautions ceases to be economically justifiable. For example, it would not be efficient to require cars to travel at walking pace (to eradicate accidents to pedestrians) or for factories to close down (to avoid all work accidents). Rather, the object is to achieve the "optimal" accident level; that is, the point beyond which it becomes more expensive to prevent accidents than to allow them to occur.[23] This means that there should be a trade-off between (1) the expected costs of an accident, (2) the costs of accident avoidance and (3) the costs of administering accident law. It also means that the socially correct degree of avoidance requires the minimisation of the sum of those three types of costs.

Given the economist's concern with efficiency, the question becomes: how is this most likely to be achieved? In the case of torts, the answer depends in large part on the comparative efficiency of alternative rules for imposing liability: strict liability, negligence, contributory negligence, comparative negligence or no-fault.

In the following pages we illustrate the economics of tort law by reference to the issue of compensation for road accidents. Using this as a case study, we examine the debate about no-fault liability from an economic perspective. This account is *not* intended as an up-to-the-minute description of the law in this area; we are concerned to illustrate the economic method of analysis, not to elucidate the legal rules. Nor do we intend to cover every dimension of the issue. Accordingly, while we examine the relative merits (in economic terms) of negligence as against no-fault liability, we do not enter into any extended comparison of negligence and strict liability.[24]

(ii) Liability for unintended torts

Automobile accidents are an example of an unintended tort in which transaction costs are high: no prior bargaining is possible because neither party knows in advance if, or with whom, an accident will occur. The legal framework may therefore have an important bearing on efficiency.

In these circumstances, economists suggest, we can derive efficient legal rules by imagining what rules the parties to an accident *would* have chosen if they could have costlessly got together before the accident. Such a fictitious outcome,

---

22　See further AM Polinsky, "Economic Analysis as a Potentially Defective Product: A Buyer's Guide to Posner's *Economic Analysis of Law*" (1974) 87 *Harvard Law Review* 1655 at 1670. Some economists, though not the Chicago school, have developed an increasing concern for other social goals. See further, for example, G Calabresi and A Melamed, "Property Rules, Liability Rules and Inalienability: One View of the Cathedral" (1982) 85 *Harvard Law Review* 1089, emphasising "distributional goals" and "other justice considerations".

23　For a fuller discussion of this point in the context of industrial injuries, see N Gunningham, *Safeguarding the Worker*, Law Book Co, 1984, Ch 12.

24　See G Calabresi, *The Costs of Accidents*, Yale UP, 1970; WM Landes and R Posner, *The Economic Structure of Tort Law*, Harvard UP, 1987; S Shavell, *Economic Analysis of Accident Law*, Harvard UP, 1987.

following Coase, *would* have been efficient, since the parties would have continued bargaining until they agreed to remedies "that lead them to scheme so as to maximise their joint benefits not their joint costs".[25] Thus, the law should "mimic" the market, establishing a liability rule which will create incentives for both parties to take the optimum amount of care, thereby generating an "efficient" outcome.[26]

There is some difficulty in applying these general principles to real world situations. For operational purposes, Chicago school economists have commonly regarded the policy goal as being the minimisation of the sum of two costs: the costs of avoiding the accident (for example, the costs of driving more slowly), and the expected cost of the accident. This takes into account losses from the accident, together with the probability that the accident will occur.[27] On this basis Chicago school economists have generally (though not unanimously) concluded that negligence is the liability rule most likely to achieve an optimum allocation of resources where both injurer and victim can influence the risk of an accident occurring. In other words, the ideal of liability for negligence can be recast in economic terms. The most famous attempt to do so is that of Judge Learned Hand in *United States v Carroll Towing Co.*[28] According to this test, liability in negligence depends on three variables:

(1) the Probability of an accident (P);

(2) the gravity of the Loss if it occurs (L); and

(3) the Burden (cost) of adequate precautions (B).

Liability depends upon whether the cost of avoiding the accident is less than the gravity of the loss, taking into account the probability of the accident. In algebraic terms, we ask whether B is less than L multiplied by P: ie is

$$B < PL.$$

As Posner has pointed out, it is easy to bring out the economic character of the Hand formula:

B, the burden of precautions, is the cost of avoiding the accident, while L, the loss if the accident occurs, is the cost of the accident itself. P times L (P X L) – the cost of the accident if it occurs, multiplied (or as is sometimes said, "discounted") by the probability that the accident will occur, is what an economist would call the "expected cost" of the accident. Expected cost is most easily

---

25   Polinsky, n 5, 39. See also T Ulen, "Rational Victims – Rational Injurers: Cognition and the Economic Analysis of Tort Law" in R Malloy and C Braun (eds), *Law and Economics: New and Critical Perspectives*, Peter Lang Publishing, 1995, 387.

26   Not all economists would accept this statement as necessarily following from the Coase theorem. According to M Kuperberg and C Beitz, *Law, Economics and Philosophy*, Rowman and Allenheld, 1983, 6, this principle ("the efficiency principle") "does not follow logically from Coase's theorem at all. Indeed, the theorem is irrelevant to the efficiency principle. ... [T]he efficiency principle is a principle of normative legal theory whereas the theorem is the conclusion of microeconomic analysis. Of course, this is not to say that the efficiency principle is incorrect, but only that the truth of the theorem (the explicit subject of Coase's article) provides no reason for accepting the principle. While Coase himself encourages readers to accept the efficiency principle, he offers no argument for it".

27   More recently, Posner has come to acknowledge that administrative costs must also be taken into account. See R Posner, *Economic Analysis of Law*, 5th ed, Aspen, 1998, Ch 6.

28   F 2d 169 (2d Cir) (1947).

understood as the average cost that will be incurred over a period of time long enough for the predicted number of accidents to be the actual number. For example, if the probability that a certain type of accident will occur is .001 (one in a thousand) and the accident cost if it does occur is $10,000, the expected accident cost is $10 ($10,000 X .001); and this is equivalent to saying that if we observe the activity that gives rise to this type of accident for a long enough period of time we will observe an average accident cost of $10, Suppose the activity in question is automobile trips from point A to point B. If there are 100,000 trips, there will be 100 accidents, assuming that our probability of .001 was correct. The total cost of the 100 accidents will be $1 million ($10,000 X 100). The average cost, which is simply the total cost ($1 million) divided by the total number of trips (100,000), will be $10. This is the same as the expected cost.

Another name for expected accident cost – for P X L, the right-hand side of the Hand formula – is the benefits from accident avoidance. If one incurs B, the burden of precautions or cost of accident avoidance, one produces a benefit – namely, avoidance of the expected accident costs. The Hand formula is simply an application to accidents of the principle of cost-benefit analysis. Negligence means failing to avoid an accident where the benefits of accident avoidance exceed the costs.

The Hand formula shows that it is possible to think about tort law in economic terms.[29]

As Swan notes, the principles embodied in the Hand formula can be found at work in a number of well-known tort cases:

For example the cost to a one-eyed man from losing the sight in his second eye is greater than the cost to a person with normal vision from losing the use of one eye alone and would thus justify more extensive precautions (*Paris v Stepney Borough Council*). The chance of a distant passer-by being injured by a cricket ball hit for a six over a seventeen foot high protective fence and a distance of seventy eight yards is so remote relative to the cost of any additional precautions involved that the owners of the cricket ground should not be found liable (*Bolton v Stone*).[30]

However, despite its apparent simplicity, the Hand formula does have some limitations. Four, in particular, are worth noting here. First, the relevant cost of accident avoidance is not total cost (as one might think from reading Hand formula), but marginal cost; that is, the additional cost that has been incurred to prevent *this* accident. Posner illustrates this point as follows:

Suppose that a person slips on a staircase and is hurt. The probability that he would slip and fall is .001, the cost of the accident is $25,000, and the cost of preventing the accident (say by installing rubber mats on each stair and by providing a guard rail) would be $50. Since $50 is more than $25, the expected accident cost, it might seem that the failure to prevent the accident was not negligent. But this conclusion is not necessarily correct. Suppose that if $10 were spent on installing rubber mats, the probability of an accident would drop by one half. The expected accident cost would then be $12.50 rather than $25. Thus it is clear that the benefits of the rubber mats in accident avoidance ($12.50) exceed

---

29   R Posner, *Tort Law – Cases and Economic Analysis*, Little Brown, 1982, 2.

30   Peter Swan "The Economics of Law: Economic Imperialism and Negligence Law" (1984) 3 *Australian Economic Review* 92 at 95.

their cost ($10). But once the mats are installed, a guard rail costing $40 would not be worth having since it would avoid only a $12.50 expected accident cost. Thus, to be a correct economic test, the Hand formula must be applied at the margin: the court must examine the incremental benefit in accident avoidance of an incremental expenditure on safety.[31]

Second, the formula only provides incentives to injurers. It does not take account of the behaviour of accident victims. If the behaviour of the victim substantially contributes to the level of accidents, then they must also be given the appropriate incentives to behave efficiently. For example:

> Suppose that a particular accident, having an expected cost of $100, could be avoided either by the injurer at a cost of $50 or by the victim at a cost of $10. Clearly, it would be more efficient for the victim to avoid than for the injurer to do so. This is a case where we want the victim to bear the full costs of the accident so that he will be induced to avoid it. We want a principle of contributory negligence whereby if the victim could have avoided the accident at a cost lower than the expected accident cost and also lower than the injurer's cost of avoidance, the injurer is not liable for the victim's loss.[32]

A third limitation of the Hand formula is that one can reduce accident levels either by encouraging more careful behaviour on the part of the participant concerned, or by reducing the amount or the nature of the activity in question. The Hand formula (and negligence tests generally) only address the first possibility, not the second. It may be that strict liability, rather than negligence, is a more effective mechanism for reducing participation levels.

Fourth, we have assumed thus far that efficiency requires the minimisation of accident avoidance costs and the expected costs of the accident. In fact, there is a further requirement for efficiency, ignored by Hand, namely the costs of administering accident law and/or a system of accident compensation. These costs can be absolutely crucial. As we shall see, it may be that a liability rule that is seemingly efficient in terms of the first two factors is so expensive to administer that it becomes inefficient overall. We set this argument out in more detail later in the chapter. Before doing this it is useful to examine the application of the Hand formula to a practical setting.

(iii)   Economics and no-fault compensation

Thus far we have explored the theoretical framework of the Chicago school economists, as it relates to unintended torts, and to automobile accidents in particular. The real test for such theories is, of course, how well they "fit" when applied to real world situations. One testing ground has been no-fault accident compensation schemes, such as those in place in Victoria, Tasmania and the Northern Territory, and proposed for New South Wales in the early 1980s by the New South Wales Law Reform Commission.[33]

---

31   Posner, n 29, 4.

32   Ibid 6.

33   *Transport Accident Act 1986* (Vic); *Motor Accidents (Liabilities and Compensation) Act 1973* (Tas); *Motor Accidents (Compensation) Act 1979* (NT); NSWLRC, *A Transport Accidents Scheme for New South Wales*, Accident Compensation Working Paper 1, May 1983.

The NSW Law Reform Commission's proposal was based on the view that the tort system, which ultimately involves contested cases through the courts, is too expensive. A no-fault system which avoids the courts and reduces the need for lawyers would be cheaper to administer. In simple terms, the idea behind a no-fault compensation scheme for automobile accidents is that the victim's right to sue for negligence is either abolished or greatly curtailed. Instead, the victim is able to claim against the motorist without having to prove negligence on the motorist's part. The motorist, in turn, is required to carry insurance against such claims. Furthermore, compensation will be paid even where the victim has been negligent and/or the motorist has not been negligent.

There are differing economic perspectives on this issue. From the Chicago school perspective it can be argued that no-fault schemes reduce or eliminate the incentives to take appropriate safety precautions. From this perspective it might be predicted that under such a system, accidents will rise to socially inefficient levels. In contrast, negligence liability (which takes into account contributory negligence) will generate the socially optimal degree of care because negligence means failing to avoid an accident where the benefits of accident avoidance exceed the costs – that is, liability is only imposed when there is a social gain from the exercise of greater care.[34]

Other economists[35] have argued that the extent to which parties to automobile accidents (whether injurers or victims) react to incentives created by liability rules can be greatly exaggerated. Drivers are required to take out compulsory insurance (thereby minimising their financial incentives) and both drivers and pedestrians *already* have a strong self-interest in avoiding personal injury. It is unlikely, therefore, that negligence liability has any substantial influence on their behaviour. Moreover, negligence law is extremely costly to administer. There are substantial barriers to accessing the legal system and cases may be settled out of court in ways that give rise to substantial injustice both in assigning fault and in compensating (and failing to compensate) accident victims. A no-fault system, on the other hand, by avoiding the need to prove fault, largely by-passes courts and lawyers, may be cheaper to administer, and might better satisfy legitimate social goals, *in addition to* efficiency (eg just and timely compensation).

The Chicago school prescription is that in the real world where there are many transaction costs, liability rules should be designed to mimic what the market would achieve. Some economists doubt that mimicking the market is the best way to achieve optimal results. An example of a sophisticated economic analysis of tort law along these lines is provided by Guido Calabresi, one of the foremost exponents of the economic analysis of law, and author of a leading text on accident compensation.[36] Calabresi's seminal contribution was to suggest how, in the presence of various types of transaction costs, a society would go about deciding a set of entitlements in respect of accidents. Calabresi has elegantly summarised his argument in terms of five propositions:

(1) that economic efficiency standing alone would dictate that set of entitlements which favours knowledgeable choices between social benefits and the social

---

34   See, for example, Swan, n 30.
35   See, for example, Maureen Brunt, "Comment: The Economics of Law" (1984) 3 *Aust Economic Review* 113.
36   Calabresi, n 24.

costs of obtaining them, and between social costs and the social costs of avoiding them; (2) that this implies, in the absence of certainty as to whether a benefit is worth its costs to society, that the cost should be put on the party or activity best located to make such a cost-benefit analysis; (3) that in particular contexts like accidents or pollution this suggests putting costs on the party or activity which can most cheaply avoid them; (4) that in the absence of certainty as to who that party or activity is, the costs should be put on the party or activity which can with the lowest transaction costs act in the market to correct an error in entitlements by inducing the party who can avoid social costs most cheaply to do so; and (5) that since we are in an area where by hypothesis markets do not work perfectly – there are transaction costs – a decision will often have to be made on whether market transactions or collective fiat is most likely to bring us closer to the Pareto optimal result the "perfect" market would reach.[37]

Central to Calabresi's argument is the notion that the costs of accidents can be minimised if the party which could avoid the accident at least cost (the "cheapest cost avoider") is made liable for the loss. That is, accident costs should be allocated to the party who has the comparative advantage in reducing risk or in achieving safety. If this is not done, the wrong party will be induced to take precautions, more resources than necessary will be devoted to achieving the same level of safety and the outcome will be economically inefficient. In the case of motor accidents, this can be readily illustrated as follows:

A careless driver's car collides with a pedestrian, inflicting damages totalling £200. It is discovered that the accident resulted from the driver's failure to fit new brakes costing £50. Clearly, road users and society as a whole would benefit if the driver had fitted new brakes, the benefit being £150 (equal to the avoided loss of £200 minus the cost of the new brakes, £50). If the driver is made legally liable for the loss, that is, he is required to pay the victim compensation of £200 should an accident occur, then clearly he would have a strong incentive to fit the new brakes. A liability rule which shifts the loss whenever it would encourage careless drivers to fit new brakes makes the cheapest solution to the individual the efficient solution.[38]

Calabresi's insight has most to contribute in circumstances where one party can be singled out as the "least cost avoider". For example, in the case of industrial accidents, the "cheapest cost avoider" is likely to be the employer, who not only controls the workplace but is in the best position to create safe working conditions, to evaluate accident risk and the expected accident losses.[39] However, even in circumstances where both parties can contribute substantially to accident reduction (and it is not clear *ex ante* which is the "least cost avoider"), it may still not be appropriate to follow the Chicago school prescription and "mimic the market" by means of liability rules.

Calabresi argues that, since mimicking the market involves the use of liability or other rules which themselves are not costless, the "optimal" result will not necessarily be the same as if transactions were costless (that is, mimicking the market may not achieve the optimal result). Moreover, the gains which might be made from "mimicking" the market (or at least moving towards that "unreachable

---

37   Calabresi and Melamed, n 22, 1096-1097. See generally Calabresi, n 24, 135-197.

38   C Veljanovski, *The Economics of Law*, Hobart Paper, Institute of Economic Affairs, 1990, 21. See generally Calabresi, n 24.

39   See further Gunningham, n 23, 285.

goal") are usually unquantifiable and based largely on guesses. As a result, "the question of whether a given law is worth its costs (in terms of better resource allocation) is rarely susceptible of empirical proof". However, this need not mean we throw up our hands and leave it to the market. On the contrary, as Calabresi says (and in sharp contrast to the Chicago school), "it is precisely the province of good government to make guesses as to what laws are likely to be worth their costs [and], ... there is no reason to assume that in the absence of conclusive information no government action is better than some action".[40]

Calabresi further argues that action in an uncertain case is more likely to be justified if goals other than resource allocation (efficiency) are served by the action. In the case of automobile accidents, for example, it may be very unclear if, or to what extent, negligence liability reduces accident levels towards the optimal level. However, it may be much more clear that an alternative policy (eg no-fault) will substantially achieve other valued social goals (eg adequate loss spreading).

We must conclude that the Chicago school framework, as applied to unintentional torts, raises far more difficulties than its proponents have acknowledged. In part, the problem lies in the highly idealised view of tort held by Posner and other Chicago school scholars. For them, administrative costs are low, all parties respond rationally to law-based incentives, the rules themselves are clearly defined, issues of evidence and fact finding do not unduly muddy the waters, judges make decisions "as if" they had economic efficiency in mind and so on.

In practice, of course, the picture is considerably more confused and complex. If behaviour in the real world is radically at variance with the assumptions of the Chicago school model, and if the administrative costs of their preferred system are substantial, then their case is considerably weakened. Moreover, if Calabresi is correct in arguing that when transaction costs lead to market imperfections, the most efficient response is often *not* to mimic the market, then the Chicago school application of Coase, is itself rendered problematic.

It may well be, at least in the area of unintended torts, that contrary to the Chicago school the value of Coase is not to provide clear answers (eg to "mimic" the market), but rather to sharpen analysis, to suggest what *kinds* of empirical data would be useful in making resource allocation decisions.

(d) The common law as a whole

We now look at the common law as a whole, and we investigate the claim that the common law does – and should – promote economic efficiency. This is both the best known and the most controversial theme in the economic analysis of law. It is most commonly associated with a number of Chicago school lawyer-economists and, in particular, Richard Posner and his influential book, *Economic Analysis of Law*.[41] However, the claim is certainly not confined to the Chicago school, and a

---

40   G Calabresi, "Transaction Costs, Resource Allocation and Liability Rules – A Comment" (1968) 11 *Journal of Law and Economics* 67 at 70.

41   Posner, n 27. See also A Kronman, "Mistake, Disclosure, Information, and the Law of Contracts" (1978) 1 *Journal of Legal Studies* 1; W Landes and R Posner, "Salvors, Finders, Good Samaritans, and Other Rescuers: An Economic Study of Law and Altruism" (1978) 7 *Journal of Legal Studies* 83; R Posner and AM Rosenfield, "Impossibility and Related Doctrines in Contract Law: An Economic Analysis" (1977) 6 *Journal of Legal Studies* 83; Landes and Posner, "A Positive Economic Analysis of Products Liability" (1985) 14 *Journal of Legal Studies* 535.

considerable proportion of law and economics scholars world-wide subscribe to it.[42]

The claim about the efficiency of the common law can be stated fairly briefly. First, at a descriptive level, they claim that the common law is *in fact* efficient. Secondly, and at a normative level, their thesis is that cases *should* be decided on the basis of efficiency considerations. In the following section we focus on the descriptive claim. We examine the normative claims later in the chapter.

(i) The descriptive claim

There are essentially three explanations offered to explain why the common law tends towards efficiency. First, some economists argue that inefficient rules generate litigation and litigation eventually generates changes in the rules. For example, if some rule of the common law prevents individuals from dealing with each other in a way that produces net benefits, those affected will try either to change the law or work around it. Eventually we are left with a common law shaped, "as if by an invisible hand", to maximise economic efficiency.

Secondly, it is argued that litigants who would benefit if the rule were made invest more in the litigation, in an attempt to persuade the court, than those who favour an inefficient rule. Since the economic stakes are higher under inefficient rules, the party that initially has the liability has a greater incentive to spend a larger amount on litigation expenses than under efficient rules.

These two explanations together are often referred to as "the economic theory of the evolution of the common law". There are, in fact, several variants of the evolutionary theme, not all of which need to be considered for present purposes.[43] In general, evolutionary claims acknowledge that inefficient rules may exist and that sometimes courts make mistakes and select inefficient outcomes. Nevertheless, they assert that the law *tends* towards efficiency, that more efficient rules persist longer than less efficient ones, or that more efficient rules replace less efficient ones more frequently than vice versa. Thus, the movement towards efficiency within the common law is primarily a *process*.

Probably the most articulate proponent of this sort of theory is Paul Rubin, who argues that:

> The presumed efficiency of the common law and the decision to use the courts to settle a dispute are related. In particular, this relationship will occur because resorting to court settlement is more likely in cases where the legal rules relevant to the dispute are inefficient, and less likely where the rules are efficient. Thus, efficient rules may evolve from in-court settlement, thereby reducing the incentive for future litigation and increasing the probability that efficient rules will persist. In short, the efficient rule situation ... is due to an evolutionary mechanism whose direction proceeds from the utility maximizing decisions of disputants rather than from the wisdom of judges.[44]

He continues:

---

42   CK Rowley, "Public Choice and the Economic Analysis of Law" in N Mercuro (ed), *Law and Economics*, Kluwer, 1989, 137.

43   See further N Mercuro and T Ryan, *Law, Economics, and Public Policy*, Greenwich, 1984, 122.

44   Paul H Rubin, "Why is the Common Law Efficient?" (1977) 6 *Journal of Legal Studies* 51.

If rules are inefficient, parties will use the courts until the rules are changed; conversely, if rules are efficient, the courts will not be used and the efficient rule will remain in force. An outside observer coming upon this legal rule would observe that the rule is efficient; but this efficiency occurs because of an evolutionary process, not because of any particular wisdom on the part of judges. If judges decide independently of efficiency we would still find efficient rules. Intelligent judges may speed up the process of attaining efficiency; they do not drive the process.[45]

The third explanation, and one very closely associated with Posner, is that judges promote efficient outcomes.[46] For example, as we saw earlier in this chapter, where transaction costs are low, the common law promotes efficiency by fostering market transactions through contract. Where transaction costs are so high as to preclude a private contract solution, then the common law will generate an outcome which "brings about an allocation of resources that simulates that which the free market would have brought about had it been operable".[47]

Posner uses the old case of *Eckert v Long Island Railroad*[48] to show that, where transaction costs are high and where market transactions are not feasible, common law doctrines "mimic the market", thereby bringing about an allocation of resources that simulates what the free market *would* have brought about in the absence of transaction costs:

> The defendant's train was going too fast and without adequate signals in a densely populated area. A small child was sitting on the tracks oblivious to the oncoming train. Eckert ran to rescue the child and managed to throw it clear but was himself killed. The court held that Eckert had not been contributorily negligent, and therefore his estate could recover damages for the railroad's negligence. For "it was not wrongful in him to make every effort in his power to rescue the child, compatible with a reasonable regard for his own safety. It was his duty to exercise his judgment as to whether he could probably save the child without serious injury to himself". If, as implied by this passage, the probability that the child would be killed if the rescue was not attempted was greater than the probability that Eckert would get himself killed saving the child, and if the child's life was at least as valuable as Eckert's life, then the expected benefit of the rescue to the railroad in reducing an expected liability cost to the child's parents was greater than the expected cost of rescue. In that event, but for prohibitive transaction costs, the railroad would have hired Eckert to attempt the rescue, so it should be required to compensate him ex post.[49]

Another example which Posner uses to show the efficiency of common law is in the different responses of the eastern and the western States in America to the problem of "fencing out" versus "fencing in". Fencing out refers to a property-rights system in which damage caused by straying cattle is actionable at law only

---

45   Rubin, n 44, 55. See also GL Priest, "The Common Law Process and the Selection of Efficient Rules" (1977) 6 *Journal of Legal Studies* 65.

46   As we shall see, "efficiency" for Posner means efficiency in terms of the Kaldor-Hicks criterion (see Chapter 11), or at least a version of the Kaldor-Hicks criterion with wealth maximisation rather than utility maximisation as the goal.

47   Mercuro and Ryan, n 43, 119.

48   1 43 NY 502 (1870).

49   Posner, n 27, 272-731.

if the owner of the crops or other goods damaged by the cattle has made reasonable efforts to fence. Fencing in refers to a system where this duty is not imposed, so that the owner of the cattle must fence them in if she or he wants to avoid liability. The former system is more efficient if the ratio of crops to cattle is low, for then it is cheaper for the farmers than ranchers to fence. If the ratio is reversed, fencing in is a more efficient system. Posner shows that in those American States where cattle farming is more common than crop farming, there are fencing-out rules – that is, the crop-growers must make reasonable efforts to keep out the cattle before they have any remedy. In other States and England, where crops are more common, then the liability is on the animal owner to keep the animals in. The argument is that the law is adopting the most efficient outcome in the local economy.[50]

Posner extends his claims about the economic efficiency of the common law to many areas of law in which the rules at first sight might not be economically determined. For Posner:

[T]he law of property (including intellectual property), of contracts and commercial law, of restitution and unjust enrichment, of criminal and family law, and of admiralty law all can be restated in economic terms that explain the principal doctrines, both substantive and remedial, in these fields of (largely) judge-made law.[51]

The claim that judges actively adopt economically efficient rules is controversial. As we saw in Chapter 5, the liberal view of judges is that they are neutral: they do not have their own agendas, and they determine cases solely by reference to the issues introduced by the parties. Why might judges adopt economically efficient rules? Does the common law, which changes only incrementally, make as much sense as Posner asserts it does? According to Posner, three factors in particular lead to the efficiency of judge-made law. First, wealth maximisation (which is what Posner means by efficiency[52]) is closely connected with utilitarianism, which was the dominant political ideology during the formative period of the common law (roughly 1800-1950). Secondly, judges are not in a good position to engage in wealth distribution and are therefore more likely to address goals they *can* achieve (such as efficiency). Thirdly, the process of common law adjudication itself leads to the survival of other rules. Posner suggests that:

Many common law doctrines are economically sensible but not economically subtle. They are commonsensical. Their articulation in economic terms is beyond the capacity of most judges and lawyers but their intuition is not.[53]

Much of this argument relies on what is known as the "as if" methodology of the Chicago school. In this approach, it is not claimed that judges necessarily consciously apply economic principles to decide cases, but rather that they "devise a set of legal rules which correspond to those which they would have chosen had

---

50   Ibid 60.

51   Ibid 271.

52   See the discussion on "The Normative Claim", below.

53   Posner, n 27, 274-275. Posner does acknowledge that economic efficiency does not provide a complete positive theory of common law.

they subscribed to a particular set of economic principles".[54] It is "as if" they behaved like economic rationalists.

(ii) Criticisms of the descriptive claim

Not everyone has found these arguments persuasive. The "economic efficiency of common law" thesis, and Posner's version of it in particular, has been subject to widespread criticism. Under this sub-heading we first consider criticisms of Posner's thesis, and then we look at criticisms of the evolutionary theory described above.

A major difficulty for Posner's thesis is that there is almost no direct evidence as to the reasons underlying judicial decisions. Most judgments (everywhere in the 19th century, and still largely today in Anglo-Australian law) are couched in formalistic terms, with no acknowledgement of their social or economic underpinnings. So, given that there is so little direct evidence one way or the other, one must ask: have Posner and his colleagues produced convincing evidence in favour of the efficiency thesis? The critics suggest they have not, and they identify a number of specific shortcomings in the thesis.

First, the approach does not follow a proper scientific method. Rather than dispassionately seeing if the theory can be falsified, Posner and his colleagues set out to marshal evidence to bolster it up. Similarly, rather than letting their theories be informed by the world, they try to make their perceptions of the world fit their theories. According to Balkin, this is akin to "shooting arrows at a board and then drawing bullseyes wherever the arrow lands".[55]

Secondly, the efficiency claim is at its most plausible with respect to 19th-century developments in the common law. This was, as Posner points out, the period when utilitarianism and market-oriented economics were at their height, and when "efficiency" considerations might plausibly have permeated judicial decision-making. However, even in this period, there is considerable evidence to suggest that in many areas the common law did *not* incline towards efficiency.[56] For example, take Lawrence Friedman's analysis of 19th-century common law liability for work accidents:

> [A] worker who had an accident on the job was usually out of luck. The fellow-servant rule [whereby a worker could not sue his/her employer if the injury arose out of the negligence of a fellow-servant] barred workers from collecting damages. But sometimes workers could fit their situations into one of the many exceptions. There was heavy litigation. The contingent-fee system financed working-class litigants. Companies settled many cases, fought some, gave up on some. They went to court from time to time and were often successful – but at a price. A losing employer had to pay damages and lawyers' fees, not to mention insurance premiums and other administrative costs. Probably less than half of the

---

54 Stephen, n 21, 195; R Posner, "Law and Economics in Common Law, Civil Law, and Developing Nations" (2004) 17 *Ratio Juris* 66 at 68.

55 JM Balkin, "Too Good to be True: The Positive Economic Theory of Law" (1987) *Columbia Law Review* 1447 at 1461.

56 See, for example, D Kennedy and F Michelman, "Are Property and Contract Efficient?" (1980) 8 *Hofstra Law Review* 711; M Kelman, "Trashing" (1984) 36 *Stanford Law Review* 293 at 312-318; M Kelman, "Misunderstanding Social Life: A Critique of the Core Premises of Law & Economics'" (1983) 33 *Journal of Legal Education* 274 at 279-283.

money paid out actually went to injured workmen. The rest was consumed by the swarm of middlemen. By 1900, the system was unpopular, it seems, with both management and labor.

... The story ... is hard to reconcile with a body of work, some of it by economists, that takes a very positive attitude toward common-law rules. The basic proposition is that these rules, generated in private lawsuits, tend toward efficiency in ways that legislation can never approach... . Observers who use cruder measures and who muck about in the dirt of actual history tend to doubt whether courts really get such magical results.[57]

More importantly, the economists fail to take account of the complexity of the actual functioning of legal institutions. As Friedman puts it:

Economic analysis (or sociological analysis, for that matter) is useless unless it confronts the legal system as it works in reality, not as it is described in the books. Theories about the way courts operate mean nothing unless they are grounded in studies of what happens in real life.[58]

Another criticism is that it is often unclear what decisions are actually efficient, and there is little reason to believe that we can identify those decisions.[59] For example, we can only determine if a particular decision is efficient if we have full knowledge of the costs which that decision will involve. As Calabresi and others have argued, often we do not.

In summary, it would seem that, at a descriptive level, Posner's arguments about the efficiency of common law are overstated. The methodology by which the theory is purportedly substantiated is dubious, the theory itself may not be testable in any rigorous way and it lacks an adequate causal basis. Empirical research which *attempts* to test the theory is scanty, and empirical questions are frequently ignored. Finally, much of the empirical evidence which does exist is not supportive of the theory.

In the light of these limitations, one might ask what value the descriptive thesis has. At best, it throws light on particular areas of law – namely those where the legal rules are directly concerned with regulating market behaviour. The paradigm case, as we saw earlier, is contract law. It may indeed be that many rules of contract law *are* designed to generate efficiency. Certainly the links between contract, which facilitates voluntary exchange, and the maximisation of economic welfare through the market, are particularly clear. However, a theory of markets and market independence (which Chicago economic theory essentially is) cannot readily be extended and applied to law and the legal system in general. As we have seen, Posner's attempt to do so has been largely unsuccessful and there is often a considerable disparity between the predictions of Chicago school economic theory, and empirical reality.

Perhaps, in assessing the "efficiency of common law" claim, more attention should be paid to the "evolutionary theory of common law" with which we began. That theory does at least suggest a mechanism by which the efficiency of certain

57   L Friedman, "On Regulation and Legal Process" in R Noll (ed), *Regulatory Policy and the Social Sciences*, U of California Press, 1985, 129-132.

58   L Friedman, n 57, 132-133. See also WLF Felstiner and P Seigelman, "Neoclassical Difficulties: Tort Deterrence for Latent Injuries" (1989) 11 *Law and Policy* 309-329.

59   VP Goldberg, "A Relational Exchange Respective and Complex Contracts" in FH Stephen (ed), *Firms, Organization and Labour*, MacMillan, 1984.

doctrines (which involve parties with a continuing interest) could emerge. Specifically, because inefficient rules impose larger costs on society than efficient ones, they thereby create incentives to use the courts more frequently when the rules are inefficient, than when they are efficient.

However, evolutionary theory has also been subjected to serious criticism. It, and Rubin's version in particular, depends on a claim that the litigation process alone, rather than the efficiency concerns of the judiciary, will generate efficient common law outcomes. Accordingly, much depends on the nature of the parties affected by specific doctrines (for example, whether there are sufficient parties with a long-term interest in precedent) and, like Posner's version, this is more plausible in some areas of law than others. That is, the evolutionary theory does not stand up as a *general* theory of law because, in non-market areas like torts, there are commonly not sufficient "repeat players" with sufficient interest to continue litigating until efficient rules are obtained.

There is also a more fundamental criticism of evolutionary theory that has been made by Kahn. He argues that, contrary to evolutionary theory, the existence of potential litigants with a continuing interest in a specific legal outcome will not necessarily result in efficiency over the long run. It all depends who those litigants are.[60] Those groups who devote the greatest resources to litigation will be those who have the greatest incentives and ability to do so.[61] They will do so irrespective of the relative efficiency or inefficiency of the existing rules.[62] Moreover, there is little doubt that those who devote the greatest resources to litigation have, over the long run, the greatest chance of success: Galanter's work on one shotters and repeat players, examined in Chapter 4, bears testament to this. Accordingly, as Kahn argues:

> Groups better able to muster resources will succeed more frequently in establishing favorable legal rules than groups less able to do so. Yet it is just this ability to muster resources, to act collectively as a group, that defines the groups likely to succeed in the political context.... If affirmative governmental (*ie*, non-judicial) actions is biased because politics is biased, then *a fortiori* common law outcomes must also be biased, because the same forces that bias politics also affect legal outcomes.[63]

It follows that common law outcomes cannot be used as a benchmark of efficiency, any more than can those arrived at through the political process.

(iii) The normative claim

Even if we were to accept that the common law is developing towards a set of economically efficient rules, that still does not tell us whether it *ought* to be doing so. Why should law or public policy promote efficiency? Should it not promote justice, redistribution or some other principle that requires us to go beyond efficiency? What, if any, is the ethical basis of efficiency?

---

60 PL Kahn, "The Politics of Unregulation" (1990) 75 *Cornell Law Review* 299 (emphasis added).

61 We will revisit this argument in Chapter 13 where we examine public choice theory.

62 See also T Webster, "Economic Efficiency and the Common Law" (2004) 32 *Atlantic Economic Journal* 39, suggesting that generally it is in a litigant's best interests to negotiate an out-of-court settlement regardless of the efficiency of the rule.

63 Kahn, n 60, 300-302.

Posner, perhaps more than any other lawyer-economist, has sought to address these questions.[64] He begins by defining efficiency as meaning wealth maximisation: the adoption of rules and laws that will maximise the aggregate wealth of the members of society without regard to the actual distribution of wealth among them.[65] This is *not* the same as utility maximisation (the more conventional definition), which takes account of concerns which are not priced by the market.

Posner argues that wealth maximisation is an ethically appealing principle on which to base a normative theory of law.[66] Indeed, according to Posner, the wealth-maximisation norm yields "a comprehensive and unitary theory of rights and duties",[67] and the "foundation for a theory of justice both distributive and corrective".[68] It is important to understand that Posner's assertion is not merely the modest one that, all other things being equal, we should handle any legal problem in the most cost-efficient way. Rather he makes the far more controversial claim that the legal system (or at least judges) should be seeking to achieve "efficiency" or "wealth maximisation", as their single over-arching goal.[69]

Posner's argument relies on the Kaldor-Hicks test of efficiency. Under this test a reallocation of resources is justified provided it would be possible for winners to compensate losers and still come out ahead. (It is important to remember that Kaldor-Hicks only requires that winners *could* compensate losers, not that they actually do so. This is why Kaldor-Hicks is also known as the "hypothetical compensation" test.) Posner embraces a modified version of this test, so that whereas Kaldor-Hicks aims to maximise utility, Posner aims to maximise wealth.

An efficiency test under which some must lose in order for others to win (albeit that the cake is bigger overall) is difficult to justify ethically. Indeed, because losers go uncompensated, the wealth maximisation principle is consistent with "quite drastic, capricious and inequitable actual redistributions of income".[70] Without some clear justification, there is no reason to believe that the wealth maximisation principle is ethically sound or that it should be applied by judges or by anyone else.

64　He is not the only one to do so, however. See, for example, L Kaplow and S Shavell, *Fairness versus Welfare*, Harvard UP, 2002, arguing that "welfare" (ie the aggregate well-being of individuals in society) should be the basis for evaluating law.

65　As Jules Coleman has noted, a number of different definitions have been employed in the efficiency of common law literature:

> Economists as well as proponents of the economic analysis of law employ at least four efficiency-related notions, including: (1) productive efficiency, (2) Pareto optimality, (3) Pareto superiority, and (4) Kaldor-Hicks efficiency. If it constitutes a suitable efficiency criterion, Posner's wealth maximisation would increase the total to at least five.

See J Coleman, "Efficiency, Utility and Wealth Maximisation" (1980) 8 *Hofstra Law Review* 509 at 512.

66　See generally the series of articles collected in R Posner's book, *The Economics of Justice*, Harvard UP, 1981.

67　R Posner, "Utilitarianism, Economics and Legal Theory" (1979) 8 *Journal of Legal Studies* 103 at 140.

68　Posner, n 67, 125.

69　R Posner, "The Ethical and Political Basis of the Efficiency Norm in Common Law Adjudication" (1980) 8 *Hofstra Law Review* 487.

70　C Veljanovski, "Wealth Maximisation, Law and Ethics" [1981] *International Review of Law and Economics* 10 at 12.

Posner's response is that, on closer examination, the actual losses that some would suffer under Kaldor-Hicks are not morally objectionable. Mercuro and Ryan have usefully summarised Posner's argument as follows:

> [S]tarting with the basic belief that systems that promote the exercise of liberty and autonomy are to be preferred to those that limit liberty and autonomy (a position which he ascribes to be broadly Kantian), Posner … suggests that the principle of consent is the ethically attractive basis for utilizing wealth maximization as a decision rule in common law adjudication. The notion of consent employed by Posner is that of ex ante compensation. Posner equates the notions of ex ante compensation and consent by pointing out that individuals would consent to wealth maximization as a criterion for establishing common law rules for adjudication provided that there is a sufficient probability that the individuals will benefit in the long run from such rules, though they may be losers in the application of a particular rule. In effect, this constitutes the Kaldor-Hicks criterion … Posner requires only that the increase in value be sufficiently large so that the losers could be fully compensated.[71]

There are two related arguments here. The first is based on a notion of consent: "everyone (or at least almost everyone) may be deemed to have consented in advance to the principles or rules that judges who seek to maximise wealth will apply".[72] Posner argues that one can presume an *implied* consent among uncompensated losers to efficient reallocations of resources and legal rights.

He illustrates what he means by consent in this context by giving the example of a company that decides to close a factory in town A and open a new one in B, where in neither location are there significant pollution, congestion or other technological externalities[73] from the plant. The move may still lower property values in A and raise them in B, making landowners in A worse off and those in B better off. Posner says that the landowners in A consented to the loss in that they were compensated when they bought the land. Specifically, the probability that the plant would move was discounted in the purchase price that they paid.[74] Posner's point is that:

> Many of the involuntary, uncompensated losses experienced in the market, or tolerated by the institutions that take the place of the market where the market cannot be made to work effectively, are fully compensated ex ante and hence consented to.[75]

For Posner, consent thus means the willingness to pay a price that discounts the risk of loss.

The second argument is based on the notion that there is a universal interest in wealth maximisation. As summarised by Ronald Dworkin, the argument is that:

---

71 Mercuro and Ryan, n 43, 125.

72 R Dworkin, "Why Efficiency?" (1980) 8 *Hofstra Law Review* 571 at 573.

73 Externalities in production exist when the production activities of one firm directly affect the production activities of another, for example, firm A discharges effluent into a river which increases the costs of firm B downstream. The essence of externalities is that their costs or benefits are not reflected in market prices, and so the decision of the consumer or firm creating the externality generally does not take its effect into account.

74 Posner, n 69, 490.

75 Ibid 492.

[T]he enforcement of [wealth maximising] principles and rules is in fact in the interests of everyone (or about everyone) including those who thereby lose lawsuits ... [for example] if negligence rules are superior from the standpoint of wealth maximization to rules of strict liability, it follows that all those who benefit from reduced driving costs – almost everyone – would be better off under a regime of negligence than a regime of strict liability. The first claim – about consent – is then supposed to follow directly: If it is in fact true that almost everyone would be better off under a regime of negligence than strict liability, then it is fair to assume that almost everyone would have chosen negligence if offered the choice between these two regimes at a suitable early time, and therefore fair to deem almost everyone to have consented to negligence even though, of course, no one has actually done so.[76]

Dworkin summarises the consent and the universal interest arguments as follows:

The first – the argument from consent – is supposed to introduce the idea of autonomy (and therefore a strain of Kant) to the case for wealth. The second – the argument from universal interest – insists on the continuing relevance of welfare to justice, and therefore is supposed to add a dose of utilitarianism. The combined arguments, Posner suggests, show that wealth maximization – at least by judges – provides the best of both these traditional theories of political morality and avoids their famous problems.[77]

(iv) Criticisms of the normative claim

Not surprisingly, Posner's argument has attracted criticism. One set of criticisms is directed at his arguments about consent and universal interest.

In respect of the first argument – the argument about consent – Ronald Dworkin suggests that Posner confuses two questions: Is it *fair* that someone should have some loss? Has he or she *consented* to bear that loss? Dworkin takes Posner's own examples to illustrate this confusion:

[Posner] imagines a case in which someone buys land which then falls in value when the biggest plant in town unexpectedly moves. He says that the loss was compensated ex ante (and hence "consented to") because "[t]he probability that the plant would move was discounted in the purchase price that they paid". The latter suggestion is mysterious. Does it assume that the price was lower because both parties to the sale expected the move? But then the plant's move would not have been unexpected. Or does it mean simply that anyone buying or selling anything knows that the unexpected may happen? In either case the argument begs the question even as an argument that it is fair that the buyer bear the loss. For it assumes that it has already been established and understood by the parties that the buyer must bear the loss – otherwise the price would not have reflected just the risk that the plant would move, but also the risk that the buyer would be required to bear the loss if it did move.

But in any event it is just wrong to say, in either case, that the buyer consented to the loss. Perhaps, though the buyer knew that the plant would very likely move and that he was getting a bargain price because the seller expected that the buyer would bear the loss if the plant did move, the buyer hoped that he

---

76   Dworkin, n 72, 574.

77   Ibid 574.

might be able to persuade some court to rescind the sale if the feared move did take place or to persuade some legislature to bail him out. It would be fair, in these circumstances, for the court to refuse rescission, but dead wrong to say that the buyer had consented to bear the loss.[78]

The second argument – the argument about universal interest – is also shown to be flawed. Arguments based on antecedent interests face the objection that it is not clear

how a person's antecedent interests should be identified or why those interests should carry moral weight after the fact. It might have been in your interest yesterday to promise to buy your friend dinner tomorrow in return for some favor, but if you did not in fact make the promise yesterday, then you do not in fact owe your friend dinner tomorrow. Analogously, Dworkin objects that the supposed fact that wealth maximization is in almost everyone's interest before any decision is made does not imply that those on whom costs are imposed by a decision have any reason to regard the imposition as morally justified.[79]

Veljanovski criticises the application of the consent and interest arguments to non-market situations. In his view, people voluntarily participate in the market because they know they will benefit from the process on some occasions. However, this cannot be presumed in a non-market context.[80]

In order to defend his argument on this point, Posner would need to show, as a minimum, that in the long run each consumer can expect to come out ahead if the wealth-maximisation rule is applied – thereby demonstrating that each person (or almost everyone) *does* have an interest in wealth maximisation. Thus even the individual who loses from one change in the rules will most likely gain from another, and experience a net gain overall.

However, as Polinsky has pointed out:

There is no assurance, however, that each person will in fact gain but only a presumption that he could expect to gain. Even after numerous changes in the law, there will in general be some individuals who are net losers.... more persons may be net gainers, but not everyone can be assured of being a net gainer unless compensation for losses is paid with respect to each change or after the bundle of changes.[81]

In summary, Posner fails to confront the crucial question: How does one ethically justify losers going uncompensated when the gainers by definition reap benefits more than sufficient to compensate them?

A second set of criticisms has been directed at the wealth-maximisation standard generally. We cannot address all of these criticisms here. Many of them are highly complex and technical.[82] However, we can indicate in general terms some of the problems which beset wealth maximisation as a normative principle.[83]

---

78   Ibid 576-577.

79   Kuperberg and Beitz, n 26, 11.

80   Veljanovski, n 70, 14.

81   AM Polinsky, "Economic Analysis as a Potentially Defective Product" (1974) 87 *Harvard Law Review* 1680.

82   See, for example, Mercuro and Ryan, n 43, 130-136.

83   In addition to the substantive problems discussed in the text, it should be noted that the vagueness and ambiguity of the wealth maximisation principle is itself a problem. See further Mercuro and Ryan, n 43, 130-132.

Wealth *maximisation* can only be pursued effectively if there is some initial delineation of rights, some prior distribution of wealth and income. One fundamental problem is that Posner's theory is incapable of identifying adequately what this distribution should be. Posner fails to provide any theory of distributive justice. Indeed, as he sees it, one of the virtues of wealth maximisation is that it strips away distributive concerns.[84] As he puts it:

> Since economics does not answer the question whether the existing distribution of income and wealth is good or bad, just or unjust, although it can tell us a great deal about the costs of altering the existing distribution, as well as about the distributive consequences of various policies: neither does it answer the ultimate question whether an efficient allocation of resources would be socially or ethically desirable.[85]

As a result, the theory suffers from a fundamental problem of circularity, in that it "attempts to deduce a structure of rights when in fact the structure of rights is needed to make such a deduction".[86]

In summary, "the only wealth maximising outcome that is ethically attractive is one based on a "just" assignment of initial rights".[87] Posner, in failing to overcome a fundamental circularity problem, and in denying that initial entitlements need to be "justly" distributed, fails to provide a normative theory with ethical significance.

A further and related difficulty lies in the way Posner measures wealth:

> Wealth is the value in dollars or dollar equivalents ... of everything in society. It is measured by what people are willing to pay for something or, if they already own it, what they demand in money to give it up. The only kind of preference that counts in a system of wealth maximization is thus one that is backed up by money – in other words, that is registered in a market.[88]

As Leff points out, for Posner:

> If you do not "buy" something, you are *unwilling* to do so. There is no place for the word or concept "unable". Thus, in this system, there is nothing which is coerced. For instance, let us say that a starving man approaches a loaf of bread held by an armed baker. Another potential buyer is there. The baker institutes an auction; he wants cash only (having too great doubts about the starveling's health to be interested in granting credit). The poor man gropes in his pockets and comes up with a dollar. The other bidder immediately takes out $1.01 and makes off with the bread. Now under Posner's definitional system we must say that the

---

84 R Posner, "Law and Economics *Is* Moral" in RP Malloy and J Evensky (eds), *Adam Smith and the Philosophy of Law and Economics*, Kluwer, 1994, 167 at 171.

85 Posner, n 27, 15. Posner's argument is that, since courts can do little to change the distribution of rights, they should concentrate on what they *can* do, namely to implement the wealth maximisation principle on the basis of the existing structure of wealth and income. In effect, they must exercise a value judgement in favour of the status quo, leaving it to the political system to address distributional questions. This argument has been undermined by Mercuro and Samuels who argue that courts, in making law, do determine who will have rights and that this constitutes the distribution of wealth in society: N Mercuro and WJ Samuels, "Wealth Maximisation and Judicial Decision-Making: The Issues Clarified" (1986) 6 *International Review of Law and Economics* 133.

86 Mercuro and Ryan, n 43, 132.

87 Veljanovski, n 70, 19.

88 Posner, n 67, 119.

"value" of the bread was no more than a dollar to the poor man because he was "unwilling" to pay more than that. An observer not bound within that particular definitional structure might find it somehow more illuminating to characterize the poor man's failure as being the result of being unable to pay more than a dollar. But one cannot, consistent with Posner's system, say any such thing. One's actual power is irrelevant... . What this all means is that Posner has not played fair with the question of power, or inequalities thereof.[89]

Again, since valuations of what are "wealth-maximising" are dependent on willingness-to-pay, it is uncertain whether a society will maximise utility, even if it is provided with more goods. Ronald Dworkin has explored one aspect of this criticism, showing that judicial reliance on the wealth maximisation principle may lead to allocative inefficiency. This can be illustrated by Leff's example above. The wealth maximising rule would call for the transfer of the bread from the poor to the rich man with no compensation paid to the poor man. But although this decision would maximise wealth, it might also lead to a reduction in utility.[90]

This short survey of some of the limitations of the wealth maximisation principle should be sufficient to indicate that the principle is unsound and incoherent, and is an inadequate foundation on which to build a normative theory of law. Most certainly it does not, as Posner claims, provide conclusive normative criteria for evaluating law. The further question is whether it should be rejected entirely, or whether (when weighed against certain other moral and political values) it provides a *partial* basis for such a theory. That is, rather than being *the* aim of the legal process, should efficiency at least be *an* aim of that process?

There is clearly a tension between equity and efficiency, and an adequate normative theory of justice must include (amongst other things) some mechanism for determining in what circumstances and to what extent one will prevail over the other. The most serious and frequent conflict is between the pursuit of efficiency and values of distributive justice. A decision which increases the size of the pie overall may also result in its being divided inequitably: in any competition based on market competence some are bound to lose out; so how, if at all, should their interests be protected?

In conclusion, Posner's wealth-maximisation principle neither provides an acceptable theory of ethics, nor does it address the question of distributive justice in any coherent manner. As such, we suggest that it lacks *any* basis as a normative theory of law. There seems to be no reason why judges should take account of it at all in the decision-making process.

This of course, is not to say that the entire concept of efficiency is worthless. There is no doubt that economics is a useful tool that can assist in the analysis of particular legal issues, one which enables us to handle those issues in the most cost-effective way. As indicated earlier, where some agreed social goal can be achieved either efficiently or inefficiently, it is self-evident that it is preferable to achieve it efficiently (assuming that this does not detract from that particular goal, or other social goals). That is, while we have argued that efficiency has no value as an independent social goal, the economic approach *is* valuable in determining

---

89   A Leff, "Economic Analysis of Law: Some Realism About Nominalism" (1974) 60 *Virginia Law Review* 451 at 478-481.

90   See further R Dworkin, "Is Wealth a Value?" (1980) 9 *Journal of Legal Studies* 191.

whether, in allocating resources among competing uses, society is getting value for money.[91]

(e) Conclusion

It would be unfortunate to leave our discussion here, for it would give an unduly negative impression of the contribution which economics can, and has, made to law. We conclude this chapter, therefore, with a brief comment on the importance of the conceptual framework by which lawyer-economists organise the legal world and we emphasise the substantial *positive* contribution made by the law and economics movement.

We have seen that the economic analysis of law has made some striking claims. Undoubtedly, the most controversial is Posner's argument that the common law can be satisfactorily explained by a single overarching principle: efficiency. Posner's message, and indeed that of the Chicago school generally, is one of great simplicity.

Perhaps the greatest attraction of Posner's work, and that of many of his Chicago colleagues, is also its greatest problem. That is, in claiming to answer almost every legal problem through such a simple explanatory framework, it promises more than it can possibly deliver.

If Posner and his colleagues were prepared to concede the limitations of the competitive market paradigm which forms the basis of their approach, and to make much more modest claims about economics' contribution to law, then their critics might more readily acknowledge the merit and value of some aspects of their analysis. As we saw earlier in this chapter, that analysis does have considerable explanatory power in some areas of law (generally those which are market related), although in others (generally those which are not) it will always be incomplete. Even in the latter case, economic analysis still has value, but only if the limitations of its assumptions, and the complexity of the real world issues it seeks to explain, are acknowledged.

Unfortunately, the more sophisticated law and economics becomes, the less clear cut become its policy implications.[92] This indeed may well explain why complex analyses such as those offered by Calabresi and Williamson, have never achieved anything like the prominence of the Chicago school approach.[93] Nevertheless, it is those frameworks which offer the best hope of integrating economic concepts with traditional forms of legal discourse, and thereby providing a richer conception of appropriate legal argumentation.

Discussion Questions

1. What do economists mean by an "economically efficient" level of tortious harm, or an "efficient" breach of contract?

---

91 This point is made by Veljanovski, n 38, 40.

92 See generally M Trebilcock, "The Prospects of Law and Economics': A Canadian Perspective" (1983) 33 *Journal of Legal Education* 288.

93 Even so, the more sophisticated forms of economic analysis are already exposing weaknesses in the "common sense" solutions often preferred by judges.

2. Imagine that an automobile manufacturer discovers a design fault in one of its models. The manufacturer knows that the fault could result in serious injury, but calculates that the likelihood of the fault manifesting itself is very small. Moreover, it would cost the company a considerable amount of money to recall and repair all vehicles affected by the fault. Accordingly, no action is taken. Should the company be liable in negligence if a motorist is injured because of the fault?

3. What are the limitations of using fault-based liability rules in motor vehicle accidents?

4. How does the transaction cost model of contract seek to improve upon the market-based model?

5. Consider the following statement by Posner:

    > [W]hen one gets to contested moral questions the power of moral discourse runs out. When one talks about abortion, or when one talks about welfare rights, or when one talks about the appropriate provision for the retarded, or when one talks about surrogate motherhood, or affirmative action, or any one of a dozen other highly controversial moral issues, moral discourse turns out not to provide any sort of solution to these problems. It merely provides a vocabulary in which people can express views that have deep emotional roots. ... I do not think they are analytically fruitful. Wealth maximisation is analytically fruitful ...[94]

    Do you agree?

6. Is wealth maximisation consistent with the liberal ideal of individual liberty?

7. Does it matter if the common law is inefficient?

8. Imagine that the Federal Government decides to relocate most of its departments from Canberra to other capital cities. The effect of this decision is to reduce property values in Canberra. Should the government be required to compensate property owners who are adversely affected?

---

94 Posner, n 84, 177.

Chapter 13

Economics and Government Regulation

(a)   Introduction

Australia, like most other advanced western democracies, is an administrative state, shaped by explicitly adopted policies which are incorporated in legislation and implemented by an array of large regulatory agencies.[1] The economy, the health and safety of the public and the work force, the environment, and a multiplicity of other social goals are all regulated (with varying degrees of success) by this means. The consequence, as Rubin observes, is that:

> [P]olicy formation has displaced the incremental operation of the common law as our primary means of social regulation, and regulatory agencies have displaced the common law courts as the primary means by which that regulation is effectuated.[2]

It follows that law students need to understand not only public law and the processes of governmental decision-making, but also their political underpinnings. Professor Patrick McAuslan has pointed out that there is a close and continuing connection between political process and public law:

> [W]e cannot hope to understand the real world of public law without at the same time understanding something of the real world of politics and government, how decisions are made, what influences are brought to bear on decision-makers, how process affects policy and policy process, how public law and political process are in many respects two sides of the same coin.[3]

In this chapter we examine economic perspectives on political decision-making and its implications for law. This chapter therefore deals with economists' contributions to the regulatory debate described in Chapter 10.

(b)   Public choice theory

Beginning in the 1960s, a group of economists began to extend the behavioural model which they had used to understand private markets, and apply this model to those who participate in political roles as voters, politicians, bureaucrats, planners

---

1   For a discussion of this point, see E Rubin, "Law and Legislation in the Administrative State" (1989) 89 *Columbia Law Review* 369.

2   Ibid 369.

3   P McAuslan, "Public Law and Public Choice" (1989) 51 *Modern Law Review* 682.

and party leaders. This enterprise has become known as "public choice" theory (or "the economic theory of regulation").[4] It is, in essence, the economic analysis of political (non-market) decision-making. Thus we can say that, while traditional economics is "the science of the private choice of private goods on the market", the economic theory of regulation is "the science of the public choice of public goods through government".[5]

Public choice theory seeks to provide a theoretical framework that allows us to understand better what we see in the political arena. The questions posed are similar to those posed by sociologists and regulatory theorists (seen in Chapter 10). For example:

- Why do many laws, which are ostensibly enacted in the public interest, operate in practice to defeat that interest?

- Why do many government programs benefit the few at the expense of the many (eg in agricultural price supports, import tariffs and quotas, minimum wage controls)?

- Why do bureaucrats often follow their own interests (the "Yes Minister" model of decision-making[6]) rather than the broader public good?

- Why is government regulation often a means by which special interest groups reap gains at the expense of public welfare?

Public choice theory purports to supply the answers by looking at who gains, and who loses, from any particular policy outcome. It is, in the words of one of its leading proponents:

[T]he avenue through which a romantic and illusory set of notions about the workings of governments and the behaviour of persons who govern has been replaced by a set of notions that embody more scepticism about what governments can do and what governors will do, notions that are surely more consistent with the political reality that we may all observe about us.[7]

Public choice takes the tools and methods of economic theory and applies them to government and collective political action. As in neo-classical (Chicago school) economics generally, the basic behavioural postulate is that individuals are self-interested, rational, utility maximisers. Thus people are assumed to behave in political decision-making processes very much as they are assumed to behave in the market place:

[F]irms seek to maximise profits, consumers seek to maximise utility, and policy makers seek to maximise political support ... Public policy makers are not

---

4   There is no clear explanation for the title "public choice". We can surmise that it describes a theory about the choices that people make in public settings – as voters, politicians, candidates, public servants, and so on. James Buchanan, one of the founders of the theory, explains the choice of title differently: "We needed a name. Somebody came up with Public Choice, which really doesn't fit very well descriptively because a lot of people think of it as a public opinion polling thing. We get questions about that. But at least it caught on": interview with James Buchanan, Federal Reserve Bank of Minneapolis, *The Region*, September 1995, <minneapolisfed.org/pubs/region/95-09/int959.cfm>.

5   L Udehn, *The Limits of Public Choice*, Routledge, 1996, 34.

6   J Lynn and A Jay (eds), *Yes Minister: The Diaries of a Cabinet Minister*, BBC, 1981-82.

7   J Buchanan, "Politics without Romance" in J Buchanan and R Tollison (eds), *The Theory of Public Choice – II*, Uni of Michigan Press, 1984, 13.

benevolent maximisers of social welfare ... but are instead motivated by their own self-interests.[8]

In both contexts, individuals seek to maximise their utility by trading with each other, but whereas in the market they trade goods and commodities, in the political sphere they trade votes and other units of political exchange.[9]

A central concern of public choice theory is to challenge the "public interest" model of government regulation. That model, which derives from the work of Arthur Pigou,[10] was the conventional wisdom of theoretical welfare economics[11] until at least the 1960s. It suggested that government regulates in the public interest to rectify "market failure".

As Shughart summarises it, the argument was that the private market economy cannot be relied on to allocate and distribute resources in "a socially optimal way":

> Left alone, private markets would produce too much environmental pollution and not enough education. Similarly, the informational disadvantages of buyers respecting the quality or performance characteristics of certain products and services leaves them vulnerable to exploitation by sellers. The suggestion is that government intervene in policy-specific ways, using taxes, subsidies, price regulation, and the like to correct these market failures: "In the Pigovian approach the state is a productive entity that produces public goods, internalizes social costs and benefits, regulates decreasing cost industries effectively, redistributes income Pareto optimally, and so forth" (McCormick and Tollison, p 3).
>
> The market failure theory of government, assuming as it does that government benignly pursues the objective of maximizing social welfare, implies that failures of policy result only from error or ignorance on the part of the policy-makers.[12]

Public choice theorists counter that such a model flies in the face of numerous well-documented examples of regulatory failure: that in reality "market failure" (which on closer examination may only be "market imperfections") is replaced by "government failure".[13] Moreover, as we shall see, they suggest that there is strong evidence that, far from performing their functions in the public interest, politicians or bureaucrats act from much baser motives. Public choice theory proposes a theoretical model that seeks to explain extensive government failure

---

8   WF Shughart II, *Antitrust Policy and Interest-Group Politics*, Quorum, 1990, 37.

9   As D Mueller, *Public Choice III*, Cambridge UP, 2003, 3, points out, public choice theorists often depict the preference-revelation process as analogous to the market (voters engage in exchange: individuals reveal their demand schedules by voting).

10 AC Pigou, *The Economics of Welfare*, 4th ed, MacMillan, 1932.

11 Welfare economics is the branch of economics which is concerned with defining economic efficiency, with evaluating the economic efficiency of particular systems of resource allocation, and with analysing the conditions under which economic policies can be said to have improved social welfare.

12 Shughart, n 8, 36-37. See also RE McCormick and R Tollison, *Politicians, Legislation, and the Economy*, Martinus Nijhof, 1981.

13 One early study of public utility regulation, for example, found that it had little or no effect on the level of electricity prices or on the rates of return to investments in that industry. Similarly, purchasers of new stock issues were found to obtain few benefits from the regulatory oversight exercised by the Securities and Exchange Commission. See GJ Stigler and C Friedland, "What Can Regulators Regulate: The Case of Electricity" (1982) 5 *Journal of Law and Economics* 1; GJ Stigler, "Public Regulation of the Securities Market" (1964) 2 *Journal of Business* 117.

and evidence that special-interest groups often used legislation to promote their own (private) interests.

In this respect, economics has not been alone. Political science and sociology, in particular, had gone down much the same path, as we saw in Chapter 7. However, those disciplines offer explanations for "government failure" which, in the view of many economists, lack scientific rigour, and explanatory and predictive power. The task for economics, therefore, has been to develop a more precise, hard-edged and scientific theory which would better illuminate the processes of political decision-making. This is the essence of the public choice enterprise.

That enterprise takes two forms. At a positive level, it offers an understanding of "the complex institutional interactions that go on in the political sector"[14] and it attempts to *explain and predict* political outcomes. At a normative level, it attempts to prescribe what political institutions *should* be adopted, suggesting a range of constitutional and deregulatory mechanisms to minimise "inefficient" state intervention.

Two particularly influential schools of thought are largely responsible for the development of the public choice approach. First, there is the "Virginia" school, which is responsible for the original and conventional version of the theory. It is closely associated with the work of Gordon Tulloch and of James Buchanan,[15] who in 1986 was awarded a Nobel Prize for his work in the area. Secondly, there is the "Chicago" school, exemplified in the work of Richard Posner, George Stigler (also a Nobel prize winner) and Sam Peltzman. This school shares Buchanan's scepticism about government and its capacity to act for the common good, but differs from the Virginia school in both its emphasis and its level of analysis. The contributions of these two schools are best understood by considering separately the positive and normative level of analysis.

(c) Positive approaches to public choice

(i) The approach of the Virginia School

Conventional public choice theory, in particular the Virginia school, analyses the behaviour of voters, politicians, members of political parties and bureaucrats, and attempts to model their behaviour in economic terms. It seeks to develop a "theory of political institutions" which incorporates theories of voting, theories of electoral and party competition and theories of bureaucracy. For example, the behaviour of parliaments and bureaucracies has been modelled to generate propositions about political behaviour. There has been particular emphasis on why voters vote and what leads them to vote as they do, on the importance of electoral competition and majority rule and on a variety of alternatives to majority rule.[16] Research has also sought to understand the importance of legislative procedural rules, such as committee structures and amending procedures, in affecting the ultimate legislative outcome.[17]

---

14 Buchanan, n 7, 11.

15 See, for example, JM Buchanan and G Tulloch, *The Calculus of Consent*, U of Michigan Press, 1962; and G Brennan and JM Buchanan, *The Reason of Rules*, Cambridge UP, 1985.

16 See generally Mueller, n 9.

17 See, for example, Shepsle and Weingast, "When do Rules of Procedure Matter?" (1984) 46 *Journal of Politics* 207.

In each case, it is postulated that individual legislators, voters, leaders and members of political parties and bureaucrats act primarily out of self-interest and that legislative and bureaucratic outcomes can be understood and explained in terms of "the rational behaviour of those engaged in legislative and bureaucratic choice under prevailing political rules".[18]

Thus it is argued that various self-interested strategies will be adopted by participants in the political process to achieve their own ends. Elected representatives will make political decisions that maximise votes so that the representative or her political party will win elections. Legislators can be expected to engage in such activities as "log-rolling" – trading votes on one issue for desired votes on another issue[19] ("you vote for my tax reforms, I'll vote for your dam"). Individuals or groups affected by government action (and with sufficient self-interest) will engage in "rent-seeking", that is, they will "devote scarce resources to the pursuit of a degree of monopoly rights granted by government".[20] Examples are an industry which lobbies government to receive protection from import competition, or a group which "seeks government aid in monopolising what would otherwise remain a competitive industry, in order to transfer consumer surplus to the producer group".[21] The problem with rent-seeking is that it involves the expenditure of resources on things such as lobbyists, lawyers, accountants and press agents rather than on more economically productive activities.[22]

Bureaucratic behaviour is viewed with equal scepticism. Because they are in charge of actually implementing government policy, bureaucrats play a crucial role in the political arena. William Niskanen, who is responsible for the most developed model of bureaucratic behaviour within a public choice perspective, has argued that the goal of bureaucratic decision-makers is to maximise their own "satisfaction". This includes variables such as salary, job security, office space, working conditions, power, patronage and public recognition.[23] Niskanen argues that the bureaucracy can manipulate the policy debate through its information advantage over the legislature, thereby distorting legislation in favour of its own interests, and that their need to maximise budgets will lead bureaucrats to engage in excessive (or sub-optimal) regulation. Similarly, as Buchanan has pointed out:

> Modern government is complex and many-sided, so much so that it would be impossible for legislatures to make more than a tiny fraction of all genuine policy decisions. Discretionary power must be granted to bureaucrats over wide ranges of decision. Further, the bureaucracy can manipulate the agenda for legislative action for the purpose of securing outcomes favorable to its own interests. The

---

18   N Mercuro and TP Ryan (eds), *Law, Economics and Public Policy*, JAI Press, 1984, 143.

19   In this way, each faction gains more from its own preferred policy than it loses in paying its share of other policies. See RD Tollison, "Public Choice and Legislation" (1988) 74 *Virginia Law Review* 339.

20   WC Mitchell, *Government As It Is*, Hobart Paper 9, IEA, 1976, n 17, 23.

21   M Kelman, "On Democracy Bashing" (1984) 74 *Virginia Law Review* 199 at 227.

22   N Mercuro and SG Medema, "Schools of Thought in Law and Economics: A Kuhnian Competition" in RP Malloy and CK Braun (eds), *Law and Economics: New and Critical Perspectives*, Lang Publishing, 1995, 94-95.

23   W Niskanen, *Bureaucracy and Representative Government*, Aldine-Atherton, 1971. For alternative public choice theories of bureaucracy, see B Weingast and M Moran, "Bureaucratic Discretion or Congressional Cartel?" (1983) 91 *Journal of Political Economy* 765; CM Rowley and R Elgin, "Government and Its Bureaucracy" in CM Rowley, CK Tollison and G Tulloch (eds), *The Political Economy of Rent-Seeking*, Kluwer, 1988.

bureaucracy can play off one set of constituents against others, insuring that budgets rise much beyond plausible efficiency limits.[24]

A crucial question for public choice theorists, and indeed for students of the political process generally, is how legislation emerges and whose interests it reflects. In answering this question, numerous writers within the social sciences have recognised the key role played by interest groups in lobbying for legislation.[25] As Jonathon Macey explains:

[I]ndividuals who want to affect the legislative process will find it advantageous to organize into political pressure groups in order to economize on the high costs of obtaining information about the welfare affects of impending legislation. Clearly, groups that have already organized for one reason or other, and therefore previously have internalized the costs of organization "will have a comparative advantage in seeking transfers and will therefore be more successful in procuring transfers as a result". Thus labor unions, trade associations, and corporations, which are already organized, will have an advantage in the political process, even though political advantage was not the reason for their initial formation.[26]

Mancur Olson, in his influential book, *The Logic of Collective Action*,[27] uses a public choice framework to analyse the dynamics of interest-group lobbying. One of the problems identified by Olson is that "unless the number of individuals in a group is quite small, or unless there is coercion or some other special device to make individuals act in their common or group interest, rational self-interested individuals will not act to achieve their common or group interests".[28]

Put another way, groups engaged in lobbying face what is called a "free rider" problem. If an interest group is successful in obtaining the legislative result it wants, this will benefit all of the group members. But, rationally, each individual member will prefer to let the other members contribute to the cost and effort of achieving that result. And each member will want to hide the size of their actual contribution, and the size of their share of the resulting benefit, from other members. In short, it is argued that interest groups face significant transaction costs in lobbying for the desired result. These costs are affected by the size of the group, especially when compared to the size of the benefit that is sought. In simple terms, the smaller the group the harder it will be for individual members to be "free riders" or to hide from other members. Indeed, in small groups individual members will realise (rationally) that there is a higher risk of failure if they do not contribute to the lobbying effort. Conversely, large groups will have greater difficulty in overcoming the free rider problem. The problem is greatest for the largest type of political group – the general voting public. So, as Macey explains:

[P]olitically successful groups will tend to be small, relative to the size of the groups taxed to pay their subsidies. The small size not only helps to overcome

---

24   Buchanan, n 7, 19.

25   See further Chapter 7.

26   J Macey, "Public Choice: The Theory of the Firm and the Theory of Market Exchange" (1988-89) 74 *Cornell Law Review* 45 at 47-48, quoting R McCormick and R Tollison, *Politicians, Legislation and the Economy*, 1981, 17.

27   M Olson, *The Logic of Collective Action*, Harvard UP, 1965.

28   Ibid 2.

free-rider effects, it also concentrates the benefits of legislative enactments so as to provide individuals with high incentives to press for legislative results.[29]

The consequence of all this is that:

> Small groups may be able to outbid larger groups even when their aggregate benefit is less than that of the larger group. Hence, actual legislative outcomes may predictably differ from the optimal.[30]

Relying on a logic similar to Olson's, James Q Wilson has developed a typology of regulatory behaviour in different interest-group contexts. Arguing that the extent to which costs and benefits are concentrated will be a crucial variable in determining regulatory outcome, he predicts:

    (i)   if the benefits of new regulation are spread across a large cross-section of the population while the costs are concentrated, then regulation will be blocked;

    (ii)   if the benefits go to a small group and the costs are diffused, the regulator tends to serve the interests of the smaller group; and

    (iii)   if the costs and benefits are concentrated between competing groups, the regulator will act as arbitrator.[31]

Legislative costs and benefits are not the only factors to be taken into account, however, and other factors may produce results that are contrary to Wilson's predictions. Macey supplies the illustration of anti-pollution legislation:

> At first blush, public choice theory would seem to predict that we would never observe environmental protection legislation because the benefits of such legislation are spread broadly over the population, while the costs are borne by a few polluters who enjoy lower production costs if they can operate their factories free of pollution controls. But keep in mind that individuals will have even less influence on the implementation and enforcement of legislation than on its initial enactment. In addition, it is clear that, for an individual with a small stake in the legislative outcome, the marginal cost of casting a vote is extremely low. The combination of these two influences should result in precisely the state of affairs that we observe: a lot of environmental legislation (it is a highly publicized problem and it costs voters little to "ask" for action on it in the electoral process) combined with significant influence by interest groups on the specific nature and implementation of the environmental programs we observe. In other words, we will get a lot of environmental legislation, but it not only will be less effective than it otherwise could be, it also will serve to benefit certain interest groups at the expense of others.[32]

One factor which is not regarded as determinative is the particular political persuasion of the legislators (that is, whether they are conservative, liberal, and so on). Public choice theory is interested in the pressure exerted by interest groups rather than the ideology of the government. As Macey sums it up, "under any form of government, there is a market for laws".[33]

---

29   Macey, n 26, 48.

30   PL Kahn, "The Politics of Unregulation" (1990) 75 *Cornell Law Review* 280 at 291.

31   JQ Wilson (ed), *The Politics of Regulation*, Basic Books, 1980, 367-370.

32   Macey, n 26, 49-50.

33   Ibid 49.

(ii)   The approach of the Chicago School

The "Chicago" school version of public choice theory is an application of market-based assumptions about utility maximisation and allocative efficiency to the realm of politics. Having said that, the difference between the two schools may appear to be one of degree. The Chicago version is concerned primarily with the efficiency of political outcomes; in contrast the Virginia school does not propose any such external standard: "the appropriateness or correctness of a public policy (or legal change) is not the improvement in an independent, observable assessment of allocative efficiency, but is instead agreement – consensus among the group".[34]

Stigler, Peltzman and Posner, writing in the Chicago school tradition, explain regulation almost entirely in terms of the supply and demand for political outcomes.[35] Legislation is seen simply as a commodity supplied by the state and demanded by private groups. In Stigler's view, various structural characteristics will determine the strength of demand for regulation. That demand will be stronger when the gainers are relatively few, expect to make large gains, have similar interests and can exclude others from sharing those gains. Those most likely to satisfy these conditions are producers:

> This follows because producer groups are typically small enough in number and their financial interests are sufficiently large that the potential benefits from organizing and lobbying for monopoly rights will exceed the associated costs. On the other hand, the more diffuse nature of consumer interests coupled with the fact that each bears only a small share of the regulatory burden means that the relatively high costs of organizing to oppose monopoly-enhancing regulations will exceed the expected gains for such groups.[36]

Accordingly, Stigler's theory resembles a "producer interest" theory, under which industry uses its lobbying advantage in the political process "to secure for itself such regulatory favors as direct cash subsidies, control over the entry of new rivals, restrictions on the outputs and prices of complementary and substitute goods, and the legitimisation of price-fixing schemes".[37]

While it is easy to see why industries should demand regulation, it is less obvious why governments should supply it. Sam Peltzman has provided an answer. Peltzman argues that politicians desire to maximise electoral majorities, and that by using regulation to benefit powerful groups, they can obtain more votes and other benefits. Thus the legislator is seen as "a political entrepreneur who actively works to gain political support by overcoming the information and organization costs that conspire against him".[38]

Achieving the optimal electoral result may be no easy matter, for politicians must steer a course that takes account of the different rewards and penalties that competing groups can offer:

---

34   Mercuro and Medema, n 22, 93.

35   GJ Stigler, "The Theory of Economic Regulation" (1971) 2 *Bell Journal of Economics* 3; RA Posner, "Theories of Economic Regulation" (1974) 5 *Bell Journal of Economics* 335; J Peltzman, "Towards a More General Theory of Regulation" (1976) 19 *Journal of Law and Economics* 211.

36   Shughart, n 8, 38. See also J Macey, "The Myth of Deregulation" (1988) 45 *Washington and Lee Law Review* 1279.

37   Shughart, n 8, 38.

38   Macey, n 26, 51.

To invoke the economists' lexicon, politicians face an opportunity cost when they pass laws. The benefits they receive in the form of increased political support from certain groups are offset by the opposition that the passage of such laws brings from other groups. Operating under these constraints, the politicians' goal is to maximize net political support.[39]

Thus for the Chicago school, on the demand side, legal rules are the outcome of political struggle among special-interest groups to redistribute wealth in their favour, while on the supply side, they reflect the efforts of politicians to maximise the political support they receive from interest groups' constituencies. That is, laws are supplied to those interest groups (or coalitions) that outbid rivals for favourable legislation.

> At the margin, a legislature will alter a rule if the resulting gain in political support from some group outweighs any expected loss in support from a rival group... . Competition among rival pressure groups with drastically differing views about what the legal landscape ought to look like leads to legislative compromise, not because compromise is in the public interest, but because it is the most effective strategy politicians have for maximizing political support.[40]

On the demand side, the transfers rarely take the form of cash. They are far more likely to be denominated

> in terms of any of the favors that can be conferred by selective use of the coercive power of the state. Domestic oil producers benefit from tariffs or import quotas on foreign oil, butter producers benefit from a tax on margarine, commercial airlines benefit from federal subsidies for airport construction, incumbent practitioners benefit from occupational licensing requirements, labor unions benefit from minimum wage laws, and so on.[41]

Similarly, on the supply side, the fee may take "the form of campaign contributions, votes, implicit promises of future favors and sometimes, outright bribes".[42]

Unsurprisingly, public choice theorists (of whatever school) conclude that representative democracy gives disproportionate emphasis to the interests of small groups who have most to gain from legislation, and that this is commonly at the expense of the larger public, who pay the price of higher taxes and higher prices for goods and services. This is consistent with empirical evidence which suggests that many regulatory programs have "large social costs, small public benefits and (often) substantial transfers from the public to some discrete group, typically the industry ostensibly controlled by the regulatory program".[43] On this view, government regulation, far from correcting market failure in the public interest, instead provides a means by which special interests profit at the public expense. Government regulation will neither reflect the interests of the median voter nor achieve liberty, efficiency or justice.

---

39 Macey, n 36, 1279.

40 Macey, n 26, 46.

41 Shughart, n 8, 41.

42 WM Landes and R Posner, "The Independent Judiciary in an Interest Group Perspective" (1975) 18 *Journal of Law and Economics* 875 at 877.

43 Kahn, n 30, 281 and references cited therein.

(d)   Normative approaches to public choice

At a normative level, the conclusion that government regulation does not serve the public interest has led to a variety of recommendations for constitutional, legal and political reform, consistent with achieving the particular liberal values that underpin the public choice tradition. Thus public choice theorists argue that appropriate political institutions can and should be designed to enhance individual liberty and freedom, to constrain the scope of government spending (and thereby reduce taxation) and to build barricades against affirmative government action.[44]

The Virginia school has particularly advocated constitutional reform and limiting government activity through precise constitutional specifications. Geoffrey Brennan and James Buchanan have argued strongly the virtue of constitutional rules to protect individuals from intrusion on their rights by special-interest groups.[45] In Buchanan's words:

> [B]asic political institutions must be re-examined and rebuilt so as to keep governments as well as citizens within limits of tolerance.[46]

In the Chicago school-strand of public choice, emphasis is placed on rolling back the state by deregulation,[47] an enterprise in respect of which it has had considerable success. Public choice arguments in favour of deregulation were embraced with enthusiasm by the conservative Reagan and Thatcher administrations during the 1980s.

(e)   Assessing public choice

How do we assess public choice theory? How satisfactory are its assumptions? To what extent is its whole policy thrust skewed by the particular values that underpin it?

Public choice has been criticised generally because it takes "a pessimistic view of democracy".[48] More specifically, critics argue that it lacks empirical support, and that other disciplines can provide equally plausible explanations (where public choice theory is consistent with the empirical evidence). Thus they have assembled evidence that legislators have motivations other than the desire to be re-elected, that voters do not operate purely out of self-interest and that other political actors may also have more benign motives than public choice theory would predict.[49] Ginsburg summarises the literature, concluding that "[i]n the light of the

---

44   For example, this might be achieved by imposing a rigid form of the non-delegation doctrine, by greater court activism to obstruct special interest deals, by adopting a more deferential standard of review of agency actions when the agency is removing regulations than when it is imposing them, or by the extension of federal antitrust law to prevent the regulation of economic activity by the States. Kahn, n 30, 282-286, and references cited therein.

45   G Brennan and JM Buchanan, *The Reason of Rules*, Cambridge UP, 1985. Curiously, this argument has some similarity with that of EP Thompson, concerning the virtues of the rule of law. See Chapter 3 above, p 67ff.

46   Buchanan, n 7.

47   Mercuro and Ryan, n 18, 144, point out that the Chicago school's emphasis has been on altering political rules through the judicial and legal processes.

48   T Ginsburg, "Ways of Criticizing Public Choice: The Uses of Empiricism and Theory in Legal Scholarship" [2002] *University of Illinois Law Rev* 1139 at 1140.

49   See, for example, D Farber and P Frickey, *Law and Public Choice: A Critical Introduction*, Uni Chicago Press, 1991, 7, 29, 33; G Jacobson, *The Politics of Congressional Elections*, Little

behavioural research, it is no longer possible to assert that self-interest is an accurate description of human behaviour".[50]

The more specific assumptions of some public choice theorists have also been criticised. In particular, Stigler's views on the factors relevant to the demand for, and supply of, regulation have been attacked as inadequate and misconceived. Fels, for example, argues that:

> The industry demand for the establishment and, more particularly, the continuation of regulation, is influenced not only by profit-maximisation but also, very importantly, by a quest for economic security or protection against the changes which an unregulated market may impose. The political supply of regulation is also influenced by factors other than the votes or political contributions which regulated industries can offer political parties. A government is judged by the electorate according to the performance of the whole economy in relation to such goals as employment, price-stability, growth and income-distribution. Yet it is business which is largely responsible for the achievement of those goals. A major concern of all government policies, therefore, is to encourage businessmen to perform well and it does this by the provision of numerous incentives which cannot be analysed in such narrow terms as vote delivery or financial contributions.[51]

The value assumptions of public choice theory have also been subjected to critical scrutiny.[52] In many ways the values of public choice reflect those of the economic analysis of law in general, and so we can take this opportunity to assess that wider ideological picture.

Much of the economic analysis of law claims to be objective, neutral and apolitical. It makes claims to being scientific, value free and rigorous in a way that by implication other social sciences are not. Many of Posner's writings are representative of this sort of argument, and Easterbrook has made similar claims about the way rigorous and scientific disciplines (like economics) will drive out less rigorous ones (like law, and other social sciences).[53]

Yet on closer examination, much of law and economics, and in particular the Chicago brand, is anything but objective. This can be illustrated both in terms of the bias which the Chicago school has in favour of the common law and against government intervention; and at the level of the other core assumptions of economic analysis and their classical liberal foundations.

We have seen in this and earlier chapters how the Chicago school expresses a strong preference for the market over government intervention and (where the unassisted market does not produce efficiency) for the common law over statute law. Two complementary arguments support that general perspective. First, that the common law promotes economic efficiency; secondly, that government regulation is inefficient, wrong-headed and wasteful (the public choice framework). As

---

(cont)

    Brown, 1984; J Mashaw, "Pro delegalisation: Why Administrations Should Make Political Decisions" (1985) 1 *Journal of Law & Economics* 1; J Olson and E Olson, "Economic Fluctuations and Congressional Elections" (1980) 24 *American Journal of Political Science* 469; See also M Kelman, n 21, 199, 237, 238.

50   Ginsburg, n 48, 1154.

51   A Fels, "The Political Economy of Regulation" (1982) 5 *University of New South Wales Law Journal* 29 at 40.

52   In addition to the references cited in the following paragraphs, see Udehn, n 5, 188-206.

53   F Easterbrook, "The Inevitability of Law and Economics" (1989) 1 *Legal Education Rev* 3.

a result, the Chicago school presents a picture of society which to an outsider, might seem surprising. It is, as Leff puts it, a society which apparently regulates its affairs in a rather bizarre fashion, in that:

> [I]t has created one grand system – the market, and those market-supportive aspects of law (notably "common", judge-made law) – which is almost flawless in achieving human happiness; it has created another – the political process, and the rest of "the law" (roughly legislation and administration) – which is apparently almost wholly pernicious of those aims.[54]

This picture is not an objective, value-free characterisation of how society operates. Rather, it is simply *presumed* that market arrangements are better able to maximise economic welfare than government intervention. This predilection for the free market is neither theoretically nor empirically established. As Edward Rubin notes, the "free market" constitutes:

> [A] master premise, an independent, unarticulated concept of a good society that silently controls the views of its proponents about both individuals and political organizations.
>
> To begin with, the free market image controls its proponents' views about the proper role of the state, and the proper scope of regulation. The role of the state, according to the free market view, is to enforce agreements between individuals according to their terms and – just as importantly, but generally less often mentioned – to create and control the money that is used for payment. Any other government involvement is an offense against the purity of the market. "Deregulation", as we use the term, refers to the removal of such involvement, a restoration of the market to its natural state ... implicit in this market vision is the idea that regulation is an unnatural act that should only be undertaken for a specified and carefully articulated reason. The free market, in other words, is a presumption, a preferred approach, while regulation must bear the burden of justification.[55]

Public choice theorists, in particular, assert the virtues of the market and of freedom from government intervention. They are also highly critical of democratic institutions and of what they term "majoritarianist democracy".[56] As Kelman observes:

> [T]he public choice literature ... is an effort to demonstrate that given certain suppositions about the way political actors (both voters and "governors") behave and given certain suppositions about the actual powers government possesses, the democratic sphere is, at its core, an arena of theft, an unmitigated disaster that should be limited carefully, tolerated only if fundamentally powerless. Not only does the democratic sphere lose the falsely idealised status that it enjoyed in the mainstream centrist picture, but it becomes the embodiment of, if not evil, then abject failure. The "market" in their view transforms private greed into social progress and harmony, mutual benefit and positive sum games; democracy transforms (indistinguishable) private greed into stagnation, wasteful rent-seeking and negative sum games ...

---

54 A Leff, "Economic Analysis of Law: Some Realism about Nominalism" (1974) 60 *Virginia Law Review* 451 at 463.

55 E Rubin, "Deregulation, Reregulation and the Myth of the Market" (1988) 45 *Washington and Lee Law Review* 1249 at 1257-1258.

56 Majoritarian democracy as contrasted with constitutional democracy. The former admits of no limits on majority rule, whereas the latter *does* impose limits on what the majority can do.

Public choice theorists contrast the beneficent market with the corrupt democratic state, unwilling even to consider the degree to which the very real corruptions of democracy we do indeed sometimes see are an aspect of the acquisitive capitalist culture they extol.[57]

This presumption concerning the undesirability of state intervention in the economy has deep roots in classical liberal ideology. It is, as Daintith points out:

> [B]ased on the liberal conception of a separation of the State from the economy, which constitute distinct worlds operating according to different principles: commandment for the State, market exchange for the economy. The State is seen as coming into the economy – from the outside. Law normally enters the scene in two guises: as public law, organising the structure of the State and expressing its command functions, and as private law, underpinning the system of market exchange with a structure of rights and duties whose observance is ultimately guaranteed by State power. Most, if not all, of the modern critiques of "instrumental law" draw directly or indirectly upon this conception. This should not surprise us, in the light ... of the continuity of the liberal tradition in modern times ...[58]

On close examination, the other core assumptions of economic analysis which we discussed in Chapter 11 also have built-in biases. These assumptions also have their roots in the central tenets of liberalism. Thus the economic analysis of law relies heavily on its liberal underpinnings and, as such, is inherently value-laden. This is not to say that it is "bad", any more than any other social science perspective which necessarily also rests on some ideology. While we can recognise the value of economic analysis we should also be aware that it is subject to misuse if its limitations and its underlying ideology are not made sufficiently explicit.

(f) Conclusion

There is no doubt that public choice analysis has been influential in understanding political behaviour and the legislative process in the USA, the UK and Australia. But public choice also has its shortcomings. It is limited by its assumptions and values, and provides explanations which are consistent with some, but by no means all, legislative and political behaviour. This is *not* to suggest that public choice theory is without merit, or indeed worse than any other social science methodology, for all methodologies are limited by their pre-empirical assumptions.[59] Rather, the central criticism of public choice is that its proponents have not recognised or acknowledged its limitations. Instead, they "tend to present their observations as conclusive, and to advance policy recommendations, with an air of certitude".[60] That is, public choice, like its parent discipline, economics, does itself a disservice by overstating its case. The uniformly bleak picture which it paints of

---

57   M Kelman, n 21, 199, 268. See also McAuslan, n 3, 681, 701.

58   T Daintith, "Law as A Policy Instrument" in T Daintith (ed), *Law as an Instrument of Economic Policy*, de Gruyter, 1987, 9.

59   See further E Rubin, "What We Expect of Legislators and What Legislators Expect of Themselves: A Critique of the Public Choice Analysis of Legislation" Paper presented at Law and Society Conference, Vail, June 1988.

60   Rubin, n 59, 4.

political institutions, and of behaviour in the public sphere, suggests that collective action *invariably* works in a perverse manner.[61]

The result is that it is unable to account for, or learn from, those circumstances where manifestly this is not the case. For example, public choice has difficulty explaining the success of deregulation initiatives. After all, if regulation was once economically optimal for legislators to enact (for example, because it benefited cartels), why does it stop being optimal? Unless, for rather convoluted reasons, it suddenly becomes sub-optimal, the answer might be that government deregulates in the public interest![62] Again, public choice is much better at explaining industry-specific regulation (where there are concentrated benefits on small groups and diffused costs on the public) than it is in explaining social regulation (where both benefits and costs are diffused).[63]

As a result of the blinkers its assumptions and ideology impose, public choice, at least in its Chicago school version, has failed to recognise that governments and agencies *can* work for the public good, and that what we need to study more carefully are the circumstances under which they work well (and under which they do not) and what makes them do so.[64]

These limitations should not be allowed to diminish what public choice has achieved. It has undoubtedly shed new light on problems which are central to both politics and sociology. It has proved invaluable in heightening awareness of the importance of small groups as beneficiaries in lobbying for special interest legislation, and of the interests that politicians may have in supplying such legislation. It provides "both a powerful critique of government policies and procedures and at the same time a way to understand why some of those policies and procedures are

---

61 This point is made by Kelman, n 21, 268.

62 This point is made by Kelman, n 21, 220. As Kahn, n 30, 286, further points out:

> After all, by should the logic of deregulation differ from the logic which explains regulation? Why, then, do deregulatory movements succeed, if special interest groups oppose them? Either the successes of the deregulatory movement indicate that some public-regarding political outcomes succeed for reasons not explained by the model, or that the political environment must have changed so that deregulation now serves the same private interests which once sought regulation. And if this is so, self-serving behaviour on occasion coincides with the public interest. The success of the deregulatory movement demonstrates the limits of the model in prescribing policy.

63 As Kahn, n 30, 308-309, points out, social regulation (environment, occupational health) is a particularly poor candidate for public choice explanations:

> By its nature, it affects many industries at once; the involvement of numerous industries and, therefore, large numbers of affected shareholders and managers, poses serious free-rider problems for an interest group trying to elicit action from its members. It usually imposes substantial compliance costs, which fall on the very parties regarded as beneficiaries under a private interest interpretation. Indeed, the magnitude of those costs were widely cited by affected industries as a reason to remove social regulation. And social regulation is unlikely to be an entry-limiting device capable of awarding monopoly power to established firms; that explanation presumes that existing firms would have monopoly power but for the competitive pressure imposed on them by potential entrants. While some parts of American industry may indeed be noncompetitive, that surely is not the rule, and in any case those industries which are competitive would have incentives to resist the imposition upon them of compliance costs unrewarded by new market power.

> Stigler's theory, in particular, has little to say when regulation takes forms other than the conferring of concentrated benefits on groups and the deferring of diffused costs.

64 See further Kelman, n 21, 268, and references therein.

being adopted".[65] It would be, as Patrick McAuslan has put it, as foolish of us to ignore public choice, as it would be to accept it uncritically.[66]

Discussion Questions

1. In 1996 the Northern Territory legislature passed legislation which permitted euthanasia. Soon afterwards a Member of the Federal Parliament introduced a Bill designed to overrule the effect of the Northern Territory's legislation. Assess this situation from the perspective of public choice theory.

2. Compare the public choice perspective on the legislative process with the perspectives discussed in Chapter 7 of this book. Which do you find more compelling? Why?

3. Imagine that Parliament introduces legislation which limits the amount of money which political parties can spend in election campaigns, and which sets limits on the amounts which parties can receive by way of contribution. In public choice terms, what are the advantages of this legislation?

---

65   McAuslan, n 3, 704.
66   Ibid 704.

Chapter 14

Law, Globalisation and Terrorism

(a) Introduction

In Chapter 3 we saw that an important aspect of the rule of law is that the state should govern according to law. This is intended as a safeguard against tyranny, dictatorship and authoritarianism. But there is another implication: that, by and large, the state is "in charge" of its own law-making and law-enforcing agendas. Liberalism regards nation states in much the same way as it regards individuals (both human beings and legal persons such as corporations), that is, as autonomous subjects having the freedom to make choices about themselves that are consistent with the free choices made by others (whether nation states or individuals respectively). These ideas underlie our system of public international law, explaining its focus on the formation and enforcement of treaties and conventions which may be viewed as contractual arrangements between nation states.

Much of what we have examined in this book is concerned with the extent to which, and the reasons why, individual choices within the domestic legal system are much more limited than this liberal ideal suggests. Can the same thing be said about nation states? Are nations truly free to determine their own destinies, free from the influences of other nations? In what ways, through processes of globalisation, have nation states and its citizens become more interconnected and interdependent through international trade, travel and communication? And, if so, what implications does this have for the lives and choices of individuals living in those nation states?

At the beginning of the 21st century, the study of "law in context" means having to consider the global context of law, an aspect that received only brief attention in earlier editions of this book. Increasingly the study of law in many areas reveals that nation states are not fully in charge of their own law-making and law-enforcement agendas. This does not mean that local laws and legal systems should be considered irrelevant, or even less relevant. Rather, it means that we must be careful not to regard domestic law as a closed system, insulated from outside influences. As one legal theorist, William Twining, puts it:

> No one can understand their local law by focusing solely on municipal domestic law of a single jurisdiction or nation state; ... the range of significant actors and processes has been extended ... .[1]

This final chapter explores some of the present and future challenges for law through a critical examination of globalisation. The focus is on how law as an

---

1   W Twining, *Globalisation and Legal Theory*, Butterworths, 2000, 221.

institution and as a system of rules is adapting to global challenges, as well as shaping and driving global change. We will explore the relationship between globalisation and law through an examination of the recent domestic legal responses to international terrorism in the wake of the 9/11 attacks in 2001.

(b) Definitions of globalisation

Definitions of globalisation abound.[2] Twining advocates a wide definition of globalisation, moving beyond a focus on purely economic matters and matters of global concerns. He is critical of the tendency to associate globalisation negatively with "extreme laissez-faire ideology and increasing American and Western hegemony".[3] Reflecting this wider conception he has defined globalisation as:

> [T]hose trends, processes and interactions which are making the world more interdependent in many complex ways, in respect of communications, cultures, language, and politics, not just the alleged development of a single world economy.[4]

How then do these forces of globalisation, and the interconnectedness which lies at its heart, interact with law?

(i) Historical aspects: Globalisation and legal precedents

The ideas captured within these differing definitions of globalisation are associated with a particular time and place. The intensification of these forces promoting interconnectedness and interdependence are tied to the latter part of the 20th century, clustering around technologically sophisticated, liberal democracies with market-based economies.

But, as historians have pointed out, universalising tendencies have a much older pedigree. David Goldman has drawn parallels between the periods of globalisation at the end of the first and second millennia, leading him to speculate that "millennial moments" seem critical to globalisation. At the close of the first millennium, religion in the spiritual form of Christianity was broadly universal in Europe, while the new religion at the end of the second millennium was belief in the market economy:

> Although lacking the traditional hallmarks of religion at first blush, the laissez-faire liberalism of contemporary economy nonetheless rates as a dominant belief and approaches the level of a religion. ... "Risk management" has overtaken faith as the solace from human fears of the unknown.[5]

---

2 The alternate spellings of the term (with "s" or "z") are emblematic of the challenges of globalisation. While writing this chapter, technological time-saving programs in the form of the Auto-Correct function in Microsoft Word changed our instinctive Australian-English spelling from "Globalisation" to US-English "Globalization". This strikes us as symbolic, a manifestation of the universalising technology-driven (and potentially repressive) tendencies of globalisation! Resistance is difficult but possible.

3 W Twining, "The province of jurisprudence re-examined" in C Dauvergne (ed), *Jurisprudence for an Interconnected Globe*, Ashgate, 2003, 24.

4 Ibid 24.

5 D Goldman, "Historical aspects of globalisation and law" in C Dauvergne (ed), *Jurisprudence for an Interconnected Globe*, Ashgate, 2003, 51 (footnotes omitted).

393

At the close of the first and second millennium, law played a critical role in globalisation. The birth of the Western legal tradition in the late 11th and early 12th centuries in Europe coincided with, and indeed promoted, globalisation.[6] As noted in Chapter 3, the rediscovery of a complete Digest of classical Roman law in 12th century Italy fostered the establishment of new institutions of learning – universities were established as new sites of scholarship, where Roman texts provided the corpus of civil law, legal scholarship and language (Latin becoming the lingua franca of law) that applied across Europe. The university itself may be viewed as an agent of globalisation, circulating scholars and Enlightenment ideas around Europe and, through European colonisation, the world.

What is significant is how key ideas travelled across national borders, influencing even predominantly customary systems of law applied in England.[7] One of the most significant universalising legacies from this period of rapid Western legal transformation was the codification of law which transformed law from largely unwritten custom and norms to legislated positive prescriptions.[8] This process reached a zenith in the 18th and 19th centuries with the adoption of comprehensive civil codes displacing unwritten localised customs across Europe.[9] While England steadfastly resisted the movement to wholesale codification, colonial societies were much more receptive to this Enlightenment project with significant uptake in British colonies (and former colonies such as the United States) especially in the criminal field. As noted in Chapter 3, the idea of codification embodied many of the liberal aspirations for law – namely coherence, certainty and predictability. It also implied that the authority for the law was vested in those who enacted statutes (the legislature), rather than those who applied and developed the common law (an unelected judiciary). Even in common law systems, like Australia, where codification seems destined to be neither complete nor comprehensive, the impetus to codify remains an article of faith for the legal community.[10] The codification movement is not confined to domestic systems of law. As Goldman noted "codification and unification of legal rules is a major characteristic of the push towards the globalisation of international economic law".[11]

---

6   Goldman, n 5, 67, has suggested that globalisation in the present era is manifesting "significant ancestral traits of the Western legal tradition". See P Parkinson, *Tradition and Change in Australian Law*, 3rd ed, Lawbook Co, 2005, 28ff.

7   England was not a civil law system; however, until the 18th century, English legal elites learned only Roman and ecclesiastical law at university. The study of English common law was left to the period of apprenticeship served at the Inns of Court in London. While critical to legal acculturation, the civil law, its concepts and techniques of reasoning were necessarily suppressed within the English common law. That said, in some areas, such as equity and canon law, the influence of civil law is manifest: see PG Stein, *Roman law in European history*, Cambridge UP, 1999, 88ff.

8   SJ Stoljar (ed), *Problems of Codification*, Australian National UP, 1977.

9   Goldman, n 5, 54.

10   This is particularly strong in the field of criminal law, see M Goode, "Constructing criminal law reform and the Model Criminal Code" (2002) 26 *Criminal Law Journal* 152. Even in this field, the lack of progress in implementation of the Model Criminal Code across the States and Territories has fostered vigorous debate on the value of this project: S Bronitt and B McSherry, *Principles of Criminal Law*, 2nd ed, Lawbook Co, 2005, 71ff; and M Gani, "Codifying the criminal law: Issues of interpretation" in S Corcoran and S Bottomley (eds), *Interpreting Statutes*, Federation Press, 2005, 222.

11   Above, n 5, 54.

The experience of European colonisation in the 18th and 19th centuries provides an illustration of many of the key features of globalisation and law. Law at this time may be viewed as a paramount agent of colonisation. During this period of global exploration and conquest, the common law and civil law systems of Britain and its European colonial rivals were transplanted to many parts of the globe. In Australia, it was the common law of England rather than French or Dutch codes that provided the legal and constitutional template for many new colonial societies. As noted in Chapter 9, the justification for the acquisition of territory by colonisers was tied to emerging doctrines of public international law, namely theories of settlement and the legal/factual fiction that Australia was *terra nullius*.

Legal historical research reveals that, while English common law was a powerful agent of globalisation, it was never a perfect copy of the laws applied in England. As noted in Chapter 9, in the colonial period, English laws were either ignored or selectively adopted to meet local societal needs. Nor can it be said that there was a uniform "colonial law" – in different parts of Empire the courts and colonial administrators adopted different and often imaginative legal responses to the problems confronting them. This explains the inconsistent legal treatment of the status and rights of Aboriginal subjects in Australia, New Zealand and other British North American colonies. The purported universality of the "English common law"– which was common to the realm and its possessions beyond the seas – belies the pluralism and diversity of the colonial legal inheritance from England.[12]

Codification on the international plane is not confined to trade law. Modern international treaties such as the United Nations Universal Declaration of Human Rights 1948 and the International Covenant on Civil and Political Rights 1966 (ICCPR) may be viewed as attempts to codify fundamental human rights into a single, authoritative charter. In relation to terrorism, we explore below how law is being marshalled in the "War on Terror" to promote a coordinated approach to terrorism offences and counter-terrorism measures, such as suppressing the financing of terrorism. As we shall see below, in relation to some core concepts such as the definition of terrorism, there is a lack of international consensus, leaving domestic states to develop their own approaches to defining the problem.

(ii)   Globalisation by law and globalisation of law

In the modern context there is a similar movement toward globalisation, with law once again playing a critical role. In this era, it has been claimed that international law stands as the "most conspicuous manifestation of legal globalisation".[13] Through the proliferation of international institutions and new supranational legal systems, the terrain of public international law has expanded greatly. From treaties promoting free trade to conventions that declare fundamental human rights, there exist international treaties touching on almost every aspect of our lives. Through a myriad of international treaties, conventions and supranational organisations, domestic legal orders are being shaped and reshaped by priorities set by political, social and economic forces beyond national borders.

---

12   See discussion of colonial legal pluralism in Chapter 9, pp 287-290.

13   D Kinley, "Globalisation and the Law" (2003) 15(4) *LegalDate* 1 at 2.

The international and transnational forces shaping legal developments may not always be apparent to law students, legal practitioners and judges in Australia, who may use their domestic legal rules without any knowledge that they owe their existence to Australia's international treaty obligations.[14] Sometimes their international origins are explicit, with domestic legislation expressly incorporating provisions of treaty into domestic law. An example here is the *Human Rights (Sexual Conduct) Act 1994* (Cth), which created a right to sexual privacy under federal law. The origin of this provision was a legal challenge, before the United Nations Human Rights Committee, that Tasmanian offences criminalising consensual homosexual activity violated the right to privacy under Art 17 of the ICCPR. In *Toonen v Australia*,[15] the United Nations Human Rights Committee held that these laws violated the right to privacy. The federal government, as a party to the ICCPR, was obliged to provide the applicant with the "effective remedy" required by the Human Rights Committee. Rather than limit the remedial legislation to an act rendering invalid the offending Tasmanian provisions, the federal legislation created a right to sexual privacy in the following terms:

Arbitrary interferences with privacy

4(1) Sexual conduct involving only consenting adults acting in private is not to be subject, by or under any law of the Commonwealth, a State or a Territory, to any arbitrary interference with privacy within the meaning of Article 17 of the International Covenant on Civil and Political Rights.

4(2) For the purposes of this section, an adult is a person who is 18 years old or more.[16]

Another example of the way in which both domestic law and the regulation of conduct within national settings is shaped by international developments can be found in modern accounting standards. In Australia the annual financial report of a company must, by law, comply with all relevant accounting standards.[17] Those standards therefore play a vital role in the process by which investors, other businesses and regulators monitor corporate behaviour. The accounting standards are formulated by a body called the Australian Accounting Standards Board (AASB), which is given this power by the *Corporations Act 2001* (Cth).[18] Since 1 January 2005 the AASB has implemented a policy of adopting the standards set by the International Accounting Standards Board, an international body that is responsible for determining International Financial Reporting Standards (IFRSs). This practice is not limited to Australia. Since 1 January 2005, publicly listed companies in the European Union have been required to prepare their financial

---

14   Through signature and ratification of international treaties, the "external affairs" power in the federal Constitution enlivens the competence of the Commonwealth to enact offences. These treaties have led to the adoption and reform of many areas of criminal law including drug offences and, in recent times, fields as diverse as sexual servitude and slavery: *Criminal Code* (Cth) ss 270.3 and 270.6 (Div 270 – Slavery, sexual servitude and deceptive recruiting).

15   (1994) 1 PLPR 50.

16   This section creates a legal sphere of sexual privacy with potential to equalise the age of consent in Australia, as well as restrict blanket criminalisation of consensual sexual acts between adults such as prostitution and homosexual sadomasochism: S Bronitt, "The right to sexual privacy, sado-masochism and the *Human Rights (Sexual Conduct) Act* 1994 (Cth)" (1995) 2(1) *Australian Journal of Human Rights* 59; see W Morgan, "Identifying evil for what it is: Tasmania, sexual perversity and the United Nations" (1994) 19 *Melbourne University Law Review* 740.

17   *Corporations Act 2001* (Cth) s 296.

18   Section 334.

statements in conformity with IFRSs. New Zealand is planning to adopt IFRSs from 2007.

The symbolic strides towards creating a system of international justice, and the interplay between international and domestic law systems, are apparent in the recent establishment of the International Criminal Court (ICC).[19] The creation of this new international forum for prosecuting for a range of international crimes has been described as "the most important positive development in international law since the formation of the United Nations".[20] The advent of the ICC does not supplant domestic jurisdiction. Rather the ICC system rests on principle of complementarity with national legal systems; thus the ICC can only assert jurisdiction where a state is unwilling or unable to genuinely carry out the investigation or prosecution.[21] Also, consistent with the idea of national autonomy, jurisdiction applies only to those states that are party to the Rome Statute creating the ICC or who have otherwise consented to its jurisdiction.[22] Australia signed the ICC Statute on 9 December 1998, enacting enabling procedural provisions and a range of international criminal offences into the federal *Criminal Code* in 2002.[23] The symbolic aspects of establishing, through the ICC, global control over crimes of global human significance should not be underestimated. However, there is a danger that these processes detach or conceal the local context of these crimes, as Mark Findlay has observed: "it could be suggested that bringing war criminals to justice for crimes against humanity is more about reinforcing world order than it is compensating victims and punishing offenders".[24]

At a general level, public international law may be viewed as a powerful agent of globalisation. That said, the influence it exerts in domestic contexts varies, not least because national legal systems do not approach and incorporate international law in the same way. Civil law systems that inherited Roman law are "monist", which means that international and domestic law are viewed holistically. Consequently sources of international law, including customary international law as well as treaties, are usually viewed as binding superior laws that prevail over inconsistent domestic law, including even provisions in national constitutions.[25] This means that rights in ratified international covenants, such as the ICCPR, can be invoked directly before domestic courts without further implementation needed by the domestic legislature. By contrast, common law systems, including Australia and the United Kingdom, are said to be "dualist", which means that the international system is distinct and thus treaties have no effect until the rights are implemented by domestic legislation.

---

19   The ICC came into force on 1 July 2002, and jurisdiction over war crimes, crimes against humanity, genocide and the crime of aggression (the unlawful use of force against a State): *ICC Statute of the International Criminal Court*, A/Conf 183/9, 17 July 1998, Art 5.

20   AJ Bellamy and M Hanson, "Justice beyond borders? Australia and the International Criminal Court" (2002) 56(3) *Australian Journal of International Affairs* 417 at 417.

21   *ICC Statute of the International Criminal Court* Art 17.

22   Ibid Art 12.

23   The international crimes covering war crimes, crimes against humanity and genocide enacted in Australia follow, but are not identical to, those contained in the ICC Statute: see Bronitt and McSherry, n 10, 860ff.

24   M Findlay, "Crime, terror and transitional cultures in a contracting globe" in C Dauvergne (ed), *Jurisprudence for an Interconnected Globe*, Ashgate, 2003, 231.

25   See generally DJ Harris, *Cases and Materials on International Law*, 6th ed, Sweet and Maxwell, 2004, Ch 3.

While Australian law maintains this strict dualism between international and domestic law, the High Court has held that international treaties may be considered, in appropriate cases, as an aid to the interpretation of statutes or as a guide to the development of the common law. Important treaties such as the ICCPR have been viewed as an expression of the fundamental values and rights that Australian law should protect. For example, in recognising Aboriginal native title, the High Court in *Mabo (No 2)* was prepared to apply principles from international law and human rights treaties to reject the legal fiction that Australia was *terra nullius*.[26] The full extent of this interpretive duty to consider international law remains controversial. The current High Court is divided over the extent to which international treaties should influence constitutional interpretation, with some members of the Court expressing the view that, since the ICCPR was not in existence when the Commonwealth Constitution was enacted in 1901, it could have no bearing on the interpretation of constitutional provisions. This view prevailed in *Coleman v Power*.[27] In this case, the defendant was convicted of using insulting words in a public place, contrary to the *Vagrants, Gaming and Other Offences Act 1931* (Qld). The majority of the High Court upheld the constitutionality of the provision, finding that the offence, though broad, did not infringe the implied freedom of political communication. What is significant is how the various judges approached the use of the ICCPR. Gleeson CJ in particular was hostile to using the ICCPR to assist with the interpretation of s 7(1)(d), arguing that the Queensland offence must be interpreted by reference to the intention of the State legislature at the time the provision was enacted: "Of one thing we can be sure, the Queensland Parliament, in 1931, did not intend to give effect to Australia's obligations under the ICCPR".[28] Furthermore, in his view, the obligation to use ICCPR standards applied only to the development of common law, and not to the interpretation of State legislation enacted before Australia ratified the ICCPR.

There is, however, a significant dissenting view. Kirby J in *Coleman v Power*, and more recently in *Al-Kateb v Godwin*,[29] has promoted the use of international law as a judicial aid to interpreting the Constitution, as well as general legislation. *Al-Kateb* concerned the meaning of "indefinite detention" under the *Migration Act 1958* (Cth). Diverging from other members of the court, especially McHugh J,[30] Kirby J argued for an approach to constitutional interpretation that recognised its wider international context:

> Whatever may have been possible in the world of 1945, the complete isolation of constitutional law from the dynamic impact of international law is neither possible nor desirable today. That is why national courts, and especially national constitutional courts such as this, have a duty, so far as possible, to interpret their constitutional texts in a way that is generally harmonious with the basic

---

26   *Mabo v Queensland (No 2)* (1992) 175 CLR 1 at 42 per Brennan J.

27   [2004] HCA 39.

28   *Coleman v Power* [2004] HCA 39 at [19] per Gleeson CJ.

29   [2004] HCA 37 at [150].

30   McHugh J held that "contrary to the view of Kirby J, courts cannot read the Constitution by reference to the provisions of international law that have become accepted since the Constitution was enacted in 1900": ibid [62].

principles of international law, including as that law states human rights and fundamental freedoms.[31]

Thus far we have considered the use of law to achieve globalisation. But law is also something that is itself being globalised. As an object of globalisation, law assumes an important role in promoting interconnectedness across the globe. So, for example, over the course of the past 50 years, there have developed common legal standards, often derived from international treaties and the jurisprudence that elaborates upon their meaning and scope. These international legal standards govern diverse fields, ranging from the law governing corporate governance, commercial transactions, to the meaning and scope of the right to a fair trial. To explore these transnational aspects of law requires legal inquiry to adopt a comparative focus. Twining suggests that globalisation requires us to "explore what it is for a concept or group of concepts or models or frames to travel far and to travel well".[32] Traversing boundaries is not limited just to geographic and jurisdictional borders, but extends to cultural boundaries.

A consistent feature of globalisation is that it is always partial and incomplete. In Twining's assessment, contemporary universalising trends, while significant, do not penetrate to every part of the globe. Twining cautions against a reading of globalisation that is focused on universal issues affecting the world as a whole, an approach that usually limits the range of interests to "climate control or world peace or humanitarian law or human rights law".[33] Globalisation is a patchy phenomenon, concluding that "some objects of globalization rhetoric are no more global than the World Series in baseball [which only fields North American teams]".[34]

Twining also cautions against the assimilation of the "global" with the "international". In his view, too much attention is focused on public international law. Globalisation must accommodate more legal pluralism than the domestic versus international legal binary suggests.[35] Between the internal legal system of nation states law and international law that governs relations between nation states there exist a range of intermediate legal orderings. These may be transnational or regional in character. A good example that spans public international law and domestic law is the legal system of the European Union (EU). Established by a series of international treaties since the 1950s, this body of supranational law has been developed by the European Court of Justice, creating directly enforceable legal rights within national legal systems. As a result, there are few areas of domestic law and policy within Europe that have not been modified by the EU legal system.

---

31 Ibid [175] per Kirby J. This approach, that views the meaning of statutory terms to change over time, not necessarily limited to the meaning intended by the legislators drafting them, has been termed the "dynamic theory of interpretation": S Corcoran, "Theories of statutory interpretation" in S Corcoran and S Bottomley (eds), *Interpreting Statutes*, 2005, Federation Press, 21ff.

32 In keeping with his broader commitment to interdisciplinary perspectives on law, W Twining, "Have Concepts, Will Travel: Analytical Jurisprudence in a Global Context" (2005) 1 *International Jo of Law in Context* 5 at 8, also advocated that this question of "travelling well" applies to crossing disciplinary boundaries – how does law fare when viewed from the external perspective of sociology or economics or psychology. See also Findlay, n 24.

33 Twining, n 3, 25.

34 Ibid 25; as Twining acknowledges, the World Series is not a good example, as it is named after its original sponsor – *The New York World* newspaper.

35 Twining, n 3, 25.

Some of these intermediate norms take the form of "soft law", developed in the shadow of international law and institutions in order to promote universal standards. The spread of codes of conduct, broadly following the same model, that are intended to promote accountable and ethical behaviour by company directors and managers is an example.[36] These norms, while not formally constituted as part of public international law, shape and define domestic law in a wide range of areas. Within states there are legal norms that exist independently of general state law, such as the customary law of Indigenous people (see Chapter 9). It is vital that exploration of the relationships between custom and law not be constrained by a comparative approach which takes the dominant legal culture as the universal default standard against which "difference" is understood.

Twining concludes that, while law as a discipline and system of governance should be more "cosmopolitan", it should not overlook local perspectives:

> Viewing law from a global perspective has its uses, not least in providing *context* and dealing with genuinely global issues. But understanding law will continue to require a detailed focus on particulars *at all levels*.[37]

To sum up, this approach requires an assessment of the interactions between the "global" and the "local" focusing on:

- **International Law** and the interaction between international law, such as treaties protecting human rights law, and domestic law;

- **Uniform and Model Laws** and the development and promotion of legal standards, outside the framework of binding international law, as part of uniform or model legislation or rules, which may be adopted "voluntarily" under domestic law. For example, corporate governance standards for public corporations;

- **Multinational Non-State Actors** and the role of powerful multinational and transnational non-state actors (corporations and non-governmental organisations) in making and enforcing legal standards in domestic law.

Drawing on the work of de Sousa Santos, Twining suggests another way of summarising these developments, distinguishing between: globalised localism and localised globalism.[38]

Globalised localism occurs where "some local phenomenon is successfully globalised". The capacity to globalise laws (and other phenomena, including culture) is most likely to be exercised by larger, economically powerful nations. The example given by Twining is the copyright laws of the United States. The detailed study done by John Braithwaite and Peter Drahos bears this out.[39]

Localised globalism occurs when laws, structures and practices within a local system change or adapt in response to influences from outside that nation state.

---

36 See, for example, the OECD (Office for Economic Co-Operation and Development), *Principles of Corporate Governance* (2004). In the UK see the Financial Services Authority, *Combined Code on Corporate Governance* (2003). In Australia see the Australian Stock Exchange Corporate Governance Council, *Principles of Good Corporate Governance and Best Practice Recommendations* (2003).

37 Twining, n 3, 27 (emphasis added).

38 Twining, n 1, 5, citing B de Sousa Santos, *Toward a New Common Sense: Law, Science and Politics in Paradigmatic Transition*, Routledge, 1995.

39 J Braithwaite and P Drahos, *Global Business Regulation*, Cambridge UP, 2000, especially Ch 7.

This is more likely to be found in less powerful countries which are forced or pressured to adapt and "modernise" their laws and practices to conform with legal templates imposed by more powerful states and multinational corporate interests. The Council of Europe Convention on Cybercrime has been very influential in the approach to reform in countries which are not signatories, including Australia.[40] It is also important to recognise the role of powerful stakeholders in the making and enforcement of these legal norms. For example, the Uniform Commercial Code definition of "fraud" in domestic US law is being applied by multinational "credit card" providers to determine whether there has been misuse of their services or systems. This "working definition" of fraud, rather than local definitions or those used in international treaties, is used by these corporate entities to determine whether or not to prosecute.

From these theoretical reflections on globalisation, we move to a more specific discussion. A useful way to explore the interaction between global phenomena and local nation-states is through a case study examining legal responses to the "War on Terror".

(c)   Case study: Legal responses to global terrorism

The "9/11" attacks on New York and the Pentagon in 2001 changed the world in many ways. In relation to domestic Australian responses, the immediate effect was to produce an unprecedented degree of consensus on how the law should be deployed and coordinated at Commonwealth, State and Territory level to combat terrorism. Since 2001, the Prime Minister and State and Territory leaders have met regularly to review national responses to terrorism.[41] The degree of political attention has generated a massive legislative response: since 9/11 more than 100 offences have been created.[42] The bombings of Australian holidaymakers in Bali in 2002 served to reinforce Australia's vulnerability to international terrorism, though as Andrew O'Neil noted: "The fact that 88 Australians were killed on *Indonesian territory* was almost overlooked in the multitude of 'post-Bali' assessments".[43] The

---

40   P Csonka, "The Council of Europe Convention on Cyber-Crime: A response to the challenge of the new age" in R Broadhurst and P Grabosky (eds), *Cyber-crime: The Challenge in Asia*, Hong Kong UP, 2005, noting that, in addition to members of the Council of Europe, the United States, Canada, Japan and South Africa also ratified. In Australia, the drafters of the Model Criminal Code section on cybercrime considered various aspects of the Convention: see S Bronitt and M Gani, "Shifting boundaries of cybercrime: From computer hacking to cyberterrorism" (2003) 27 *Criminal Law Journal* 303.

41   The first national response was the *Commonwealth, State and Territories Agreement on Terrorism and Transnational Crime* (2002), which introduced a raft of new laws to combat terrorism. Model forensic procedures, drug offences and computer offences were identified as a matter of national priority for law reform. In addition to promoting consistency in the substantive criminal law, the Agreement foreshadowed the need for more effective cross-border cooperation in criminal investigation. See S Bronitt "Constitutional rhetoric versus criminal justice realities: Unbalanced responses to terrorism?" (2003) 14(2) *Public Law Review* 76, which notes that many of the reforms announced under the agreement were being contemplated before the events of 9/11.

42   B McSherry, "Terrorism offences in the *Criminal Code* (Cth): Broadening the boundaries of Australian criminal laws" (2004) 27(2) *University of New South Wales Law Journal* 354 at 356.

43   A O'Neil, "The evolving nature of international terrorism and Australia's response" in D Chappell and P Wilson (eds), *Issues in Australian Crime and Criminal Justice*, LexisNexis Butterworths, 2005, 377 (emphasis in original).

federal government swiftly responded by enacting a new offence of "harming Australians", offences that had both extraterritorial and retrospective application.

Many commentators have expressed concern that the legal responses to terrorism – based on broad offences and expanded powers of the state – depart from traditional liberal rule of law standards.[44] Not only are these counter-terrorism laws regarded as excessively broad and vague, they have also derogated from key procedural safeguards.[45] The political justification for these laws is that "exceptional times demand exceptional measures"!

The following case study explores the threats to liberalism through a critical examination of recent federal laws enacted to deal with terrorism.

(i)   9/11 laws: The limits of harm prevention

A critical element of liberal philosophy that aims to promote liberty and restrain the arbitrary exercise of state power is the "harm principle", previously discussed in Chapter 2. The harm caused by terrorism is manifest, ranging from acts of serious violence to the wanton destruction of property. The proscription of this type of physical harm by state law is relatively uncontroversial, having long been deemed as crimes and torts by our legal system. Indeed the key definition of "terrorist act" for the purpose of the federal *Criminal Code* (Cth) is defined as conduct involving serious physical harm, or serious property damage, or a person's death, or endangerment of a person's life, or serious risk to public health, or serious interference, disruption or destruction of an electronic system.[46] The terrorist dimension is grafted onto this conventional criminal conduct by highlighting particular motivations behind the action. Thus, under s 100.1(1) Definitions of the *Criminal Code* (Cth) the "terrorist act" also must involve an action or threat of action done with the intention of:

> (c) advancing a political, religious or ideological cause; and
> > (i)   coercing, or influencing by intimidation, the government of the Commonwealth or a State, Territory or foreign country, or of part of a State, Territory or foreign country; or
> > (ii) intimidating the public or a section of the public.[47]

The difficulty for liberalism lies in accommodating the legal proscription of behaviours which have the *potential* to harm or cause fear within individuals and the wider community. Harm is an elastic concept, with considerable controversy over whether it includes indirect and less tangible forms of harm. A focus on *potential* harm can justify the criminalisation of a wider range of conduct that "signifies" a predilection or propensity to doing harm. By widening the definition of harm, the ability of the harm principle to be protective of individual liberty is thereby weakened. Consistent with this concern, the common law was initially wary of criminalising preparatory criminal activity, though eventually it did

---

44   See J Hocking, *Terror Laws: ASIO, Counter-terrorism and the Threat to Democracy*, University of New South Wales Press, 2004.

45   Bronitt and McSherry, n 10, 871ff.

46   *Criminal Code* (Cth) s 100.1(1) Definitions, *Terrorist act*.

47   *Criminal Code* (Cth). The approach derogates from the standard criminal law in several respects. Motive is usually irrelevant to liability but here is the core of culpability, with the politics and religion of the defendant likely to assume a prominent focus in criminal trials: Bronitt and McSherry, n 10, 891ff.

recognise offences based on attempt, incitement or conspiracy.[48] Until statute created "possession" offences, the common law similarly refused to recognise indictments where the alleged offence was that the accused simply possessed an article or thing involved in crime. By the late 20th century, this liberal hesitancy was abandoned, and parliament has created many offences (particularly in the field of drug law) that criminalise possession and less direct forms of involvement in criminal activity. With intense political pressure to prevent terrorism, the "net-widening" trend in the criminal law has only intensified.

Rather than rely on existing offences (such as laws concerning attempt, incitement or conspiracy) to respond to terrorism activity, 9/11 brought a raft of new offences that target conduct that manifests a *potential* for terrorism.[49] These include:

- possession of things connected with terrorist acts;[50]
- collecting or making documents likely to facilitate terrorist acts;[51]
- other acts done in preparation for, or planning, terrorist acts;[52]
- directing the activities of a terrorist organisation;[53]
- membership of a terrorist (prescribed) organisation or association with one;[54]
- recruiting for a terrorist organisation;[55]
- providing or receiving training connected with terrorist acts, training a terrorist organisation or receiving training from a terrorist organisation;[56]
- offering support (including financial support) to terrorist organisations.[57]

In late 2005, further amendments to the terrorism offences were made to redefine sedition as an offence criminalising incitement of violence against the community to replace the existing sedition offence.[58] The new sedition offence, which carries a penalty of imprisonment for seven years, makes it an offence to:

- urge another person to overthrow by force or violence the Constitution, the State, Territory or federal government, or the lawful authority of the government of the Commonwealth;[59]
- urge another person to interfere by force or violence with lawful processes for an election of a member of a House of the Parliament;[60]

---

48 Ibid Ch 8, 399ff.

49 N Hancock "Terrorism: Legislating for security", Parliament of Australia, Department of Parliamentary Library, 2002, *Research Note 25*.

50 *Criminal Code* (Cth) Part 5.3 – Terrorism, s 101.4.

51 Ibid s 101.5.

52 Ibid s 101.6.

53 Ibid s 102.2.

54 Ibid ss 102.3 and 102.8.

55 Ibid s 102.4.

56 Ibid ss 101.2, and 102.5.

57 Ibid ss 102.6, 102.7, 103.1.

58 Schedule 7 to the *Anti-Terrorism Act (No 2) 2005* (Cth) amends the Commonwealth *Criminal Code* to rename Div 80 – Treason to "Treason and Sedition", and insert the new offences; the amendment commences on 14 June 2006 unless proclaimed earlier: *Criminal Code Act 1995* (Cth) Note 3. The provision is subject to the widest category of extraterritorial jurisdiction: s 80.4.

59 *Criminal Code* (Cth) s 80.2(1) (recklessness applies).

60 Ibid s 80.2(3) (recklessness applies).

- urge a group or groups (whether distinguished by race, religion, nationality or political opinion) to use force or violence against another group or other groups (as so distinguished); and the use of the force or violence would threaten the peace, order and good government of the Commonwealth;[61]

- urge another person to engage in conduct; and the first mentioned person intends the conduct to assist an organisation or country; and the organisation or country is at war with the Commonwealth, whether or not the existence of a state of war has been declared; and is specified to be an enemy at war with the Commonwealth;[62]

- urge another person to engage in conduct; and the first mentioned person intends the conduct to assist an organisation or country; and the organisation or country is engaged in armed hostilities against the Australian Defence Force.[63]

Offences like sedition and seditious libel have until recently been regarded as a "dead-letter". "Political" crimes have an unsavoury pedigree in Australia. Over the past two centuries, sedition charges have been used to repress unpopular political minorities including, most famously, the political activities of members of the Australian Communist Party in the 1940s.[64] The danger with the new federal sedition offence, like its predecessors, is that it has a potentially chilling effect on political and press comment; indeed, many submissions on the federal Bill raised concerns about its potential incompatibility with the implied constitutional freedom of political communication. The federal government sought to allay these concerns by the inclusion of a "good faith" defence. The defence operates where the defendant can establish that he or she:

- tried to show in good faith that the Sovereign, the Governor-General, the Governor of a State, the Administrator of a Territory, an adviser of any of the above, or a person responsible for the government of another country are mistaken in any of his or her counsels, policies or actions; or

- pointed out in good faith errors or defects with a view to reforming those errors or defects in the government, the Constitution, legislation, or the administration of justice; or

- urged in good faith another person to attempt to lawfully procure a change to any matter established by law, policy or practice; or

- pointed out in good faith any matters that are producing, or have a tendency to produce, feelings of ill-will or hostility between different groups, in order to bring about the removal of those matters; or

---

61   Ibid s 80.2(5) (recklessness applies).

62   Ibid s 80.2(7) (recklessness does not expressly apply).

63   Ibid s 80.2(8) (recklessness does not expressly apply).

64   *R v Sharkey* (1949) 79 CLR 121; *Burns v Ransley* (1949) 79 CLR 101. See Bronitt and McSherry, n 10, 779, where the authors note: "Except for its brief renaissance to combat Communism in the late 1940s, leading to the prosecution of agitators such as Burns and Sharkey, the offence of sedition seems to be a dead-letter. This may be contrasted with the widespread use of seditious libel charges during the colonial period to deal with individuals, including prominent lawyers and newspaper editors, who criticised various institutions of government, including governors and judges". For a review of the use of these charges during the colonial period: see G Woods, *A History of Criminal Law in New South Wales*, Federation Press, 2002, 50-56.

- does anything in good faith in connection with an industrial dispute or an industrial matter.[65]

The symbolic dimension of criminalising sedition is highly significant. Politicians must be seen to be fighting terrorism threats effectively, though it should be noted that under the modern criminal law sedition offences are largely legally redundant – inciting individuals or groups to use force or violence (in the typical form of an unlawful assault) is already a crime under existing State and Territory laws.[66] In such cases, the state could use ordinary crimes such as incitement and, in cases where there is a racial aspect to the incitement, racial vilification offences may also be available to prosecutors: for example, *Anti-Discrimination Act 1977* (NSW) s 20D (see further discussion of these offences in Chapter 9 at p 299ff).

Some terrorist offences have no real or direct link to *actual* terrorist activity, though they are nevertheless prescribed because they contribute to fear or panic within the community. These include:

- perpetrating hoax offences through the postal service;[67] or
- using a carriage service for a hoax threat.[68]

The danger in moving beyond the criminalisation of tangible direct harms is that the state is criminalising a person's status, rather than their conduct. This is a proposition that liberal theorists strenuously reject.[69] Status offences such as vagrancy, being a habitual offender or prostitute (or "consorting" with such criminal classes); and being found drunk in public have been removed from the criminal statute books in most jurisdictions. The introduction of associating with terrorists has clear historical parallels with these 19th century status offences.[70] The reforms adopted in late 2005 also broadened the scope of a terrorist organisation further, extending it to include advocacy – raising concerns about interference with legitimate criticism of state policy and freedom of expression.[71]

---

65 *Criminal Code* (Cth) s 80.3. The good faith defence applies to all of the treason and sedition offences, whereas a defence for the provision of humanitarian aid applies to just parts of the sedition offence: s 80.2(9).

66 While such threats and incitement could be prosecuted under the general criminal law, the racial motivation behind such conduct would be deemed legally irrelevant to the issue of culpability: HREOC, *Racist Violence*, AGPS, 1991, 276. It could, however, influence the severity of the sentence imposed.

67 *Criminal Code* (Cth) ss 471.10, 471.11.

68 Ibid s 474.16.

69 An important premise behind the rule of law is that the state punishes criminal conduct, not criminal "types", a feature associated with Soviet and Nazi regimes: F Allen, *The Habits of Legality – Criminal Justice and the Rule of Law*, Oxford UP, 1996, 15.

70 Alex Steel has traced the moral panic around the emergence of "razor gangs" in New South Wales in the 1920s and 1930s, which led to the introduction of a general crime of consorting with criminals or prostitutes: "Consorting in New South Wales: Substantive offence or police power?" (2003) 26(3) *University of New South Wales Law Journal* 567 at 582ff.

71 Before the Governor-General can specify an organisation is a terrorist organisation the Minister must be satisfied on reasonable grounds that it is directly or indirectly engaged in, preparing, planning, assisting in or fostering the doing of a terrorist act or that the organisation *advocates* the doing of a terrorist act (whether or not a terrorist act has occurred or will occur): *Criminal Code* (Cth) s 102.1(2). Schedule 1 to the *Anti-Terrorism Act (No 2) 2005* (Cth) inserts a definition of *advocates* into the *Criminal Code* Div 102 – Terrorist Organisations: s 102.1(1A) In this Division, an organisation advocates the doing of a terrorist act if: (a) the organisation directly or indirectly counsels or urges the doing of a terrorist act; or (b) the organisation directly or indirectly provides instruction on the doing of a terrorist act; or (c) the organisation directly praises the doing of a terrorist act.

(ii)   9/11: Globalisation of crime and transnational criminal law

9/11 provides a new impetus to international coordination and cooperation to fight terrorism globally. Although terrorism is not a new phenomenon, after 9/11 political scientists have begun to speculate whether there is a form of "new" terrorism that is distinct from earlier forms of political violence. The point of departure post-9/11 is claimed to be the global dimensions of terrorism and the rise of mass casualty, which is linked to the increasing hold of religious ideology over terrorist groups.[72] The extent to which these threats are qualitatively and quantitatively different remains controversial,[73] and human rights organisations have expressed concern that the threat of terrorism is being used as a justification for quashing legitimate political dissent or religious minorities in many countries.[74] The International Commission of Jurists (ICJ) has voiced concern over this opportunism in the Berlin Declaration:

> Since September 2001 many states have adopted new counter-terrorism measures that are in breach of their international obligations. In some countries, the post-September 2001 climate of insecurity has been exploited to justify long-standing human rights violations carried out in the name of national security.[75]

It is important not to overstate the novelty of terrorism. Terrorism can and should be addressed, wherever possible, under existing laws: as the ICJ has recommended:

> In combating terrorism, states should apply and where necessary adapt existing criminal laws rather than create new, broadly defined offences or resort to extreme administrative measures, especially those involving deprivation of liberty.[76]

The global dimension of "new" terrorism may simply be a reflection of general trends toward the "globalisation of crime".[77] Through increased personal mobility

---

72 O'Neil, n 43, 378. O'Neil argues that the nature of terrorism has changed: it is global rather than regional; it is internationally networked; it views itself as something apart from, rather than within, the political process, cf IRA and Basque movements; and that new terrorists are less discriminating and far more lethal, having "fewer moral scruples than the terrorists of yesteryear about initiating mass casualty attacks targeting civilian populations": 383.

73 Bronitt, n 41, noting that many of the reforms announced under the agreement were being contemplated before the events of September 11. A recent European human rights watchdog similarly noted that of the 57 initiatives announced at an EU Summit to combat terrorism in the wake of the Madrid bombings in 2004, 27 of the proposals have "little or nothing to do with tackling terrorism – they deal with crime in general and surveillance", <http://www.statewatch.org/news/2004/mar/swscoreboard.pdf> (accessed 1 April 2005).

74 See, for example, Amnesty International EU Office, "Human rights dissolving at the borders? Counter-terrorism and EU criminal law", AI Index IOR 61/013/2005, 31 May 2005; <http://web.amnesty.org/library/Index/ENGIOR610132005> (accessed 30 September 2005); and Human Rights Watch, "In the name of counter-terrorism: Human rights abuses worldwide" *A Human Rights Watch Briefing Paper for the 59th Session of the United Nations Commission on Human Rights*, 25 March 2003.

75 The International Commission of Jurists, *Declaration on Upholding Human Rights and the Rule of Law in Combating Terrorism (The Berlin Declaration)*, adopted 28 August 2004, 2.

76 Ibid. A similar recommendation was made by the UK Privy Counsellor Review Committee (the Newton Committee) which proposed ordinary criminal justice and security provisions are preferred for dealing with terrorism crime: *Anti-Terrorism, Crime and Security Act 2001 Review: Report*, London, 18 December 2003, <http://www.homeoffice.gov.uk/docs3/newton_committee_report_2003.pdf>.

77 See generally M Findlay, *Globalisation of Crime*, Cambridge UP, 1999 and Findlay, n 24.

and improved communications technology, opportunities for new forms of criminal behaviour, which include terrorist activity, have been created.[78] Further-more, in common with organised crime, terrorists can exploit geo-political and legal boundaries, fragmenting illegal activities and locating themselves in jurisdictions where law enforcement is weak or less hostile to their cause.[79] Responding to these concerns, nation states are engaging in increased levels of cooperation through international and regional agreements concerning uniform laws and cross-border law enforcement. This cooperation is occurring not only in the field of terrorism, but also in relation to combating organised crime and cyber-crime.

The global and transnational dimensions of Australia's legal responses to terrorism are reflected in the extended reach of the key terrorist offences. Although there is no agreed definition of "terrorism" under international law,[80] some domestic definitions have been internationally influential. The Australian defini-tion of terrorist act (see above) is modelled directly on the definition in the *Terrorism Act 2000* (UK), developed before the 9/11 attacks. The Australian definition adds a further transnational dimension. Under the federal *Criminal Code* (Cth) the terrorist act must be done, or the threat made, with the intention, inter alia, of coercing or intimidating the "government of the Commonwealth or a State, Territory *or foreign country*".[81] While this definition of terrorism bears similarity to conventional political crimes such as treason and sedition, the extension to *any* foreign country is a clear manifestation of the globalisation of security. The recognition that the security of Australia is now dependent upon the security of other states (not just allies) justifies the adoption of expanded offences and powers that promote *global* rather than exclusively *national* security. With the adoption of such far-reaching definitions (in both senses of the term), there is a further blurring of the traditional distinction between internal and external security.

Terrorism is viewed as a global threat transcending national sovereign boundaries. The result is that there are increased political pressures to enact terrorism offences that have extraterritorial effect.[82] The traditional view that "crime is local" has been displaced by the view that "crime is global", leading to extraterritorial provisions being adopted particularly in the field of federal criminal

---

78   See J Travis, "Building knowledge about crime and justice in the global age: Infrastructure first" *Address to the Fifth Biennial Conference of International Perspectives on Crime, Justice and Public Order*, Bologna, Italy, 8 June 2000, 2-3.

79   N Passas, "Cross-border crime and the interface between legal and illegal actors" in PC van Duyne, K von Lampe and N Passas (eds), *Upperworld and Underworld In Cross-Border Crime*, Wolf Legal Publishers, 2002.

80   The difficulty for international law is the need to devise terrorism in ways that do not interfere with liberationist movements that are recognized by the right of self-determination. As a consequence, international treaties and conventions have focused on specific, common terrorist activity, such as hijacking; discussed in Bronitt and McSherry, n 10, 883-884.

81   *Criminal Code* (Cth) s 101(1)(b) and (c) (emphasis added). The approach derogates from the standard criminal law in several respects. Motive is usually irrelevant to liability but here is the core of culpability, with the politics and religion of the defendant likely to assume a prominent focus in criminal trials: Bronitt and McSherry, n 10, 891ff.

82   The standard test of jurisdiction in the criminal law is based on territoriality or territorial nexus, that is, the crime has to have occurred or have consequences or some link with the territory, discussed in Bronitt and McSherry, n 10, 86ff. Extending criminal law beyond borders has always been "exceptional", reserved for a narrow range of crimes recognised as having universal jurisdiction under international law, such as piracy or war crimes.

law.[83] Bronitt and McSherry have concluded that the existing safeguards to prevent the over-extension of criminal jurisdiction are likely to be ineffective:

> Even where parliament has extended jurisdiction, the permission of the Attorney-General is required to institute proceedings against a non-citizen/resident of Australia in relation to conduct that occurs wholly in a foreign country. Notwithstanding these safeguards, the domestic pressures to be seen to be fighting crime at the international level may be difficult to resist. The process of normalisation of extra-territoriality in the criminal law will be fostered and legitimated by the large (and increasing) number of international treaties dealing with transnational and global crime. This is apparent in relation to drug laws ..., and terrorism and cybercrime offences ...[84]

The question remains whether broadening the scope of federal criminal jurisdiction and the domestic substantive laws to combat terrorism is warranted. A good example of jurisdictional over-reach is the legal response to the Bali bombings that killed 88 Australians on 12 October 2002. The bombings demanded a swift response legislatively, even though the events occurred on foreign soil. A new part was inserted into the *Criminal Code* (Cth) (Part 5.4). Division 104 is titled "Harming Australians" and creates a range of extraterritorial offences against the person including murder, manslaughter and causing serious injury to Australian citizens or residents of Australia.[85] The most serious offence, murder, adopts the maximum penalty of life imprisonment. Though the perpetrators of the Bali bombings were prosecuted under terrorism laws in Indonesia, the symbolic importance of legislating to safeguard Australians overseas from harm proved to be politically irresistible.

As well as having extraterritorial effect, these new offences challenge liberalism in other ways. The federal offences above were expressly intended to have retrospective effect.[86] An important element of the rule of law is that a person should only be punished for conduct that was prohibited at the time the offence was committed: this is embodied in the Latin maxims of *nullum crimen sine lege* (no crime without law) and *nulla poena sine lege* (no punishment without law). These long-standing liberal ideals are embodied in numerous international human rights treaties,[87] as well as domestic Bills of Rights.[88] Without a national Bill of

---

83   Determining the scope of criminal jurisdiction was traditionally left to the courts. A new approach has been introduced following the adoption of model rules inserted into the *Criminal Code* (Cth), which permit parliament to stipulate in advance the extent and conditions of extraterritorial jurisdiction: s 14.1; discussed in Bronitt and McSherry, n 10, 857.

84   Bronitt and McSherry, n 10, 857-858.

85   There are four offences in Div 104: murder of an Australian citizen or a resident of Australia (s 104.1); manslaughter of an Australian citizen or a resident of Australia (s 104.2); intentionally causing serious harm to an Australian citizen or a resident of Australia (s 104.3) and recklessly causing serious harm to an Australian citizen or a resident of Australia (s 104.4). The offences attract the following maximum penalties: murder, life imprisonment; manslaughter, 25 years imprisonment; intentionally causing serious harm, 20 years imprisonment; and recklessly causing serious harm, 15 years imprisonment.

86   The provisions are specified to apply retrospectively, from 1 October 2002, as the drafters intended to use them to prosecute those involved with the 12 October Bali bombings: Parliament of the Commonwealth of Australia, House of Representatives, *Criminal Code Amendment (Offences Against Australians) Bill 2002, Second Reading Speech.*

87   ICCPR Art 15; *Convention for the Protection of Human Rights and Fundamental Freedoms* (also known as the European Convention on Human Rights or ECHR) Art 7.

88   *Human Rights Act 2004* (ACT) s 24; s 1 of the *Human Rights Act 1988* (UK) incorporates the ECHR rights (as listed in Sch 1) into UK domestic law.

Rights that can restrain federal law, there are no legislative restrictions on the adoption of retrospective criminal laws in Australia.[89] This position may be contrasted with Indonesia, where retrospective criminal laws used to prosecute the Bali bombers were ruled to be unconstitutional![90]

(iii) 9/11 Law-making: Balancing security and liberty

Although there are many new powers to combat terrorism at both federal and State levels, the tide of counter-terrorism law reform seems not to be abating. Traditional State-federal rivalry over "law and order" issues has been put aside in an unprecedented effort to coordinate a national response to terrorism. In addition to generating retrospective and extraterritorial offences, the Bali bombings also expanded the scope of federal legislative power through the referral of powers from the States to the Commonwealth to legislate in respect of counter-terrorism. The subsequent bombings in Madrid and London in 2004 and 2005 both produced immediate internal reviews of security laws, and further expansion of the powers of intelligence agencies (such as ASIO) and law enforcement agencies.[91] At a meeting of the Council of Australian Governments in 2005, Commonwealth, State and Territory governments agreed to a legislative package that included preventative detention for terrorist suspects and new offences relating to inciting terrorist violence.[92]

The perceived exigency of the situation – that Australians may be subject to imminent terrorist attack both internally or externally – severely challenges the liberal democratic processes of law-making. Under these conditions there is limited opportunity for reviewing the adequacy of existing laws or to critically examine the likely effect of proposed reforms. Reform is driven by popular and political perceptions that stronger laws are needed, with little attention given to the

---

89   In *Polyukhovich v Commonwealth* (1991) 172 CLR 501, the High Court upheld the validity of the *War Crimes Act 1945* (Cth) as a proper exercise of the Commonwealth's external affairs power in the Constitution pursuant to s 51(vi), (xxiv). The majority concluded that the legislation was a valid exercise of these powers, notwithstanding the fact that it had extraterritorial effect and applied to past conduct of persons who at the relevant time had no connection with Australia. There are systems of parliamentary scrutiny which monitor new legislation for, amongst other things, retrospective operation; for example, the Australian Senate's Scrutiny of Bills Committee.

90   The bombers were charged under special terrorist offences enacted after the bombings. The Constitutional Court held that these laws were invalid, incompatible with the Indonesian Constitution's prohibition of retrospective criminal laws: S Butt and D Hansell, "Case Note: The Masykur Abdul Kadir Case: Indonesian Constitutional Court No 013/PUU-I/2003 (Bali Bombing case)" (2004) 6(2) *Asian Law* 176; see also M Kirby, "Terrorism and the democratic response: A tribute to the European Court of Human Rights", *Robert Schuman Lecture*, The Australian National University, Canberra, 11 November 2004, <http://www.hcourt.gov.au/speeches/kirbyj/kirbyj_11nov04.html>.

91   The *Anti-terrorism Act 2004* (Cth) reverses the presumption in favour of bail in relation to specified terrorist offences, fixes the non-parole period for these offences at three-quarters of the relevant sentence, and also permits extensions of the period of investigation available for terrorist offences.

92   The *Anti-Terrorism Act (No 2) 2005* (Cth) is very wide ranging, amending provisions relating to: the definition of a terrorist organisation (Sch 1); financing terrorism (Sch 3); control orders and preventative detention orders (Sch 4); powers to stop, question and search persons in relation to terrorist acts (Sch 5); power to obtain information and documents (Sch 6); sedition (Sch 7); optical surveillance devices at airports and on board aircraft (Sch 8); financial transaction reporting (Sch 9) and ASIO powers etc (Sch 10). The amendments modify 16 Commonwealth Acts.

possibility that wider powers may not be effective or, indeed, may be counter-productive. There is certainly no time available to involve national law reform bodies.[93] As a result, the process of parliamentary scrutiny of legislation has been only effective at blunting the worst excesses of the political response.[94]

The introduction of preventative detention of suspects in late 2005 is a good illustration of measures that not only undermine liberal values, but are also likely to be counterproductive. Under these laws suspects may be detained in order to prevent a terrorist offence and also to preserve evidence.[95] The basis for issuing a preventative detention order is satisfaction that there are reasonable grounds to *suspect* that the subject will engage in an imminent terrorist act or has done a preparatory act, or possesses a thing that is connected with a terrorist act and satisfaction of the reasonable utility and necessity of the detention in preventing the terrorist act from occurring.[96] There is no requirement of a conviction and no legal hearing at which the evidence against the suspect can be challenged. There is a clear danger that this type of detention is a form of arbitrary detention and tantamount to extrajudicial punishment.[97] Detention is regulated by legislation, and involves some element of independent administrative oversight. In our view, however, the faith in administrative and judicial oversight as providing a "check and balance" mechanism can be misplaced: in existing areas where coercive law enforcement activity is subject to independent authorisation by judicial officers or members of the Administrative Appeals Tribunal, such as warrants and authori-sations relating to the use of telecommunications interception, surveillance devices and controlled operations, there is concern that the request by the law enforcement officers is rarely (if ever) refused.[98] Also there is a constitutional objection about judicial involvement in these decisions since the oversight function is in the nature

---

93 Since the early 1990s, criminal law reform in Australia has been dominated by the work of the Model Criminal Code Officers Committee (MCCOC). Yet the work of the MCCOC played no role in developing the package of new terrorism offences inserted into Ch 5 of the *Criminal Code* (Cth) in 2002. As McSherry has noted, "the new offences were developed and enacted without attention to the foundational work of the MCCOC": McSherry, n 42, 356.

94 The amendments implementing preventative detention and sedition in late 2005, the Anti-Terrorism Bill (No 2) 2005, were adopted with indecent haste. Despite allowing only one week for public submissions, the Senate Legal and Constitutional Committee received submissions from 294 individuals and organisations. At the close of submissions the Senate committee had only 11 business days to review and make recommendations on the Bill. Not surprisingly, few significant changes were made to the Bill before its enactment.

95 *Anti-Terrorism Act (No 2) 2005* (Cth) Sch 4 – Control orders and preventative detention orders, s 105.1 – Object: The object of this Division is to allow a person to be taken into custody and detained for a short period of time in order to: (a) prevent an imminent terrorist act occurring; or (b) preserve evidence of, or relating to, a recent terrorist act. Note: Section 105.42 provides that, while a person is being detained under a preventative detention order, the person may only be questioned for very limited purposes.. Further, there is a proposal to permit further detention beyond the initial 48 hours to 14 days under mirror legislation at State and Territory level: <http://www.pm.gov.au/news/media_releases/media_Release1551.html> (accessed 6 October 2005).

96 *Criminal Code* (Cth) s 105.4(4).

97 The common law has developed remedies against arbitrary detention including the writ of habeas corpus to permit subjects to challenge the legality of their detention. This process will enable scrutiny of the grounds for detention under the relevant legislation. Note, however, that the Bill now envisages the ability to review the decision to detain.

98 In 2002-03, there were 3058 telecommunications interception warrants issued and only nine refused/ withdrawn. The implications of these data are discussed in S Bronitt and J Stellios, "Telecommunications interception in Australia: Recent trends and regulatory prospects" (2005) 29 *Telecommunications Policy* 875 at 882 ff.

of an administrative function, though being exercised by judicial officers, raising doubts as to its compatibility with the separation of powers doctrine.[99]

Examples of similar terror laws introduced in other countries, such as the UK, are often used as precedents for reforms in Australia,[100] though such claims typically overlook the successful human rights challenges to these powers in those jurisdictions. The introduction of preventative detention in Australia raises particular concern in light of the failed policy of internment in Northern Ireland in the early 1970s, where more than 2000 people (overwhelmingly young Catholic males) were held in internment camps between 1971 and 1974. To minimise the risk of arbitrary detention, internment orders issued from 1973 onwards did include a quasi-judicial element – the orders of internment were to be reviewed by an independent "Commissioner" who was a person of legal experience. However, as an official inquiry ordered by the UK government later revealed, the procedures were farcical and unsatisfactory: "the quasi-judicial procedures are a veneer to an enquiry which, to be effective, inevitably, has no relationship to common law procedures".[101] Ultimately, the policy of internment was counterproductive, damaging the legitimacy of local government and state authority in the province, as well as mobilising many within the community in support of violent political struggle. As Kieran McEvoy's study concluded:

> Apart from the political fallout, in purely military terms internment was an unmitigated disaster. The degree and intensity of the violence in the aftermath internment has not been matched either before or since. The principal justification for internment had been to take the principal players out of action and then make further inroads on their operations by gaining intelligence through interrogations. In the seven months prior to internment, eleven soldiers, and seventeen civilians died; in the five months following internment, thirty-two British soldiers, five members of the Ulster Defence Regiment, and ninety-seven civilians were either shot dead or blown up. The intended objectives of internment had clearly not been achieved.[102]

The denial of due process, derogating from the ordinary process of prosecution, and limiting access to the courts severely damages the legitimacy of the state and the law enforcement agencies tasked with using these powers. Paddy Hillyard, in a recent essay to note the launch of a new European civil liberties network, reflected on the lessons from Northern Ireland in the 1970s:

> The lessons from Ireland are clear. Widespread violation of human rights in the so called "war against terrorism" is counterproductive. It erodes democracy by undermining the very principles on which social order is based and alienates the

---

99   The High Court has held that such powers may be exercised personae designatae (personal capacity rule) which allows individual judges to perform certain functions so long as they are appointed to do so in their capacity as individuals and not as judges: *Drake v Minister for Immigration and Ethnic Affairs* (1979) 46 FLR 409; *Hilton v Wells* (1985) 157 CLR 57; *Grollo v Palmer* (1995) 184 CLR 348.

100   O'Neil, n 43, 390.

101   Lord Gardiner, The *Report of a Committee to Consider in the Context of Civil Liberties and Human Rights, Measures to Deal with Terrorism in Northern Ireland* Cmnd 5847 (HMSO 1975), discussed in K McEvoy, *Paramilitary Imprisonment in Northern Ireland*, Oxford UP, 2001, 214ff.

102   McEvoy, n 101, 214-215.

communities from whom the authorities need support in dealing with political violence.[103]

In the Australian context, preventative detention will be much shorter, measured in days, rather than months – 48 hours under the federal schemes and 14 days under the complementary State and Territory schemes. However, there must be doubts as to whether terrorist threats can be effectively neutralised by the detention of terrorist suspects for such short periods. The legitimacy of using ordinary criminal processes and offences against people who intend serious harm against people or property, combined with their imprisonment after conviction, will likely be a more effective response to terrorism in the long term. Rather than place faith in administrative detention, preventative strategies should be based on strengthening multiculturalism and interfaith and cross-cultural dialogue.

The fear of terrorism can also promote historical blindness and the view that the rights of some individuals can be sacrificed for the interests of the community. Utilitarianism has provided the justification for many of these admittedly "draconian" laws – this theory is discussed in Chapter 2. It promotes a balancing approach where state legal action must strike a balance between national security and respect for fundamental liberal values.[104] As the federal Attorney-General, Philip Ruddock has pointed out:

> There will always be a trade-off between national security and individual rights. The task of government is to recognise these trade-offs and preserve our security without compromising basic rights and liberties.[105]

But the implicit liberalism in this "balanced" approach is misleading. It has been rejected by many scholars as an appropriate model for policy development in this field.[106] There are considerable problems with applying the utilitarian calculus to terrorism. How do we calculate and weigh the harms threatened to the majority, particularly when they move beyond physical harm to less tangible and direct interests, such as a community's need to *feel* secure? Promoting the happiness of the majority necessarily tips the balance heavily in favour of the state over the citizen. As Greg Carne has pointed out:

> The national security aspect in the balance is inevitably given special weighting, producing a structural inequality in that "balance". These considerations suggest a general unsuitability of the balancing paradigm for reconciling national security and democratic interests.[107]

---

103 P Hillyard, "The 'war on terror': Lessons from Ireland" (2005) *European Civil Liberties Network*, p 4, <http://www.ecln.org>.

104 The balanced approach was adopted in the Senate Committee on Constitutional and Legal Affairs, *Inquiry into the Security Legislation Amendment (Terrorism) Bill 2002 [No 2] and Related Bills*, Interim Report, tabled 3 May 2002. It is also adopted by G Williams, "Australian values and the war on terrorism", *Australian Financial Review*, 7 February 2003, 6-7 (edited version of National Press Club Address, 29 January 2003) and in G Williams, *The Case For An Australian Bill of Rights: Freedom in the War on Terror*, University of New South Wales Press, 2004.

105 P Ruddock, "The commonwealth response to September 11: The rule of law and national security", *National Forum in the War on Terrorism and the Rule of Law*, New South Wales Parliament House, 10 November 2003, paras 28-29.

106 For criticism of these balancing models, see Bronitt, n 41, and M Gani, "Upping the ante in the 'War on Terror'" in Patty Fawkner (ed), *A Fair Go in an Age of Terror*, David Lovell Publishing, 2004, 80-91; and G Carne, "Brigitte and the French connection: Security carte blanche or al la carte" (2004) 9(2) *Deakin Law Review* 573 at 613-614.

107 Carne, n 106, 613-614.

The logic of utilitarian approaches leads some criminal law scholars to suggest that even torture, under some form of judicial supervision, may be justified to avert imminent terrorist attacks.[108] Sometimes this is justified as a form of self-defence (a doctrine which extends to defence of others), but, in reality, this action is not likely to be directed against the perpetrator, but rather against the suspected terrorist's associates or family members. A further point of distinction here is that the defensive action is not being performed by a private citizen, but by law enforcement officials, thus invoking what amounts to a wider defence of necessity. The criminal law defence of necessity, which admits that there will be circumstances where a person may legitimately break the law, involves the weighing of lesser evils. There is little case law on the defence, though the courts have held that necessity and duress are unavailable in murder cases – the courts are seemingly hostile to utilitarian calculations in cases that have involved the intentional sacrifice of one person's life to ensure the survival of many. Recognising necessity in torture cases would deny the autonomy and moral existence of the subject as a human being.[109] Even if the torture is "regulated" so as to avoid the risk of death,[110] the victim of torture is subjected to not only to serious pain but experiences a form of moral death.[111] Respect for human life and human dignity is a paramount value and, in modern times, the law has not been willing to entertain legal argument about the relative value of one human life over many.

Beyond these liberal and moral arguments against utilitarianism, a leading criminal justice scholar, John Kleinig, claims that there are practical problems with the torture calculus. How "imminent" does the threat need to be to justify this action? How many lives need to be threatened: "Do we need to be talking about 3 million lives or will 1 million do, 100 thousand, 100, 10, or even 1?".[112] In most liberal democracies torture has been banished from the panoply of state powers to investigate crime and protect national security. The revival of interest in "legitimate" forms of torture can be viewed as part of a wider trend to trade liberal

---

108 In America, this has been proposed by Harvard law professor, Alan Dershowitz, *Why Terrorism Works: Understanding the Threat, Responding to the Challenge*, Yale UP, 2002. A similarly controversial view was proposed by M Bagaric and J Clarke, "Not enough official torture in the world? The circumstances in which torture is morally justifiable" (2005) 39(3) *University of San Francisco Law Review* 1. It is not surprising that the father of utilitarian philosophy, Jeremy Bentham, wrote an essay on the utility of torture, concluding that its use depended in each case on its "overall utility": see W Twining and P Twining, "Bentham on torture" (1973) 24 *Northern Ireland Law Quarterly* 307; discussed in J Kleinig, "Ticking bombs and torture warrants" (2005) 10(2) *Deakin Law Review* 614 at 614. In the modern law, torture is strictly prohibited, as it is subject to an absolute ban under international human rights law and prohibited under the *Criminal Code* (Cth) ss 268.13 Crime against humanity – torture, 268.25 War crime – torture (War crimes that are grave breaches of the Geneva Conventions), 268.73 War crime – torture (committed in the course of an armed conflict that is not an international armed conflict).

109 D Manderson, "Another modest proposal" (2005) 10(2) *Deakin Law Review* 640 at 651.

110 Kleinig notes, n 108, 625, that Dershowitz proposed that the torture under warrant should be medically supervised and involved only the insertion of a sterilised needle under the fingernail.

111 As Manderson points out "our societies have, at least since the Enlightenment, feared pain more than death, believed that human dignity requires absolute protection under all circumstances, and thought torture a more serious act than execution": n 109, 649. This is reflected in the hierarchy of executions, the most painful reserved for those guilty of treason and *petit* treason (a wife who killed her husband) who would be burned alive at the stake which persisted in England until 1790. These punishment practices are detailed on the Proceedings of the Old Bailey website: <http://www.oldbaileyonline.org/history/crime/punishment.html#death> (accessed 6 April 2005).

112 Kleinig, n 108, 618.

values for security and the idea that state officials need to be able to act with impunity.

An interesting development in this debate about the balance between security and liberty is the emergence of a "right to security" as a fundamental human right.[113] Indeed, the federal Attorney-General, Philip Ruddock is a strong proponent of this approach, recently claiming that the right to life, liberty and security of the person is the basis for anti-terrorism laws:

> In combating terrorism, we should focus on creating "human security" legislation that protects both national security and civil liberties.[114]

In this way liberalism has been turned back on itself, with national security now being packaged itself as a right which is paramount – this priority arising because security is a necessary precondition for the enjoyment of all other human rights.[115] But as Miriam Gani has persuasively pointed out, this is in fact an inversion of the values behind the concept of human security, which has rested upon restraining rather than expanding the powers of the state vis-à-vis its citizens.[116] Arguments since 9/11 have tended to conflate the nation's security and the security of the citizen. A cursory review of the case law under the "right to security" in international human rights law would reveal a basic concern with confining the power of the state to coerce its citizens through powers of arrest and detention.[117] National security interests, where considered relevant under international human rights law, are viewed simply as competing public interests that may place some necessary and proportionate restriction on the exercise of a particular human right.[118] It would seem that, in this new era, fundamental human rights related to liberty and security can acquire radically new meanings.

The balancing model and its advocates fail to recognise that the interests at stake are not inversely related. Normatively speaking, when threats to liberty posed by terrorism are grave, values such as the rule of law and due process ought to become *more* (not less) important to maintaining the legitimacy of state action. Similarly, from an empirical perspective, there is little compelling evidence that requiring higher standards of due process and protection of human rights impedes effective law enforcement or counter-terrorism activity. In the end, the use of balancing metaphors simply encourages sloppy reasoning and poor policy development.

---

113 The right to life, liberty and security of the person is protected by the Art 3 of the United Nations Universal Declaration of Human Rights and Art 9 of the ICCPR.

114 "Australia's legislative response to the ongoing threat of terrorism" (2004) 27(2) *University of New South Wales Law Journal* 254 at 254.

115 This "disconcerting twist" in the Attorney-General's speeches is reviewed by Gani, n 106, 80-91.

116 Ibid.

117 The case law is reviewed in *The Right To Liberty and Security of the Person*, Human Rights Handbooks, No 5, <http://www.coe.int/T/E/Human_rights/hrhb5.pdf> (accessed 6 April 2005). The right to liberty and security of person under Art 9 of the ICCPR "guarantees against arbitrariness in relation to arrest and detention", rather than some broader right to safety: see N O'Neill, S Rice and R Douglas, *Retreat from Injustice: Human Rights in Australia*, 2nd ed, Federation Press, 2004, 214.

118 This is apparent in the international human rights decisions examining whether surveillance for national security or crime prevention and law enforcement purposes amounts to arbitrary interference with privacy: for example, *Klass v Federal Republic of Germany* [1978] 2 EHRR 214, in which the European Court of Human Rights set out the circumstances under which secret surveillance will be justifiable under the doctrines of necessity and proportionality: at 222.

What, then, are the alternatives to balancing models? We suggest an approach to terrorism that places human rights compliance at the forefront of policy formation. Choices between competing values cannot be avoided, but giving human rights such prominence ensures that limitations and restrictions on fundamental rights are permissible only if they are *proven* to be necessary, reasonable and proportionate.[119] Thus far, legislative and policy debate has been strikingly resistant to taking human rights seriously or to adopting an "evidence-based" approach to reform.[120]

(iv)   9/11 laws: Rule of law and executive lawlessness?

As noted in Chapter 3, a critical element of the rule of law is the idea that the executive and individual public officials are not exempt from the law. Also, consistent with the separation of powers, the exercise of executive power should be subject to independent judicial review. However, terrorism and national security present a significant challenge to these fundamental liberal legal values. In a political climate characterised by a "War on Terror", there are doubts whether legislatures are capable of producing statutes that impose effective limits on the exercise of executive power. Recent national security and terrorism legislation in Australia has been criticised for its vague wording, and conferral of a wide margin of discretion on intelligence and law enforcement agencies.[121]

The prospect of any rigorous and independent judicial review of executive power seems remote in this context. Even before 9/11 the courts have tended to regard executive action in the interests of national security as non-justiciable or legally "off-limits".[122] The involvement of judges in the intelligence-gathering or, indeed, normal investigative processes raises constitutional problems from the perspective of the separation of powers, as noted above. Even assuming such objections can be overcome in the name of promoting "checks and balances", there is a danger that judicial officers will simply "rubber stamp" the exercise of executive powers in cases involving national security. In those few cases where executive power have been tested before the courts, judges tend to defer to the executive's assessment of the threat to national security, unwilling to "second-guess" the merits of these decisions. As a result, judicial review is limited to an examination of the decision-making process for procedural flaws.

---

119 H Fenwick, "The *Anti-Terrorism, Crime and Security Act 2001*: A proportionate response to 11 September?" (2002) 65 *Modern Law Review* 724.

120 Bronitt, n 41.

121 Jenny Hocking has suggested, in relation to the legislative and procedural overhaul introduced after 9/11 in Australia, that "the ambiguity of key terms has been the result not of poor legislative drafting but of a studied and deliberate attempt to allow for 'flexibility' in the application of the Act ... It is this linguistic imprecision that leaves open the possibility of an abuse of executive power through the discretionary interpretation and application of these laws, and the possibility of a form of racial or religious profiling in their implementation": "Protecting democracy by preserving justice: 'Even for the feared and hated'" (2004) 27(2) *University of New South Wales Law Journal* 319 at 323.

122 See *Liversidge v Anderson* [1942] AC 207, where the House of Lords reviewed the powers to detain individuals under wartime regulations in the interest of public safety and defence of the realm. See AWB Simpson, *In the Highest Degree Odious: Detention Without Trial in Wartime Britain*, Oxford UP, 1992.

David Dyzenhaus poses the question: "why do courts resile from the rule of law in national security cases"?[123] The answer, according to Dyzenhaus, lies in the contested nature of the rule of law itself and the fact that judges are torn between two competing conceptions of their role. On the one hand, there is the positivist model, which states that law does not contain broader values and principles relating to human dignity and freedom. The judicial role is simply to apply the law as found. In the absence of a clear legislative mandate, it is illegitimate for judges to appoint themselves as guardians of liberal or moral values which they deem to be fundamental. On this view, judicial review of the powers to control, detain or investigate individuals under national security laws would focus narrowly on the question of legality, whether the powers were exercised within the terms of the legislation. Should laws prove to be overbroad or unjust, it is for the democratic legislative process to repeal or modify them. The alternate model envisages a rule of law that extends beyond statutes, to include a broader range of legal sources, principles and values. On this view, the judicial role assumes more intrusive forms of merit-based review, which would utilise a wider range of standards against which the legality of executive action would be judged (including standards derived from international human rights law). Dyzenhaus summarises the effect of this judicial tension over their role as follows:

> On the one hand, they [the judges] recognize that their role in legal order is to uphold the rule of law, where law includes more than statute law. On the other hand, they still cling to a formal conception of the separation of powers which deprives them of the resources to uphold the rule of law. They resolve this tension by claiming that they are upholding the rule of law, at the same time as they tell the executive that it is a law unto itself.

It may not be a surprise to find that the rule of law does not live up to its liberal rhetoric and that it is the judiciary, as much as the executive or the legislature, that has carved out this "pocket of lawlessness".[124] The danger is that this culture of impunity around national security is spreading into a wider range of areas. Political, social and even economic interests are amenable to repackaging as matters of "national security". As John Kleinig has observed, national *security* tends to elide into wider claims of national *interest*:

> [A]ppeals to national security are themselves deeply problematic. I do not of course want to underestimate the damage that terrorism can and does do. But invocations of national security can be greatly overdone. ... One of the difficulties here is that the idea of national security – never entirely clear-cut – has undergone considerable expansion, to the point, I think, at which it can no longer bear the moral weight that it is accorded. Whereas it was once seen primarily in terms of the security of borders – in which an attempt at conquest constituted a threat to national security – it has now been expanded to cover almost any threat to national *interests*. National security interests may be challenged by contagious disease and economic events overseas no less than by North Korean nuclear capability.[125]

---

123 D Dyzenhaus, "Humpty dumpty rules or the rule of law: Legal theory and the adjudication of national security" (2003) 28 *Australian Journal of Legal Philosophy* 1.

124 Ibid 29.

125 Kleinig, n 108, 624.

National security and terrorism are said to justify "exceptional" legal responses, including the suspension or limitations upon the ordinary due process of law. In an age of terrorism, the contours of "national security" have become increasingly hazy and politically malleable. In this environment of pervasive insecurity, the real danger is that these "legal exceptions" will gradually legitimise, irreversibly establishing themselves as the "legal norm".

(d) Conclusion

Globalisation has many impacts on law. Not only is it promoting a particular economic paradigm based on international free trade, it is also marshalling a global alliance against terrorism.[126] Law is an agent of globalisation, promoting closer interaction between peoples, political elites and business entities. The result is that domestic law itself is becoming more international and transnational. At the apex is the creation of supranational courts of justice established by international treaties, which include, at the international level, the ICC, and at regional level, courts such as the European Union's Court of Justice and the European Court of Human Rights.

These new institutions constitute new legal orders that interact, and sometimes compete, with domestic legal systems. Globalisation operates not only at this macro-level through creating demand for more supranational law and international cooperation. At the micro-level, globalisation also affects local law and order priorities. For example, reforms to public order law in Australia, particularly the creation of "move on" powers to deal with gangs, have been directly influenced by "zero tolerance" policing strategies introduced in the United States in the 1990s.[127] In New South Wales, new police powers were introduced without any inquiry into the adequacy of existing laws, or indeed empirical research that there was a serious (as opposed to perceived) problem of gang-related crime. The danger is that transnational comparisons are not always valid, with the result that legal transplants may have unintended and counterproductive effects, as well as being incompatible with existing legal and constitutional traditions.[128]

Public order issues can also be repackaged as threats to national security. A recent example of the "War on Terror" combining with local "law and order" politics is the beach violence between "Middle Eastern" and "Australian" gangs in New South Wales in December 2005. Focusing on a series of violent confrontations at Cronulla, the NSW Parliament introduced and passed on the same day an emergency package of powers for police, allowing them to "lock down" suburbs. Without the involvement of any judicial officer or court, senior police can declare an area they define as "locked down", in which case the following powers apply. Police may close licensed premises; to declare an emergency alcohol-free zone for up to 48 hours; set up roadblocks and employ stop and search (without warrant) powers to persons, vehicles, and anything in the possession of those persons; seize

---

126 Findlay, n 24, 231-247.

127 The theories behind zero tolerance policing, and the New South Wales reforms are critically reviewed in Bronitt and McSherry, n 10, 741-748.

128 The anti-gang laws in the United States have been controversial there too, having been struck down by the US Supreme Court as constitutionally void for vagueness under the due process clause: see Bronitt and McSherry, n 10, 748.

and detain any vehicle, mobile phone or similar device. Outside the exercise of locked down areas, the amendments also empower any police officer to stop a vehicle if the officer has reasonable grounds for believing there is large-scale public disorder occurring or threatening to and that it is reasonably necessary.[129] In the immediate aftermath of the violence, charges of riot and violent disorder were laid, though the overwhelming majority related to minor traffic infringements.[130] Most significantly, as noted above, these extraordinary police powers were enacted hastily, without proper review of the adequacy of existing laws or objective analysis of the underlying causes of these disturbances.[131] The moral panic[132] apparent in the responses of legislators reveals the tendency to assimilate local public order problems with terrorist violence overseas, and to construct disorderly conduct and "suspect communities" as significant threats to national security.[133]

These trends are sometimes presented as the emergence of a single world culture and economy, and a global justice system. This approach overlooks the paradoxical aspects of globalisation, namely that efforts to promote universality across cultures (which include legal cultures) tend to provoke resistance.[134] This is manifest not only in the anti-globalisation movements, but also through political claims that local and regional interests (including borders) must be respected and protected. This explains why a feature of 9/11 laws has been to increase controls over borders, fostering new laws against "people smuggling", and the political and media labelling of refugees as threats to both territorial and national security.[135] Responding to and feeding these perceived threats, the Australian government toughened its provisions governing migration, enacting a wide range of offences

---

129 *Law Enforcement (Powers and Responsibilities) Act 2002* (NSW) ss 87B, 87C, 87D, 87E, 87I, 87J, 87K, 87L, 87M, 87N, respectively, inserted by Sch 1 to the *Law Enforcement Legislation Amendment (Public Safety) Act 2005* (NSW).

130 Andrew Clennell, "Labor soft after riots: Debnam", *Sydney Morning Herald*, 13 January 2006, p 1.

131 The *Law Enforcement Legislation Amendment (Public Safety) Act 2005* (NSW) was introduced, assented to and commenced on the same day: 15 December 2005.

132 The term "moral panic" is famously associated with Stanley Cohen's classic sociological study of youth gang violence between "Mods" and "Rockers" in England in the 1960s: *Folk Devils and Moral Panics*, Paladin, 1973. It applies when "[a] condition, episode, person or group of persons emerges to become defined as a threat to societal values and interests", and distinctively exerts a strong and often disproportionate influence on legal and social policy makers: 9. In Australia and the UK, moral panics about crime and disorder often focus on public order law (particularly street crime by juveniles) which in turn generate special police powers and new offences: see further Bronitt and McSherry, n 10, Ch 14.

133 Criminal justice reform is rarely evidence-based. Much reform is driven by the politics of law and order, rather than careful consideration of the available data on crime and what constitute effective law enforcement policy: see generally D Weatherburn, *Law and Order in Australia: Rhetoric and Reality*, Federation Press, 2004. Some commentators have observed that criminal justice reform is directed by "law and order commonsense" rather than informed expert opinion, leading to an "uncivil politics of law and order" in Australia: R Hogg and D Brown, *Rethinking Law and Order*, Pluto Press, 1998, Ch 1.

134 "Globalisation is paradoxical in the way it unifies and delineates, internationalizes and localizes": Findlay, n 24, 235.

135 People smuggling has shifted from its earlier focus on criminal violations of immigration laws, to a new focus on potential threats to national security: S Pickering, "The production of sovereignty and the rise of transversal policing: People smuggling and federal policing" (2004) 37(1) *Australian and New Zealand Journal of Criminology* 362.

relating to people smuggling. As Sharon Pickering concludes, through this "mundane process of criminalisation" the State's liberal commitment to the rule of law and human rights is threatened, producing deviancy by the state itself, and fostering a new category of criminality called "state crime".[136]

This resistance to the universality of globalisation can generate powerful counter-movements. An example of this in the legal context is the attack on the purported universality of human rights across cultures. There has been significant debate, within both political and legal academic circles about the cultural biases of human rights, and whether it attaches too much priority to a narrow set of Western liberal values based on individual, as opposed to communal rights and "Asian values".[137]

Globalisation promotes free trade and consumerism as a "universal" good. It also repackages local and regional conflict as international terrorism, and prioritises transnational criminal activity, principally drug trafficking, organised crime and cybercrime, as the most serious and harmful. Criminal activity that actually presents a direct harm to individuals and communities, such as domestic violence, wilful environmental damage or corporate crime, is likely to remain a globalisation blindspot. The differential treatment of these crimes, locally and globally, is not a product of the seriousness of the harm or even whether the activity is criminalised. Rather, as Mark Findlay concludes, "[i]t is the social context of crime that holds the key to its significance. Whether it be a local or global context, the story remains the same".[138]

Questions

1. There have been several periods of globalisation. During an earlier period of globalisation, it is claimed that the Roman law, and more broadly western European legal values, played a critical role in globalisation. What legal values and legal cultures are driving globalisation today? In what way are they the same, and in what way are they different? Are there any alternatives to the present drivers of legal globalisation?

2. What are the critical elements that promote the conditions for globalisation? What do you think motivates individuals, communities, corporations and states to be more "cosmopolitan"?

3. Consider the following statement:

    The "War on Drugs" was followed by the "War on Terror". By literalising metaphors, politicians have provided a justification for invoking wider powers to deal with drug traffickers and terrorists.

    Do you think that military analogies are useful? What are implications for the law and human rights, particularly in relation to powers used in relation to the prevention, disruption and investigation of these activities?

---

136 S Pickering, *Refugees and State Crime*, Federation Press, 2005, Ch 7.

137 See generally K Jayasuriya (ed), *Law, Capitalism and Power in Asia*, Routledge, 1999; HJ Steiner and P Alston, *International Human Rights in Context: Law, Politics and Morals*, 2nd ed, Oxford UP, 2000, 538ff.

138 Above n 24, 242.

4.   Consider the following statement:

> Conventional criminal justice processes such as arrest, prosecution, trial and punishment of offenders are being gradually displaced by increased surveillance and emphasis on disruption tactics, and the risk management of dangerous persons as well as "suspect" communities.

Beyond the terrorism powers reviewed in this chapter, what other laws and regulations (not confined to the criminal justice sphere) conform with this assessment?

5.   Divide the class into two groups.

Group One, develop arguments in support of the following:

> A constitutional Bill of Rights in Australia is urgently needed. It would impose effective and reasonable limits on the scope and type of laws that could be enacted to deal with terrorism.

Group Two, develop arguments in support of the following:

> A constitutional Bill of Rights in Australia would not impose any significant limits on the present "War on Terror". Too much faith is placed in the capacity of the courts to safeguard the rule of law and human rights.

Reconvene the class. Consider and debate the arguments developed by the two groups.

Some further reading: G Williams, *The Case for an Australian Bill of Rights: Freedom in the War on Terror*, UNSW Press, 2004.

6.   Andrew O'Neil has rejected claims that the federal government's legal responses to terrorism were draconian in the following terms:

> First, if one accepts the need for a counter-terrorist strategy, then one also needs to accept that pursuing such a strategy will inevitably entail the derogation of certain civil liberties. No country throughout history has implemented a counter-terrorist strategy that has not impacted in some way on civil liberties. Due legal process is a prominent part of our democratic way of life, but its importance is not absolute. For instances, if law enforcement agencies representing a democratically elected government reasonably conclude that they have grounds for detaining an individual whom they believe may be involved in, or have knowledge of, a terrorist plot that has the potential to kill Australian citizens and/or damage property and infrastructure, then given the urgency of preventing an attack from taking place it is hard to see why they should not have this discretionary power. (footnotes omitted)[139]

Do you agree? Is this "trade off" of due process for more security inevitable? Are there any limits to the types of preventative action that the state might take? How does the law in other areas seek to constrain the exercise of "discretionary power" by law enforcement officials?

---

139   O'Neil, n 43, 389.

Index

Also available from The Federation Press:

Australian Constitutional Law and Theory
Fourth edition

Tony Blackshield and George Williams

Blackshield and Williams is well established as the leading modern work on Australia's Constitution. The text has been thoroughly revised, updated and restructured in this new edition which continues the work's authoritative status.

Reviews of previous editions:

> *The book is much more than a casebook. It contains a wide range of materials, including excerpts from a broad range of writers and commentators. The contents of the book do provide, as the authors claim in their preface, 'the materials and commentary needed to understand the doctrines and theories behind the law'.*
>
> Sir Anthony Mason AC KBE

> *A book of many useful and original insights. The authors helpfully stand back from the detail and reflect on the big questions – which is, after all, what constitutional law is usually about.*
>
> Justice Michael Kirby AC CMG

> *[T]he most comprehensive treatment of Australian constitutional law available today.*
>
> Ethos

> *Overwhelmingly well-researched, the book is a must for the library of all lawyers and law students.*
>
> Law Society of South Australia

> *[T]he book will be of immense interest and utility to all readers. It is a mine of well-presented information.*
>
> Law Society of Tasmania Newsletter

> *This is a book which one should own, read and revere.*
>
> Law Institute Journal

> *Every glowing review of* Australian Constitutional Law and theory *... is richly deserved, for the book is scholarly, informative, challenging and innovative.*
>
> Alternative Law Journal

2006 • 1 86287 585 5 • paperback • 1520 pp • $125

The Hidden Gender of Law

Second edition

Regina Graycar & Jenny Morgan

This innovative book starts from the premise that women's lives are central to the operation of law and that legal categories and legal doctrines have been developed in such a way that women have been disadvantaged. While the book's authors are Australian and it draws extensively on Australian examples, it has much to say to anyone seeking to use the law to pursue equality and eradicate disadvantage, in Canada and elsewhere. The Hidden Gender of Law makes a wonderful contribution to reconceptualising law in the twenty-first century.

The Hon Madame Justice Claire L'Héureux-Dubé,
Supreme Court of Canada

[A]n understanding of the problems posed by Graycar and Morgan is a most important step along the road to equal justice for women and, ultimately, to equal justice for all.

Justice Mary Gaudron, High Court of Australia

"[T]ruly international... It successfully presents feminist legal theory as a dynamic set of ideas, moving and changing with the times, neither static nor unitary ... a book which deserves considerable credit and attention, for its fine blend of creativity and practicality."

Feminist Legal Studies

"[A] student text, and an introduction to feminist legal studies, while simultaneously managing to be an important contribution to feminist legal theory. ... What makes this book special is that the authors have drawn together an impressive array of primary and secondary material that exposes the gendered nature of the barriers and of law generally, while simultaneously breaking them down."

International Journal of the Sociology of Law

[T]he level of scholarship and analysis on the part of Graycar and Morgan is very high. ... strongly recommended.

Peter Barr, Balance (Law Society NT)

This is a good book. For anyone with questions about feminism, or about law, or the seductive power of rhetoric and doctrine, this book has value.

Sydney Law Review

[Q]uite simply, a tour de force.

Canadian Journal of Women and the Law

A starting point for becoming a new sort of practitioner.

New Zealand Universities Law Review

The contents is an easy-to-use look-up guide covering sub-topics as diverse as women's unpaid work, nervous shock, abortion, breast implant surgery, child custody, violence against women and pornography. ... Each topic is discussed within the context of current Australian statistics and attitudes.

Michaela Ryan, Law Institute of Victoria Journal

2002 · ISBN 1 86287 340 2 · paperback · 512 pp · $66

Achieving Social Justice

Indigenous Rights and Australia's Future

Larissa Behrendt

Larissa Behrendt attacks the chasm which has grown between Indigenous lives and aspirations in Australia, and the psychological *terra nullius* which continues, despite *Mabo*, to pervade so much of Australia's mythology and policy.

Writing with great power and clarity, Behrendt proposes practical short-term reforms, as well as longer term aspirational initiatives leading to institutional change that will facilitate greater rights protection and the exercise of self-determination including:

- a preamble to the Constitution
- a treaty
- the national self-image
- economic redistribution
- alternative institutional forms
- regional framework agreements
- a more energised politics
- Constitutional protection

A magnificent synthesis of Indigenous history and insights ... based in profound scholarship yet highly readable and accessible, it deserves the widest possible readership

Dr William Jonas AM

[A] remarkably lucid and readable book

Professor Ann Curthoys

A clear and unambiguous statement of what is wrong with the status quo from an Aboriginal perspective. It helps to define the unfinished business of reconciliation.

Fred Chaney AO

Behrendt provides perhaps the clearest articulation we have of what Indigenous Australians want and need – and how it might be achieved. This book will be debated, dissected, applauded and disagreed with in the years to come, and certainly quoted ... compulsory reading for anyone working or interested in Indigenous law and policy. ...

Most of the critical contemporary issues in Indigenous law and policy in Australia are discussed in the book ... most of the significant contributions to the debate are interpreted and responded to.

Behrendt writes with an honesty and clarity that is sometimes lost in the Indigenous law and policy debate, and offers constructive proposals ...

QUT Law Journal

2003 · ISBN 1 86287 450 6 · paperback · 208pp · $29.95